History and Identity

This introduction to contemporary historical theory and practice shows how issues of identity have shaped how we write history. Stefan Berger charts how a new self-reflexivity about what is involved in the process of writing history entered the historical profession and the part that historians have played in debates about the past and its meaningfulness for the present. He introduces key trends in the theory of history such as postmodernism, poststructuralism, constructivism, narrativism and the linguistic turn and reveals, in turn, the ways in which they have transformed how historians have written history over the last four decades. The book ranges widely from more traditional forms of history writing, such as political, social, economic, labour and cultural history, to the emergence of more recent fields, including gender history, historical anthropology, the history of memory, visual history, the history of material culture, and comparative, transnational and global history.

STEFAN BERGER is a leading figure in the history of historiography and historical theory with more than thirty years' experience teaching courses at the Universities of Cardiff, Glamorgan, Manchester and Bochum. His publications include *The Past as History: National Identity and Historical Consciousness in Modern Europe* (2015), *Writing the Nation: A Global Perspective* (2007) and *The Search for Normality. National Identity and Historical Consciousness in Germany since 1800* (2003). He serves as series editor for the Bloomsbury Academic book series 'Writing History: Theory and Practice'.

History and Identity

How Historical Theory Shapes Historical Practice

STEFAN BERGER
Ruhr-Universität Bochum, Institute for Social Movements

CAMBRIDGE
UNIVERSITY PRESS

CAMBRIDGE
UNIVERSITY PRESS

University Printing House, Cambridge CB2 8BS, United Kingdom

One Liberty Plaza, 20th Floor, New York, NY 10006, USA

477 Williamstown Road, Port Melbourne, VIC 3207, Australia

314–321, 3rd Floor, Plot 3, Splendor Forum, Jasola District Centre, New Delhi – 110025, India

103 Penang Road, #05–06/07, Visioncrest Commercial, Singapore 238467

Cambridge University Press is part of the University of Cambridge.

It furthers the University's mission by disseminating knowledge in the pursuit of education, learning, and research at the highest international levels of excellence.

www.cambridge.org
Information on this title: www.cambridge.org/highereducation/isbn/9781107011403
DOI: 10.1017/9780511984525

First published 2022

A catalogue record for this publication is available from the British Library.

ISBN 978-1-107-01140-3 Hardback
ISBN 978-1-107-64884-5 Paperback

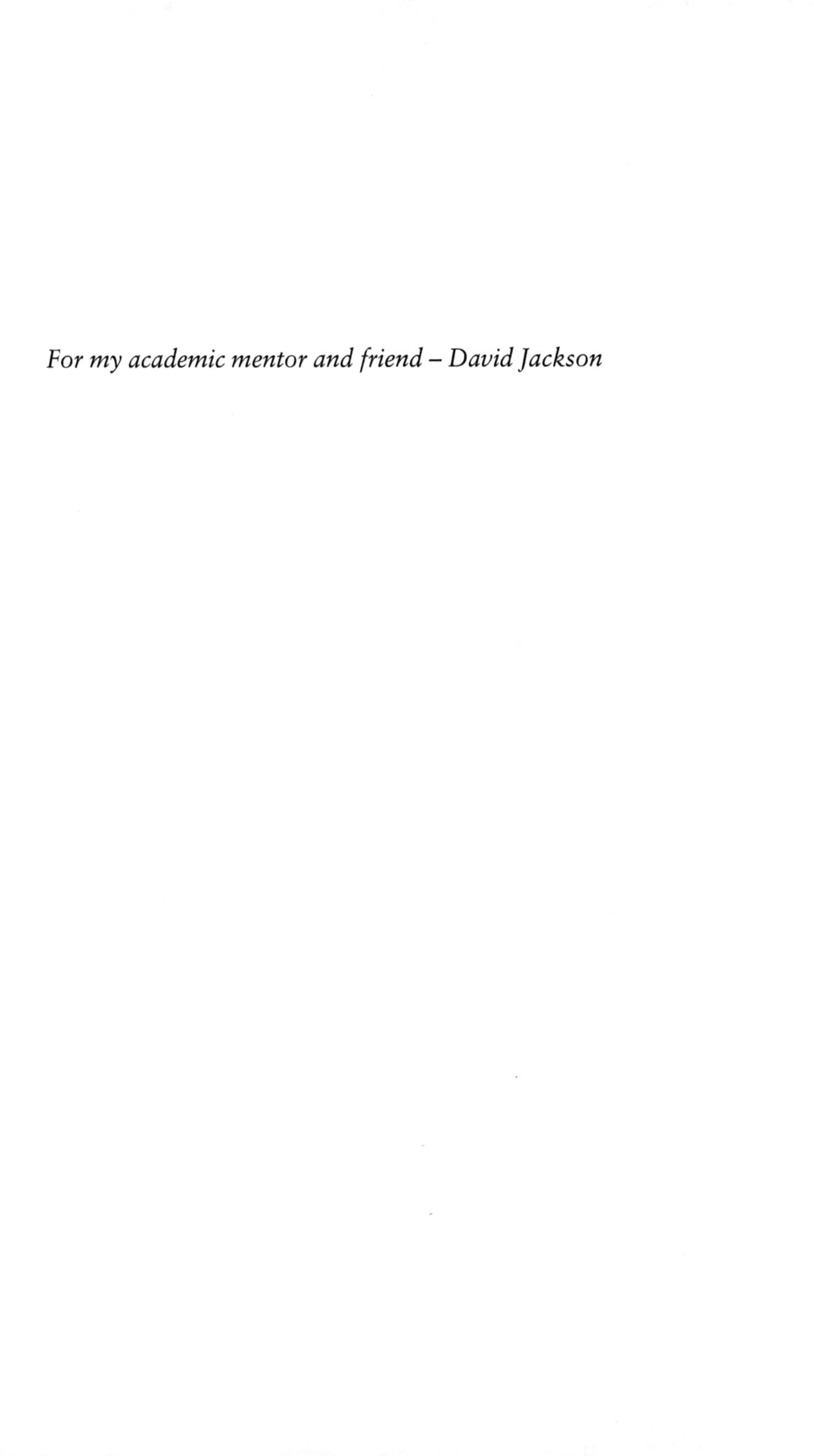

For my academic mentor and friend – David Jackson

Contents

List of Figures — *page* viii
Preface — xi

1 Introduction: History and Identity — 1
2 The New Political History — 34
3 The New Social, Economic and Labour History — 59
4 The New Cultural History — 80
5 Gender History — 105
6 Historical Anthropology — 129
7 The History of Memory — 152
8 The History of Concepts — 179
9 The Visual Turn — 203
10 The History of Material Culture — 235
11 Transnational, Comparative and Global History — 261
12 Conclusion: Problematising History and Identity — 284

Notes — 310
Bibliography — 397
Index — 478

Figures

1.1	Hayden White	*page* 14
1.2	Michel Foucault	19
1.3	Mikhail Bakhtin	22
2.1	Revolutionary Festival of the Supreme Being, 1794,	49
3.1	Chromolithograph after 'American Progress' by John Gast	67
4.1	Woodcut from 'Le Roman de Melusine'	97
5.1	Mother India poster	115
6.1	A cock fight in Bali	131
6.2	Rough music during the Yorkshire custom of 'Riding the Stang'	142
6.3	Uyghurs celebrating in traditional costume	145
6.4	A Native American shaman	148
8.1	Britain's Day poster, 1918	188
9.1	Press conference for the 'Velazquez, Rembrandt, Vermeer: Parallel Vision' exhibition	204
9.2	The panopticon	208
9.3	*The King Governs by Himself*, by Charles LeBrun	209
9.4	*The Bard*, by John All	212
9.5	A Maasai warrior	214
9.6	Steelworker Andy Lopata and his son reading *Steel Labor*	217
9.7	'Lenin lived. Lenin lives. Long live Lenin': Soviet propaganda poster	219
9.8	*The Freedman, American* by John Quincy Adams Ward	221
9.9	'Migrant Mother' by Dorothea Lange	223
9.10	*The Homeland in Danger (The Recruitment of Volunteer Soldiers)*, by Guillaume Guillon-Lethière	224
9.11	A white doctor vaccinating African girls	226
9.12	Official programme of a woman's suffrage procession, Washington, DC	230
9.13	War memorial, Neue Wache, Berlin	232

10.1 Mosaic of Empress Theodora and her retinue 240
10.2 Highway 127 yard sale in Kentucky, USA 245
10.3 US Longhorn cattle 245
10.4 Assembly Building and Reflecting Pool, Chandigarh, India 252
10.5 Headgear of Zeche Zollverein in Essen, Germany 254
10.6 Madhukeshwara Temple, Banavasi, south India 258
11.1 Toussaint L'Ouverture 263
11.2 Visa stamps on a passport 277
12.1 The expulsion of the Jews from England, 1290 297

Preface

I have never been able to conceive of writing history without reflecting on the practice of what is involved in this exercise. Inversely, I have never been able to read in the theory of history without reflecting on the meaning for the actual practice of history writing. This book is the outcome of both interests that is truly one interest. I should also add that my primary interest is in the history of historiography, in which I have worked over the past thirty years – with a special emphasis on the relationship between historical writing and national identity formation. But I have always also been a practicising social historian, writing, often comparatively and transnationally, on labour movements, social movements, nationalism, deindustrialisation processes and their impact on industrial communities. Reading and reflecting on the writing of history theorists and philosophers of history has always helped me in conceptualising those social histories and also the histories of history writing that I have written since I began life as an academic historian in the 1980s – the period that is the starting point also for this book. Much of the literature that I discuss here hence has accompanied me during my own lifetime, and therefore this book is also, in more ways than one, a reflection on thirty-five years of reading history through the eyes of a professional historian with a keen interest in the theory of history.

In the process of writing this book I have, as usual, benefited enormously from the critical advice of many colleagues and friends. In particular I would like to thank Antoon de Baets, Lucian Hölscher, Tim Le Cain and Chris Lorenz for commenting on drafts of chapters of this book. I have also discussed aspects of the book, during its long gestation period, with Berber Bevernage, Nicola Brauch, Mario Carretero, Anna Clark, Heiko Feldner, Maria Grever, Georg G. Iggers, Wulf Kansteiner, Jürgen Kocka, Joep Leerssen, Alf Lüdtke, Stuart Macintyre, Guy Marchal, Philipp Müller, Bill Niven, Kevin Passmore, Kalle Pihlainen, Tyson Retz, Ann Rigney, Jörn Rüsen, Nick Stargardt, Marek Tamm, Jo Tollebeek and Edward Wang, and

I have benefited tremendously from those conversations. There are undoubtedly others I have forgotten to mention and I apologise to them. My friend and mentor David Jackson, Professor Emeritus from Cardiff University, has been kind enough to look through the entire manuscript. The book has profited not only from many of his astute comments as a literary specialist, but also from his grammatical and stylistic interventions. I am greatly indebted to him, not only for this, but for providing important guidance during my early career at Cardiff University in the 1990s. Many thanks also to the University of Technology, Sydney, and to Northwestern Normal University at Changchun, both of which provided me with research fellowships that helped me to complete parts of the book. I also wish to thank the two anonymous reviewers for Cambridge University Press for their careful reading of the manuscript and many helpful suggestions. Of course, thanks are also due to my own institution, Ruhr-Universität Bochum, where many colleagues have provided an intellectually stimulating and friendly atmosphere. Several terms of research leave, granted by the university, also contributed to the finalisation of this book. A final big thank you goes to Michael Watson at Cambridge University Press, who never stopped believing in the project during its long years of gestation, and who has commented on all chapters of the book. Without his constant encouragement to complete the book, which I started, as an idea, about ten years ago, it is highly likely that it would never have seen the light of day. As always, the remaining shortcomings of the book are entirely my own.

1 Introduction: History and Identity

Introduction

'... perhaps we should think of history writing, not as something that engages in the building of national identities, but rather as something that critiques all historical identity-claims, and in doing so, as a by-product, opens a space for constitutional allegiances and behavioural norms that stand at a remove from what is *simply* given to us by the past.'[1]

Allan Megill's idea of thinking of history writing as 'something that critiques all historical identity-claims' is one that, by implication, highlights the strong correlation between the development of professional history writing since the late eighteenth century and the formation of modern national identities. This book will review key developments in the history of historiography over recent decades, both in traditional historical fields, such as political, social and cultural history, and in more recent sub-fields, such as gender history, memory history, visual history, the history of material culture and global history, among others, in order to investigate to what extent the new history that has been emerging is one that is indeed characterised by critiquing historical identity claims, or, at the very least, being more self-reflexive about those claims. In this chapter I will begin by providing an overview of the manifold links between the writing of history and the construction of collective identities of nations, classes, ethnicities, religions, genders and a host of spatial sub- and transnational identities.[2] This link was built into professional historical writing from its inception in the eighteenth century. As I argue in the second part of this chapter, such links were challenged by diverse developments in the theory of history writing during the 1960s and 1970s. These developments are connected to a range of thinkers who are not easily grouped together under one label. For that reason I discuss them individually rather than as a united body of theory, even if certain linkages between them will also be discussed. In the third and final part of this chapter, I will comment briefly on the way in which this body of theories has percolated through to the historical profession and led to the making of a new history writing since the 1980s. I introduce some of this new history writing in subsequent chapters of this volume.

The Writing of History and Its Link to Building Collective Identities

Before the eighteenth century, history had often been a sub-discipline of theology at the universities in Europe, i.e. subservient to explaining the history of the Church and of Divine providence in the world.[3] History writing, in other words, was tied to the promotion of religious identity. During the Enlightenment, it became a more secular affair, although the ruptures with religion were usually gradual and should not be exaggerated.[4] Many Enlightenment historians, following their universalising aspirations, sought to trace the emergence of progress through world history, often identifying particular cultures or civilisations in different parts of the world as carriers of progress through the ages. Several authors were not shy to locate the most recent champion of progress in their own nation. Voltaire, for example, in his history of Louis XIV, declared the French nation the most advanced in its customs and habits, whilst his Scottish colleagues William Robertson and Adam Ferguson thought of Scottish commerce and industry as well as Scottish legal and historical thought as marching at the forefront of contemporary progress.[5] By linking the idea of progress to the idea of national character and national development, Enlightenment historians were already pinning history writing to the promotion of national identity.[6] This relationship became ever stronger as the eighteenth century gave way to the nineteenth. The modern historical profession, as we know it today, began to form institutions, networks and communities that allowed historians to set themselves up as the only ones who could speak authoritatively about the past. Their long years of training and practice in the archives and libraries and their methodological and theoretical rigour allegedly gave them a superior vantage point from which to understand the past.[7] This claim was never entirely successful, as many academics from neighbouring disciplines as well as authors operating outside academia continued to write history that was, at certain times and in certain places, more popular and more influential than academic history writing. I will have to come back to some of these cases in later chapters. But certainly, for about a century, between 1850 and 1950, professional historians rose to prominence, because both those in power and those seeking it sought to harness their professional standing to their own causes, which were often identitarian ones linked to nation-building. In an age of nascent nationalism, historians became prophets of the nation-state, both of existing nation-states, of nations at the core of empires and of nations seeking sovereignty from multinational states or empires.[8] 'Methodological nationalism'[9] thus became a central hallmark of the historical profession during the nineteenth and the first half of the twentieth century.

The link to nation, however, has by no means been the only collective identitarian link that historians forged. I have already referred above to the older links between religion and historical writing. These continued into the modern era, with church and ecclesiastical history remaining an important sub-genre through the long nineteenth century and churchmen playing an influential role among historians in different parts of the world.[10] To this day, religious identity remains an important focus of historical writing wherever diverse world religions are prominent. Religion has played a key role in many of the conflicts of the twentieth century. One thinks, for example, of the civil wars in Ireland, Spain and Yugoslavia. With the rise of political Islam in the last third of the twentieth century, historical writing in many parts of the *umma* underpinned religious identity, whereas outside the Islamic world, it has been used to serve Islamophobic identitarian discourses. Christian fundamentalism today is strong not only in the United States, but also in parts of Latin America, Asia and Africa. Here too we see history being used in the service of religious communities. In most cases such history is not state-sponsored (with exceptions such as the Islamic Republic of Iran) and it often finds a home outside university history departments, but it still speaks to the resilience of the link between religious identity and historical writing up to the present day.[11]

With the advent of Social Darwinism in the last third of the nineteenth century, historical writing also began to be linked to biology through the controversial concept of race. Whilst some of the most popular propagandists of the idea of the impact of race on historical developments, such as Joseph Arthur de Gobineau and Houston Steward Chamberlain, were not professional historians, racism certainly struck a chord among many reputable university historians. The case of the Liberal historian Edward Augustus Freeman in England, whose racism was directed against black people and Irishmen alike, is as famous as that of the German liberal conservative historian Heinrich von Treitschke, whose anti-Semitism sparked the Anti-Semitism Dispute in Germany in 1878.[12] After the First World War, a new form of racialised history, one oriented towards the people understood as a racial unit, came to the fore. This occurred especially in some of the countries that had lost the war, above all in Germany, but also in Hungary. In Germany, so-called *Volksgeschichte* attracted young radical right-wing historians who rose to prominence in the Third Reich and sought to justify forms of ethnic cleansing and genocide in Eastern Europe as well as the expansion of the German Reich on its western and eastern borders.[13] The link to nation had already led a considerable number of historians to justify violence and war in the nineteenth century. In the twentieth the link between historical writing and race made an even more substantial group of historians into indirect apologists for genocide and, outside Europe, in particular in the United States and South Africa, into outright apologists for apartheid regimes.[14] It should, however, also be noted that the link between racial identity and historical writing could serve a range of emancipatory agendas, i.e. in the historical writings on black identities in the USA or in the diverse writings on 'first nations' across different parts of the world.[15] Here race was used not in a racist sense but in an attempt to liberate oppressed ethnic minorities from discrimination and social injustice.

In the nineteenth and twentieth centuries history writing forged another strong identitarian link to class. Karl Marx and Friedrich Engels' historical materialism amounted to a philosophy of history linking, as it did, class formation to specific historical periods. According to them, history started with an 'original communist society' and moved on to a slave-holding society and then to feudalism before arriving at capitalism. It would come to an end with the overthrow of capitalism and the advent of communism. Humankind would at last be liberated from all forms of exploitation. Marxism's critique of the inequalities produced by capitalism rang a bell with many labour movements across Europe, but it was never the only show in town: religious socialism, ethical socialism, anarchism and liberal socialism were all based on different sets of ideas. Yet at least a large part of the labour movement everywhere adopted the language of class in an attempt to improve the situation of the workers in the industrialised areas of Europe. Whilst the nineteenth-century labour movement had few supporters among professional historians, who tended to be liberals or conservatives of various shades when it came to politics, labour movement intellectuals, who were at the same time political activists, wrote histories of class and of the labour movement across Europe. Their writing was explicitly meant to strengthen the class identity of class-conscious workers. In its turn this would bolster the organisations of the labour movement, i.e. political parties, trade unions and cooperatives.[16] Only in a few countries, e.g. Britain, did historians sympathetic to class discourse, such as R. H. Tawney and G. D. H. Cole, occupy university positions in the interwar period.[17] They were often at the forefront of developing forms of labour and social history which contested the dominance of political history writing. In most countries, however, the rise of social and labour history only occurred after the Second World War. (See Chapter 3.)

Whilst identitarian links to the histories of nation, religion, race and class have been prominent, historians also forged strong links to subnational and transnational spatial entities. Thus, much historical writing underpinned local and regional identities, as well as so-called pan-histories, like pan-Germanism, pan-Slavism, pan-Iberianism and pan-Scandinavianism. In addition, European histories and histories of empire have all sought to forge strong identities around those transnational concepts of belonging. Histories of particular cities or regions often preceded the flowering of national histories in the nineteenth century and they have remained strong throughout the modern period.[18] Studies devoted to pan-movements sought to establish commonalities in macro-regions spanning more than one nation.[19] European histories were already conceptualised in the nineteenth century in order to build a European identity vis-à-vis diverse non-European 'others'.[20] In all nineteenth-century empires history was firmly institutionalised at the universities, and many of the histories produced there were meant to forge strong identitarian ties with and across the empires.[21] There is also a distinguished tradition of global history writing that sometimes rivalled and sometimes strengthened national historical accounts.[22]

The most successful identitarian link ever forged by historical writing was, however, that with the nation. Although the age of the nation was shorter than the age of empire or the age of cities, historical master narratives were far more important in underpinning nations than either empires or cities. Conceptualisations of the nation were uniquely able to subsume all other identitarian discourses under the language of the nation. Regions became the building blocks of nations in many national histories.[23] Pan-histories served to justify nations' imperial ambitions, whilst European histories became spatial fields in which particular European missions of specific nations could be exemplified. Imperial histories glorified imperial nations, as can be seen, for example, in J. R. Seeley's conceptualisation of a 'Greater Britain'.[24] Global histories could also be related to national missions in the world. Class histories, for their part, were comprehensively nationalised, the nation-state widely being seen as the framework in which the liberation of the working classes would have to take place.[25] Racial histories claimed that particular races formed the core of nations, e.g. the 'Aryan race' in National Socialist Germany. Religious history identified nations strongly with particular religions or religious denominations. In Europe one thinks of Catholicism and Poland as well as Spain, Orthodoxy and Romania as well as Russia, Protestantism and Germany as well as England and Scandinavia.[26]

This strong historiographical nationalism turned into hypernationalism in the first half of the twentieth century, dominated, as that was, by the two world wars, a series of genocides, in particular the Holocaust, and unprecedented forms of ethnic cleansing as well as diverse fascist regimes of terror. Historical writing, tied to identitarian concerns, played an important role in justifying all of them. At the end of the Second World War hypernationalism and hypernationalist historiographies had left Europe devastated and exhausted – with tens of millions of dead soldiers and civilians and cities reduced to heaps of rubble. In the immediate post-war period historians struggled to restabilise traditional national historical narratives in the light of the upheaval which had occurred between 1914 and 1945. The search for good national traditions on which to build post-war national identities was only partially successful and met with increasing criticism. The long 1960s amounted to a 'delayed break' with traditional historiographical nationalism. Historians began to take a more critical look at national histories.[27]

This more critical perspective was closely related to institutional changes in the historical profession. Across the Western world the massive extension of higher education resulted in thousands of new jobs in history departments.[28] It became increasingly impossible for the gate-keepers of the profession to ensure that the discipline retained its political-ideological homogeneity. An increased plurality of forms of history writing associated with different identitarian concerns came to the fore. Political history's long dominance ended. In many places social history, especially labour history, now became powerful. It was linked to left-wing political identities. The promotion of class discourses was one way of situating history in the political conflicts of the turbulent 1960s and early 1970s. Class was inscribed into nation. Class discourses underpinned hopes for the eventual demise of capitalism by providing a historical tradition of past challenges to the capitalist system. In that political context E. P. Thompson's *The Making of the English Working Class*, first published in 1963, became an international bestseller.[29]

The fact that a distinctly left-wing political project became linked to historical writing in the 1960s was a sign that the traditional link between identitarian politics and historical writing had not been weakened by the change from political to social history. The same is true of the rise of women's history that accompanied the forward march of the women's movement in the 1960s and 1970s. Much of it dealt with the discovery of women's agency and women's identity in the past. Women had been systematically written out of history by a male profession.[30] At worst, they had been depicted as being the reason for all the misfortune of nations, races and religions.[31] Many histories had been thoroughly gendered, all the positive virtues being normally associated with allegedly male values and actions and all the negative ones reserved for their female equivalents. At best historians had recognised that both women and men had to fulfil their roles according to middle-class gender norms established as general norms in the West during the eighteenth and nineteenth centuries. Feminist, women's and gender historians thus had an incredibly rich historical field to investigate, and over the decades the canvas has become much more colourful than it was in the 1960s. Having said that, much of this work (see Chapter 5) was strongly linked to identitarian concerns. The same is true of sexual identities: here the rise of LGBTI (lesbian, gay, bisexual, transsexual and intersexual)[32] histories was massively in line with strengthening LGBTI identities. Once again many of the histories emphasised long periods of discrimination and persecution, whilst at the same time highlighting the agency of people with LGBTI identities. As Leila Rupp wrote in a book which she hoped would help put LGBTI history into the history curricula in higher education: 'For contemporary students who identify as transgender or genderqueer, knowing this history can go a long way toward fostering self-acceptance and, we hope, creating a more acceptable environment.'[33]

In the left-wing political atmosphere of the 1960s and 1970s, attempts to highlight minority and oppressed identities coincided with a far more critical attitude towards apologetic national history writing and a more trenchant critique of colonialism and imperialism. The latter built on the reception of anti-colonial and postcolonial historical writing that, since the late nineteenth century, had emanated from both the colonial peripheries and its centres. Franz Fanon's *Wretched of the Earth*, first published in 1961 (in French), became a classic of socialist revolutionary anti-colonial literature and set the tone for a strong link between anti-colonial as well as postcolonial identities and historical writing. It would eventually lead to a questioning of Western understandings of history. Fanon had already written: 'So, comrades, let us not pay tribute to Europe by creating states, institutions, and societies that draw their inspiration from it.'[34] However, history writing, as it was practised in the West, had been a very successful colonial export in the nineteenth century and first half of the twentieth. Colonial powers set up academies and universities in their colonies and imported Western sciences, including the 'science' of history.[35] Japan, which became a colonial power in the first half of the twentieth century and is often referred to as 'West in the East', adapted from the West what it regarded as the core of modernity. In terms of history writing, it learnt from the West, in particular from the German schools of historical writing considered to be the most advanced in the world before 1914.[36]

Learning from the West, however, did not mean copying it. Rather, it took the form of adapting in a multitude of different ways Western practices and ideas. Here we should think not so much of countries that export vs. those that import, but rather of circulations and mutual influences. We can observe the strong link between identitarian politics and historical writing in many of these forms of colonial and postcolonial history writing. Japanese imperialism and hypernationalism in the first half of the twentieth century did, after all, underpin much historical writing.[37] The anti-colonial struggle was likewise strengthened by a good deal of historical writing that took up and adapted the language of historiographical nationalism from the West. Anti-colonial historians tied historical writing to national independence struggles and decolonisation. In Africa, for example, history was explicitly written to give newly decolonised states self-confidence and pride. As Martin S. Shanguhija and Toyin Falola have written: 'There was a need to furnish Africa and Africans with a historiography that gave purpose and meaning to former colonial subjects and their newfound sense of belonging.'[38] Where anti-colonial struggles were infused by left-wing ideologies, class narratives united with national(ist) narratives, just as they had done in left-wing class historiographies in the West. In the course of the twentieth century a globalised historical profession came into being imbued with the core principles of a Western understanding of history.

The rise of postcolonialism from the 1980s onwards, which figures in many subsequent chapters, has problematised these forms of Westernised universalisation without finding a solution to Dipesh Chakrabarty's famous statement that Western thought, whilst remaining 'indispensable', was at the same time 'inadequate'.[39] In its move from the margins of India and the postcolonial world to the metropolitan centres of academic knowledge production in the USA and Europe, postcolonialism has contributed much to the problematisation of Eurocentrism.[40] But it has also moved towards establishing a project primarily concerned with establishing cultural difference between the West and 'the rest'. In so doing it has at times lost sight of the other important project with which postcolonialism started, namely giving a voice to the subaltern classes in the postcolonial world. In the contemporary globalised world, their disadvantaged position continues. Moving them back to the centre of the postcolonial project requires renewed attention to developing the political economy without losing sight of the importance of establishing cultural differences.[41] In subsequent chapters I will attempt, where possible, to look beyond the borders of the West and incorporate non-Western historiographies. But, of course, many of the theoretical and conceptual underpinnings of histories I discuss still have Western origins. They were, after all, formulated in the centres of knowledge production in the West. A certain Western-centrism perhaps is unavoidable in our discussion.

Questioning Historiography's Link to the Building of Collective Identities: Developments in the Theory of History during the 1960s and 1970s

By the 1970s, historical writing was underpinning intersecting and intermingling collective identities. Since all collective identities are always situational, depending on context, sometimes one seemed more prominent than the other and was emphasised more in historical writing.[42] The critical national tradition that emerged in the West from the 1960s onwards questioned the link between nationalism and historical writing but was much more willing to accept a link between it and class consciousness. It tended to be strongly tied to an understanding of history as a form of Enlightenment drawing on Enlightenment traditions from the eighteenth century onwards.[43] It is no coincidence that one of Germany's foremost 'critical' historians, Jürgen Kocka, published one of his essay collections under the title 'History and Enlightenment'.[44] As I have argued above, Enlightenment history was itself infused with identitarian concerns, and most historians in the 1960s and 1970s retained this link. The only change was that their concern moved from nationalist concerns to a series of progressive political ones that had to do with the emancipation of hitherto oppressed identities, such as workers, women, the colonised and a whole range of minority ethnic and sexual identities.

Theorists of history who championed the link between enlightened progressive concerns and historical writing also tended to uphold the link between historical writing and the formation of collective identities. One of the most internationally prominent was the German philosopher of history, Jörn Rüsen. For him it was unthinkable to engage in historical writing without thinking about identity: 'The question of identity is a fundamental fact of human culture. It demands a response. Historical thinking is an essential medium for that response.'[45] Rüsen was very much aware of the strong link between identity, historical consciousness and ethnocentrism. Historical writing has constructed exclusionary mechanisms that created both an individual and a collective 'self' allegedly more valuable and worth more than the 'other'. In this fashion, historical consciousness served a range of inhumane ends. Yet there was, according to Rüsen, no way of escaping the question of identity. Hence he has spent decades developing a universal theory of humanism which would reconcile the values of a universal humanity with those of cultural diversity and difference.[46] The notion that there are elements of a universal human nature common to all cultures and civilisations is something that a small band of anthropologists, psychologists and even some historians have been exploring.[47] Positing an 'otherness' that does not necessarily deteriorate into inhumanity and co-exists with the re-affirmation of the value of all human beings is, for Rüsen, an identitarian theory entirely in line with Kantian Enlightenment philosophy of history.[48] It is undoubtedly a noble ideal for historians to aspire to and Rüsen's theory of history constitutes, in my view, the most developed and sophisticated theoretical frame for such an ideal of historical understanding and practice.

Rüsen is one of a range of thinkers who have gone in search of identities that do not depend on negative and often violent forms of 'othering'. Inspired by psychoanalysis, Jessica Benjamin, for example, has attempted to use intersubjective theory to argue that the self does not have to appear at the end of a process where the identity of 'self' splits itself off from the identity of 'others'. She defines the 'essence of intersubjective theory' thus: 'where objects were, subjects must be'. She finds solace in humanity's 'marvellous capacity for identification with others to either further or impede our recognition of others, to bridge or obfuscate differences between us'.[49] Of these two sides of 'identification', she underlines the need to develop the one that would allow identity to emerge from complex encounters with 'others', i.e. would in effect be based on a constructive and accepting engagement with 'others'. In her view, the mutual constitution of 'self' and 'other' is interrelated in an ongoing learning process that lies at the core of what she calls 'the intersubjective project'.[50] Following on from Benjamin, it is possible to argue that a better understanding of 'self' and 'other' in history requires a positionality that incorporates both. Historical writing would thus still be attached to identity-building, but in ways that incorporate rather than vilify 'the other' and that seek to learn from 'the other' in the hope of also learning something about the self. Things go wrong, according to Benjamin, when polarity replaces mutuality and a politics of domination twists the 'bonds of love' that otherwise hold humanity together. Much of her work is devoted to studying those 'bonds of love' which, she claims, have been distorted by the production of social orders that rest on hierarchies of nation, race, class and gender in which subjects adhering to one particular identity deny others other forms or inflections of identity. This is arguably in line with what

Rüsen has in mind when he talks about balancing the need for different identities with a tolerant universalist ethos. Historical writing based on crude essentialised definitions of 'self' and 'others' along a normative line that neatly separates 'self'-equals-good from 'others'-equals-bad would not be commensurate with such a universalist ethos.

Rüsen's work is an example of a line of thinking that maintains the link between historical writing and identity formation but seeks to counter the negative exclusivist, ethnocentrist and intolerant results produced in the past by that link. His enlightened cosmopolitan universalism is related to his adamant defence of the 'science' of history (*Wissenschaft*) that has rigorous methodological foundations which are universally valid, in order to allow for a meaningful discourse about the past to take place between and across different human cultures.[51] His theory of history rests on the understanding of a 'scientific history' which became dominant in the course of the nineteenth century. It is associated with the nineteenth-century German philosopher of history, Johann Gustav Droysen, who has been a source of great inspiration for Rüsen.[52] Rüsen's belief in the rationality of a universally valid historical reasoning makes him critical of those trends in the theory of history that challenge this belief, namely poststructuralism, narrativism, constructivism and postcolonialism.[53]

Ultimately, however, these developments in the theory of history shook the foundations of any historical 'scientificity', and they also reframed the long-established link between historical writing and the construction of collective identities.[54] Indeed, they have worked as a de facto challenge to Rüsen's cosmopolitan universalism. These developments have not been unitary; rather they have been associated with a range of theorists with very different concerns and understandings of history. These theorists are sometimes very inadequately lumped together under the label 'postmodernism'.[55] I shall avoid this label, wherever possible, as it is not helpful in understanding the differences and nuances existing between individual thinkers and as it has become a term of intellectual stereotyping used either to validate or to devalidate particular positions in historical theory.[56]

It is true that these theories share certain common characteristics. Thus, all of them were united by a new attention to language, which is why we find frequent references in the literature to 'discourse analysis' and the 'linguistic turn'.[57] But overall, as Ethan Kleinberg has pointed out, they also mark out quite distinct and often incompatible theoretical positions.[58] In relation to Jacques Derrida's project of deconstruction, Kleinberg argues that it has haunted history writing like a ghostly spectre and that he, more than any of the other theorists discussed here, has been declared by many historians, including those favourably inclined to many of the theoreticians subsequently discussed, as being incompatible with the project of history writing. Whilst I share Kleinberg's view of the more limited influence of Derrida on the historical profession in comparison with many of the other theorists discussed here, I would still maintain that, taken together, these theories have shifted the ground on which the historical profession stood until the 1970s. Many of the histories discussed in subsequent chapters were influenced either directly by those theorists or by a wide range of mediators in the historical profession who took up and popularised the ideas of those theorists and of those who subsequently built on them. Whilst most historians want to retain, for good reason I would say, a difference between 'history' and 'fiction',[59] they have, under the combined impact of those theories, become far more self-reflective about what is involved in the practice of writing history. In the remainder of this introduction, I illustrate how those theories challenged the scientificity of historical writing and its links to collective identity formation, and ultimately how they contributed to a more self-reflexive way of thinking about collective identities through the practice of writing history.

Let us start with Hayden White. (Figure 1.1.) White's depiction of historical writing as literature put a big question mark behind the 'scientificity' of historical practice. Other theorists of history had already stressed the link between historical writing and literature. Thus, for example, Siegfried Kracauer had argued that modernist literature, represented by Virginia Woolf and Marcel Proust, had shown historians how to find ways to tell stories about the past that were no longer linear and continuous.[60] But White went considerably further. If what went on in the past could no longer be reconstructed by historians as it had actually happened, to paraphrase Leopold von Ranke's famous quote, and if historians could only choose between different ways of narrating that past, then the scientific nature of the historical discipline, as it was still commonly understood in the 1960s and 1970s, was in grave doubt. According to White, historians choose to narrate their histories in different story forms related to diverse aesthetical and political ways of presenting the past. He distinguished

Figure 1.1 Hayden White (1928–2018), photograph taken at a conference in Göttingen, 2011. © Babette Tischleder.

four basic narrative forms: romantic, tragic, comic and satirical. The romantic form suits stories about the struggle between good and evil, the search for liberty, progress and heroes seeking to redeem themselves. The tragic form, in contrast, tends to focus on some kind of downfall and failure that often carries lessons for the readers of history. The comic form seeks to restore a certain harmony to the past by reconciling those forces that opposed each other, whilst the satirical form is the one chosen by the most pessimistic historians, who see no hope of learning from the past and instead emphasise the passing of time as mere repetition of the same processes. In these narratives, human beings are deemed incapable of shaping historical processes and are primarily their victims.[61] The bottom line of White's famous *Metahistory* is that the same story can be told in different forms and it will then carry different messages and meanings. Historians, in other words, cannot make any 'objective' statements about the past, as all statements are related to metahistorical assumptions about the nature of historical reality.[62]

Different ways of narrating a story can be related to different perspectives on history.[63] Chris Lorenz has argued that truth claims are interpretative and revisable within rational scientific discourse. A 'fact' only exists within a specific framework of description and presupposes normative choices. This makes for a possible plurality of true statements without reducing a scientific statement to its functional uses in politics. The nature of all historical knowledge is ultimately perspectival.[64] Lorenz in this way tries to rescue 'scientific history' by integrating White's thinking on narrativity, normativity and relativity of historical thinking into an understanding of the past that goes beyond historians' traditional truth claims.[65] He underlines how fruitful White's rediscovery of literary and rhetorical aspects in the writing of history were. Whilst also confirming the importance of recognising the narrative structures of historical arguments, he is adamant that it did not necessarily follow that history amounted to yet another fiction. What still marks out historical writing is the intention to persuade audiences that its representation of the past is truthful. A number of disciplinary factors have indeed prevented historians from just inventing the past.[66] Ever since White began publishing on the narrative foundations of historical writing, theories of narrativity have blossomed and have made historians more attentive to the narrative structures of their own historical writing.[67] He has also inspired others to develop their own theories of narrativity. Frank Ankersmit, for example, has been particularly influential in developing a narrativist philosophy of history that has been widely discussed in the theory of history.[68]

Even if considerable confusion regarding diverse concepts of narrative and their application to the analysis of historical writing still persists,[69] diverse theories of narrativity have nevertheless led to a rethinking of the 'scientificity' of historical practice. They have also increased the awareness that historians have a choice in how they narrate their particular histories. That choice has to do with aesthetics, normative values and politics.[70] Choosing to narrate a history in support of a particular identity becomes an exercise in constructing that identity rather than presuming that this identity is rooted in the past and therefore essential, unchangeable and continuous. Knowing this will make for a practice of historical writing that is aware of the constructed nature of all such writing and will therefore also lead to a higher self-reflexivity about the link between the practice of the historian and the promotion of particular collective identities. White's concept of the 'practical past', which he elucidated in his last collection of essays, seeks to establish through history writing an ethical discourse about the past that has meaning in contemporary debates.[71] History writing, according to White, should neither be antiquarian, in the Nietzschean sense,[72] nor be pursuing unethical aims. White was, throughout his life, an intensely political scholar pursuing a wide range of broadly progressive political agendas which he no doubt deemed to be in line with an ethical discourse about the past. But those agendas, discourses and histories ultimately, for him, always were a matter of aesthetics, political stance and normative choice rather than rooted in the past itself.[73]

Historians have undoubtedly been guilty of both charges – antiquarianism and a lack of ethics. There is no shortage of examples of historians who have written history either for its own sake or in the interests of unethical causes. Indeed, in his book *The Writing of History*, first published in French in 1975, Michel de Certeau, the theorist of everyday life,[74] linked historical writing firmly to the legitimation of political power and highlighted in particular its usefulness in justifying forms of colonialism. It can write indigenous populations out of history by denying them any form of agency.[75] In many instances historians were paid to narrate their histories in a particular narrative mode. In others they did so out of personal conviction. History writing, de Certeau noted, went on in many different places and was related to many different ambitions in society. Hence it always came in the plural. Historians worked from traces left from the past. Turning them into documents, historians manipulated them according to certain rules of the profession, using language and narrative to create facts out of the materials of the past. De Certeau's conclusions, just as White's, point to the need to problematise the ways in which historical writing served political and often identitarian causes. De Certeau's own history writing, some of which will be discussed in Chapter 6, always underlined the importance of studying 'practices'. In that he echoed the work of Bourdieu, discussed below. De Certeau was interested in linking practices of everyday life to the creativeness and inventiveness of human beings when it came to giving meaning to their lives, which they partly did through the construction of identities. Out of a given repertoire of cultural meanings, they re-appropriated and re-contextualised older practices with their associated meanings and produced new ones. They were often used as strategies of social groups to position themselves vis-à-vis others in the struggle for better material resources and more freedom. De Certeau's work, like White's, thus also points to the political orientations towards the past.[76]

As regards the long-standing identitarian concerns of historical writing, I would like to posit here that re-appropriations of culture for the construction of social identities, like an ethical discourse about the past, involve a high degree of self-reflexivity about that link between the practice of historical writing and identity formation. That link does not necessarily have to be given up, but historians should ask themselves how their practice is related to collective identity formation in the contemporary world. Furthermore, theories of narrativity make it necessary to accept the validity of different positions with regard to constructions of collective identity through history. It is not a matter of establishing one position 'truthfully' through science. Rather, historians, in formulating different positions, take part in political debates and conflicts that result in agonistic forms of politics, where political adversaries, who accept each other as such and are willing to stay within democratic political frameworks, formulate different competitive visions about the future of societies – on the basis of their understanding of the past.[77] Identitarian concerns are part and parcel of such political conflicts, but they are a matter of choice and construction. They undergo historical change, rather than being an integral and essential, non-changeable and permanent part of who we are as human beings.

Some historical theorists, who follow White, such as Kalle Pihlainen, have argued that choosing a narrative does not lie in the historical subject itself but in a kind of Sartrean 'decisionism'. The author decides to frame a historical story in a particular mode that fits his or her normative predilections and politics.[78] Such a position does contribute to a genuine pluralisation of the historical profession and highlights the links between particular versions of the past and choices in contemporary politics. If we feel uncomfortable about ending up on the wilder shores of relativity about the past, Imre Lakatos' theory of sophisticated falsification may help us. It acknowledges that the testing of 'facts' always boils down to comparing *collections* of theories *with each other* (that he called 'scientific research programmes'). Hence it might come as a useful corrective of reducing the historical sciences to a mere choice between different narratives linked to different politics. And yet the corrective has its own internal limits. As philosophers of science, such as Paul Feyerabend and Imre Lakatos have pointed out, it is impossible in principle to say that something is obviously false.[79] Hence, we are left in a situation where 'sophisticated falsification' might help us avoid the worst cases of historical relativism, but we also have to recognise that in many cases, it does not present a magic way out of the possibility of casting most histories in different narratives and diverse interpretations. Marek Tamm has argued that any claims to truth and objectivity are rooted not in the texts produced by historians but in the communicative relationship between the historians and their audiences. A 'truth pact' (Tamm) between the historians and their readers acknowledges that truth claims no longer correspond to historical reality. Instead they are mediated by a disciplinary consensus on methods of inquiry, cognitive values and epistemic virtues that allow for a rational quality control of historical works.[80]

Relating these thoughts on the limits of relativism to the concern with the question of the relationship between historical writing and collective identity formation, we can insist, with Chris Lorenz, first, on the deep relationship between historical representations and constructions of identity. Secondly, we can insist on the feasibility and legitimacy of developing several perspectives on the evolution of historical identities, and, thirdly, we can underline the relationship of such different perspectives to political choices made by historians that are related to their own positionality and (self-constructed) identity. Whilst these choices are never determined by the evidence, they are, in Lorenz's argument, restricted by the evidence and respect for the evidence has to remain at the heart of the professional self-understanding of historical practice.[81] This insight into the restrictive role of evidence, however, offers no basis for claims regarding the objectivity of historical writing but only to an acceptance of the positionality of all historical writing, which rules out the formulation of essentialised collective identities through historical writing. Where there are only different positions, there cannot be an essence.

White's emphasis on language and narrative as constituting and arranging the past is shared by Michel Foucault's insistence that history amounts to a discursive construction that is itself based on discursive practices in the past.[82] (Figure 1.2.) The past cannot be retrieved through historical writing. The languages of the past are related to power relationships that determine not only what remains of the past but also how to frame what remains into discursive formations. Foucault's various historical explorations into the relationship between knowledge and power showed up time and again how individuals were subjected to dominance by states and/or other individuals or groups.[83]

Figure 1.2 Michel Foucault (1926–84). © Bettman Collection, Getty Images.

Power relationships, according to Foucault, were productive of 'reality'.[84] Knowledge forms, called epistemes by Foucault, created over time particular social orders and power hierarchies which, in turn, determined what was sayable about the past. In *The Order of Things*, first published in French in 1966, he distinguishes between three epistemes: the Renaissance, the Classical and the Modern episteme, each with its defined time line: 1450–1650, 1650–1800, 1800 to his present.[85] According to Foucault, historical writing has to be about the recovery of plural readings of the past. An archaeology of the past is committed to uncovering those perspectives that have hitherto been dispossessed and powerless. Critical history writing has to be about decentring the past and leaving no privileged centre.[86] If the past is a construction hiding different perspectives and power relationships, then there cannot be a truthful reconstruction of the past. Instead we are left with a plurality of stories that have meaning for those engaging in the establishment of or challenge to epistemic knowledge. Foucault's work demonstrates how the discursive formation of identities could be both the source of oppression and the means of liberation. In any case, constructions of identities through language were never innocent but always connected to the strivings for power. Not surprising, therefore,

Foucault posits that 'the purpose of history, guided by genealogy, is not to discover the roots of our identity, but to commit itself to its dissipation'.[87] Foucault's work, like that of White, can be read less as a call to challenge the relationship between collective identity formation and historical writing and more as an invitation to pluralise it and make it more self-reflective, and thereby to destabilise and ultimately explode it. Overall, then, history writing is related either to constructing or deconstructing identities for a whole range of different subjectivities, battling for the discursive high ground and ultimately for power – once again, I would add, ideally in an agonistic democratic political frame.

Understanding history writing as a political battleground, where historians choose a past in order to frame a vision for the future, reveals the normative choices on which our interpretations of the past are based. At the same time, it avoids the kind of essentialisation of identity that we have already discussed above in relation to national history, national identity and a whole host of other collective identities. Such essentialisation has in the past led to the establishment of grand narratives. These have always been related to power. It was Jean-François Lyotard who, in his seminal *The Postmodern Condition*, published in 1979 in the French original, criticised the 'grand narratives' of Western modernity and called for the abandonment of any attempts to construct all-encompassing universal theories of knowledge. Instead, he suggested a multiplicity of different discourses, all with their own rationality and normativity.[88] Many professional historians, in following a more self-reflective practice, have subsequently become wary of contributing to the 'grand narratives' analysed by Lyotard. The overall tendency to deconstruct 'grand narratives' rather than construct them demonstrates how historians, under the impact of thinkers such as Lyotard, White and Foucault, have become increasingly attentive to the ways in which histories have underpinned particular power and knowledge regimes.[89]

Theories of social constructivism, not necessarily related to White and Foucault, had a similar effect. They mostly referred back to a seminal publication by Peter L. Berger and Thomas Luckmann rather than anything penned by narrativists or poststructuralists.[90] Nowhere has this arguably been more the case than in the realm of national identities. Under the impact of the important publications of Eric Hobsbawm, Terence Ranger and Benedict Anderson, generations of scholars of nationalism have examined the diverse ways in which national identities have in the past been constructed and reconstructed. Studies of how traditions have been invented and communities imagined have gone a long way towards deconstructing the mythologies of national essences.[91]

Guided by yet another methodological and theoretical perspective very different from those adopted by narrativism, discourse analysis and constructivism, some of the theoretical insights of the French sociologist Pierre Bourdieu have also contributed to the greater self-reflexivity of historians about the relationship of their work to the construction of collective identities. Bourdieu's theory of 'cultural reproduction' has highlighted how a particular group, in his case the French bourgeoisie, managed to strengthen its dominant position in society without appearing to be biased in the way that societal controls of advancement operate. Members of particular social groups and, by implication, their identities reproduce social hierarchies through mechanisms and institutions which at first sight seem to be autonomous. Bourdieu's concept of 'habitus' has drawn attention to everyday practices through which those social hierarchies are reproduced. These practices are rooted in ideas and values, but also in physical and bodily functions. Together, they establish which public behaviour is preferred in particular societies.[92] The 'habitus' in particular 'fields'[93] establishes who is successful and who is not. In Bourdieu's thinking the 'habitus' is related to particular forms of 'capital'. Thus, he speaks of 'cultural capital', 'social capital', 'symbolical capital'. This capital can be invested by individuals and social groups in order to gain social advantages. They may even use it strategically in order to achieve processes of 'distinction'. Social identities, Bourdieu argues, are rooted in such 'distinctions', which are constructed by members of social groups in order to achieve a comparative advantage in relation to other social groups.[94] Especially in the new cultural history that came to the fore in history writing during the 1980s (see Chapter 4), Bourdieu's emphasis on the examination of practices that reveal how social groups have constituted social identities in a way that gave them a comparative advantage in society has had a major influence on historians.[95] In contrast, grand narratives about those social groups and their identities, to which historians contributed, have been very good at hiding the processes by which they achieved or at the very least aspired to social power.

Grand narratives related to collective identities veer towards closure. They have a beginning, and evolve towards an end, which may lie in the future. The work of Mikhail Bakhtin takes issue with such linear conceptions of history. His concept of 'unfinalisability', when applied to history, leads to a re-affirmation of the open-endedness of the past.[96] (See Figure 1.3.) In his view, the historical dialogue about the meaning of the past for the present stays forever open and can never be finalised. Dialogues about the past between different subject positions create a polyphony of voices and any understanding of the past needs to be based on this polyphony which is itself the product of a multitude of perspectives and identities. Bakhtin's polyphonic concept of truth emphasises the need to engage with and address different voices from those that are one's own, since an understanding of the past can only be reached through an open-ended dialogue with other voices.[97] Bakhtin's emphasis on heteroglossia, i.e. the primacy of context over text, as well as his insistence on the hybrid nature of language (polyglossia), further relativises truth statements of grand narratives and contributes to a greater self-reflexivity on the part of practising historians.[98] Any text, Bakhtin argues, can only be properly understood in relation to other texts that engage with it. Such intertextuality is, according to Bakhtin, the basis of voice-creation, and the possible number of voices emerging from texts in conversation with other texts is potentially

Figure 1.3 Mikhail Bakhtin (1895–1975). © The History Collection/Alamy Stock Foto.

innumerable.[99] History as an open-ended dialogue rather than a grand narrative aiming at closure is an idea that has further contributed to distancing historians from simple identitarian projects. The polyphony of voices, if taken seriously, de-essentialises the relationship between writing history and constructing collective identities and makes it a matter of political and moral choice.

Although Bakhtin was more concerned with literature than with history, his theoretical insights also have influenced historians. The same is true of Roland Barthes whose famous article on 'the death of the author', first published in 1968, questioned the received wisdom that a text reflected its author's intentions.[100] Instead, Barthes argued that the author's main tool, language, created such a multitude of meanings that, together with the impossibility of knowing the author's mind at the time of writing, it was impossible to reconstruct any one 'truthful' meaning that the author had intended. If meaning was no longer located in the author, Barthes concluded, it must be located in the readers whose textual analyses produce multiple meanings. Such plurality in effect made any text 'reversible', i.e. it could be read in different and even contradictory ways. It was all a question of interpretation.[101]

Bakhtin's insistence on 'polyphony', 'unfinalisability', 'heteroglossia' and 'polyglossia' as well as Barthes' championing of multiple meanings and multiple interpretations, although hugely different, chimed rather well with a tradition in historical writing that has always been sceptical about the claims made by historism[102] and positivism as to objectivity, emphasising instead the relativism of all historical knowledge. The American historians Charles Beard and Carl Becker are good examples of this. Both championed highly pragmatic attitudes towards the past viewing it from their present. They emphasised its practical value in giving orientation in the present whilst upholding the possibility of different positions both in the present and vis-à-vis the past.[103] Marc Bloch in his magisterial *The Historian's Craft* argued that history was all about understanding the present: 'This faculty of understanding the living, is, in very truth, the master quality of the historian.'[104] They all thus preceded E. H. Carr's famous call, echoing Benedetto Croce, that one should understand all historical writing as contemporary history, since historians always re-interpreted the past from their own standpoints in the present.[105] The philosopher of history Artur Danto had claimed, as early as the 1960s, that all narratives about the past are organised according to the historian's perspective, as this is inevitably rooted in the present. This perspectivalism of historical knowledge, in his view, makes it necessary to understand all historical sentences as provisional and open towards the future.[106] Historical writing could draw also on those traditions of perspectival relativism that ultimately fed into the same anti-essentialist stances about collective identity alluded to by Bakhtin and Barthes.

Jacques Lacan and Jacques Derrida were other important theorists whose writings aimed at undermining the promotion of fixed and essential collective identities through historical writing. Lacan combined the linguistics of Ferdinand de Saussure and Freudian psychoanalysis to arrive at the conclusion that identities are based on an illusion. Lacanian psychoanalysis was fundamentally concerned with destroying the notion of the possibility of fixed identities.[107] From here it was but a short step to Derrida's 'deconstruction' of what he called general 'god terms', such as Reason, Nature or Identity – concepts that are allegedly eternal, unchanging and true. They needed to be deconstructed by introducing what Derrida called 'différance', i.e. the recognition that meaning can only be attributed to something within a wider context of meanings in the plural. His method of deconstruction sought to read texts as sites of contestation and struggle in which a hierarchy of meaning was imposed that could never entirely eradicate alternative meanings, as dominant meanings already always contained their binary opposites. From this dispersed nature of meaning follows that concepts such as 'collective identity' can never be entirely identical with themselves but instead they are caught in a system of differences which decentre the concepts themselves. 'God terms', Derrida argued, include binary oppositions, in the case of collective identity, the opposition between 'self' and 'other'. He underlined the falseness of such binary oppositions and instead pointed to the simple fact that the opposite always is already part of the overall phenomenon. In describing the 'self', we have to assume a range of 'others'. Derrida ultimately concludes that deconstruction is liberating us from the logocentrism of modernity and setting us free to define and normativise the world around us. This, however, can never only be done in one way, so that the political process consists of several ways of doing this that are competing with each other.[108] Related to collective identities it means they only come in the plural and are undergoing permanent change in their constitution and meaning. According to Ethan Kleinberg, 'the unheimlich realization that history and identity are moving targets is revealed by [Derridaean] deconstruction'.[109] Kleinberg himself has argued how useful deconstruction is for historical practice, even if he would be the first to admit that of all the theories unduly lumped together under the label of postmodernism, Derrida's ideas were deemed to be most unsuitable for historical practice and hence had far less influence than those of Foucault.[110]

Nevertheless, Lacan's and Derrida's, just as Foucault's, undermining of the concept of collective identity has had a huge impact on an array of influential feminist theorists, including Julia Kristeva, Hélène Cixous and Judith Butler, whose work, especially that of Butler, amounted to a radical rejection of essentialised forms of gender identities (see Chapter 5). Butler argued that gender identity was ultimately a fiction, constructed for a particular political purpose.[111] Lacan, Derrida and Foucault also inspired many postcolonial thinkers on the issue of collective identity. Thus, Edward Said, often regarded as a founding figure in postcolonial studies, was deeply concerned about the construction of homogenised reductive collective identities which used binary oppositions to stereotype and exclude 'the other' from identity discourses. He also produced powerful counter-narratives to such exclusionary identitarian discourses, identifying, as is well known, with the Palestinian cause in the Middle East. Exploring ways in which humans could live in tolerant forms of co-existence that acknowledge the heterogeneity of possible identitarian choices was something that haunted many of his writings. As he famously put it:

> I think the one thing that I find, I guess, the most – I wouldn't say repellent but I would say antagonistic – for me is identity. The notion of a single identity. And so multiple identity, the polyphony of many voices playing off against each other, without, as I say, the need to reconcile them, just to hold them together, is what my work is all about.[112]

Another important postcolonial thinker who dealt with the issue of collective identities was Homi Bhabha. His notion of 'hybridity', when applied to collective identity, meant that identities were always to be seen as 'hybrids' that already incorporated parts of the 'other' into the 'self' – especially in colonial and postcolonial constructions of identity.[113]

Not only gender and postcolonial discourses on collective identity took their cue from Lacan, Derrida and Foucault; so, too, did those concerned with the waning of class identities. Here the work of Ernesto Laclau and Chantal Mouffe was particularly important. In the 1980s they began to argue that a social identity such as class was as 'unfixed' as all collective identities. Class, they insisted, cannot be captured in terms of an essence but only in terms of discursive fields in which different political factions struggle for hegemony – a term Laclau and Mouffe adapted from the works of the Italian Marxist theoretician, Antonio Gramsci.[114] The ongoing deconstruction of essentialised forms of identity in gender, postcolonial and social theory led some theorists, such as Stuart Hall, to argue that it would make sense to replace the language of identity, which always veered towards essentialisms, with the language of identification. The latter, according to Hall, allowed more self-reflection about the constructed and fluid nature of collective identities and their utilisation as political tools designed to achieve specific aims and objectives at certain historical junctures.[115] His search for a non-essentialist strategic identity politics made constructions of collective identity temporary and changeable phenomena brought into being through discursive practices. Collective identities are themselves the site of multiple and contradictory struggles and therefore always already fragmented. Culture, for him, is the realm in which these struggles over meaning are carried out and by which humans attempt to make sense of the social world.[116]

This chipping away at discourses of identity led to the emergence of historical work that severely questioned the analytical usefulness of the concept of identity. Thus, for example, Frederick Cooper and Rogers Brubaker criticised collective identity discourses, arguing they reified essentialised collectives then taken for granted as really existing phenomena that have an agency of their own.[117] For his part, the German historian Lutz Niethammer has traced the usage of collective identity discourses back to fascist and communist ideologues of the interwar period, arguing that identity is an extremely vague analytical category which also has dubious political credentials.[118] Even if Cooper, Brubaker and Niethammer have not really been influenced by the likes of Lacan and Derrida, their indictment of identity discourses certainly helped sharpen the scepticism of historians towards such discourses. Chris Lorenz has spoken about a 'great divide' between scholars sceptical about 'collective identity' and those wanting to make use of it politically and analytically. He himself proposes an inbetween position that would continue to use notions of 'collective identity', both analytically and politically, but with the proviso that we should not think of collective identities as having absolute power over groups or possessing essences that members of the group cannot escape. Collective identities would then be binding upon group members only to a degree and would always be available in the plural. Seen in this way, we have, I would argue, already arrived at highly self-reflective, anti-essentialist and pluralistic usages of identity discourses. One can agree with Chris Lorenz, who pleads for using the concept of collective identity 'as political subjects and as analysts of the past and present'.[119]

The very different bodies of theory associated with theories of narrativism, re-appropriation, discourse analysis, historical archaeology, constructivism, historical relativism practice theory, heteroglossia, the reversibility of meaning, deconstruction, hybridity, hegemony and ideas around identification have all, in hugely different ways, contributed to a more self-reflective historical practice on the part of professional historians. It has encouraged historians to deconstruct the relationship between historical practice and collective identity formation rather than contribute to its construction. At the very least, it has led to more self-reflexive and plural ways of constructing collective identities through histories. Rather than promoting collective identities, the 'new histories' that emerged in the wake of the historical theories discussed above problematise them, as will be shown in subsequent chapters. These 'new histories' are far more willing to accept rival historical narratives underpinning different constructions of collective identities that are often related to specific political projects. Rather than essentialising collective identity, they are insisting on the constructed nature of these identities that are related to normative values.

Elsewhere I have described such genuine pluralisation of perspectives as 'happy ecclecticism'.[120] It has had implications for the pluralisation of methods in historical writing. When social historians of the 1960s and 1970s were fighting against political historians for dominance within the historical discipline, they often argued with Thomas Kuhn that science progresses through a series of paradigm changes.[121] As one paradigm rises, another declines. According to Kuhn, several paradigms can exist next to each other; a paradigm only becomes hegemonic when its enemies fail to attract a new generation of scholars.

Nevertheless, Kuhn's notion can easily be instrumentalised as a theory of scientific progress in which a more progressive school replaces another, more backward one. Whilst this would amount to a banalisation of his theory, it has at times been used in this way by those who wanted to establish their kind of history as the only legitimate new form of history. A good example of this is the Bielefeld school of social history in Germany. It used Kuhn to argue that social history had replaced political history as the new paradigm which allegedly had become the only way of doing history in the 1970s.[122] Declaring one paradigm the dominant one thus served the purpose of repressing all others. It was an exercise that was bound to fail, but only after much acrimonious debate. Cultural history and everyday life history/history from below were the first to challenge social history's new-found dominance, and subsequently a proliferation of historical turns has led to a multiplicity of different approaches to the past. The visual turn, the spatial turn, memory history, material culture history, conceptual history – these are just some of the 'new histories' that have been prominent since the 1990s and are still enriching the historical field today. We will discuss later their perspectives and narrativisations of the past in relation to the construction of collective identities. Indeed, the present book can be read as an introduction to these 'new histories'. Discussions of them will, however, be guided throughout by the core argument of this volume, namely that they are based on a more self-reflective relationship between historical writing and collective identity formation.

The Impact of Theories of History on the Historical Profession and the Structure of the Book

Of course, it is important not to overemphasise the role of theories in the writing of history. Historians often remain wary of theory. The historical profession is still characterised by a strong empirical bent.[123] If anything, we have seen a return to empiricism in recent years, although, as Gabrielle Spiegel has pointed out, there is no need to posit an antinomy between empiricism and theories of narrativism, constructionism and the linguistic turn.[124] With regard to theory, historians are bricoleurs who use theories in eclectic ways.[125] But my argument here is not about theory per se. Instead I would like to propose that the wide-ranging theoretical perspectives discussed in this introduction have percolated down to the practice of historical writing in manifold ways.[126] Practising historians, like Peter C. Hoffer, have given much attention to what he memorably called the historians' paradox.[127] Historians, under the impact of developments in the philosophy of history, could no longer claim that they were in possession of the truth, but in a world of fake news it was all the more urgent to look for ways of verifying what had been going on in the past. Hence Hoffer, in his book, provides a 'philosophy of history for working historians'[128] that may be able to square the circle and allow for the study of history as the basis of arguments about the past. Overall, I hope to show in this volume that working historians, influenced by some of the theories discussed in this chapter, have pluralised our understanding of the past, both in its methods and its content, and by making it more self-reflexive about its relationship to the construction of collective identities.

Whilst only a minority of practising historians have ever studied the historical thinkers mentioned above, their ideas have still been discussed in the wider historical profession thanks to a huge variety of theory primers and popularisers of their thought. In this way, their ideas have become influential among historians. In a widely discussed manifesto entitled *Theses on Theory and History*, the theorists of history Ethan Kleinberg, Joan Wallach Scott and Gary Wilder have called on historians to abandon the long-standing dominance of empiricist and positivist positions. A closer connection between theory and historical practice, they argue, would lead to a 'critical history' – one seeking to intervene much more actively in contemporary society.[129] In my view historians have already gone a long way further down this road than Kleinberg, Scott and Wilder have been willing to recognise. Thus, for example, few historians nowadays would claim that language is a mirror reflecting social reality. Instead, it is widely seen as contributing in a major way to constituting and constructing that reality.[130] Kleinberg, Scott and Wilder surely are right in appealing to historians to be more receptive to historical theory. Yet I would argue that they underestimate the degree to which a considerable number of practising historians have already been influenced by theory. This book reviews the work of some of those who have certainly taken theoretical perspectives on board, albeit often not wholesale but rather as bricoleurs using theory to make sense of their empirical material. The extent to which the past is constructed is still hotly contested, but that an element of construction is part of historical writing today is very widely accepted among historians. Whilst few historians have bought wholesale the historical thinking of theorists of history discussed in this introduction, many have come to appreciate the anti-essentialist aspirations of their work. Their thinking undermined foundationalist stories framed around master narratives of nation, race, class or religion.[131] The radical insistence on the many histories rather than the one has helped highlight the positionality of any author and to make all readings of the past, by their very nature, provisional.[132] It also feeds into discussions about an 'ontological turn' in the historical sciences, enabling them to escape from the Western-centrism of historism and allowing for a racial historisation of different non-Western worlds and different non-modern worlds within the West. Such an 'ontological turn', as Greg Anderson has argued, encourages a pluralisation of historical understanding that is 'more ethically defensible, more theoretically robust and more historically meaningful.'[133]

Overall, then, an increasing body of historical work has problematised the strong link between historical writing and collective identity formation that has been a legacy of historical writing for a very long time and had been strengthened by the growing scientificity of the historical discipline in the nineteenth century. Today, as the subsequent pages will show, much historical writing is devoted to deconstructing collective identities and demonstrating why certain of those identities were forged and how they have changed over time. Historians now stress the instability of collective identities and their essential contestedness. They promote themselves as critical commentators on historical cultures and regard it as their task to explode the certainties and clear-drawn boundaries of collective identities. Instead, they seek to introduce ambiguities, contradictions and uncertainties. And even where historians are still engaged in bolstering identities, as in gender history, black history and indigenous history, they do so with a far more self-reflexive positionality. They explain how and why they promote not essentialised and non-changing, but constructed and evolving forms of 'identification' (in Hall's sense) that have often been oppressed in the past and are therefore in need of being strengthened. Building on the work of the theorists discussed in this chapter, gender, black, indigenous and other historians who relate their histories to ongoing struggles for emancipation, on balance, have, on the whole, avoided socio-biological essentialisms that would root a politics of identity in an essentialised experience that is biologically given and that would argue that only someone who is a woman, black or indigenous can know what it is like to be that identity and therefore only they have a right to write their histories. Such a politics of identity has no doubt built powerful social movements in the past, but it makes for poor history, as knowledge is not rooted in physique, and categories of difference, such as class, race, gender and nation, should not result in a denial of the possibility to produce knowledge about those categories from outside its ascriptions. Laura Lee Downs has argued that deconstruction and postmodernism have helped such attempts at hermetically sealed identity politics by showing how every text is ultimately indeterminate and undecidable, and she has looked for different epistemological grounds on which to deny such identity politics and historiographies that underpin it.[134] Whilst her discussion of Jessica Benjamin and Carolyn Steedman should be seen as a welcome correction to the wilder shores of identity politics, her work nevertheless still builds on poststructuralist insights and much of the body of theories discussed above.

I see her text as being fundamentally different from the problematisation of identity politics conducted by Francis Fukuyama. He attacked such politics in order to call for a return to national master narratives that would underpin an alleged national consensus.[135] Fukuyama, like Downs, is critical of forms of identity politics that demand privileged treatment of one particular group over others. He criticises the adherents to identity politics for drawing tight boundaries around 'their' particular group and for only allowing its members to participate in a discourse about the group. This made communication between groups near-impossible. However, his conclusion to do away with such identity politics and instead return to an alleged overriding concern for national cohesion and unity would simply return us to the regimes of discrimination and silencing of marginal groups that gave rise to identity politics in the first place. It intends to veil again what has been unveiled, namely the power relationships that make our societies unequal. It is a right-wing attempt to re-install the dominance of old white heterosexual men over all those groups, black people, ethnic minorities, LGBTI groups, women and the socially disadvantaged, who have been fighting for recognition by constructing their identities. As I have argued above, with reference to Stuart Hall, the concept of 'identification' is a useful one to avoid essentialising and totalising identities without throwing the baby out with the bath water. It opens the path towards a self-reflective and playful, open and dialogic construction of collective identities that thinks of the other as an adversary to be engaged with rather than an enemy to be eliminated. It also would allow the writing of histories that supported self-reflective constructions of collective identities in the pursuit of specific emancipatory agendas.

There have, of course, also been significant resistances to such a changing self-understanding of the historical profession. Many members of the historical profession across the globe still regard themselves as prophets of the nation or guardians of other specific collective identities, be they those of religion, class, race, gender or particular sub- or transnational forms of spatial collective identities. Where professional historians have abandoned the quest for essentialised forms of identity formation, they have often simply been replaced by 'amateurs', i.e. authors working not as professional historians, but often as independent authors, journalists or publicists. Nevertheless, I think that we can observe an overarching trend in the history of historiography over the past forty years – a move towards a history which understands itself as a radical critique of the idea and politics of collective identities and which seeks to move to greater levels of self-reflection about the constructed nature of such identities. This has been visible over a wide range of sub-fields that have developed since the 1980s. I will review those in subsequent chapters. The next three chapters will be about forms of historical writing that preceded the watershed theoretical developments of the 1960s and 1970s, such as political history, social and economic history and cultural history. The following six chapters will be about some of the most important new sub-fields that have emerged since the 1980s, starting off with gender history and moving to historical anthropology, memory history, conceptual history, the visual turn and material culture history all the way to transnational approaches to history writing and the recent success of global history. Throughout I will look at how different conceptualisations of history have problematised the relationship between historical writing and collective identity formation. At the same time the chapters of this book can and should also be read as introductions to particular subfields of historical writing that have been prominent over recent years.

I do, however, want to end this introduction by being myself watchful not to construe an all-too Whiggish history of historiography, i.e. one which postulates a forward march of history writing towards greater self-reflexivity and a happy eclecticism. I have already referred to the ongoing pursuit – albeit increasingly not by professional historians – of constructing identities through histories. There has also been no shortage of historians sceptical, critical and downright denunciatory of the theories I have been discussing here.[136] Furthermore, new turns and developments in historical writing are as certain as the Amen is in church. The multi-directionality of historiography that has been its key characteristic in the past will also be a key feature in the future. As Geoff Eley has written in his engaging story of the development of historical writing during his lifetime: 'I see absolutely no reason why the "cultural turn" should be the end of the story or the final chapter in some whiggish romance of ever-improving historiographical sophistication. Something else, I'm sure, is lying in wait.'[137] What I trace in the subsequent pages of this book is just one trend visible in some of the historical writing that forms the totality of historical writing today. I happen to believe that it is one that historians, or those who train to become historians, should take note of and build on, but undoubtedly many among my colleagues would disagree. For me an adherence to anti-essentialism and to greater self-reflexivity about the link between historical writing and collective identity formation does indeed make for histories that are less poisonous and murderous and are therefore more capable of fostering historical learning. In this sense my book is based on a normative choice about what history should be about.

Further Reading

Stefan Berger (with Christoph Conrad), *The Past as History: National Identity and Historical Consciousness in Modern Europe*, Basingstoke: Palgrave Macmillan, 2015.

Stefan Berger, Heiko Feldner and Kevin Passmore (eds.), *Writing History: Theory and Practice*, 3rd edn, London: Bloomsbury, 2020.

Heidrun Friese (ed.), *Identities: Time, Difference and Boundaries*, Oxford: Berghahn Books, 2002.

Jürgen Straub (ed.), *Narration, Identity and Historical Consciousness*, Oxford: Berghahn Books, 2005.

Marek Tamm and Peter Burke (eds.), *Debating New Approaches to History*, London: Bloomsbury, 2019.

Daniel Woolf, *A Global History of History*, Cambridge: Cambridge University Press, 2011.

2 *The New Political History*

Introduction

'[It] is surely a highly practical truth that history is simply past politics and that politics are simply present history.'[1] Freeman's famous aphorism points to the dominance of political history in nineteenth-century historiographies. Many historians regarded it as their most noble task to write the history of states, governments and inter-state power relations. I will start this chapter by briefly reminding the reader how strongly this political history was associated with concerns about collective identities, above all those of national identity. In the twentieth century, and in particular after 1945, with the advances of, first, social history (see Chapter 3), and, subsequently, cultural history (see Chapter 4), political history began to look old-fashioned, outdated and backward, even though, during the first half of the twentieth century, it still retained a strong position at the universities. Although, even after 1945, it continued to play an influential role, by the 1970s it increasingly did not seem to be at the cutting edge of the discipline's thematic, methodological and theoretical concerns. The second part of this chapter will discuss the crisis of political history. More recently, however, the new set of ideas associated with some of the theorists discussed in the previous chapter have reshaped it. Indeed, the so-called cultural history of politics has led to its renaissance since the 1980s. In the third part of this chapter, I will discuss how this new political history impacted on its older mission to underpin collective identities. I shall argue that it is far more self-reflexive about the links between political history writing and the construction of collective identities. In fact, much of it is about the deconstruction of identities. I shall discuss some specific examples taken from fields of political history where this development has been particularly strong. These include, first, attempts to inject more popular politics into traditional high politics approaches. Secondly, they encompass concerns with political languages that reflect the impact of theories perceiving the past in terms of discursive formations. Thirdly, I shall review the hugely influential body of work that has analysed the impact of religion on the political sphere in an attempt to illustrate how cultural and intellectual history have reshaped the understanding of the political. Finally, I will consider the literature written about the glocalisation of politics, as this has also reframed the political in a major way by drawing attention to the different spatial levels on which the political was constituted (see also Chapter 11 on global history). This also included a decentring of the long-dominant national political perspective. Other fields of the new political history could also have been discussed here, but for reasons of space I will restrict myself to those four.

Traditional Political History and Its Links to Identity Politics

The Greek national historian Spyridon Lambros (1851–1919) famously remarked that the historian's pen was far more important for constructing national identities than the guns of the military.[2] The pens of many nineteenth- and twentieth-century historians were particularly busy in newly formed nineteenth-century nation-states like Germany or Italy and in those parts of empires where national movements strove to free themselves from a perceived imperial yoke. But it was also important in more traditional nation-states, where the new nationalism emanating from the French revolution made it necessary to reconceptualise nation and national identity and bring them in line with modernity. Christopher L. Hill has demonstrated in his comparison of France, the USA and Japan how national historiographies in all three countries were geared towards constructing a national identity that would bring nation in line with concepts of modernity.[3] Nation-formation through historical writing took place within the development of a global modernity that had to be written into national histories.

Political history was the privileged genre of historical writing where such concerns with collective national identity were located. The nation was represented by and identified with its governments. The fate of nations rested with their rulers. Hence much political history concentrated on high politics. Political historians of England, for example, focused on the progress of parliamentary government from the time of Magna Carta to the present day. They paid much attention to the conflicts between king and parliament, and in accordance with the so-called Whig approach to historiography they interpreted the gradual and reformist evolution of parliamentary government in England as the best form of government in the world. The English mother of parliaments and constitutional government had allegedly produced the preconditions for England's rise to great nation status. This remarkably homogenous national master narrative rested on a political interpretation of England's history from the Middle Ages to the present day. It came in two versions, a small-England and a Greater Britain one. Political historians either could focus on the development of constitutional history internal to England and eventually to Britain, or they could highlight the development of the greatest modern empire infused with the values of Britishness.[4]

The over-concentration on rulers and famous men (and they were largely men) characterised many historiographies in the nineteenth and twentieth centuries. In Germany the so-called Prussian school of historiography interpreted the political history of Prussia as fulfilment of the Prussians' national mission to unify Germany.[5] Swedish historians overwhelmingly focused on the role of the Swedish kings and their governments in shaping the fate of Sweden – its rise to great power status in early modern Europe and its demise in the eighteenth century.[6] In France the political histories of the revolutions, from the 'Great Revolution' of 1789 to a succession of revolutions in the nineteenth century, anchored the republican master narrative in the midst of French national identity that remained dominant for almost the entire twentieth century.[7] In the United States political historians focused on how post-independence politicians had shaped the building of the 'city on the hill', i.e. the formation of the United States and its rise to the status of a great political power before the First World War. Focusing on the history of political institutions, the majority of early American professional historians wrote a national story of evolving liberty.[8] Meiji Japan even instituted a Historiography Office as a governmental department, from which political histories were written glorifying the new Meiji rulers and constructing a political history that perceived the Meiji as the latest reincarnation of a long modernising trend in Japanese history witnessing its rise to great power status by the beginning of the twentieth century.[9] Nineteenth-century Mexican historiography developed three different modalities of national historical consciousness. Rodrigo Díaz-Maldonado described them as will, experience and memory.[10]

Where national narratives could be hung on continuous state histories, political history focused on narrating the story of these states and their governments as well as their alleged national missions. However, in many parts of Europe and the wider world, political historians could not do this. In those cases where empires and multinational states witnessed the emergence of national movements, historians close to them focused on the loss of statehood and indicated an alleged yoke of foreign oppression. Reminding their readers of the former greatness of lost nation-states was, for them, one way of calling for them to be restored after a successful struggle against imperial domination. Thus, Norwegian historians harked back to the greatness of the Norwegian kingdom before it was suppressed by the Danes. Greek and Bulgarian historians wrote the history of ancient Greece and of the empire of Constantinople as well as the early Bulgarian kingdom in order to remind the adherents of their respective national movements of an alleged proud and glorious past that awaited its re-awakening.[11] Slovak historians recalled the greatness of the medieval Moravian empire in order to justify their struggle against the Habsburg empire.[12] In each case, political history played an important part in justifying political demands for an independent nation-state.

In Europe, political history in pursuit of nation-building generally harked back to the medieval period, using it to underpin the alleged origins of either an existing or a yet to be created nation-state. In pursuit of building national collective identities, political historians manufactured the Middle Ages in order to produce usable medievalisms.[13] Anti- and postcolonial historical writing in non-Western contexts followed a similar logic. Here political historians focused on pre-colonial histories in order to demonstrate the greatness of a national past waiting to be restored after the nation had rid itself of the colonial yoke. Chinese historians wrote the history of the pre-colonial Chinese dynastic empires back to the mythical 'Yellow emperor' about 5,000 years BC. This allegedly made China the oldest nation-state in the world. Indian historians were part and parcel of the communalist divide that eventually split the Indian national movement and was to produce separate nation-states on the Indian subcontinent: India, Pakistan and Bangladesh. But whether they celebrated the Hindu Gupta kingdom (fourth to sixth century AD) or glorified the Muslim

Mughal emperors (sixteenth to nineteenth century AD), this recalling of the great political rulers of the past served the purpose of foreshadowing a great political future that was to follow renewed national independence once colonialism had been defeated. In Senegal, Cheikh Anta Diop, the founding father of the Dakar school of historical writing, portrayed the foundations of the Athenian polis as the cradle of European civilisation and located it in the Nile delta of Africa. Black Athene was to challenge the European myth of origin and translocate it to Africa. Political historians in black Africa also focused on black independent kingdoms and their histories before the onset of European colonialism in order to demonstrate that the Eurocentric view of Africa as a continent without history was false.[14]

The strong global affinities of political histories to the construction of national identities included overt attention to religion and religious history. Representatives of churches became flag-bearers of nations. Greek and Bulgarian Orthodox priests struggled against the Ottoman empire. Polish Catholic priests fought Russian, German and Austro-Hungarian imperialism and kept alive the spirit of the Polish nation after it disappeared from the map of Europe for more than a century between 1793 and 1918. The Protestant spirit was an important ingredient in the politics that shaped all Scandinavian nations, Britain and Germany. In all the Protestant nations of Europe as well as in the United States, political history paid due attention to the evolution of Protestantism as the backbone of national character. Germany was, of course, divided between Protestantism and Catholicism and, in the late nineteenth century, rival Catholic and Protestant master narratives emerged. These posited a strong link between religion and the shape of the political nation. Outside Europe and North America, anti- and postcolonial historiographies were similarly inclined to emphasise the religious underpinnings of political histories. Shintoism in Japan, Buddhism in China and Sri Lanka, Islam and Hinduism in Pakistan and India, Catholicism in Latin America – everywhere the politics of nations were closely associated with religions.[15]

The Crisis of Political History

There have been prominent critics of the long dominance of political history in the nineteenth and twentieth centuries and its links to forging collective identities. Jakob Burckhardt, for example, wrote his version of cultural history in an attempt to counter the German nationalist historiography of his time.[16] Members of the first generation of Annales historians had been traumatised by the hypernationalism of the First World War. Marc Bloch developed comparative history in order to move away from national(ist) perspectives in scholarship. Lucien Febvre wrote about the river Rhine as a borderland between Germany and France, reflecting on the divisions it had produced, but also on the contact zone it constituted. Henri Pirenne, an ardent admirer of German scholarship before the First World War and a prisoner of war in Germany during it, detoxed his Belgian national history by getting rid of its ethnic ingredients. He presented his native Belgium as a bridge between Romance and Germanic cultures, thereby expressing his desire to overcome national(ist) rivalries and enmities.[17] In the USA, Ellen Fitzpatrick has highlighted a long tradition in American historiography that has been critical of the ways in which American history was written as the history of formal politics and governing elites. Rather than seeing the watershed of the 1960s and 1970s in American historiography as something that could build on few traditions, her book-length study is full of examples of historical work that had critiqued nationalist and self-celebratory American histories and rejected narratives of American history as the gradual unfolding of liberty, equality and abundance. According to her, a range of historians, from the 1880s onwards through to the interwar years and the immediate post-Second World War period, should be seen as precursors of the 'new American history' of the 1960s and 1970s, which inserted the experiences of ordinary men and women into history writing, shone a spotlight on hitherto forgotten groups, wrote history from the bottom up and emphasised the importance of conflict rather than consensus in American history. Fitzpatrick's book is a stark reminder that the new history in the USA, and I would argue also elsewhere, could build on traditions that preceded the watershed decades of the 1960s and 1970s.[18]

Yet historiographical hypernationalism continued to be rampant in interwar Europe, above all in Germany. Even when Europe lay in ruins after 1945, the link between political history and the construction of national identities was so strong that in virtually every country historians sought not to overcome the national orientation of political history writing but to stabilise national historical identities that had become fragile.[19] In communist Eastern Europe traditional national storylines were simply painted red.[20] In the USA, Canada and Australia, the end of the Second World War brought heroic and triumphant confirmations of established national historical narratives, underpinned by political histories celebrating the superiority of their respective liberal and parliamentary political systems.[21] In Japan political historians presented a whole host of apologies for Japanese imperialism whilst highlighting Japan as victim of the first use of nuclear bombs and otherwise legitimating the elite's new-found conversion to liberal democratic procedures.[22] In the colonial world, participation of colonial troops in the Second World War heightened the desire to construct national histories that would underpin demands for independence and freedom from colonial rule.[23]

Political history often continued to stand at the forefront of attempts to sustain strong national identities well into the second half of the twentieth century. In the German Historians' Controversy of the 1980s, many conservative political historians, above all Michael Stürmer, who was a close political adviser of the German chancellor Helmut Kohl, worried about the decline of national identity in West Germany and sought to promote a history that could, once again, bolster such national identity.[24] In Italy, political historians, above all Renzo de Felice, aimed at the rehabilitation of Italian fascism as cornerstone of a far more positive conservative look at modern Italian history.[25] In Britain, Euroscepticism was strong among conservative political historians. Thus, for example, one of the most influential public historians, David Starkey, lamented the demise of national history and national identity in what he perceived as the threat of Europeanisation: 'Maybe we have a future as a series of disparate regions of the European Union ... But where ... an English history fits in ... a sense of England that once existed, that once mattered, that was once glorious – I'm really not sure.'[26] In 2016 the campaigners for Brexit could build on such historical sentiments, reminding their supporters of the British empire and the Second World War as alleged glory moments of a proud and independent nation that would never surrender to being subservient to Brussels.[27] In communist Eastern Europe the demise of communism in the late 1980s and early 1990s produced a flurry of interest among political historians in re-establishing traditional national(ist) master narratives.[28] In both Catalonia and Scotland political historians have been bolstering powerful movements of independence from Spain and Britain respectively.[29] These examples of the continued influence of political history on shaping national(ist) collective identities could be multiplied across the world. These tendencies should not be ignored, as they continue to have strong political implications. They underpin recent right-wing populist movements from Trump's America to the Rassemblement National in France and the Alternative für Deutschland in Germany, not to mention the BJP history politics in India, Russian history politics under Vladimir Putin, or the charge of a 'black armband history' by right-wing historians in Australia seeking to bolster a positive national identity among white Australians.[30]

Yet I would argue that those attempts to write history in the service of collective national(ist) identities have been relying increasingly, albeit not exclusively, on historical narratives produced outside professional history writing at the universities and academies. At the universities, political history has arguably had a hard time since the 1960s and 1970s, and political historians have often expressed the feeling that their sub-discipline has been in crisis. Susan Pedersen, for example, has written: 'political history for some decades has had difficulties attracting able graduate students, who are understandably drawn to research areas seen to be more "cutting edge"'.[31] However, there have been many cutting-edge developments in political history, as is, incidentally, also readily conceded by Pedersen. Hence, in the remainder of this chapter I would like to highlight developments in the professional writing of political history that have gone a long way to problematising its links with collective national identity. A new political history has been in the making from the 1980s onwards which has been part and parcel of the pluralisation of the historical sciences.

Remaking Political History

The remaking of political history since the 1980s took a variety of different forms, and I would like to discuss four prominent ones here. First, the previous over-concentration on high politics was replaced with a stronger concern for popular politics. Historians increasingly explored the links between popular politics and high politics. Secondly, under the impact of theories of narrativity and discourse theories, discussed in Chapter 1, political historians have paid much greater attention to the languages of politics, leading them to deconstruct the ways in which those languages constituted power relationships and collective identities. Thirdly, political historians began to rethink the relationship between politics and religion, challenging the thesis that the age of modernity had seen a progressive secularisation in which religion played an increasingly insignificant role in political processes. In rediscovering religion, political historians problematised the previous links, mentioned above, between religion and the forging of political identities. Fourthly, political historians investigated the history of political transfers as an important means to highlight the interconnectedness of politics across nation-state boundaries, thereby contributing in vital ways towards more self-reflexivity among historians about national storylines. Overall, as Jon Lawrence has observed, recent trends in political history writing have left the field looking highly fractured,[32] but these fractures, I would argue, represent the outcome of a genuine pluralisation of political history writing that included greater self-reflexivity about its relationship to constructing collective national identities.

Inserting Popular Politics into High Politics

In the post-1968 world, political historians had to grapple with a new understanding of politics that had emerged from the global 1968 movement,[33] i.e. one that emphasised a much wider understanding of what constituted 'the political'. No longer could politics be defined exclusively as high politics with its attention to political and administrative elites and their intrigues. Popular politics, with its emphasis on the everyday and on mass politics as well as social movements, now increasingly came to the attention of political historians as they subscribed to the view that many everyday aspects of human relationships were intensely political and therefore deserved the attention of political historians.

Such a new understanding of politics from below meant that the new political history was much less focused on high politics, yet state structures, power, domination, authority and legitimacy remained central concerns of the new political history. Jon Lawrence, a representative of the new political history in Britain, has argued strongly in favour of a 'reintegrated approach to political history' which combines attention to high politics with a concern for popular politics.[34] Moving away from a high-politics focus significantly extended the remit of political history, of which the borders to other forms of history became far more porous.

From the 1980s onwards political history had much greater overlaps to social history, cultural history, gender history, transnational and global history. Indeed, the new history emerging from the 1980s was one in which strict sub-field divisions have been disappearing as rapidly as new fields of enquiry have emerged.

British political history, for example, became far less concerned with the narrow band of usually male political leaders who allegedly had determined policy.[35] Instead it increasingly highlighted the impact of popular radicalism and liberalism which significantly shaped the British parliamentary system in the second half of the nineteenth century.[36] Political historians also paid more attention to the influence of mass media on mass politics. In realising the importance of social factors for contextualising developments in politics, political historians, like Duncan Tanner, moved political history closer to social history.[37] At the same time politics became a prism through which social structures could be analysed if proper attention was given to issues of class, gender, religion and ethnicity. British political historians now examined constituency politics, electioneering and party activism as well as the diverse cultural norms and expectations that had an impact on political actors. Jon Lawrence's examination of how gender and class norms were influential in reshaping urban British Conservatism in the late nineteenth and early twentieth century is a good example of this new orientation in political history writing.[38]

Generally speaking there has been far greater emphasis in the new political history writing on political culture, political rhetoric and political ideas. Reconstructing political cultures gave due attention to how they were linked to collective identities in the past. Thereby the new political history heightened levels of self-reflection about that link. Politics in the new political history emerged as a competitive, conflict-driven system producing sets of diverse political identities. The process of 'governance' itself became the focus of attention – with Foucault's ideas on governmentality looming large over the new political history.[39] It avoided state-centric conceptualisations of the political, emphasised the political as communicative space and drew attention to politics in the public sphere. Political history was about the reconstruction of different positionalities and subjectivities in the past that were battling for political control. Power relations were more diffuse but still central as questions of how specific political platforms won popular appeal in the past were being explored by political historians. Histories of political culture focusing on the links between power and identity construction undermined consensual views of the past and showed them up for what they had been: pieces of a discursive battle between different political visions resting on contested interpretations of the past. A cultural history of politics has reshaped political history across wide parts of Western historiography.[40] In Germany, for example, we immediately think of Thomas Mergel's studies on Weimar parliamentarism as a symbolical constitution of politics,[41] or of Johannes Paulmann's re-examination of international diplomacy as a highly symbolic and ritualistic political practice.[42] Overall, a new cultural history of politics pluralised our understanding of the past, revealing diverse links between interpretations of that past and political projects using those pasts in order to construct specific futures.

This is not just the case for British and wider Western political histories but equally true for historians of non-Western histories that have been deeply influenced by postcolonial theories since the 1970s. Postcolonial thinkers often had a close theoretical affiliation with the theories discussed in the first chapter of this volume. Thus, Foucauldian discourse analysis was central to Edward Said's pioneering study of orientalism,[43] as well as Gayatri Chakravorty Spivak's equally path-breaking studies on the voices of the subalterns.[44] Postcolonialism had different roots and origins in different parts of the world: Franz Fanon, C. L. R. James, Edward Said and the Subaltern Studies Group on the Indian subcontinent were all important starting points for postcolonialism. One of the Subaltern Studies Group's most important historians, Ranajit Guha, analysed the discursive hegemony of the colonialist and imperialist imagination through the speech acts of the colonisers.[45] Other members of the group worked with and through the archives of the colonial power, in order to ask what the impact of the colonial regime of power was on the experience of the subaltern and how the latter responded to the impositions of the colonial regime. Their emphasis on colonising politics, always relating coloniser and colonised to one another, underscored the dialogic and open-ended historical process also highlighted by Bakthin's theories that I discussed in Chapter 1.

Postcolonial theory had a massive influence on the writing of all kinds of histories – especially histories of the non-Western world, which is also why it will figure in many of the subsequent chapters of this volume. Postcolonial political histories were taking issue with a long-standing tradition in Western history writing to categorise non-Western societies as pre-political, thereby universalising their own understanding of what constituted politics. Dipesh Chakrabarty thus argued that political actors were not only governments, parliaments and political parties, but that gods and spirits should equally be regarded as political actors when discussing the politics of Indian peasants.[46] Postcolonial political histories were often characterised by the search for how the political constituted forms of identity in the struggles between colonisers and indigenous populations. By problematising these identities and asking about their constructed nature, postcolonial political histories made a vital contribution to more self-reflective approaches to history writing as identitarian project. Like the new political histories in the West, postcolonial histories that concerned themselves with politics often combined an interest in political history from below with traditional questions of high politics, regarding power, domination and political change. We can witness this already with one of the classics of postcolonial writing, Franz Fanon's *Wretched of the Earth*, where the author argues that national political leaders involved in colonial struggles need to recognise the revolutionary potential from below – emerging from the subaltern classes in colonialised spaces. What Fanon calls the 'spontaneity' of the politics from below needs to be channelled, through education, into supporting the politics from above formulated by national political leaders.[47] Fanon's prescription for the anti-colonial struggle has at the same time been methodological advice for historians of the politics of anti-colonialism in the non-Western world: the history of the politics from above cannot be looked at in isolation from the politics from below.

The emphasis on national liberation in postcolonial theory has produced a particularly strong body of histories in the realm of the political history of nationalism. If we take Declan Kiberd's book *Inventing Ireland* as an example, we can see how he puts at the centre of the invention of Ireland a process that he describes as 'deanglicisation'. It amounted to a nationalist programme of cultural revival subscribed to by cultural-political organisations such as the Gaelic League.[48] Nationalist movements in the era of decolonisation have also been a focus of Partha Chatterjee's work on Indian nationalism.[49] How national identities have been constructed and deconstructed over time stands at the heart of those postcolonial studies on nationalism.

Thereby they have actively contributed to a more self-reflective understanding of the links between historical writing and national identity formation that was such an important part of political history writing in the modern period. At times, postcolonial historians also actively strove to contribute to the formation of particular collective identities as part and parcel of struggles for emancipation, but they did so more in the way of 'identification' as strategic tool, as Stuart Hall had suggested. (See Chapter 1.) In this way, they promoted a de-essentialised and self-reflective form of collective identity in anti-colonial, anti-racist and social struggles of diverse subaltern groups. The struggle of many postcolonial African historians to write against the colonialist assumption that Africa was a continent without history is a case in point. Putting Africa on the map of historiography also meant giving Africans a historical collective identity, but historians such as Jacob Ade Ajayi, one of the founders of the Ibadan school of history in Nigeria, did so with a high degree of professional self-reflectivity about such links between historical writing and collective identity formation.[50]

Popular politics and high politics were not only connected in studies of nationalism. Discussion of cultural representations of colonialism in relation to their impact on state power and high politics can be found, for example, in Bernard Cohn's trenchant analysis of how British power in imperial India was represented and constructed. Dissecting the political cultures of colonial rule, he has highlighted the impact of the Indian Mutiny of 1857 on constructions of British authority and on the construction of what became its mirror opposite, Mughal India. Focusing on the colonial spectacle, such as the Imperial Assemblage of 1877, where Queen Victoria was proclaimed 'Empress of India', and the governor general, Lord Lytton, acted as master of ceremonies, Cohn provides a political map of the construction of political authority underpinning the power of British colonial rule in India.[51]

In a different but equally relevant way, Mrinalini Sinha brings together cultural history and political history into a cultural history of politics of India in her study of masculinity as a system of symbolical representation which negotiates regimes of power. At the heart of her examination is the analysis of power and identity in colonial India during the end of the nineteenth century. For the British colonisers, denying the masculinity of the Indian population was one way of preventing an extension of native participation in the administration and rule of the empire. The trope of the 'effeminate Bengali' became an important weapon excluding Indians from law courts sitting in judgement over white Europeans, from colonial administration and from military service. The colonial counter-image of the 'manly Englishman' was in turn critiqued by subaltern voices intent on challenging the exclusionary practices of white British imperialists. A native Indian elite adapted the discourse of manliness and merged it with the discourse on modernity to seek entitlement to colonial offices and political advancement in order to participate in the power regimes of British imperialism. Regaining Indian manliness thus became an important tool in the struggle to fight discrimination and ultimately British colonial rule over India.[52]

The Languages of Politics

The emphasis of new political historians on cultural history was one way of combining the politics from below with the politics from above. Another was the new political historians' declared interest in intellectual history, in particular their concern with ideas and knowledge production. Here we can observe the influence of conceptual history, both Reinhard Koselleck's 'Begriffsgeschichte', emanating from Germany,[53] and the works associated with the so-called Cambridge school around Quentin Skinner, J. G. A. Pocock and J. W. Burrow.[54] (See Chapter 8 for more detail.) Many political historians were inspired by conceptual history and cannibalised its theoretical reflections into new ways of writing political history – with due attention to political discourse, speech acts and the social context of texts that had been brought centre stage by the theorists discussed in Chapter 1. In other words, new political historians became more interested in the wider debates that shaped the political world and transformed political practice. Naturally, this drew them to forms of political communication. At the University of Bielefeld, for example, a group of historians have examined the role of political communication and language in great detail, making use of conceptual history to explore the various layers of meaning inherent in political communication.[55]

Gareth Stedman Jones, a political historian of nineteenth-century British radicalism, including Chartism, wrote a series of penetrating historical analyses in the 1970s and early 1980s that were published in book form under the telling title *Languages of Class* (1983), where he persistently asks how political discourse was constructed. According to Stedman Jones, the language of nineteenth-century political radicalism cannot be reduced to class consciousness that was derived from a particular social structure. He paid due attention to the narratives constructing class in the nineteenth century, for example in his classic essay on 'Re-thinking Chartism', where he highlights the linguistic origins of the dynamics of Chartist radicalism.[56] Dror Wahrman did not so much focus on the construction of the working class through language as on the making of the middle class through narratives about what allegedly constituted this class.[57] The discursive construction of identities beyond class, strongly influenced by Foucauldian discourse analysis, stood at the heart of works by Patrick Joyce and James Vernon, who looked at narratives about the 'people' as a new way of constructing political solidarities through language that found expression in popular political culture.[58] Other political historians of nineteenth-century Britain followed suit and increasingly underlined the role of language and narrative in shaping the major political forces of the century. Eugenio Biagini, to give just one example, has shown how the influence of working-class radicals in the Gladstonian Liberal Party fostered the languages of humanitarianism and internationalism that eventually came to characterise wide sections of the party at the beginning of the twentieth century.[59]

The new political history had major repercussions not just in British but in a range of other national historiographies. In French history, for example, Mona Ozouf and François Furet as well as Lynn Hunt argued that the 'Great French Revolution' of 1789, in many ways the central anchor point of French national identity until today, had its roots not in social structures but in political narratives.[60] Political representations and the construction of political identities through language remade the French nation in the late eighteenth and early nineteenth century. Social structures did not determine politics, but politics worked through cultural representations which constituted the social. We will return to these questions about the relationship between the political and the social in the next chapter on social history. But let us consider here the impact of Mona Ozouf's work on revolutionary festivals published in the late 1980s.[61] (See Figure 2.1.) Ozouf highlights the symbolical character of these festivals and examines their political functions and meanings. They were, she argues, attempts to unify the revolutionary polity characterised by a strong desire to create unanimity among that polity by introducing

Figure 2.1 Revolutionary Festival of the Supreme Being, 8 June 1794, nineteenth-century engraving. © Universal Images Group, photo 12/Getty Images.

a variety of exclusionary practices. She underlines the religious qualities of the festivals, their emphasis on 'the sacred', which was one way of reintroducing religion into studies of the revolution. Her overriding interest in representation through the visual and through language led her to a close examination of the revolutionary discourse. Wary of the socio-economic determinism of Marxist and Marxisant social history, which had dominated the study of the French revolution until the 1970s, Ozouf highlights the agency of the political revolutionaries, their utopianism and their obsession with inventing a new national narrative. In Ozouf's work we find the concern of new political historians to bring together high politics and popular politics. Her 2005 book *Varennes: the Death of the Monarchy* closely examines the flight of King Louis XVI to Varennes and its consequences.[62] It is, however, not only about high political history, the king and his circle of advisers, but also about public opinion. Through the spectre of political culture, Ozouf interprets the concept of the monarchy as having been irreparably damaged by the flight to Varennes. The monarchy, she argues, was desacralised after Varennes; the first step was taken on the road to regicide.[63]

New political historians in Britain, France and elsewhere, paying attention to the languages of politics, tended to emphasise the diversity of political ideas and customs and sought to reconstruct their meaning. Their main question was what politics meant for contemporaries at any given moment in time. This made collective identities a key concern for the new political historians. Political identities were often examined in relation to other identities, including those of nation, class, race, ethnicity, culture and gender. Thus, for example, Kathleen Wilson, in her *The Sense of the People* (1995), examined the impact of race, class and gender on understandings of imperialism in eighteenth-century England.[64] Similarly, the pathbreaking volume of Catherine Hall, Keith McClelland and Jane Rendall on *Defining the Victorian Nation* looked at the politics of the Reform Act of 1867 in light of issues of race, class and gender.[65] Catherine Hall's magisterial *Civilizing Subjects* (2002) again interpreted the manifold relationships between metropole and colony in English imagination in light of the complex negotiation of identities around master narratives of class, race, and gender.[66] For the interwar period of the twentieth century, historians such as Ross McKibbin and Alison Light have examined the political languages of national reconciliation as a way of explaining the Conservative political dominance over interwar politics in Britain.[67] These are just some British examples of a whole body of work, associated with the new political history that problematised the politics of collective identity. Increasingly, new political historians also paid more attention to the role of emotions in politics. Thus, for example, Martin Francis' work on the 'emotional economy' of post-Second World War politics in Britain highlighted the role of emotions in Conservative political culture.[68]

Whilst the attention to language has been seminal for the emergence of the new political history, more recently a range of historians have pointed to the limits of reducing the political entirely to language, communication and representation. Instead they have picked up the importance of material objects in history and pointed to the relevance and agency of the material in history. (See Chapter 10 for more detail on material culture history.) Thus historians have begun to consider how things have had agency in the past and how material objects constituted the political in diverse ways. Histories of commodities were in the forefront of demonstrating how things impacted on political processes and understandings.[69] Things, political historians have pointed out, influenced governmentality processes. The development of technologies especially, but also the material behind forms of knowledge production, such as files or maps, have had a major influence on politics.[70] The new attention to things has brought political historians to consider practices and ways of doing politics. Here they often take their cue from Bourdieu's theories on practices discussed in Chapter 1. Practices integrate human action, materiality and knowledge as well as communication and language. As these practices are often situated at the border of the public and the private, and the interface of public sphere and state, they also reinforce the new political history's concern with bridging the former gulf between high politics and popular politics.

Politics and Religion

The new interest in representations, languages, symbols and narratives, combined with investigations of practices, has contributed to the revival of an interest in religion among political historians. Modernisation theories after the end of the Second World War highlighted the long-term decline of religion as a political force, which is why many political historians abandoned the field of religious history that had traditionally been an important one for them, not just in early modern history, where the maxim of 'cuius regio, eius religio' underlined the direct relevance of religion for politics. Religious elites have been part and parcel of governing elites and organised religion has been an important element of both high and popular politics well into the twenty-first century in different parts of the world. If the new political history turned to popular politics, as described above, those with an interest in religion now also turned more to popular religion, i.e. congregations and lay circles rather than high clergy and office holders within the church. The politics of religion took a cultural turn as historians examined religion as a form of culture that was discursively constructed. Studying religion at the grassroots showed how diverse political commitments were perpetuated through religious practices. Thus, for example, Boyd Hilton's *The Age of Atonement* (1988) examined the world of British evangelical Christianity to underline its impact on the politics of liberal Tories like Pitt, Peel and Gladstone.[71] As the new political historians were strongly interested in forms of social control, religion was cast as one way of achieving this control, both in the state and at the level of the private home. Investigating the religion of the people, i.e. how people received orthodoxies and adapted them to everyday life, was one way of examining how religious identities were forged and which politics emerged out of such forging of political identities. Jon Parry's *Democracy and Religion*, for example, shows that mid-Victorian political discourse cannot be understood properly without its religious dimension. Religious differences were at the heart of debates surrounding Liberalism. They go a long way towards explaining the electoral defeat of Liberalism in 1874.[72] Religious symbols, rituals, ceremonies, processions, pilgrimages, rites – all were investigated to show how religion impacted on political belonging. Lee Trepanier's book on the importance of symbols in church–state relations in Russia is a good example of this attentiveness to representations.[73] Of special interest were the manifold conflicts between different religions, as it was here that issues of otherness and alterity became crucially important. The battles between Protestantism and Catholicism in Northern Ireland have had lavish attention from political historians producing whole libraries of work.[74] Finally, the transnationalisation of political history, discussed below, found an important transmitter of ideas and practices in religious institutions, in particular missionaries and their encounters with non-Christian religions and cultures. Jonathan Spence's *The Memory Palace of Matteo Ricci* sketches how an Italian Catholic met representatives of Chinese civilisation not only with great respect but also with a deep desire to mediate between Christianity and Confucianism. Ricci's commentaries on China were to have an important impact on European thinking about China.[75] To give another example, a variety of different Irish, American and British reform movements, dealing, for example, with the abolition of slavery or Catholic emancipation, were deeply rooted in religious identities. For many activists in these movements, their political engagement followed directly from their religious beliefs.[76] At another level, religious languages have been examined in diverse forms of secular politics, in both its totalitarian and its democratic forms. Politics itself has been viewed as religion with its own forms of 'veneration' and 'sacralisation'.[77]

The Glocalisation of Political History

The Dutch political historian Henk te Velde has written about the long and symbiotic relationship between political history writing and the promotion of nationalism in the Netherlands to conclude that things have changed: 'The writing of national political history is still common practice in almost every country but its legitimation is no longer based on a patriotic duty, not in Western Europe at least.'[78] Te Velde has played a key role in developing a very productive historical method to overcome the strong ties of political history to the nation-state and to move towards a greater self-reflectiveness among practising political historians about this link. I am talking about the idea of studying transnational 'political transfers'.[79] Te Velde and others have been questioning the idea that national political phenomena necessarily have only national explanations. In their research they have been looking beyond the borders of the nation-state in order to investigate forms of political transfer from one nation-state to others which were then circulated, adopted, adapted, and in the process of adaptation changed and transformed. In this way national political frameworks are constituted in transnational ways. Foreign inspirations and foreign examples have been vital in constituting the political nation. Political practices have not been confined to the nation-state; they have been migrating between national political frameworks. New insights into political history can be won if the historians are ready to abandon their exclusive focus on one, usually their own, nation-state. Thus, for example, the history of parliaments cannot be adequately understood without taking into account transnational influences: the Westminster parliament served as model for many continental parliamentary systems, even if, in the end, very few of them ended up looking exactly like Westminster.[80] The same arguably goes for the history of democracy generally and all of its political institutions.[81] Political parties are another good example of institutions that cannot be analysed in a national political framework alone. International contacts and perceptions, especially between political parties belonging to the same political families – liberalism, socialism, nationalism, conservatism, Catholicism – were commonplace and significantly influenced the shape and outlook of national political parties.[82] Transnational political transfers shaped not only political parties but a whole range of other political social movements, from the environmental movement to the peace movement, and further to the women's movement and moral movements, such as the anti-slavery movement.[83]

Pasi Ihalainen's recent book on the *Springs of Democracy* is a good example of the merits of such a transnational and comparative approach to political history. Analysing in great detail the debates on democracy, parliamentarism and revolution in Britain, Germany, Sweden and Finland between 1917 and 1919, he manages to demonstrate how transnational debates impacted national politics in all four countries and led to very different results that were partly the result of different national frameworks and historical contexts. In Britain, with a long tradition of putting parliament at the centre of national development, the restoration of parliamentary authority progressed relatively smoothly, whereas in Germany, the beginnings of parliamentary democracy were burdened with the loss of the First World War and the widespread perception of parliamentarism as a foreign imposition. The reception of Western political models also caused major social ruptures in Sweden, but there it was possible to implement a series of social reforms which would see the country embark on its road towards becoming a model social democratic country that began in the interwar years. In neighbouring Finland parliamentary legitimacy was seriously challenged by the strong reception of Bolshevik revolutionary discourse within the strong Social Democratic Party, which led the country into a bloody civil war, after which a republican compromise could only be found on the basis of much outside, Entente, pressure and a domestic politics of social reform that ironically saw the losers of the civil war as major winners of interwar Finnish politics.[84]

Transnational political transfers do not deny the importance of the national sphere for political history, but the notion underlines how that national sphere is never exclusively nationally constituted. National political traditions have a transnational frame. Hence it adds to a subtler understanding of the constitution of political practices within nation-states and relativises the importance of the national frame for those practices. Hence it is an important method of making the historian more aware of the constructedness of the national in political history, thereby producing greater self-reflexivity between the writing of political history and national(ist) commitments.

If we take, for example, Sean Scalmer's study on nineteenth-century political oratory in Australia, the USA and Britain, we can see how transnational political history is contributing to a more self-reflective understanding of what constitutes national political traditions. Scalmer shows that the development of mass democracy was intimately connected with the rise of public forms of oratory across different national contexts. The author traces the origins of 'stumping' to the south-western states of the USA and analyses its rise to national importance, before following the remarkable transnational career of stumping and its spread to Australia and Britain through a series of biographical sketches of famous stump orators in all three countries, notably Davy Crockett, Henry Clay,

Charles Gavan Duffy, Graham Berry and William Gladstone. All of these political characters combined a remarkable talent for public oratory with elements of personal magnetism. Scalmer understands stump oratory as performance and hence pays special attention to how things were said and what characteristics marked stumping: it was rough, sometimes vulgar, always plain and manly, and stood for the ambitions of the self-made man with humble origins, refusing to be deferential to his social superiors in the unequal democracy of the early United States. The author also takes a special interest in the representations of stump oratory, for it was through such representations, be it in visual art or newspapers, that it became defined, popularised and widely practised across very different social and historical contexts. The transnational approach that Scalmer adopts is particularly intriguing as it shows stumping as a transnational practice that is adopted and adapted in different parts of the world at different times.[85]

Scalmer's book is focused on the Anglo-world, where transnational forms of political activism have been extremely prominent.[86] This Anglo-world is a reminder of the importance of the histories of empire in constituting spaces for political transfers. Next to the Anglo-world, there is a Francophone world, a Hispanic world, a Lusophone world, a Chinese world, and possibly others which all need to be explored in terms of the political transfers they engendered, and ultimately they also need to be compared. Furthermore questions need to be asked about transfers between those different linguistic and cultural worlds related to political empires.

With a renewed interest in the histories of empire from the 1980s onwards,[87] it has been impossible to write those histories without a transnational dimension. In particular the mutual influences between metropole and periphery have, time and again, been at the heart of studies on empire. It is by now well established that the one cannot be constituted without the other. Christopher Bayly, in his magisterial *Imperial Meridian*, discusses the manifold interconnections within the British empire and between the latter and the wider world in the period 1780 to 1830 by making use of two bodies of historical theories that have both shunned the national.[88] On the one hand, he takes recourse to Imanuel Wallerstein's world systems theory and the macro-approaches that they entail.[89] On the other hand, he refers back to culturalist micro-history approaches which are frequently related to historical anthropology, discussed in Chapter 6, and which often use methods connected with Clifford Geertz's 'thick description'.[90] In Bayly's history, European and non-European history are each related to the other in ways that avoid essentialising both and thereby falling into the trap of orientalising or occidentalising one or the other. What is at the heart of Bayly's book is a global political struggle over land and labour, at the end of which Britain emerges victorious as the most successful European power on the globe. Under British imperial leadership mercantilist imperialism is replaced by free trade capitalism. The decentring of national history is a necessary consequence of this form of imperial history. The making of the modern world can only be understood through interconnections and interdependence. The local and the global, as Arjun Appadurai has emphasised in his writing, are so deeply intertwined that they need to be seen together rather than divided neatly into different spatially organised histories.[91] (See Chapter 11 for more detail.)

Comparative histories of empires can have a similar function of decentring identitarian claims connected to historical writing. If we take the comparison of the relationship between European empires and nation-formation, such comparison points to the long-standing nonsense of opposing empires to nation-states. Nation-building took place within imperial cores and was meant to preserve and extend empires rather than replace them with nation-states. Jürgen Osterhammel has distinguished four different types of nineteenth-century nation-state formation – a typology which also underpins the strong interconnectedness of empires with nation-building.[92] But nation-building in imperial nations took place because it was perceived by imperial elites as a political and economic asset. The 'empire state'[93] was as able to develop nations and nationalisms as the nation-state. In the management of migrations, communication systems and urban developments and in the construction of economic ties and political solidarities, the empire state was as competent as the nation-state. Inter-imperial rivalries also played an important role in nation-building. The politics of language, ethnicity and race in the nineteenth century cannot be adequately understood without taking into account the manifold linkages between nation and empire.[94]

Conclusion: the New Political History and Its Weakening Links to Questions of Identity

This chapter has shown how the new political history has decisively reconfigured the meaning of the political in history writing. As James

Epstein has written: 'Less concerned with the formal processes of government and institutions of the state, the new political history has turned more often to the symbolic investments of actions and communication, to questions about how meanings are produced, received and sustained.'[95] We have traced the move away from the history of high politics and towards the languages of politics, popular politics and the history of political culture broadly defined. The emphasis has been increasingly on the intersections between 'high politics' and 'popular politics'. We have briefly alluded to how the new concern with the popular and with culture has affected what used to be a vital part of political history, namely the history of religion, before we turned our attention to the tendencies to move political history away from national and towards transnational frameworks. The increasing popularity of transnational methods and the attention paid to political transfers is putting a huge question mark behind the earlier symbiotic relationship between political history and the construction of collective national identities. We started the chapter by briefly reviewing this tradition and we have analysed how this link produced a sense of crisis in the field of political history during the 1960s and 1970s. Although we have also pointed to the persistence of a tradition of political history that seeks to underpin national(ist) identities, the most innovative work in the field that contributed to its revival points in a different direction. Here the deconstruction of collective identities is far more the outcome of historical work than their construction. Political history writing today, in many of its variants, is arguably making a valuable contribution to achieving greater self-reflexivity about the links of history writing to collective identity formation. In the next chapter we will explore how social history, during the 1960s and 1970s widely regarded as successor to political history as the most dominant and popular form of history writing, has fared in its positioning towards the formation of collective identities.

Further Reading

Dipesh Chakrabarty, *Provincializing Europe: Postcolonial Thought and Historical Difference*, 2nd edn, Princetion: Princeton University Press, 2008.

Jon Lawrence and Alexandre Campsie, 'Political History', in: Stefan Berger, Heiko Feldner and Kevin Passmore (eds.), *Writing History: Theory and Practice*, 3rd edn, London: Bloomsbury, 2020, pp. 323–42.

Mark H. Leff, 'Revisioning US Political History', in: *American Historical Review* 100 (1995), pp. 829–53.

Willibald Steinmetz, Ingrid Gilcher-Holtey and Heinz-Gerhard Haupt (eds.), *Writing Political History Today*, Frankfurt am Main: Campus, 2013.

Henk te Velde, 'Political Transfer: an Introduction', in: *European Review of History* 12:2 (2005), pp. 205–21.

3 The New Social, Economic and Labour History

Introduction

'The great impulse to unite historiography with the social sciences occurred after the Second World War. The extraordinary disasters of the previous four decades all demanded a new effort among informed experts to address crises that ran across the social, economic, political and cultural-oriented disciplines ... a new generation of historians from far more diverse backgrounds [expanded] the profession's emphasis on social history.'[1]

As this quote from John L. Harvey underlines, social history, and by implication economic and labour histories, were latecomers to the field of professional history writing. As a comprehensive 'history of society' that analysed, above all, demographic, economic and social processes and dealt with the conflicts arising from different kinds of societies at different times and places, it had to establish itself against the dominance of political history in the nineteenth century. In the first part of this chapter, I shall look at this battle and trace the rise to prominence of social, economic and labour histories. Whilst this did not occur at the same time everywhere, the period between the 1950s and the 1970s can be seen as the highpoint of social, economic and labour histories. From then on, as I shall analyse in the second part of this chapter, social, economic and labour historians were heavily criticised from different quarters and soon found themselves in crisis. However, they have also reacted in productive ways to this crisis and have looked for ways to rejuvenate and reinvent their respective sub-disciplines. Just as I traced the emergence of a 'new political history' in the last chapter, I shall now look for instances of a 'new social, economic and labour history', before referring to what I believe to be some of the most innovative ways of rethinking all three sub-disciplines. Throughout, I shall once again pay special attention to the relationship of social, economic and labour histories to concerns about collective identities.

Early Social Histories and Their Rise to Prominence in the Twentieth Century

In the nineteenth century social histories were strongest where historical narratives could not easily be hung on continuous national political histories, i.e. where there was either no statehood at all, or where that statehood had been interrupted. In such cases historians often referred to 'the people', seeing them as carriers of the nation, in either a cultural/ethnic or a political sense.[2] A further correlation can be found between the early rise of social history and liberal democratic politics. Because of the emphasis on 'the people' one encounters in liberal democracies, such as Britain and the United States, the social carried a stronger weight there than in more authoritarian illiberal regimes. Economic history, like social history, was most successful in establishing itself where it could buy into national historical master narratives. Thus, in Germany, under the influence of the Historical School of Economics, historians showed how Germany's economic development had contributed to unification and Germany's rise to great power status before the First World War. The leading scholar of the Younger Historical School, Gustav Schmoller, heavily criticised the development of Manchester capitalism in England. Instead he championed a more ethical and social variant of capitalist development, one that became associated with the so-called 'socialists of the chair' (*Kathedersozialisten*) – a group of academics arguing for social reforms to alleviate the worst excesses of uncontrolled capitalism.[3] In England economic historians such as William Cunningham, who published the first English economic history in 1882, contributed to establishing the master narrative of England as the motherland of the Industrial Revolution.[4] The development of economic history as a sub-field brought with it a strong empirical orientation, an emphasis on statistics, and extremely detailed studies of particular aspects of the economy that often did not relate economic developments to wider social, political and cultural contexts. Economic histories thus sometimes resembled large quantitative data collections. John Clapham's three-volume *Economic History of Modern Britain*, published between 1926 and 1938, belongs to this category.[5]

In the interwar period economic history became more established in a number of countries. In Britain the founding of the Economic History Society and its journal *Economic History Review* in 1926/7 was characteristic of a wider trend. British social history also thrived in the early parts of the twentieth century. Sydney and Beatrice Webb, the founders of the London School of Economics, wrote extensively on social welfare and trade unionism,[6] whilst John and Barbara Hammond wrote a three-volume history of the labouring poor in London.[7] In the interwar period R. H. Tawney, a Christian socialist and Labour Party parliamentary candidate, championed social and economic history. In one of his best-known works, *Religion and the Rise of Capitalism* (1926), he argued against Max Weber that capitalism did not have its origins in religion and that it in fact amounted to a moral perversion of Christian teaching, putting greed before morality.[8] At about the same time social history also made major advances in France – with the rise of the Annales school of historical writing.[9] Already before the First World War the strong influence of French sociology, in particular Émile Durckheim, on historical writing found expression in Henri Berr's important journal *Revue de Synthèse Historique*, founded in 1900. This influence continued after 1918 but it was now powerfully augmented by the geography of Paul Vidal de la Blache. The father figures of the Annales, Henri Pirenne, Lucien Febvre and Marc Bloch, paid due attention to social, economic and geographical processes and determinants in historical developments, favouring a form of structural history with strong materialist dimensions, quantitative approaches and an eye for collective representations.

Social and economic historians, like Tawney or some of the French Annalistes, intended to provide social criticisms of their own contemporary societies. Arguably, labour history was the most strongly politicised form of social history. It rose to prominence in close association with the labour movements founded across the Western world during the second half of the nineteenth century. Its first practitioners were almost invariably labour movement activists such as Jean Jaurès in France, Eduard Bernstein in Germany, Filippo Turati in Italy and Robert Grimm in Switzerland.[10] They often sought to write the labour movement and the working classes into their respective national histories. Hence, their form of history writing was strongly connected to constructing and strengthening collective identities, in particular class identities. In the USA, social history also adopted progressive political causes. Here the so-called 'Progressive Historians' produced a range of historical studies that amounted to calls for social reform to remedy the ills of industrialisation.[11]

In the Soviet Union after the Bolshevik revolution of 1917, in communist Eastern Europe after the Second World War, and in those parts of the world that turned to communism during the Cold War, history writing was strongly tied to producing classed nations.[12] In the Soviet Union the *Short Course in the History of the USSR*, penned by Vasilievich Shestakov and published in 1937, characteristically started with the words: 'The USSR is the land of socialism. There is only one socialist country on the globe – it is our motherland.'[13] Not only the USSR as a whole but also many of the independent Soviet republics developed their own national master narratives under Stalin's tutelage.[14] After 1945 other communist historiographies emulated the regimes' desire to combine a commitment to socialism with traditional historiographical nationalism. In a fascinating study of the emergence of a communist historical profession in Albania after 1945, Idrit Idrizi has demonstrated how much it adhered to constructing a grand national master narrative for communist Albania and how the profession was related symbiotically to political power.[15] In China, after 1949, communist historians, under direct Soviet influence, merged a commitment to working-class and peasant emancipation with a national one. They painted old nationalist paradigms in Chinese history red.[16] In the non-communist global south, Marxist historiographies tied history writing to emancipatory national concerns. In Brazil, for example, Marxist historians, from the 1930s onwards, have addressed the question of the consequences of colonisation for the trajectory of the Brazilian nation-state within the framework of a global commercial capitalism.[17]

In the Western world Britain was a pioneer of an early professionalised labour history, with labour historians close to the Labour Party occupying important academic positions. At Oxford University, G. D. H. Cole was a leading socialist intellectual, who trained a whole generation of labour and social historians. They in turn influenced the direction of British historiography in the post-war era.[18] In the interwar years many British intellectuals, including historians, felt drawn to communism. The Communist Party Historians' Group, formed in the 1930s, lasted until the aftermath of the crushing of Hungarian reform communism in 1956.[19] It included some of the country's most prominent social, economic and labour historians, such as Eric Hobsbawm, Maurice Dobb, E. P. and Dorothy Thompson, Raphael Samuel, Christopher Hill, George Rudé, Dona Torr, Viktor Kiernan, Rodney Hilton, John Saville, Roydon Harrison and A. L. Morton – all household names in British historiography. They combined the writing of social, economic and labour history – as Marxists, invariably giving primacy to economic developments. Collectively they helped to make social, economic and labour history the most attractive form of history writing among a radical cohort of post-war British historians. In the neo-Marxist climate of the 1960s many younger historians had the feeling that they were engaging with the most exciting and cutting-edge form of historical writing. Theirs was a self-consciously left-wing committed oppositional history which countered official and established orthodoxies in order to bolster left-of -centre class identities. Some, like Morton, managed to connect Marxist social history with an endeavour to rewrite the national historical master narrative, for example in his seminal *People's History of England*, first published in 1938.[20]

Even among more mainstream historians, social, economic and labour history became popular in the years after 1945. Harold Perkin, the founder of the Social History Society in Britain in 1976 and the holder of the first chair of social history at the University of Lancaster, championed a social history that would be able to depict the development of society in its totality. He attempted this most notably in his 1969 monograph on *The Origins of Modern English Society, 1780–1880*.[21] Henry Pelling became one of the most influential post-war labour historians, exercising considerable sway over a group of historians who eventually were to unite in the Society for the Study of Labour History, established in 1960. It was one of the first attempts internationally to institutionalise labour history. Its *Bulletin for the Study of Labour History*, today's *Labour History Review*, has become one of the leading journals in the field.[22] The foundation of the journal *Past and Present* in 1952 was an attempt to maintain a dialogue between Marxist and non-Marxist social historians in what was perceived as a joint effort to write the history of society rather than the history of high politics.

Not everywhere was the rise of social, economic and labour history connected to strong left-wing sympathies. In Germany, for example, a right-wing, racist, völkisch form of social history writing, the so-called

Volksgeschichte, augmented the traditional state orientation of conservative political historians in the interwar years. In it, young right-wing radical historians, lamenting the loss of the First World War, denounced the Versailles Treaty and hated the Weimar Republic. In a social history inflected by race they found a theoretical framework with which to replace the statism of an older generation. Hans Rothfels at the University of Königsberg became the doyen of a young generation of rising stars, including Werner Conze and Theodor Schieder, the two fathers of West German 'Strukturgeschichte' (history of structures), who endorsed this racialised form of social history that rose to full prominence during the Third Reich.[23] Many of these historians, as well as a good portion of traditional statist conservative historians, supported the National Socialist regime with its expansionist and racist aims of re-ordering Europe during the Second World War.[24] After 1945 many continued their careers unharmed by their association with National Socialism. Among them were some who abandoned their commitment to *Volksgeschichte* and finally began to develop a form of social history in which they laid to rest their earlier political predilections and endorsed liberal democracy. Conze and Schieder, for example, now engaged with the Annales tradition, even if they completely misunderstood it.[25] They did encourage their pupils to move more towards the direction of social history, go to the USA and make other international contacts in order to locate German historiography in the mainstream of post-war Western historiography. Despite this, the German variant of structural social history remained deeply rooted in a conservative scepticism about modernity.[26]

These developments in the UK and Germany typify two very different trajectories. Yet both bear witness to the fact that in many parts of the world social history replaced political history as the dominant form of history writing in the decades from the 1950s to the 1970s. In the English-speaking world E. H. Carr's immensely influential *What Is History?* summed up the prevailing feeling: 'the more sociological history becomes, and the more historical sociology becomes, the better for both'.[27] For their part, the second generation of the Annales, under the undisputed leadership of Fernand Braudel, created an international 'monde braudelien' that seemed to many to be at the cutting edge of social and economic history writing.[28] As Eric Hobsbawm recalls in his autobiography, Paris was the place for historians to be in the 1950s.[29] The strong structuralist element in the social sciences that affected

Braudel and the Annales was derived from Claude Lévi-Strauss, a massively influential figure in social history writing in France and elsewhere.[30] He and his followers believed that social structures conditioned societies to such an extent that individual agency was rather meaningless. Social history was for them a history of structures that had no place for the people. Nevertheless, the immense success of the Bielefeld school in Germany and of social historians like Peter Stearns in the USA, Stuart Macintyre in Australia or Hanna Batatu in Iraq indicated the global success of social history. It was also emulated in other parts of the world. Thus, in Latin America, where it soon became 'the "new establishment"',[31] Marxist-inspired social and economic histories blossomed during the 1980s. In Japan, social and economic history, also deeply influenced by Marxist thinking, took a turn to the local in the 1960s. Here, detailed studies of local social and economic conditions ran alongside many others, which began to explore ordinary people's lives.[32] In India, where 'economic history reigned supreme in the late 1960s and 1970s', the country's transition to capitalism was the subject of passionate controversies.[33]

At the high point of social science history, much attention was paid to economic structures, the economy being widely seen as the basis for social developments. Both Marx and Weber had alloted a vital, in the case of Marx even primary, role to economic processes in conditioning politics, society and culture. Economic history retained its earlier strong attachment to quantitative data and mechanistic mathematical model-building. The investigation of overseas trade, trade cycles, business histories, histories of particular sectors of industry, prices, GNP, population development – all these areas became popular subjects for study and all were guided by basic assumptions about the rationality of human beings trying to maximise profit. Economic history was also believed to have the practical value of being able to present Western industrialisation as a model for developing countries.[34] By the 1970s, in many parts of the world, it appeared as though social and economic history would carry all before it. Young historians were excited by the project of developing a comprehensive understanding of the dynamics of longer-term societal developments. Whether Marxists or not, they shared a commitment to social, economic and labour history. Everywhere books on the strong interrelationship between sociology and history proliferated.[35] In 1971, Eric Hobsbawm argued in his seminal essay 'From Social History to the History of Society', that social causes were the driving forces in history and that social history opened up the possibility of writing the totality of society.[36] Only ten years later, however, many historians saw such totalising assumptions and macro-historical ambitions as a problem rather than a promise.

The Crisis of Social History in the 1970s and 1980s

Ironically it was soon after social historians had celebrated their victory over their rivals in political history that social history itself came under fire from diverse quarters. Political historians attacked social historians for their alleged structuralist determinism. Outside the West, political history, e.g. in the Ibadan school in Nigeria, continued to underpin nationalist and anti-colonialist ambitions.[37] During the 1970s and 1980s social history also came under attack from a range of historians identifying with history from below and cultural history. I will discuss cultural history more extensively in the next chapter. Suffice it to say here that the new cultural history, as it gained momentum during the 1980s, was deeply influenced by some of the theories discussed in Chapter 1. Cultural historians argued that social history's emphasis on structures and functions paid too little attention to symbols, representations, ideas and cultural factors that influenced historical processes. A much-cited critique came in 1979 from the pen of the Marxist historian Tony Judt. He argued that social history had become a 'clown in regal purple'. In his view, it was mistaking method for theory and reduced social life to statistics and modernisation. It was guilty of an uncritical commitment to the idea of progress in history.[38]

One important strand in social history in the post-1945 world had indeed been strongly influenced by the modernisation theories established by Talcott Parsons and his pupils in the United States, theories which built on the works of one of the classics of sociology, Max Weber.[39] Parsons advocated a functionalist structuralism that viewed society as a collection of interconnected functional groups. He developed a theory of social action which reduced people to their social functions in a regulatory system that mediated social conflict (more or less successfully). Another strand of social history was more Marxist in orientation. Both Marxists and Weberians shared a strong commitment to functionalism and structuralism.[40] Both also shared the idea of progress in history. Social historians thus often wrote histories that sought to explain how (usually Western) societies had become more modern during the nineteenth and twentieth centuries, or how (usually non-Western) societies had missed opportunities to modernise. (See Figure 3.1.) Marxists, in particular, saw economics as determining everything else in society. This conviction was enshrined in the 'base-superstructure' model of Marxist thinking, according to which the economy was the 'base' on which cultural, social and political superstructures developed.[41] This gave pride of place to economic history. Post-war social history was also committed to forms of scientificity, i.e. the belief that history was a science that established truthfully how structures had determined events in the past. Weber's idea of studying society by means of 'ideal types' was to have a strong influence on social history.[42] It contributed to what its critics later would label reductionist methodology, i.e. one which downplayed people's agency.

Figure 3.1 Identifying progress with national history was particularly prominent in the United States, in historiography and in the arts. Chromolithograph after *American Progress* by John Gast. © Library of Congress, Corbis Historical Collection/Getty Images.

Economic history becamc more and more technical and specialist during the second half of the twentieth century. Especially in the USA, it developed its own econometric theories based on highly specialist mathematical and statistical knowledge. Ordinary historians were thus increasingly incapable of understanding the arguments put forward by an econometrics-oriented economic history. Employing deductive methods of neoclassical economics and often propagating its dubious and strongly normative assumptions about human nature, economic historians developed computer-technology-based models and fell in love with interpolations, simulations and 'back-projections' (what growth rates there might have been even if data are non-existent). They created massive new data sets and positioned themselves against what they described as impressionistically written older economic history. As a result, economic history lost touch with more general history and became an inward-looking sub-discipline only loosely attached to other fields of history writing. As it lost its appeal for general historians, it was also incapable of winning support among economists, for many of whom it remained too simplistic, introduced too few variables and therefore was not scientific enough. Over time, more mainstream historians regarded an econometrics-oriented economic history as an irrelevance. Taking on board the insights of de Certeau that in history writing quantification served, above all, to create an illusion of objectivity,[43] new cultural approaches to economic history turned away from quantitative approaches or at the very least viewed them with scepticism. As a result of all these developments, economic history inevitably suffered. Chairs of economic history were not replaced, and the whole sub-discipline went into a steep decline from the 1980s onwards.[44] This development was exacerbated by the increasing scepticism about forms of scientificity in historical writing which were genereated by the reception of the diverse theories discussed in Chapter 1. As economic history moved furthest in the direction of an alleged 'hard science' and was quite unreflective in its use of languages and concepts, it looked increasingly old fashioned in its approaches to historical writing.

Representatives of a history from below, of everyday life history and of microhistory picked this up and criticised what they saw as forms of a lifeless, bloodless structural economic and social history, in which human beings hardly figured at all as meaningful agents. Instead they set out to recover the ordinariness of people's lives, their everyday experiences, their hopes, aspirations and fears. This emphasis on the everyday demanded new approaches and access to new sources. State archives, the traditional hunting grounds of political historians, contained little of value for histories of everyday life. Hence, at least in contemporary history, historians turned to oral history as one of the means of creating the sources with which to recover everyday experiences.[45] Oral history eventually became an established part of professional history writing at the universities. Its beginnings, like that of everyday-life history, lie outside academia. A host of lay historians, including school teachers, labour movement activists and members of the professions, made it their goal to recover worlds not covered by traditional forms of academic history writing.[46] The pioneer of British oral history, George Ewart Evans, was a school teacher and never occupied a university position.[47] Over time, the category of 'experience' was much discussed, as historians pointed out that every story about an experience was itself already a representation and a narrativisation of that experience and should not be mistaken for an actual experience. Under the influence of the narrativity theories discussed in Chapter 1, the history of everyday life became a thriving sub-discipline of historical anthropology in many parts of the world.[48] With its emphasis on participant observation and 'thick description' (Clifford Geertz), anthropology appeared to many historians from below to be a discipline that had developed a range of methods that should also be applied to history.[49] (See Chapter 6.)

Apart from their championing of oral history, historians from below sought to use archival records and read them against the grain of their provenance. Thus, for example, records of court proceedings and police records could often be used to access forms of deviancy associated with people who themselves rarely left records. But, of course, historians of everyday life also eagerly hunted down the ego-documents of those who did not normally leave any records. To give a few examples of historians committed to history-from-below approaches, let me briefly discuss the work of Carlo Ginzburg, Lyndal Roper, Alf Lüdtke and Lutz Niethammer. Ginzburg used the records of the Inquisition to piece together the world view of Menocchio, a miller in northern Italy, who was twice tried for heresy, in 1583 and in 1599. As his hearings before the Inquisitional Court had been transcribed verbatim, this provided Ginzburg with a unique window on to a subordinate culture that usually only transmits its ideas, experiences and feelings orally.[50] De Certeau, Bakhtin and Foucault were among the theoreticians who influenced Ginzburg's historical writing. Roper also extensively used official court records and Inquisition records to explore witchcraft, magic and sexuality in the early modern German lands. Her essays emphasise the irreducible individual subjectivity of historical actors that historians can recapture by studying the everyday and psychological processes. Her interest in the sexuality of men and women led her to argue for the inclusion of the corporeal aspects of the body in an analysis of people's sexualities since, in her view, they could not simply be reduced to discursive practices. In explaining early modern psyches she put ordinary women centre stage.[51] Although Roper engages strongly with the work of Foucault, her own approach goes beyond a Foucauldian discourse analysis, building instead on the practice theories of de Certeau and Bakhtin. (See Chapter 1.) Lüdtke explored the lives of industrial workers and what he came to call their 'Eigensinn' in their everyday lives. To do this he used company records, police records and ego documents.[52] The translator of Lüdtke's work into English defines *Eigensinn* as 'wilfulness, spontaneous self-will, a kind of self-affirmation, an act of (re)appropriating alienated social relations on and off the shop-floor by self-assertive prankishness, demarcating a space of one's own'.[53] Following Bourdieu and Foucault, Lüdtke was intensely interested in the discourses and practices of governmentality as well as the practices employed by the subalterns to undermine them. Another German historian, Lutz Niethammer, pioneered a major oral history project in the 1980s. It investigated the lives of ordinary people in the Ruhr region, the country's industrial powerhouse, as they transitioned from Weimar to National Socialism and later to the early Federal Republic. His aim was to assess the relevance of political caesuras if measured against the experiences and life worlds of ordinary men and women.[54]

A transnational history workshop movement made a major contribution to those histories from below. Its guiding spirit in Britain was Raphael Samuel,[55] one of the co-founders of the *History Workshop Journal*. Established in 1976, it became one of the earliest intellectual centres for a politically committed left-wing history from below.[56] It was soon emulated in other countries, including Germany, where first *Geschichtswerkstatt* and later *Werkstatt Geschichte* resembled the British journal even in its name.[57] History workshops were institutions which initially shunned universities and academies and were in turn shunned by them. Their aim was to mobilise parts of civil society, including trade unionists, working-class education circles, teachers, members of the professions and everyone who identified with the broad left in an attempt to write a new history from below that would help uncover hitherto untold stories of class, gender and race. As much of its work was linked to the ambition of achieving more gender, race and class equality, one of its central concerns was bolstering the collective identities of women, the working class and minority ethnic groups. Its histories have underpinned feminist agendas, as well as those for more racial equality and more social justice. It mobilised history as a resource for politically left-wing projects and was thus as committed to underpinning collective identities as the old political history outlined in the previous chapter. It was no coincidence that the subtitle of *History Workshop Journal* in its early years was 'a journal for socialist history'. This was changed to 'socialist and feminist history' in 1982. Eventually, in 1995, the subtitle was dropped altogether – a sign that by the mid-1990s the history-from-below approaches had become more professionalised and institutionalised. Arguably they have today entered the mainstream of professional history writing.

Many historians of everyday life were sceptical about labour history's traditional concern with organised labour movements. They argued that the latter at best played a marginal role in the lives of ordinary workers. They also maintained that by focusing on organised labour, the old labour history had neglected the vast majority of workers and their experiences. Indeed, alongside structural social and economic history, labour history also experienced a crisis. The popularity of labour history in the 1960s and 1970s was associated with a left-wing political climate, the global student movement of 1968 and the New Left. Looking for struggles in the past that could inspire the struggles of the present made it appear relevant and cutting-edge to many young historians coming of age in the 1960s. When Eric Hobsbawm argued in 1978 that the 'forward march of labour' had been 'halted', this was an admission that a politically highly charged labour history had reached a dead-end.[58] Marxists had long seen class conflict as the motor driving all social change. However, with the global rise of neoliberalism and the non-revolutionary nature of whatever was left of an industrial working class in the increasingly post-industrial West, historians lost interest in past class struggles. Future generations of historians would spend less time exploring the worlds of organised labour, as these worlds did not excite them any more in their present.

As many class histories and organisational histories of labour movements seemed to speak less and less to present-day concerns, this did not affect the popularity of the works produced by the labour historian E. P. Thompson. His classic *The Making of the English Working Class* (1963) was also an organisational history in many respects, of the London Corresponding Society and other small circles of working-class radicals seeking to bring about social change in early nineteenth-century England. Thompson saw them as the precursors of left-wing political movements in his own present. *The Making* was an inspiration to generations of historians from below, since Thompson had stressed that not structures but the agency of ordinary working people in their daily interactions had literally made the English working class. His work inspired manifold excursions into the ordinary world of workers – not just in the Western world.[59] But here we are already moving into the new social history that emerged from the 1980s onwards.

I have already indicated how some of the major works written by historians of everyday life or microhistory had been inspired by some of the theories discussed in Chapter 1. Key critics of the 'old' social history, such as the British historian Patrick Joyce, argued that the 'old' structuralist social history, committed, as it was, to modernisation theory, could no longer be defended and that a 'new' social history had to be reconceptualised along narrativist, discursive and representational lines.[60] In the ensuing debate, Geoff Eley and Keith Nield responded to Joyce with the plea that social historians should embrace the insights of some of the theorists discussed in Chapter 1. At the same time they were critical of Joyce for abandoning 'the social' as a prime field of historical investigation.[61] Under the impact of these theoretical debates the fields of social, economic and labour history began to change.

The New Social, Economic and Labour Histories since the 1980s and Their Contribution to More Self-reflexive Collective Identities

Thompsonian ideas had a huge influence on the Subaltern Studies Group that emerged in India during the 1980s. Its members often focused on Indian workers and their everyday lives and struggles. Dipesh Chakrabarty, for example, investigated the jute workers of Calcutta between 1890 and 1940. Whilst coming from a Marxist tradition, he nevertheless criticised any form of economic determinism and avoided teleological assumptions about progress in history. Strongly influenced by Foucault's writings, Chakrabarty traced the emergence of the complex interrelationship between the jute workers' communal and class identities. Attentive to the pre-capitalist and pre-bourgeois contexts in which the jute workers operated, he examined connections that were based on family, kinship, community, religion and village life. His interest focused on the significance of the everyday and its impact on how workers came to think of themselves and the world surrounding them.[62] He is only one of many examples one could cite of the way in which postcolonial perspectives have enriched the field of social history in recent years.

Elsewhere, social, economic and labour historians were also rethinking their commitment to structuralism and functionalism. A younger generation of social historians now viewed modernisation theories with considerable scepticism. Many sought to apply insights gained from the theorists discussed in Chapter 1 leading to a cultural turn of social history. Thus, for example, Thomas Welskopp sought to reshape German labour history by emphasising the importance of representations, symbols and narratives in the making of early Social Democracy in Germany.[63] US labour historians also took a cultural turn in the 1970s and 1980s, emphasising either a long history of workers' militancy, or the co-option of the American working classes into the capitalist system.[64] Robert E. Weir's book on the cultures of the Knights of Labor is a good example of a new labour history which took on board insights from narrativism and discourse analysis. Thus he sets out to analyse the specific culture of solidarity and resistance that marked the Knights and set them apart from ordinary 'bread and butter' unionism. Weir talks about rituals, literature, song, imagery, sports, demonstrations and unionism as a quasi-religion. He traces a specific cultural understanding of class espoused by the Knights and put into practice through the agency of ordinary working people.[65]

Labour history has, over recent decades, moved away from the purely organisational histories of trade unionism, political parties, co-operatives and other institutions of the labour movement and instead moved towards histories of work, nutrition, leisure, sport, education, literature, sexuality, drinking, crime and a host of other areas associated with workers' lives. Arguably, the financial crisis of 2007/8 has heightened interest in the alternatives to capitalism and brought a new generation of students again closer to labour history. Many feel it is time to reconnect the global histories of work and working-class lives with the story of working-class politics, even if the politics of labour was much wider than the story of the labour movement, which was, at best, an important part of it.[66]

Whilst labour and social historians came to acknowledge the importance of representations, language and narrative, they also insisted that historians should pay due attention to practices and to material things. We will discuss the new materialism in Chapter 10, but let me here give a few examples of how the new social history has combined attention to narrativity with an emphasis on practices. Many historians were deeply influenced by Pierre Bourdieu's theory of practice since it allowed them to combine their attentiveness to language and linguistic construction with the categories of agency, experience and social action. (See Chapter 1 for more detail.) Whereas Foucault's epistemes could appear to be rather timeless structures, which made it difficult to explain social change, Bourdieu's theory of practice, by paying greater attention to agency, seemed better able to account for historical evolution.[67] Many of the contributions in Victoria Bonnell and Lynn Hunt's seminal edited collection of 1999 stressed the importance of studying not only discourses but also practices. Meaning and action were intertwined in complex ways which needed to be unravelled by historians. Practice could explain how particular readings and representations were translated into action through processes involving power and authority.[68]

If, from the 1980s onwards, social history has found ways of re-inventing itself by turning to culture and experience, the same is true for economic history. Economic historians moved away from econometrics and began studying representations rather than 'hard facts'. Neoclassical formalism and rational choice theories became less and less attractive. Instead they began to discover a hermeneutic tradition and the diverse theories of narrativity discussed in Chapter 1. The 'new economic history' stressed the heterogeneity of markets. They underlined that there always have been forms of production and consumption that did not conform to the idea of the market. They emphasised the extent to which economic transactions were related to trust, customs, routines, habits and reputation. They worked out the enormous role played by institutions and knowledge information systems in economic processes. They looked at how economic processes were gendered and paid attention to the agency of economic actors. They stressed how economic facts were often discursively constructed and based on an intersubjective understanding of economic processes.[69] If we take, for example, Craig Muldrew's *The Economy of Obligation*, he investigates economic processes through the lenses of social and cultural practices. He interprets markets as much culturally as economically and shows how credit has had multiple cultural meanings that changed over the course of the sixteenth century. Muldrew emphasises that it is impossible to understand economic developments without taking into account cultural factors such as trust, sociability, reputation and neighbourliness. Economic change went hand in hand with ethical values. Economic history thus needed to engage with literary analyses, i.e. the interaction of texts that could be interpreted differently by diverse actors recalling the theories of polyglossia and the reversibility of texts associated with the work of Bakhtin and Lacan discussed in Chapter 1.[70]

As key representative of the cultural turn in economic history in Britain Pat Hudson writes:

> The future for economic history looks bright because it is able to draw upon a wider and more sophisticated range of economic theory and method than in the past. It is also less eurocentric and more global in orientation than in its earlier hey day. It is placing new stress upon the cultural, social and institutional framework of economic activity, and it draws increasingly upon the tools of anthropology, ethnography and cultural history, alongside economics, to analyse those aspects of material life that conventional economists have rarely reached.[71]

In looking at the production, distribution and consumption of goods in the context of social, cultural and political factors, the 'new economic history' has moved towards a more holistic approach. It recognises that economic processes cannot be looked at in isolation. Ironically, this approach has also led to a proliferation of sub-fields often rooted in an older economic history: business history, transport history, demographic history, urban history and agricultural history, to mention but a few.[72]

Where an older social, economic and labour history sought to underpin class and national identities by rooting them in a supposedly objective social reality, the new histories, informed, as they were, by many of the theories discussed in Chapter 1, were far more self-reflective about the link between history writing and identity formation. Accepting the constructed nature of historical reality and the roles that narratives played in the processes of construction, the new histories highlighted the multiplicity of identities informing historical actors and actions. If identities were forever shifting, then collectivities, such as those based on class, could no longer be taken for granted. Instead they had to be deconstructed through historical writing, which contributed in turn to a far more 'self-reflexive social history' in which 'collectivities will not be taken for granted, but will be explained in terms of social and cultural practice'.[73] If social, economic and labour histories were written less with a view to forging particular class identities and more with a view to deconstructing them, they underlined how those identities were constituted in manifold ways. In particular, they paid attention to the interrelatedness of class with gender, race/ethnicity, religion and migration. Working-class solidarity was no longer self-evident and the making of solidaristic cultures needed to be explained. Women were no longer neglected in the study of wage labour. Once historians came to study the work of women, the gendered nature of the whole process of production became far more obvious. Representations of femininity and masculinity were now studied in relation to representations of class. Kathleen Canning, for example, produced a pathbreaking study on female textile workers in imperial Germany in which she showed that they negotiated the simultaneous complex demands of work and family, of the public and the private sphere. She highlighted their social practices and their agency in the historical process, and recovered their work identities and cultures. Her work combined this perspective 'from below' with a thoughtful analysis of how social policy reacted to female factory work and in turn shaped women's work in factories. This classic has contributed much to rethinking class formation and the development of the Western welfare state.[74]

Investigations of the relationship between class and ethnicity also had the effect of undermining essentialist ideas about class identities. Just as gender historians discovered a female working class, historians of race and ethnicity discovered a non-white working class and asked about the relationship between race and class.[75] They demonstrated how white and non-white workers experienced work differently and were treated differently by employers and the state. Class identities, they showed, were not only gendered, they were also negotiated through race. In many situations, they underlined how racial difference made class solidarity more difficult, since a solidaristic white working class often defended its privileges against non-white fellow workers.[76] Historians of ethnic/racial identities paid much attention to the constructedness of race, just as labour historians had paid attention to the constructedness of class. Because of their work, it is now firmly established that it was not necessarily skin colour that determined whiteness. The Irish or Italians, they showed, could also be 'blackened' and put on the same social level as free African Americans in the industrial cities of the northern United States.[77] Across the Atlantic, in Europe, the racialisation/ethnicisation of class was also a common phenomenon. Thus, historians of race/ethnicity highlighted how the English and the Germans declared the Irish in England and the Poles in Germany an ethnic and foreign 'other' and how, consequently, it was difficult to build class alliances across those ethnic borders.[78]

Historians of religion added another dimension to the complexities of class formation. Both the Irish in England and the Poles in Germany, they demonstrated, were often strongly aligned with the Catholic Church and their Catholicism inflected their understandings of class significantly. Where organised religion was hostile to predominantly socialist labour movements, they underlined that it was difficult to forge class alliances.[79] Catholicism in particular built its own labour movement, complete with trade unions, political parties and co-operatives, and here historians have highlighted the existence of strong Catholic class identities, even if the church discouraged their construction and preferred to speak the corporate language of estates instead.[80] Socialists and those adhering to religious identities could certainly find common ground with each other, but they were always trying to demarcate their respective identitites from one another.[81] Historians have thus underlined in diverse contexts how gender, ethnicity/race and religion have had an impact on the discursive construction of class and the practices of class politics emanating from it. They have also pointed to a proliferation of other identities, including those of generation and nation, all of which have impacted on our understanding of the practices of class and class politics.[82]

Conclusion

In a wonderfully personal account of historiographical developments over the past half century that interweaves autobiography with historical theory, Geoff Eley emphasised the impact made by some of the theories discussed in Chapter 1 on the writing of history. He championed the merger of cultural and social history in an encompassing history of society that incorporates the Marxist perspectives of the 1960s and 1970s, the micro-historical challenges and the theories around narrativity, social practice and the agency of ordinary people as they lived their everyday lives.[83] When Eley writes, 'between social history and cultural history, there is really no need to choose',[84] I share his argument. It reflects the argument I have been making in this chapter, namely that the 'new social history' is one that is infused with cultural history and the theories that led to the rise of the new cultural history that we will discuss in the next chapter.

In Chapter 2 on political history I stressed traditional political history's inclination to support a range of conservative political agendas, including its underwriting of diverse nationalist identities in the nineteenth and the first half of the twentieth century. As social history rose to prominence, it was opposed not only to political history on methodological grounds. Social history's rejection of its methodology was bound up with arguments about progressive political agendas such as social reform and the emancipation of the working classes. Social historians, as we have emphasised, studied social inequality as a means of calling for ways to end it. They made visible social groups that had long remained invisible, especially workers and artisans. The ideas of Marx and Weber have played a crucial role here.

The rise of social history was tightly connected with the rise of economic history, as many social and economic historians came to see the economy as the basis on which social and cultural processes unfolded. This was, of course, particularly true for Marxist historians, but it was also more widely shared among those with no particular affinity to Marx. Studying industrialisation and social change meant studying structures and processes in a teleological frame that inexorably pushed societies towards modernity. Such a structural social history, tied to modernisation theory, was soon criticised for disregarding human agency and being overly deterministic and teleological. As a result a 'new social history' emerged, that, like the new political history, deconstructed its earlier alliances with constructing forms of national and social identities. Approaches originating in cultural history were often adapted to social history in order to move it away from its earlier structuralist and determinist frameworks.

The links between history writing and identity formation were initially strong in social, economic and labour history, but their renewal found ways of being far more self-reflexive about the link between historical writing and identity formation. Overall, the new social, economic and labour historians demonstrated that class identities were always negotiated, relational, situational, shifting and constantly in the process of being remade. Hence their histories showed how identities were remade and how those identity constructions led to social practices, but they no longer underpinned those identities. By encouraging the reader to reflect on the constructed nature of all forms of identity, they contributed to de-essentialising identities in the contemporary world. In the next chapter we shall discuss directly the development of cultural history – a sub-field of historical writing that, like political and social history, had a long tradition in historical writing, but also one that was significantly reshaped under the theoretical developments of the 1960s and 1970s.

Further Reading

Lynn Abrams, *Oral History Theory*, London: Routledge, 2010.

Geoff Eley, *A Crooked Line: From Cultural History to the History of Society*, Ann Arbor: University of Michigan Press, 2005.

Pat Hudson, *History by Numbers: an Introduction to Quantitative Approaches*, London: Arnold, 2000.

Jan Lucassen (ed.), *Global Labour History: a State of the Art*, Bern: Peter Lang, 2006.

Alf Lüdtke (ed.), *The History of Everday Life: Reconstructing Historical Experiences and Ways of Life*, Princeton: Princeton University Press, 1989.

Hans Medick, 'Missionaries in a Row-Boat: Ethnological Ways of Knowing as a Challenge to Social History', in: *Comparative Studies in Society and History* 29 (1987), 76–98.

Steve Rigby, *Marxism and History: a Critical Introduction*, 2nd edn, Manchester: Manchester University Press, 1998.

Adrian Wilson (ed.), *Rethinking Social History*, Manchester: Manchester University Press, 1993.

4 *The New Cultural History*

Introduction

'In many ways, what we have seen over the past thirty years has been little more than the working out of the agenda of the New Cultural History in different directions.'[1]

Tracey Loughran's sweeping statement points to the importance of the New Cultural History for many historiographical developments in historical writing. I shall review some of them in chapters 5–11. In the current chapter I concern myself solely with the rise of the new cultural history from the 1980s onwards. It largely coincided with the impact of the linguistic and narrative turn on history writing – theories I discussed in detail in Chapter 1. There are, of course, older forms of cultural history, associated, for example, with histories of high culture, cultural sociology, the Annales school and cultural studies. In the first part of this chapter I will review these traditions since they have, in various forms, fed into the boom of cultural history towards the end of the twentieth century. However, what is frequently referred to as the cultural turn in history is unthinkable without the linguistic turn. Attention to language, narrativity and symbols was crucial for the success of cultural approaches to the past. The 'new cultural history', the subject of this chapter's second part, has spread and proliferated into many different sub-fields and contributed to the extension of what can be studied historically. In the third and final part of this chapter I will provide a few examples of prominent sub-fields, such as the history of emotions, the history of the body, the history of violence, especially collective violence, and the history of nationalism. What unites all cultural history approaches is their insistence on history as a process significantly shaped by actors. Human beings have tried to make sense of the world around them by their cultural practices and representations, constructing their identities discursively and through a range of recorded practices. The task of cultural historians is, therefore, to retrace the surviving inscriptions of these discourses and practices.

Like political, social, economic and labour history, cultural history was strongly connected to the forging of collective identities. Given the importance of the notion of culture to definitions of national identity in the nineteenth century, it is not surprising that, once again, this link was a strong one. As we shall see, the symbiotic relationship of the new cultural history with narrativism, discourse analysis and practice theory led to deconstructions of the relationship between history writing and national identity formation and a far more self-reflexive way of thinking about it.

Cultural historians were never exclusively concerned with the nation and national identities. They equally turned to class and class identities, and began deconstructing the older shibboleths to be found in identitarian forms of social history underpinning heroic notions of class, class struggle and class consciousness. As I have already in the previous chapter discussed how the new cultural history has contributed to reconceptualising histories of class and labour, I will not discuss this again here. Instead I will highlight how the 'new cultural history' underpinned a variety of identities that faced massive discrimination in the past and that were associated with the new social movements that rose to prominence in the 1970s and 1980s. Movements for racial equality, women's movements, gay, lesbian, bisexual and queer activists – they were all prominent in promoting a form of history writing that highlighted these discriminations and injustices suffered in the past in order to build on it demands for emancipation, liberation and the right to live their lives as equal citizens. Like class historians almost a century earlier, race, women's and LGBTI historians wrote a cultural history which had emancipatory and identitarian agendas. However, coming equipped with the theoretical arsenal provided by the 'new cultural history', many of them were keen to highlight the constructed nature of all identities and because of this, even if they remained tied to emancipatory and progressive agendas, included a self-reflective element in their histories.

Traditions of Writing Cultural History

Culture was an important concept in Enlightenment historiography, carrying a double meaning. On the one hand, it stood for the self-perfection of individual capacities and virtues through education (what in German is expressed through the idea(l) of *Bildung*). On the other hand, it was also an entity possessing agency in the realm of universal history. Cultures, in the plural, with their relations to peoples and languages, often formed the basis for universal histories.[2] Strong national(ist) sentiments among historians produced histories that championed the historian's own culture above all others. Thus, a Western-centric bias among Western historians posited a division between allegedly higher Western cultures and lower non-Western ones. At the extreme end of such thinking, Africa became the continent without history. There culture was frozen in a timeless essence akin to a natural state of being. African cultures were therefore not studied by historians anymore but by representatives of a new discipline, ethnology, which focused on so-called 'primitive cultures'. In the West, cultures were universalised, as famously happened in French republicanism after 1789, or they were particularised, i.e. identified with specific languages, cultural practices and constructions of ethnic groups, as was common in most Western nation-states in the nineteenth century. Culture was an important tool in generating the fiction of ethnic homogeneity that underpinned the various attempts to construct nations.[3] Once ethnicity became a biological destiny with the emergence of diverse race theories in the context of Social Darwinism from the last third of the nineteenth century onwards, the concept of culture also underpinned these theories.[4]

At the cradle of ideas of 'national cultures' stood Johann Gottfried Herder, for whom the fundamental unit in world history was the nation. For him, nations possessed collective personalities made up of culture and language.[5] Cultural history was, however, not necessarily tied to projects of nation-building. It could also relate to 'historical meso-regions' that transcended the nation-state.[6] In Scandinavia notions of a common culture shared by all Scandinavian nations underpinned pan-Scandinavian historical writing.[7] Culture also played a central role in pan-Germanism, pan-Slavism, Yugoslavism, Iberianism and pan-Turanism. Cultural historians could commit to the nation-state or to transnational entities. They could even be searching for universal ideals and aspirations. Deeply influenced by Italian Renaissance culture, Jakob Burckhardt, in what is often seen as his major work, sought to depict how the ideal of modern man as an individual subjectivity emerged during the Italian Renaissance. At the same time he made this into a universal aspiration of humankind. In one of the all-time best-selling books in cultural history, his ambition as a cultural historian was nothing less than to establish the mental attitudes and structures of thinking that lay behind the Renaissance.[8] The outcome was deeply Eurocentric and even racist.[9] One of the founding figures of cultural history, Burckhardt identified three forces driving historical development forward: the state, religion and culture. Of those three, only culture sought to exercise some form of coercive power. It alone was therefore a force for the liberation of (white) individualities and subjectivities.[10]

Burckhardt was a towering figure in nineteenth-century cultural history and had a huge impact on the self-understanding of cultural historians elsewhere. The same can be said of the founding generation of the Annales school. I have discussed their contribution to social history in Chapter 3. Both social and cultural historians have looked to them as shapers of their respective sub-disciplines, with cultural historians often referring to the Annalistes' concern with mentalities, i.e. particular mindsets through which people made sense of the world around them.[11] The proximity of this idea to Burckhardt's search for mental attitudes is obvious. But the Annales school widened his concern with elite culture so as to include popular culture and ordinary men and women, a concern which had already characterised the work of the Dutch cultural historian Johan Huizinga. In his magnum opus, *The Waning of the Middle Ages*, he, like Burckhardt, sought to understand the spirit of an age, in his case the transition period of the late Middle Ages.[12] He wrote on chivalry and heroism but also on religiosity and death, love and compassion. Cultural motifs and themes abounded in his description of medieval urban life.[13] A similar concern with understanding collectives rather than individuals can be found in the writings of the founding generation of the Annales. Thus Lucien Febvre spoke of civilisations having mental tools to make sense of the world which the historians needed to understand. His study on Rabelais, first published in 1942, was not a biography of an individual, but an exploration of the beginnings (and limits) of free thought (i.e. the questioning of Christian orthodoxies) in sixteenth-century France. Marc Bloch's study on the 'royal touch', first published in French in 1924, was an attempt to understand how people in the Middle Ages made sense of the world around them by referring to the miraculous powers of kings.[14] The study of popular beliefs, concepts and mentalities continued with the post-Second World War generation of Annales historians. Philippe Ariès, for example, wrote a history of childhood that sought to trace the emergence, between the late medieval period and the eighteenth century, of the idea of a separate phase of human development, called childhood.[15]

Alongside the nineteenth-century traditions, represented by Herder and Burckhardt, and the twentieth-century Annaliste historiography, a third major influence on cultural historians came from Anglophone cultural studies, associated with names such as Raymond Williams and Stuart Hall. Williams' article on the etymology of the word 'culture' in his hugely influential book *Keywords* is one of the most often cited starting points for discussions on culture in the English-speaking world and beyond. Writing in 1976, Williams saw three contemporary meanings of culture: first, 'a general process of intellectual, spiritual and aesthetic development', secondly, 'a particular way of life' in time and space, and, thirdly, 'the works and practices of intellectual and especially artistic activity'.[16] His particular brand of cultural Marxism built on the Annalistes' concern with the everyday, for he also emphasised that 'culture is ordinary'.[17] Influenced by the writings of Antonio Gramsci, Williams connected the world of culture tightly to the world of social and economic processes, but without giving primacy to the latter and by emphasising the dynamic, interconnected relationship between cultural, economic and social factors.

Similarly situated in an unorthodox cultural Marxism was the seminal work of the cultural theorist Stuart Hall, who was closely associated with the journals *New Left Review* and *Marxism Today*, and headed the famous Birmingham Centre for Contemporary Cultural Studies in the 1970s. (On Hall see Chapter 1.) Strongly influenced by the ideas of Gramsci and Foucault, he came to understand culture as a site of social intervention. Always conscious of the impact of power relationships on culture, he wrote pioneering works on cultural identity, especially in relation to race. Here he underlined the ways in which these identities had been constructed culturally over time. In so doing he contributed to a greater awareness of the way in which they were never given but always the result of cultural processes aligned with power relationships.[18] His 'encoding/decoding model of communication' became more influential in media studies than in history,[19] but cultural historians also often referred back to many of Hall's pathbreaking ideas about the role of culture in human society.[20] Other major figures in the Anglophone turn to cultural history included Richard Hoggart and E. P. Thompson, who has been discussed in the previous chapter.[21] Thompson's emphasis on the role of culture in constructing class identities, like Hoggart's broadening of traditional understandings of culture, fed directly into the cultural turn of the 1980s.

The Cultural Turn in Historical Writing

All these traditions of writing cultural history fed into the turn to culture inspired by the poststructuralist theories of the 1960s and 1970s, some of which I discussed in Chapter 1.[22] The strong emphasis of the older cultural history on subjectivity, interpretation, language and meaning as well as representation was highly adaptable to a poststructuralist-informed cultural history.[23] Given the many continuities between older forms of cultural history and the 'new cultural history', Alison Moore suggested that the narrative of rupture that is associated with the notion of a 'new cultural history' should be taken with more than a grain of salt.[24] However, something new was arguably happening: in the wake of poststructuralism cultural historians denied the possibility of history reconstructing historical reality. Instead, they focused on how historical reality was represented and constructed through signs, texts and symbols. Representations referred to the construction of meaning. Characteristically, one of the foremost new cultural historians in France, Roger Chartier, wrote that it was the principal aim of his studies 'to note how, in different times and places, a specific social reality was constructed, how people conceived of it and how they interpreted it to others'.[25] Methodologically, cultural historians often built on the work of Wilhelm Dilthey who, at the beginning of the twentieth century, had developed his hermeneutical approach around notions of understanding rather than explanation.[26] Paul Ricoeur, for example, called on historians to decipher 'the hidden meaning in the apparent meaning' and unfold 'the levels of meaning implied in the literal meaning'.[27] Ricoeur belonged to those history theorists who came to the fore in the 1960s and 1970s and reshaped the historical dicipline in subsequent decades. (On Ricoeur see Chapter 1.) His influence has been particularly visible in cultural history, as was Hayden White's emphasis on narrativity and imagination in historical writing. Initially cultural historians demarcated their position firmly from older forms of social history. In a seminal article, often cited by new cultural historians, Lawrence Stone called on fellow historians to abandon their concern with social structures. They should, he argued, turn to human existence itself. In his view 'the culture of the group, and even the will of the individual, are potentially at least as important agents of change as the impersonal forces of material output and demographic growth.'[28] Ten years later, Lynn Hunt published a seminal collection of essays in which she formulated some of the key theoretical concerns of the 'new cultural history' and gave plentiful examples of its historiographical practice.[29]

From the 2000s onwards, new cultural historians sought to embed their concern with language, symbols and discourse in social practice. Drawing on the social theories of Pierre Bordieu and Anthony Giddens, they arrived at histories that both captured the structures of social interaction and emphasised the agency of individual historical actors.[30] This new concern with sociological theories also led to a revision of some of the more literary concerns of the new cultural historians. Thus, Lynn Hunt, one of those spearheading the new cultural turn, already worried, five years after publishing *The New Cultural History*, about the impact of postmodernism on the writing of history – together with Joyce Appleby and Margaret Jacob. Whilst, in 1989, she praised some of the insights of postmodern thinkers and emphasised their relevance for the practice of writing history, she now was concerned about the wilder shores of relativism on which it would be impossible to refute those deliberately falsifying history, including holocaust denial. For her and her co-editors, it was important to find grounds on which history could still tell apart true and false stories, even if they had to admit that to speak about truth in history was deeply problematic.[31] The turn to sociology was one way of finding new firmer ground under their feet. Another five years on, in 1999, Lynn Hunt co-edited another seminal collection entitled *Beyond the Cultural Turn*. Here, together with sociologist Victoria Bonnell, she explored new ways of writing cultural history that would steer a middle way between accepting many of the insights of the body of theories discussed in Chapter 1 and refuting a complete relativism in historical writing.[32]

New cultural historians were, above all, concerned with the ordinary, the everyday, the working folk rather than with elite groups and elite culture. This move had been well prepared by Raymond Willians and the cultural Marxists referred to above. Furthermore, the new cultural historians understood cultural history as a history of the processes and practices that produced culture. These processes, they claimed, were always situational and relational. If we look, for example, at the six-volume *Cultural History of Women*, which extends from antiquity to the present day, one sees how the authors looked at the life cycle of people, their bodies and sexualities, popular belief systems, including religion, as well as the impact of medicine and illness on ordinary people's lives. They looked at the diversity of women's private lives, investigated their public lives, studied the presence of women in the world of work and examined the long struggle to gain access to education. Examining the diverse ways in which women were subject to male regimes of power whilst themselves also sometimes exerting power, they highlighted the representation of women throughout the ages.[33] Questions regarding the collective identity of women are to the fore in many of the chapters in the *Cultural History of Women*. Highlighting the discrimination and oppression faced by women as well as their agency in fighting against patriarchal systems, they justify the politics of women's emancipation. However, unlike an older women's history that combined the construction of identity with the formulation of essences, the new cultural history of women is very aware of the constructed nature of gender (through discourses and social practices). In this sense it avoids essentialising women and gender and instead remains highly self-reflexive about women's identities and how these have been continuously constructed in power relationships that in turn define the position of women (and men) in society. In this sense we have here the continuation of an emancipatory agenda in history writing that makes use of Hall's concept of 'identification' (see Chapter 1). Susan Pedersen has called this the 'transformative presence' of feminist history writing:

> If we take feminism to be that cast of mind that insists that the differences and inequalities between the sexes are the result of historical processes and are not blindly 'natural,' we can understand why feminist history has always had a dual mission – on the one hand to recover the lives, experiences, and mentalities of women from the condescension and obscurity in which they have been so unnaturally placed, and on the other to re-examine and rewrite the entire historical narrative to reveal the construction and workings of gender.[34]

I will return to this theme in the next chapter which examines women's, gender and feminist history writing.

The new cultural history that emerged in the West during the 1980s had major repercussions in the Subaltern Studies School of historical writing. The emphasis on subjectivities and individualities allowed Subaltern historians to stress the agency of colonial and postcolonial subjects. In African history, for example, an emphasis on the culture of ritual practices helped reconfigure histories of the slave trade.[35] Through culture and customs, African colonial subjects were able to negotiate their position in colonial society with the colonisers. As Megan Vaughan has pointed out, historians of Africa such as Jan Vansina[36] had long employed the techniques of cultural history in their studies of long-term African political traditions.[37] Studying the culture of ritual also found repercussions in Mexican history. Thus, for example, Claudio Lomnitz's book on death in Mexico underlined the importance of cultural constructions of death for Mexican national identity.[38]

Postcolonial cultural histories have been particularly alert to the construction of racial identities and their impact on racial discrimination from the discovery of the non-European world by Europeans in the sixteenth century down to the present day. Ramón Grosfoguel, for example, has attempted to rethink the global position of Puerto Ricans and of Puerto Rico from the position of coloniality in a world system that interlinked modernity, capitalism and coloniality in intrinsic and multiple ways. The postcolonial subject, he argued, was constructed as racially inferior over centuries and its representation in culture was a long struggle between attempts to stabilise a racial order in support of a particular vision of capitalist-colonial modernity and opposition to that order from the postcolonial subjects themselves.[39] Postcolonial cultural histories have also emphasised the extent to which the culture of ordinary people was influenced by popular beliefs and cultural practices. Thus, for example, Shahid Amin has analysed Indian peasants' religious beliefs and practices and how they impacted on their perception of Gandhi. He concludes that the peasants attributed to the Indian national leader occult powers derived from ancient beliefs in the occult power of Indian gods.[40] Race and cultures of racism have not only influenced in multiple ways the writings on colonial and postcolonial subjects, but they have also impacted on the literature on the metropoles. In English cultural history, historians such as Bill Schwartz have emphasised the degree to which definitions of white English racial, gender and national identities can only be properly understood against the background of England's imperial past.[41]

The cultural turn in historical writing produced a greater awareness of the way in which national cultures are constructions rooted in nationalist ambitions. Cultural transfer studies have attempted to denationalise historical writing by drawing attention to cultural transfers in history, i.e. cultural practices that moved from one place to another and changed in transit. Whilst being closely related to political transfer studies discussed in Chapter 2 on political history, these histories focus not on political but on cultural transfers. Cultural practices were adapted and newly contextualised in a variety of different ways, thereby producing melanges of different cultural practices often described in terms of hybridity and creolisation – picking up the ideas of Homi Bhabha mentioned in Chapter 1 above.[42] The fiction of cultural and ethnic homogeneity was contrasted with historical processes of cultures emerging out of adaptations. The nationalising process of the nineteenth century often produced conscious forgetfulness about such adaptations. Nationalists attempted to present culture as unchanging, and part of an ethnic or even racial set-up of a particular people that marked an essentialised national core. By historically retracing the processes of cultural transfer and adaptation, historians showed how spatial identities emerged and developed in constant exchange with other spatial identities.[43]

The history of cultural transfer broke up the picture of homogenous and internally stable national cultures by demonstrating that they depended on a dialectical process through which foreign elements were selectively appropriated. Cultural transfer historians called into question national modes of argumentation, relativised national yardsticks and broke up national explanatory frameworks. National identity appears in their works as a process of cultural appropriation and mediation, and what is imagined as 'one's own' is bound up with what is conceived of as 'the other', be it in negative or in positive terms. That 'other' often appeared, at one and the same time, attractive and dangerous. As a rule, therefore, appropriation and rejection are two sides of the same coin. Research on cultural transfers thus contributes to exposing the absurdity of notions of national character and of national cultures composed of national essences. This research thus makes visible the process of creation and evolution of plurally constituted national cultures. National memory comprises innumerable fragments of cultural assets, a goodly proportion of which are imported and adapted.

Borders are of particular importance for research on cultural transfers.[44] On the one hand, a border can mean demarcation, putting off limits that which is defined as not belonging. On the other hand, borders can indicate preparedness for exchange and appropriation – a transmission belt of 'the other' on the way to its adoption as one's own. Border territories may variously be understood as sites of confrontation, intolerance and the collision of fundamentally incompatible 'national' values and normative horizons.[45] But they can also be terrains of an altogether different kind. Thus, delineations between 'national cultures' are blurred, for there is exchange between the mutually 'other' and foreign. Not every transfer is immediately recognisable as such. Once the foreign has been embedded in indigenous discursive and agential contexts, its foreign-ness tends to disappear. The archaeological capacities of the historian are required to bring the connections to light once more. The transmitters and the means of transmission must first be identified. Transmitters shared a transnational consciousness which permitted them to raise their sights above and beyond the merely national. This kind of international orientation was facilitated by personal contacts, lengthy stays abroad and opportunities for institutional co-operation. Together with Bénédicte Zimmermann, Michael Werner has developed a theoretical and methodological framework for cultural transfer studies that has inspired many studies in cultural history.[46]

The theories of cultural transfer were developed in relation to Franco-German history in the second half of the 1980s,[47] but they have implications for a very wide range of geographical and chronological fields. Take, for example, the transatlantic slave trade, where black people were brutally uprooted from their places of origin, violently displaced across the Atlantic and inserted into an altogether different culture. In the plantations of the new world, their African cultures, extremely varied in themselves depending on where the slaves came from, had to be adapted in multiple ways to their new circumstances in order to produce new meanings. Ritual and bodily practices were transformed in this process of producing forms of cultural hybridity. The culture of the slaves cannot be traced back to some form of 'pure' origin, but rather it is rooted in complex, ambiguous and contradictory ways of adapting beliefs and practices that they brought from one place to another. This process of constructing culture involved mixing and creolisation. Paul Gilroy's analysis of the Black Atlantic emphasises its historical evolution, its constitution amidst a range of power relationships that have been constantly remaking black and white cultures alike. American, British and Caribbean identities are thus intertwined and interconnected in manifold ways. Those hybrid identities which are characteristic and constitutive of modernity cannot be understood with reference to origins, but only by understanding displacement, diaspora and slavery. Gilroy's book thus unmasks forms of cultural nationalism and identitarian claims that are rooted in some form of cultural essence.[48] Instead, in his book *After Empire*, he proposes a 'new humanism' based on the experience of oppression and suffering, one which denies all notions of cultural identity that draw categorical borders between diverse groups of people. Influenced by his teacher Stuart Hall, discussed in Chapter 1, Gilroy understands collective identities as never fixed and closed but always under construction.[49]

Gilroy has conceptualised race in a way that allows for 'identification' in Hall's sense and combines it with a vision of multiculturalism that has direct political repercussions.[50] On the one hand, he insists on the importance of formulating a proud racial identity for those who are racially oppressed, even if such identities can never be built on ethnic absolutes and essences.[51] Instead, such identity construction aims at ending centuries-old forms of discrimination against non-white populations, by questioning the racial categories of white and black themselves and by providing resources for hybrid and multicultural identitites in the present. Such conceptualisations of race allow black historians today to act as 'engaged historians'[52] and use their professional expertise to rally support for contemporary movements, such as the Black Lives Matter movement in the United States.[53] Once again, the theoretical framework employed, inspired by various theories discussed in Chapter 1 above, is one that emphasises not essences but constructions of identity that are forever shifting over time and place. It therefore provides an emancipatory identitarian agenda that is highly self-reflexive about its own political agenda. Similar to the agendas of feminist cultural historians, discussed above, race historians have attempted to combine emancipatory identitarian concerns with the avoidance of essentialist claims that would lead to the construction of new exclusionary practices.

Another perspective that has had a huge influence on cultural historians is that of alterity. It goes back to Bakhtin who had already argued that being outside a particular culture was key to understanding it.[54] Homi Bhabha's claim that new cultural perspectives can only be developed from a position of marginality and alterity go in a similar direction.[55] These ideas ring true, especially with historians dealing with subjects that have been marginal in history, such as women's history, the history of particular racial groups, and also the histories of those whose sexual orientation differed from the heterosexual mainstream. LGBTI historians have written cultural histories that, first, highlighted the presence of LGBTI identities throughout history and, secondly, underlined that those with LGBTI orientations have been struggling against much discrimination, persecution and oppression, in order to get accepted in society and live out their sexual orientations. From their position of marginality and alterity they have also developed new cultural perspectives capable of redefining understandings of sexuality in our contemporary societies. Historical anthropologists like Stephen Murray and Will Roscoe have traced the practice of homosexual relationships and cultures in black Africa before the European colonists stamped it out.[56] Throughout all continents and times, LGBTI groups have lived their various sexualities in the face of oppression,[57] which is an indirect way of establishing identitarian concerns with a view of fostering a contemporary emancipatory agenda that, like the agendas on racial and women's equality, remains acutely aware of the constructed nature of the identities in question. The new cultural history, on the one hand, was involved in identitarian projects and, on the other, attempted to avoid essentialisation and to be open about the constructed nature of all identities and their respective political connotations.

In the final part of this chapter, I will give some examples of subfields of the new cultural history that have been particularly fruitful in recent years: histories of emotions and bodies, histories of violence, and histories of nationalism.

Promising New Avenues in the New Cultural History

Anna Green has pointed out that many of the most famous cultural histories, which have appeared over recent decades, have focused on 'curious, rebellious, purposeful' individuals. From this she concludes:

'It is time for the rediscovery of individuality within cultural history.'[58] Yet, as she herself then goes on to elaborate, any such individuality is always a construction, as individuality is part and parcel of a discursive field, where it is closely bound up with performativity in a specific given situation. The performative turn in historical writing, drawing on the theories of Erving Goffman, John Austin and Pierre Bourdieu, looks at human culture as a performance, through which identities are constructed.[59] As Peter Burke has pointed out, the notion of culture as performance developed out of an older idea that society resembled the theatre. Many of the thinkers discussed in Chapter 1 did indeed use ideas related to the theatre. Hayden White spoke of emplotment. (See Chapter 1.) Michel Foucault was fascinated by the 'theatre of terror' in his writings on executions. Michel de Certeau wrote about medieval reports on possessed nuns as 'spectacle'. Peter Burke therefore related the performative turn to the rise of postmodern ideas in historical writing.[60] He also explicitly noted how studies on collective identities have used the new attention to performance to question essentialism in those collective identities. Performances of national and class loyalty, of ethnic and gender identities could be analysed to demonstrate how these changed according to specific situations and times. The performative turn thus moved attention away from fixity and towards fluidity.[61] With reference to Bourdieu, cultural historians began to analyse the gap between the perfomative 'script' and the actual 'practices' of the performance that could vary considerably. Collective identities worked through code-switching, hybridity, diglossia and syncretism and could never be reduced to fixed essences. What Peter Burke calls 'occasionalism' has thus contributed in a major way to historians discussing collective identities in a more self-reflexive manner.[62] Analysing in detail how performances have shaped collective identities differently at different times and in different situations heightens the consciousness of how individualities and their identities are never givens but always forged through cultural processes, and therefore never absolutes but always relative to given situations and subject to change. Any essentialisation of identity is indeed very difficult to achieve through this lens of cultural history.

One of the early pioneers of cultural history in France was Alain Corbin who made the historicity of the senses his big topic. Taking his cue from Foucault, who had famously commented that feelings, contrary to popular belief, were not eternal but that they had a history,

Corbin looked at the sense of smell and the sense of hearing.[63] Smell and sound, Corbin argued, are historically constructed and relate to regimes of power that can determine their meaning. Rival conceptualisations did, however, mean that such power was always contested. Through giving meaning to smells and sounds, it was possible to attribute to social groups both physical and moral qualities. Women, workers, peasants and whole ethnicities came to be defined by a certain smell or sound. The senses had to be regulated by governments, they became the subject of medical discourse, and individual households invested heavily to prevent, for example, the emergence of certain odours. The bourgeoisie discovered fragrances that were associated with good smell. Hygiene, erotic appeal and morality were all soon associated with particular smells. Corbin was also one of the first to write a history of the sea, analysing the anxieties and phantasies as well as interests and leisure pursuits that human beings associated with the sea.[64] Up until the mid-eighteenth century, Europeans perceived it largely as a hostile and inhospitable place – the counterpart of human civilisation. Under the double impact of new ideas in medicine, which promoted the sea as being good for health, and of European Romanticism, which provided intellectual and moral value to the sea, it became a magical and spiritual place. Soon seaside resorts abounded on the coasts of Europe. Corbin's books were sensitive to the fact that the history of our senses had a social and a gender dimension. Representation of the senses ordered societies into different social hierarchies.

Corbin's history of the senses paved the way for an emerging sub-field, the history of emotions, which has risen to prominence over the past twenty years. Whilst Peter Burke could ask in 2005: 'Is There a Cultural History of Emotions?',[65] fifteen years later, few historians doubt that the answer to this question is an emphatic 'yes'. Indeed, from about the turn of the millennium onwards the history of emotions has become a booming field of historical investigation – with new journals and book series devoted to it and new research centres being founded in different parts of the world. Of course, we can also trace the concern for emotions in history back to older historiographies. In the midst of the Second World War, Lucien Febvre already called for a history of emotions.[66] Cultural historians, above all Johan Huizinga, dealt explicitly with the topic of emotions.[67] Yet, as Piroska Nagy has argued, the breakthrough which established a sub-field of the history of emotions with its own conceptual, methodological and theoretical debates took place only from the late 1970s onwards and was directly related to the influence of poststructuralist theories and the cultural turn in history writing.[68] From Peter and Carol Stearns' call for a sub-discipline of 'emotionology'[69] to Carolyn Pedwell's attempt to 'de-colonise empathy',[70] there has been no shortage of attempts to put emotions centre stage in historical writing. Drawing on insights from a wide variety of neighbouring disciplines, above all psychology, anthropology and sociology, historians of emotions have either examined particular emotions, e.g. shame, sorrow, anger, hatred, happiness, love, or viewed emotions as an analytical category with which to understand better particular historical developments, processes or events. Social constructivist approaches had a huge influence on generations of historians examining how affective phenomena have had very different connotations in diverse cultures across the globe.[71] Yet there have also been those, like William M. Reddy, who have warned that Foucault's discourses and Bourdieu's practice theory cannot capture the full force, significance and meaning of emotions in history. Yet Reddy admits that his 'concept of emotives builds on poststructuralist insights about language but goes beyond them'. Testing the limits of what he calls 'simplistic constructivism' and relativism, he points to a basic universalism of affects that are, if not the same, at least very similar, in all cultures. They cannot, he argues, be constructed from nothing but are rooted in physiological and psychological realities. Acknowledging this, however, does not lead him to re-endorse essentialist ideas about identity. His 'emotives' have the power to shape collective group identities, but they are not 'natural'.[72] The interesting thing about emotions, he argues, is who controls them and how the power over emotions, always contested, affects change in societies. Hence Reddy's important critique of a simplistic constructivism does not re-instate essentialism; on the contrary, he insists, with many of the thinkers discussed in Chapter 1, on the need to overcome historical writing that fosters such essentialism underpinning collective identities.

Whereas earlier histories of emotions focused on textual discourses about emotions, more recent ones have incorporated diverse forms of visualisations of emotions. (See Chapter 9.) This has involved studying objects that were given emotional value and impacted on people's emotions. Furthermore, the sub-field has moved from studying discursive representations of emotions to a concern with their bodily basis. I have already noted at several points how historians moved from a history of discourses to one of social practices. Similarly, I also see in the history of emotions a growing concern with emotions as social practices. Historians increasingly ask what emotions actually do in particular circumstances. The focus can be on individual selves and their developments, on small communities, like villages, or also on larger ones, like nations. As Ute Frevert has argued, the study of emotions should link subjectivities to social, economic and political structures and developments.[73] Emotions are crucial to the construction of individual selves and form the basis of modern subjectivities. They are constantly being performed, manipulated and instrumentalised by diverse actors in history. Examining their history thus not only provides the challenge to historise 'emotions as bodily feelings',[74] it also provides answers to some of the most pressing political concerns of the contemporary world. It is no coincidence that the history of emotions rose to prominence at a time when, during the 1970s and 1980s, people in the West were infatuated with the self and with identity. The history of emotions allows for the unpacking and deconstructing of selves and identities and therefore also for a more self-reflexive way of conceptualising them both throughout history. It thus is, as a sub-field, directly related to problematising and creating greater awareness about the construction of identities through history writing.

Like so much history writing, the history of emotions emerged in the Western world and tends to work with Western norms and concepts. It is, however, also becoming increasingly popular in the non-Western world. The question will have to be answered whether the conceptualisation and theoretical frameworks to be found in the history of emotions will be changed by these studies on non-Western contexts. We already have some wonderful comparative studies done on how emotions cross the boundary between West and East. Thus, for example, William Reddy's *The Making of Romantic Love* is an outstanding comparison of the relationship between longing and sexuality in medieval Europe, India and Japan. Examining the conceptualisation of that relationship by European aristocrats, troubadors and romance writers (see Figure 4.1), he concludes that the European notion of romantic love was constructed as a means of overcoming the condemnation of sex by Christian religion as sinful and shameful. Turning his attention from medieval Christian contexts to Buddhist and Hindu sources in

Japan and Bengal, Reddy argues that here there was no need to differentiate between love defined as a 'longing for attachment' and sex, since both were only thinkable within a larger spiritual realm that did not identify sex with lustful sin. His immensely differentiated and sophisticated argument underlines to what extent a history of emotions can historise emotions and show how they were culturally constructed over time in different ways and according to diverse contexts.[75]

The history of emotions arguably cannot be written without taking into account the wider history of the body – another prominent subfield in cultural history associated with the problematisation of essentialised forms of collective identity. Thus, it is no coincidence that gender historians were among the earliest advocates of a history of

Figure 4.1 Woodcut illustration from the medieval French romance 'Le Roman de Melusine'. © Fine Art, Corbis Historical Collection/Getty Images.

the (female and male) body and its role in producing gender identities.[76] Histories of gender, reproduction and sexuality belonged to some of the earliest body histories in the 1990s, and many of them were strongly influenced by the writings of Foucault who, of course, was himself intensely interested in the construction of deviant bodies. Many body histories chose subjects to do with medicine, psychology, criminality and diverse therapeutic approaches that aimed at optimising and 'normalising' bodies.[77] Most of these works were characterised by a strong determination to do away with any biologist explanation of the body. Much of this scholarship underlines the extent to which the discrimination and persecution of 'deviant' bodies directly resulted from specific normative constructions of the body. Collective identities, it was argued, rested on such constructions, which often excluded all those who did not fit them. National identity was itself related to bodily ideals of health, fitness and beauty,[78] just as racial identity was based on assumptions about 'white' or 'black' or 'Jewish' bodies.[79] Foucault's influence did not end there. His writings on biopolitics and governmentality have produced work on racism and the construction of 'colour lines'. The body of the colonised and the body of the coloniser were written into practices of colonial subjugation and resistance alike.[80] Since different spaces produced diverse bodily experiences, the urban body was constructed in distinctly different ways from the rural one.[81]

In Chapter 1, I showed how the idea of space was related to the construction of identities. The history of the body has revealed in manifold ways how bodies were a vital field for the construction of such spatial identities. Whilst early works deconstructed discourses about the body, increasing attention has focused on its materiality. Historians have begun asking pertinent questions about how that materiality was constructed. Thus, for example, the body of the worker in industrial societies was, it is claimed, produced through scientific research, associated, for example, with the sociology of work and human resources management. Such research investigated eating habits, leisure pursuits and practices at the workplace in order to optimise the bodies of workers and thereby increase their productivity.[82] Many histories also concentrated on recording resistance to attempts, often associated with a politics of social engineering, to produce such optimised bodies in order to make capitalism more lucrative. Bourdieu's concept of the 'habitus', referred to in Chapter 1, was often used in studies on how the body was moulded to fit particular forms of class, national, racial, religious or gender identities. The history of sport, religious history and the history of social movements have all benefited from paying attention to bodies and the way in which identities were constructed through and with bodies.[83] The same is true for the history of historiography: the modalities of body politics shaped the nineteenth-century discipline in multiple ways, re-inforcing a dislike for female bodies and their alleged inability for academic work. It prioritised heterosexual male bodies as the only adequate ones for the writing of history. Ideas about the body thus directly excluded women from 'scientific' history writing.[84]

The history of (bodily) emotions can be usefully applied to traditional fields of historical writing, including histories of international conflict and revolutions. Rob Boddice wrote that emotions 'were central to the experience and the course of revolutions and counter-revolutions'.[85] The body also frequently served as a weapon in political struggles, most notably in the hunger strikes carried out by political prisoners. This brings us to another sub-field of historical inquiry that in recent years has flourished under the influence of cultural paradigms – the history of violence. Cultural historians have increasingly understood violence as being rooted in specific cultures and have tried to understand it as a form of communication. Much work has commented on the decline of interpersonal violence in the West as part and parcel of Norbert Elias' 'civilising process'. Many scholars have argued that the decline in interpersonal violence has resulted from changes in the conceptualisations of male honour, and the rise of individualism.[86] Others attempted to make sense of the enormous violence of the first half of the twentieth century, with its two world wars, the Shoa and the Armenian genocide.[87] As Stefanos Geroulanos and Todd Meyers have shown, the First World War completely reconfigured the human body as a self-regulating system. The sites of meaning associated with the body subsequently influenced a whole range of disciplines, from psychology to political thought and further to medicine and cybernetics.[88] The influence of violence on the human body has been extensively studied,[89] as has the attempt to curb violence through diverse ideas to do with humanitarianism and human rights.[90] Violence has been discussed as an effective means of excluding minorities – not just in the modern period. David Niremberg's study on 'communities of violence' in the Middle Ages, for example, has argued convincingly that collective communities have repeatedly dramatised the exclusion of others through spectacles and rituals of purification that need to be studied by cultural historians.[91] Bakhtin's insights into the role of violence in festivals and carnivalesque-type festivities inspired many of those studies. Bob Scribner's work on popular culture in the German lands during the Reformation is a good example of how Bakhtin's insights were used to make sense of religious practices aimed at constructing religious identities.[92] Furthermore, Pierre Bourdieu's theory of 'symbolic violence'[93] and Michel Foucault's reflections on disciplining and punishing and on the 'microphysics of power' have inspired further explorations in this area.[94] A cultural understanding of violence has heightened our understanding of violence as a phenomenon associated with particular forms of human culture and constructions of specific identities. It has made us warier and more self-reflexive about such identities and their power to engender diverse forms of violence. Strong identities underpinned by histories and historical consciousness have in the past been used to justifying violence, including terrorism, war and genocide. Ethnic, racial, political, religious and class violence was often directly related to such strong identities.[95] Zygmunt Baumann saw one of the characteristics of modernity in its desire to get rid of identitarian ambivalences and he perceived this desire as the origin of modernity's violence against anything perceived as 'other'.[96] This is precisely one of the reasons why many of the new cultural histories that have emerged from the 1980s onwards have been wary of such identitarian concerns of historical writing.

A fourth prominent field in historical writing that has been redefined by cultural history approaches is that of nationalism studies. Early nationalism studies, represented by scholars like Friedrich Meinecke, Carlton Hayes and Elie Kedourie, studied, above all, ideas and ideologies associated with nationalism. Later on, writers influenced by either Marxism or Weberian ideas of modernisation instead investigated the social and economic functions nationalism fulfilled. The writings of Ernest Gellner, Eric Hobsbawm and Miroslav Hroch can be seen as examples of this trend. Historians such as John Breuilly asked about the ways in which nationalism was linked to power and served the interests of those in power. In the case of nationalism scholars such as A. D. Smith and John Hutchinson we see a cultural turn. They were interested in looking at the production of representations, symbols and layers of meaning in nationalist movements. Nationalism was no longer seen merely as a set of ideas or an ideology fulfilling a modernising function in societies. Instead, scholars now paid much more attention to the ways in which it was constructed by specific actors and represented through cultural practices by various agents in history who often rivalled each other in their conceptualisations of the nation. By focusing on the processes of cultural construction of nations and nationalisms, this scholarship contributed to a more self-reflective understanding of the object of their study. Eric Hobsbawm and Terence Ranger's celebrated edited collection on *The Invention of Tradition* highlighted to what extent culture has always been constructed in the interest of certain people and in conjunction with power. Culture was to be seen not as an unchangeable given, but as something that is made. Historians writing about nationalism took their cue from the 'invention of tradition' and 'imagined communities'. (See Chapter 1.) Many were questioning the essential existence of national(ist) identities, as their works revealed to what extent such essentialist constructions have been bound up with the formation of specific identities serving specific political interests.[97]

I have already observed how the turn to culture and cultural identities had a distinct political edge in the 1980s, as various groups such as women, LGBT groups and black and ethnic minority people, including indigenous groups, claimed the right to their respective cultural identity and used forms of cultural history writing to underpin these identities. Laying claim to a particular culture was about re-asserting the rights of that specific culture. The multiplication of histories underpinning 'identifications' (Stuart Hall, see Chapter 1) of minority concerns from the 1980s onwards was related to the increasing disillusionment in class emancipation and the achievement of social equality through a politics of class. Hence the end of the 'forward march of labour' discussed in the Chapter 3 in relation to the crisis of labour history marks the beginning of the rise of cultural identities among various minority groups.

Sometimes these groups have been prone to essentialising their identities. Black historians, for example, have claimed they alone could write black history. Similar claims for 'their' groups have been made by queer, transgender and first nations' historians. This stance is highly reminiscent of nineteenth-century nationalist historians' conviction that the history of their respective nations could only be written by historians coming from that particular nation. In other words, it is an assumption based on the belief in essentialised identities. Any such assumptions are incompatible with the theoretical presuppositions of the new cultural history and its rootedness in the narrativist and poststructuralist theories of the 1960s and 1970s, which were precisely about de-essentialising rather than re-essentialising historical writing. As Richard Biernacki has argued in an influential collection of essays entitled *Beyond the Cultural Turn*, 'research attuned to difference rather than essence is what keeps investigators aware that every concept of analysis ... is only a device for "seeing as"'.[98] I share this view.

In fact, in many places around the globe culture has been a key political battleground. Culture has been appropriated not just by left-of-centre social movements but also by right-wing political movements. The Tea Party in the USA and Thatcherism in the UK claimed that multiculturalism was a threat to their respective identities. White heterosexual Christians in America and the UK have claimed that their specific culture is threatened by minorities hijacking culture for their particularist concerns.[99] For their part, indigenous 'first nation' groups in Australia, Canada and the USA have brought legal claims for land on the basis of their cultural rights. In Australia this led to an explosion of indigenous history writing seeking to underpin the emancipatory agendas of the 'first nations'. In response, right-wing historians such as Geoffrey Blainey and Keith Windschuttle began writing against what they called a 'black armbands' history that, in their view, was unnecessarily abandoning a more heroic and patriotic white Australian history. The Australian 'history wars' are a good example of how right-wing and left-liberal political concerns around issues of identity continue to be relevant well into the twenty-first century.[100]

The political right has long sought to harness history to its diverse causes, but since the 1960s it has found it increasingly difficult to capture the universities and academies. With prominent exceptions, they have been bastions of a more self-reflexive and left-liberal history writing informed by the theories discussed in Chapter 1. What clearly differentiates right-wing and left-wing attempts to use cultural history for identitarian ends is that the political right is more essentialist about the identities it seeks to boost, whereas the left is, on balance, social constructivist. Taking its cue from Stuart Hall's notion of 'identification', this has contributed to a more self-reflective advocacy of particular identities. Whereas left-wing histories wish to harness ideas of (constructed) collective identity to further an emancipatory identitarian tradition traceable to the class and labour histories of the late nineteenth century, right-wing histories defend older essentialised forms of collective identity centred on nation, race, religion and gender. The politics of a historiographical practice of constructing collective identies on the left and the right is thus very different and should not be seen as two sides of the same coin.

Conclusion: From the Victory of Cultural History to the Proliferation of Culturally Informed Histories

In many respects cultural history seems, from the 1980s on, to have carried everything in front of it. The chapters on political and social history have both ended with examples of how those fields of history writing have been reconfigured by cultural history. In this chapter I have traced its deep roots in the nineteenth century but also emphasised how the poststructuralist and narrativist ideas of the 1960s and 1970s gave it a new meaning and orientation. Cultural history has also produced exciting sub-fields, such as the history of emotions, the history of the body, the history of violence and the history of nationalism. Many of the cultural histories being written today are deconstructing identities rather than constructing them. Those historians who still are intent on constructing them are wary of essentialising those identities, with some exceptions, mainly on the political right. In subsequent chapters, I will discuss other fields of historical writing that are often closely related to the cultural turn in history writing and have, in parts at least, emanated from it. Many of them have contributed further to de-essentialising the strong link between history writing and collective identity formation.

Further Reading

Katie Barclay, *The History of Emotions: a Student Guide to Methods and Sources*, Basingstoke: Palgrave Macmillan, 2020.

Rob Boddice, *The History of Emotions*, Manchester: Manchester University Press, 2018.

Victoria E. Bonnell and Lynn Hunt (eds.), *Beyond the Cultural Turn: New Directions in the Study of Society and Culture*, Berkeley: University of California Press, 1999.

Peter Burke, 'Performing History: the Importance of Occasions', in: *Rethinking History* 9:1 (2005), 35–52.

Anna Green, *Cultural History*, Basingstoke: Palgrave Macmillan, 2008.

Stuart Hall, 'The Question of Cultural Identity', in: Stuart Hall, David Held and Anthony McGrew (eds.), *Modernity and Its Futures*, Cambridge: Polity Press, 1992, 274–316.

Lynn Hunt (ed.), *The New Cultural History*, Berkeley: University of California Press, 1989.

Lawrence Stone, 'The Revival of Narrative: Reflections on a New Old History, in: *Past and Present* 85 (1979), 3–24.

Michael Werner and Bénédicte Zimmermann, 'Beyond Comparison: "Histoire Croisée" and the Challenge of Reflexivity', *History and Theory* 45:1 (2006), 30–50.

5 *Gender History*

Introduction

So far I have traced how a range of diverse theories of history originating in the 1960s and 1970s, in their different ways, from the 1980s onwards, reconfigured traditional forms of historical writing such as political, social and cultural history. This body of theories, not coherent in itself, although exhibiting many overlaps, undermined the strong ties that historical writing still often retained to essentialised forms of collective identity building. Subsequent chapters will evaluate how these ideas have also shaped new fields of investigation which have become prominent since the 1980s. I will start with the field of gender history that has risen to prominence often in close alliance with poststructuralism. Its transformatory ambitions for the field of history writing as a whole have been immense. Karen Offen, for example, describes 'the potential of women's and gender history ... as a revolutionary development in the politics of historical knowledge'. Arguing that the 'analysis of gender relations through historical time has brought us ... the opportunity to revisit and rethink many basic male-centred "master narratives"', she concludes: 'Without a knowledge of, or better yet, expertise in, women's and gender history, no historian can pretend to be "up to date" in the field of history.'[1] Gender history set out to reconfigure the field of history writing and the body of theories discussed in Chapter 1 played a crucial role in underpinning this ambition. After a brief section on the tradition of writing women's history, which was itself strongly connected to the writing of social history in the 1960s and 1970s, much of the present chapter will concentrate on discussing the ambitions and agendas pursued by gender history, as it emerged from the 1980s onwards. The chapter concludes with some remarks on the relationship between gender history and identity formation, arguing that the deconstruction and de-essentialising of gender identities has been at the very heart of key publications in the field of gender history.

The Long Struggle to Give Women a Voice in History

In Western and non-Western worlds alike, women have, for centuries, been centrally engaged in the writing of histories. Famous examples include Gulbadan Begum, the author of a history of the Mughal emperors in the sixteenth century, and Mercy Otis Warren, who, in 1805, published a history of the American revolution.[2] The increasing professionalisation of historical writing in the nineteenth century was, however, accompanied by the growing exclusion of women from the profession. They remained active in a variety of different genres, but increasingly did so outside the universities and academies. There men produced 'true' and 'scientific' histories. Women at best stood beside their husbands, fathers and brothers, but their labour in co-researching and co-writing their books was rarely acknowledged.[3]

The exclusion of women from professional history writing was representative of the exclusion of women from the public sphere in patriarchal societies more generally. In the face of such discriminatory practices a women's movement formed that struggled for the emancipation of women, for voting rights, for the right of education and for the general inclusion of women in public life. Much historical writing by women sought to support the women's movement. Ivy Pinchbeck's *Women Workers and the Industrial Revolution, 1750–1850*, first published in 1930, wrote the experience of women and women workers into the Industrial Revolution.[4] Alice Clark looked at working women before the Industrial Revolution. Eileen Power examined medieval English nunneries. Olive Schreiner investigated the relationship between women and labour.[5] Mary Beard analysed programmatically the importance of women in historical processes and developments. Léon Abensour wrote a history of feminism from its earliest beginnings to his present.[6] In Japan the feminist historian Itsue Takamure published in 1953 her seminal *Study on Matrilocal Marriage*, in which she argued that before the introduction of the Confucian patriarchal family idea somewhere between the fifth and the eighth century, women in Japan had chosen their sexual partners freely in order to father their children.[7]

In my discussions of the development of political, social and cultural history above, I noted time and again the importance institutions had for historical writing. They also played an important role in women's history. The Webbs, for example, with their feminist concerns, founded the London School of Economics in 1895 with the explicit aim of institutionalising co-education in higher education. It would also be a place where women's history could flourish.[8] The first women's movement in the late nineteenth century and second-wave feminism in the 1960s and 1970s gave a major boost to women's history and the rediscovery of women and women's agency in history. Women's study courses were established in many universities. Feminist historians stressed the importance to their own development and consciousness of women's liberation groups. To them they owed their refusal to accept gender-role divisions as natural.[9] Simone de Beauvoir's *Second Sex*, published in French in 1949, inspired many feminist historians. Tracing, as it did, the enslavement of women from the agrarian societies of prehistory down to the twentieth century, it functioned as a rallying cry for change.[10] One of the key slogans to emerge from the politics of the left in the 1970s, 'the personal is the political', was directly relevant to women writing histories about women. It found expression in Carolyn Steedman's iconic publication *Landscape for a Good Woman*, which interweaves the story of her upbringing in 1950s London with reflections on women's role in a patriarchal and classed family structure and society.[11] Women's history came from the margins and many of its practitioners found a home in adult education departments or on the fringes of universities. From the beginning it was also remarkably interdisciplinary, with women from sociology like Leonore Davidoff, from social policy like Pat Thane, or from education like Penny Summerfield all playing an important role.[12]

Initially the concern was very much with rediscovering the agency of women in the past: sources were retrieved, publishing houses, archives and libraries established, and works by the pioneers of the first women's movement in the nineteenth century reprinted.[13] Gender historians often faced the difficulty of finding sources on which a history of women, their experience and their agency could be based. Some of the gender historians in the non-Western world were most innovative in accessing unusual sources. In China, for example, gender historians looked, among other things, at poetry, autobiography, youth books, letters and philosophy, in order to recall women's lives in imperial China from the eighth to the nineteenth century.[14] In Nigeria, pioneers of gender history, such as Bolanle Awe, born in 1933, set up in 1987 the Women's Research and Documentation Centre expressly to gather resources for the study of women and gender. Placing special emphasis on oral evidence, Awe looked towards poems, folk tales, fables, legends and mythical stories in her endeavour to recover the experience of Nigerian women. Given the centrality of poetry to Yoruba life, she argued that poems are a particularly rich source that should be used more widely by historians. Exploring the past leadership role of women such as the Queen of Daura, Awe called on fellow historians to give women a voice in the past as a means of demanding a greater voice for Nigerian women in the present. Inspired by Awe, other Nigerian women historians, e.g. Adetoun Agunseye, began recording the history of pre-colonial women in Africa as well as the impact of colonialism on women's status in African societies. Awe was also an early critic of what she saw as Western universalism in much of Western women's and gender history. Insisting on the importance of the local and the national experience of women, she distrusted easy universalisms with their assumption that women were exploited everywhere by patriarchy. In an edited collection, *Nigerian Women in Historical Perspective*, Awe argued for the need to investigate both the subjugation of women and their agency in the past, in issues such as warfare, politics, agriculture and trade, in order to understand better Nigeria's pre-colonial, colonial and postcolonial development.[15] In a similar vein Lynn Thomas has pointed out that the women who resisted the ban on infibulation in 1950s Kenya did so out of a conscious long-term resistance against Westernising, universalising arguments that clitorectomy was a form of patriarchal oppression.[16]

Western women's historians often eyed the postcolonial nationalism of a historian like Awe suspiciously. The feminists who (re)discovered women's history in the West in the 1960s and 1970s were often on the political left. Many of them were active in a variety of different social movements, including the peace movement, the civil rights movement, the reproductive rights movement and the environmental movement. Their engagement for women and their writing of women's history were part and parcel of that intense political struggle.[17] Influenced by the 'New Left' and by 1968, they felt an affinity to people's and labour history and preferably wrote about working-class women, who, they argued, had been doubly disadvantaged. Confronting both male power and the power of capital, feminist labour historians thus related class analysis to gender analysis. The sexual division of labour, they argued, had to be linked to the class struggle in order to make sense of categories such as class.[18] In 1983 Barbara Taylor directly discussed the relationship of socialism and feminism in her book *Eve and the New Jerusalem*.[19] If feminist historians inserted gender into class, they also put gender into race. How black women negotiated issues of race, class and gender was told masterfully by Jacqueline Jones' *Labor of Love, Labor of Sorrow*, first published in 1985.[20] And Catherine Hall has written about how the British empire produced racialised, classed and gendered selves, both in the metropole and in the colony. Empires were, she argued, genuinely transnational spaces in which ideas about gender, class and race circulated freely.[21]

Socialist feminist history was more prominent in countries where left-wing politics coalesced around issues of class, as was the case in Britain. One of the most prominent expositions of the intimate relationship between gender and class formation was Leonore Davidoff and Catherine Hall's study on *Family Fortunes*.[22] Its authors argued that the middle-class family with its specific gender roles for men and women was crucial in shaping industrial capitalism in the hundred years between the mid-eighteenth and the mid-nineteenth century. Notions of class and gender shaped the political economy of the household and in turn provided a new foundation for English society. By paying close attention to gendered subjectivities, Davidoff and Hall were able to reveal underlying social structures and cultural representations. Among US feminist historians there was less interest in the relationship between gender and class formation. Instead, many there identified the divide between men and women as the most important divide, thereby sidelining the importance of class or race conflicts. Building on feminist anthropology, they argued that the gendered divide of space – public for men, private for women – was part and parcel of all human cultures and societies.[23] The main struggle thus had to be that against being confined as women to the private sphere. Adopting a separate-spheres model of social development meant that historians often only investigated the sphere of women. Arguably they discovered many bonds of sisterhood and solidarity, but they lost sight of how interrelated the spheres of men and women were and how issues of power and conflict lay embedded in that relationship. The separate-spheres model tended to cast women in the role of victims, thus denying them agency and contributing to new silences about how women had successfully negotiated their roles vis-à-vis men.[24]

From Women's to Gender Histories: Agendas and Ambitions

The movement from women's history to gender history was an attempt to break the binaries created by the separate-spheres model and move out of a ghetto where women historians were responsible for women's history whilst the rest of history was still all about men and still largely written by men. Joan Wallach Scott's article 'Gender: a Useful Category of Historical Analysis', first published in the *American Historical Review* in 1986,[25] argued that it was no longer enough to research women in history. Indeed, she identified a danger in doing so: women's history, she maintained, was easily compartmentalised into its own little field, where it could be isolated and would remain an insignificant side-show to the 'real' male histories. Instead, Scott made extensive use of poststructuralist theory and its insistence that social reality was, above all, rooted in linguistic construction and symbolic representation. Using these insights she called on fellow historians to take account of how the construction of gendered identities impacted on all fields of history, from the history of kings and queens to histories of warfare and diplomatic histories, and further to social and cultural histories. Whatever historians studied, the gender dimension of the subject should become an integral part of their study. The field of history itself had to change under the view that gender and gender regimes were important to each and every historical inquiry and subject. All social relationships, she argued, were rooted in the construction of differences between male and female. Using Foucault, Scott argued that these gender constructions signified power relationships in the organisation of the social. Normative ideas of gender were present in a whole range of areas, from religion to education and from science to the law, not to mention politics. Alternative or deviant ideas about gender, although oppressed and censured, could be retrieved by the historian interested in the relationship between gender order, power and the organisation of the social.

The turn to gender also led to the discovery of men as a subject of historical writing. From the 1990s onwards 'men's studies' blossomed as scores of historians attempted to analyse the diverse ways in which men had been socially defined in different parts of the world at different times.[26] Men's studies showed how male and female gender identities had been mutually constituted. The one could not be understood without the other. Ideals of masculinity were intricately related to public honour codes and a variety of representations in wider public cultures more generally. As Robert Nye argued in a pathbreaking book on male codes of honour, ideas about honour were inscribed on to the male body and male sociability reflected those ideas.[27] Gender orders controlled men every bit as tightly as they controlled women. With regard to the public culture of empire, John Tosh, for example, has demonstrated how an aggressive masculinity was bound up with British imperial ambitions and practices and stabilised those gender identities against a perceived threat at home.[28] Mark E. Kann has pointed to the importance of tropes of masculinity for the generation of the founding fathers in the USA and stressed their impact on forging the nation-state in a highly gendered and patriarchal way.[29] Since then a wealth of other work has demonstrated the close link between constructions of masculinity and the shaping of national discourses in many parts of the world. The often intricate interdependencies between dominant and marginalised masculinities were an especially important aspect of nation-building processes. Nations were de- and re-masculinised in an astonishing variety of different spatial and non-spatial contexts.[30]

The move from women's histories to gender histories was intimately connected with the distinction made between sex and gender. Whereas sex had been thought of as biologically determined and unchanging, gender was seen as socially constructed and undergoing change over time. However, by the 2000s, gender theorists were increasingly challenging this dichotomy, arguing that sexuality was itself socially constructed and undergoing historical change. Building once again on the writings of Foucault, Judith Butler argued: 'If the immutable character of sex is contested, perhaps this construct called "sex" is as culturally constructed as gender; indeed, perhaps it was always already gender, with the consequence that the distinction between sex and gender turns out to be no distinction at all.'[31]

The concern with gender and sexuality meant that the history of sexualities developed strongly into its own sub-field. The influence of Foucault's *History of Sexuality* loomed large over the entire field and threw its long shadow over a discipline that saw sexuality as socially constructed.[32] Foucault had pointed the way by showing how sexual norms were constructed through a scientific discourse that excluded and criminalised everything deviant. He had emphasised a process of limitation and normativisation of sexualities. Subsequently historians of sexuality have emphasised how our modern ideas about sexuality were deeply rooted in medieval and early modern discourses and practices.[33] The medicalisation of deviant sexualities has been discussed in great depth, as has the scientific discourse on sexualities.

The connection made by Foucault between sexualities and power was further explored. Foucault had a particular interest in the exclusion of male homosexuality, but soon scores of books also looked at female homosexuality. In 1990 a new journal dedicated to the history of sexuality, the *Journal for the History of Sexuality*, was published by the University of Texas Press. Historians of sexuality were quick to emulate gender historians, arguing that they were not content to occupy a niche existence where they would pursue endless investigations into diverse sexual practices and the construction of sexual identities. They argued that sexualities impacted on all spheres of social life and therefore had wide implications for the constitution of the social, the cultural, the political and the economic. In other words, general history could not be understood without a proper understanding of sexualities in history. The development of histories of sexuality has been closely aligned with histories of the body and histories of fashion and clothing. The strong concern with deviancy has produced whole libraries on the histories of homosexuality, leaving heterosexuality almost an under-researched topic. Much interest has also been paid to the impact of age on sexualities.[34]

As Foucault had already pointed out, there was no shortage of discourses on sexuality despite the fact that it was widely regarded as belonging to the innermost circle of the private. Hence, it was only a short step from studying sexualities to analysing private lives, something that had, for a long time, been deemed unworthy of historical study. The interest in marriage, household and family was reflected in the desire to move the areas occupied by women out of historical obscurity. Gender historians emphasised that it was important to look not just at the world of production, but also at the work of reproduction. The education and socialisation of children in the household and the home as location of production, especially in working-class households, now moved centre stage. At the same time the distinction between 'private' and 'public' was questioned. Was the education of children not a public concern, and did the positioning of men and women in the household not have political consequences? Was the private not political? The multi-volume *History of Private Life* showed how fruitful the study of the private sphere had become. It analysed changes to gender orders and introduced diverse historical actors: fathers, mothers, parents, children, brothers and sisters, domestic servants, neighbours and relatives.

Familial relationships, sexualities, feelings and bodies were central in the depiction of the life cycle from birth via marriage to death.[35]

Another sub-field of historical inquiry strongly influenced by gender history has been the history of the body. (See also Chapter 4.) Already in 2001 Roy Porter could write about the history of the body having become the 'historiographical dish of the day'.[36] At the beginning of this massive new interest in the history of the body stood, once again, Michel Foucault. He had pointed out how bodies were determined not by biology but by history and that they therefore had to be properly historised. His notion of 'biopower' refers to practices and knowledges that regulated, defined, categorised and measured the body in order to provide norms of what was healthy and productive.[37] Disciplinary regimes surrounding dress codes, dieting and exercising were adopted and implemented in order to make bodies adhere to those norms. Ideas of the body were linked to ideas about self and identity in the making of the modern subject. Catherine Gallagher and Thomas Laqueur's *The Making of the Modern Body* pioneered scholarship that saw the body as defined no longer by biology but by narrative construction. This in turn posed the problem of who had the power to determine which narrative was most credible and adhered to, i.e. who ultimately had the power to set the norms governing the body, and, by extension, modern subjectivity. The body itself was inherently unstable and multi-faceted in the meanings ascribed to it. It was declared to be the historians' task to uncover the processes of meaning-making and relate them to questions of power.[38] As Roger Cooter has pointed out, the discursive turn in the history of the body produced a range of counter-reactions.[39] Caroline Walker Bynum had already asked in 1995: 'Why all the Fuss about the Body', and called on historians not to dissolve the body into language and speech acts, but instead to take seriously the materialist corporeal existence of bodies and their experiences.[40] From here some of the research on the body moved back to forms of biological essentialism, taking its cue from neuroscience and its attempts to reduce the body to molecular and neuronal 'truth'.[41] Other research moved to 'presentationalism' with its insistence that the presence and materiality of the body come before language.[42] Most promising of all, and here I concur with Cooter, were attempts which sought to develop further Foucauldian ideas on biosubjectivities, i.e. subjectivities constituted around notions of biological processes. Nikolas Rose, for example, has argued that forms of social citizenship, characteristic of the industrialised nation-states of the nineteenth and first half of the twentieth century, have been increasingly replaced by 'bio-citizenships'. These circle around medicalised individualised bodies, in the postmodern, post-industrial and increasingly globalised world of the twenty-first century.[43]

A poststructuralist move to gender analysis institutionalised and paved the way for new sub-fields in history, such as histories of sexualities, of private lives and of bodies. It also impacted enormously on other fields of historical writing, e.g. political history. The history of civil society, for example, was reconstituted through the insertion of gender into studies of the emergence of civil society in the eighteenth century, a development first postulated and traced by Jürgen Habermas.[44] Gender historians had been quick to point out that the public sphere, as conceptualised during the European Enlightenments, excluded women and established male forms of bondage and 'brotherhood'. Soon historians such as Isabell Hull investigated how gender orders underpinned constructions of liberal democracy and the bourgeois public sphere in the nineteenth century.[45] This turn did not just occur in Europe and the West. As Mrinalini Sinha has shown for India, the so-called Mayo controversy, which was ignited by the publication of Katherine Mayo's 1927 book *Mother India*, led to an indictment of the shortcomings of the colonial British state and a reconfiguration of the relationship between state and the communalist public sphere in India. Towards the end of the 1920s there was a moment when Indian women were reconfigured as citizens with individual rights vis-à-vis the state, rather than being deemed objects who were dominated by the patriarchal logic of a communalist civil society.[46] (See Figure 5.1.)

Gender historians have reconstituted other mainstream fields in historical writing, e.g. the history of empire. Ann Laura Stoler, for example, has argued that the racial stratification of colonial orders was tightly interrelated with constructions of gender and sexuality. Colonial worlds were shaped not only by high politics and diplomatic conferences, but also by the management of sexualities and the organisation of domestic life. Indeed, Stoler made it clear how the idea of European superiority depended on notions of manliness and femininity that were as important in managing empires as guns. Analysing the political construction of the binary coloniser/colonised, Stoler historised the range of private and public practices that constituted racial hierarchies in the Dutch West Indies. The diversity of topics that she

Figure 5.1 Images of 'Mother India' are everywhere in popular representations of India, including this poster for the 1957 film *Mother India*, starring Nargis. © LMPC, Getty Images.

examined is breathtaking: gender, sexuality, miscegenation, images of childhood (raising and abandoning children) and womanhood, rape, eugenics and many more. In her view, sexual and racial politics were closely intertwined. Inserting gender into race allowed her to analyse in depth the categories employed and the meanings given to actions in the making of gendered (and classed) racial identities.[47]

Building on Foucault, Stoler and many other historians have pointed to the close relationship between scientific knowledge and the construction of gender, sexuality and race. Hence it is not surprising to find that they have also paid close attention to the history of science. Londa

Schiebinger, for example, has analysed how even the birth of the natural sciences in the seventeenth century, which on the surface was connected to the ideals of objectivity, was accompanied by ideas about gender (and race) dichotomies that would influence the entire scientific thinking in the West. Scientific knowledge was constructed against the background of colonial encounters and specific gender orders.[48] Lisa Bloom, in her study on how the expedition of Peary to the North Pole constructed both geographical and anthropological knowledge, confirmed the intricate ways in which gender as well as race and nationalism was woven into the fabric of scientific truths.[49]

In economic history, gender historians have not only explored women as entrepreneurs and industrialists, they have also examined in detail how they were involved in a range of professional services and how, as consumers, they shaped societies. Nancy Folbre, for example, has argued that the development of economic ideas from the Middle Ages to the present day has been highly gendered. Self-interest, seen as the prime motivating factor behind capitalist economies, worked through different constructions of what women's and men's self-interest was. In eighteenth-century economic thinking, ideas about economic growth were deeply intertwined with notions of population growth which directly pointed to women and their 'rights' over reproduction. Dealing with the marketisation of sexual desire and a whole range of other ideas about markets, competition and free trade, Folbre concluded that our whole tradition of economic thought is shot through with constructions of gender orders.[50] To give another example: Jan Luiten van Zanden has led a research team which successfully introduced the issue of gender inequalities into New Institutional Economics and applied it to history. Setting out to test Amartya Sen's 'capability approach', which posits a positive correlation between greater autonomous decision-making of women as economic entrepreneurs and improvements to economic performance, van Zanden and his collaborators have studied family systems and family relationships as the basis of economic activity across different regional settings between the middle of the nineteenth century and the present day. They conclude that economic development has been severely hampered by discriminating against half of the human population through existing gender hierarchies.[51]

Nationalism studies have also been deeply influenced by gender perspectives. Nations were widely conceptualised as families, with specific roles for men and women. If these gender norms were intact and performed well, the nation was depicted as thriving. By contrast, failure to adhere to the bourgeois gender order resulted in its decline and disappearance. Furthermore, gendered representations of nations defined 'others', in particular enemies, and constructed a positive sense of self that could be juxtaposed with 'others'. Access to both the material and immaterial resources of the nation was via particular ideas of gender order.[52] Scholars studying particular nations have investigated how nations were culturally constructed through the lens of gender.[53] Thus, in the Indonesian province of Aceh, a particular gender order was found to underpin female forms of agency in Islamic movements against the Indonesian state. Reviewing long-standing matrifocal ideas and values within the Islamic culture of Aceh, Jacqueline Aquino Siapno concluded that patriarchal Islam has been strengthened by the defensive posture it was forced to take up when the Indonesian state sought to repress the strong Islamic identity of the people of Aceh.[54]

Gender has also been influential in reconfiguring the history of warfare which, throughout modernity, has been closely aligned to the emergence of modern nation-states.[55] The military as a male affair and the construction of gender orders inside the military and through the militarisation of societies has been extensively examined, in particular, but not exclusively, in relation to the two world wars.[56] The gendered images of soldiers and warriors have been analysed,[57] as have questions about how male and female bodies suffered in war, and how military values penetrated civil societies.[58] Carrying weapons has been analysed as a privilege of manliness.[59] The gendered relationship between home fronts and the 'real' frontline where armies met has also been discussed.[60] Wars constituted national emergencies and thus often provided openings for challenging and reconstituting gender orders. They saw the mobilisation of women in social protests – often related to shortages of food and clothing.[61] They were also related to states granting more rights to women. Thus voting rights were extended to women in two waves, the one after the First and the second after the Second World War.[62] How did war frame gender relations and gender symbols? To what extend did women have agency in wars and were not merely victims of male violence?[63] These questions have, in recent years, transformed the history of warfare, as they transformed other fields of history writing.

Many of the books that have reshaped whole fields of historical writing by applying the category of gender to them have underlined the intersectionality of gender: it needs to be understood in relation to race, class and a whole host of other identitarian concepts that overlap and influence each other. Knowledge about gender identities and their historical evolution has thus developed alongside the exploration of other identities. Influenced by poststructuralism and narrativism, gender historians did not take them as given, but instead set out to historise those identities by showing how they were constructed by a web of power relationships that prioritised some constructions over others in an ongoing contest about the meaning of social phenomena. Gender history was therefore closely related to the dissolution of stable, given and essentialised identities. Instead they pointed to the ongoing making, unmaking and remaking of gender identities, as I shall explore in the last sub-section of this chapter.

Gender Histories and the (Un)Making of Identities

As I noted when discussing the origins of women's history, discovering women in history often meant discovering the history of women's movements and of feminisms. This was a history of resistance against patriarchy. It portrayed women as victims of patriarchy but also as agents willing to protest and work for change.[64] The activists fighting for women's rights were presented as direct precursors of the contemporary women's movement. Recalling and celebrating the past struggles strengthened the identity of feminists in the present and contributed to a struggle that was being carried out in the here and now. History was a resource and a weapon in an ongoing battle for emancipation, perceived also as a struggle of and for identity. Historians of the women's movements became public historians engaged in social movements trying to win and extend rights for women. Initially their work focused on the national frame as it was within it that rights could be won. However, with the rise of globalisation around the turn of the twenty-first century and the growing popularity of global and transnational history, studies on women's and feminist movements increasingly highlighted transnational concerns and networks, the internationalism of women activists and the exchange of ideas across national borders.[65] Seeking to insert gender into transnational and global history (see also Chapter 11), gender historians have begun to explore 'how cross-border connections and global developments have shaped diverse women's lives' and how they gendered social, cultural, political and economic relations.[66] Breaking out of nation-based investigations into women's lives and the impact of constructions of gender, they sought to subvert the grand narrative of globalisation by inserting gender. Especially the gender historians' emphasis on perspectives from below, e.g. subaltern, indigenous and community perspectives, succeeded in destabilising binaries in the field of global history, perhaps most importantly that between the local and the global. Drawing attention to the gendered nature of the global inequalities of power, gender historians have pointed to ways in which, in the imperial archives, women have been silenced.[67] And they gendered the study of transnational networks, the constructions of metropole and periphery in global history. They effectively brought together the local and the global in women's agency across a wide variety of different fields. Especially in the field of the history of imperialism and imperial racism, gender historians made an important contribution to transnational history.[68] A global survey of women's and gender history demonstrated how it influenced much historical writing across a broad time span in history and it underlined how regionally specific women's and gender history has been, whilst at the same time having been a truly global phenomenon.[69] Even rather traditional fields of historical writing, such as the history of international relations and high politics, have benefited enormously from adopting a gender perspective.[70] This transnationalisation of women's and gender history did not necessarily reject the older national frame. On the contrary, it often managed to shed a sharper light on the national frame by pointing out to what extent national phenomena could only be properly understood by paying attention to 'its connections, interactions and relations to other nations and supra-national institutions alike'.[71] Thus, critique of gender hierarchies, belief in the possibility of historical change and the construction of a collective identity for women stood at the forefront of research on women's and feminist movements.[72]

Writing women's history was one way of boosting women's identity. At the same time developing an identity as 'woman' also encouraged historians to dig deeper into women's history. As Carroll Smith-Rosenberg wrote about her experience in the 1960s: 'Self-conscious feminism strengthened the resolve of those who insisted upon restructuring the scholarly canon to make the study of women's roles and visions, power and oppression central to historical analysis.'[73] The women's movements as social movements and historical writing seemed symbiotically related. By focusing on the history of women, feminist historians would demonstrate the position of women as victims in history, and this status of victimhood would only strengthen their identity politics aimed at the liberation of women in the present. Parts of the male-dominated historical profession, often still strongly tied to historist and objectivist understandings of what 'historical science' is, rejected this overtly political side of women's and gender history as 'bias' and 'presentism'. Françoise Thébaud has argued that the rejection of feminist history by French historians stemmed from such strong distrust of history writing tied to clear political agendas.[74] In many parts of the world women and gender historians were subsequently at the forefront of those advocating a different understanding of history, questioning notions of 'objectivity' and 'truth', and instead pointing to the normativity and politics of all scientific endeavours, even if they followed the methodological ground rules of their respective 'sciences'. Adherence to source criticism as an objectifying tool might well hide political concerns, but it did not get rid of them. By redefining the relationship between the political and the profession of writing history, women and gender historians drew on the body of theories discussed in Chapter 1 and they thus contributed in a major way to changing the self-understanding of historians as professionals.

Having said that, women's and gender historians themselves ultimately came to warn about the dangers of flattening the history of women into a one-dimensional lament about oppression out of which arose the cry for emancipation. Recovering the full depth of women's experiences in the past would, they argued, necessitate the recognition of the diversity of women's experiences across different times and cultures. The category of 'woman' itself had to be pluralised, diversified and inserted into many different historical contexts.[75] Thus black women had different identities from white women. Working-class women's experiences could not be equated with middle-class ones. Time and space had to be taken into account to understand fully the range of women's identities. 'Woman' was not a universal category applicable to all times and places. Chandra Talpade Mohanty, for example, has pointed to the many differences among women living their lives under diverse colonial regimes.[76] Out of a position of understanding women in the plural that rejected the temptation of some feminisms to construct their own orientalisms arose highly complex, interrelated and different forms of identity politics through historical writing. Terms such as 'oppression' and 'liberation' had very different meanings when looked at from different parts of the world, or, indeed, when looked at in terms of class, ethnicity or sexual orientation. In short, women had many histories which needed to be told from a variety of different and sometimes mutually incompatible perspectives.[77]

Gender symbols have hardly ever been static and one-dimensional. They were fluid and ambiguous, prone to be interpreted in different ways by different historical actors. Natalie Zemon Davis, one of the first to analyse systematically gender symbols and their roles in cultural systems in the early modern period, argued that their indeterminacy gave women more leeway for interpretation and action. As early as 1975 she wrote: 'Our goal is to discover the range in sex roles and in sexual symbolism in different societies and periods, to find out what meaning they had and how they functioned to maintain the social order or to promote its change.'[78]

Under the weight of such pluralisations of the meaning of 'woman', it became increasingly impossible to construct woman as a unified subject with a homogeneous and monolithic identity. As already noted, women's historians had long recognised that gender identities were relational to a whole host of other identities. The concept of 'intersectionality' now developed a more systematic way of studying these relationships.[79] Alice Kessler-Harris, for example, pointed out that one cannot understand the concept of 'labour' without taking into account its relation to that of 'gender'. She showed how the male breadwinner model was instrumental in coding the idea of 'labour' in the Western industrial world by allocating particular roles to men in the economic world, whilst leaving the household, family and motherhood to women.[80] Similarly, the concept of 'race' only becomes fully comprehensible when we look at its close proximity to 'gender': there was a 'politics of the womb' in colonial and postcolonial settings, where procreation was closely aligned with the production of racial hierarchies.[81] The Spanish colonisers in Latin America, for example, carefully managed their descendants and made distinctions between the sons and daughters they had fathered with indigenous women as they constructed racial categories for economic, political, religious and cultural reasons.[82] Finally, let us consider the relationality of 'gender' to religion. Here, Lata Mani has shown how the debate on widow-burning (sati) in colonial India did not only position Western colonialists, seeking a ban against what they perceived as a barbaric and inhumane practice, against Hindu traditionalists. Many of the Indians who also opposed sati did so, not because they sympathised with Western humanitarian ideals, but because they saw in sati a practice introduced into Hinduism through Islamic influences. Hence, they harked back to older and allegedly 'purer' Hindu traditions that did not know sati. In other words, the conflicts surrounding sati were complicated by different religious understandings of this practice within the Hindu community.[83]

The intersectional nature of gender became more visible under a constructivist paradigm in gender history that also played a vital role in de-essentialising our understanding of the roles that have been performed by men and women in history. When constructivism came to incorporate sexuality, the de-essentialising of gender identities was taken one step further. African gender historians have pointed out that gender constructions in African cultures could be very flexible in the pre-colonial period. 'Male daughters' and 'female husbands' were not uncommon in Igboland, and whilst there was an understanding of the anatomical sexual differences between men and women, these were not necessarily put into a strict binary hierarchy. Seniority, for example, was more important than sexuality.[84] Gender identities were no longer biologically determined in natural and unchanging ways that were the same the world over. Women's and men's identities were historically contingent and underwent multiple changes across varying cultures and times. Collective identities could no longer be understood as stable, coherent and producing a sense of inner self, but instead were dissolved into a myriad of representations, readings and linguistic constructions.[85] Social positions did not determine identities; instead these identities were discursively constructed, performed and embodied through cultural processes and activities.[86] Subjects, as Judith Butler has argued, are constructed through discourse, but they also develop the faculties to rewrite those discursive scripts and develop forms of agency that would allow them to change their subject position by giving it new meanings.[87] Gender identities, in other words, are work-in-progress undergoing constant change. The binaries they produce between male and female constantly shiver under the attempt to keep them strictly separate, when in fact they constantly collapse into each other.

Queer studies and queer theory have been extremely influential in demonstrating how bodies were defined sexually in a binary way that made heterosexuality compulsory and established a binary gender system that systematically sidelined, criminalised and excluded any form of deviant sexuality.[88] The LGBTI movement draws on the expertise of historians to commemorate key events in its history, such as the Stonewall protests in New York in 1969 – widely seen as being of crucial symbolic significance in the global fight for gay rights.[89] LGBTI historiography often refers to a seminal texts such as, for example, John D'Emilio's *Sexual Politics, Sexual Communities*, first published in1983,[90] as establishing a sub-discipline of LGBTI history in the 1970s and 1980s. In the USA, a host of local studies followed that commented on and added to the broad canvas painted by D'Emilio.[91] Heavily influenced by both feminism and poststructuralism, LGBTI histories have since explored many aspects of the oppression of sexual deviancy and the resistance to such oppression, as well as the desire of LGBTI communities to live out and express their sexualities. Whilst studies on the USA and other Western states dominate the field, there is, by now, considerable research on postcolonial spaces. Thus, for example, Afsaneh Najmabadi showed how it was the modernising and nationalising twentieth-century Iranian state that made heterosexual love the unquestioned norm and ended centuries-old homosexual practices between men and male youths (*amrads*) who were, just like women, deemed to be sexually desirable.[92] The field has also increasingly made the internal conflicts and debates within the LGBTI community the topic of studies.

Whilst I cannot here go into detail about what is by now a distinguished history of LGBTI histories with its own research centres and research journals as well as book series and associations,[93] I would like to draw attention to the claim made by Howard H. Chiang that many LGBTI historians have in fact contributed to essentialising LGBTI identities, regardless of their commitment to social constructivist frameworks, by presenting the experiences of LGBTI people in coherent and continuous ways around a set of qualities that are ascribed to them.[94] Chiang's call on fellow LGBTI historians to learn from the conceptualisation of histories provided by postcolonial scholars such as Gayatri Chakravorty Spivak and Gyan Prakash, in order to highlight contestations, discontinuities, struggles, contradictions and ambiguities in the framing of LGBTI identities, is certainly a point worth considering. However, it should not distract from the fact that most engaged historians in the field write their histories and other public utterances in support of the LGBTI movement and that they do so with the explicit aim of de-essentialising sexual identities. Their 'identification' (for Stuart Hall's concept see Chapter 1) with the cause is thus linked to the recognition of the constructed and non-essentialist nature of all forms of collective identities. Hence, LGBTI histories, alongside the other histories discussed in this volume, have played an important role in breaking the link between historical writing and the construction of fixed identities.

In his controversial book on the staging of sexual differences in the West from ancient times to the twentieth century, Thomas Laqueur has argued that sexual organs had not been clearly aligned with gender identities well into the eighteenth century. Hence, it was only then that ideas about the sexual nature of humanity changed so fundamentally as to replace the 'one-sex model' with the more familiar binary model that distinguishes between male and female identities.[95] Once again, his argument underlines the importance of perceiving sexual identities not as biological or unchanging, but as undergoing profound historical changes and being essentially contested.

The move from women's to gender history brought a recognition that there was no easy path from social experience to social identity. Much depended on the languages that constructed women's social experiences. Hence gender history sought to recuperate the discourses about femininity and later also masculinity that constituted identities as male and female. In a seminal article on 'The Evidence of Experience', Joan W. Scott used the theories of Michel Foucault, Michel de Certeau and a range of other theorists discussed in Chapter 1 to support her claim that 'experience' was never authentic and original. Any appeal to 'the evidence of experience' in history writing, she argued, 'reproduces rather than contests given ideological systems'.[96] Experience, she continued, can never be the source for explanations and an authoritative voice emerging from the historical evidence. Historians have instead to ask and to explain how an experience is related to knowledge production. In her words: 'To think about experience . . . is to historicise it as well as to historicise the identities it produces.'[97] This leads the writing of history away from being 'largely a foundationalist discourse' that takes for granted, does not question and sees as permanent and transcendent 'primary premises, categories and presumptions'.[98] One of those premises, according to Scott, is the category of 'experience'. It amounted to a revolution in historical writing when she asked 'whether history can exist without foundations'.[99] Problematising the category of experience allowed her to ask 'how conceptions of selves (of subjects and their identities) are produced',[100] which was a major step on the road to questioning the link between historical writing and collective identity formation and, in particular, the essentialism often built into this link. Furthermore, Scott's insight that 'identity is a contested terrain, the site of multiple and conflicting claims'[101] allowed historians to escape the unifying tendencies of the category of 'experience' and ask why, under certain conditions, some discursive constructions of experience had become more powerful than others. Scott drew here on the important work of Denise Riley, whose book *Am I that Name?* (1988) had shown how the experiences of women were not constructed on the basis of womanhood alone but were dependent on a whole set of other identities related to systems of domination and power.[102] Instead of taking collective identities for granted, Scott called on historians 'to understand the operations of the complex and changing discursive processes by which identities are ascribed, resisted, or embraced and which processes themselves are unremarked and indeed achieve their effect because they are not noticed'.[103]

Ever since Scott's landmark intervention, there has been a debate in gender history and in the theory of history as to whether experiences are discursively constructed, as she suggested, or whether they are rooted in pre-linguistic forms of social reality and only made meaningful in different ways through language.[104] From the 2000s onwards, the dissolution of experiences and social identities in discourses led to attempts to recover the materiality of experiences that were rooted in such discourses, as we already observed with cultural history more generally. (See Chapter 4.) Subsequently, discourse was much more linked to practice and to the materialities of the lived experience (see Chapter 10) also in gender histories. This, however, did not change the earlier recognition that gender identities were never fixed and static but always situational, relational and changing over time and space. Gender is not something that individuals have but something that they perform and embody. These performances and embodiments vary greatly. The agency of ordinary men and women consists of their (limited) choices about how they perform their gender roles in different situations.

Conclusion

When, in a review of Léonie Villard's *La femme anglaise au XIXe siècle et son évolution d'après le roman anglais contemporain*, Virginia Woolf reminded her readers that 'it has been common knowledge for ages that women exist, bear children, have no beards, and seldom go bald, but save in these respects, and in others where they are said to be identical with men, we know little of them and have little sound evidence upon which to base our conclusions',[105] it was a feminist call to arms to find out more about one half of the world's human population. I started this chapter by arguing that women have been writing about other women for a long time, even if they had been largely excluded from professional history writing since its birth in the nineteenth century. However, at the time Woolf was writing, i.e. in the interwar period, a first wave of professional female historians began to write about women and their experiences. A new feminist wave, beginning in the 1960s, gave another major boost to women's history by providing important conceptual models such as the 'separate-spheres' model discussed above and by linking the experience of women to the experience of class.

In the second section I then traced the move from women's to gender history, a step that led to the discovery of 'men's studies' and also to the constitution of new, booming fields of inquiry such as the histories of sexualities, private lives and bodies. Furthermore, gender history recast established fields of history such as political history, the history of empire, the history of science, economic history, nationalism studies and the history of warfare. The success of gender history in reconstituting the field of history writing can be measured by the simple fact that today hardly any historian would doubt the simple statement that gender 'has shaped human history'.[106] The centrality of gender to historical analysis is visible in all fields and themes – from nation and empire to the state and public sphere, and from economic processes to social interactions. Gender analysis has contributed to rethinking both the state and the functioning of societies across a wide range of geographical areas and times. Gender history has shown gender to be central to constructions of social and political order.

Paying greater attention to issues of gender has contributed in a major way to pluralise histories. It has shown how gender structured local and global processes in manifold, often contradictory and non-linear ways. Times and spaces have always been gendered but never in a unitary way. Plural conceptualisations of the categories of 'woman' and 'man' have often been competing with one another. They made the construction of fixed and essentialised collective identities more problematic and fostered a deep mistrust in identitarian master narratives emerging out of the writing of histories.

In the last part of this chapter I talked about how women's history sought to strengthen female identities as part of a political project. I outlined how this political project, far from being abandoned, has been made more complex by gender history: the recovery of the full range and depth of women's experiences meant an acceptance that there was no universal category of 'woman'. The intersectionality of gender identities with those of race, class and religion highlighted that they were all work in progress, inherently unstable and always in the process of transformation. Given the many histories and the many identities, it made more sense to tell many small narratives that stood next to each other, contradicted and augmented each other at the same time. This has become characteristic of the new history since the 1980s more generally and we will also be able to observe this fractured nature of historical knowledge as basis for an acceptance of plural forms of identity construction in subsequent chapters. I will continue with the sub-field of historical anthropology which emerged out of the history of everyday life. The latter, like women's history, also had its beginnings in the 1960s and 1970s and was in fact closely bound up with the rediscovery of women in history.

Further Reading

Judith Butler, *Gender Trouble: Feminism and the Subversion of Identity*, London: Routledge, 1990.

Kathleen Canning, *Gender History in Practice: Historical Perspective on Bodies, Class and Citizenship*, Ithaca, NY: Cornell University Press, 2006.

Laura Lee Downs, *Writing Gender History*, 2nd edn, London: Bloomsbury, 2010.

Teresa A. Meade and Merry E. Wiesner-Hanks (eds.), *Companion to Gender History*, Oxford: Blackwell, 2004.

Clare Midgley, Alison Twells and Julie Carlier (eds.), *Women in Transnational History: Connecting the Local and the Global*, Routledge: London, 2016.

Karen Offen and Chen Yan (eds.), Women's History at the Cutting Edge, special issue of *Women's History Review* 27:1 (2018).

Sonya O .Rose, *What Is Gender History?*, Cambridge: Polity Press, 2010.

Leila J. Rupp and Susan K. Freeman, *US Lesbian, Gay, Bisexual and Transgender History*, Madison: University of Wisconsin Press, 2014.

Joan W. Scott, 'Gender: a Useful Category of Historical Analysis', in: *American Historical Review* 91:5 (1986), 1053–75.

6 *Historical Anthropology*

Introduction

Gender history, as discussed in the last chapter, was almost symbiotically related to the body of theories discussed in Chapter 1. Their impact was also felt by historians keen to write the history of the everyday life of ordinary men and women. People's history as history which sets out to explore the lives of ordinary people has a long and distinguished track record. In many parts of Europe it goes back to the late nineteenth and early twentieth century. In Western Europe, the 1960s witnessed a revival of neo-Marxism, which contributed to movements keen to recover the stories of underprivileged classes who had not made it into the mainstream history books. The history workshop movement in England, *microstoria* in Italy, *Alltagsgeschichte* in Germany and many parallel movements across the Western world all sought to recover marginalised experiences and voices. In the non-Western world postcolonial history has been one of the most successful forms of history from below on a global level. Unorthodox Marxist historians often embraced aspects of the history theories discussed in Chapter 1 in an attempt to set the tone for a history from below that soon came under the influence of anthropology. Historical anthropology, a term most directly used in Germany,[1] moved towards producing what Foucault had termed 'archaeology of knowledge',[2] i.e. analyses of how power operated in everyday human interactions. Methodologically Clifford Geertz's ideas about 'thick description' informed many histories from below.[3] Geertz's cultural anthropology aimed at recovering 'an historically transmitted pattern of meanings embodied in symbols, a system of inherited conceptions expressed in symbolic forms by means of which men communicate, perpetuate and develop their knowledge about and attitudes toward life'.[4] Anthropology promised that it would liberate history from the power of metanarratives, which had been at the very epicentre of the criticism levelled by narrativism, constructionism and the linguistic turn. By championing close observation of social life and paying attention to the symbolical behaviour of social actors, historical anthropology aimed to stay closer to its historical subjects and avoid the grand narratives. Causal explanation was to give way to the interpretation of meanings. All of this contributed in complex and varied ways to the acceptance of pluralisation in the historical profession and the breaking up of notions of essential collective identities.

People's Histories before the Linguistic Turn

The writings of Karl Marx were undoubtedly an important influence on many historians seeking to recover the lives of those routinely forgotten by high political history. His historical and dialectical materialism had constructed the working class as a major agent in world history. Marxist historians were among the earliest historians seeking to write about workers and those not belonging to the politically powerful. In the interwar period of the twentieth century, the Annales school, whose representatives developed a deep interest in anthropology, insisted on using as sources for historians not only written texts, but also all possible human traces left from the past.[5] Both Lucien Febvre and Marc Bloch, the founding figures of the Annales, agreed that all human traces were of interest to historians who should not restrict themselves to written records.[6] After the Second World War, the second and third generations of Annales historians in France continued and deepened the anthropological investigations into everyday lifeworlds.[7] François Dosse has commented that 'the third generation of the Annales ... has shifted its discourse towards historical anthropology'.[8] They did so, he pointed out, under the banner of 'mentalités' (mentalities). Another important influence on those seeking to merge their interests in history and anthropology was the sociologist Norbert Elias.[9] Elias' keen interest in customs, mores and life-styles gelled well with those, in France and elsewhere, championing historical anthropology. Across the Atlantic, Howard Zinn wrote the history of the American people with an eye for anthropological concerns, tracing the interconnectedness of their struggles with their everyday lifeworlds.[10] In Germany Jürgen Habermas argued as early as 1958 that historians could only fully understand the diversity of humanity if they paid attention to socio-cultural constructions that humans had created of themselves. As anthropologists had long experience of studying human beings as 'non-determined', historians should take a leaf out of their book.[11]

Indeed, the moment of anthropology in history came at precisely the time when the links between sociology and history appeared vulnerable and when historians were turning away from the macro and from big sociological theories about how societies functioned. Cultural anthropologists, above all Clifford Geertz, but also Marshall Sahlins, Margaret Mead and Victor Turner, provided new theoretical insights for historians keen to explore the micro and the everyday.[12] Geertz and Sahlins were both hugely influenced by semiotics and the linguistic turn, in particular the linguistic theories by Ferdinand de Saussure and some of the poststructuralist theorists who built their edifice on de Saussure's insights.[13] Geertz treated cock-fighting on Bali as a text which could be read and interpreted by the anthropologist who had in front of him or her a drama related to a cultural system deeply interconnected to power structures. (See Figure 6.1.) Cock-fighting thus told the anthropologist something about the role of spectacle underpinning or undermining state

Figure 6.1 A cock-fight in Bali, 14 September 1946. © Bert Hardy/Stringer, Picture Post/Getty Images.

power.[14] Sahlins saw broader cultural orders as equivalent to de Saussure's language (langue: language as a system with all the rules that make up a language), whilst he argued that cultures as distinct and specific human projects are the equivalent of de Saussure's speech (parole: how the abstract rules of a language are put into practice by its speakers). Culture as structure becomes the overarching edifice in which culture as speech acts move and may, in turn, change the entire overarching structure.[15] It was no coincidence that Sahlins was working at the University of Chicago, where, already from the 1950s onwards, a whole host of scholars had been pioneering work of historical anthropology. In particular, the Committee on the Comparative Study of New Nations, which drew together, among others, scholars like McKim Marriot, Robert Redfield, Edward Shils, Milton Singer and Aristide Zolberg, was to act as a major inspiration for others interested in exploring the linkages between anthropology and history.[16] The fact that they focused on nations already underlined an interest in collective identities that was to play an influential role in many fields of work subsequently populated by historical anthropologists.

Among the proponents of an early historical anthropology was also Alan Macfarlane. Trained at Cambridge University as both a historian and an anthropologist and influenced by the Annales school, he wrote extensively on English history, using anthropological methods and insights.[17] In his Frazer Memorial Lecture, delivered at the University of Liverpool in 1973, Macfarlane made a programmatic call for bringing anthropology and history closer together. Turning to anthropological practice, i.e. 'studying small, semi-enclosed, communities', would, he argued, allow history to achieve that old dream of the profession of studying the totality of a given society. Turning to anthropology would make it possible for historians 'to understand the strange' and distance themselves from the 'over-familiar'. The task of historical anthropologists was more difficult than that of conventional ones: they needed more imagination as they could rely only on past records whereas conventional anthropologists could go out among the living to collect their data. Nevertheless, the task facing both was the same: 'In both anthropology and history we have to create a total, ideal, model of the world that exists behind the fragments that we observe. This arrangement of the pieces into something larger than themselves is a creative, imaginative act, and depends entirely on the sensitivity and assumptions of the observer.'[18] This is a very interesting passage, for

Macfarlane points to knowledge being constructed by the historical anthropologist whilst he is still referring to a total world that is out there and has to be reconstituted through historical anthropology. This confidence that scholars had the ability and the means to do that authoritatively and conclusively would get lost among the generation of historical anthropologists after narrativism and the linguistic turn, as we shall see below.

From History Workshop Movements to Historical Anthropology

Historical anthropology was to find some of its strongest proponents among the diverse history-from-below schools that emerged out of the political ferment of the 1960s.[19] The history workshop movement in Britain and elsewhere started with the deliberate aim of democratising history. Its advocates built on the long tradition of people's histories referred to above and were an integral part of the turn to social history in the 1960s and 1970s. (See Chapter 3.) Starting in 1967, the British history workshop movement organised twenty-eight history workshops and founded the *History Workshop Journal* (*HWJ*), which is today one of the leading international history journals. During the 1970s many local groups sprang up across Britain. Committed to the political left, to socialism and feminism, they initially focused on topics such as Chartism or workers' control or the women's movement. New-found topics and new-found methods, in particular oral history, were meant to pluralise a historical profession that was still, by and large, dominated by political history.[20] In the editorial in the first issue of *HWJ*, the editors emphasised the politically emancipatory aims of their kind of history: 'history is a source of inspiration and understanding . . . we believe that history should become common property'.[21]

Similar movements committed to a left-wing emancipatory political agenda and the pluralisation of historical writing sprang up in the United States, Australia, South Africa and, outside the Anglo-world, in France, Italy, Germany and many other places during the 1970s and 1980s.[22] In Italy *microstoria* developed out of theoretical concerns with what its founders, Giovanni Levi, Simona Cerutti and Carlo Ginzburg, perceived to be overgeneralisations typical of the dominant macro-social histories of the 1970s.[23] Over recent decades, micro-history has developed into a major sub-field of historical writing with its own theoretical and empirical concerns, very different from 1970s-type social histories. It explicitly acknowledges the fragmentary character of the past which means that historians can access it only through a multiplicity of different interpretations. Taking their cue from Walter Benjamin's famous call on historians to brush history against the grain of the sources, they have in their works attempted to make the best of often meagre traces in order to tell stories from the perspective of those at the bottom of society.[24] In his most recent book, co-authored with Bruce Lincoln, Ginzburg, for example, analyses the mythical figure of the werewolf, which plays an important role in several societies, in a comparative and multi-perspectival way, unravelling competing interpretations of the same phenomenon over different times and places.[25] Yet, micro-historians have been, time and again, discussing the precise relationship between the micro and the macro. More recently, they have investigated how to insert their concerns into the writing of global history.[26]

In Germany two of the leading figures in the history workshop movement, Thomas Lindenberger and Michael Wildt, taking their inspiration from Michel de Certeau, argued that history from below is powerful enough to be able to contest the desire of a history from above to centralise, totalise and streamline the many histories into one authoritative history. The narrative and performative nature of history radically pluralises the past and allows a variety of different social actors to tell stories that have the power to decentre privileged readings of that past.[27]

In France, Jacques Rancière has been an outspoken proponent of a historical practice that gave a voice to the hitherto voiceless. In his own research on the French working class, he delved into the archives to emerge with the voices of tailors, shoemakers, printers and ironworkers who were trying, after long working days, to find answers to questions that concerned them by prolonging their nights for study and discussion.[28] Through their letters, diaries, poems and proclamations, Rancière sought to recover a polyphony of voices that one could not reduce to a single movement, like a labour movement, or to issues of class, like the working class. Highlighting fragmentation and individual lifeworlds of experience, he aimed at recovering people who had been repressed at their time of living and subsequently by a historiography that had preferred the voices of the powerful. Calling for a heretical history, he accused professional historians of writing an academic history that hid the dark underbelly of history rather than revealing it.[29] He shared with Hayden White a deep interest in the narratives of the voiceless and considered their recovery to be as much a literary task as a historical one. Even more than White, he stressed the political dimensions of excluding and recovering those voices.[30] His own history very much explored the past from the perspective of the below and the margins – something highly characteristic of history workshop traditions all over the world.

Leaving big social theory behind, many in the history workshop movement turned to anthropology. In Germany Hans Medick talked about a 'missionaries in the row boat' approach that included 'ethnological modes of thinking'.[31] In 1993, he, together with Alf Lüdtke, Regina Schulte, Richard von Dülmen and others, founded the journal *Historische Anthropologie*, which has become one of the most prominent history journals in Germany today. In the editorial in its first issue, the editors set out their agenda of historical anthropology. Its emphasis on the practices of the everyday would not be dominated by macro-structures, and would focus instead on ordinary people and the materiality of their conditions as well as the sense-making processes of their lifeworlds. A comprehensive concept of culture was central to their undertaking and needed greater interdisciplinary efforts. They expressed a strong interest in comparative cultural studies, which they saw as capable of decentring common assumptions about alleged anthropological constants and universalisms. Eurocentrism and ethnocentrism were to be avoided. At the centre of historical anthropology's interest stood the 'multiplicity of "social logics"', although the editors were also keen to stress that cultural relativism would have to be limited by the acceptance of the physical and mental integrity of the other. What is of particular interest in the context of the present study is the editors' highlighting of historical anthropology's ability to reveal the construction and contribute to the deconstruction of identities.[32] It underlines my argument that historical anthropology was closely related to attempts to break the link between historical writing and collective identity formation, or, at least, to contribute to more self-reflective attitudes of historians towards that link. During the 1990s, outside Germany too, diverse forms of historical anthropology became the leading methodological light of the different history workshop movements. For André Burguière, a leading French historical anthropologist, the 'historiography of habits' and the 'exploration of the ordinary' became the prime concern for this field of history writing.[33]

The concern with anthropology and the everyday was also strong in the development of the Subaltern Studies Group in India.[34] Under the mentorship of Ranajit Guha and inspired by the writings of Antonio Gramsci, Subaltern Studies scholars explored the history of the lives of the subaltern classes in India and South-East Asia more generally, making good use of anthropological approaches.[35] Even before the advent of the Subaltern Studies Group, historical anthropologists such as Bernard S. Cohn pointed out, as early as 1957, that 'one of the primary subject matters of an historical anthropology or an anthropological history is . . . the colonial situation'.[36] Categories and concepts that had been crucial for both history and anthropology, he argued, had emerged in the wake of colonialism. This concern with the colonial archive and its functions in knowledge production was one eagerly picked up by postcolonial scholars. Guha himself and, above all, Gayatri C. Spivak developed a set of techniques with which they related archival evidence to systems of domination under colonial rule.[37] Archives were no longer mere repositories of documents from the past. Instead, they were now read themselves as discursive constructions which did not contain but rather constructed and structured the hegemonic discourses formulated by the colonisers. A range of scholars influenced by postcolonial thought has subsequently attempted to deconstruct the 'colonial lexicons' left by the colonisers.[38] They have explicated the ways in which these lexicons have constructed stable, bounded and authentic identities around both the colonised and the coloniser that were related to the construction of essentialised and unified collective identities. Reading those lexicons against the grain not only revealed a range of disparate subversions of the dominant discourses, they also highlighted the existence of indeterminable, ambiguous, fragmentary and fluid subjectivities that cannot be subsumed and contained under one totality.

If we take, for example, the work of Ann Laura Stoler, her first book on the plantation belt of Sumatra already illustrated her commitment to historical anthropology. Focusing on life in the village of Simpang Lima, she analysed employment patterns as sources of discord and disharmony in village life. Her account of the control of this largely indentured labour force and its resistance to diverse forms of exploitation owed much to Marxist categories and ideas, but it was already inflected by poststructuralist, especially Foucauldian, insights. Her century-long story of planters' exploitative designs and workers' resistance to them related coloniser and colonised in manifold ways and provided a range of different perspectives, including a gender one, on this relationship.[39] Ann Laura Stoler's second book on *Race and the Education of Desire* was centrally concerned with Foucault's work, as its subtitle *Foucault's History of Sexuality and the Colonial Order of Things* indicates. Exploring sexuality and racism as constitutive of nineteenth-century European bourgeois identity, she argued that the colonial experience acted as a laboratory for testing the European social order. Drawing on Foucault's insights, she investigated how both constructions of race and sexuality were invented in the colonies. Critiquing Foucault for excluding the racialised body from his exploration of sexuality, she insisted on the importance of the sexualities ascribed to the colonised. Their alleged permissiveness, lasciviousness and engagement in sexual acts deemed perverse served the function of delineating non-deviant, non-depraved, normal forms of sexuality that were in line with bourgeois morality.[40] Stoler's third book was still very much concerned with the intimate relationships between the colonisers and the colonised. The rules for the moral and sexual conduct of European male colonisers, she claimed, very much sought to uphold notions of European superiority over the 'savage' colonised. Racial, gender and class markers were present everywhere in the diverse attempts to constitute imperial subjectivities in colonial contexts. Yet colonisers living for generations in these contexts often could not live up to the moral ideas and ideals generated by the dynamic interrelationship between metropoles and peripheries. As a result, a substantial (unwanted) mixing of 'races' across the colonial world produced a new class of 'mixed blood' origin which constructed its own cultural identities. Stoler throughout was extremely adapt at relating the private lives of colonisers and colonised to constructions of racial and sexual identity.[41]

With her next book on the *Archival Grain*, she turned full-scale to the question, discussed above, of how to read colonial archives. Stoler explored diverse ways of reading them against the grain of the discourse they constructed, i.e. in ways that were capable of extracting from them the 'minor histories' of counter-hegemonic discourses. Here strategies for reading the colonial archives were predicated on the idea that, first of all, historians have to lay bare the way in which the documents already form a hegemonic narrative, as it is only from that position that counter-hegemonic readings become possible at all. Influenced by Derrida's reading of the archives,[42] she outlined how, despite colonial governance having structured the archives, historians, making good use of historical anthropology, had nevertheless revealed the fragmentary and ambiguous structure of the colonial that was the location for many contestations. The case studies assembled in this volume were designed to convince scholars of colonialism and imperialism that they should use the archives, not as an institution from which to extract historical knowledge, but as a site for anthropological fieldwork.[43] In her most recent book, *Duress: Imperial Durabilities in Our Times*, Stoler coined the concept of duress as meaning 'a relation of actualised and anticipated violence', in order to show how the legacies of imperialism still determine many aspects of contemporary politics, underlining how empire left traces that are still in need of being uncovered in order better to understand the present.[44] Overall, I have discussed at length Stoler's work on historical anthropology over the best part of thirty years, because it seems to me to be paradigmatic of many aspects of historical anthropology over the years: its rootedness in an undogmatic Marxism; its commitment to retrieving those voices from history that had hitherto been marginalised; its productive engagement with the set of theories that I introduced in Chapter 1 of this book; its concern with collective identities revealing how previous historical writing had constructed them as essentialist and foundational; and its insistence that these constructed identities had always been fragmentary, ambiguous and contested.

Stoler's trajectory is thus entirely in line with what Geoff Eley described as the 'crooked line' taken by historians like himself and Stoler from Marxist social history to a productive engagement with the body of theories discussed in Chapter 1.[45] Foucauldian theorisations of power structures, critical views on processes of 'othering', a turn towards intersectionality, and a deep concern with identity politics all stem from the theoretical engagements with some of these theories. Looking at history 'from the margins' was, for many historical anthropologists, the best recipe for pluralising our perspectives on the past, for avoiding Eurocentrism and for drawing attention to the consequences of formal and informal power structures in societies.[46] The Gramscian concept of 'hegemony'[47] was widely used, as was the Thompsonian idea of 'moral economy'[48] – indicating the influence of undogmatic Marxism on historical anthropology. E. P. Thompson, of course, had himself reflected intensely on the relationship between social history and anthropology.[49] In the wake of his musings, historical anthropologists argued that it was possible to go beyond macro-social theories and instead uncover the complex ambiguities underlying the cultural processes of the everyday.[50] Ideas of diversity, performance and resistance were widely used in works of historical anthropology. Such a perspective on history that we commonly find among historical anthropologists emphasised the plurality of possible conceptions of the past and the multiple variations of knowledge about the past. Alternative interpretations of the past thus became part and parcel of the *conditio humana*. What was needed, historical anthropologists argued, was a playful acceptance of and openness towards the ultimate indeterminedness of the past.

The key starting point for historical anthropology was anthropology's turn to culture in the decades between the 1950s and the 1970s.[51] Anthropologists like Geertz pointed out that all societies created forms of orientation through culture.[52] Identities hence were related not to essences but to constructions through culture, which changed over time and were different in different places. Interested in explaining cultural change, William Sewell, for example, investigated the impact of the new justification of private property, which, in his view, went back to the changes brought about by the French revolution. In the nineteenth century, however, workers, he argued, could not acquire property, and, at times, they could not even pay for basic rent and food. The disparity between cultural expectations and practices helped to create organisations aimed at defending workers.[53] Sewell drew attention to practices and to how cultural values and expectations led to specific practices. In this, his work was closely related to Pierre Bourdieu's attempt to develop a theory of practice capable of incorporating the lived experiences of the everyday with all their ambiguities and indeterminacies, whilst at the same time not denying the role played by intentionality and agency in the production of everyday experiences.[54] (See Chapter 1.)

The increasing number of works exploring the intersections of culture and social practices could draw not only on Bourdieu but also on Michel de Certeau's ideas on the practices of everyday life. De Certeau in fact entered into a prolonged dialogue with Bourdieu in his own work, seeking to relate the specifics of the everyday to more general expressions of culture.[55] His theory of everyday life saw it anchored in repetitive, unconscious routine practices produced by institutional strategies and structures of power implemented from above. He was interested in particular in the creative 'tactics' (a concept meant as a counterpoint to Bourdieu's 'strategies' from above) adopted by individuals from below navigating this frame for the everyday. This frame was, he argued, appropriated and re-employed through the actions of ordinary people. The French title of his book speaks of the 'invention of the everyday' (*l'invention du quotidian*), arguing that people had the power to make limited choices as 'consumers', choices which in turn influenced the frame of the everyday, even if they always had to move inside the frame. Unlike representatives of the Frankfurt school such as Theodor W. Adorno, de Certeau did not view the realm of mass consumption as irretrievably corrupted and degraded. He recognised that in the sphere of mass consumption there still lay the germ of active and creative remaking. As 'consumers', people were not the mere objects and victims of commodity fetishism: they could also become 'poachers'. In other words, they had the power to subvert the meanings of the institutional frames and could mobilise creative forms of resistance to them. The structures and the frames imposed from above could thus never totally control the everyday and hence always left a space for resistance. De Certeau's concept of 'anti-discipline' was related to Foucault's emphasis on disciplining regimes. Like Foucault, de Certeau had taken a linguistic turn to the interpretation of the social. Re-appropriations of consumption were like speech acts that could be read by the historian and unearthed in an archaeology of the everyday. As the production, consumption and enactment of those cultures of the everyday were closely interrelated, the whole system of culture could only be illuminated by examining the multiple modes of actions at work within the wider system. Hence de Certeau drew attention once again to practices and performances, and his own works were full of analogies to drama and the stage, especially his book on a group of seventeenth-century nuns in the small town of Loudon who were allegedly possessed by the devil.[56] The individual who acts in the everyday is, according to de Certeau, not a rational, stable and unitary being: 'Each individual is a locus in which an incoherent (and often contradictory) plurality of … relational determinations interact.'[57] Such a non-identitical subject also does not adhere uniformly to one collective identity. S/he cannot become the unitary carrier of or agent on behalf of collectives, be they classes or nations or other collective subjects. De Certeau's construction of the individual in the everyday thus also warns historians not to fall into the trap of forging, through their writing, uniform and essentialised collective identities. However, de Certeau at the same time insisted that the cultures of the everyday constructed identities through the practices of adopting, adapting, modifying and resisting the structures of the everyday, albeit in fluid, uneven, contradictory, ambiguous and heteronomous ways.[58]

De Certeau's work was inspirational for generations of historical anthropologists, many of whom turned to the sphere of culture, especially cultures of the everyday. Sewell, in his attempt to theorise the concept of culture, attempted to distinguish between culture as theory and culture as practice. Theorising culture with the help of cultural anthropology led him to emphasise that culture should be understood as structure, structuring human behaviour. Yet culture should also be seen as a practice, i.e. as a performance of a world of beliefs, rituals and daily enactments that changed over time and place. The constant production and reproduction of culture made it impossible to fix it. It was fragmented, fluid, changeable – a contested process drawing attention to which agents attempted to fix it and who constructed borders and boundaries vis-à-vis other attempts to fix it. The constructions of identities based on culture thus were stripped of all essences and were revealed as constructions that stood in relation to changing power positions. The performance of these identities was rooted in everyday practices that in turn impacted on our abstract understanding of culture.[59] Such cultural relativism went hand in hand with a perception of culture as an autonomous entity that did not depend on social and economic structures. Thus, E. P. Thompson, for example, argued against social and economic reductionism in explaining eighteenth-century riots, and instead highlighted the role of culture in providing insights into crowd behaviour.[60] Historians such as Thompson, but also, in North America, Natalie Zemon Davis, in their classical writings on rough music and charivari as cultural expressions of rebellion, were influenced strongly by Bakhtin and a range of anthropologists, especially Claude Lévi-Strauss and Arnold van Gennep.[61] (See Figure 6.2.)

Robert Darnton's equally iconic essay on 'the Great Cat Massacre' drew directly on Geertz's cultural anthropology. Darnton and Geertz had been colleagues at Princeton University and had taught a joint

Figure 6.2 Rough music during an old Yorkshire custom known as 'Riding the Stang', which could express all sorts of displeasure felt towards different people. From: *Picturesque History of Yorkshire*, published c. 1900. © Universal History Archive/Universal Images Group via Getty Images.

seminar on history and anthropology for several years. As anthropologists were interested in the otherness of cultures, so Darnton was interested in the otherness of the past. Just as Geertz read the Balinese cock-fight as a text, so Darnton too read as texts historical incidents that came to him via the archives. In 'The Great Cat Massacre' he dealt with Paris-based apprentices who, angry at being kept awake at night by howling cats, decided to hunt them down, court-martial them and hang them. His reading of this incident made him relate the events to labour relations in 1730s Paris and the role of everyday violence in society at the time. He showed how cat killings, especially killing the cat of the master's wife, was one way by which apprentices could voice their grievances about their masters and show their hostility. In the drama and spectacle of cat killings they celebrated a riotous moment of freedom from their masters' control. It was a form of everyday resistance that Darnton, unlike Thompson, did not seek to relate to the emergence of class consciousness, because for him, the macro-sociological concept of class already did violence to the intricacies and specificities of the stories of the past. His articles on French cultural history rejected sociological grand narratives and instead engaged in reading texts as miniatures that nevertheless provided valuable insights into how historical anthropologists could recover and render meaningful the everyday voices and actions from the past.[62]

Historical anthropologists' concern with culture was de-essentialised thanks to their engagement with poststructuralist theory. Many scholars discursively (de-)constructed culture, arguing that it had no essences in a world existing solely on linguistic structures. The poetics of historical anthropology became, for some, the object of study.[63] Drawing attention to the actual act of writing historical anthropology and to the production of texts, scholars now argued that writing involved much more than putting into practice method and technique: it involved elements of construction and invention that were strongly related to the political, social and cultural contexts of text production. It was thus actively involved in the cultural production of meaning and part and parcel of a complex web of knowledge systems that make up the epistemic structure of discursive regimes of power. The Foucauldian emphasis on epistemic ruptures dividing different ages from one another pointed to the impact of discourses in stabilising existing epistemes.[64] A new attention to language was to characterise many works in historical anthropology. Its practitioners concluded that culture was neither unitary nor coherent. Instead, they argued that it carried political implications and was thus inherently contested. The cultural concepts with which people attempted to make sense of the world around them, the epistemologies they developed and the social categories they used were all rooted in specific linguistic constructions that rarely went unchallenged.[65] Culture was no longer fixed; it was a fluid concept and changed its shape under the influence of performative power relationships. Edna Bay's study on the kingdom of Dahomey, which lasted in Africa from the seventeenth to the nineteenth century, thus examines the construction of gendered power hierarchies through language. She concluded that their purpose was to justify the creation of a female warrior guard which had great influence in the slave-trading aristocracy of the kingdom.[66]

Such poststructuralist-inspired studies of cultural systems analysed the self-positionings of historical actors and their readings of the past. These were never coherent and evolved from contestation, negotiation and change over time. This fluidity of diverse constructions of meaning drew attention to the human existences as performances carried out in specific locations and temporalities.[67] A classic case has been Rhys Isaac's book on ante-bellum Virginian social life in the USA. Drawing, among others, on Geertz, he portrayed social life in Virginia as a 'series of performances' and described them in great detail. They included the ceremonies that characterised the everyday of the Virginian gentry household – from tea drinking to hosting dinner parties. He furthermore combined this with an account of legal, military and political rituals, all of which he related back to performances on the theatre stage. His main argument about the transformation of Virginia in the second half of the eighteenth century was about the evangelical counter-culture that challenged and ultimately replaced the hitherto dominant gentry culture that had dominated Virginia down to the second half of the eighteenth century.[68]

Subsequently, many historical anthropologists have concentrated on the life cycle of human beings and on the ordinary within this life cycle, i.e. on births and deaths, on youth, marriage, old age, illness, food, clothing, home, violence, rituals and sexuality. Ildikó Bellér-Hann's historical anthropology of the Uyghurs in China between the late nineteenth century and the onset of communism in 1949 is a good example of studies of the ordinary everyday as experienced by a specific group, in this case an ethnically Turkic, religiously Muslim sedentary oasis-dwelling population in eastern China. Making good use of both Uyghur texts as well as texts produced by those visiting and writing about the Uyghur communities, Bellér-Hann constructed a kaleidoscopic, fluid and situational story of a community riven by internal contradictions and contestations that still managed to construct a sense of identity around the key concepts of 'community' and 'reciprocity'. One of the chapters in this book is specifically dedicated to rituals associated with the life cycle of the Uyghurs, whilst others deal with religious practices and customs as well as representations impacting on economic and social organisation.[69] (See Figure 6.3.)

Studies on the life cycle have also been important in re-interpreting early modern societies with the help of insights from historical anthropology. Building on the work of Victor Turner, David Cressy, for example, has examined a range of religious and social rituals surrounding birth, marriage and death between the early sixteenth and the early eighteenth century. Drawing on a wide range of sources, including

Figure 6.3 Uyghurs celebrating in traditional costume at a desert scenic spot in Yopurga county on 2 May 2016. © Visual China Group, Getty Images.

sermons, court proceedings, medical books, marriage manuals, parish records and literary texts as well as ego-documents, such as diaries and letters, he managed to throw a new light on the early modern household by paying due attention to life-cycle rituals. Relating these rituals to the reinforcement of social order, he paid due attention to contestations which sought to undermine or modify and alter this social order. Ambiguity and dissent figured prominently in his rich descriptions of rituals in the life cycle of the early modern household. Accounts of everyday life, Cressy showed, cannot be understood without paying due attention to the protocols of tradition and the controversies surrounding them, as well as the full range of rituals of the life cycle. Understanding the workings of English society in the early modern period thus needed an anthropological investigation of precisely those rituals that he read as statements and interventions in religious and political debates.[70]

Historical anthropologists dealt with diverse cultural realms. Prominent among them were religion, superstition and magic. The emphasis here was on practices and behavioural patterns, as well as social and power relations. A classic in the historical anthropology of religion was Keith Thomas' *Religion and the Decline of Magic*, first published in 1971. He was inspired by anthropologists' writings on Africa, in particular by Edward E. Evans-Pritchard's work that understood witchcraft as an important social force in central African societies.[71] Natalie Zemon Davis' work on the wars of religion in sixteenth-century France was also instrumental in drawing attention to the value for historians of anthropological insights. She interpreted mutual lynchings of Catholics and Protestants as ritual murders meant to cleanse the community of heresy.[72] From the 1980s onwards, the link between anthropological methods and historical writings on religion grew stronger and stronger. To give a more recent example: Roman Loimeier's historical anthropology of Muslim Africa dealt with a great variety of different contexts over a long period of time, in which African Muslims situated their religious identity vis-à-vis a great many other identities relating to themselves and others. The dialogical and fractured, multi-faceted nature of Muslim Africa is due to the dynamics of historical change which affected power relationships in Muslim empires, the control over long-distance trade routes, the impact of diverse religious-political movements and the interrelationship with non-African societies.[73]

Above all, historical anthropology has de-essentialised humanity and human identities by pointing out that there is no unchanging essence at the heart of human behaviour and that human actions are generated within the triangle of social practices, symbolic forms and power relations.[74] Christoph Wulf has argued: 'Anthropology presupposes a plurality of cultures and assumes that cultures are not closed systems; rather, they are dynamic, able to permeate each other, and they have an indeterminate future.'[75] In the study of the relationship between frontiers and identities, for example, insights from historical anthropology have loomed large. Collective identities at the border were shaped by frames set by nation-states and empires, but the people living at the border, time and again, sought to negotiate and, if necessary, subvert these frames by means of contesting representations, and by seeking alternative forms of seeing the borders through everyday practices and symbolic actions. In this way, border identities emerge as constructed in multiple and at times mutually incompatible ways that have always been situational, fluid and contested. No essential and foundational collective identity existed in borderlands.[76]

In line with these assumptions, historical anthropology has frequently stressed the importance of mimetic processes, which are not based on simple copying and repetition, but involve transforming that which serves as a model and, in the process, producing something new. Mimesis has been described by Gunter Gebauer and Christoph Wulf as a key concept for the human sciences, as it is an integral part of the simulation and symbolisation of the world.[77] All images that make the world stand in mimetic relation to other images. If symbolical worlds are mimetically produced, they always relate to other worlds similarly produced. As they can be in competition and are always in a relation to diffused power relations, this makes mimesis an intensely political concept. Axel Michaels and Christoph Wulf's edited collection on the *Images of the Body in India* is a practical attempt to make use of the concept of mimesis to account for the diverse ways in which systems of meanings were inscribed on to bodies that were culturally created, rather than being biologically constituted. Margrit Pernau's article in this collection, for example, looks at the way in which bodies were culturally constituted in transnational ways through knowledge circulation in the field of medicine. Focusing on Unani medicine (practised widely in South Asia and based on the ancient Greek idea of the four humours which had to be balanced out in order to ensure the health of the individual), she demonstrates how one (of many) constructions of the Indian body was due to such transnational circulations of knowledge systems.[78] (See Figure 6.4.)

Pernau's article underlines how authors who have been inspired by historical anthropology have also been deeply involved in decentring a Western perspective in historical writing, thereby contributing to the provincialisation of Europe.[79] Influenced by theories about historical narratives, Steven Feierman, for example, has examined the issue of public healing on the northern Rwandan frontier, showing how Western colonisers attempted to repress African practices of healing. These practices could not be accommodated by Western narratives following rational forms. They simply did not make sense in the narrative repertoires available to Western colonisers. Hence, in their narratives, healers and healing simply disappeared. They were not only physically repressed; they were also silenced in discourse. Recapturing healing rituals can thus rely not on texts but on rhythmic performances which combine music and dance and are still available in oral narratives provided by African 'voices'. However, Feierman also points out that we

Figure 6.4 'An Indian Medicine Man or Shaman with Elaborate Body Painting Performing a Ritual Dance'. Wood engraving. © Wellcome Collection. Attribution 4.0 International (CC BY 4.0).

cannot simply sustain a dichotomy between coloniser and colonised, since their worlds were in effect intermingled in manifold ways. Out of such insights developed an intense interest in questions of hybridity. According to Feierman, the very destructiveness of colonial power relations meant that everything that survives is necessarily hybrid. This makes it very difficult to recover authentic African voices: the 'European sources hang like a veil between the historian and the African actors of this period'. The gaps in our understanding of the African past can only be filled by means of an extremely self-reflective approach to the sources, both European and African. In particular, historians seek to actualise the marginal(ised) memories that survive in these sources, even if they do not seem to make sense if looked at through the layers of textual meaning produced by the colonisers' narratives.[80] A strong emphasis on hybridity has also characterised other work done by postcolonial historical anthropologists. Take, for example, John Pemberton's book on ceremonies associated with Javanese kingship. It demonstrates to what extent these practices, for a long time described as authentically Javanese, in fact emerged out of intense collaboration between indigenous elites and Dutch colonisers.[81] Historians need to arrive at different meanings and configurations by making familiar texts and objects unfamiliar, thus decentring the layers of Western narratives that dominate our mainstream interpretations of the past. Such decentring and such making unfamiliar are precisely what historical anthropology, especially of the subaltern studies variant, has been trying to do over the past four decades.

This defamiliarisation of the familiar had a deep impact on reconceptualising some familiar Western concepts. Take, for example, the concept of class. By studying a single small village in Württemberg from the beginning of the eighteenth century to the late nineteenth century, David Sabean managed to reconceptualise the concept of class by homing in on the close interrelationship between class and marriage. His painstaking reconstruction of village life showed how the agricultural revolution resulted in overpopulation and increased economic inequality within the village. In turn, it led to marriage patterns in which the richer sections no longer intermarried with the poorer ones. This then led to the emergence of an elite that could subsequently be constructed in terms of class. Such an ethnographic analysis, by paying due attention to discourses, is thus resulting in the production of new meanings of the idea of class in nineteenth-century German history.[82]

Conclusion

The influence historical anthropology has had on history writing is immense. Lynn Hunt, in her influential book *The New Cultural History*, first published in 1989, argued: 'At the moment, the anthropological model reigns supreme in cultural approaches' to history writing.[83] As I have shown in this chapter, the historians' turn to anthropology in the 1980s sprang from many historians' increasing unease about structural social history. In particular, those historians who had been part of the attempt to recover a 'history from below' now began to merge their often neo-Marxist concerns with ideas derived from poststructuralism, narrativism and constructivism, in order to arrive at theories of culture that were capable of explaining social development without reference to structural determinism. In this sense culture gave agency back to ordinary people and unearthed locally produced knowledge capable of opposing and resisting dominant knowledge systems. Historical anthropology was also able to question essentialised constructions of identity and point to the indeterminate, contested and changing nature of these historical identities. Anthropological approaches to history have pointed to our limited ability to understand past cultures, thus sharpening our awareness of the differences between past and present. There is no easy way from that past to our present. No collective identity emerges teleologically from the past to burst unmediated into our present. At the same time historical anthropologists have themselves already asked questions about how our own cultures are always contested, plural, and made up, not of straight lines, but of cul-de-sacs, roundabouts, pathways not taken and blocked-off roads. Drawing on a wide range of traditions, from people's histories to the Annales, they have thus made an important contribution to a more self-reflective and playful history writing, one that is aware of its relationship to the construction of identities and extremely wary of it. Historical anthropology, like gender history, dealt with in the last chapter, is firmly rooted in the cultural turn of the historical sciences that was related to diverse theories discussed above in Chapter 1. The same is true for memory history, which will be discussed in the next chapter.

Further Reading

Brian Keith Axel (ed.), *From the Margins: Historical Anthropology and Its Futures*, Durham, NC: Duke University Press, 2002.

Alexandre Coello de la Rosa and Josep Luís Mateo Dieste, In *Praise of Historical Anthropology: Perspectives, Methods and Applications to the Study of Power and Colonialism*, London: Routledge, 2020.

Michel de Certeau, *The Practice of Everyday Life*, Berkeley: University of California Press, 1988.

Saurabh Dube, *Historical Anthropology*, Oxford: Oxford University Press, 2009.

Don Kalb and Herman Tak (eds.), *Critical Junctions: Anthropology and History beyond the Cultural Turn*, Oxford: Berghahn Books, 2005.

Alf Lüdtke (ed.), *The History of Everyday Life: Reconstructing Historical Experiences and Ways of Life*, Princeton: Princeton University Press, 1989.

Hans Medick, 'Missionaries in the Row Boat? Ethnological Ways of Knowing as a Challenge to Social History', in: *Comparative Studies in Society and History* 29 (1987), 76–98.

William M. Reddy, 'Anthropology and the History of Culture', in: Lloyd Kramer and Sarah Maza (eds.), *A Companion to Western Historical Thought*, Oxford: Blackwell, 2002, 277–96.

Christoph Wulf, 'On Historical Anthropology: an Introduction', in: *The Senses and Society* 11:1 (2016), 7–23.

7 *The History of Memory*

Introduction

The new histories that we have so far discussed are all characterised by an understanding of historical writing as an attempt to reconstruct and represent the past. They recognise that there is a plurality of legitimate ways of contesting historical interpretations. Historians of memory, by and large, share this view, not least because the object of their study, memory, is invariably contested. They belong to a much wider field, now called memory studies, which is fast becoming a separate discipline,[1] although, to date, there are, to my knowledge, no departments of memory studies and few professorships or other academic positions specifically in memory studies. Historians of memory, by working closely with memory scholars from other disciplines, are more multi- and interdisciplinary than many other historians.[2] The conceptual arsenal developed by memory studies is truly awesome. Already in the opening issue of the flagship journal *Memory Studies*, Henry L. Roediger and James V. Wertsch listed:

> active cultural memory, archival cultural memory, autobiographical memory, collective memory, context-dependent memory, cultural memory, discovered memory, dynamic memory, emotional memory, episodic memory, explicit memory, false memory, fear-dependent memory, flashbulb memory, general political memory, historical memory, implicit memory, involuntary memory, meta-memory, narrative memory, particular political memory, personal semantic memory, public autobiographical memory, reconstructed memory, recovered memory, self-memory, semantic memory, social memory, tacit memory, transactive memory, traumatic memory, unconscious memory and working memory.[3]

To this I could add today a range of other concepts of memory. I shall start this chapter by asking how the field of memory studies has influenced histories of memory and their perspectives on the past.

Historians of memory have recognised that memories of the past have an important impact on the diverse ways in which the past becomes both meaning and powerful in the present and in which it is capable of shaping the future. Memory work and historical writing thus draw closer together in that both tend to be future-oriented and about re-inscribing stories of the past into the present.[4] But the historical writing about memory is also about analysing how memory works in its retelling of the past. Memory history has consequently been deeply intertwined with the rise of memory debates in many different societies worldwide. In the second part of this chapter I shall review some of these debates in order to show how memory histories have often contributed to relativising identitarian claims about the past and contributed to a greater self-reflexivity among historians about what they are doing when they write history.

Historians of memory have paid particular attention to what is variously called 'collective memory', 'social memory' or 'cultural memory'. Taking their cue from diverse theoretical inspirations to be discussed in the next section of this chapter, historians of memory often refer to forms of material and immaterial heritage as having symbolic significance within a given society. They start from the assumption that our understandings of the past derive from both an individual and a collective engagement with what comes to us as stories and remnants of the past. Memory is not so much a reliving or re-activating of past experiences as a reconfiguring and re-interpreting of that experience. It is thus unthinkable without experience, but is equally unthinkable without narrativity and emplotment. The memory of an event is intrinsically different from the event itself. Memory historians have been primarily interested not in how truthful a particular memory is but rather in what that memory tells us about the historical consciousness of a given group of people in society. In the final part of this chapter I shall introduce three memory regimes that have developed very different forms of historical consciousness – antagonistic, cosmopolitan and agonistic. Memory history, I shall argue, can play an effective role in contributing to an agonistic memory culture, i.e. one which seeks to repoliticise memory and rebut the renewed rise of antagonistic memory regimes, thus contributing to the robust defence of pluralist democratic political cultures.[5]

Historians of Memory and the Field of Memory Studies

The development of the sub-field 'history of memory' has much to do with the outstanding international success of Pierre Nora's 'Realms of Memory' project, which, in seven volumes, focuses on the material and immaterial places shaping French historical consciousness.[6] Nora's idea of exploring the French nation's 'collective memory' went back to the theories of French interwar sociologist Maurice Halbwachs, who championed the idea that individual memory worked through 'social frames' that made individuals part of collectives, such as nations, and produced 'collective memory'.[7] Both Halbwachs and Nora identified with the traditions of the Annales school in France and its desire to write a history informed by geography, anthropology and culture. (See Chapters 3, 4 and 6.) Halbwachs, murdered by Nazi guards in Buchenwald, had been forgotten by the international scholarly community until Nora revived his concept of 'collective memory'. It was no coincidence that this happened in the 1980s, at a time when French national identity, with its strong attachment to republicanism and the resistance to German occupation during the Second World War, came under increasing attack. The debates surrounding the role of the French revolution of 1789 in forging French national identity, as well as the debates about the widespread collaboration of the French under German occupation during the Second World War, destabilised these two important pillars of French historical identity constructions. In this situation Nora lamented the disappearance of living memorial cultures which held the French community together. They were, he argued, replaced by dead historical cultures coldly dissecting the myths of past national communities. This amounted to a rallying call to historians of memory to help reconstruct notions of national community via memory history. In other words, Nora's project was a classic identitarian one. And the innumerable projects on 'realms of memory', national, regional, transnational, related to specific political ideologies or religious denominations, that happened across the globe in the wake of Nora's volumes, often also spoke to these identitarian concerns.[8]

However, it was precisely these identitarian concerns that were also heavily criticised by many memory scholars. Lucette Valensi, in the

French flagship journal *Annales*, accused Nora of pretending to deconstruct national myths but in reality only reviving them through the back door. She argued that his project was not so much the replacement of national history as a monumental attempt to present a new national history that could create stability in the rough waters that the national historical master narrative of France had entered in the 1980s.[9] Furthermore, Nora's sharp distinction between objective history and subjective memory, which owed much to Halbwachs, was criticised by poststructuralist thinkers who pointed out that historians were only one among a range of other memory groups constructing forms of collective memory.[10] And Nora's selection of memory places betrayed very much a top-down official and positive memory of the French state, which was entirely in line with his desire to establish a new national master narrative. In fact, in his project he posits the idea of a singular and homogeneous French memory community that ignores the contentiousness and diversity of national memory cultures. Problematic aspects of the French past found at best a marginal place in his seven volumes. Thus, women, social movements, colonialism and elements from a history-from-below approach were distinctly underrepresented, as was local and regional history. Whilst his volumes no doubt emphasised the diversity and polyphony of French national history, the concept of France itself was never questioned and counter-memories were mostly notable through their absence. The nation remained a given to which a lost thematic unity had to be restored, albeit in a kaleidoscopic form.[11]

It is interesting to reflect for a moment on the differences between Nora's project and the memory project carried out by Raphael Samuel, whose two-volume *Theatres of Memory* can be seen, in many respects, as a counter-project to Nora's.[12] Interested in the details of the everyday, Samuel welcomed the rise in interest in historical memory among wide sections of the population. He emphasised the malleability of historical consciousness, which he saw not at all one-sidedly determined by reactionary right-wing politics. The interest in the heritage of the everyday and local was, in his view, impossible to subsume under one single ideology. Hence Samuel, a major figure in the British and international history workshop movements,[13] thought of historical consciousness as being forged in an open-ended cacophony of voices in which performances of the past played a particularly important role in determining how that past was mobilised and whose political interest would benefit from such mobilisation. Unlike Nora, he refused to draw a neat line between memory and history, emphasising instead their symbiotic relationship. He therefore called on fellow historians to engage with the heritage boom and influence it in a direction that was in line with the left-wing ideas that he and the history workshop movement in Britain more generally came to be associated with.[14] This was a politics of memory conscious of and self-reflective about the indeterminate, fluid and contested nature, as well as the multiple inner contradictions, of collective forms of memory.

Historiographical developments since the 1990s have pushed the sub-discipline of memory history in an entirely different direction from the one intended by Nora. In recent decades two of the leading theoreticians of memory have been the Egyptologist Jan Assmann and the literary scholar Aleida Assmann.[15] Their conceptualisation of memory rests on the foundations laid by Halbwachs but was also inspired by figures such as the German cultural and art historian Aby Warburg.[16] However, unlike Nora, they have not been primarily concerned with using memory to bolster a weakening national identity. Coming out of left-of-centre German intellectual discourses that, at least in the Federal Republic during the 1980s, were far more sceptical about scholarship helping to strengthen national identity,[17] they became champions of transnational and cosmopolitan forms of memory. Strong champions of the idea of European unity as represented by the European Union (EU), they advocated cosmopolitan approaches to memory.

The idea of cosmopolitan memory was championed by, among others, Daniel Levy and Natan Sznaider, who have worked on the memory of the holocaust in transnational perspective.[18] Whilst earlier debates on holocaust memorials were very much centred around the national texture of memory,[19] Levy and Sznaider argued that memorialisation of the holocaust became a prime example of how memory could work in the direction of cosmopolitanism, as it led to the championing of universal human rights and liberal freedoms as a defence against the kind of dictatorial barbarity that had led to the holocaust. Subsequently cosmopolitan memory became an important building block in ideas about 'transitional justice' put forward by, among others, Elazar Barkan.[20] Barkan, as director of the Institute for the Study of Human Rights at Columbia University in New York, has become a key player in the promotion of the idea that engaging with history in a cosmopolitan memory frame has an important role to play in attempts to reconcile former enemies in places that have seen violence, ethnic cleansing, massacres, war and genocide.[21] These ideas of 'transitional justice' built on the work of Paul Ricoeur, the author of a seminal book on *Memory, History, Forgetting*, first published in French in 2000. He was particularly concerned about the relationship between memory and history, chiding the historiographical profession for its lack of self-reflexivity about that relationship and pointing to similarities between historiography and literature. His engagement with narrativist theorists, especially Hayden White, and Lacanian psychoanalysis led him also to talk about the need to work through the past through acts of remembering, which, for individuals, as for societies, was a necessary step on the road to reconciliation with self and others.[22]

The idea of transnational cosmopolitan memory having a crucial place in overcoming nationalist politics and leading to reconciliation has also been championed in diverse ways by Kwame Anthony Appiah and by Paul Gilroy. Appiah's notion of 'cosmopolitan patriotism' or 'rooted cosmompolitanism' was meant to avoid the pitfalls of both nationalist and humanist essentialisms and open up a space for the controversial discussion of political differences between people of diverse political, religious and ideological orientation. On the one hand, Appiah confirmed the importance of being rooted in concrete communities and their social networks and specific cultures, but, on the other, he also underlined that such rootedness is important for other individuals and communities as well. It was therefore necessary to accept diverse political, religious, ethnic and gender identities. In that acceptance of others, 'rooted cosmopolitanism' is cosmopolitan, and it is precisely such acceptance which leads to a sustained questioning of essentialised forms of identity through an awareness of which specific developments led to the formation of different cultures and communities.[23] Thus, historians writing the histories of their communities from the perspective of 'rooted cosmopolitanism' will fulfil the function of providing collective historical identities to their communities, but they do so with the recognition that others will do the same for their communities which will have to be accepted in their otherness.

Gilroy in his book *Postcolonial Melancholia* started off by critiquing what he calls 'armoured cosmopolitanism', by which he understands justifying military intervention in other people's territories on dubious humanitarian grounds. He described it as a fig-leaf for Western imperialism – sometimes using the same tropes of a civilising mission that were common to Western imperialist endeavours in the nineteenth century. Subsequently he contrasted this 'armoured cosmopolitanism' with a cosmopolitanism from below that he identified, above all, with multiculturalism, i.e. the valuing of cultural otherness as enriching and improving a society. Such cosmopolitanism from below would, he argued, ultimately lead to greater self-reflexivity as people would become aware of their own cultures' preconceptions and develop an empathy for other cultures from which a constructive hybridity of cultures can emerge. Cultural estrangement and reconceptualisation of what constitutes one's own culture are processes which also work in the direction of undermining essentialised notions of identity.[24]

Scholars working on postcolonial memory have contributed substantially towards the project of decolonising Western imperial mindscapes, for example in colonial museums.[25] Removing colonial artefacts from museums, contextualising anew colonial objects in museums and restoring stolen colonial objects back to their now postcolonial 'homes' are just some of the many strategies that have been pursued in the name of a postcolonial memory politics critical of the ongoing vestiges of imperialism and colonialism in the contemporary world. Its aim has been to recast the colonial and imperial identities of the West still visible in well-meaning attempts to recast those identities in a more self-critical and nuanced way, such as the conceptualisation of the Quai Branly Museum in Paris that opened its doors in 2006.[26] Much scholarship on postcolonial memory has drawn attention to the violent and exploitative nature of Western colonialism that does not form an adequate part of the memorial landscape in the West today. In an edited collection that attempts to 'postcolonialise' the French realms of memory, a distinguished list of authors has called attention to how colonial memory has been intricately connected to many forms of French national memory, both in France itself and in France's overseas possessions, the *Outre-Mer*. Official national memory, the authors in this collection argue, has for a long time silenced and suppressed colonialism. Their articles work as a clarion call to provide new readings of the past which would anchor the colonial more firmly in the national memoryscape of France. Acknowledging material and immaterial realms of memory, the authors in this collection dealt both with new memory sites of a multicultural society not previously canonised in national memory and with iconic sites of that canon that have not so far been read through the postcolonial lens such as the Pantheon in Paris. The editors explicitly aimed at extending the 'conversation at the intersection of memory studies and postcolonialism'.[27] Outside the core countries of the West, the meeting of minds in postcolonial theory and memory studies has also produced works that have unearthed silenced histories and memories. A case in point is that of the so-called 'comfort women' in Korea – forced sex workers for imperial Japanese troops during the Second World War. Dealing with multiple contending representations of these women, Sarah Soh asked uncomfortable questions about the past and the present, keeping a clear eye on future questions surrounding contemporary forms of indentured sex labour. Working with survivors' life stories and the existing, by now broad, historiography on this topic, she portrayed the fate of the comfort women as primarily the result of gendered structural violence inherent in patriarchal societies.[28]

If the memory of colonialism has loomed large over memory history, so has the history of war. Among pioneering historians of memory, the British historian Jay Winter has been a prominent champion of using the memory of war in order to promote policies of reconciliation. His own celebrated work on the memory of the First World War has highlighted how that memory had for a long time served the nationalist politics of nation-states and had, to some extent, prepared the road to the Second World War.[29] He drew lessons from his memory history for his own times by becoming involved, as founding director, in the making of a museum of the First World War in Peronne, France that has been described as an archetypal peace museum.[30] It acts as another champion of cosmopolitan memory, focusing, as it does, on soldiers as victims of war and highlighting suffering in war on all sides of the conflict. The transnational cosmopolitan message of the museum could not be clearer: there are no winners in war.

Different conceptions of transnational cosmopolitan memory have thus been increasingly replacing the old national(ist) memory frames, at least as far as scholarship on memory is concerned. The memory frames themselves, however, were still very much dominated by official, top-down, state-led corporate interests. John Bodnar warned that in the struggle between a vernacular citizens' memory of the everyday and the memory produced by interest groups and the state, the latter, throughout the twentieth century, had been increasingly successful in the United States in dominating public commemorations and shaping national memory.[31] But since the publication of his book in 1992 a move away from top-down nation-state-directed national memory and national commemorations in the public realm has also been visible. Jennifer Allen has drawn attention to a mnemonic shift towards more bottom-up, local, social movement-based memories from the last quarter of the twentieth century onwards.[32] After reviewing the older top-down forms of national commemorations in an age of nationalism, Allen analysed a variety of grassroots, bottom-up initiatives that, from the 1980s onwards, destabilised the state-driven official commemoration cultures. She drew attention to the new memorial practices first appearing in Germany, citing the activities of Joseph Beuys and his 7,000 oaks project, the Beuys-inspired Omnibus for Direct Democracy project, which started a short-lived boom in mobile monuments, and, above all the 'stumbling stones' (*Stolpersteine*) initiative of Günter Demnig, as examples of bottom-up initiatives that were first described by James Young as 'counter-monuments'.[33] According to Andreas Huyssen they were mainly based on uncovering and making visible the 'voids' in a more localised memory landscape.[34] They were adept at recovering the 'traces' of the past that had long been ephemeral to the national memory landscape.[35] From their German national origins, these innovative attempts to recast memory landscapes from the bottom up travelled to many other places – a process which Allen followed to South Africa, Austria, Argentina, the United States and Russia.[36] Allen argued that there is a new 'transnational restive mnemonics' in the making, and that it has been so successful that states have begun to co-opt grassroots movements in commemorative efforts.[37] She saw in these developments 'the beginning of a global memory movement'[38] that took its cue from Michel de Certeau's ideas around the practice of everyday life. It was informed by an ethics of radical plurality that did away with any attempt at prioritising homogeneous master narratives around national and other collective identities. It brought into the open the radical plurality of the past that was constructed around fluid and discursive commemorative practices that could not be streamlined by essentialised and totalising collective identities. Yet Allen also ends her article with the fear that the rise of new nationalisms across the globe might threaten the forward march of this new mnemonic practice. I shall return to this fear in the final section of this chapter.

Arguably cosmopolitan approaches to memory have, since the 1990s, dominated the field of memory studies in many parts of the world. The huge popularity of this sub-field has recently been underlined by the success of the Memory Studies Association, founded in 2015 and, after only four years, counting in the thousands members who have been attracted to hugely successful conferences in Copenhagen in 2017, Madrid in 2019, and Warsaw in 2021.[39] The leading journal in the field, *Memory Studies*, is also aligned to the Association in which historians form only one disciplinary strand. Much stronger are representatives from literary studies, the social sciences and anthropology/ethnology. Thus, for example, the literary scholar Michael Rothberg has put forward the idea that memory is always 'multi-directional'.[40] Emphasising how the situatedness of memory in concrete situations and contexts can lead to very different meanings produced by the same memory, he highlighted the fluidity of memory discourses and their malleability in diverse political and social contexts. He also pointed out how memory conflicts between different memories do not necessarily lead to one memory dominating all others. Rather, he argued, memories cross-reference each other and borrow from each other. Memory in this way becomes inherently dialogic with other memory. Such dialogical acts of remembrance also problematise any direct link between a specific memory and a specific identity. Thus, for example, American identity is built not only on American memory, but on a dialogue with many other forms of national, as well as other spatial and non-spatial forms of memory that make American memory multi-directional and contested. Recognising this multi-directionality of memory enhances self-reflexivity about memory discourses and questions essentialist constructions of identity.

The social scientist Jeffrey Olick has emphasised, in an article co-written with Daniel Levy, how memory can never be fixed in its relation to particular identities and is instead inherently unstable, changing over time.[41] By stressing the role of meaning-making through memory Olick also, early on, highlighted the role of those who construct memory. Building explicitly on the theoretical work of Mikhail Bakhtin, Olick's own work on holocaust memory has attempted to trace the dialogic nature of holocaust commemoration over time. Later events, he contends, always 'communicate' with earlier ones in ways that are producing a cacophony of pluralist voices.[42] Much of his writing is a warning against the reification of collective memory and its tendency to ossify around essentialised identity discourses. Instead his work has contributed to a wider understanding of cultural memory as grounded in specific practices that lead to processes of intersubjective sense-making. As he makes clear in *Sins of the Fathers*, identities rely on narrative and storytelling, yet the storytellers have different interests, their stories have varying effects, and they derive their power from diverse sources; in other words, they are extremely heterogeneous. Storytelling performs the 'us' in collective memory in multiple and sometimes mutually contradictory ways.[43] Other memory scholars have emphasised the close interrelationship between the theories of narrativity, discussed in Chapter 1, and memory. According to James Wertsch, collective memories adhere to 'schematic narrative templates' that structure and organise the memories of groups. Events that happened in the past are emplotted according to these templates. Hayden White's influence on Wertsch is obvious here.[44] In relation to national collective memories, Wertsch argued that national literature, customs, politics and ideas were constructed through these templates.[45] The strong emphasis on the construction of memories in memory studies has led to a situation where, at least before the 2000s, fewer scholars have studied the reception of memory cultures among the consumers of this culture. As early as 1997 Alon Confino critiqued this situation.[46]

Overall, then, the development of the field of memory studies has led most historians of memory to write history that is directed against nationalist and other forms of memory based on essentialist identitarian beliefs and ideas. Thus, recent nationalist developments in history politics in Ukraine have provoked a counter-reaction among memory historians. They launched a major project of rewriting the national history of Ukraine in ways that would counter simplistic and nationalist functionalisations of that history, even if the project itself has been riddled with theoretical, methodological and political problems.[47] In particular, the concept of transnational cosmopolitan memory and a range of related concepts reviewed above have steered historians to encourage their readers to develop a more self-reflexive attitude towards questions of history writing and the constructions of collective identities. They allowed them to see through the constructed character of identities and recognise their changing nature over place and time. They also enabled them to commit themselves to approaches towards the past that are more playful in relation to what meaning that past has for contemporary identities. They also furthered a belief in the essential contestedness of memories that is reflected in the frequent memory debates held in the public realm. In the next section I will review some paradigmatic memory debates from the 1990s down to the present day in order to show how they successfully undermined beliefs in essentialist identities.

Memory Historians and Memory Debates

Debates about a wide variety of past events and how one should remember them occur the world over. Often those debates focus on traumatic past events, including wars and genocides. Frequently, however, they also home in on political protests such as revolutions or student protests, and on the struggles waged by social movements such as the civil rights movement in the USA or the global women's movement. As Jakob Tanner has pointed out, social movements and protest cultures have been using narratives and narrativist theory, in particular forms of storytelling, in order to underpin their calls for social change.[48] 'Making Movement History' has been an important resource for a variety of different social movements.[49]

Here I will briefly introduce five memory debates and explore the extent to which historians of memory contributed to raising, among fellow historians, a greater self-reflexivity about the link in those memory debates with essentialised collective identities. The five chosen debates are, first, debates surrounding the memory of communism in East-Central and Eastern Europe after the collapse of communism in the late 1980s and early 1990s. Secondly, I will look at simultaneous debates surrounding the role of anti-Semitism and the holocaust in the collective identities of East-Central and Eastern European nations. Thirdly, I will investigate the memory debates surrounding the Second World War in Europe. Fourthly, I will analyse the interconnected memory debates surrounding the civil war and the civil rights movement in the USA since the 1990s, followed, finally, by a review of the memory cultures surrounding apartheid in post-apartheid South Africa. As we shall see, in all five debates controversies raged about the extent to which memory underpinned or undermined essentialist understandings of collective identity. I will examine to what extent histories of memory positioned themselves within those debates.

Ever since communism collapsed in East-Central and Eastern Europe in the late 1980s and early 1990s, the societies that during the Cold War lay behind the Iron Curtain have witnessed major controversies about the question of how communism should be remembered. The rise of strong nationalist memory cultures in many of the formerly communist nations often used the communist past as an effective 'other'. Communism, nationalists argued, was a foreign ideological force underpinned by the military power of the Soviet Union that had subjugated the nation to its rule. Only after the end of communism could those nations return to their (positive) national traditions and values. There are many examples of such post-communist nationalist memory discourses across East-Central and Eastern Europe. A prominent one is the so-called House of Terror in Budapest – a museum, established in 2002, in which historians of memory have contributed to a narrative that sees the Hungarian nation as the innocent victim of totalitarian foreign ideologies.[50] German fascism and Soviet communism are the perpetrators in a storyline in which the Hungarian nation appears solely as victim. The message to the visitors of the museum is clear: only a strong, proud and self-reliant Hungarian nation can in future defend itself against such dangers. The nation has to return to traditional national values and ideas in order to find the inner strength that will, in future, allow it to repel all of its enemies. Whilst there are historians working inside and outside the House of Terror who subscribe to this view, much memory history produced on post-communist Hungary and on post-communist East-Central and Eastern Europe more generally has attempted to counter these facile politically motivated attempts to functionalise memory in the service of Hungarian or other East European nationalisms.[51]

James Mark's *The Unfinished Revolution*, for example, looks at the after-life of communism in East-Central Europe after its official end around 1990. His analysis of the History Commission in Romania and the Institute of National Memory in Poland, as well as his interpretation of many of the museums, monuments and mass graves excavations, shows how political elites instrumentalised the memory of communism for their own, often nationalist, purposes.[52] As Attila Pók has pointed out in a review of memory histories of communism after 1989, many historians have warned of the ways in which an anti-communist memory discourse is combined with calls for a more nationalist political orientation. Anti-communism was, for post-communist regimes in Eastern Europe, the lowest common denominator on which to build, through memory, new identities.[53]

In other parts of the world, such as China, Vietnam, Laos and Cuba, communist governments are still in place that have abandoned central ideals of communism but still have to negotiate an often precarious and difficult memory politics vis-à-vis their communist pasts. Those regimes do not favour an anti-communist memorial landscape. Instead, they have found highly diverse strategies for how to incorporate the communist past into a post-communist present in which the Communist Party still clings to political power.[54]

In East-Central Europe, however, post-communist anti-communist nationalism was the driving force behind establishing, in 2008/9, 23 August as the day of remembrance of the crimes of communism within the EU. This date, 23 August, is the day in 1939 on which the Hitler–Stalin pact was signed that divided East-Central and Eastern Europe into zones of interest and influence between Soviet communism and German fascism. Whilst this day is commemorated in many East-Central and Eastern European states, it is hardly marked at all in Western Europe. By contrast, 27 January – the date on which the annihilation camp in Auschwitz was liberated by the advancing Red Army in 1945 and the day on which the EU officially remembers the holocaust – is of major importance to the memory debates in the EU's Western member states, reflecting the predominance of cosmopolitan memory there – as opposed to the antagonistic nationalist memory in East-Central and Eastern Europe. The core Western members of the EU have repeatedly insisted throughout the enlargement process to Eastern Europe that the new East-Central and Eastern European nation-states must adhere to this holocaust-focused cosmopolitan form of transnational memory, often to the chagrin of dominant memory cultures there. This heavy emphasis reflects attempts by the EU, which pre-date the collapse of communism, to build a European identity, among other things, on the transnational and cosmopolitan memory of the holocaust.[55] In Eastern Europe, however, such perspectives were criticised for highlighting too strongly the role of the Red Army as liberators. Many in Eastern Europe were also unhappy about commemorative practices that underlined the role of East European societies as collaborators of the Nazis in the holocaust, which, they felt, marginalised their prominent self-positioning as victims of Soviet communist oppression.

Historians of memory have played an influential role in countering this dominant victim-memory discourse in East-Central and Eastern Europe by contributing to an awareness that anti-Semitism was deeply ingrained in their nationalist cultures before the Second World War.

Only these long-term anti-Semitic traditions, they argued, would be capable of explaining why so many citizens in East-Central and Eastern European countries willingly and proactively participated in the National Socialist holocaust. Jan Gross' book on Jedwabne is a case in point.[56] Gross narrates in meticulous detail how home-grown Polish anti-Semitism felt justified during the German occupation of Poland to commit a murderous pogrom in the village of Jedwabne in July 1941, in which 1,600 Jews were slaughtered by their Polish neighbours. The outcry over Gross' book in Poland was enormous[57] and arguably contributed to a much greater self-reflexivity in Polish society about the consequences of Polish anti-Semitism. It questioned the essentialist victim-centred nationalism that has become a hallmark of right-wing political forces in post-communist Poland, including the current governing party, PiS, which has been at the forefront of the so-called Polish 'culture wars'. The government even attempted to introduce a law that would make it a punishable offence to claim that Poles had any share in National Socialist crimes during the Second World War, including the holocaust. This caused an international uproar, not just among historians, and ended in a tactical retreat by the PiS government.[58]

Nikolay Koposov's recent comprehensive analysis of memory laws in Western and Eastern Europe confirms the impression that the memory clocks tick differently in Western and Eastern Europe.[59] Both memory cultures, Koposov argued, focus on the Second World War and on victims, but, overall, the differences are more striking. In the West the memory of the holocaust as a universal symbol of evil dominates. It is combined with a national-heritage paradigm that allows Western memory discourses to combine a focus on the holocaust with the espousal of a positive patriotic national memory. Its humanistic sympathy with the victims of violence and its association of culture with humanity have led Western governments to champion memory laws in order to prevent holocaust denial or denial of genocides outside the cosmopolitan Western consensus about the memory of the first half of the twentieth century. However, Koposov also shows how such laws, transferred to the entirely different context of Eastern Europe and Russia, served to promote nationalism and right-wing populism. The prominent self-victimisation of societies in East-Central and Eastern Europe is protected by memory laws against a more critical examination of the extent to which nations and populations in Eastern Europe were also, in certain conditions and circumstances, perpetrators. Whereas anti-fascist and anti-racist traditions were vital motivating factors behind the adoption of memory laws in Western Europe, anti-totalitarianism was the most powerful motivation behind the adoption of memory laws in Eastern Europe. It is widely used there to promote a manipulative history politics that whitewashes traditional nationalist master narratives externalising guilt to non-national 'others'. Russian memory laws, for example, criminalise any criticism of Russia's policies and actions during the Second World War and legally protect the reputation of Stalinism. Whilst memory laws in the West were supposed to end memory debates regarded as being outside the pale of what should reasonably be discussed within an intersubjective agreement on cosmopolitan humanist values, memory laws in the East became the instrument with which governments declared their own (usually nationalist and right-wing) memory politics to be the only legitimate one. Koposov's meticulous analysis is a warning against the instrumentalisation of memory by governments for their own nationalist and right-wing purposes and therefore inherently also a warning against an essentialist identity politics.

The debates on communism and on anti-Semitism in East-Central and Eastern Europe are closely aligned, as Koposov has pointed out, with debates about the Second World War and its eventual outcome. Indeed, contrary to Tony Judt's prognosis that the Second World War would cease to be the anchor-point of European memory culture in the post-Cold War world,[60] there is no sign of it being replaced by anything else. In the 2016 British campaign to leave the EU, the so-called 'Brexiteers', i.e. those wishing to leave, heavily used imagery and vocabulary from the Second World War to persuade the British people that their future lay outside the EU. 'Brussels', as the capital of the EU, was routinely compared to National Socialist Berlin. Just as Great Britain had repelled the National Socialists and were ultimately victorious in the Second World War, they would now repel the similarly monstrous EU, behind which still lurked the German desire to achieve hegemony in Europe. Posters in front of houses proclaimed that 'our boys' who died in the Second World War did not die for the EU.[61] The memory of national unity in the Second World War was thus mobilised behind efforts to leave the EU and instead seek a nationalist future for the UK. Apart from the Second World War, the First World War, the legacies of the British empire, the Cold War and the long-standing ambiguities of the UK's relationship with the EU (summed up by the continental view of the UK as the 'awkward partner') since joining the community in 1973 all also played an important part in rooting the Brexit campaign in history.[62] Whilst much of this memory rhetoric is mobilised by right-wing politicians and journalists, some nationalist and Eurosceptic historians have joined their ranks. In fact, as Andrew Bonnell had already pointed out in 1999, Europhobia was an important part of what he called 'the new Tory historiography'.[63]

However, the majority of memory historians have been busy deconstructing the memory discourses of the right and pointing out that such memorialisations are yet another example of how the past is politically functionalised for a specific political project. Ben Wellings and Chris Gifford, for example, have argued convincingly that the Euroscepticism that lay behind Brexit was rooted in three very particular perceptions of the past: first, a specific view of the development of English parliamentary democracy; secondly, a specific view of empire; and thirdly, a specific view of the world wars of the twentieth century. Wellings and Gifford proceeded to analyse how memories of the past have shaped the memory discourses of the Brexiteers. By doing this they also pointed to the need to counter such memory discourses with others that would result in a more pro-European attitude among the British people.[64] As Wellings has also argued, much of English nationalism after 1945 was directed against European integration and in favour of keeping the UK's 'wider categories of belonging' to its former empire.[65] As long as British war memory celebrated the Second World War itself as 'Britain's finest hour', it had, unlike its continental neighbours, little reason to familiarise itself with a narrative that celebrated the EU for bringing peace to Europe, a narrative for which the EU won the Nobel Peace Prize in 2012.[66] Instead, in the UK it gave rise to a memory discourse that saw the country continuously fighting the battles of the Second World War all over again, only now not against a Nazi Germany but against an alleged German-dominated Europe. The high levels of Germanophobia in Britain after German reunification in 1990 were, as John Ramsden has pointed out, a marker of how ingrained this connection between the Second World War and anti-Germanism is in British memory discourses.[67]

Gurminder Bhambra has supported Wellings and Gifford's argument about the importance of empire for memory discourses surrounding Brexit. She has argued that forgetfulness about empire and the multiculturalism that empire brought to the UK is a major source of the deep hostility to migration, foreigners and ethnic minorities inside the UK. It was also a major motivating factor for people voting 'Leave'.[68] Empire, itself, as the distinguished historian of empire Linda Colley has pointed out, does not necessarily set the UK apart from other European nation-states, since the experience of empire is one that is common to many of them.[69] The way in which after-lives of empire have influenced memory politics in different parts of Europe has, however, not yet been sufficiently explored. Those who have begun asking questions about how the memory of empire is today influencing a very wide range of issues across many nation-states in the Western metropoles have rightly emphasised that the starting point has to be 'the domestic self-image of the nations that masked their insecurities behind a confident imperial swagger'.[70] By deconstructing those self-images, historians of memory have been making an important contribution to public memory debates right across former imperial powers. In the UK historians have pointed out that discourses on empire were revived at the same time as the Thatcher governments in the 1980s were pushing against the declinist narrative about British post-war development.[71] Whilst there were historians such as Niall Ferguson who acted as apologists of empire, there was no shortage of historians of the British empire who criticised his stance.[72]

If memory debates in Britain have raged around Brexit, with many historians of memory taking the role of encouraging greater self-reflexivity and questioning assumptions about an essentialised British identity, then the right-wing discourse on the Second World War predominantly reflects a white British experience of war. It excludes from memory the many black Britons and black members of Commonwealth countries fighting alongside Britain in the war.[73] It is a good example of how the issue of race is never far removed from the issue of national identity. A similar trend can be observed in the USA, where the involvement of black soldiers in the American army in both world wars increased calls on behalf of the black community to end discriminatory practices and battle racism at home. It was, however, only in the 1960s that the civil rights movement in the USA fully came into its own and was able to end the most blatant forms of racism and discrimination. However, this remains an ongoing struggle in American society, where there is considerable evidence that racism more generally and Ku Klux Klan activities in particular have in recent years been on the rise again. In this situation memory debates have come to the fore. Thus the recent debates surrounding the memorials to generals and politicians who fought for the slave-holding south in the American civil war, or the debates surrounding the significance of Martin Luther King Day, arguably America's most publicly celebrated national memorial day, have been exceptionally prominent.

Historians of memory such as Sarah E. Gardner show how those defending Confederate monuments in the south cannot hide behind claims that they wish simply to honour the dead, since such commemorative practices stand in a long tradition of celebrating a society built on racial oppression.[74] Confederate monuments were built and became popular alongside the establishment of the Jim Crow system in the southern states of the USA which denied African Americans equal rights in the American polity. The monuments celebrated the institution of slavery and underpinned the rule of white supremacists across the American south. A new wave of Confederate monuments was erected across the south at precisely the moment when the Jim Crow system came under attack. Thus the carvings of three of the most famous Confederate generals on Stone Mountain in Georgia were completed in 1963, the moment when the civil rights movement was at its heights. Larger than the carvings at Mount Rushmore, they sent out a clear message: retain white supremacy and defeat the civil rights movement.

Whilst historians of memory dealing with the American civil war have been in the forefront of those undermining the essentialist identities of white supremacists and their memory of that war, they have at the same time celebrated the memory of the civil rights movement in the USA. Thereby they contributed to making it the central anchor point of the fight for racial justice in the country today. As Renee Christine Romano and Leigh Raiford wrote in 2006: 'some of the most heated battles in the area of the black freedom struggle . . . revolve around *how* the civil rights movement should be remembered'.[75] Historians of memory have followed these memory battles which have seen the production of films and theatre plays, the creation of monuments, the staging of art exhibitions and a wide variety of community celebrations. Scholars have also contributed, alongside local activists, to recreating major movement events, such as the Freedom Rides of 1961 and the Selma to Montgomery march of 1965. They played an important role in the setting up of at least sixteen museums dedicated specifically to the memory of the civil rights movement. Their examination of the stories that various groups tell about the movement is an attempt to generate greater self-reflexivity about the movement and its role in American society. It is a classic case of how memory historians have been dealing with the past in order to problematise it and raise the issue of how memories of that past have influenced the decisions people make in the present as well as their imaginings of the future. Romano and Raiford, for example, have identified a 'civil rights movement consensus memory' and their volume charts 'how this memory is challenged or perpetuated, and by whom'.[76] In this way, they have contributed to an ongoing debate about how to give meaning to a movement that continues to be extremely relevant for identity debates in the USA.

If the issue of race remains central to memory debates in the USA, this is also true for memory debates in South Africa. Here the Truth and Reconcilation Committee (TRC) that was set up after the end of the apartheid regime has often been portrayed as an exemplary case of cosmopolitan memory culture working towards the reconciliation of two formerly hostile groups.[77] The TRC, itself following the example of Chile and its reconciliation commission of 1990/1 which produced an extensive report into human rights abuses under the dictatorship of the Chilean generals, has been widely seen as a model for other reconciliation processes around the world. However, how successful has this model cosmopolitan approach to memory been in actually achieving reconciliation? The whites of South Africa continue to vote with their feet, leaving the country in great numbers. Those who remain barricade themselves in gated communities in the richer suburb of the South African cities, which remain over-proportionately white, whilst in the countryside the remaining white farmers are armed to the hilt and busy announcing on billboards that every trespasser will be shot on sight. Black radicals in the ruling ANC are in the meantime advocating an inverse anti-white racism, not least to paper over their own failure to combat rampant corruption and to achieve more racial equality for the millions of black South Africans still living below the poverty line – without access to education and without the means to escape the dreadful shantytowns that still mar the geographies of all South African cities. Histories on the memory and commemoration of apartheid in South Africa have contributed to exploring the diverse ways in which memory has been used in order to achieve recognition for the victims of apartheid. At the same time those debates have played their part in post-apartheid South Africa's attempts to build its future on a multi-racial vision that is all the more resilient because it remembers its racist past. Many excellent books have been written on the impact of memory and storytelling on post-apartheid South Africa.[78] Annie Coombes' *History after Apartheid*, for example, analysed how the construction of new public histories in museums and around memorial sites in South Africa in the 1990s has contributed to changing ideas about community and nation in a deliberate attempt to transform a history of violent social conflict into a future-oriented nation-building process.[79] Her case studies involved an examination of apartheid monuments and their fate in post-apartheid South Africa, an analysis of post-apartheid museums such as the District 6 Museum in Cape Town and an in-depth look at memorial sites such as Robben Island. She also paid a lot of attention to contemporary fine art in South Africa. All of this she combined into a book that encouraged self-reflexivity about a process which has attempted to commemorate and give space, especially to the victims of apartheid, whilst at the same time moving forward to the creation of a new South Africa. The complex memory culture of post-apartheid South Africa, the topic of her book, thus also warned her readers against replacing the essentialist white supremacist identity of white South Africans under apartheid with any form of essentialised post-apartheid identities.

My five all-too-brief examples of global memory debates have underlined how historians of memory have been overwhelmingly engaged in deconstructing nationalist and racist memory cultures. They have contributed to transnational cosmopolitan forms of memory in countries such as Hungary, Poland, Britain, the USA and South Africa. Yet it is noticeable that in many places across the world their historical memory discourses have not been very successful in winning the memory battles against contemporary nationalist and racist memory discourses. The latter have been influential in helping get Donald Trump elected to the White House. They have helped Boris Johnson to become British Prime Minister as the foremost activist on behalf of Brexit. They have provided arguments for all those right-wing nationalist, anti-European political parties and movements, which, from the Rassemblement National in France to the Alternative für Deutschland (AfD) in Germany, are threatening the politics of European integration and democratic government in parts of Western Europe. They have also had an important mobilising function for right-wing authoritarian governments in Poland and Hungary seeking to silence a democratic opposition. And they have been instrumental in attempts to recast the memory landscape and politics of India under its Prime Minister Narendra Modi. Over the past decade all of these movements have been in the ascendant.

Indeed, they have prompted prominent erstwhile champions of transnational cosmopolitan memory such as Aleida Assmann to ask self-critically whether they have sidelined and marginalised national memory too early. In response to right-wing vernacular nationalism, Assman pleaded that the left had to rediscover national memory. The left, according to her, has to work towards developing a concept of national memory that is in line with the values of liberal democracy, humanitarianism and a positive recognition of the other.[80] I am not convinced that a return to national memory is necessarily the right answer to the rise of right-wing nationalisms. For a start, I am not persuaded that national memory was ever completely sidelined, as important memory debates over the past forty years have still been fought most ferociously at the national level, even in Germany. Furthermore, I would emphasise the need to enhance and further transnational forms of memory as a counterpoint to the nationalist narrowing of memory lenses. Hence I would like, in the last section of this chapter, to ask whether alternative memory regimes to the cosmopolitan ones, which do not return to the nation but remain transnational, would be more successful in challenging the nationalist and racist memory discourses currently popular? For the past five years, the concept of 'agonistic memory' has been discussed as a possible means of developing more effective memory discourses with the power to engage with and defeat these nationalist and racist discourses with which right-wing populist governments operate. Is 'agonistic memory' a means to further self-reflexivity and undermine essentialised identities to an even greater and more effective extent than we have seen with 'cosmopolitan memory'?

Collective Memory, Experience and Emplotment: Agonistic Perspectives on the Past

Anna Cento Bull and Hans Lauge Hansen argued in a much-cited article that appeared in 2016 that it was time to move from a cosmopolitan memory frame to an agonistic one.[81] This claim then informed a considerable amount of research on 'agonistic memory' and underpinned a three-year Horizon 2020 programme entitled 'Unsettling Remembering and Social Cohesion in Contemporary Europe' (UNREST). Between 2016 and 2019, this programme explored European memory cultures of war.[82] When it comes to the memory of war in Europe, it concluded that cosmopolitan forms of memory dominate in museums and official memory discourses, whilst antagonistic, mainly nationalist, forms of memory are still to be found, especially in East-Central and Eastern Europe and in the UK. In fact, it found that those antagonistic discourses are also on the rise in Western Europe. Hence the project recommended an agonistic approach to memory and attempted to put such an approach into practice through staging of a theatre play and curating an exhibition on war.[83]

In a nutshell, agonism, unlike the nationalist and the cosmopolitan modes of remembrance, does not divide memory according to normative categories into 'good' and 'bad'. Instead, it seeks to put radical historist perspectives in place that seek to understand, not only victims, but also perpetrators and bystanders in an attempt to reconstruct the memory of all groups in society. Antagonistic memory, by contrast, identifies wholeheartedly with a positively framed national/ideological 'us' that is contrasted with a negative 'them'. It essentialises identities in order to identify more strongly with them. Cosmopolitan memory also constructs a positive 'us' but that 'us' is identified with the values of human rights and liberal democratic rights. This is contrasted with a negative 'them' in the form of totalitarianisms which suppress both human rights and liberal democracy and are responsible for acts of mass violence. This approach is again in danger of essentialising a positive 'us' in the form of liberal democracy and human rights and a negative 'them'. An agonistic memory mode, in contrast, avoids any essentialisation of identities and instead promotes greater self-reflexivity about how certain groups ended up doing what they did. It therefore ultimately aims at understanding historical actors and emphasises that memory discourses need to reflect this understanding of different groups in society. Such understanding can then become the basis for normative political choices based not on essentialisms but on mutual recognition that these choices are constructions resting on interests, experiences and emotions. The mutual recognition of the 'other' as a political adversary rather than an enemy to be destroyed is a key precondition for agonistic memory politics.

Whereas both antagonistic and cosmopolitan modes of remembering result in a binary narrrativisation that distinguishes villains (anti-nationalist forces and totalitarian ideologies respectively) from heroes (pro-nationalist forces, liberal democrats and champions of human rights respectively), cosmopolitan memory is also characterised by a strong focus on the victims. Remembering victims of totalitarianisms is the key means employed to safeguard the values of liberal democracy and human rights. By contrast, agonistic memory is characterised by a more radical multi-perspectivity of memories of perpetrators, victims and bystanders. Antagonistic modes of remembering are unreflexive and monologic, oriented purely towards the 'we' group that remembers its heroes and the good national 'us' in contrast to the bad 'them'. Cosmopolitan memory, by contrast, is more self-reflexive and allows for dialogue, yet it still strives for ultimate closure, i.e. the dialogue aims at producing a consensus which concludes the dialogue. Once they have reached closure such memory cultures become hegemonic and repressive in that they do not allow any deviation from the consensual agreement about the frame of the respective memory culture. Agonistic memory, by contrast, is open-endedly dialogic in a Bakthinian sense of a polyphony of voices constantly in discussion with each other.[84] Here there is no end to self-reflexivity. Instead, self-reflexivity leads to a constant undermining of fixed meanings in memory and to a narrative openness vis-à-vis the construction and reconstruction of identities.

All three modes of memory have an important affective side that mobilises emotions in those individuals doing the remembering. Antagonistic memory frames rely on the passion of belonging to a pre-defined essentialised 'us', typically one's own nation, against an equally defined essentialised 'them', typically 'enemy' nations. Thus, for example, Italian visitors to a First World War museum in Kobarid, Slovenia, felt the emotional need to identify strongly with the Italian soldiers in that war, thereby displaying strong antagonistic memory frames.[85] Cosmopolitan memory frames, by contrast, seek to produce compassion for the victims in order to mobilise emotions in favour of the desired commitment to human rights and liberal democracy. The Oskar Schindler factory in Krakow, for example, hosts an exhibition on the city's history under German occupation during the Second World War that engenders strong feelings of identification with the Polish victims of German aggression, thereby fostering a mix of cosmopolitan and antagonistic memory frames.[86] Agonistic memory frames, in opposition to both antagonistic and cosmopolitan frames, seek to produce passions for greater social justice and global solidarity, hope for social change and commitment to defending democratic structures in politics and society. However, these passions, as Mihaela Mihai has argued, are tamed by understanding and contextualisation, and therefore 'permeable by judgement'.[87] Agonistic approaches are not averse to working with emotions felt for victims, but they would temper this with a critical historical understanding of the underlying causes and recognise that these can lead to forms of othering that produce in turn both perpetratorship and victimhood. Passions such as animosity and hatred need to be historically understood and not just morally condemned. Understanding the perpetrators does not mean empathising with them. Instead, it leads to forms of understanding that might contribute to underpinning humanistic visions of solidarity, since compassion with victims is morally easier than attempts to understand perpetrators. Agonistic interventions would aim to complicate emotional messages of memories and allow for moral ambiguities that make use of emotions as a cognitive resource. Rather than resting on a binary construction where emotions are divided into 'good' and 'bad', agonistic memory frames work with more complex and less morally charged understandings of emotions. In a historical museum setting, for example, the visitors' emotional engagement has been widely seen as key to engaging them and making them understand the properly contextualised history that is on display.[88] Artwork has often been used sucessfully in museums to achieve exactly this emotional engagement. As Cristian Cercel has argued, the artwork at the Bundeswehr Military Museum in Dresden is used very effectively to produce agonistic interventions in the museum.[89] In the case of 'hot memories', i.e. those memories still highly contested in their meanings, an affective element is often encountered, as studies on the exhumation of bodies of people killed in wars and civil wars clearly demonstrate. Whether and how they work in the direction of fostering antagonistic, cosmopolitan or agonistic memory frames very much depends on the specific local context.[90]

Most historians of memory today adhere to cosmopolitan frames of memory. Among the minority championing agonistic modes of remembering are also those who, like me, have been seeking to build bridges to the advocates of cosmopolitan memory. It seems to me that the cosmopolitan commitment to dialogue, multi-perspectivity and reconciliation, in conjunction with the championing of the values of liberal democracy and human rights, are important universal benchmarks for a history of memory that should not be given up lightly. At the same time, its one-sided victim-centredness and its desire to arrive at a closure of debate prevent historians of memory from a more radical historisation of the past and block any recognition that debates about the past can never arrive at a conclusion after which all debate stops. Historians adopting agonistic approaches to memory insist on the perpetual political conflict underlying memory debates. Their work, as engaged historians,[91] contributes to a politics that is passionate about transnational and intranational solidarity and aims to counter the memory politics of a nationalist right that relies on a revival of antagonistic memory politics. Whereas cosmopolitan perspectives on memory discourses are self-reflexive in the sense that they are dialogic and they accept controversy, their self-reflexivity ends once they have arrived at an intersubjective truth. From the moment agreement has been reached it gains an absolute, universal and often essentialised value. Thus, for example, the commitment to human rights becomes a normative value not to be discussed any further, even if it serves inhumane and imperialist ends. In contrast, historians committed to agonistic perspectives on memory are perpetually self-reflexive and committed to never-ending controversiality, as they see the political need to struggle for political values, including those of human rights. In their view there can be no intersubjective truth. It is replaced by the need constantly to fight for political norms and values. This means engaging political adversaries rather than excluding them from debate.

Conclusion

The history of memory and memory studies more generally continues to be one of the most booming fields of study in the humanities. As Patrick Hutton, as early as 2000, perceptively wrote: ‘memory today is our inspiration, and in the future, I think, history as an art of memory will be remembered as the historiographical signature of our times’.[92] As we have seen in this chapter, historians of memory have often engaged in projects that investigate the role of key concepts in memorial landscapes such as nation, class and race. They have thus been involved in a constructive dialogue with another new sub-field of historical writing that is deeply related to the cultural turn in historical writing in the 1980s and that we shall examine next: the history of concepts.

Further Reading

Aleida Assman, *Cultural Memory and Western Civilisation: Functions, Media, Archives*, Cambridge: Cambridge University Press, 2011.

Jan Assmann, *Cultural Memory and Early Civilisation: Writing: Remembrance and Political Imagination*, Cambridge: Cambridge University Press, 2011.

Stefan Berger and Bill Niven (eds.), *Writing the History of Memory*, London: Bloomsbury, 2014.

Stefan Berger and Jeffrey Olick (eds.), *A Cultural History of Memory*, 6 vols., London: Bloomsbury, 2020.

Stefan Berger and Wulf Kansteiner (eds.), *Agonistic Memory and the Legacy of 20th Century Wars in Europe*, Basingstoke: Palgrave Macmillan, 2022.

Siobhan Kattagoo (ed.), *The Ashgate Companion to Memory Studies*, Farnham: Ashgate, 2015.

Nikolay Koposov, Memory Laws, Memory Wars: the Politics of the Past in Europe and Russia, Cambridge: Cambridge University Press, 2018.

Jeffrey K. Olick, *The Sins of the Fathers: Germany, Memory, Method*, Chicago: University of Chicago Press, 2017.

Michael Rothberg, *Multidirectional Memory: Remembering the Holocaust in the Age of Decolonisation*, Stanford: Stanford University Press, 2009.

8 *The History of Concepts*

Introduction

The rise of the history of concepts to a flourishing field of inquiry, practised almost everywhere on the globe,[1] is a sign that many historians now use concepts, ideas and language far more self-reflexively than ever before. After all, one cannot study how concepts have shaped specific discourses and practices without being aware of the way in which they often have been constructed with an eye to bolstering collective identities. Conceptual history is frequently portrayed as growing out of the history of ideas and seen as being closely related to intellectual history and to the history of political thought, as well as to the history of discourses and a history of semantics more generally. For that reason I will start this chapter with a brief look back at the history of ideas, out of which all of these different sub-fields of historical writing emerged. Subsequently I will focus on, first, the origins of the history of concepts in the work of Reinhart Koselleck and, secondly, the historians associated with the 'Cambridge school', in particular Quentin Skinner and J. G. A. Pocock, who have been pursuing a related, albeit different project. Although both approaches share similar premises, they remained separate, and attempts to bring them closer together have by and large failed.[2] Skinner explicitly rejected Koselleck's approach; Pocock was not really familiar with Koselleck's work, despite his claim to be interested in him; and Koselleck remained intellectually aloof of his Anglophone colleagues and their writings.[3] Nevertheless, building on all three, many historians have contributed in different ways to an understanding of texts as literary and linguistic constructions rooted in a particular time and place. The rest of this chapter will discuss a variety of examples of how this history of concepts has, over recent years, provided a more self-reflexive attitude among many historians towards the relationship between historical writing and collective identity formation.

The History of Ideas: Its Origins and Trajectories

The history of ideas has often been the history of philosophical and political thought, in particular the thought of canonical thinkers. The influential American historian Arthur Lovejoy published *The Great Chain of Being* in 1936. In this book he introduced the concept of 'unit ideas', i.e. universal and timeless ideas that operated in changing historical constellations at different times and places.[4] Lovejoy, who, in 1940, also founded the *Journal of the History of Ideas*, was mainly interested in 'great thinkers' and canonical 'styles of thinking'. E. H. Carr unwittingly underlined how powerful this history of ideas approach was in historiography. In his seminal book, first published in 1961, on *What Is History?* he meant to shift the profession to adopt social history as new paradigm (see Chapter 3 above). Yet what in this book drove the historical process were not social structures but great thinkers, including Descartes, Rousseau, Hegel, Marx and Freud. Through the power of their thought, Carr argued, they had moved humankind into modernity.[5] Nevertheless, from the 1970s onwards this distinguished tradition of writing the history of ideas was heavily criticised from a number of different directions. There were those, foremost among them Annales historians and their international followers as well as historical anthropologists (see Chapter 7), who berated this approach for being interested only in the canon of classical thinkers. Instead, the critics argued, historians needed to turn their attention to the mentalities of ordinary people and to the everyday. A major critique also came from Michel Foucault, discussed in Chapter 1, who ridiculed the idea that there was something like a free exchange of ideas between autonomous individuals endowed with reason. Instead, he asked what power relationships were visible in the exchange of ideas: who was allowed to speak about what and in which way? What rules governed 'reasonable' assumptions about what was normal and what was deviant? He called on historians to look for the often hidden rules that governed discourses.

The critique of traditional ways of writing the history of ideas resulted in a fundamental rethinking of this sub-field in historical writing. One of the foremost contemporary intellectual historians, Donald Kelley, argued as early as 1990 that it had become impossible to discuss the history of ideas as if historians occupied a 'spiritual forum in which ideas are endlessly debated'.[6] Individual authors, he argued, were not sovereign intellects seeking for knowledge and truth regardless of their societal and cultural circumstances. Out of crisis came renewal. Different approaches tried to put the old history of ideas on to new foundations. Intellectual history, the history of political thought and a variety of other approaches all sought to develop historical semantics that would avoid the pitfalls of the older history of ideas.[7] Subsequently I will examine two such approaches that have had enormous international repercussions. First, I will deal with the history of concepts associated, above all, with the work of Reinhart Koselleck. Secondly, I will discuss the so-called Cambridge school of intellectual history, a group of historians initially based at the University of Cambridge, of whom Quentin Skinner and J. G. A. Pocock are the most important representatives.

Reinhart Koselleck as the Founding Figure of Conceptual History Approaches

In the English-speaking world Koselleck is best known for his theoretical articles translated and collected in two volumes. They had a remarkable success in terms of their wider reception by the historiographical community, making him arguably into the best-known German historian today.[8] His intense reflection, ongoing over several decades, on the importance of concepts for an understanding of history was grounded in his co-editorship, with Otto Brunner and Werner Conze, of the multi-volume *Historical Basic Concepts*.[9] For Koselleck a 'basic concept' was one capable of condensing linguistically complex layers of meanings, experiences and contexts into one word. These concepts represented a discursive formation that could be modified over time and that shaped the political, social, economic and cultural world just as this world had shaped the concepts. One of Koselleck's central findings was that, in the second half of the eighteenth century, concepts had become more future-oriented. They justified conceptions of a particular future, often with reference to specific pasts. Koselleck coined the term 'saddle period' (*Sattelzeit*) to refer to the century roughly between 1750 and 1850 when, according to him, the modern conceptual universe, as we know it, came into being. The present time from the second half of the eighteenth century onwards was constructed as a future-oriented modernity (*Neuzeit*, in German). 'Spaces of experience' (*Erfahrungsräume*) opened up 'horizons of expectation'

(*Erwartungshorizonte*). 'Entimed concepts' and, consequently, 'movement concepts' came to the fore. History became a linear process of time, moving into the future and expressed by a processual language, reflected in terms such as democratisation or nationalisation.[10] More recently, Christian Geulen has suggested that we might want to consider a second 'saddle period' lasting from the late nineteenth century to the 1970s, which was characterised by scientisation, popularisation, spatialisation and volatilisation. According to him, a proper understanding of the twentieth century would require an awareness of this second 'saddle period'.[11]

Apart from the time conceptions of concepts becoming linear and progressive, concepts also became more democratic between 1750 and 1850. No longer used only by a social and intellectual elite, they were now available to an ever-larger number of people coming from different social classes. This democratisation of concepts was directly linked to another new feature of concepts after 1750 – their ideologisation. By this Koselleck meant that concepts now became tools with which groups and movements in society pushed through their interests. This development was related to the politicisation of concepts. Increasingly, groups and movements employed them as slogans in political struggles.[12] Concepts were thus strongly related to questions of power and social conflict.

If history was moving, in a linear way, in one direction, then the many histories were reduced to one, and the future became 'plannable'. In other words, on the basis of a true understanding of the one historical process it should be possible to plan the future. This was the hope of Karl Marx whose writings were based on the belief in a historical process evolving over time and ending up of necessity in the communist society of the future. Koselleck's work can be read as revealing, through an analysis of multi-directional and multi-layered concepts, the ideological nature of this belief and thereby restoring plurality to the past and emphasising the openness of future horizons. As the past could be moulded differently, so, too, the present, at any given moment in time, held at the ready several futures. Which of these futures was realised depended on the power of its conceptual underpinnings as well as on the social, political, economic and cultural contexts of the historical moment in time. From this perspective, one of Koselleck's pupils, Lucian Hölscher, has developed his idea of writing 'histories of the future' (*historische Zukunftsforschung*, in German). It aims at reconstructing what eventually did not happen but what was thinkable and sayable in the past. Such histories of the future allow the contemporary observer to relativise the linearity of the past and realise its contingencies: in other words, the openness of the past and the present at any given moment in time.[13]

Koselleck's and subsequently Hölscher's critique of modernity was thus one which aimed, above all, at the restoration of a certain contingency of the historical process that, in their view, was not reducible to a single linear process.[14] If Koselleck insisted on the plurality of possible pasts and futures, he also retained his distance from the relativism with which he identified the ideas of Hayden White. Against relativism he formulated his famous dictum of the 'veto rights of the sources'. What he meant by this was that the available historical sources, whilst limiting what was sayable about the past, did not tell us what we should say about the past. Thereby he emphasised the role of the historian as constructor and interpreter of that past – something that, in fact, brought him closer to White than he might have wanted. Subsequently not only Koselleck, but many other conceptual historians have been strongly influenced by narrativism, poststructuralism and constructionism, i.e. the body of theories discussed in Chapter 1 of this volume.[15]

Another of Koselleck's ideas that has become influential in conceptual history and has contributed in diverse ways to the de-essentialising of our understandings of the past is the notion of 'temporal layers' (*Zeitschichten*). Every concept, Kosellek argued, contained many such layers from diverse times, and it was the task of conceptual historians to peel back those layers in order to understand how different temporalities had influenced concepts over time. Any understanding of the past, he argued, would have to take into account that this past resembled a quarry from which particular futures had been constructed. Only a rigid and full historisation of the 'basic concepts' that had shaped these discursive formations would allow a true understanding of the past.[16] Andreas Huyssen, noting his indebtedness to Koselleck, has developed this line of thought further. He argued that layers of time form variants of a palimpsestic memory. Older time layers are still present in the contemporary, whilst others have sunk into oblivion, but can still be revealed by peeling back younger layers of time.[17]

The Cambridge School and Conceptual History

The Cambridge school is an umbrella term with which to refer to a group of historians who all taught at the University of Cambridge and were concerned with the history of political ideas from the early modern era. Its two most famous representatives are Quentin Skinner and J. G. A. Pocock, but John Dunn, Raymond Geuss, Peter Laslett, David Runciman and James Tully are also often subsumed under the Cambridge school. Peter Laslett, in particular, produced, as early as 1960, a highly influential interpretation of John Locke's *Two Treatises of Government*, in which he argued that Locke's writings could only be understood properly by radically historising them. Laslett questioned the standard interpretation of Locke's work as justification of the English revolution of 1688 by showing that the text had been produced ten years before that revolution – at the height of Charles II's absolutist regime.[18] Laslett and others in the group argued that the political ideas of the early modern era should not be interpreted in the light of later developments but had to be understood in their own social, cultural and political contexts. Later on, Skinner did for Thomas Hobbes what Laslett had done for Locke. Situating Hobbes in the context of wider debates on rhetoric in Renaissance England, Skinner showed how Hobbes' *Leviathan* could not be understood without taking note of its important context.[19] He argued that there was no 'perennialism' in the history of ideas, i.e. there were no ideas that were essentially the same and had been discussed by philosophers since the dawn of time. Instead, he pleaded for a radical historisation of the history of ideas that would put texts into the context of other texts written at the time. This would mean moving away from regarding the history of ideas as a progression of iconical texts standing on their own and outside time.[20]

Skinner insisted, incidentally very much like Koselleck, that 'speech acts' were vital for an understanding of how discourse worked in any given era.[21] Hence, texts could not be analysed on their own terms, but only against the background of their discursive and social contexts. His interest in the rhetorical structures of language was shaped to no small extent by his reception of the history of concepts.[22] His examinations of the performativity, intentionality and purpose of speech acts have pointed to the importance of specific norms and discourses that underlay conceptual beliefs at any given time. Concepts were, according to Skinner, vital for participants in debates, as they allowed them to position themselves. Rhetorical means and speech acts were vital for accounting for conceptual change. Having studied in particular the concepts 'state' and 'liberty', Skinner traced conceptual changes through rhetorical devices in particular writers such as Hobbes (referred to above), and emphasised the contingency of conceptual changes in history.[23] His interest in excavating the production of meaning in texts is strongly related to investigating the history of concepts, although it is hardly the same. Skinner's work has persistently challenged the belief in the universalism and timelessness of ideas, in their status as perennial truth and expressions of unchanging forms of morality. In this sense, he has, like conceptual historians, but with different methodological emphasis, contributed to questioning and undermining attempts to construct fixed collective identities in and through history.[24]

In his two-volume work *The Foundations of Modern Political Thought*, published in 1978, Skinner sought to put these ideas into practice by tracing changing habits of political thought. He took into consideration an enormous amount of writing from legal texts and histories to philosophies and religious tracts. Liberty, republicanism, constitutionalism, religious freedom, resistance to absolutism, theories of revolution, sovereignty, natural and divine law – all figure prominently in 1,300 pages that span the medieval and early modern period, something which in itself was highly unusual in a day and age that tended to separate the medieval world from that of the Renaissance and the early modern. Skinner's radical historisation of the emergence of the idea of the *Homo politicus* in the historical period he investigated unearthed the foundations of what would become the discipline of the history of political thought. Skinner laid bare in these volumes a kind of prehistory of the political thought of Locke and Hobbes, who are not themselves part of the analysis of these books but can only be understood against the background of developments in earlier centuries.[25] So influential was Skinner's book in the history of political thought that thirty years after its first appearance a volume was published that aimed to rethink the history of political thought starting from Skinner's seminal work.[26]

Very much like Skinner, Pocock also insisted that authors had to be understood within the wider social structures within which they wrote. Their scripts could only be constituted within the conceptual worlds that were available to them at their time. Hence his prime interest was in conceptual and linguistic structures and not in the intentions of specific authors.[27] Influenced by structuralist linguistics, especially the ideas of Ferdinand de Saussure (see Chapter 1), he set out to examine political languages and their development over longer periods. In his book *The Machiavellian Moment*, for example, he traced the language of republicanism from its rediscovery in Renaissance Florence down to seventeenth-century English republicanism and further to the founding fathers of the United States in the eighteenth century.[28] Unlike Skinner, he did not ultimately believe in the possibility of recapturing authors' intentions by studying their speech acts in relation to other speech acts as performative argumentative interventions. Much more influenced by his teacher Herbert Butterfield's radical rejection of the linear progressive view of history entailed in the Whig approach to British history, Pocock was sceptical of any attempt to fix meaning and arrange it in a linear progression of time.[29] His scepticism about authorial intentions also derived from his insistence that texts bore multiple meanings and could not be read only in one particular way. In his *Barbarism and Religion*, which amounts virtually to an intellectual history of the eighteenth century, he put different conceptualisations of 'the Enlightenment' into conversation with each other. He conclusion was that it was only possible to speak of 'the Englightenments' in the plural, as the traditions were too diverse to be put under one singular, unified concept. At the centre of his investigations stood Edward Gibbon, whose work reflected many of those traditions and hence, like a burning glass, provided access to them.[30] Pocock and Skinner are often put together under the rubric 'contextualism', since both insist on the ultimate importance of contexts for understanding, although never fixing, the meaning of texts.[31] Historians may attempt to reconstruct the landscape in which particular ideas were generated through language, but they still have to insist on the ultimate historicity and alterity of these ideas and landscapes.

Although the Cambridge school's enterprise was quite distinct from that of the history of concepts, both shared an interest in radical historisation, in language and in putting texts, ideas and concepts into their contexts, as well as relating texts to actions. With regard to the latter, they very much followed R. G. Collingwood's argument that the history of thought should be studied in close conjunction with the history of actions. According to Collingwood, if this were done, all history could be understood as the history of thought.[32] Wary of universalisms and truth claims, Skinner and Pocock shared a desire to make readers of history realise the plurality of possible meanings encoded in texts. Both inspired a range of authors who wrote the history of concepts and ideas in order to problematise the essentialising claims historians had made in relation to collective identities. Many of them were also strongly influenced by the body of theories discussed in Chapter 1.

Conceptual Histories and Their Impact on Deconstructing Collective Identities

Following the pathbreaking work of Koselleck, Skinner and Pocock, Margrit Pernau and Imke Rajamani have pointed out that much more attention needs to be paid to the way concepts have been capable (or not, as the case may be) of mobilising passions through the argumentative and aesthetic force that they developed.[33] Furthermore, a closer look at the narrative structuring of concepts is also necessary in order to evaluate how they have acted and performed over time and how they impacted, not just on texts, but on a whole variety of material objects, including iconic buildings, artwork, photography and film, as well as on political symbols, and non-literal and non-oral forms of language. As a result, the history of concepts, over recent years, has started to build bridges to visual history and the new material culture history (see Chapters 9 and 10). Visualisations of the nation in the form of national figures such as Britannia, Germania or Marianne, or in the form of animals representing nations, such as the American eagle or the British lion, for example, lend themselves to being combined with a conceptual analysis of those iconic symbols of nationhood.[34] (See Figure 8.1.) Similarly, aspects of the materiality of thought production, e.g. the history of the book, have received a huge amount of attention. Robert Darnton, for example, has written about how books largely unknown to us today, and certainly not part of the canon of 'great thinkers', became best-sellers in pre-revolutionary France because of the way in which the book industry functioned.[35] Mary Elizabeth Berry, to give another example, traced the impact of the material side of information making, i.e. the production of books, maps and taxation surveys, back to constructions of nation in early modern Japan.[36] Conceptual analysis of reading practices and examinations of practices employed in producing particular styles of books have to be seen as powerful attempts to historise the material side of ideas. In an intriguing book, Anthony Grafton, for example, has written the history of the footnote, showing how, in the practice of footnoting, a particular

Figure 8.1 The American eagle and the British lion in a poster advertising Britain's Day and showing Uncle Sam and Britannia arm in arm, 7 December 1918. © Galerie Bildwelt, Hulton Archive/Getty Images.R

scientific style became established and came to underpin a specific understanding of scientific inquiry.[37]

Whilst the history of concepts has, over recent years, been building bridges to visual and material culture history, it has also become a more international affair. Koselleck and Skinner were very largely operating within national containers. The *Geschichtliche Grundbegriffe* were about Germany and Skinner's explorations were all about England. When it comes to concepts, national languages and nation-states are, of course, far from irrelevant, but conceptual historians have started to look at transfers and translations precisely in order to destabilise the alleged naturalness of national containers. Historians such as Pim den Boer have started to question the strength of the national in forging key concepts and instead pointed to the importance of transnational contacts in the making of key concepts.[38] Connotations to other cultures were almost always inherent in those concepts. Jörn Leonhard's study of the concept of liberalism has shown how many transnational links have significantly shaped the idea of liberalism over many centuries.[39] The same can be said of Annabel Patterson's work on early modern liberalism, which explored how liberal traditions were conveyed from Britain to the American colonies. Influenced strongly by poststructuralist ideas discussed in Chapter 1, she detailed how liberalism arose in direct response to a set of perceived injustices relating to questions of equality. Hers is also a politically committed history in the sense of Hayden White's 'practical past' (see Chapter 1), for she leaves no doubt that its aim is to strengthen a liberal agenda in the contemporary world.[40] Postcolonial perspectives on liberalism have, on the other hand, investigated the ways in which theorists of liberalism have conceptualised liberalism so as to include ideas about civilisations, ethnicities, and races that excluded non-white, non-Western peoples from the liberal agenda.[41] This did not, however, prevent Indian intellectuals from adopting various Western theories of liberalism and adapting them to the political conditions of the subcontinent. They produced what Christopher Bayly has termed a 'liberalism of fear' and a strong communitarian orientation of Indian liberalism, seeking to salvage badly divided communities through the ideals of a reconceptualised liberalism.[42] Liberalism remained very differently inflected in India. The liberalism espoused by the political elites was subject to various challenges from plebeian liberalisms that critiqued the capitalist social order in India.[43] Rethinking the concept of liberalism from the margins of the British empire has made it possible to resituate debates around liberalism in the global West.[44] Overall, the transnational and comparative turn in conceptual history has contributed to de-essentialising collective identities and raising greater self-awareness about the transnational construction, through concepts, of such collective identities.[45]

Looking at larger geopolitical regions that have been constructed in the past, such as the Balkans and Scandinavia, conceptual historians have analysed how those terms came into being, and how their usage changed over time. They have also paid attention to the many contestations surrounding the conceptualisations of such macro-regions, thus de-naturalising the use of such spatial entities and the collective identities often associated with them. With regards to the Balkans, Maria Todorova has demonstrated how this concept involved strong temporal frames which sought to define the region in terms of 'backwardness', 'stagnation' and 'delay', thereby contrasting it with other concepts such as 'the West', which were associated with 'progress' and 'development'.[46] Enlightenment thinkers had mapped the world according to their concepts of 'civilisation', and in this mapping, the Balkans and Eastern Europe did not score highly on the scoreboard of civilisation.[47] Both spatial and temporal concepts were necessary to define the space called 'the Balkans'. It was related to a whole host of other concepts, such as 'pan-Slavism', various national concepts of nations that were part of the Balkans, micro-spatial concepts, associated with cities and smaller regions within these nations, as well as imperial concepts incorporating the Balkans, especially those related to the Ottoman and Habsburg empires. Furthermore, many non-spatial concepts such as class, ethnicity, gender and religion interacted with spatial ones in often highly complex and multi-directional ways. Regions such as the Balkans thus require us to reflect on multiple boundaries and time regimes, all of which operate simultaneously. This awareness prompts the historian to think about how concepts constructed both space and time and associated regional identities.

National conceptual worlds have constructed transnational regions in different ways. Romanians, for their part, preferred the concept 'South-Eastern Europe' to 'the Balkans', whilst Croats and Slovenes used the concept 'the Balkans' as a form of negative othering. All of these conceptual battles were directly related to political struggles and conflicts over collective identities.[48] Often the question of political hegemony over transnational regions played an important role in this. Diverse thinkers on the Balkans formulated special roles and missions for specific nations in the Balkans.[49] Defining a region such as the Balkans internally invariably went hand in hand with defining it externally against its manifold 'others', and this led to a variety of overlapping concepts such as 'the Balkans', 'East-Central Europe', 'the Mediterranean' or 'South-Eastern Europe'. Studying the interrelationship of these conceptualisations and their relationship to physical, geographical space, to questions of mentality and cultures through to questions of power and politics, goes a long way towards historising collective identity formation in South-Eastern Europe, and illustrates how politically contested and conflictual such identity constructions have always been. Transnational regional concepts are thus always 'essentially contested concepts' and relational to a set of other regional concepts. Their meanings cannot be fixed.[50]

Transnational spatial concepts could also be important for framing national identities. Thus Martina Steber and Riccardo Bavaj have identified the concept 'the West' as 'a central concept in German public discourse'. Tracing the mental mappings of that concept, they have identified a range of narratives which rejected or endorsed 'the West' as a normative value Germany either had to combat or embrace. Pointing out that concepts often need to be examined in the light of their counter-concepts, in this case 'the East', they traced the usage of the concept back to the post-Napoleonic era. They explored how the concept had, from the nineteenth century to the present day, exhibited so many facets that it seemed to have been in particular demand at times of crisis and decline of the nation-state.[51] Spatial metaphors have been increasingly analysed, using the toolbox of conceptual history, as particular spatial units, be they regions, nations or empires, and have been described metaphorically as melting pots, transition zones or bridges between cultures.[52]

If we move on to conceptualisations of Europe, the history of concepts has been in the forefront of problematising homogenising ideas about a collective European identity. Helge Jordheim has pointed out that significant asynchronicities are at work in the intellectual and social development of this concept. To understand those asynchronicities properly, what is needed is attention to the way in which different languages and cultures are entangled and interconnected, as this would reveal specificities and commonalities across different linguistic and cultural spaces.[53] Through conceptual history European identity has become a kaleidoscope in which the different pieces of language, culture and politics are forever being re-assembled to contest the multiple meanings of Europe.

Language was the basis on which national identities were forged in the nineteenth century. A multilingual Europe is still struggling with understanding how its multiple languages have produced differing and similar concepts, not least in constant dialogue with one another. A European identity, Patrick Pasture has recently argued, cannot be forged unless we understand how different spaces in Europe interacted with each other.[54] Such a close examination is the basis for relativising essentialist identity claims and leads invariably to greater self-reflexivity about the construction of such identities through language and concepts and their subsequent contestedness. The extent to which Europe has travelled along a common path and the extent to which circumstances there differed is reflected in the presence or absence, over time, of particular concepts in different parts of Europe. Conceptual histories of Europe will therefore invariably contribute to undermine homogeneous forms of European identity. A longue durée view of conceptual history has often been helpful in analysing how concepts have moved from the lingua franca of Europe – Latin – into the diverse vernacular languages. It has highlighted how different linguistic paths in Europe led to different appropriations of Latin concepts.[55]

Histories of Europe, academic, popular and exhibited (as was recently the case in the House of European History in Brussels), have shaped our temporal and spatial understanding of Europe. Jan Ifversen examined the narrative templates that historians of Europe have used in order to forge European identity and concluded that they often used templates derived from national history writing.[56] This is the case with so-called 'container histories', i.e. those that assemble various national histories (usually those of large nations in Europe) in order to constitute a European history. Such borrowing from national templates is also true of the dominant modes of emplotment of European history in recent years. They include, first, the rise of Europe narrative in the post-1945 period, which puts the European Union centre stage; secondly, the fall of Europe narrative in the pre-1945 period, which ends in total war, unprecedented destruction of the continent and genocide; and, finally, the decline of Europe narrative, which bemoans the loss of power of a continent reduced to a mere shadow of its former self after two world wars. At least some narratives seem to take comfort from the argument that Europe has supposedly been able to universalise its values, which others, however, denounce as a new form of European imperialism. National diversity and tolerance of differences seem to be the lowest common denominator in attempts to write a European history in the contemporary world. Ifversen has traced the forging of a mythical Europe based on the pursuit of peace, prosperity and democracy, and also a long pan-European history that he sees represented in much historical writing about Europe. As he noted in his review of the exhibition at the House of European History in Brussels, such narratives contain a high dosage of Eurocentrism that excludes, rather than incorporates, the non-European elements that have gone into the making of Europe.[57]

Not only in Europe but also across the world, conceptual historians have paid particular attention to spaces that were multilingual and multinational. In Africa multilingualism is particularly marked within virtually all sub-Saharan nation-states, where most people speak several languages, many of which are primarily oral and not written. This poses special challenges for conceptual history in terms of the translatability of concepts. African intellectuals constantly needed to translate one local language into another as well as various local languages into the dominant imperial languages, especially English and French (next to German and Dutch).[58] In peripheral spaces, be it of nations or empires, multilingualism was as prominent as it was in large cities, which often acted as hubs of powerful nation-states and empires. Multilingualism was also the norm in university towns and in professions characterised by high mobility, such as seamen, merchants and scholars. Paying attention to languages has also led conceptual historians to discuss the homogenisation of languages, which often only took place very late in the day, when national standards were imposed on languages that were often characterised by a confusing variety of linguistic characteristics.[59] Global languages, such as English, developed manifold vernacular variations at precisely the same time as national languages were being standardised.[60] Thus, linguistic heterogeneity has made historians recognise how important translations are if one is to achieve any deeper understanding of the development of concepts. In the natural sciences, economics, law, politics, and across a whole range of professions, translations have influenced our understanding of particular phenomena and shaped the conceptual world. Translations have tried to convey the meanings associated with a concept in one language into another language. If this was not done well, specific meanings of a concept in one language were lost, as the concept into which it was translated carried different connotations and meanings in a different linguistic context.[61] Translations, in their attempts to familiarise target audiences with something 'foreign', could either hide that foreignness or highlight it. Since translations rarely faithfully reproduced meanings, they instead produced something else in the course of the translation process. It is precisely that difference that makes the study of translations interesting for comparative conceptual historians who want to investigate how translations have shaped national and transnational understandings of concepts.[62]

Conceptual historians who have paid attention to peripheral spaces have pointed out how these peripheries have been continuously confronted with the universalising ambitions of 'centres', which have been prone to posit their own particularisms as universalisms. Peripheral spaces, in order to maintain their own particularisms, either appropriated these concepts provided by centres to fit and accommodate their needs,[63] or, where it was impossible to accommodate them, challenged their universalising tendencies.[64] The asymmetrical translation of core concepts from the centres to the peripheries meant that, within the peripheries, quasi-autonomous conceptual universes were constructed to counter the centres' universalisms. The centres, for their part, ignored the conceptual universes at the peripheries until the moment arrived when they wanted to claim intellectual hegemony over those peripheries. In that event these encounters led to sometimes violent clashes between different conceptual worlds. The essentialising, universalising and basically ahistorical conceptualisations of the centre ran up against the counter-conceptualisations of the peripheries, which were far more immune to an ahistorical and universalising conceptualisation of key concepts than were the centres. By paying attention to specific spatial contexts, peripheries were able to de-essentialise key concepts forged in and sometimes imposed upon peripheries.[65] If we think, for example, of the ways in which key concepts of Western social thought, constitutionalism, parliamentarism, the rule of law, the welfare state, have circulated between 'centres' and 'peripheries', we can trace the ways in which these concepts have been adapted, transformed, rejected and re-appropriated in diverse ways in different parts of the world.[66] Conceptual historians such as Pasi Ihalainen have been very adept at tracing the way in which Western models of parliamentarism and constitutional government circulated at critical junctures such as during the revolutionary upheaval at the end of the First World War, and have produced very different results. Whilst in Britain parliamentary legitimacy was restored, in Germany and Finland the end of the war led to revolution, whereas Sweden, for its part, embarked on the long road towards the social democratisation of its political culture.[67] The intense politicisation and ideologisation of languages and key concepts has alternated with periods of depoliticisation. Both the politicisation and the depoliticisation of languages and key concepts were most effective wherever they were not premeditated and more indirect rather than direct.[68]

During the Cold War, the USA was the centre of the so-called 'Western world', standing against the so-called 'communist world' led by the Soviet Union. Re-assessing the concept 'Cold War' enables one to recognise how different actors in diverse societal fields understood and used the meaning of this concept in order to forward and back up their own visions of world order and domestic political understandings, depending on whether they derived from the centre or the periphery.[69] Thus, a conceptual history of the Cold War pluralises our understanding of it and helps deconstruct one of the key master narratives of the second half of the twentieth century. Many Western concepts derived from European and North American history have benefited in several ways from adopting a conceptual history approach. Explaining the rise of the USA to the rank of a world power since the end of the nineteenth century, Frank Ninkovich made good use of the history of concepts by putting the concept of globalisation and the USA's response to it centre stage.[70] In legal history, Edoardo Zimmermann argued that concepts of an 'American model' had important repercussions for constitutional cultures in Latin America.[71] Philip Gleason, in analysing the place occupied by ethnicity and ethnic conflict in American twentieth-century history, paid attention to the concepts of 'pluralism' and 'assimilation' in order to show the dialectical nature of these two ideas usually depicted as mirror opposites.[72]

Overall, regarding spatial concepts and their associated collective identities, we have seen how conceptual historians have contributed to deconstructing the production of spatial frameworks on different levels, regional, national and transnational. Concepts allowed specific spatial social orders to emerge and justified the specific power structures sustaining them. The same is also true for non-spatial concepts to which historians of concepts have also devoted much attention. With the rise of social history, few concepts were as important in guiding armies of researchers as that of class. (See Chapter 3.) As argued in Chapter 4, the new cultural history challenged these conceptualisations of class by using the arsenal of poststructuralist theories discussed in Chapter 1. This, in turn, prompted attempts to defend unifying concepts, such as class, by taking on board and working constructively with some of the key insights achieved by the new cultural history.[73] The rethinking of the concept of class has led many, like Mike Savage, to pay greater attention to ideas of 'space', 'place', 'gender', 'religion' and 'ethnicity', which are often combined with an interest in social mobility, historical demography and political mobilisation.[74] The study of how class was constructed under specific local and intersectional conditions moved centre stage. Thus, for example, the concept of 'class' was introduced into Korea during and after the 1920s, where it was used extensively to counter the liberal colonialist regime of Japan. Thus, for example, tenants resisting landlords made effective use of the concept of class. In interwar Korea concepts of class, opposed to the imperialist concept of individualism and at the very least ambiguous towards the national concept, constituted the social in radically new ways.[75]

In the field of the history of religion, conceptual historians have analysed changes in religious ideas as well as changes in the idea of religion itself. Piety, belief and ritualism are all religious ideas that have been scrutinised by historians interested in tracing the multiple meanings inherent in these concepts. Lucian Hölscher has explored how religious concepts have interacted with a range of other secular concepts, including those of 'community', 'state' and 'people'.[76] Practices and institutions have shaped semantic constructions that differ across diverse languages and societies and result in diverse conceptualisations of religion within these societies. As those concepts in turn resulted in the forging of specific institutions and social practices, their examination led to a radical historisation of religious identities. Whereas, for example, in Germany, 'church' is understood, above all, as a hierarchical social organisation, in France 'church' is understood predominantly as a community of believers. The concept of 'confession', Hölscher argued, was a vital instrument in defining, bordering and ultimately dissolving religious conflicts in the German lands. According to him, the German term 'confession' (*Konfession*) has no real conceptual equivalent in other languages. They rely on other terms such as 'denomination' or 'communauté religieuse'.[77] Comparing the conceptual world of religion across different societies contributes to a deeper understanding of similiarities and differences and relativises the claims about collective identity made on behalf of religions. To give another example: a conceptual approach to the history of religion has also been visible in Talal Assad's *Genealogies of Religion*.[78] The concepts of religion, he argued, are necessarily always contested as they are the product of culturally specific discourses that change over time. He demonstrated how at various junctures in the history of post-Reformation Christian religions, diverse meanings of religions served the purpose of disciplining believers and asserting the authority of institutions over them. At the same time concepts of religion could be used by the enemies of religion to fight against its influence in society. Asad also drew attention to the importance of power imbalances between different religious cultures, in his case Christianity and Islam. These, in his view, had an important role in shaping over time the concepts of diverse religions.

In the meeting of non-Western and Western religions in the post-Reformation era, concepts of race often interrelated with concepts of religion. In the case of American history they have both been described as foundational, and, according to James Carson, the Judeo-Christian underpinnings of conceptualisations of race go a long way towards understanding their long purchase and dreadful consequences.[79] Elazar Barkan, in his study of the concept of race in interwar Britain and the USA, has shown how political beliefs were far more important than scientific evidence in determining it. Science could be used to underpin a great variety of political beliefs. Barkan's study confirms the close links between concepts and political interests. Indeed it was the growing presence of those groups, often deemed racially inferior, among the scientific community that also brought to the fore anti-racist political beliefs. No other factor was more important in moving towards a more culturalist and societal understanding of race than the opposition to National Socialism, and specifically its racism. It effectively sidelined the biological understanding of race.[80] Yet the conceptual history of race in the USA is not one that has seen cultural concepts of race eradicate racism and end race discrimination. It is true that new conceptualisations of race allowed the civil rights movements to achieve important successes against racism, but at least from the 1980s onwards, under the Reagan administration, we also witness a vicious backlash that opened up multiple spaces for the rejuvenation of racism.[81] The conceptual battle over race is thus far from being politically over in the USA today, as campaigns such as 'Black Lives Matter' clearly indicate.[82]

Conceptual historians have also shown an interest in the concepts 'woman' and 'man' and tried to dissolve the dichotomous construction of gender identities which resulted from these two central binary ascriptions. The political nature of those concepts has been highlighted in relation to struggles over voting rights, household duties and a whole range of other public and private concerns, all of which have been highly gendered. Such conceptual histories of gender have increasingly decentred the white middle-class heterosexual ideal of woman- and manhood. Instead, they have problematised the naturalisation of the concepts of 'woman' and 'man' – pointing to specific constructions of woman- and manhood that have occurred at different times and in different places. Thus, postcolonial feminist writing emphasised how colonialism and imperialism spread European and Western concepts of 'woman' and 'man' and sought to apply them to colonial contexts, often justifying colonialism by describing colonial subjects as feminine and thus in need of male guidance through the coloniser.[83] In South Africa, on the North-Eastern Cape, the concept of work was highly gendered among both the Xhosa population and the Moravian Protestant missionaries. The latter sought to introduce Western forms of work ethic primarily to the men of the Xhosa, who were to embrace agricultural technology as a first step to becoming sedentary farmers and lead the way towards Christian understandings of modernity. In the conceptual world of the male Xhosa, however, such technologies were clearly female, as the world of work was associated with the world of women, whereas maleness was associated with courage, warriordom and strategic thinking. Consequently, the conceptual world of the Christian missionaries clashed with the conceptual world of the Xhosa.[84] And, to take another example from Africa: among Bagisu men in eastern Uganda circumcision was an important ritual of collective male identity mixed with ethno-national belonging. The abduction and forced circumcision of men refusing to be circumcised made a powerful statement that it was impossible to be Bagisu without being circumcised. The concepts of 'manhood' and 'being Bagisu' were crucial markers of collective identity that necessitated complex rituals of circumcision, whcih themselves established hierarchies and positionings within the Bagisu community.[85]

Non-spatial conceptual histories that have contributed to the deconstruction of collective identities extend to conceptual histories of democracy.[86] In our contemporary world the prima facie commitment to democracy is overwhelmingly strong. Only the most hard-boiled dictator would today reject any pretence of being the head of a democratic regime. Fascists in the interwar period sometimes claimed that, by fulfilling the will of the people, they were in fact pursuing a higher form of democracy. Communists, ever since taking over the government, first in Russia in 1917 and subsequently in half of the world during the Cold War period of the twentieth century, always claimed that their 'people's democracies' were far superior to the capitalist liberal democracies of the West. Those behind the recent authoritarian turn in countries as diverse as Russia under Putin, India under Modri, Hungary under Orban and Poland under the rule of the PiS would all deny that their authoritarian moves are undermining democracy, however much they actually do precisely that. A nation such as Britain often claims to be the first democracy, citing 'Magna Carta' in the thirteenth century and a long history of parliamentary government as proof that an ingrained democratic sentiment is part of the national character.[87] In the recent Brexit campaign conducted by politicians intent on leaving the European Union, this claim that they were the representatives of a democratic Britain standing against an undemocratic European Union was one of their central arguments (next to others, such as xenophobia and nostalgia for empire). Nations with a less glorious record with regard to democratic government, such as Germany, do nevertheless pride themselves on having learnt the lessons of the past and in now being model democrats.

Understanding the power of the concept of democracy in the twenty-first century and its relationship to the construction of collective identities needs a conceptual approach which shows how democracy was constructed at different times and in different places in order to be in line with modernity, national character and progress. Older conceptualisations tended to be negative about democracy. Aristotle famously described it as a chaotic and violent form of mob rule – a view that many aristocratic and middle-class observers of the French revolution of 1789 shared.[88] It was only in the course of the nineteenth century that concepts of democracy emancipated themselves from primarily negative associations,[89] and it was only in the course of the twentieth century that a distinction drawn between democracy and the two other ideologies that marked that century, fascism and communism, made it into the ideological hegemon that it is today. More recently, Achille Mbembe has analysed the dark side of liberal democracies, which, he argued, could only develop democracies in the Western centres, because they had colonial and imperial peripheries where democratic values did not count. According to Mbembe, a continuity of racist thinking is deeply ingrained in the alleged universalism of liberal Western democracies.[90] Thus, like all concepts, the concept of 'democracy' is ideologised, politicised, contested and legitimatory. Historically, conceptualisations of democracy have certainly not been incompatible with racism, imperialism and misogyny. Far from following a linear trajectory, they have been characterised by breaks, countertendencies and perennial battles over meaning.

With all of the concepts that have been investigated by conceptual historians, spatial and non-spatial alike, disagreement over their meaning has been an integral part of the development of the concepts themselves. It is characteristic of concepts that they cannot be determined once and for all; they remain sites of contestation.[91] In other words, each and every concept is endowed with a range of plausible conceptualisations and is thus inherently pluralistic in its meanings. Recognising the ultimate indeterminacy of concepts helps counter essentialised forms of collective identity that rely on determining concepts and making them resistant to change. This contestedness of concepts is invariably increased by their inter-conceptuality, i.e. the relatedness of particular concepts to other concepts which produces conceptual fields in which boundaries and meanings are fixed differently depending on how these concepts relate to each other. As Michael Freeden has put it: scholars should 'approach concepts ... as constantly bumping into one another, cutting across each other, chipping away at each other, adding and dropping conceptualisations, and all along in those processes changing the meaning each separate concept carries'.[92]

Conceptual historians, in their concern with discourses and the power they possess, have pointed to both the oppressive and the liberating potential that lies within concepts. Their very indeterminacy makes it ultimately impossible to impose meanings on them and prevent counter-concepts from being formulated.[93] Writing about colonial Bioko (Equatorial Guinea), Ana Lúcia Sá traces the use of concepts such as 'land' and 'indigenous' made by a group of local Bubi farmers calling themselves 'sons of the country'. Submitting a petition to the colonial government, they appropriated these Western concepts in order to express their hope that land taken away from them in order to satisfy colonial settlers would be handed back to them. In this way their use of translated concepts became a way of striving to undo past and present injustices.[94]

Conclusion

The history of concepts, together with a set of related approaches, such as critical discourse analysis and the study of ideologies, has problematised the use of language in the past. It has questioned the relationship between language and social reality, pointing out that the latter is constituted on the basis of linguistic concepts. It is thus related to the linguistic turn in historical studies discussed in Chapter 1. It claims that an understanding of the social, cultural, economic and political worlds around us is impossible without studying concepts and the linguistic forms through which they are shaped and become a meaningful practice. For various spatial and non-spatial collective identities, conceptual history has provided an awareness that the meanings associated with those identities have not only changed over time and space but have invariably been subject to contestations and power struggles. Such an awareness works towards preventing any essentialisation of these identities, contributing instead to their radical historisation. In particular the transnational and comparative turn in conceptual history has alerted us to the travelling nature of concepts that change both their meaning and their significance when crossing language and cultural borders. Translations and transfers have never produced uncontested universalisms, and investigations into the processes of translation and transfer can help us understand how and why particular concepts developed powerfully whilst others withered away.[95] This in turn makes us realise how concepts contributed to the plurality of possible identifications in history across space and time. As Margrit Pernau and Dominic Sachsenmaier have written:

> globally oriented conceptual history can point to a world of linguistic entanglements – a world in which the "West" was not an unmoved mover but rather subject to outside influence and change, just as other parts of the world were. Moreover, the field can show which interpretation of a concept gained influence at which particular time – across national, semi-colonial and colonial boundaries.[96]

Further Reading

Axel Fleisch and Rhiannon Stephens (eds.), *Doing Conceptual History in Africa*, Oxford: Berghahn Books, 2016.

Iain Hampsher-Monk, Karen Tilmans and Frank van Vree (eds.), *History of Concepts: Comparative Approaches*, Amsterdam: University of Amsterdam Press, 1998.

Margrit Pernau and Dominic Sachsenmaier (eds.), *Global Conceptual History: a Reader*, London: Bloomsbury, 2016.

Javier Fernández Sebastian (ed.), *Political Concepts and Time: New Approaches to Conceptual History*, Santander: Cantabria University Press, 2011.

Willibald Steinmetz, Michael Freeden and Javier Fernández-Sebastián (eds.), *Conceptual History in the European Space*, Oxford:Berghahn Books, 2017.

9 *The Visual Turn*

Introduction

Whereas the 'conceptual turn' in historical writing has focused on texts (and contexts), the 'new cultural history' has brought with it the desire to extend the historians' subject matter beyond textual artefacts from the past and include a wide range of visual material. They have felt a greater need to concern themselves with images, not only as illustrations, but also as historical sources and evidence in their own right. Some historians, often those working on the borderlines between art history and history, have emphasised that images bring the historians and their audiences 'face to face with history'.[1] This visual turn in history involves a recognition that images are at least as ambiguous and polysemic as texts and that they cannot be understood without acquiring a deep understanding of how to read them, something which often demands different interpretative techniques from the ones needed for reading a text. This recognition of ambiguity and of the ultimate indeterminacy of meaning has also led visual historians to champion forms of self-reflexivity that made them aware of the extent to which images have been crucial in fostering forms of collective identity in the past. Subsequently much of visual history was about deconstructing these images and showing how the construction of collective identities through history relied on images' performative power. In what follows I would like to give a brief account of the rise of historical attention to the visual before focusing on a range of examples that demonstrate how visual history has contributed to undermining the link between historical writing and collective identity formation.

From Texts to Visuals

Professional historical writing was traditionally characterised by an almost exclusive concentration on written sources from the past.

Historians went into libraries and archives, where they consulted written texts in order to reconstruct what had happened in the past. A separate sub-genre of historical writing, the history of art, had emerged alongside the historical sciences. Art historians dealt centrally with visual material, but they focused on great works of art, masterpieces that they, above all, described in aesthetic and timeless frames, i.e. without too much attention to the social contexts of art. In the nineteenth century art historians were part and parcel of the national turn of the humanities, grouping art into so-called 'national schools' and ascribing national characteristics to particular forms of art and specific artists. Recently, the ideological nature of such ascriptions has been a topic of books and of art exhibitions, such as the one held in the Prado in 2019 entitled 'Velázquez, Rembrandt, Vermeer: Parallel Visions'. (See Figure 9.1.) Such exhibitions and books have drawn attention to 'the extent to which discourses on art and the visual image are still nationally framed',[2] and serve the purpose to underpin the formation of national collective identities.

Figure 9.1 Press conference presenting the exhibition 'Velazquez, Rembrandt, Vermeer: Parallel Vision' at the Prado Museum, 21 June 2019. © Europa Press News, Europa Press/Getty Images.

It was only under the influence of, first, social and, then, cultural history that art historians turned to look at the social conditions under which art was produced and at the historically specific cultural meanings transported by art. Thus, for example, Michael Baxandall's *Painting and Experience in Fifteenth-Century Italy* explored the ways in which artists were contracted to paint and the diverse social practices that explained why particular art schools developed at particular times.[3] In his wake many others have explored how the figure of the artist was constructed, how studios developed, how commissions of art worked, how the art market thrived and how art critics became ever more powerful.[4] Svetlana Alpers' pathbreakting *The Art of Describing* analysed Dutch seventeenth-century painting by drawing attention to new skills, for example in map-making, new technologies, such as microscopes and the camera obscura, and new knowledge about the operation of the eye and its ability to see things.[5] Both books were representative of a move away from the timeless genius of the artist to a social and cultural contextualisation of art.

Not all images produced in the past were classed as art, and art historians such as James Elkins have long denounced art history's snobbery in ignoring the vast array of images it classed as aesthetically of no or low value.[6] Thus it was arguably not primarily art history that made mainstream history turn to the visual but the development of new visual media in the twentieth and twenty-first centuries, above all photography, graphic novels, film, television and the internet. In 1964 Kenneth Winetrout already stated that television had produced 'the new age of the visible'.[7] Similarly, Marshall McLuhan, in his volume on media theory published in the same year, had seen his contemporaries as being particularly influenced by visual culture. McLuhan talked about the appearance of 'visual man'.[8] Historians became interested in understanding how images work, in what contexts they were used, what purposes they fulfilled and what 'agency' they possessed. Especially the agency of images in their specific contexts and their performative power became the subject of much discussion – with authors stressing how images had the power of constituting the one who looked at them. In other words, the gaze was not only from the observer to the image but also from the image to the observer. The images were looking back and were aiming to produce meaning in the observer.[9]

Historians interested in visuals have, over time, included more and more types of material in their analyses. These include paintings, sculptures, posters, photography, film, TV, images on the internet, advertising, caricature, cartoons, postcards, and a diverse range of everyday objects, ranging from stamps, steam engines and silk shawls, to rickshaws, mugs and glassware. Whereas, initially, many historians using visual material focused on publicly available material that was used by official or civic institutions, the field has seen an increasing interest in private collections and everyday visual material, e.g. snapshots made by tourists with their smartphone cameras or photographs contained in family archives.[10] The material can be fictional or non-fictional. It can be related to types of media or to types of spectacle. Each type of visual material has its own challenges – methodologically and theoretically. History departments at universities have been slow in incorporating the teaching of those challenges and of visual material more generally into their curricula. This is not surprising, as most historians have been trained for centuries to deal primarily, almost exclusively, with textual sources. However, within the past two decades we can see a change here, as a new generation of historians has also been introducing the visual turn into their teaching. What seems clear is that there is no fixed canon of theories or methods with which to approach visual history. Iconographic and iconological methods stand next to semiotic ones, and the influence of diverse sociological theories, from Pierre Bourdieu to Bruno Latour, has been strong. The writings of Roland Barthes and Michel Foucault also figure prominently in visual histories.[11] Walter Benjamin's idea that every historical era had particular techniques of reproduction that guided the way in which images were understood has had a particularly strong influence on visual historians.[12]

A first major challenge has been to draw historians away from reading visual material only in terms of the content or the message supposedly conveyed by the image. Instead, historians had to take seriously the aesthetics of visual objects, including their materiality, which often determined their aesthetic value and impacted on the messages carried by images. Their aesthetic value has its own semantic status and is constitutive for their meanings. Secondly, historians had to learn that images are always multi-layered and characterised by a high degree of indeterminacy. The settings in which visuals were seen and presented had to be taken into account – some were extraordinarily formal, like museums, cinemas and the great world fairs of modernity, whilst others were rather informal, e.g. window-shopping and other everyday visual experiences. Thirdly, historians have to be aware that images, just like texts, have been circulating across nations, empires and continents and can thus only be understood properly if questions of reception, adaptation and hybridity are taken into account. Indeed, some visual historians have moved away entirely from an object-fetishism and instead have started to examine visual history as a dynamic process of seeing and being seen and thus remaking the world around us.[13]

The connection between the study of images and the study of power was established by Michel Foucault's archaeology of surveillance, which he connected above all with Jeremy Bentham's panopticon, an image of total control.[14] (See Figure 9.2.) Medieval images often depicted God as all-powerful, the only one who could see into the souls and hearts of people and whose hand was acting invisibly in the world.[15] In the early modern world of absolutism, the sovereign was equally depicted as all-powerful. The absolute king, e.g. Louis XIV in France, realised how important images were to re-inforce the notion of an all-powerful and all-seeing king who derived his authority directly from God.[16] (See Figure 9.3.) Nicholas Mirzoeff's discussion of slave-holding plantations in eighteenth-century North America is an ambitious attempt to connect different historical power regimes to visualisations – British nineteenth-century imperialism, twentieth-century fascism and the counter-insurgency strategies of the West in the wake of 9/11 with the USA taking the front seat. He discusses not only the visualisations of those in power, but also the counter-visualisations of the oppressed and powerless.[17] In an age of democracy, the visibility of the many increasingly moved centre stage in visualisations, as visibility became a form of 'social capital' (on Bourdieu's concept see Chapter 1 above) that can be used effectively in political contests.[18]

If seeing has always been related to power, there have been many different ways of seeing. Thus Martin Jay has distinguished perspectivalism, which he associated with Cartesian thought, the art of observation, which he charted back to Francis Bacon, and proliferation, which he traced to Leibniz – all of which form a plurality of ways of seeing in modern culture.[19] This emphasis on the plurality and ultimate heterogeneity of regimes of seeing can also be found in Jonathan Crary's

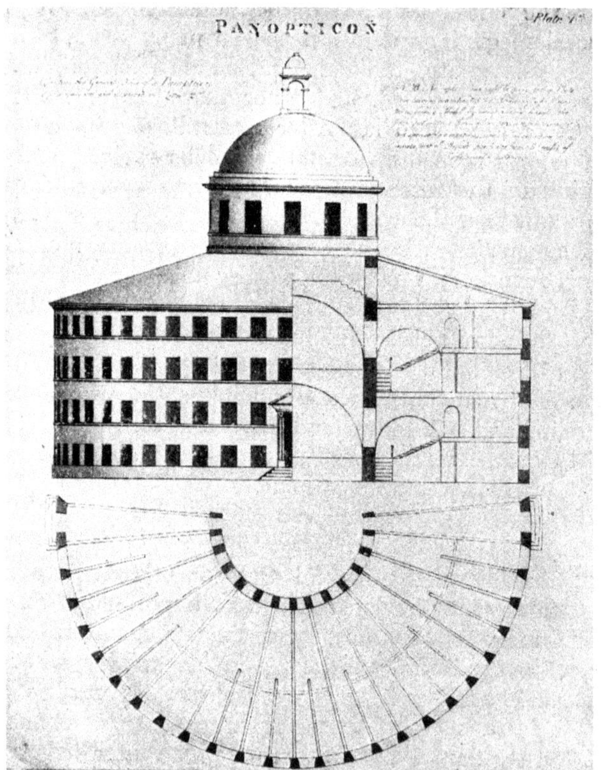

Figure 9.2 Drawing of a prison design called a panopticon, from the book *Management of the Poor* by Jeremy Bentham, 1796. Bentham's design shows a prison where each prisoner is housed in such a way as to prevent them from being aware of whether or not they are, at any given moment, under observation by the prison staff. © Mansell, The LIFE Picture Collection/Getty Images.

attempt to counter arguments about an increasing objectivity of visual images since the time of the Renaissance. Crary pointed to a rupture in the early nineteenth century, from when the idea of visual subjectivity has ruled our ideas about what can be represented through images.[20] If a plurality of different ways of seeing is built into seeing itself, historians examining ways of seeing have to be, by the very definition of seeing, aware of the impossibility of determining how images can or should be seen. Historical writing thus is revealed as perspectival and

Figure 9.3 *The King Governs by Himself*, 1661. Ceiling painting by Charles LeBrun depicting the absolutist aspirations of Louis XIV. © Heritage Images, Hulton Fine Art Collection/Getty Images.

subject to revision in the constructions it makes of the past – a central concern for the body of theories discussed in Chapter 1.

Just like memory history, discussed in Chapter 7 above, has become a disciplinary facet of a new transdisciplinary field of study entitled memory studies, visual history is part of a wider field called visual studies or visual culture, which is as transdisciplinary as memory studies and derives much inspiration from sociology and other social sciences and humanities-based disciplines. One of its flagship journals, now entitled *Visual Studies*, was in fact called *Visual Sociology* before 2002. Bruno Latour's association of scientific modernity with a new visual regime that 'redefines both what it is to see, and what there is to see',[21] had a major influence in boosting visual studies across a wide field of disciplines. Historians followed W. J. T. Mitchell in exploring how visual culture constructed the social in a broad variety of different contexts,[22] and how visual regimes produced assumptions of what was normal and what was deviant, thereby producing specific normative regimes.[23] Finally, Jean Baudrillard's analysis of the First Gulf War (1990–1) as a media event had a major impact on visual historians.[24] Baudrillard argued that the media had visualised the destruction of war in aestheticised forms that begged questions about simulation and the authenticity of 'real' pictures. His hugely successful book spurred on more historians to study in depth the power of the pictorial in a wide variety of subject matters, for it seemed to underline the omnipresence and domination of the visual. Real war led to a war of images that was by no means restricted to the Gulf War. One of the major historical debates in Germany during the 1990s concerned the famous exhibition on the crimes of the German Wehrmacht during the Second World War, and specifically the question of what actually could be seen on some of those pictures.[25] All of these theoretical and political developments contributed to a much greater interest in images among historians. As pictures often represented and spoke to collective identities, those themes in particular that were directly related to the forging of those identities were prominently represented in the scholarship on visualisations.

Deconstructing the Nation and the Visual Turn

A very early and to this day fascinating example of exploring national history through visual images is a project conducted by Peter Lord at the Centre for Advanced Welsh and Celtic Studies at the University of Wales, Aberystwyth between 1994 and 2003. It resulted in three volumes exploring visual images of Wales, one of the stateless nations in Europe to this day, from medieval times to the 1960s.[26] Lord's project demonstrated how the national identity of Wales was formed in distinction to and conversation with, in particular, English, Irish and French influences. The national was constituted in conversation with the foreign. If Lord's work can be understood as constituting the nation, it did so in highly self-reflective ways, seeking to avoid forms of othering that have often been a prominent part of nation-building exercises. Furthermore, the second volume of the trilogy in particular highlighted how Welshness was not eternal and unchanging but rather constructed in specific ways at particular times and places, often serving diverse interests. Thus, for example, the bardic tradition and the depiction of Welsh bards and druids not only fostered a conviction that the Welsh were the first and true Britons, but also cemented the belief in the English being hostile and inimical to the Welsh. (See Figure 9.4.) Lord's project thus reveals and deconstructs images of the nation and relates them to various ideological and chronological standpoints down the centuries.

Of late, many national histories have taken a deconstructionist stance, highlighting the complex and contested ways in which images were used to construct different visions of nationality. A recent textbook on the history of modern China explicitly set out to discuss the importance of images for topics such as Qing court ritual, rebellion and war, the history of urbanisation and of rural life, sports history, the Chinese diaspora, the Cultural Revolution, propaganda and environmentalism.[27] Images, the editors argue, are not mere illustrations of our text-based knowledge of the past. Rather, they had a dynamic of their own that shaped the past – often in much more powerful ways than did texts. The book drew attention to the contested nature of images and the difficulties of making images conform to any one specific meaning given to them. Habits of seeing changed over time and place. As the editors write: 'Visual culture is ... deeply related to social identity.'[28]

Drawing on the 58,000-item-strong Maynard L. Parker photographic collection at the Huntington Library, Jennifer A. Watts and her collaborators have underlined the extent to which the post-war American dream of endless consumption produced images of privacy, leisure

Figure 9.4 *The Bard*, by John All, engraving, 1784. This print was made as a frontispiece for Edward Jones' *Musical and Poetical Relations of the Welsh Bards*. The imagery comes from Thomas Gray's 'The Bard: a Pindaric Ode', which tells how the invading army of Edward I of England pushed the Welsh bard on to a cliff. Here we see the windblown figure continuing to play his harp as soldiers stand far below by the river Conway. © Gift of Georgiana W. Sargent, in memory of John Osborne Sargent, 1924, Metropolitan Museum, New York.

time and domesticity that were constitutive of notions of Americanness, and were at the same time heavily classed, raced and gendered. Parker's camera was astute in constructing visions of modernity in architecture and everyday life that underpinned a way of life in the early decades of the Cold War.[29] Watts has also pointed out how regional identities in America, such as identities in and around Los Angeles, have been constructed to a large extent through the power of photography and visual images. She described photography as 'the rose-coloured glasses through which the country could glimpse this new city or, as some have claimed, this new civilisation. A flood of photographic imagery flowed from the region and around the globe in snapshot albums, postcards and the illustrated press.'[30] Visual tropes that she found to be particularly appealing included references to the climate, i.e. the 'land of sunshine', the exotic landscape dotted by yuccas, banana and orange trees as well as the pampas grass, and the architectural relics associated, above all, with the Spanish missions in the region. The imagery was both classed and raced in the sense that the images were meant to appeal to white middle-class people coming from the east or mid-west of the United States. Multi-ethnic and multi-cultural images were part of the visual appeal of Los Angeles – there were constant references to Mexican dancers, Chinese merchants and Indian basket-makers – but it is also clear that some types, e.g. the Spanish señorita, were more favoured by the cameras than others, e.g. the Mexican labourer. Picturing ancient Native Americans was intended to give the region a heritage, whereas their still-living descendants were excluded from the ocular gaze. Overall, Watts' essay and book are perfect examples of how historians have begun to deconstruct both national and regional constructions of collective identities by being attentive to the images doing the constructions.

In a volume entitled *The Colonising Camera* a range of historians look at the way in which photography and film have contributed to the making of Namibian history.[31] The essays in this collection show how the photography produced by the colonisers, first the Germans and later the South Africans, projected a colonial modernity against an indigenous primitivism. Photography thus was complicit in producing cultures of colonialism, but it did so in complex and often contradictory ways. Ethnicities and landscapes were constructed by the camera in messy and fuzzy ways that remained open to multiple readings. Imperial knowledge production through photography was intensely contested not only by different empires but also, at times, by the colonised, who learnt to use cameras and images to counter those of their colonial adversaries. Thus, once again, the reader is reminded of the multiplicity of constructions and counter-constructions of colonial and postcolonial identities through images. Intriguingly the postcolonial independent state of Namibia that emerged after 1990 produced a host of images reproducing earlier colonial attempts to differentiate between 'civilising' and 'primitive' forces. The 'simple ways of life' of some 'backward' people in the new-found nation state were now constructed as standing in the way of economic and social development. Thus, for example, electrification, associated with progress and modernity, had to triumph, according to the Namibian ruling party, over 'traditional' forces, i.e. 'tribes', in this case the Himba people, who opposed the hydro-electric scheme on the Kunene river that destroyed the traditional burial grounds of their ancestors. Old idioms were thus cast into new power relationships and visualised in ways strikingly reminiscent of older colonial images.[32] (See Figure 9.5.)

Figure 9.5 The camera is still often capturing Africans in ways that are prone to stereotyping. Here, a Maasai warrior holding spears. © DeAgostini Getty Images.

As Richard Vokes and Darren Newbury have argued, 'the camera became a key technology for the establishment of colonial concepts of African history, European constructs of African "traditions", and even widespread ideas about how certain African peoples represented previous "evolutionary stages".'[33] Yet, as they continue to argue, 'none of these visual constructs of African pasts was ever entirely stable'. Contestations came from local historical and oral traditions. African interlocutors shaped the way in which the colonisers' cameras captured images, and there always remained the possibility of counter-readings of the images taken by the colonisers' cameras. Last but not least, Africans themselves have used the camera to unsettle and question colonial images. Images of the past were intricately bound up with images of the future, as photography was also producing narratives of progress which contrasted the pre-modern past with the modern future that was inevitably represented by the colonisers. In postcolonial African states governments, political parties and a wide range of civil society actors all used images produced by cameras in order to position themselves in the political struggle of how to connect the pre-colonial and colonial pasts with the imagined postcolonial futures, clad, like colonialism's images, in the clothes of progress and civilisation. During the Cold War, global imaginaries produced by organisations such as the World Health Organisation or the United Nations and ideological imaginaries produced by the adversaries in the global Cold War all tied images of African pasts to scenarios of African futures. Nationalist image-making in Africa in the postcolonial period was intricately tied up with the visualisation of modern and bright futures. Anti-colonialist guerrilla movements, like the Front for the Liberation of Mozambique (FRELIMO), used photography extensively in order to project a self-image of a nationalist movement capable of uniting a fragile alliance of ethnic and regional groups under the banner of national liberation. The images produced by FRELIMO-trained photographers were aimed both at national integration and at an international audience in support of anti-imperialism.[34] National Development Plans have been presented by several nation-states in Africa in recent years, and every time they have been accompanied by a host of images signalling visions of the future that had been borrowed and adapted from places allegedly marching at the head of global modernity, architecturally and in terms of building modern economies and societies.[35] Historians pointing to those intriguing continuities in the visions of progress and modernity between colonial and postcolonial national image-making in African postcolonial nation-states have contributed to a higher self-reflexivity about the connections between constructing national collective identities and the production of images.

Deconstructing Class and the Visual Turn

The same can be said about visual histories of class. Carol Quirke's book on how news photography was instrumental in shaping images of American working-class lives around the middle of the twentieth century is based on a close reading of more than a hundred photographs immaculately contextualising the images and the stories they were telling (and, in many cases, hiding).[36] Both employers and trade unions, she argued, were attracted to the medium of photography, as it seemed ideally suited to represent 'truthfully' the situation of the working class and of working America. Whilst radical unionists used heroic images of the working class to promote their political aims, Quirke drew attention to the fact that mainstream images in news photography promoted conformity to American values, consumerism and loyalty to the big corporations that shaped the image of American industry. Thus, *LIFE* magazine's 1937 portrayal of the working week of the steelworker Andy Lopata depicted him as a hard-working American, well cared for by his wife. (See Figure 9.6.) A family man, he enjoyed modest wealth thanks to the powerful vision of the American captains of industry, and his union ensured that he got a share of the spoils. Happy in his own carefully constricted world, the images did not in any way suggest conflict between labour and capital. And this despite the fact that, as Quirke showed, Lopata was eventually fired by his bosses for his activism on behalf of his union. Quirke's book is a wonderful example of how a visual history of class can demonstrate the diverse ways in which class was constructed through imagery by different actors and how it could be either emphasised or hidden. Class, she concluded, is not a social fact but more a social construction that can take different forms, many of which have been powerfully transported through images.

The labour movement has long used images in its struggle on behalf of the working classes. Many of those images represented workers, and those representations in turn spoke to the aspirations and aims of a self-styled working-class movement. British trade union banners were

Figure 9.6 Steelworker Andy Lopata and his son reading the newspaper *Steel Labor*, which was a paper belonging to the moderate American trade union confederation Congress of Industrial Organisations (CIO). © Alfred Eisenstaedt/The Picture LIFE Collection via Getty Images.

a particularly marked visual demonstration of the unions' self-confidence in shaping a brighter future for its members.[37] Annie Ravenhill-Johnson has shown to what extent the visual images produced by British trade unions were informed by the reception of an elite culture and its penchant for classicism. This hankering after access to a culture often denied to workers was a sign of the aspirations of a movement that was to a considerable extent an educational movement. It also meant, however, that this movement bought into the values of a middle-class culture that could blunt the labour movement's desire to overcome the bourgeois social order. Ravenhill-Johnson's careful analysis of the images of emblems and banners shows the extent to which the labour movement was part of a British imperial imagination in the nineteenth and early twentieth century and the degree to which it bought into very traditional patriarchal gender norms.[38] Her deconstruction of images of the labour movement makes readers more aware of how they were vital in forging a solidaristic culture of labour, but how, at the same time, they transported messages that were in opposition to some of the proposed aims and ambitions of the labour movement.

In his study of the American Knights of Labor (KoL), Robert Weir has pointed to the importance of material culture, including a host of images in the form of banners, placards, pins, tools, bookmarks and playing cards, for promoting a culture of labour that aimed to construct solidarity among all workers – regardless of skill and profession. These visual images were part of a wider culture of songs, storytelling, poetry and a whole host of rituals that gave the KoL strength in its political and industrial battles.[39] Like sections of the British labour movement, parts of the American labour movement constructed ideas of class-based solidarity around a host of powerful images.

In the Soviet Union images of class were state-sponsored and meant to forge the key collective identity of the new communist state after 1917. (See Figure 9.7.) Victoria Bonnell's *Iconography of Power* has demonstrated how political artists in the Soviet Union sought to shape the collective self-understanding of the Soviet citizens and how they were themselves shaped by the political, cultural and social developments of the Soviet Union in the period between 1917 and 1953.[40] Examining a hagiography of class as well as a demonology of those forces constructed as enemies of class emancipation, i.e. capitalism, imperialism and social democracy, Bonnell paid close attention to the aesthetics of the posters and to small details indicating sometimes significant changes to the way in which class identities were promoted. Thus, for example, she demonstrated how images of the backward Russian peasants dominating Soviet posters in the early years gave way to an iconography of the collective farm worker, in which peasants were incorporated into the classed identities of the 'motherland of the proletariat'. Overall, her deconstruction of the way in which class identities were made and remade in the Soviet Union highlights the shifting nature of collective class identities and their relationship to the communist centre of power seeking to control the making of collective class identities in support of their domestic and global ambitions as a world power.

Not only the study of class identities promoted by labour movements and communist states, but also the study of work and its impact on

Figure 9.7 'Lenin lived. Lenin lives. Long live Lenin.' Soviet propaganda poster by Viktor Semenovich Ivanov (1909–68). © Universal History Archives/Getty Images.

class identities has benefited enormously from turning to visual history. Thus, for example, Josef Ehmer and Catharina Lis' edited collection on *The Idea of Work in Europe from Antiquity to Modern Times* has a whole section dedicated to visual representations of work. Between the sixteenth and the eighteenth century, as Peter Burke points out here, it became fashionable to paint or otherwise visually depict working-class women in artwork usually consumed by the middle classes. Whilst some of the images had erotic overtones, the interest in the genre, according to Burke, had more to do with the exotic and picturesque that was often expressed by these images, in a world in which the middle-class consumers of the images rarely encountered working women in their daily lives.[41] Depicting working women in images was thus one way of delineating and ultimately cementing class boundaries in early modern Europe.

The visualisations of the private homes of working men and women are capable of revealing manifold stories about the making of collective identities through both work and non-work.[42] Photography has been capable of depicting homes as spaces that are both eminently material and highly discursive. Nitin Varma, co-operating with the graphic artist Theresa Grieben, has portrayed the Anglo-Indian home in the early nineteenth century. He underlines the importance of that space in constructing visions of class, race and gender.[43]

Deconstructing Race/Ethnicity and the Visual Turn

Histories of race and ethnicity, just like histories of nation and class, have increasingly put visual representations centre stage – often also producing greater self-reflexivity about constructions of racial and ethnic identities. Thus, for example, June Namias, in her exploration of the stories of white women and men held captive by Native American tribes on the American frontier, has made good use of artwork and illustrations to show how notions of ethnicity, race and gender played out in the encounters between white Americans and Native Americans. She identified different archetypes of white captives' narratives – the 'survivor', the 'Amazon' and the 'frail flower' narratives among women and, among men, the 'heroes' and 'white Indian' narratives. Many of the narratives she examined dealt with sexuality, as intimate relationships between whites and Native Americans were especially fascinating, transgressing the carefully constructed borders of ethnicity.[44] By highlighting the extent to which ethnic and racial identities were forged in and through encounters, Namias also raised awareness about the constructed nature of such ethnic/racial ascriptions.

The same can be said of an astute analysis of John Quincy Adams Ward's sculpture *The Freedman*, first exhibited in New York City in the middle of the American civil war in 1863. (See Figure 9.8.) Kirk Savage has shown how Ward managed to create a sculpture that broke with the dominant visual and narrative tropes of depicting the

Figure 9.8 *The Freedman, American*, by John Quincy Adams Ward, sculpture, 1863, cast 1891. © Sepia Times/Universal Images Group via Getty Images.

emancipation of American slaves.[45] Whereas it was usually seen as a benevolent act of the white northern elites, especially in the person of Abraham Lincoln, Ward's sculpture alluded to a more active role played by the slaves themselves. After all, by fleeing the south and joining the Union army, they had weakened the south's economy and re-inforced the fighting power of the north. *The Freedman* neither is begging for his freedom, nor is he shown as a figure in despair, two of the most popular tropes handed down from the abolitionist images. Idealising black manhood on the threshold of freedom took the perspective of the slaves and sidelined white moral leadership. *The Freedman*, Kirk argued, was all about the promise of emancipation. This is the reason why it had such widespread appeal in the 1860s. Yet it is also the reason why it ultimately did not become an icon of the civil war and the American national imagination, as this promise was all but forgotten in the Reconstruction period following the end of the civil war. Unlike Thomas Ball's *Freedman's Memorial to Lincoln*, which depicted the black man in his traditional pose as destitute beggar, Ward's sculpture never became a national monument in the United States.

Ethnicity was closely associated with nationality, as most nineteenth-century constructions of nationality relied on assumptions of ethnic homogeneity. In a fascinating analysis of more than three thousand images from a very wide range of genres, ranging from photography, postcards, films and magazines to tourist brochures and advertising, Sarah Dellmann has explored how Dutchness was constructed through a range of stereotypical ethnic clichés. Anthropological discourses surrounding 'dress' and 'race' produced a range of images that constructed Dutch ethnicity and nationality from the eighteenth century onwards. The author showed that, next to anthropology, geography was key in providing images of Dutchness that related nationality and ethnicity to landscape.[46] Readers of Dellmann's book will come away with a much-heightened sense of how competing and divergent constructions of ethnicity and race were at the heart of the nineteenth-century discourse on nationality in the Netherlands.

More than ten years before Dellmann's exploration of ethnic images and their meaning for the construction of a Dutch national identity, Ardis Cameron, in a pathbreaking volume entitled *Looking for America*, had performed a similar exercise for the USA, assembling a range of articles by different authors who all used visual sources to demonstrate to what extent ethnic identities intermingled with gender and class identities to produce American national identities.[47] Cameron herself discussed the emergence of discourses of physiognomy in the nineteenth century that were to classify bodies in terms of ethnicity and class. Habits of seeing were established that created hierarchies of ethnic and social typologies.[48] More recently, Don Nardo has pointed out how Dorothea Lange's iconic photo of a 'Migrant Mother' with her two children taken in a migrant workers' camp in Nipomo, California, came to epitomise the misery of the Great Depression and helped those who implemented the New Deal in response to the economic crisis.[49] (See Figure 9.9.)

Photographs were vital in defining race, as Shawn Smith's analysis of photographs of the 'American negro' underlined. The photos had been on display at the world exhibition in Paris in 1900, telling tales about race and nation in an America where many whites wanted to see

Figure 9.9 'Migrant Mother' by Dorothea Lange (1895–1964), silver print, 1936. Commissioned by the Resettlement Administration. © Graphica Artis/ Getty Images.

Americanness exclusively in terms of a Protestant Anglo-Saxon legacy.[50] Stuart Cosgrove looked at the zoot-suit as a particular form of ethnic clothing that signalled a form of ethnic identity for young blacks and Mexican-Americans alike in the 1940s. For them it was an alternative claim as to what it meant to be American – a sign of their own exclusion and a claim to belonging that led directly to the so-called zoot-suit riots, which are read by Cosgrove as a struggle over what it meant to be an American citizen.[51] Just as 'all-American families' were made to a considerable extent through the images produced in magazines and films, ethnic minorities had to negotiate their way into the canon of what it meant to be American. Family photography, images of class and sex, the role of visual images for the making of trade unionism in America, visual images of Jewishness and their relationship to Americanness are just some of the other examples of how visual history can shed light on how America was made at the seams of ethnicity, race, class and gender constructions. Many historians who have addressed these issues were indebted to some of the theorists mentioned in Chapter 1, including M. M. Bakthin and Michel Foucault. Visualising ethnicities that underpinned conceptualisations of nation was about the power to authorise specific 'social perceptions and conceptualisations'.[52] Looking, then, has always been an intensely political act and bound up with political decisions and inclusions as well as exclusions.

This is also clear when looking at the ways in which 'men of colour' negotiated the revolutionary politics of late eighteenth and

Figure 9.10 Detail of *The Homeland in Danger (The Recruitment of Volunteer Soldiers)*, by Guillaume Guillon-Lethière (1760–1832), 1799. The artist is identifying himself with the endangered French revolution but also inserts men of colour into his painting. © DEA/G. Dagli Orti/De Agostini via Getty Images.

nineteenth-century France. The Haitian painter Guillaume Guillon-Lethière came face to face with his Creole identity at several key junctures in his life as a revolutionary nationalist in the decades between his passionate endorsement of revolutionary values in 1789 and his death in 1832. (See Figure 9.10.) Celebrating in some of his work the Haitian revolution that had pitched blacks against whites, he nevertheless, through that same work, re-inscribed the narratives of white superiority, having transferred his own allegiance in 1789 to the construction of an overwhelmingly white fatherland.[53] Just as people of colour elsewhere have a long history of using images in the struggle for emancipation, freedom and equality, images have also been crucial in establishing the human rights of the indigenous population in Australia. Jane Lydon has powerfully shown how, for a very long time, constructions of race held back the recognition of indigenous people as fellow human beings.[54]

Europeans travelling to Africa in ever-growing numbers during the second half of the nineteenth century often took their cameras with them and produced a range of ethnographic surveys that constructed typologies of races.[55] Phrenology and a range of other sciences were used to categorise individual bodies into racial collectives and thereby fix collective identities and appearances. Colonial and world exhibitions used visual imagery to order the evolutionary process and relate it to racial characteristics. Outward racial indicators were transformed into inner characteristics. In India, typologies of caste were also thus racialised by the European colonisers.[56] Similarly the encounter between a colonising Europe and the Andean world was interlaced with constructions of race, in which photographs played a vital role in producing images of the Andes.[57] Deborah Poole's book on the 'visual economy' of the Andean image world, heavily influenced by the writings of Michel Foucault, underlined how class, nation, empire and modernity were constructed in interrelated ways, under regimes of power that set the frames for visualisations. Vision was crucial in constituting race as a historical and biological fact. The lens of the camera, Poole showed, was 'a means to invent new racial and cultural identities'.[58] Yet here as well as in India and in Africa, this racial seeing was from the outset influenced by Andean, Indian and African ways of seeing, as the Europeans in the Andes, India and Africa were heavily dependent on Andean, Indian and African interlocutors, often elites who had a strong interest in portraying themselves and others in

Figure 9.11 A white doctor vaccinating African girls, all wearing European clothes, at a mission station. Process print by Meisenbach after a photograph. © Meisenbach, Wellcome Collection. The Wellcome Trust.

a particular light.[59] It has also been noted how racial seeing has significantly influenced visual representations of Europe in the European metropole, often producing synergies between national and European imaginations through the 'other' of the colonial world.[60] Thus, a certain messiness entered all attempts to fix the ocular impression, producing ambiguities and contradictions in the colonial gaze and its attempts to produce clear-cut boundaries between the 'races'. Thus the imperial knowledge produced by photography was not so much authoritative (however much it wanted to be), as intensely unstable. Yet early colonial photography not only served the purpose of classifying the black races. It was also meant to attract more white settlers into Africa. For this purpose it was vitally important to show how colonisation was making headway in modernising an allegedly 'backward' continent. Hence, the superiority of the white races was underlined by images showing Europeans teaching Africans how to do things, e.g. building railways and dams or constructing administrative and political systems, implementing immunisation programmes, or institutionalising Western-style education.[61] (See Figure 9.11.) The legitimatory lens of the colonial camera was later replaced by the equally legitimatory lens of the postcolonial state, which proudly celebrated black African identities and their imagined futures.[62] During the Cold War images of race were used on both sides of the ideological divide to summon up visions of a capitalist and communist future that would bring progress to Africa.[63] In African history, but also in the history of former colonial powers in Africa, images of race coded diverse forms of collective identity from the mid-nineteenth century to the present day.

Deconstructing Religion and the Visual Turn

Medieval historians exploring the visual world of the Middle Ages in Europe have been particularly interested in the way in which images constituted the theological and anthropological way of seeing the world.[64] The cult of religious images, such as icons and reliquaries, iconophobia, forms of idolatry, religious paintings, ritual objects, animated statues and bleeding crosses have all been examined in order to understand how religious identity formed the world view of different people from the Christianisation of the Roman empire to the present day. Historians have pointed out that religious images had an extraordinary power to intervene in the social world. They challenged authority, justified violence and instigated debate. In his book *The Forge of Vision: a Visual History of Modern Christianity* David Morgan studied the history of Christianity from the sixteenth century to the present day through an examination of the way in which Christians have visualised their beliefs in diverse contexts.[65]

Serge Gruzinski has pointed out how religious images were vital for the colonisation of the Americas, in his particular case mainly Mexico, by Spaniards. They were used extensively for the Christianisation of the indigenous populations but also for communicating with the latter. Visualisation was not a one-way street, as the indigenous populations used counter-images to refute the claims of the colonisers to religious, political and economic domination. Gruzinski underlined the Spaniards' initial curiosity about indigenous religious objects and practices, but he also showed how that curiosity gave way eventually to a complete rejection of anything indigenous as 'develish' and 'heathen', so that the brute force used against the indigenous population could be justified. War became a war against indigenous images, a war to eradicate this alien culture and often, of course, the people themselves who had produced it. The replacement of what the Europeans came to call 'idols' with Christian images was a means of asserting European authority over indigenous people. Yet in private, often clandestine, circumstances, the latter retained their religious beliefs, practices and images and gave them from one generation to the next. The religious orders active in Latin America taught the indigenous people they converted how to produce Christian religious images, and in the process of this knowledge transfer, some fusion took place between indigenous and European practices. Gruzinski highlighted that the indigenous population was incredibly receptive to the Christian images brought by the Europeans, partly because they came to believe in their powers. In the end, the most effective Westernisation of the indigenous imagery was produced by the indigenous people themselves, although Gruzinski also traced indigenous opposition to Spanish domination, including resistance that turned Christian images against the colonisers.[66] Gruzinski's analysis of a war of and over religious images underlines the importance of images in constructing religious identities in the process of colonisation and anti-colonial struggle in Latin America.

Missionaries in Christian missions in Africa and elsewhere in the non-Western world have often grasped the importance of photography for promoting their own work in the West and for helping them with the task of converting the 'savages' and turning them into morally upright Christians in the modern Western mould. Thus, for example, missionaries would produce photographs of enslaved children in Ghana in order to appeal to Western audiences to send money in order to allow the missionaries to buy those children's freedom and give them a Christian education and upbringing.[67] Paul Jenkins' work on missionary photography in West Africa has highlighted two thematic groups of photos connected to each other in binary ways. First, photos depicting the life of the mission demonstrated how it morally uplifted the lives of the indigenous people. Secondly, photos showing scenes from indigenous life wavered between invoking in the Western spectator feelings of empathy and emotions connected to the alien other, and affirming the strange and 'unnatural' nature of such lives. Overall, the photographic evidence examined by Jenkins underlined the extent to which missionary activities resulted in a 'history of interaction between Church and indigenous culture in which both have changed, and not necessarily in the way foreseen by the missionaries'.[68] Missionaries' photographs would also frequently capture the building of schools and hospitals by missionary societies – images that were used to depict visions of progress but also at the same time to mobilise more funding in the metropoles for missionary activities.[69] Central to the missionaries' use of photography was the construction of 'conversion narratives' that were frequently in line with a Westernising form of humanitarianism.[70] The Society for the Propagation of the Gospel pursued a photographic project in the West Indies that highlighted the responsibility of the Christian missionaries for the economic and social welfare of the black population who, through Christianity, were to be immunised against the perceived twin evils of nationalism and communism.[71] Missions were at the heart of the colonising experience in Africa, and the missionaries' production of images was a powerful way of seeing Africa.

If the Christian missionaries' gaze had been part and parcel of the colonial gaze in Latin America and Africa, visual histories of Christian images can also be usefully applied to the history of the West itself and the construction of religious identities there. Thus, for example, Benjamin Städter has examined the presence of Christian images in the West German media from the end of the Second World War to the 1970s and found no evidence of their disappearance during this period. What he did find, however, was their increasing pluralisation and their application to secular meanings. Thus, the religious imagery survived and persisted even in a society that grew more and more secular in the period under examination. It is an interesting example of the power, endurance and changeability of religious images which, increasingly in the West, no longer necessarily stand for religious identities but have taken on a life of their own and evoke secularised meanings in different contexts.[72]

Deconstructing Gender and the Visual Turn

The French revolution of 1789, seen by some historians as the birthplace of the modern nation-state, also saw the proliferation of images of women depicting a wide range of revolutionary and republican virtues – above all, liberty, equality, republicanism and nationalism. Joan Landes, one of the pioneers of gender history in the 1980s, turned to these images in 2001 in order to show how they underpinned male attempts to exclude women from the public sphere. Looking in particular at allegory and caricature, she examined a wide range of popular prints circulated between the late

1780s and the 1790s, and argued that the visual and the political rhetoric, so powerfully intertwined, proved instrumental in cementing a male-dominated gender regime in *la patrie*. Although women were never completely banished from the public sphere, the images of the female body representing revolutionary values not only were capable of arousing (sexual) passion among the male fraternity, but also effectively excluded women from a public sphere thought of as an exclusively male sphere by the overwhelming majority of revolutionary men. But it was not just the virtuous republic that was clad in female clothing. The old and decrepit female body was also used extensively to represent aristocratic corruption and debauchery. At the same time, the image of the beautiful young and strong woman was an ideal representation of the republican nation, as it offered a metaphor for a unified community that hid the effective exclusion of one half of that community. Using visual history Landes effectively problematised the emerging bourgeois gender order in the nineteenth-century nation-state, drawing attention to the importance of gendered

Figure 9.12 Official programme of a woman's suffrage procession in Washington, DC, 3 March 1913. Several of the features here are reminiscent of trade union banners, including the medievalism and also the path leading to liberty/liberation. © VCG Wilson/Corbis via Getty Images.

images for the constitution of the male public sphere and the making of both male and female identities in the bourgeois nation-state.[73]

In examining the banners of the suffragist movement, Lisa Tickner has examined how one of the most clichéd gender stereotypes – women engaged in needlework – has helped transform the public images of women.[74] The banners were used to decorate meeting halls and public platforms, and were carried in protest marches. (See Figure 9.12.) Modelled to a certain degree on the older tradition of trade union banners that had underwritten constructions of class since the 1820s (see above), the banners of the women's suffrage movement were aesthetically and materially quite different. That difference was at times exploited by the enemies of both movements, but ultimately the images that were spread through the use of banners served emancipatory movements in both cases.

The performance of gender was also time and again crucial in the staging of colonialism. Visual evidence has been used very effectively to demonstrate the gendered nature of colonialisms. Examples abound, but to mention just one: Wolfram Hartmann's exploration of a range of homo-erotic photographs from the Dickman Collection in the National Archives of Namibia. The manly world of the colonial frontier, complete with safaris, hunting and campsites, was revealed in Dickman's photographic collection as a world that raised 'interesting questions about desire, representation, masculinity and colonialism'.[75] René Dickman was a colonial officer and administrator, of Belgian origin, in the service of the South African colonial state in Namibia in the 1920s and 1930s. According to Hartmann, the photographic evidence left by him showed how the confrontation with the colonial 'other' unsettled gender identities and had to be reconstructed, leaving behind a range of ambiguities.

The gendering of diverse nationalisms has, for some time, been a blossoming sub-field in the history of nationalism.[76] Visual histories of the gendered imagination of nations have contributed much to this field. Thus, for example, Sumathi Ramaswamy has explored how the visual image of the Hindu goddess Bharat Mata (Mother India) drawn upon a map of India has become the ubiquitous symbol of the sacrality of the nation and thereby the most powerful merger between Indian nationalism and the Hindu religion.[77] Nineteenth-century territorialised nationalism was the starting point for the extraordinarily successful transposing of the goddess on to the map of India, serving as a means to emotionalise territorial images such as maps, giving them a strong affective side. 'Barefoot cartographers', Ramaswamy argued, were crucial in ensuring the mass distribution of the dual image of India and Bharat Mata in the twentieth century. Going up to the present day, Ramaswamy's book is a powerful deconstruction of one of the central iconographies of Hindu nationalism today, and this makes her book, in Hayden White's sense (see Chapter 1), part of a 'practical past'.

In a much-cited edited collection on *Gender and Germanness*, Mariatte Denman examined images of madonnas and mourning mothers in post-Second World War West Germany. She showed how, through those images, ideals of family and womanhood that had their roots in the National Socialist period were turned into visual narratives of the victimhood of the German nation that effectively pushed stories of perpetratorship into the background.[78] In making men responsible for war, women, and in particular mourning mothers, came to stand for a de-historised suffering that was transferred to the nation, and made it possible for Germans to see themselves first and foremost as victims of the Second World War. Combining her in-depth analysis of images with insights from Roland Barthes' writings on myths (see

Figure 9.13 War memorial at Neue Wache, Berlin. © Stock Editorial/Getty Images.

Chapter 1), Denman demonstrated how these images still struck a chord in post-Cold War Germany. Thus, Helmut Kohl chose a blown-up version of Käthe Kollwitz's *Pietà* as the central image for the war memorial at the Neue Wache in Berlin. (See Figure 9.13.) As with Ramaswamy's work on India, Denman's work on Germany thus comments on the relevance of constructions of collective identities in the past for the present day.

Whilst Denman concentrated on the work of artists and images to be found in popular culture in post-war Germany, other historians have focused on film. They have indicated how much the history of film contributed to the visual turn in historical thinking and writing. Examining the images produced by the West German post-war Heimatfilm, Ingeborg Majer O'Sickey pointed to the amazing continuities inherent in this genre, not only in terms of actors, but also in terms of the messages conveyed by the genre in National Socialist Germany and in the early Federal Republic. Vulnerable animals of the forest, such as the little deer Bambi, became images of femininity that had to be protected, because they were always in danger of falling prey to the male gaze. Images of womanhood and femininity in a kind of alternative Heimat movie only began to change in the 1990s, when stronger, more self-confident women appeared on cinema screens and the earlier gendered images were deconstructed through film.[79]

Conclusion

As indicated by the above examples, ranging widely over visual histories of nation, ethnicity, race, class, religion and gender, historians have played a prominent role in seeking to unravel how images constructed a diverse range of collective identities. They thus effectively contributed to a de-essentialisation of those constructions of collective identities.[80] If seeing itself was a biological faculty, visualising was a cultural and social action. The aim of visual historians has been to reconstruct the multiple ways of seeing and how those acts of seeing were related to underpinning particular social and cultural identities.

The making of images involved intent; in other words, those who created and paid for the images wanted to convey a particular message. However, we have also seen that, time and again, images could be read differently by those consuming them. Many involuntary meanings have been attributed to images. Highlighting the plurality of ways of seeing has been another way of demonstrating that identities could never be fixed through images but remained forever fluid. This fluidity had much to do with the power wielded over images by a highly diverse set of actors from the state and from civil society, all of whom mobilised identitarian images that, time and again, took on a life of their own, as they were remoulded, re-interpreted and remade over the course of time. Visual historians, often making use of theoretical frameworks discussed in the first chapter of this book, have thus contributed in substantial ways to breaking the link between history writing and essentialised forms of collective identity formation. As we shall see in the next chapter, the same is true for historians of material culture.

Further Reading

Gil Bartholeyns, 'History of Visual Culture', in: Marek Tamm and Peter Burke (eds.), *Debating New Approaches to History*, London: Bloomsbury, 2019, 247–76.

Horst Bredekamp, *Image Acts: a Systematic Approach to Visual Agency*, Berlin: De Gruyter, 2018.

Ian Heywood and Barry Sandywell (eds.), *The Handbook of Visual Culture*, London: Bloomsbury, 2011.

Richard Howells and Joaquim Negreiros (eds.), *Visual Culture*, Cambridge: Polity Press, 2012.

Nicholas Mirzoeff, *An Introduction to Visual Culture*, London: Routledge, 1999.

10 *The History of Material Culture*

Introduction

Cultural historians intent on moving beyond text rediscovered, not only images, but also material objects as primary sources for historical research. All sorts of material objects, from houses and clothing to toothbrushes and money, have become the focus of major historical studies seeking to explore the relationship between people and things. Sometimes things also include other living things, such as animals and plants. Things are of the past and they can tell stories about the past. Just as we found in the case of images in the previous chapter, things themselves possess agency – through their materiality they create and shape experiences and are involved in constructing identities.[1] Humans and things have a reciprocal relationship. Humans value things because they are meaningful to them and speak to their sense of self; in other words, they speak to who we think we are and, in many ways, make us into who we are. As Tim LeCain put it:

> humans do not just manipulate a clearly separate and distinct material environment that exists beyond the bounds of our genes, bodies, brains and minds. Rather, this material environment is the very stuff out of which the changing and evolving amalgam that we call human emerges ... [M]aterial things ... helped to create who we are in all dimensions: biological, social and cultural.[2]

Material things from the past are routes to past experiences and identities. In this chapter I will, first, discuss some of the major theoretical and methodological frames used by historians of material culture. Subsequently I will give examples of how some of these historians have used their histories of material culture to challenge notions of essentialised and fixed collective identities. In the strikingly transdisciplinary field of material culture studies, archaeologists like Ian Hodder, sociologists like Tony Bennett and historians like Patrick

Joyce have been trailblazers on the way to being far more self-reflective about how scholarship is constructing and deconstructing the objects of their examinations, including those related to collective identities.[3]

What Is in a Thing?

'Material culture ... refers to the entire complex of relationships between objects, their meanings and people.'[4] In this definition of material culture, made by two of the leading practitioners of the history of material culture, the 'meanings' are situated between the objects and the people, thereby indicating how meanings cannot be reduced to the meanings people give to them.[5] Acknowledging the material presence of the past means accepting the agency of things, including the bones of bodies killed in the past. Both Paco Ferrándiz's studies on the memorial battles being waged in present-day Spain, surrounding the dead of the civil war, and Ewa Domanska's reflections on the presence of disappeared persons in Argentinian memory politics illustrate this.[6] Most historians of material culture today are convinced that objects speak for themselves; in other words, their very materiality produces meaning outside human cognition. Where does their understanding of the relationship between humans and the things that surround them come from?

A concern with material culture is as old as humankind, but, as Anne Gerittsen and Giorgio de Riello have argued, the successful professionalisation of historical writing in the nineteenth century sidelined an interest in material culture and prioritised the archive and the written text over any other historical evidence.[7] In Britain, for example, the so-called antiquarian scholarship, which preceded professional historical writing, paid a lot of attention to material objects. Antiquarians gathered many objects for their local and regional histories, and their explorations into ancient pre-modern cultures, such as the Romano-British one, rested on these collections of things. These 'antiquities' often became nationalised in the course of the seventeenth and eighteenth centuries, making objects into things that began to signify Englishness or Britishness, as the case may be.[8] The more history as an academic discipline became institutionalised and professionalised, the more material culture became the preserve of archaeologists and anthropologists, i.e. sciences where written evidence was supposed to be rare. Historians were concerned with the past as it was collected in the form of texts and preserved in archives.[9] It was only from the 1980s onwards that this belief was challenged. Arjun Appadurai's much-lauded edited collection *The Social Life of Things*, published in 1986, was an example of how diverse scholars drew attention to the importance of considering objects and their 'social lives'.[10] Asa Briggs' study on *Victorian Things*, first published in 1988, confirmed a trend among historians to turn to the material worlds of everyday objects.[11] In many cases the emphasis was on commodities.[12] Much subsequent work focused on the history of consumption and the role of objects for people's identities as consumers in a modern consumer society from the early modern times to the present day.[13] The pathbreaking work of Sidney Minz on sugar consumption set the scene for a whole string of histories of particular commodities, often to do with food, clothing and housing. Minz traced the way in which the consumption of sugar changed from a luxury article for the rich to an everyday article for the great mass of consumers. Attentive to the symbolical aspects of sugar consumption, he analysed the multiple meanings of social rituals associated with its consumption.[14]

Like many of the 'new histories' discussed in previous chapters, the history of material culture was also characterised by strong doses of transdisciplinarity. I have already mentioned the important role of anthropology. Cultural and human geographers were prominent among the scholarship examining the interrelationship between things and human actions.[15] In literary studies Bill Brown has developed 'thing theory': drawing on Martin Heidegger's distinction between 'objects' and 'things', he looked at how things were related to a multiplicity of human identities.[16] Lyn Pykett has drawn attention to the fascination with things during the Victorian age, arguing that new approaches to its culture and literature were possible through paying more attention to diverse aspects of this obsession of the Victorians with material things.[17] In political philosophy, Jane Bennett has been writing about 'enchanted materialism', effectively countering Max Weber's famous thesis about the interrelationship of modernity with processes of disenchantment.[18] In sociology, Alex Preda argued that the discipline needs to take more seriously things as active social agents that are constitutive for societies and have the ability to stabilise, reproduce but also undermine social order.[19] Momin Rahman and Anne Witz drew attention to the usefulness for feminist thinking on gender and sexuality of new concepts of materiality that they traced back to poststructuralist engagements with material culture.[20]

The turn of historians to material culture made it necessary to acquire new skills. Reading was no longer enough. As with visual history, discussed in the previous chapter, the turn to material culture necessitated much broader aesthetic, visual and haptic competences that were all crucial for the historian's ability to interpret objects. The turn to material culture was in many ways a critical response to the linguistic turn and its emphasis on language producing contested social realities. If everything was text and if nothing existed outside texts,[21] the materiality of things was in danger of disappearing. Some historians began to argue that humans made experiences with things, that they interacted with objects and that the material world around them mattered for their understanding of that world. They looked to linguists who argued that language developed in a direct relation to humans making experiences with objects. New insights from the neurosciences were also hugely influential in bolstering the belief that, not only language development, but the development of the human self, too, could not be reduced to texts.[22]

Having said this, most historians of material culture also recognised that material things rarely exist completely independently of text. In some sense they were not so much refuting many of the insights of proponents of the linguistic turn as building on these insights in order to move to an understanding where both the material world and texts about the material world could be used to understand more fully how the past was shaped. As the human engagement with things has an impact on language and ideas, the need is less to juxtapose language and matter than to think both together and look at embodied practices and the nexus between materiality and discursivity. The aim of historical endeavours has to be to unearth the intimate connections existing between the cultural and the material. In this sense, the history of material culture is, like the 'linguistic turn', rooted in the cultural turn of the human sciences in the 1980s.[23] If we take the example of the history of the body once again,[24] the material turn has opened new vistas on to material practices connected to bodies and the material-based nature of human encounters, but these material practices had to be brought into dialogue with the diverse representations of the body that had been discursively produced.[25]

Historians of material culture began to see texts themselves as material objects, and researchers took the materiality of texts in diverse media more seriously when writing about them.[26] They paid attention to things such as what typeface was used, what quality the paper had, what the binding was like, how printed works were illustrated and what the relationship between printed word and illustration was – and many other details that refer to the object character of books, newspapers and other genres in which texts were produced. Questions of the production, distribution, ownership, reception, cost and value of these texts moved into the foreground of exploration. To give one example among many of how artefacts made global connections possible, the history of the materiality of books traced their global circulation through translations, receptions, copying and adaptations.

Medieval historians of Europe have recently pointed out how the making of transregional gender identities was made, in no small part, through the circulation of objects.[27] Women of high aristocratic birth usually travelled across the borders of kingdoms or dukedoms to marry, taking with them a range of objects that thus circulated from one historical context to another. These included textiles, religious ceremonial items, manuscripts, jewellery, paintings and many everyday items, but also livestock such as horses, and skills brought by master artisans travelling with their aristocratic mistresses. As connectors, translators and bridge-builders between different places and cultures, they had a powerful influence on the transregional creation of styles and the circulation of skills in different parts of Europe. Empress Theodora of Byzantium and Eleanor of Aquitaine are famous examples of widely travelled aristocratic women who, on their travels, left and acquired objects which in their new homelands developed an agency of their own. (See Figure 10.1.)

Historians of material culture have described human relationships with things in all their complexity. Humans consumed things and exchanged them; they destroyed them and collected them; they named them and classified them. In other words, they provided an 'order of things' already alluded to in Foucault's famous text, first published in French in 1966.[28] However, representatives of the linguistic turn had paid more attention to what Foucault had to say about words and discourse than what he had to say about 'things'. Historians of material culture now re-read Foucault, unearthing his close attention to material culture. They pointed out that things

Figure 10.1 Empress Theodora and her retinue. Bzyantine mosaic in the apse of the Basilica of San Vitale, Ravenna. Detail. © DEA/A. De Gregorio/De Agostini via Getty Images.

existed in relation to human thinking about things. Things influenced that thinking and that thinking in turn ascribed different meanings to them.[29]

Things often have specific meanings in specific societies and cultural contexts in which the thingness is clear to members of the same society or cultural context. It becomes far more complicated if a thing intervenes in the relations between people belonging to different societies and cultural contexts. Then, unequal power relationships between these different societies may further complicate matters.[30] Objects may reveal, but they may also hide, power relationships. Given that many material objects connected regions across time and space, the meaning of a thing may well be re-appropriated and re-inscribed; it may become contested and the object of differing claims. Yet, such perspectives on things still often give pride of place to humans, who, in different circumstances, form a different (albeit sometimes related) relationship to things. Yet, as they considered the relationship between humans and their environment, historians of material culture grew increasingly convinced that human agency needed to be decentred. A more materialist understanding of history, many argued, required a less anthropocentric understanding of the past. Who we are as humans, they asserted, has less to do with our minds and our creativity and more to do with the material things all around us. And these things existed in their own right; they did not need humans. As Bruno Latour, a hugely influential theorist for historians of material culture, famously put it:

> Things-in-themselves? But they are fine, thank you very much ... You complain about things that have not been honoured by your vision? ... But if you missed the galloping freedom of the zebras in the savannah this morning, then so much the worse for you; the zebras will not be sorry that you were not there ... Things in themselves lack nothing, just as Africa did not lack whites before their arrival.[31]

Drawing heavily on Latour's actor-network theory, Ben Anderson and John Wylie, among others, pointed to what they called the imperatives of matter in the 'material imagination' and showed how these are dispersed, repeated and diverge in ever-changing constellations. Underlining the organising potential of materiality, they distinguished between three different types of materiality: turbulent, interrogative and excessive. All of them heavily limited the agency of human beings.[32] Also heavily influenced by Latour, 'non-representational theory' has emphasised how things and humans form hybrid assemblages endowed with a sense of agency and even personhood. The material and the social thus cannot be separated any more. In his magisterial attempt to summarise the ambitions of 'non-representational theory', Nigel Thrift has insisted that it is impossible to think of identities, whether individual or collective, as homogenous and whole. Looking at diverse forms of embodied, corporeal action in everyday life that establish manifold and contested meanings would, he argued, allow scholars working with 'non-representational theory' to highlight how materiality was at the heart of many social and cultural developments and also form the basis for an affective 'ethics of hope'. This Thrift sees as the basis of contemporary political action.[33]

Latour and others problematised the anthropocentrism of current thinking about agency in the world. Problematising the Anthropocene, i.e. the contemporary age in which humans think that the world moves round them, became part and parcel of what historians of material culture were about.[34] Relativising the importance of the human mind and of human agency in history – moving towards posthuman history[35] – also influenced a range of historians who, in their histories, had focused on humanity. The postcolonial historian Dipesh Chakrabarty, for example, admitted that he was deeply impressed by the work of those who had challenged the human-centredness of the historical profession, even if he did conclude: 'histories of intrahuman (in)justice will remain relevant and necessary. But we will probably have to think of them in the much larger context of the history of life, how earth-history connects to it, and where humans figure in it overall.'[36] Historians of material culture argued that humans had been, for historians, too long at the centre of interest. This was due to centuries-old Christian traditions of prioritising the allegedly immaterial mind and soul of humans. The idealist presumptions of Hegelian philosophy and, in the twentieth century, Collingwood's philosophy of history, together with the postmodernist idea that the world can be reduced to texts produced by humans, were just secularised variants of this religious belief. Instead, historians of material culture asserted the right of things to be regarded as creative and destructive forces in history in their own right.[37] Chris Otter, in his book on changes in the nineteenth-century British diet, used the British example to show how the modern global food system came about and how it led directly to the contemporary world food crisis. Linking the human desire for more meat and carbohydrates with an ecologically destructive system of food production highlights the ultimately destructive and exploitative relationship between humans and the material world around them.[38] Historians argued that the very materiality of things, their shape, function and decoration, had the power to create and shape the world around them, including human identities. Things and objects, including biological things, had to be taken seriously as active agents. Human identity was not a construction of human minds, but was at least to some extent constructed out of objects and through objects and in the co-evolution, through processes of domestication, with biological things.[39]

In fact, many historians of material culture have argued compellingly for abandoning the distinction between the natural and the human-made, as the two have been so closely intertwined that one can only speak about one if, at the same time, one also refers to the other. According to Latour, all subjects and objects are already always hybrids. The social and the technical are mixed up with the natural and the cultural in ways that make it impossible draw neat boundaries around any of those concepts. Materiality, discursivity, the real and the imagined have to be thought together without falling back on to new essentialisms.[40] If this is the case, then human culture, including collective identities, emerges with and from the material and discursive worlds around us. Decentring humans from our histories would not, however, necessarily lead to a new form of anti-humanism. According to LeCain, rather the reverse is true. His plea for a 'neo-materialist humanism' as 'a richer and more inclusive humanism'[41] echoes through much of the literature of the new materialism. Its advocates argue that greater self-reflexivity about the relationship between humans and the world around them would lead humans to lead a more responsible life vis-à-vis their environments. They would recognise that they could only fulfil their potential as humans in tandem with, rather than against, the material world surrounding them.

Historians of material culture have also pointed out that material artefacts often existed for a very long time – sometimes centuries. This raises questions about their origins and their original use, but also about how their usage changed over time and how this affected the meanings they carried. The malleability of meanings and agencies related to objects undermines any notion that an object has an essential and non-changing identity. As objects relate to human identities, this highlights also the degree to which these human identities were forever changing. Studying things means presenting the past in ways that highlight stranded, failed or never completed projects of the past to which these objects, properly contextualised, belong. Objects thus complicate the past and make it less likely that it can be streamlined and homogenised in master narratives which underpin collective identities. Precisely because things can never be fully controlled by human cognition, in their afterlife they might point to past futures that have not come to fruition. Things may talk about relationships to constructions of identity no longer persisting in the present. Therefore, Olsen talks about the 'unruly agency' of things and of 'undisciplined things'.[42] Although many things persist in their materiality longer than the humans they interact with, it is precisely the longevity of things that adds instability. Not only do they themselves change over time, they are also used differently and acquire different meanings for different people and generations. If they are exchanged and change place this often adds to the instability of their meaning, as it adds layers of usages and interpretations that are increased with restorative work performed on the objects in question. Things have many lives – parallel lives and succeeding lives. Even if the maker's intention can be clearly established, which is often very difficult, this intention can be appropriated in diverse ways by others depending on time and place.

Many historians who turned to things focused on everyday objects and their meaning for people in their everyday lives. Hence, histories of material culture have often been closely aligned with everyday life histories and historical anthropology, discussed in Chapter 6. This is hardly surprising, given that anthropology, because of its earlier concerns with material culture, was one of the inspirations for historians of material culture. The concern with the everyday, as we have noted above, already undermined the earlier concern of historical writing with grand narratives related to collective identities. Historical anthropology was no longer prima facie about national, ethnic and class identities, but more about how people lived their everyday lives and how they used objects to give meaning to them. In an article on garage sales in America, Gretchen Hermann has pointed out that the objects sold there often had great personal value for those selling them. The purchasers then were equally keen to show that the objects would find a good new home with them because they cherished the object more because of the personal meaning invested in it.[43] (See Figure 10.2.) Hermann's article reflected an ever-growing interest among historians in personal identities and how things shaped them. However, the personal identities of people were often related to the construction of larger identities – as women, as workers, as members of religious congregations and, yes, also as members of imagined national and ethnic communities. If objects were endowed with aesthetic and cultural value, they were used as markers of distinction, and Pierre Bourdieu's writings on distinction and taste had already clearly signalled the importance of things for the reproduction and delineation of social classes. Things and their performance signalled social status.[44] Hence the history of material culture also had things to say about how collective identities were constructed in the past.

Figure 10.2 Highway 127 yard sale in Kentucky, USA. It boasts thousands of personal vendors every year. © Education Images/Universal Images Group via Getty Images.

Figure 10.3 US Longhorn cattle. © Andy Cross/*Denver Post* via Getty Images.

Things and Their Impact on the Construction of Collective Identities

In discussing American and Japanese national identities, LeCain demonstrated how these identities were constructed in a close and constant exchange with their material environments. Thus the American ideas of the west and the frontier, so crucial to constructions of American identity, were forged through the 'Longhorn' – the epitome of the American open-range cattle industry, without which many of the central tenets of what it meant to be American could not have been sustained. Similarly LeCain pointed out that the silkworm, as the basis of the Japanese silk industry, was instrumental in developing Japan's industrial potential and made it possible for Japan to develop ideas of being the West in the East, i.e. of catching up in terms of modernity and industrial development with the West and becoming part of it. Japan's and America's encounter with a third material object, copper, enabled both the Japanese and the Americans to perceive themselves as representing industrial modernity, since copper allowed them to develop powerful navies and light their cities with electricity. The encounter with copper, in both the USA and Japan, remade the world that had been made through the encounter with the Longhorn and the silkworm respectively, remaking American and Japanese identities respectively. Americans and Japanese sacrificed Longhorns and silkworms and gave up their ways of life associated with these animals and industries, because the material power of a metal, copper, was remaking ways of life and ways of defining Americannness and Japaneseness.[45]

A new materially grounded history has contributed in other ways to the reconceptualisation of national histories. Mark Fiege's *The Republic of Nature*, for example, has re-interpreted central chapters in American history by drawing attention to their materialist underpinnings. The Salem witch trials, for example, cannot be understood without taking into account the early settlers' inability to produce the agricultural crops needed to sustain their existence. Unable to understand their failure, they turned to witchcraft as an explanation of why the land was not bearing the fruit they had been hoping to reap through their self-assured techniques of agricultural production. Their failure to understand their biophysical environment thus directly produced one of the most iconic events in early American history. The Gettysburg battle of the American civil war, Fiege argued, was won by Union troops against the Confederacy because they had superior supplies. Union soldiers were better equipped and better fed due to a hinterland of canals, railroad and port cities that allowed them to be in much better shape than those of the Confederacy. Material things rather than human power or the ingenuity of the minds of generals decided one of the defining battles in American history.[46]

Fiege is a prominent US environmental historian. The phenomenal growth of environmental history over recent years has established a thriving sub-field of historical writing that is closely aligned with the material turn in historical studies. Starting in the 1970s environmental historians have explored a wide array of topics, including the history of pollution, landscape history, animal history, natural history (and its commodification), the history of rivers, forests and bacteria, and the history of human waste, to mention just a few prominent themes. It would have been perfectly feasible to add a whole chapter on environmental history in this volume, as it certainly has acquired a new urgency and a new popularity with the public discussions on climate and environmental change that accelerated from the 1990s onwards.[47] Environmental perspectives have increasingly been informing theories of history, most prominently in the discussions surrounding 'the Anthropocene', i.e. the idea of humans shaping an entire geological era through their interference with geology and climate.[48] Environmental historians have been at the forefront of redirecting history away from the idea that it consists only of the history of human intentions. Instead environmental historians have heightened our awareness about the manifold interconnections between humans and the non-human world. These interactions shaped human identities in a variety of different ways, as the biophysical environment shaped human experiences without ever determining them completely. Many environmental histories have thus contributed to de-essentialising the relationship between nature and culture. Whilst there is no ecological determinism in history, environmental change has to be brought together with cultural and social change in order to understand the exchanges and flows between nature and culture that transformed human identities over time and place. Without a proper understanding of ecological factors and ecosystems it is near impossible to account for historical developments, including the contested nature of human identities.

Thus, environmental historians in the USA have pointed out the extent to which the conquering of 'wild' nature has become part and parcel of American national identity and its central narrative of a land of progress and modernity. Frederic Jackson Turner's notion of the 'frontier' nation has been problematised by environmental historians who highlighted the negative impact of deforestation, the mass extinction of animals and the genocide of America's first nations on American eco-systems. Destructive farming techniques, the manipulation of waterways and the destruction of regional ecologies gave a different twist to the familiar triumphalist story of the 'frontier' nation, as did the highlighting of ecological imperialism, i.e. the stress put on the import of non-native animals, plants and diseases, with their negative impact on indigenous species, including human populations. In this new look at the national master narrative, it was not great men who made America. Instead, it was ecological developments that allowed the specific course of history to take its turn. The agency of things was intricately related to the agency of humans. The traditional national narrative had also classed the 'native Indian American', itself a colonialist construction, as 'primitive', for living in close harmony with nature. By contrast, the all-conquering white American hero had mastered nature, and this mastery, called 'civilisation', gave him a superior edge vis-à-vis the 'Indian American'. As environmental historians recast the story of the 'Indian Americans' to make them the heroes of sustainable living in harmony with the nature around them, they simply took over the binary construction of the old American master narrative and turned it on its head – something subsequently critiqued by postcolonial scholarship on Native Americans. Only a blurring of the boundaries between the natural and cultural made it possible to see how binary constructions of identity had essentialised both America's first nations and the white settlers who came to think of themselves as Americans.[49]

The history of indigeneity and of indigenous peoples has been another sub-field of historical writing that has been thriving over recent years.[50] Under the influence of postcolonial and poststructuralist theories but also increasingly the new materialist history, they have exploded the binary constructions that have for so long essentialised indigenous identities. Indigenous people were neither 'primitives' clinging on to superstition, irrationality and savage customs, nor were they the ones living always in harmony and a non-exploitative relationship with nature. Racialised, gendered and classed concepts have long stereotyped indigeneity and produced a whole host of cultural constructions of 'the indigenous', which tried to get rid of the fluidity and ambiguity of any attempt to define indigeneity. The recent reluctance to ascribe an identity to 'the indigenous' from the outside is a clear sign of the intention to focus on the multiple and contested definitions of indigeneity. Like environmental history and the history from below, indigenous history emerged in the 1970s from the desire to give a voice to the voiceless and to see their history through their own eyes. Historians took the perspective of the oppressed and the persecuted, highlighting their agency, including their resistance to domination. Their histories contributed to building the foundations of an identity politics of indigenous peoples that, on the one hand, demanded recognition and support, but on the other hand, at least with the best of that history, also produced forms of identitification, in Stuart Hall's sense (see Chapter 1), which was highly self-reflective about the construction of identities, in particular avoiding essentialisms.

Elsewhere, historians of first nations and ethnic minorities have made extensive use of the history of material culture to tell counter-narratives about collective identities. Indigenous historians of New Zealand, for example, studied tattooing as a form of cultural collective memory and resistance to colonial domination.[51] Historians of New Zealand have also presented things as intriguing 'pathways into the country's colonial history'.[52] Objects, today contained in museums and art galleries,[53] but also occupying treasured places on family mantelpieces and part of the everyday environment, such as tin billies, roads and buildings, all tell multiple tales about encounters between colonialist and Māori cultures. They reveal materially grounded practices which led to the building of institutions and social structures that were an integral part of the making of colonial and postcolonial New Zealand. Roads, for example, were vital in opening up Māori territories to colonialisation. Changes to race and gender relations were contained in objects that took on new meanings as they changed hands over time and place. Colonial practices as well as anti-colonial resistances around the transfer of lands were recorded in Māori Land Court Record books. The Māori New Testament speaks of religious encounters, and many objects have stories of circulation and transfers to tell that link the history of New Zealand to places such as China, South Africa, the United States and Australia. The sensual and intimate character of many of these objects and the emotional value they carried add substantially to the representational and symbolic value of the material objects, throwing light on colonial and postcolonial identities in New Zealand.

Historians have similarly used objects to tell stories about postcolonial national identities. Drawing on the work of anthropologist Victor Turner, Kathleen Adams, a historian of Indonesia, has shown how the multivocality of objects, in her case a traditional Toraja house structure, called tongkonan, built by a small ethnic minority in Indonesia, has made it impossible to relate that object in an unequivocal and essentialised way to specific constructions of Indonesian national identity. This is not for lack of trying. But the object's multivocal nature has time and again evaded fixations of meaning and essentialisation.[54]

Histories of the 'black continent' have often been haunted by the colonial image of African history as being predominantly a history of different tribes. Histories working with material culture approaches have been able to undermine this construction of the dominance of tribal allegiances and identities in sub-Saharan Africa. The work of Ann Brower Stahl on the frontier region of Banda in central Ghana analysed in detail how, over a period of almost seven hundred years, different interpretations of the region's history have relied on anthropological, archaeological and historical evidence to produce different lineages, all of which end in a differently conceptualised present. Stahl used archaeological evidence to show how the region was formed by networks of exchange that were both regional and global, and involved, over time, trade routes of the Niger, the Atlantic and the British colonial empire. The material remains that were at the heart of Stahl's analysis allowed her to look at diverse aspects of daily life that constituted distinctions between different groups of people. These in turn were at the heart of social and cultural power relationships in the region. Through material artefacts, she recuperated local voices and family histories, in order to comment on beliefs and rituals that brought to life a community that was part and parcel of global historical processes that cannot be adequately described in terms of the 'tribal' paradigm.[55]

Another example of a national history that has been re-interpreted using material culture approaches is that of China. Frank Dikötter, in his study on the reception of Western objects in China,[56] has shown to what extent they were enthusiastically received, copied and consumed, not only by an elite but also by mass consumers. He demonstrated how they became an integral part of something later constructed as specifically Chinese. In other words, objects imported from different cultural context were made into something that was 'one's own'. Dikötter built on Michel de Certeau's theoretical insights (see Chapter 1) about how the ordinary usage of objects in different cultural contexts did not necessarily lead to uniformisation but can equally result in adaptations that are both diverse and specific.[57] This allowed him to highlight how a very pragmatic approach to foreign objects and a willingness to assimilate them into Chinese culture made China capable of adapting modernity where it found it. His object history is thus a good example of how histories of material culture can decentre essentialised notions of national identity and national self, and instead demonstrate the extent to which these alleged national cultures rely on the reception of elements coming from outside.

Design history, i.e. the history of objects made by designers, has also been usefully related to questions of national identity. Javier Gimeno-Martinez noted how, from the fifteenth century onwards, particular fashion items were associated with specific national identities.[58] Costumes became national symbols represented in folk art and painting, collected and displayed in museums. Gimeno-Martinez analysed in detail how nation-states actively promoted national design schools in order to associate nations with a particular design often seen as internationally desirable. To this day, one can find references to the particular quality and beauty of, for example, Italian, Danish or Swedish design, when it comes to fashion, furniture or technical objects, such as cars. The design of national emblems and bank notes are other examples he discussed extensively. However, he also noted how ideas about national design were not just promoted by states from above. They also emerged powerfully from the midst of civil society. Here he used examples of companies like IKEA, whose global power as a furniture giant is closely associated with the promotion of Swedishness in design. Finally, he also pointed to the impact multiculturalism has had on design. In a world where migration and diaspora have impacted on many national territories, design histories have provided us with various examples of fusion and transfer when it comes to objects and their design.

Next to design history, architectural history has played an important role in highlighting the manifold ways in which things were related to

Figure 10.4 Assembly Building and Reflecting Pool, Chandigarh, India. © Glasshouse Images, The Image Bank via Getty Images

the contested constructions of national identity. Examining the long history of designing capitals in line with specific national and imperial designs and master narratives, Lawrence Vale paid special attention to the design of parliamentary complexes in Washington, DC, Canberra, Brasilia, Ankara, New Delhi and Chandigarh, before turning to four examples of postcolonial capitals in Papua New Guinea, Sri Lanka, Kuwait and Bangladesh.[59] (See Figure 10.4.) Designers, architects and politicians take centre stage in this book, as they often co-operated and sometimes clashed over particular ways of constructing and reading national identity through material objects. Vale highlighted the degree to which the design of key political buildings in national capitals was undertaken in transnational conversation with other buildings. In particular, he underlined the impact both of imperial cores on imperial peripheries and of imperial peripheries on each other. The parliamentary complexes built by diverse political regimes reveal a great deal about the different nationalist ideologies of the regimes in question, and the material culture history that is foregrounded here is one that actively deconstructs the way in which buildings carry (usually contested) meanings related to constructions of national identity.

Historians of national identity have often noted how the national was associated with particular territorial, geographical definitions. Swiss national identity was unthinkable without the mountains; the sea played a major role in imaginations of nation in all maritime nations; and what would the German nation be without forests, or the USA without the 'wild' landscapes of 'the West'? The same strong link between space, territory and identity is true for regions, and Helen Berry has demonstrated the extent to which a history of material culture can throw light on regional identities – in her case the regional identity of the north-east of England.[60] Berry noted how a history of material objects can be written in pursuit of the construction of an essentialised, unchanging construction of region. Alternative stories and change over time tend to be excluded. Against the backdrop of such authoritative constructions of a regional identity by a history from above, Berry considered the use of material culture in histories from below. Such histories from below had attempted to reconsider histories of local places in many parts of the world since the 1970s and they had tried to give a voice to those who had remained voiceless in the top-down exclusionary narratives. They had, in other words, disrupted homogenising top-down storylines. In my own attempt to assemble the mnemohistory of the Ruhr region in Germany, the history of material culture certainly took pride of place: the motorways criss-crossing the region, the canals, the rivers, the parks, the smoke produced by the chimneystacks of the Ruhr, industrial buildings, slagheaps, religious items, things brought by the tens of thousands of migrants to the region, objects used by miners and steelworkers in their daily work in the hundreds of mines and steelworks that once were a byword for the region, coal, iron, steel, civic architecture, working-class housing estates, food, such as Currywurst and Döner Kebab, beer in a region once boasting hundreds of breweries, football, pubs, discounter stores, weapons (the production of which also made the region famous), strike banners, and political pins and posters – all feature prominently there. (See Figure 10.5.) The materiality of the memory landscape of the Ruhr allows for a decentred and kaleidoscopic portrayal of contested and competing identity narratives that can be related to politics and the unequal distribution of power between different groups populating the Ruhr. In this way, a memory history of material culture contributes to problematising regional identity constructions and promoting greater self-awareness of how those

Figure 10.5 Headgear of Zeche Zollverein in Essen, Germany. UNESCO world heritage site. This iconic site for industrial heritage in the Ruhr area of Germany has become the symbol of a widespread heritagisation underpinning the anchoring of a strong regional identity in the industrial past of the region, which needs to be questioned by a regional history intent on pluralising and problematising this strong link between collective identity constructions and heritigisation. © Dirk Herdramm/EyeEm via Getty Images.

constructions have been associated with different political, social and cultural interests.[61]

Not only national and regional identities, but also class identities, were forged in dialogue with things and materiality. Thus, as Thomas Andrews has argued, class solidarities were forged in direct contact with the materials with which workers worked – in his case coal. The material nature of coal and the methods of its extraction from under the ground go a long way to explaining how a sense of common class identity emerged among miners.[62] Everyday material objects also shaped nineteenth-century middle-class identities. As Manuel Charpy argued, the development of locks, alarm and intercom systems allowed the middle classes to put a safe distance between themselves and the street.[63] Middle-class dress in the nineteenth century had to be impractical, as its intention was to signal the ability of its wearers to remain idle or, at best, to engage in intellectual work. Top hats for men and corsets for women imposed body languages that signalled arrogance in the case of the top hat and dependency on others to get dressed/undressed in the case of the corset. Yet, especially with regard to the corset, Valerie Steele has shown that its history cannot be reduced to a history of the male oppression of women. Undoubtedly, that was one side of the story, but not all advocates of women's liberation were enemies of the corset. At the same time, many medical practitioners, far removed from the goals of women's liberation, argued that the corset was adversely affecting women's ability to reproduce. Hence, in the case of just one single item of fashion, Steele showed how it could be used in highly contested ways to further a range of highly gendered and conflicting identities at different times and in different places.[64]

Clothing often spoke to gendered class identities. White clothes became a symbol of middle-class cleanliness. Fragile and complex materials indicated that one had the time and money to care for them properly.[65] Like clothes, furniture also regulated middle-class lifestyles.[66] Particular types of furniture signalled specific ways of behaving. Thus, the middle-class desire to copy furniture that was believed to be aristocratic underlined the extent to which the middle classes were keen to model themselves on those who were once their social superiors. Arranging furniture in an orderly fashion signalled the middle-class ability to keep social order. Middle-class houses became spaces where public and private, male and female, upstairs and downstairs became neatly ordered and separated. Middle-class girls were taught such order through dolls' houses and mini-kitchens. Within such middle-class households dress codes also determined the relations between the mistress and master of the house and their servants. Power relationships were expressed through clothing. Self-observation and self-fashioning became an obsession in middle-class households, indicated by the popularity of writing desks with many secret compartments, which often held writings about oneself that one did not want to be publicly known, photographs and personal memorabilia, as well as collected objects, including jewellery, artwork and hairstyles, which constructed a sense of self. Other social groups chose to distinguish themselves from the middle classes by adopting their own sense of style through objects. Once again, clothing took pride of place. Unkempt hair and baggy clothing signalled bohemian rejection of bourgeois dress codes and values. Workers' blue overalls and cloth caps indicated a separate social group, even if the tradition of the 'Sunday best' amounted to a nod in the direction of middle-class dress codes.[67]

Histories of material objects have helped us better to understand constructions of class; they have also massively advanced our decoding of the construction of gendered identities. Stacey Alaimo and Susan Hekmans edited a voluminous tome in 2008 with the aim of bringing about a 'material turn' in feminist theory. The linguistic turn, they argued, had been vital for feminist theory and a better understanding of the development of gender relations. However, they were also adamant that it was accompanied by a 'retreat from materiality' that had negative effects on the understanding of gender regimes. In relation to the human body, they argued that it is not enough to talk about it as a discursive construct. What was needed, they argued, was to take seriously the material nature of bodies and to talk about bodily experiences. We need to understand what material processes went on within bodies and how those related to power over bodies. Careful contextualisation of the materiality of bodily experiences can further our understanding of the contested sites of gender constructions in history.[68] Karen Barad, in tracing how the human was materialised over time, turned to the performativity of the natural world, of which humans are a part.[69] Her 'agential realism' reconciled materiality and nature with a non-essential, changing understanding of collective identities, including gender identities.

There are, by now, many examples of how historians of material culture have re-interpreted gender identities. As Hannah Greig, Jane Hamlett and Leonie Hanna have written: 'ideas about gender and the material world are closely connected. Gender informs things and, in turn, the things people own inform conceptions and perceptions of gender in wide-ranging ways.'[70] Attention to the 'gendering of the material world', they argued, 'can allow us to connect cultural ideas of masculinity and feminity with the everyday practices of everyday life and individual experience'.[71] Stella Moss' treatment of how the spatial arrangement in pubs and the objects encountered in specific places in pubs contributed to the gendered social behaviour of pub-goers is a good example of this link between the analysis of objects and a deeper understanding of gendered experiences.[72] How gender identities were interrelated with identities of race, class and nation in the clothing of the colonised in colonial Sri Lanka is another fascinating example of how the materiality of bodies and dresses fostered a contested, contradictory and changing sense of self. Highlighting the playfulness of those identities, Nira Wickramasinghe positioned dress as a creative and political act, the multiple meanings of which can be analysed by careful historical contextualisation and investigation.[73]

The history of material culture can also be usefully applied to religious identities. Take, for example, Uthara Suvrathan's discussion of sacred landscapes in Banavasi, south India during ancient and early medieval times.[74] She found manifold interactions between a great number of religious practices. Local religious cults intermingled with more mainstream Buddhist and Hinduist traditions. Suvrathan investigated Brahmanical, elite and pan-Indian religious practices (referred to as 'Great Tradition'), but also analysed village, folk and lower caste traditions (what she calls 'Little Tradition'). Relating evidence from inscriptions to archaeological evidence of religious sites, involving religious objects, she examined architectural styles and designs, paying particular attention to overlaps, the emergence of new cults out of older ones, adaptations, appropriations and contestations. All of this she carefully contextualised in the power structures evident at different times in Banavasi. Objects like naga (snake) stones from the 'Little Tradition' point to the persistence of local folk traditions as resistance of local religious practices against dominant ones. Suvathran concluded that Banavasi should be seen as 'shared space for numerous religious traditions ... Instead of looking at the multiplicity of religious traditions solely in terms of conflict or even necessarily incorporation ... we can see Banavasi as a stage, where the availability of resources and patronage allowed for shared religious space.'[75] In a communalist India, where essentialised forms of religious identity still kill on an almost daily basis, such insights do truly serve to deconstruct deadly claims about collective identity. (See Figure 10.6.)

I have noted above that the history of material culture has often been related to the history of the everyday, and yet we have also seen over recent years that material history has turned global. A major public success with global repercussions was Neil MacGregor's BBC broadcast 'A History of the World in 100 Objects'.[76] MacGregor, at the time director of the British Museum in London, followed a simple idea: to explore human civilisations by discussing objects and things that spoke about those civilisations. In the first of these one hundred 15-minute programmes, first broadcast in 2010, MacGregor expressed his conviction that listeners 'will find ... that their own histories quickly intersect

Figure 10.6 Madhukeshwara Temple, Banavasi, south India. © Amith Nag/ 500 Px Plus via Getty Images.

with everybody else's, and when that happens you no longer have a history of a particular people or nation, but a story of endless connections'.[77] MacGregor's attempt to use the history of material culture to defuse ideas about an essentialist, particularist identity and instead further the recognition of the global connectedness of the world underlines the desire of historians of objects to problematise and deconstruct essentialist ideas about identity. An accompanying interactive website asked listeners to submit their own objects, thereby opening a pathway for people to engage with these ideas about the connectedness of global historical cultures. Four million people listened to the broadcasts and the podcasts were downloaded more than ten million times. The accompanying book was an instant bestseller.[78] A touring exhibition, organised in 2016, visited Abu Dhabi, Japan, China, Taiwan and Australia.

Another, more academic endeavour to bring the history of material culture together with global history is Giorgio Riello's *Cotton: the Fabric that Made the Modern World*.[79] This is a history of objects related to cotton manufacture, which involved global exchanges from around 1000 AD to the present day. Its impressive geographical as well as chronological reach underlined the extent to which the world was an interconnected place in which developments in one place and at one time had manifold repercussions for developments in another place at the same and different times. It is part and parcel of the history of material culture but also part and parcel of transnational, global and comparative history, the subject of our last substantive chapter. The latter, as we shall see, has done much to tell stories that have the power to de-essentialise collective identities and show how they have always been forged in conversation with others, how they changed over time and how they were related to specific power structures and interests.

Conclusion

'The things we interact with are an inescapable part of who we are.'[80] If our environments make us who we are, then it makes no sense toproduce historical narratives about unchanging and essentialist identities, as such identities have always been related to changing environmental factors. In this way the history of material culture has been 're-casting established historical narratives in new and exciting ways'.[81] Emerging out of a renewed engagement of cultural history with anthropology and archaeology, the history of things was also a reaction to the linguistic turn. As we have seen, it did not so much reject the importance of language but sought to build on insights from the linguistic turn in order to foreground what historians of things argued was the forgotten impact of materiality. Attributing various degrees of agency to objects, historians of material culture explored the diverse ways in which those objects moulded identities, e.g. as consumers, as members of nations or regions, as belonging to social classes, ethnic groups or religious communities, as men and women and those belonging to different gender constructions. The unruliness and instability of objects made it impossible to stabilise those identities. Instead they were constantly being remoulded through processes of adaptation, appropriation, transfer and exchange. If tracing the histories of objects through time and space points to the importance of such processes, they are the same processes that are also highlighted by transnational, global and comparative historians, as we shall see in the next chapter.

Further Reading

Annabel Cooper, Lachy Paterson and Angela Wanhalla (eds.), *The Lives of Colonial Objects*, Dunedin: Otago University Press, 2015.

Anne Gerritsen and Giorgio Riello (eds.), *Writing Material Culture History*, London: Bloomsbury, 2015.

Karen Harvey (ed.), *History and Material Culture*, London: Routledge, 2009.

Timothy J. LeCain, *The Matter of History: How Things Create the Past*, Cambridge: Cambridge University Press, 2017.

Laurel Thatcher Ulrich, Ivan Gaskell, Sara J. Schechner and Sarah Anne Carter, *Tangible Things: Making History through Objects*, Oxford: Oxford University Press, 2015.

11 *Transnational, Comparative and Global History*

Introduction

At present, no history seems more popular than global history. Chairs of global history are sprouting from the ground like mushrooms, and multi-volume global histories have sought to summarise the knowledge produced by the ever-increasing armies of global historians.[1] The reasons for this global presence are manifold: an ongoing intensification of globalisation processes that started towards the end of the twentieth century, the end of the Cold War with its transatlantic Western-centric world view, and the rise of China as major global power.[2] Unsurprisingly, many global historians come from specialisms in non-Western histories, especially the histories of Asia and Africa. To some observers globalisation seemed to make the national container increasingly redundant. In their view, it was impelling historians towards world history.[3] Kenneth Pomeranz, in his presidential address to the American Historical Assocation, published in 2014, with his reflections on changing perceptions of space, time and place, looked for 'histories for a less national age'.[4] Criticising the historiographical nationalism exhibited in the past, a new generation of historians set sail for global history armed with the methodological dispositions of comparison and transnational exchanges and circulations.[5] Comparison was the older method already practised by Marc Bloch and Otto Hintze in the interwar period. When theorists of transnational exchanges and circulations came on to the scene from the late 1980s onwards, they were extremely critical of comparative approaches. However, global histories have used both methods successfully to demonstrate how many historical processes could only be understood in a global dimension.[6]

Historians have been making major progress in transcending national tunnel vision, even if many have, in the process, been reluctant, for good reason, to throw out national perspectives altogether. Some have warned against underestimating the continued hold of the national imagination over the historical landscape and have pointed to various national history wars (often intertwined with national memory wars) in different parts of the world.[7] Nevertheless, the profession has made significant advances in overcoming historiographical nationalism. In the first part of this chapter, I will trace the development of this particular kind of history writing from the beginnings of professional history writing to the present day in order to show that it, like many of the sub-fields already discussed, has deep roots in past historiographical practices. In the second part of the chapter, I will provide examples from recent historical writings to demonstrate how comparative, transnational and global approaches have helped foster greater self-reflexivity about the link between history writing and collective identity formation.

The Long Practice of Comparative, Transnational and Global History Writing

Enlightenment historiography already took a strong interest in global history, or, as many called it at the time, universal history.[8] It allowed the historian to trace the story of the progress of humankind through the ages. Subsequently, a recurring interest in global perspectives went hand in hand with periods of intense globalisation and the development of theories, such as Marxism or theories of imperialism, which took such processes of globalisation seriously. The foundation of the International Committee of the Historical Sciences and the origins of the World History Conferences are good examples of a renewed interest in world history scholarship around 1900.[9] Late nineteenth-century orientalist scholarship was also strongly transnational in its orientation.[10] The nineteenth-century philologist, religious studies scholar and historian Ernest Renan's desire to use comparison to order the world was part and parcel of the orientalist agenda of imposing Western standards as yardsticks for global development.[11] Comparison was thus a crucial method in relegating non-Western societies to concepts of backwardness. It justified a developmental colonialism and imperialism that was only problematised with the onset of postcolonial scholarship.[12]

In a completely different vein, W. E. B. Du Bois' writings on black America, from his 1896 dissertation on the transatlantic slave trade down to his autobiography published posthumously in 1968, are good examples of how transnational perspectives informed early attempts to reshape the dominant white national narrative in the USA and transform it into a more cosmopolitan one that could incorporate 'black folk'.[13] Nico Slate has discussed such transnational forms of 'colored cosmopolitanism' that sought to build transnational solidarities without reifying 'race' as an essentialist category.[14] Another example is C. L. R. James' *The Black Jacobins* – a groundbreaking study of how transnational connections between revolutionary ideas in France and Haiti brought about the slave-led revolution of 1791, which eventually led to the independence of Haiti in 1804.[15] (See Figure 11.1.) Black

Figure 11.1 Toussaint L'Ouverture (1743–1803), Haitian revolutionary and statesman. © Time Life Pictures/Mansell/The LIFE Picture Collection via Getty Images.

historians wishing to strengthen proud black identities in order to develop different national historical master narratives and a more cosmopolitan transcontinental identity were early pioneers of global history.

Notable practitioners of global history after 1945 also included Arnold Toynbee and William McNeill. Toynbee's *A Study of History*, on which he worked for almost thirty years, represents a type of world history in which the author follows the rise and decline of diverse civilisations, emphasising the importance of non-Western ones.[16] McNeill, in his influential *The Rise of the West*, first published in 1963, argued, contrary to Toynbee, that civilisations are not so much distinct entities in world history as interconnecting ones. In his view, it was the ability of the Western civilisations to facilitate contact with other civilisations that was the basis on which the West rose to dominance.[17] According to McNeill, transnationalism was a major driver of historical change. In subsequent publications, such as *Plagues and Peoples*, he extended his transnational concerns to environmental history, the history of medicine and military history.[18] Intriguingly he also wrote a biography of Toynbee.[19] Several universities in the USA, above all the University of Chicago, became drivers of a renewed interest in global history in the post-war period after 1945.[20] Peter Stearns inspired generations of historians with his version of global history.[21] Eric Hobsbawm wove different parts of the world together in broad-brush paintings that nevertheless stayed attentive to local differences.[22] The Marxist-inspired history that he represented had a long tradition of analysing transnational connections and interdependencies, with a strong focus on economic, social and political structures.[23] Immanuel Wallerstein's world systems theory, influenced by Marxist dependency theory, Fernand Braudel's writings and postcolonial writings on Africa (Wallerstein worked as an Africa specialist towards the beginning of his career), divided the world into capitalist core, semi-periphery and periphery, and sought to write history as a history of interconnections.[24]

The end of the Cold War gave transnational history a further boost. In 1991 Ian Tyrrell argued that the national container should no longer remain the dominant unit of analysis for American historians, because it veiled the genocidal politics towards indigenous people in the Americas and continued to prioritise progressive narratives about the emergence of an allegedly unique American democracy. The dominant narrative of American national history, he argued, could only be broken if historians were to operate through and take seriously the interrelatedness of diverse geographical scales – the local, the national and the transnational.[25] The subsequent rise of courses at American universities on 'America and the World' signalled the shift from an American-centred American history to one aware of America's manifold global entanglements.[26]

Transnational history also developed a critical edge towards comparative history. Thus, a group of Franco-German scholars, above all Michel Espagne, Michael Werner and Bénédicte Zimmermann, championed an alternative that they described as 'connected histoires'. It would look for ways in which historical writing 'can combine empirical and reflexive concerns into a dynamic and flexible approach'.[27] Drawing attention to the relational character of historical developments allowed historians to highlight how different languages, traditions, disciplinary terminologies and conceptualisations led to a multiplicity of identitarian constructions – a recognition that in itself would prevent them essentialising those identities. They could also point to antecedents among the first generation of Annalistes, especially Lucien Febvre, whose book on the river Rhine as a border river, first published in 1931, had highlighted the many transfers and circulations across the Rhine between France and Germany, and had thereby also destabilised notions of fixed, whole and homogenous national identities on either side of the Rhine.[28]

Those who championed connected or entangled histories argued that comparative history artificially isolated units of comparison, often nations, without realising that these were not autonomous entities but porous containers that had multiple contacts with each other. Other containers influenced how they looked. Instead of comparing, they insisted that it was necessary to study transfers, flows, circulations and contacts. Only this would effectively undermine methodological nationalism and lead to forms of historical writing that would highlight how the nation was always a construction dependent on borrowing, adaptation and hybridity. The notion of the circulation of ideas, concepts and practices was hugely influential in rethinking history in terms of imports and exports.[29] Whilst transnational historians were undoubtedly right in highlighting a weakness of many comparative studies, other scholars pointed out that this did not invalidate the comparative method as such.[30] It just meant that comparative historians would have to pay due attention to such transfers and take them into account when comparing developments between two or more cases.[31] As Liise Lehtsalu has written: 'With the rise of transregional, transnational and global histories, comparative method has become a staple in the historian's toolbox.'[32] Following Sven Beckert, we can understand transnational history as 'the interconnectedness of human history as a whole, and while it acknowledges the extraordinary importance of states, empires and the like, it pays attention to networks, processes, beliefs and institutions that transcend these politically defined spaces'.[33] Then we can also see how this interconnectedness forms the basis for comparison. The transnational and transregional turn in historical writing is thus, not so much about sidelining comparison and replacing it with transfer studies, as about combining both approaches.[34]

Enriched by theoretical debates surrounding cultural transfers in history,[35] global history experienced a veritable explosion of studies from the 1990s onwards. They focused on diverse themes such as technological change, the environment, migration, the production and consumption of goods, and the spread of ideas, faiths and diseases. What unites these studies is a desire to overcome national borders and an insight that historical explanation can gain from moving beyond national frameworks. An emphasis on polyphony (Bakhtin, see Chapter 1) and multiperspectivity combined with an animus against holistic and essentialised perspectives in historical writing. Using insights derived from Bourdieu, Latour and Anthony Giddens, global historians, such as Angelika Epple, argued for the use of practice theory, in order to shed light on why global transformations happened in the way they did.[36] Much of recent global history has also tried to overcome Western-centric models of development based on modernisation theories and viewing Western development as the model for all other societies and cultures. Arif Dirlik, for example, has promoted transnational perspectives in history writing as a means of questioning Western categories that claimed to be universalisms. If the intellectual parameters of understanding the world have been set in the West, and if the history of colonialism and imperialism has imposed them on the rest of the world, then transnational history is the way to historise those universalisms as European parochialisms. Historical decolonisation thus starts with attention to the transnational.[37] A closer look at the eighteenth century reveals a world of empires interconnected in constant exchanges of goods and ideas.[38] They can only be understood if those multiple points of contact are taken into account and if the isolated study of separate empires is overcome. Global history has brought about a remarkable renaissance in the histories of empire. The same is true of economic history and the history of migration, where historians highlighted the degree to which the histories of migration and of economics had been Western-centric. Thus, Western histories of migration, classically focusing, as they did, on the transatlantic space, tended to ignore or belittle the impact made by empires, colonial violence, racism and exploitation on migratory processes. In global economic history, the 'great divergence debate' is but one of several examples of how attention to global processes has led economic historians to question Western-centric assumptions and tell more complex and often more contingent stories about economic development.[39]

Transnational history is not the same as global history. Whilst the latter is invariably transnational, the former does not necessarily have to be global. Historians can study transnational circulations and interconnections at a more modest level. Global history is also not the same as world history. The latter has often been criticised for employing totalising concepts indiscriminately and additively telling the story of everything. However, over recent years, world history has also significantly revamped itself and it seems difficult nowadays to draw clear lines between world history and global history.[40]

Related to the boom in world and global history are the fields of 'deep history' and 'big history'. The former is often connected to Daniel Lord Smail's 2008 publication *On Deep History and the Brain.*[41] It amounts to an argument to take seriously the 1.8 million years in which the human brain developed and not to restrict the study of the human past to literate societies. Smail explicitly argues for the co-evolution of culture and nature. They are always intertwined so that there is no human nature that is not culturally inflected. Picking up the anti-essentialist views about identity inherent in poststructuralism, Smail argues that contemporary understandings of human evolution in biology follow a similar anti-essentialist logic.[42] Identities are not a given rooted in biological processes, yet understanding the evolutionary processes of the brain throughout human history means writing the history of biocultures through neurohistory – through taking seriously the materiality of the brain and the body. This, Smail argues, would allow a new look at human emotions, experiences and behaviour. It also necessitates new cross-disciplinary interactions between disciplines such as biology, chemistry, neuroscience, psychology, linguistics, palaeontology, archaeology, anthropology and history. In a follow-up volume, co-edited by Smail and Andrew Shryock, representatives from many different disciplines explore the diverse benefits of studying 'deep history'.[43] Overcoming the dichotomy between what is human and what is natural is described here as a major challenge for the historical sciences. The editors see the construction of this dichotomy based on centuries of logocentric thinking that posited a hierarchy in which the human stood above nature. Encouraging historians to look at bigger timescales means developing a range of concepts with which those longue-durée timescales can be studied. These include energy, ecosystems, scale, goods, food, the human body, language, migration and kinship. They are all concepts that travel well through time and space and appeal to universal processes that impacted on past developments and the construction of past identities.

Combining human history with natural history is part and parcel of 'deep history' and is also a key axiom of 'big history', which is associated with names such as David Christian, Fred Spier, Cynthia Stokes Brown and Eric Chaisson.[44] In fact, for 'big historians' 'deep history' does not go back far enough as it remains largely concerned with humanoid development. 'Big history' instead covers a range of 14 billion years, from the big bang to our times. It amounts to a history of the universe and is even more cross-disciplinary than 'deep history', involving cosmology, astronomy, geology, evolutionary biology, nuclear physics, geography and all the disciplines mentioned above as well as others. It is an explicit counter-reaction to what 'big historians' criticise as extreme fragmentation of historical scholarship. 'Big history' insists that human history is part and parcel of a much bigger picture related, above all, to cosmology and natural history. Attempting to divide 14 billion years of history into distinct periods with key thresholds, 'big historians' have been talking a lot about complexity and conditions for complexity, about energy streams and collective learning, in order to give a unified and coherent account of everything. Like 'deep history' it is intent on overcoming the nature vs. nurture divide. Instead it asks large unifying questions about the past which seek to explain how the universe works. Rooted in an older universal history, 'big history' has been intent on contributing towards developing global identities, i.e. allowing for identifications with the globe in its trials and tribulations with human intervention. On this cosmic canvas human history is presented as only a small part of the history of the biosphere, the earth and the planetary systems. Discovering the place of humans in the natural world is, according to most 'big historians', a humbling experience, underlining, above all, the ecological embeddedness of human history. 'Big history' encourages self-reflection about the place of humans in time and space and about human adaptability to environmental change. It is often strongly ethically anchored in that it reflects on the impending ecological disasters awaiting humankind, as humans, like no other species before, have changed the biosphere of the planet. 'Big history' has thus played an important role in identifying the 'Anthropocene' as a distinct era in world history and in problematising it. (See also Chapter 10.) Reflecting on human identity in the most fundamental sense of human survival, 'big history' connects very different fields of human knowledge in order to account for the universality of human experience and its relationship to the natural world. Since the formation of its own scholarly association, the International Big History Association, in 2011,[45] it has gone from strength to strength – with ever more university and school courses being developed and taught in this subject area. In 2020 a *Companion to Big History* attempted to summarise the achievements and agendas of big history, drawing attention to the many disciplinary contexts as well as the possibility of combining 'big history' with attention to the micro and the local in history.[46] I find this attempt to localise and specify 'big history' particularly intriguing as it avoids the pitfalls of making 'big history' into yet another grand master narrative seeking to forge a unified identity. Instead attention to the micro and the local is a way of underlining the extent to which myriads of variations on global themes existed and how the manifold, ambiguous and contradictory constructions of identifications underpinned all attempts by humans to make sense of their place and their being in this world. In the *Companion to Big History* David Christian interestingly pays homage to Fernand Braudel and the Annales tradition in historical writing as being of prime importance in kindling his interest in geography and material life.[47]

Braudel's work on the Mediterranean has transcended borders, geographically and chronologically, and it is this endeavour that is shared by deep, big, universal, global and transnational histories. In their concern with borders, they theorised borders as objects of historical studies. A border can mean demarcation, putting off limits what is defined as not belonging, but it can also indicate preparedness for exchange and appropriation – a transmission belt of 'the other' on the way to adopting it as one's own. Border territories may be understood either as sites of confrontation, intolerance and the collision of fundamentally incompatible 'national' values and normative horizons or as terrains of exchange and fruitful dialogue.[48] Concepts such as Mary Louise Pratt's 'contact zones'[49] or Homi Bhabha's 'interstitial spaces'[50] were influential in encouraging scholars to look at border zones and diasporas transnationally in order to find out how collective identities had been constructed, challenged and redefined at the border or in diaspora situations. One pioneering example of the study of borders in a transnational way is Gloria Anzaldúa' work on *Borderlands/La Frontera.*[51] She analysed the complex multiple identities of Mexican-Americans living in the borderlands between the USA and Mexico, underlining how limited the national container was in understanding the identities forged at the border. Postcolonial studies have emphasised how postcolonial elites have implemented forms of postcolonial nationhood that instituted repressive border regimes, which interrupted more entangled lives across borders going back to colonial times.[52] Since then many other studies have focused on borderlands and border cities. Their complex ethnic and religious make-up and the power relationships between different national groups have fascinated historians, who have often been able to point to the importance of identitarian claims and constructions of these claims in regions and places literally between nations. The town of Harbin in north China and the surrounding region of Manchuria, in which Russian influences were strong in the nineteenth and early twentieth century, is a perfect example of such an in-between place.[53]

Decentring Collective Identities by Comparing, Pointing to Transfers and Circulations, and Paying Attention to Global Processes

Jack Goody's comparison of pre-modern family structures across a great variety of European and Asian societies has thrown up surprising similarities between Asia and Europe, thereby problematising forms of supposedly distinct Asian vs. European identities.[54] Goody's focus on the family is in itself indicative of the desire felt by many transnational histories to focus on units of analysis below the nation: apart from family, one can also mention village structures, regions and individuals. Decentring the nation by analysing how non-national collective identities have framed the lives of individuals was one way of deconstructing national identities and their power over the historians' imagination.

The study of intercultural transfers has also become a prominent way of relativising national contexts and underlining how the modern world was remade through a series of transnational contacts. Thomas Adam has focused on five aspects of the making of the modern world: consumer co-operatives, housing, eugenics, education and non-violent social action.[55] In all of those areas he traced the importance of circulations between different parts of the world vital in creating the reform movements that shaped debates on these areas of social organisation. The adaptation and modification of circulating concepts, their dilution and hybridisation with other concepts, are very much to the fore in Adam's book, as are the individual activists who often played a vital role in bringing about those circulations. One of the most intriguing aspects of such studies is the deconstruction of ways in which borrowings and adaptations have, over time, become hidden in narratives that conceal their integration into narratives of national originality and authenticity.

Another way in which transnational history can deconstruct and de-essentialise national identities is by pointing to the importance of transnational actors in constructing these identities. Thus, for example, Silke Strickrodt has pointed out how slave returnees from Brazil to Lagos were the ones who standardised the Yoruba language (largely by translating the Bible from English) and subsequently moulded many forms of cultural nationalism in Nigeria.[56] Migratory connections between places geographically far apart led to what Benedict Anderson called 'long-distance nationalism', i.e. the ability of migrants to take their experiences from the places they had been transplanted to and adapt them to their countries of origin.[57] Many of the national movements of the nineteenth century were in effect highly transnational affairs. Thus Eric Pécout, for example, has pointed out how the armies of the Italian Risorgimento were made up of troops that came from many parts of the globe.[58] It was thus no mere coincidence that the hero of the Risorgimento, Garibaldi, fought for national liberation on two continents. The solidarity campaigns supporting the national movements of Greece and Poland in the nineteenth century were transnational affairs, and many volunteers flocked to Greece from all over Europe to take up the Greeks' national struggle. Whilst transnational and global history is often and even mainly engaged in countering national and nationalist perspectives in historical writing, in certain parts of the world, such as East Asia, national(ist) historians either vociferously attacked transnational and global perspectives as unpatriotic,[59] or tried to make them compatible with a more national(ist) perspective. Indeed, Chinese global history often starts from highly ethno-centric perspectives.[60] Hence, as Dominic Sachsenmaier has underlined, it is important to compare and constrast different national traditions of writing global history, paying attention to transnational circulations but also to remaining divergences.[61]

Transnational histories of Europe are also not necessarily immune to constructions of identity through history. Especially within the framework of the European Union from the second half of the twentieth century onwards, historians have sought to construct a common European identity by highlighting a range of features supposedly common to all European societies.[62] Historians seeking to underpin and foster a European collective identity[63] have been at loggerheads with other historians who seek to maintain and foster national identities against an alleged threat from the European Union.[64] Furthermore, a third group of historians has underlined how historians should not lend their pen again to forging a spatial collective identity as too many of them had done in the nineteenth and twentieth centuries.[65] Jörn Leonhard has disentangled the different ways of writing European history since the nineteenth century and related them to diverse political ambitions. He urges historians to use comparative and transnational methods in order to write a less Eurocentric history but one still capable of analysing and explaining characteristics of European historical development.[66]

European history became the focus of identitarian concerns in the context of the European Union's attempts to foster greater unity and stronger feelings of identity with the European project. Another continent where the writing of history was deeply connected with identitarian concerns was Africa. There generations of anti-colonialist and anti-imperialist historians, such as Cheikh Anta Diop and Abdoulaye Ly, wrote transnational African history, first and foremost to put Africa on the map and counter the Western-centric nineteenth-century idea that it was the continent without history. Problems with written sources and with an alleged marginality of Africa in world history had to be overcome, and generations of African historians wrote history as an integral part of the ongoing struggle of decolonisation which included the rehabilitation of African civilisations. Raising black consciousness and underpinning African identities became two of the most important aims pursued by an engaged black African history writing in the second half of the twentieth century. This could be done through transnational history. Africanists in the West and in Africa played a major role in putting Africa back on to the map of world history – something that allows a new generation of younger global historians of Africa to investigate Africa's global links to other parts of the world whilst being less concerned with identitarian themes.[67]

Attacking theories of exceptionalism in Africa and elsewhere was a very effective way of overcoming identitarian forms of historical writing. National(ist) histories had long rested on assumptions of national peculiarity, be it 'American exceptionalism',[68] the German *Sonderweg*,[69] or the idea of Britain as 'first industrial nation'.[70] However, it is noticeable that the alleged peculiarities were often established without substantial comparison and on the basis of assuming peculiarity. Actual comparisons instead falsified constructions of allegedly peculiar national identities. Neville Kirk's book comparing the development of American and British labour movements, for example, went a long way towards undermining assumptions about American 'exceptionalism'.[71] The whole *Sonderweg* debate in German history from the 1980s to the 2000s questioned earlier assumptions of German peculiarity.[72] And the comparative histories of industrialisation have altogether abandoned the national frame, arguing that industrialisation should be understood as a regional, not a national phenomenon.[73] In meso-regions such as the Balkans, nationalist histories ruled supreme for a long time and were rekindled in the wake of the collapse of communism around 1990 and during the Yugoslav wars in the 1990s. Writing an 'entangled history of the Balkans' is thus a project that challenges historiographical nationalism, deconstructs national myths and de-essentialises understanding of national identity by pointing to the manifold circulations within the Balkans and between the Balkans and the outside world.[74] Overall, comparisons, entanglements and transnationalism as well as transregionalism serve as antidotes to the construction of national histories which underpin national identities.

Whilst comparative history often undermined attempts to naturalise spatial collective identities, be they regional, national or transnational, it also highlighted the constructed nature of class identities. Already Werner Sombart's iconic article which asked the question 'Why was there no socialism in the United States?' used a comparative question to highlight the fact that Marxist class politics had developed, albeit in different ways, across Europe but not in the United States.[75] Sombart thus instigated an ongoing debate on how class was constructed – by whom and under what specific circumstances. Comparative labour historians have made linkages of the strong reception of Marxism in European working-class parties with the degree of state repression that these parties faced. The more repression, the more likely it was that they would turn to Marxism as an explanatory framework for social and political developments.[76] John Breuilly traced the emergence of liberal labour movements in Britain and Germany, and went on to explain why in Britain a liberal labour movement succeeded, whereas in Germany it soon lost out to a rising socialist movement.[77] Comparing class identities of workers in one country could, he argued, be explained better by comparing them with class identities in others.

Under the impact of poststructuralist theories outlined in Chapter 1, labour historians began to question the usefulness of grand theories, whether Marxist or Weberian, that had had a major impact on the construction of class identities through historical analysis. Questioning the naturalness of class identities became second nature to a revamped labour history that did not take class for granted and sought to explain how workers sometimes came to perceive themselves in terms of class.[78] Global labour history, as it emerged from the 1990s onwards, further undermined key assumptions of Western ideas about class that were not reproduced outside the West. Hence it started a fundamental rethinking of key categories in labour history, including 'class', 'wage worker', 'sharecropping', 'slavery' and 'free and unfree labour'.[79] Transnational labour history in the Americas, as Leon Fink has argued, began to understand

> global processes, historically conceived, to be fundamental to labour's history, be it capital or labor mobility, imperial and neo-imperial political economies, or the mobilization of labor internationally and/or across borders. The transnational also opens new avenues for understanding – over time and space – changes in the concepts, policies and practices of states ...

and the ways in which the popular classes resist, react and use both the nation state and the non-state entities to advance their interests.[80]

No other historical approaches have been so adept at testing, modifying and falsifying historical explanations for collective identity formation than comparison, transnationalism and global history. Nor have any other methods demonstrated so effectively the range of possible situational and changing identities. It has thus allowed historians to gain a vantage point outside one particular regional, national or transnational history and made history a less identitarian undertaking.

Labour historians were not the only ones to question the ties between historical writing and collective identity formation – through comparison, transnationalism and by going global. The same is true for historians of ethnicity and race. As Robin Kelley has argued, the diasporic nature of black studies, Chicano/a studies and Asian-American studies meant that they invariably had to contest the bounded site of national history. Historical scholarship on black people in the USA from H. Ford Douglass in the nineteenth century down to today had to counter the (dominant) racist and nationalist historiography and provide an alternative form of cosmopolitan nation-building, often referring to a glorious African past of American blacks. They wove transnationalism into black American history from its earliest moments onwards. In their search for freedom, justice and self-determination, black engaged historians, supporting the civil rights movement of black people in America, were questioning the identitarian boundaries of white America and thereby contributing to a greater self-reflexivity of what it might mean to be American.[81]

Paul Gilroy's *The Black Atlantic* was an early example of how transnational history established race as being at the very heart of modern subjectivities.[82] Describing the black Atlantic as a 'non-traditional tradition, an irreducibly modern, ex-centric, unstable and asymmetrical cultural ensemble', Gilroy traced the making of diasporic slave identities that were inherently transnational and situated between Jamaica, England and Africa.[83] Subsequent scholarship produced many fine works that highlighted the importance of transnational forms of resistance waged by an enslaved population against a dominant political order.[84] Marilyn Lake, for example, examined how notions of progressive national development were thoroughly racialised in the United States, South Africa and Australia.[85] In a book-length study that Lake published with Henry Reynolds, they expanded on this idea and demonstrated how we can only understand the concept of whiteness by studying the transnational connections that established the meanings of whiteness, albeit with wide variations, across different continents and cultures. The making and unmaking of racial identities is at the centre of their exploration of the emergence of a global colour line.[86] Madeline Y. Hsu has highlighted how racial and cultural boundaries between Asian Americans and other Americans excluded the former from being regarded as an integral part of the nation, despite the inclusionary claims of the dominant national narrative in the USA. Like Du Bois' histories, her history of race deconstructed the dominant national historical master narrative by examining racial boundaries experienced by Asian Americans in their everyday lives in the USA. Territorial space, power relationships and the construction of collective identities ultimately came to locate Asian Americans outside the boundaries of the nation.[87] Indeed, as Radhika Viyas Mongia has argued, the modern nation-state was founded on a conscious 'blurring of the vocabularies of nationality and race'. From this perspective it makes no sense to differentiate between nation and race, as the global context of racism (and colonialism) is always already inscribed into the language of the nation-state. The passport, Mongia argued, was a 'concrete technology' that reflected strategies of nationalisation.[88] (See Figure 11.2.)

If we turn to gender identities, we can see how comparative and transnational global approaches have equally helped in questioning the naturalisation of gender orders and opened a space for discussing the fluidity, intersectionality and constructedness of gender orders across time and place.[89] Empire, for example, is impossible to understand without comprehending how gender was constructed in and through empires. Inversely, the imperialist constructions of racism impacted on understandings of gender – even among those transnational feminists who sought to build bridges between white and non-white women activists.[90] The emergence of an 'imperial feminism' cast a long shadow over the Western-centric assumptions of feminism.[91] But transnational networks of women were not simply confined to imperialist and nationalist contexts. The proletarian socialist and communist women's movements were also a significant force in the nineteenth and twentieth centuries.[92] The women's movements knew many transnational activists' biographies that transgressed borders and circulated across

Figure 11.2 The passport indicates national belonging. This inside of a passport with its visa stamps highlights the ability of the holder of the passport to move about the globe, a privilege that many people do not have, either because they have no passport or because the passport does not allow them to travel. © Gen Sadakane/EyeEM via Getty Images.

cultural and national borders.[93] Translation became a 'crucial practice' in this 'transnational women's movement' around 1900 and played a vital role in globalising the space for women's movements and their differing understandings of what feminism might mean.[94] Indeed, the figure of the transnational activist is a well-known one in a wide range of transnational social movements that aimed at building identities: national identities, in the case of national movements, class identities, in the case of workers' movements, or women's identities, in the case of women's movements. Memory studies scholars are beginning to investigate how the memory of activism has been a resource for movements and their specific societal aims.[95] In this way they are contributing to greater self-reflexivity about the link between particular constructions of memories about the past and the strengthening of identities within specific social movements in the present. The impact of the welfare state on the gendering of specific state policies, women's suffrage, the development of male and female sexualities, cultural specificities in the emergence of gender relations at different times and places, and the gendered nature of international relations have all been examined in transnational ways.[96] Yet, despite all this, the editors of *Women in Transnational History* have argued that transnational histories are not yet sufficiently gendered, as women continue to be marginalised within those histories.[97]

In the hands of global historians, transnational and comparative approaches have led to a stringent questioning of Western-centrism in historical writing, as I noted when reviewing some of the writings on race and gender. Edward Said's critique of orientalism in Western thinking highlighted how the West had constructed an image of its 'other', the Orient, with an eye to establishing particular historical parameters such as modernisation and development, where the West was allegedly superior to its 'other'.[98] Postcolonial perspectives that took their cue from Said have subsequently pointed out how 'the other' was relegated to the 'waiting room of history',[99] as it could never hope to catch up with the West. The distinction between civilised parts of the world, basically 'the West', and barbarous ones, 'the rest', was crucial in making 'civility ... a marker of global order'.[100] These historical perspectives championed by the West were thus a means of keeping 'the rest' in a subordinate position. Subverting Western identities and their semi-colonial outlook has been one of the key achievements of postcolonial scholarship over the past four decades. Thus, for example, in *Tensions of Empire* Ann Laura Stoler and Frederick Cooper argued that it is impossible to understand either the colonial or the European world without analysing the transnational connections that remade both many times over. The 'metropolitan–colonial connections', they argued, are vital in understanding how both Western and colonial as well as postcolonial identities have been shaped. The very concept of universalism, they concluded, emerged from that encounter and is in need of being decentred from its Western bias – something only possible if one reads metropolitan–colonial encounters from the perspective of the colonial margins.[101] This is precisely what Cemil Aydin's *The Politics of Anti-Westernism in Asia* is doing. Examining the agency of Ottoman pan-Islamic and Japanese pan-Asian intellectuals and their evolving critiques of the West between the second half of the nineteenth century and the end of the Second World War, Aydin succeeds in showing how anti-Westernism was rooted in the growing doubts about the legitimacy of a Western-centric universalism that seemed to betray its own standards and norms. It was not Western liberalism or imperialism as such that formed the focus of the critique, but the inability of the West to maintain its own global standards in the metropolitan–colonial encounters.[102]

The advances made by transnational global history have been directly related to globalisation processes and the forging of transnational global identities that have become a lived reality for many people across the world, including many scholars. This also raises the possibility that history projects serve new identitarian purposes – a danger recognised by key representatives of transnational history. As Pierre-Yves Saunier has pointed out, just as historiographic nationalism served the interest of the nation-state, transnational history has to be highly self-reflexive in its endeavours if it wants to avoid becoming the handmaiden of contemporary globalisation processes.[103] In 2014 Lynn Hunt, in her *Writing History in the Global Era*, argued that global historians needed to be aware of the grand narratives they were weaving.[104] Overarching historical narratives, she showed, had been linked to the exercise of political and cultural power for a long time. Tying globalisation to modernisation narratives would lead down the cul-de-sac of yet another teleology that global history should stay clear of. Instead, it should remain alert to the multiple stories inherent in globalisation processes and emphasise the political contestation at the heart of battles surrounding globalisation narratives. Global history, in other words, had to be highly self-reflexive about its own presentist traps. This also means recognising that not everything can be related to flows and circulations. Processes of globalisation had been historically accompanied by the building of borders, fences and walls, physical and mental ones. The move towards global orders is characterised by this tension between crossing and building borders.

In the first issue of the *Yearbook of Transnational History*, published in 2018, Thomas Adam described the prime aim of transnational history as 'recovering history as a universal project'.[105] Indeed, there is a long tradition of transnational histories seeking to demonstrate the connectedness of all human beings and their belonging to one humanity. Inversely, attempts to separate humans into nations, races and other categories that rely on othering processes were seen as running counter to the commitment of transnational approaches. Fernand Braudel's masterpiece on the Mediterranean can be read as a transnational history, showing, as it does, the connectedness of the Muslim and Christian worlds in the Mediterranean.[106] His involvement in the UNESCO-sponsored *History of Mankind* was also inspired by ideas about showing how the world benefited from peaceful global interactions and exchanges.[107] UNESCO's project was 'born out of the perceived need to restore a lost sense of common humanity after 1945'.[108] Rooted in post-war liberal optimism about history's edifying and educational function, it reconceptualised history away from a history of political elites, state formations and wars in the direction of a cultural history, in which material culture, communication, the history of science, environmental history and everyday politics all featured prominently. It promoted a new peaceful univeralism that was ultimately defeated by the impossibilitiy of finding consensus around notions of universalism in the singular.

Many practitioners of transnational history, albeit not all, sought to contribute to a post-national future in which a universal cosmopolitanism promotes a tolerant and democratic multiculturalism. These sentiments are undoubtedly often well-meaning. However, what is the content of such universalism? In the Enlightenment universalism was a thinly veiled claim to superiority of a particular set of Western-centric values and ideas, located often in particular national histories. If endorsing universalism is reduced to endorsing contemporary forms of globalisation, history has simply found a new focus for identitarian projects rather than continuously undermining such projects. Furthermore, I would argue that national perspectives on history are not so much invalidated as enriched by transnational perspectives. Whilst the transnational works through the adoption of both supra- and sub-national perspectives,[109] it also helps one to understand national developments better. Thus, for example, in the case of the United States, transnational history has been employed to comprehend US national history in new ways.[110] Furthermore, transnational history is not so much about sidelining national history as about highlighting its historical power, including its power to bring about transnational circulations. Matthias Middell and Katja Naumann have pointed out that transnational history does not deny the importance of the nation-state: 'On the contrary, it emphasises its capacity to control and channel border-transcending movements.'[111] Transnational histories, they argue, have to take into account different spatial orders and look for the impact of those orders on processes of globalisation: 'we need histories that describe the meshing and shifting of different spatial references, narratives in which historical agency is emphasised, and interpretations acknowledging that the changing patters of spatialisation are processes fraught with tension'.[112] Their plea is in line with the insights produced by the spatial turn in the historical sciences since the 1990s, which has dynamised and temporalised our understanding of spatial order – often with reference to the body of theories discussed in Chapter 1.[113] Furthermore, the very process of deconstructing the nation as the epicentre of historical writing involves a recognition of the powerful hold the national imagination has over people's collective identitification. As Antoinette Burton has remarked, the nation continues to be an important lens through which to deconstruct and maybe reconstruct in a more self-reflective way notions of racialised, gendered and classed identities in a range of territorial scales, from the local to the colonial, imperial and global.[114]

If transnational histories have pointed to the continued importance of the national frame, they have also been criticised for reifying the national container in historical writing. In prioritising the national over other territorial scales, the concept of the transnational presupposes that the national scale is the most important. In response to those critiques historians have championed ideas of a translocal history – an approach that often picked up the concept of micro-history that we discussed in Chapter 6. But historians have also pointed out that the national container has a role to play in our understanding of global processes. There is no need to throw the baby out with the bath water. Rather, global, transnational and comparative histories point to the interconnectedness of different spatial scales. As Pierre-Yves Saunier has put it: 'a transnational perspective shows how deeply the national fabric and the local or national political debate are intertwined with issues, actors and processes that cut through what we are used to conceiving as local or national'.[115] Hence a range of projects have been trying to write global and world history from the perspective of particular nation-states.[116]

Conclusion

Fiona Paisley and Pamela Scully, in their outstanding book *Writing Transnational History*, 'see the contribution of transnational history as a methodological commitment to critical historical practice'. For them transnational history is about revealing the unequal power relationships which produce particular sets of identities, nationalised, racialised, gendered, and inflected by imperialisms and localisms. Reframing such identititarian constructions through the transnational highlights 'marginalised spaces and subjectivities'. It defamiliarises dominant narratives about identity and reveals scales of identity formation that question authoritative stories on nation, empire, class, race and gender.[117] This emphasis on deconstructing identity formations and drawing attention to the ways in which identities have been constructed in order to sustain dominant regimes of power has had the effect of making historians more self-reflexive about the position they take vis-à-vis specific sets of identities. The influence of poststructuralist theories reviewed in Chapter 1 has often been strong on transnational scholarship. Thus, for example, Gilles Deleuze and Félix Guattari's idea of the rhizome as a metaphor for understanding diversity and multiplicity has been instrumental in transnational scholarship and its attempt to think the world in a more decentred and pluralist way.[118] Rhizomatic structures of knowledge, practices and power relationships have been far more able to depict flows and ties and explain multiple origins and circulations. Notions of cross-fertilisation and creolisation, so important in transnational scholarship, can take their starting point from rhizomatic structures that avoid the clear hierarchies so characteristic of Western-centric histories. Overall, the transnational and global turn can be seen as being rooted in 'poststructuralist reactions to the new global conditions that characterise the present'.[119]

Further reading

Sven Beckert and Dominic Sachsenmaier (eds.), *Global History Globally: Research and Practice around the World*, London: Bloomsbury, 2018.

Stefan Berger, 'Comparative and Transnational History', in: Stefan Berger, Heiko Feldner and Kevin Passmore (eds.), *Writing History: Theory and Practice*, 3rd edn, London: Bloomsbury, 2020, pp. 290–313.

Akira Iriye, *Global and Transnational History: the Past, Present and Future*, Basingstoke: Palgrave Macmillan, 2013.

Fiona Paisley and Pamela Scully, *Writing Transnational History*, London: Bloomsbury, 2019.

Willibald Steinmetz (ed.), *The Force of Comparison: a New Perspective on Modern European History and the Contemporary World*, Oxford: Berghahn Books, 2019.

Michael Werner and Bénédicte Zimmermann, 'Beyond Comparison: "Histoire Croisée" and the Challenge of Reflexivity', *History and Theory* 45:1 (2006), pp. 30–50.

12 Conclusion: Problematising History and Identity

Introduction

Michael Bentley in the introduction to his *Modern Historiography*, published in 1999, emphasised the break that occurred with the advent of postmodernism in the 1970s. He observed pervasive changes in the writing of history: 'Postmodernism has made a major difference to historical projects now underway but does not yet itself have a historiography: we shall see much more clearly its historical ramifications in thirty or forty years' time. It has, all the same, a presence and a vocabulary that readers need to encounter ...'[1] Twenty years later I have provided an account of the impact made by postmodernism and have added a range of other theories such as constructivism and narrativism that cannot easily be subsumed under the label of postmodernism. I have shown that this wider body of theories did indeed have a major influence on historical writing.

This result is not affected by recent attempts in the theory of history to move beyond narrativism and representationalism.[2] The various post-narrativist and post-representationalist theories that have emerged do not replace narrativism and representationalism; they seek to build on them. In his own elaborate attempt to move beyond narrativism, Jouni-Matti Kuukkanen has underlined the importance of narrativism, and what he sees as its three key elements, namely representationalism, constructivism and holism.[3] He finds himself in agreement with basic narrativist assumptions that historical narratives are important in stabilising or, alternatively, challenging contemporary social orders. His critique of representationalism and holism are intended to prevent professional history sinking into total relativism. Instead, he seeks to build a theory of history in which rational discussions about the justifications of historical explanations are still possible.[4] In other words, he aims at restoring the borderlines between history and fiction. Historical narratives, according to Kuukkanen, cannot represent historical reality – something White and Ankersmit still believed possible – because historical reality is only constructed by historical arguments. Yet these historical arguments, Kuukkanen further claims, are evidence-based and lay claim to being epistemologically superior to others. They follow an epistemic rationality and uphold epistemological standards. If, as post-narrativists argue, the past only exists in research-based arguments, i.e. if it never existed as a present for its contemporaries, then the past cannot be represented, pace White and Ankersmit. Ultimately, however, I would argue that post-narrative theory does not so much reject narrativism as make it more usable for historical practice. Furthermore, post-narrativists stress, even more than narrativists do, that every historical argument only exists in a framework of discussion, and always engages with and is situated in other arguments. As such, every historical argument is related to a particular moment in time and irretrievably connected to the present. History cannot be narrated in any other mode than a presentist one.[5]

My investigation into the historiography of the past forty years has focused in particular on the impact of a diverse body of narrativist, constructivist and poststructuralist theories on the levels of self-reflexivity to be found in historical writing in so much as they deal with constructions of collective identities. In his book on *Why History?*, Donald Bloxham takes the reader through two thousand years of Western history writing trying to delineate different motivations in the writing and consumption of history.[6] Writing identity history is one of these motivations, and it is one, in his view, strongly related to other motivations, like history as moral lesson, history as exemplum, history as promoter of tolerance and emancipation. I chose to focus on identity histories, as I believe that these have had a major impact on how people have come to understand themselves in terms of being members of wider 'imagined communities'[7] – nations, cultures, ethnicities, races, classes, religions and genders. Charles Maier, in his attempt to reconceptualise the twentieth century, has argued that the period between the 1860s and the 1970s witnessed an ever closer alignment between governance and forms of collective identity.[8] I have argued that historians, through their writings, have for a long time promoted such collective identities and that the theoretical underpinnings of history writing were no safeguard against identitarian commitments. Rather the opposite was the case: the presumed scientificity of their endeavours protected them from self-questioning. It was only with the emergence of the body of theories discussed in Chapter 1 that a new self-reflexivity about what was involved in the process of writing history entered the historical profession. Mark Poster wrote that 'in a mediated world, historians need the self-reflexivity afforded by theoretical questioning'.[9] Robert Berkhofer set important markers as to how such self-reflexivity led them away from grand narratives, including the grand narratives that have underpinned collective identities ever since the foundation of the historical profession.[10] He called on historians to abandon their quest for objectivity, and instead recognise their position as arbiters of knowledge that fulfilled social functions. Their power over words, in Berkhofer's view, amounted to power over their readers' minds.

If historians through their work intervene in the social world, they have to be, at the very least, aware of doing so. The theories discussed in chapter one above, if applied to historical practice, prevent them from falling prey to their own objectivist illusions. Instead, they can still participate in debates about the past and its meaningfulness for the present in democratic polities and civil societies in which histories construct powerful collective identities, amounting to interventions in the social sphere. And where historians encounter dictatorships, censorship and oppression, their voices form a powerful reminder that histories have a role to play in fostering plural perspectives on the past – something non-democratic regimes tend to dislike and persecute.[11] Thus, Marjorie Dryburgh, for example, pointed to the power of oral life histories, remembering occupied Manchuria, in re-introducing ambiguities that the communist regime had been trying to iron out with their prescribed national master narrative and a simplistic 'speaking bitterness' narrative.[12] If historians decided, as an increasing number did from the 1980s onwards, to deconstruct and debunk the mythologies of constructions of collective identities, then this was also a deliberate intervention in the social sphere. Building on the insights of some of the theorists discussed in Chapter 1, Joan W. Scott comprehensively refuted the notion, associated with the work of Frances Fukuyama, that the end of communism had brought the end of history. She started by reminding her readers

> that there is a paradox at the heart of the historians' practice: the reality to which the historian's interpretation refers is produced by that interpretation,

yet the legitimacy of the interpretation is said to rest on its faithfulness to a reality that lies outside, or exists prior to, interpretation. History functions through an inextricable connection between reality and interpretation that is nonetheless denied by positing reality and interpretation as separate and separable entities. The historian's inevitable dilemma consists in the need simultaneously to avow interpretation and to disavow the productive role interpretation plays in the construction of knowledge.[13]

In being self-reflective about how their work as historians helps to shape the social spheres and the identifications of individuals within them, historians keep history open towards the future. History will not come to an end as long as there are different interpreters of the past.

The New Histories and Their Relationship to Identifications as Basis for Social Interventions

The aim of this volume has been two-fold. On the one hand, it wishes to introduce its readers to changes in some of the oldest and most-established sub-fields of historical writing, such as political, social and cultural history, and furthermore, to inform them about some of the sub-fields that have prominently emerged over recent decades, such as gender history, historical anthropology, memory history, conceptual history, material culture history, visual history and transnational history. Others I mention less prominently, such as the history of emotions, the history of the body, the history of the environment, or the history of science. They are present, but they could easily have formed separate sub-chapters, too.

On the other hand, this volume has also argued throughout that the new history emerging from the 1980s onwards has been more self-reflective about the relationship between historical writing and collective identity formation than its predecessors. My claim is that the body of theories introduced in Chapter 1 has had a considerable impact on the historical profession in that they have undermined the link between scientific historical writing and truth claims, thereby pointing to the constructed nature of all histories and the possibility of telling more than one truthful story about the same event. This willingness to accept different and even contrasting interpretations as truthful has re-inforced historians' rethinking of their works' relationship to the construction of diverse collective identities. If some engaged historians have continued to use history in the struggle to boost specific identities, be they those of women, black people, ethnic minorities or LGBTI groups, they have, by and large, I would argue, done so in more self-reflective and less essentialist ways than previous historians in their constructions of national or class identities. Sometimes making explicit use of Stuart Hall's concept of 'identification',[14] these engaged historians de-essentialised their constructed histories and made them visible, not as historical truth, but as interventions in an ongoing political struggle. There were, of course, also histories that followed the older trajectory of using the scientific clout of professional history writing in order to support totalising, holistic and essentialist identities, but these have not been the subject of my investigation.

Overall, Chapter 1 introduced readers to trends in the theory of history that had a profound impact on the ways in which historians have written history over the past four decades. Given the complexity of many of the theoretical debates, I attempted to be as accessible as possible for an audience of history professionals and students of history who have an interest in history theory without being experts in it. Intellectually and politically, it seems to me important to translate some of the implications of this body of theoretical work. In subsequent chapters I show how it has influenced the writing of practising historians in ways that have undermined and reconfigured the close link between historical writing and collective identity formation that was so strong from the beginnings of professional historical writing to the 1970s.

I have traced the longstanding ties between the modern historical profession and attempts to bolster a range of collective identities, including national, religious, class, ethnic, racial and gender identities. Spatial and non-spatial forms of collective identity were often intricately woven together in histories that amounted to interventions in the social world, even if the power and authority of those histories rested on presumptions of their disinterested objectivity. The 'delayed break' with historiographical nationalism and the emergence of a 'critical' historiography from the 1960s onwards, I argue, brought greater openness about the social positionings of historians in pursuit of emancipatory aims, whether focused on class, women's, racial or sexual liberation. Nevertheless, a form of historical writing often associated with social history continued to bolster collective identities.[15] In fact, in the theory of history associated with such 'critical' social history the link between historical writing and collective identity formation was strongly maintained, as I showed in Chapter 1 with reference to the work of Jörn Rüsen. This link was only challenged by a body of heterogeneous and sometimes mutually contradictory theories associated with terms such as postmodernism, poststructuralism, constructivism, narrativism and the linguistic turn. Hayden White's writings rocked the foundations of the historical discipline's claims to being a science, whilst at the same time calling on historians to use their talents as writers of historical literature to pursue projects of political interventions in society. If, as Chris Lorenz has insisted, narrative choices were restricted by evidence, theories of narrativism have underpinned a growing awareness in the historical profession that multiple narratives about the past underlie multiple visions of the future that are part and parcel of political conflicts in democratically constituted societies. Re-appropriations of cultural meanings, Michel de Certeau reminded his readers, were strategies for power struggles in which historical work was deeply engaged. Like White's 'metahistory', Michel Foucault' 'historical archaeology' emphasised how history, as a discursive construction of the past, was always related to power struggles and the stabilisation or destabilisation of social orders. It was possible for historians, Foucault argued, to recover the plural meanings of the past and thus undermine the grand narratives that rested on dominant readings of that past. Coming from a very different perspective, Pierre Bourdieu has argued that such dominant narratives were at the heart of forms of cultural reproduction that led to the formation of a particular habitus on the basis of a cultural capital that boosted social identities.

However much historians had wanted in the past to provide narratives that were in the service of dominant political, economic, social and cultural orders, they could never entirely silence the polyphony of voices coming to us from the past. Hence, Mikhail Bakhtin spoke of the 'unfinalisability' of history and the open-endedness of the past, and Roland Barthes demonstrated how texts always contained multiple meanings. Based on Jacques Lacan's argument about identities being based on illusions, Jacques Derrida built his edifice of deconstruction as a system of creating differences that would decentre the self and pluralise meanings. For collective identities this meant that they could no longer be seen as fixed and essential, but instead as undergoing constant changes and transformations and being based on hybrid constructions of 'self' and 'other'. Gender theorists, e.g. Judith Butler, postcolonial thinkers, e.g. Homi Bhabha, and theorists of class, e.g. Ernesto Laclau and Chantal Mouffe, were strongly influenced by deconstruction. I have shown how all these theorists inspired a new generation of historians to write new histories more aware of the relationship between historical writing and collective identity formation, and leading to a serious questioning of the analytical usefulness of concepts of collective identity.[16] Slowly but surely, a 'happy eclecticism' emerged in the historical profession.[17] It was based on some of the insights derived by the historical theorists, mentioned above, whose ideas had percolated to practising historians, often through the work of historical primers seeking to distil philosophical works into doses acceptable to historians, or via distinguished representatives of various sub-fields of historical writing who espoused the virtues of those theories for practising historians.[18] In this way, essentialist languages of identity were replaced by constructed languages of 'identification' (Stuart Hall), as scholars searched for non-essentialist strategic forms of collective identity politics.

Older Histories Remade: Political, Social and Cultural History

In Chapter 2, I traced the impact of those new theoretical foundations on one of the oldest and most established forms of historical writing, political history. After demonstrating how diverse forms of traditional political history writing were linked to essentialist forms of nationalist collective identity politics, I argued that it was no coincidence that the crisis of political history came at precisely the moment when traditional national paradigms came under increasing scrutiny in the 1960s and 1970s. Building on longer-standing critiques of historiographical nationalism, such as those provided by Jacob Burckhardt and the first generation of the Annales historians in the interwar period, I have shown how the 'new political history' set out to remake political history writing along four axes. First, it discovered popular politics, the everyday and the emergence of mass politics, and sought to connect an older history interested in elites with popular politics. An emphasis on political culture and what Foucault had termed regimes of governmentality followed.[19] Postcolonial historians began to write history that paid attention to the 'subaltern', extending the realm of the political and, at the same time, questioning some of the Western-centric conceptualisations of the political.[20] Whilst some of the postcolonial writing was in the service of national self-liberation, it nevertheless tended to be highly self-reflective about its strategic interventions in contemporary social struggles. Secondly, the 'new political history' put a heavy emphasis on the languages of politics – something which linked it to the history of concepts discussed in Chapter 8 of this book. Historians examined the production of meaning through language in relation to the construction of collective identities. Under the influence of Bourdieu, they began to move from discourses to practices, taking seriously the material cultures that influenced particular political cultures (see also Chapter 10). Thirdly, the 'new political history', in seeking links to other fields of history writing, sought to evade a self-referential posture that had characterised the older political history's fixation with high politics. I used the example of the political history of religion to underline that point. Fourthly and finally, the 'new political history' contributed to the 'glocalisation'[21] of political history by highlighting the importance of political transfers of ideas and practices from one locality to another. Subsequently a transregional and transnational dimension characterised much of the 'new political history' and thus contributed also to the decentring of collective identities (see also Chapter 11).

The third chapter dealt with social, economic and labour history. I argued that it was the main strand of history writing which challenged the dominance of political history writing in the 1960s and 1970s. Much of it was infused with structuralism and its totalising assumptions built around master narratives of modernisation and class structures. This was also the reason why, soon after reaching its highpoint in the 1970s, it was challenged from diverse directions. An older political history fought a rearguard action against social history, but more damaging to it was the attack on it conducted by historians previously sympathetic to social history. New cultural historians, historians from below, an international history workshop movement and oral historians were in the forefront of those seeking to challenge the commitment of social history to simplistic stories of progress and modernisation. New categories, including those of subjectivity, experience, representation and narrativisation, challenged the social historians' macro-social theories. Making use of many of the theories discussed in Chapter 1, historians now criticised the scientificity of social science history, claiming that it came with a deadening inability to create narratives that could inspire and engage wider audiences. David Harlan, for example, called on fellow historians to use the arsenal of poststructuralist theories to write history as a moral reflection on the present, and thus fulfil a contemporary social function.[22]

Out of these debates, I argued, emerged a new social, economic and labour history less concerned with labour movements and social structures and more intent on exploring the worlds of ordinary workers and subaltern classes. The influence of postcolonialism and unorthodox Marxists such as E. P. Thompson was strong.[23] More concerned with representations, symbols and narratives than structures, the new social history sought inspiration from the new cultural history. The study of discourses and practices now became the staple diet of new social historians. They became far more self-reflexive about their commitment to collective identity formations such as class. De-essentialising class identities meant that scores of new social historians invested heavily in showing how diversely these identities were constructed under specific conditions in different parts of the world and in close association with constructions of gender, race and religious identities.

If the new cultural history had been vital in remaking social history, it had also recalibrated its own sub-field, cultural history, the subject of Chapter 4. In the 1980s the cultural turn in historical writing became associated with poststructuralist, postcolonial and constructivist theories. James W. Cook has pointed out that we should not understand the 'cultural turn' as something that had been achieved, was now closed and written in stone, but as a process of 'turning' that has to be ongoing.[24] Attention to impersonal structures was replaced by interest in human everyday experiences situated in relational and situational processes that were changing over time. The new cultural history, I argued, was still linked in various ways to a variety of different emancipatory agendas, grouped around gender, race, ethnicity and class, but it was more self-reflective about producing 'identifications' that were part and parcel of wider political struggles. The intense study of cultural transfers and theories of alterity, associated with Mikhail Bakhtin, produced concepts such as creolisation and hybridity that inspired generations of new cultural historians to investigate collective identities at and across borders, physical and mental ones.[25] De-essentialising those identities and revealing them as processual tools in social struggles became a key concern of new cultural historians who developed a range of promising new sub-fields, including the history of emotions, the history of the body and the history of violence I discussed in Chapter 4. The historiographical turn to culture was accompanied by calls from various marginalised sub-groups in society for the right to cultural identity, but also by politically right-wing attempts to foster traditional nationalist identities through cultural history. I have shown how both tendencies, in turn, brought with them the danger of new essentialisms incompatible with the body of theories discussed in Chapter 1. Nevertheless, the new cultural histories were, in the main, in line with those theories and led directly to the proliferation of 'new histories' discussed in Chapters 5–11.

History Keeps Turning . . .

Starting off with gender history, I noted the centuries-old struggle to give women a voice in history. Under the influence of the new cultural history, women's history was transformed into gender history. I noted the strong influence of poststructuralist theories, e.g. in the seminal work of Joan Wallach Scott.[26] The new cultural histories of gender and sexualities not only discovered men's studies but also investigated the construction of gender and sexual identities over time and place. Here gender histories overlapped with histories of private lives and histories of the body. Taking their cue from Michel Foucault's important work in the history of sexuality, the sub-field of the history of sexualities explored the full variety of sexual identities and forged important links to other fields of historical writing, including political history, the history of empire, the history of sciences, economic history, the history of nationalism and the history of warfare. Gender histories, I have shown, were vital in de-essentialing gender and sexual identities by questioning the binary construction of the categories 'men' and 'women' and investigating the relational character of gender constructions with notions of race, class and religion. Moving from an interest in the discursive construction of gender to a concern with embodied experiences,[27] gender historians began to understand gender identities as an ongoing work in progress, diverse at different times and places.

Emerging out of women's history, people's histories, histories from below, history workshop movements and micro-histories, historical anthropology followed anthropology in seeking a more grounded and situated knowledge committed to retrieving from the past the voices of the underprivileged and the subaltern. Anthropologists such as Clifford Geertz, Marshal Sahlins and Alan Macfarlane inspired historians looking for ways out of the cage of macro-social theories. For many, I have shown, the turn to historical anthropology was also a turn away from the link between history writing and dominant forms of essentialised constructions of collective identity. An interest in narrativism and poststructuralism (once again, the writings of Foucault were central here) led to a concern with rewriting history from the margins that would strengthen counter-hegemonic narratives. A playful openness towards the indeterminacy of the past led historical anthropologists to search for diversity, plurality, performativity and resistances to dominant practices. Theories of the everyday and its relatedness to structures of power, e.g. those of Michel de Certeau and Pierre Bourdieu, led historical anthropologists to view the past as a stage on which the agency of ordinary people and their performance played a vital role in giving the evolving drama of the past multiple directions. Stressing the fluidity of cultural systems, historical anthropologists insisted that cultures could not be fixed and related to essences. In their attention to the life cycle of human existences, to religion and magic, they contributed to a de-essentialisation of collective identities. Foundationalisms were replaced by a series of mimetic processes that transformed what it copied and produced something new in the process. Historical anthropologists thus also decentred a Western-centric universalist perspective and defamiliarised the familiar.

The history of memory was directly rooted in the interest in questions of representation and construction that came with the new cultural history. Highlighting contestation as a central ingredient of the history of memory, Chapter 7 traced the emergence of memory studies as a strongly transdisciplinary field in which history was one among many disciplines engaged upon the deconstruction of how memories had constituted collective identities in the past and present. If, originally, the history of memory was strongly related to national frames, the sub-field has been moving towards investigating (and often promoting) cosmopolitan and transnational forms of memory more recently. Such cosmopolitanism, I have demonstrated, was based on a greater self-reflexivity on the part of memory scholars about the link between memory and the construction of collective identities. Memory activists, including memory scholars, played an important role as agents in a range of transnational memory debates in which political attempts to link essentialised identities to constructions of memory were questioned.[28]

In many of the 'new histories' explored in the first seven chapters I have found a deep concern with concepts, of the political, the social, the cultural, and of gender, the everyday and of memory. Hence it is little surprising that concepts themselves became the focus of an increasingly popular sub-field of historical studies. Chapter 8 discussed different approaches to conceptual history and their relationship to a more self-reflexive historical practice when it comes to the construction of collective identities. I focused on two of the most influential schools in the history of concepts. First, I examined Reinhart Koselleck's idea of 'basic concepts' in history, one that he adorned in his theoretical writings with a whole string of influential and thought-provoking concepts, such as 'saddle time', the relationship between 'spaces of experiences' and 'horizons of expectations', 'histories of the future' and 'temporal layers'. They all were widely received by historians who sought to develop the history of concepts over the past forty years. Secondly, I investigated the so-called Cambridge school of intellectual history, homing in on two of its most influential historians, Quentin Skinner and J. G. A. Pocock. I showed how Skinner's writing on the history of political thought was heavily influenced by speech act theory. It sought to extract the production of meaning by properly contextualising texts and no longer understanding them as timeless wisdom. Pocock was more sceptical about authorial intention and the possibility of fixing meaning and understanding. Their 'contextualism',[29] I argued, amounted to a radical historisation of the history of political thought that, like Koselleck's ideas, amounted to a comprehensive deconstruction of conceptual attempts to forge collective identities around concepts of nation, class, race, religion and gender. By looking at the contextual narrative structuring of concepts and their performance in differing situations, conceptual historians problematised conceptual containers that had attempted to essentialise and fix collective identities in the past.

As the history of concepts was closely related to vernacular languages, I showed how it started from looking closely at concepts in one particular language. Over time, however, conceptual historians moved to a transnational history of concepts, paying due attention to transfers and translations between different languages. The construction of historical macro-regions such as the Balkans and Scandinavia was only possible against the background of conceptual battles about the meaning of these transnational entities. The same is true, I argued, when we look at conceptualisations of Europe. There the history of concepts has presented us with a kaleidoscopic view of interacting and contradictory concepts that did not allow a homogeneous and unilinear concept of Europe to emerge. Instead, the history of concepts provides us with multiple narrative frameworks, producing a variety of Europes. I have shown how historians of concepts have also been adept at exploring the conceptual contestation between peripheral spaces and the universalising ambitions of centres, be it in continental perspectives (even Europe had its centres and peripheries) or in imperial perspectives (colonisers and colonised). Conceptual historians demonstrated that concepts of nation, class, religion, race, gender and democracy are based on contested meanings. Producing their own counter-concepts, these concepts were characterised by plurality and ultimately indeterminacy. They have no essence and function in constant relationship with a host of other concepts in the search for the construction of meaning through language.

The heavy emphasis on language in the history of concepts, but also in all 'new histories' inspired by forms of narrativism, poststructuralism and constructivism produced a backlash in the form of the visual and material culture turns in historical writing discussed in Chapters 9 and 10 respectively. The visual turn highlighted the plurality and heterogeneity, in other words, the 'perspectivism', of interpretations of images.[30] It rested on bodies of theories discussed in Chapter 1 and developed further by theorists of the visual, including Bruno Latour and Jean Baudrillard. I have shown how visual histories of specific nations, European, Asian, American and African, began to problematise the use of images in the construction of collective national identities. Visual histories of social classes pointed to the power of images in stabilising and questioning social orders. Labour movements that challenged the capitalist economic system used images to produce conceptualisations of class as a collective willing and able to provide an alternative vision of social order, whilst anti-labour forces equally used images to convey their messages defending the capitalist order. Similarly, visual representations of work cemented class boundaries and related constructions of class to a host of other collective identities, including race and gender. Narratives of race, of whiteness, blackness, indigeneity were themselves visually constructed through sculpture, art, photography and film. Using examples from the Americas, Australia and Africa, I showed how ways of seeing race involved interlocutors and circulations that produced unstable narratives. These narratives trembled under the weight of their ambiguities and contradictions.

During the Middle Ages and in the modern world, visualising religious beliefs was, as I have shown, part and parcel of the formation of religious identities. Collective identities, like ethnicities and race, have been intricately intertwined with state-building processes and the self-positionings of a universalising church that go back deep into the Middle Ages. Influenced by Foucault, medievalists like Geraldine Heng have talked about medieval forms of 'race-making' in relation to anti-Jewish policies in thirteenth-century England, as well as in relation to the Crusades' political theology, which, according to Heng, amounted to a racist knowledge system. (See Figure 12.1.) Whiteness, she argued, became part and parcel of a Christian-European identity during the second half of the thirteenth century.[31] I explored the complicity of images of the Christian religion with colonising and racialising ambitions through work on Latin America and Africa, but I also pointed to the importance of secularised Christian images for an understanding of the post-Second World War identities

Figure 12.1 Miniature showing the expulsion of the Jews following the Edict of Expulsion of Edward I of England (18 July 1290), highlighting the violence against Jews that was the consequence of the racialisation of religious belonging that is discussed by Geraldine Heng's book. © The British Library Board, Marginal illustration from the Rochester Chronicle, Cotton Nero D. II., folio 183 v.

of Western metropoles. Finally, I highlighted how visual histories of gender have revealed women's exclusion from the public sphere and traced the women's movements' attempts to challenge the existing patriarchal gender order. In particular, the heavy gendering of diverse nationalisms has been a fruitful area for undermining the construction of collective identities in many parts of the world. Understanding the visual as a form of cultural and social action allowed historians to reconstruct multiple ways of seeing as the basis for differentiating between dominant and counter-narratives locked in ongoing contestations that make it impossible to fix the construction of collective identities.

Images were not just representations; they had a material base. I have shown how historians were discovering the materiality of images and of a wide range of objects that they found to be endowed with agency. The history of material culture saw objects as routes to past experiences and collective identities. They allowed greater self-reflexivity about the constructions of such experiences and identities. Located at the heart of a triangle seeking to relate objects, meanings and people to each other, histories of material culture were critical of the over-concentration on language of many of the new histories emerging in the wake of post-structuralist theories. At the same time, however, I have shown how historians of material culture built on ideas about the discursive construction of objects. Characteristically, many historians of material culture, like historians exploring discourses, started from Michel Foucault's claim that language and things produced social orders. Like many of the new histories, the history of material culture, as I have demonstrated, was strongly transdisciplinary in orientation, seeking inspiration from anthropology, architecture, design, sociology and many other disciplines concerned with objects. Giving agency to things, I argued further, meant decentring human agency and problematising the Anthropocene[32] as an age in which humans have ordered the world around them in hierarchical relation to themselves and their mental faculties. Historians of material culture have instead called for an understanding of historical processes that would abandon the long-standing logocentrist[33] opposition between the natural world and a world made by humans. The longevity of many things over times and places, I argued, highlighted the multiplicity of meanings produced by them. It gave them a certain unruly and undisciplined agency that undermined constructions of fixed and stable collective identities.

Following on from Bourdieu, historians of material culture have explored the relationship of things to the production of social distinctions. In Chapter 10 I gave multiple examples of how histories of objects have deconstructed notions of homogeneous and essentialised collective identities. Material culture has been crucial in reconceptualising national histories in the USA, Japan, China, New Zealand and Indonesia, and I am sure many other examples could have been added. But not only national histories were reconceptualised through material objects. The same is true for regional histories. Here I presented the examples of the north-east of England and the Ruhr region of Germany. Furthermore, things have been vital in constructing class, gender and religious identities through dress, furniture, hairstyles, bodily adornments, housing, tools, natural resources, artwork and many other objects. The transnational turn in material culture histories pointed to circulations and transfers that undermined constructions of homogenised collective identities.

Indeed, many of the new histories discussed in Chapters 5–10 participated in the transnational turn in historical writing that moved history away from its long prioritisation of the national container. Although one should not underestimate the extent to which methodological nationalism still continues to perpetuate national imaginaries in scholarship,[34] Chapter 11 examined this transnational turn in its own right and highlighted its links to the emergence of global history as one of the most booming and fashionable fields in historical writing in recent years. Theoretical debates between the proponents of comparison and the advocates of cultural transfers have resulted in a sharpening of the theoretical arsenal of the key methods in global history. I discuss a wide variety of examples showing how global history has contributed to questioning previous constructions of essentialised and homogeneous collective identities. I have shown how the study of borders and migrations has been particularly influential in highlighting the role of transfers and circulations in the shifting and contested constructions of such identities. A global labour history, I concluded, has decentred Western concepts of class and enriched our understanding of how diverse work regimes underpinned a wide variety of constructed collective identities among the subaltern classes of the world. Comparative and transnational histories of race have challenged collective identities constructed on the exclusion by race. They have identified a global colour line, whilst global histories of gender have underlined the intersectionality and diversity of gender orders around the globe. Strong postcolonial perspectives on global history produced a transnational understanding of regimes of colonialism that highlighted the inability of the West to maintain its own moral standards and thereby undermined their legitimacy. Global historians have also been highly aware of their own potential role in legitimating contemporary processes of globalisation. They have called for the need to be self-reflexive about their own positioning in existing power regimes. Whilst global history has ended the long reification of the nation (without denying its crucial importance in many histories), I argued that it should be wary of reifying the global as a privileged site for historical investigations of the future. In its desire to highlight the constructed nature of collective identities and its theoretical anchoring in the body of theories discussed in Chapter 1, global history has been quite exemplary in achieving high levels of self-reflexivity, even if I did also briefly refer to forms of global history that do still justify new nationalisms and dominant economic and social orders.

The Struggle over and with History will Continue

In analysing the making of the 'new history' since the 1980s, I focused on academic history writing that betrayed the influence of the body of theories discussed in Chapter 1. Most of its practitioners are cosmopolitan in orientation and lean politically to the left. They are prominently represented within the global academy and have often occupied influential positions within nationally and transnationally constituted professional associations. Hence, I find it justified to talk about a global development of the historical profession towards more self-reflexive ways of writing history, especially vis-à-vis its relationship to the construction of collective identities. Yet I already concluded my first chapter with a warning not to mistake the argument of the book with a new kind of Whiggish progressivism that posits a progressive march of the historical profession towards greater self-reflexivity and the deconstruction of all forms of collective identity formation. Within the academy, many who under the influence of poststructuralism, narrativism and constructivism, started to dismantle dominant narratives, were keen to promote counter-narratives that sought to empower hitherto marginalised groups in society: women, LGBTI groups, ethnic minorities, indigenous populations and those suffering social, racial and religious discrimination. Indeed, an 'engaged'[35] scholarship has often directly supported social movements championing the rights of these marginalised groups (women's movements, civil rights movements, indigenous rights movements, LGBTI movements, etc.). Such engaged scholarship upheld and fostered constructions of collective identities, albeit mostly in the sense of Stuart Hall's concept of 'identification' discussed in Chapter 1. In other words, the historians in question were aware of the constructed and political nature of these identity claims and did not seek to underpin ideas of their naturalness, homogeneity and non-changing character. The construction of collective identities was a situational and relational weapon in a political struggle for rights and recognition against dominant power structures seeking to deny such rights and recognition. The new histories thus did not bring about an end to identity history; they practised identity histories in a more self-reflective mode.

It should also be recognised that in many historical professions around the world, historians remain committed to writing a more traditional history that seeks to stem the tide and is committed to an ongoing essentialisation of collective identities around national, class, religious, ethnic and gender identities.[36] I have not dealt with this work, because it does not seem to me to be among the most innovative and cutting-edge. This says nothing, of course, about its influence. In the ongoing Australian history wars, which began in the 1990s, the political goals of John Howard's Liberal-National government to boost white Australian nationalism and criticise those who had problematised it, especially vis-à-vis the treatment of Australia's indigenous population in the past, were supported by a minority of prominent historians such as Geoffrey Blainey and Keith Windschuttle. The vast majority of (mainly white) Australian historians steadfastly opposed any attempts to whitewash the terrible catastrophes that their white forefathers had brought upon the native population.[37] Nevertheless, in broader historical culture, the political support of the Liberal government bolstered the whiteness of Australia's national identity that continued to produce forms of racism and refused to accept responsibility for the history of the colonisation of a non-white Australia.[38] In Hungary, to give another example, the Fidesz government of Victor Orbán has founded two new institutions for historical research which many have accused of being official history institutes charged with the task of rewriting Hungarian national history in a way that fits the political outlook of Orbán and his allies. The Veritas Research Institute, on its website, endorses unbiased research, but it has found it difficult to escape the whiff of being a government-funded institution. Similarly, the Research Institute and Archives for the History of the Hungarian Regime Change has come directly under the Prime Minister's Office, indicating that the legacy of the post-communist transition is a history with special political relevance for the Orbán regime. The Fidesz government has also prominently sought to influence the teaching of Hungarian history in school in the direction of a more nationalist orientation. The government founded a publishing house to churn out history books that were in line with its history politics. New memorial days celebrating the Hungarians' exceptional national achievements were introduced.[39] Not only do governments use historians in their political ambitions. At crisis moments, historians can still achieve remarkable influence over the direction of nation-states. This is exemplified by the case of the Estonian historians in the transition period in the late 1980s and early 1990s. In the new-found independent nation-state of Estonia their interpretations laid the foundations for the political orientation of the state and their legacy has survived to the present day.[40] Historians interact with a whole host of other actors to produce a vibrant history politics that, to a remarkable extent, remains focused on contested national collective identities.[41]

If there are still more than enough professional historians lending their pens to constructions of collective identities, it is also noticeable that historical writers outside the academy have taken up this task in areas where the academy itself has, by and large, abandoned it. The attempts by the Indian Prime Minister Narendra Modi to strengthen Hindu nationalism in India have relied on publicists and freelance writers to produce history books that have been popular and often achieved considerable media attention and high circulation figures due to government and nationalist support. University-based historians overwhelmingly distanced themselves from those attempts. They countered the government measures seeking to restrict the independence of Indian universities and, through legal proceedings, to prevent academic freedom of expression where it threatened its Hindu nationalist agenda.[42] Popular forms of history writing, often involving non-professional historians, are not new phenomena. In various parts of the world they have exercised a strong influence.[43] However, where the high priests of a history with capital 'H', who still claim the high ground of extracting objective truth about the past from the archives, have been willing to serve at the altar of collective identities, popular historians are less needed or needed only as auxiliary forces. At a time when the body of theories I referred to in Chapter 1 has largely exploded the certainties of history with a capital 'H' and unclothed its high priests, the latter have become wary of serving collective identities or are doing so only with strong doses of self-reflexivity about their positioning in political struggles. This gave popular, non-professional historians not only reasons to claim that their truths were as valid of those of the professional historians, it also made it possible for those in political power to draw on them to promote the kind of collective identities they wanted to promote through historical writing. Examples from different parts of the world of nationalist governments relying on the espousal of nationalist histories by publicists and writers outside the gates of the academy could easily be multiplied. The same is true for the espousal of religious fundamentalism and for an essentialised class discourse on the wilder shores of a radical left that, unlike religious and nationalist fundamentalism, today seems almost completely marginalised politically.

If we have to admit that the construction of essentialised, homogeneous and totalising collective identities through historical narratives is not a thing of the past, do we also have to ask ourselves to what extent professional historians have left a gap for others – publicists, journalists and freelance writers – who have not been shy in putting their pens in the service of collective identity formation? Where university historians have been withdrawing to their ivory towers, remaining aloof from debates about collective identities in wider society, this would indeed be a serious charge. However, many of the historians I discussed are politically engaged, seeking to use their historical insights to intervene in contemporary debates. Their interventions have mostly been in the spirit of what Joan W. Scott, building on the work of Jacques Rancière, has powerfully called the 'historicisation of identity':

> If instead of asking how women were treated in some former time, we ask how and in what circumstances the difference of their sex came to matter in their treatment, then we have provided the basis for an analysis of 'women' that is not a rediscovery of ourselves in the past . . . If we ask not how African Americans . . . were treated under slavery, but how and under what

circumstances race came to justify forced labor, we understand the oppression of slaves but have to ask different questions about how racism constructs black identity today. Or if we document not the long history of homophobia, but the ways and times and terms in which certain sexual practices were pathologized and others normalized, we historicize rather than naturalize both homosexuality and heterosexuality. Or, to take up the matter of national identity again, if we ask not what it means to be an American, but how Americanness has been defined – and by whom – over time, we can write the history of the United States not as the realization of an essence, but as the story of ongoing political contestation around terms and practices that are at once durable and changeable.[44]

This is precisely what historians of gender, race, sexuality, nation and other collective identities have increasingly done over the past three decades, and it amounts to a politics of identity that is highly self-reflexive about its constructions of collective identities through historical narratives.

Thus, we have seen an increasing trend for professional historians engaging with the public in the form of exhibitions curated by academics, or where academics, at the very least, had important positions on advisory bodies. Whereas a public historian like A. J. P. Taylor was slighted in the 1960s for appearing on television,[45] today many historians are keen to talk to the media, including newspapers, radio, television and film, in order to spread their sometimes highly specialised research findings to wider audiences and bring out the political and societal implications of their work. In some countries, such as Britain, the government has pushed so-called impact agendas that have encouraged academics to bring out the societal relevance of their research and seek to influence debates and policies. However, the impact agenda has also been criticised as a tool to further the commodification of British higher education along the lines of New Public Management ideals and to functionalise research in instrumentalist ways.[46] The government's power in many countries to fund research in particular areas and not in others certainly has an impact on what kind of research finds an airing in wider arenas. In the same vein, the power of the media to produce certain kinds of histories and not others also had an impact on what was presented to wider publics. Why is it, one may ask, that rather conservative historians such as David Starkey and Niall Ferguson have been dominating the television programmes in Britain with high-profile series on Tudor kings and queens and the history of empire that play to very traditional and politically conservative tropes in British society? At the European level, the research programmes of the European Union – over recent years in the form of Horizon 2020 (now Horizon Europe) programmes – have also had a strongly functionalist approach in seeking answers from researchers to what were seen by the EU to be politically pressing problems. Whilst this has produced a range of engaged histories, and whilst it has been important to retain scholarly autonomy over what should and should not be funded, there remains an agenda-setting function for EU politics in terms of what is defined as relevant research and what is not.

One sign that history has been reaching out to wider publics is the rise of public history over recent years. History, like almost never before, has been present in many parts of the world. Historical markets, graphic novels, industrial ruins, historical re-enactment, living history, dark history, themed historical city walks – the consumption of history is popular, and doing history seems to provide many people with emotional, sensual and corporeal experiences that are meaningful to their personal selves. Indeed, the question has been asked whether empathy and emotional engagement are not necessary prerequisites for all historical learning.[47] Tourism has discovered this attractiveness of the past, and from industrial heritage and war heritage to medieval heritage and prehistoric heritage, there is hardly an area of history that is not commodified and commercialised today in pursuit of paying customers. Historical learning is often not top of the agenda in these undertakings. We still know far too little about how millions of ordinary people engage with history around the globe. But it would be fair to assume that for many people their engagement with the past is identity-related. Performing the past is one way of eradicating the difference between the past and the present and creating the illusion of similarity. Thus, many kinds of public history run counter to the tendency of professional history writing to stress the alterity of the past and to be more self-reflexive about identifications and the relation of historical writing to the construction of collective identities. In a large survey of the uses of the past in American people's lives, Roy Rosenzweig and David Thelen found that people used the past in manifold and often contradictory ways to make sense of themselves and the ways they lived. Identity was thus high on the agenda of why people developed an interest in the past, even if that identity was often related not so much to grand narratives about collectives such as nations and classes, but rather to local issues and concerns.[48]

Within the historical profession, public history is becoming increasingly well established, not least because many students hope that it is something practical that will offer them better opportunities in the job market. That is why the textbooks and handbooks of the new subdiscipline often stress the practical side of public history.[49] National associations for public history have been founded in many countries. New journals such as *International Public History* have been established (in 2018). An International Federation for Public History, founded in 2010, is providing a forum for transnational exchanges. Museums, archives, heritage centres, preservation movements, theatres, film companies, community and company histories, and digital histories all offer a wide field for public historians. Public history is actively interested in incorporating a wider public into the practice of historical work. It is thus genuinely collaborative, seeking to engage the public on the premise 'that people are active agents in creating histories'.[50] They are seeking to bring about a more participatory historical culture, and it seems to me that the overwhelming majority of them are attempting to move public history precisely in the direction of greater self-reflexivity and types of historical learning that allow for self-reflective identitification rather than essentialised identity. Problem-oriented historical learning seems to be high on the agenda of public history. Civil engagement and greater social justice as well as the fostering of democratic cultures are themes close to the heart of many public historians. Many of them stress the importance of dealing historically and locally with a range of ethical dilemmas where it is vital that people can make informed decisions on the basis of a solid consideration about the past.[51] Of course, a great deal of public history is contracted history, where those who pay (as in the case of companies) determine at least to a certain extent the outcome of historical research. But even in these cases, those who pay have to be aware that a semblance of independence is a vital precondition for the credibility of the contracted research. The historical methods of public history are manifold and build on those previously championed by history-from-below approaches like oral history. There is, in any case, a considerable continuity between a history from below, as championed in the 1960s and 1970s, and public history. Public historians are at the forefront of communicating history to wider publics. Yet historians, like other scholars in the social sciences and humanities, pay increasing attention to communicating the results of their research to wider audiences through outreach activities and through involving stakeholder groups – putting themselves in a long tradition of engaged history writing.[52]

The vociferous debates surrounding the publication of Jo Guldi and David Armitage's *History Manifesto* in 2014 centred on their charge that historians had lost the role of public arbiters that they had supposedly once possessed.[53] According to Guldi and Armitage, the historians' voices were never more needed than in the present that they see characterised by a crisis of global governance consisting of unregulated financial markets, climate change and questions about the survival of the human species. Scientific long-term thinking that they associate with scholars such as the Webbs, R. H. Tawney, Fernand Braudel and Eric Hobsbawm, they argue, has been replaced with professional 'short-termism'. This they see rooted in an over-concentration on micro-history combined with the, in their view, destructive potential of postmodernism, which has led the profession to lose its public role. However, as the manifold examples given above demonstrate, there has been no shortage of public engagement among historians. As Deborah Cohen and Peter Mandler pointed out in their response to the manifesto, historians already occupy manifold public roles and enjoy the attention of sizeable audiences: 'It is precisely the diversity of our discipline, its rich, humane traditions that speak to the multiple audiences on all the scales in which humans feel and think, that have made us an indispensable part of the educational and cultural landscape over the past generation.'[54] The new histories that have been the subject of this volume have, I argue, been part and parcel of the diversifying tendencies that have enriched our understanding of the past, problematised history's relationship to the construction of collective identities, and intervened in contemporary social and political debates through various conceptualisations of 'practical pasts'.[55]

I could provide many examples of historians working as public intellectuals. Let me just mention briefly two impressive ones. Georg G. Iggers had to flee National Socialist Germany when he was a young boy. Making his career as a historian in the USA, his experience of racial discrimination was one factor why he decided, early on, to join the civil rights struggle of African Americans, working at African-American institutions of higher education and being active on behalf of the National Association for the Advancement of Colored People

(NAACP). Specialising in intellectual history, he became best-known for his book on *The Conception of German History* which sought to explain why German historiography, with few exceptions, had become the handmaiden of statist, conservative, nationalist and, in the context of the Third Reich, even racialist politics.[56] The book was an important intervention also in the remaking of the German historical profession and its political alignments during the 1960s and 1970s. Iggers was active in the campaign against the Vietnam war, advising conscientious objectors. Although highly critical of communism, he nevertheless sought to contribute to attempts to end the Cold War by building bridges between historians on either side of the Cold War divide, and later to historians in communist China. One of his last initiatives before his death in 2017 was the attempt to end the isolation of Cuban historians and bring them back into the world community of historians.[57]

Another example of a public intellectual, this time from Britain, is Catherine Hall. Family life – she was married to Stuart Hall until his death in 2014 – had initially drawn her away from academic life. But when she picked up academic work again, it was consistently characterised by promoting feminist and anti-racist positions through insights derived from historical study. The impact of gendered subjectivities on class societies like Britain[58] and the decolonisation of British national history were two of the big themes she explored, and both had enormous repercussions for questions of gender and race in contemporary Britain. In edited collections such as *Cultures of Empire* and *At Home with the Empire*,[59] she explored the extent to which the histories of colonialism and the history of the island nation were intricately linked. In her monograph *Macaulay and Son*,[60] she revealed how the architect of one of the most influential national master narratives of England was at the same time embroiled in the history of slavery and empire. The legacies of racism and the violence of enslavement also led her to direct the Legacies of British Slave-Ownership project. It provided a huge database containing the identities of slave-owning families in the British Caribbean between 1763 and 1833.[61] The project showed how the wealth of many of the wealthiest people in Britain today was built on slavery.

Many other examples of historians as engaged public intellectuals could be added. They are a sign that history has a role to play in producing identifications, in the sense that we defined them with

Stuart Hall's work in Chapter 1. But they are also often a sign of the historians' growing self-reflexivity about forms of collective identity – in the case of Iggers, those of race, nation and ideology, and in the case of Hall, those of race, class and gender. As François Dosse wrote at the end of the introduction to his masterful history of the Annales school in France: 'History remains a science under construction in the image of our society from which it cannot be separated. And so the struggle for history continues.'[62] That struggle is a struggle of constructed narratives that will forever remain plural and contested. The recent strong interest in the history of temporalities has increased this tendency. Explorations into how historians have dealt with the issue of historical time and the recognition that different time regimes exist contemporaneously highlighted the constructed nature of all historical writing. As Matthew Champion wrote: 'The history of temporaralities is, in this mode, a self-reflexive history that must be alert to the temporal forms of historical analysis and representations, and to the temporal assumptions and habits that shape fields and objects of knowledge.'[63] Multiple contemporaneous temporalities are pluralising perspectives on the past, making it more difficult to streamline the past into homogeneous identitarian master narratives. In his reflections on the changing role of historians over the past half-century, Stuart Woolf ended on a depressing note, arguing that they have become more defensive about their profession and uncertain about the direction they are going in.[64] However, whilst I do not disagree with any of the developments so cogently analysed by Woolf, I do not share his sense of loss. Rather, I hope that this book is testimony to the profession's transformation in the direction of a more self-reflective and more socially engaged practice of historical writing. In a beautiful reflection on the relationship between history, theory and poetry, Andrew Zimmermann, following Heidegger, argued that writing and thinking are always related to versifying rather than verifying.[65]

Notes

1 Introduction: History and Identity

1. Allan Megill, 'Historical Representations: Identity, Allegiance', in: Stefan Berger, Linas Eriksonas and Andrew Mycock (eds.), *Narrating the Nation: Representations in History, Media and the Arts*, Oxford: Berghahn Books, 2008, 32.
2. The centrality of issues of identity in many different types of histories is discussed by the contributions in Heidrun Friese (ed.), *Identities: Time, Difference and Boundaries*, Oxford: Berghahn Books, 2002.
3. Thomas Sizgorich, 'Religious History', in: Sara Foot and Chase F. Robinson (eds.), *The Oxford History of Historical Writing, vol. II: 400–1400*, Oxford: Oxford University Press, 2012, 604–28. See also Gabrielle M. Spiegel, 'Historical Thought in Medieval Europe', in: Lloyd Kramer and Sarah Maza (eds.), *A Companion to Western Historical Thought*, Oxford: Blackwell, 2002, 78–98.
4. John Sandberg, 'Religion and the Enlightenment(s)', in: *History Compass* 8:11 (2010), 1291–8.
5. Chantal Grell, *L'histoire entre erudition et philosophie: étude sur la conaissance historique à l'âge des Lumières*, Paris: Presses Universitaires de France, 1993; Murray Pittock, 'History and the Teleology of Civility in the Scottish Enlightenment', in: Peter France and Susan Manning (eds.), *Enlightenment and Emancipation*, Lewisburg, PA: Bucknell University Press, 2006, 90.
6. On Enlightenment history writing and its ties to the idea of progress see Johnson Kent Wright, 'Historical Thought in the Era of the Enlightenment', in: Kramer and Maza (eds.), *Companion*, 123–42.
7. On all processes of the institutionalisation and professionalisation of historical writing see Ilaria Porciani and Lutz Raphael (eds.), *Atlas of European Historiography: the Making of a Profession, 1800–2005*, Basingstoke: Palgrave Macmillan, 2010; Ilaria Porciani and Jo Tollebeek (eds.), *Setting the Standards: Institutions, Networks and Communities of National Historiography*, Basingstoke: Palgrave

Macmillan, 2012; Rolf Thorstendahl, *The Rise and Propagation of Historical Professionalism*, London: Routledge, 2015.

8. On the complex relationship between empires and nations in Europe during the long nineteenth century see Stefan Berger and Alexei Miller (eds.), *Nationalizing Empires*, Budapest: Central European University Press, 2015.
9. Andreas Wimmer and Nina Glick-Schiller, 'Methodological Nationalism and Beyond: Nation-State Building, Migration and the Social Sciences', in: *Global Networks* 2:4 (2002), 301–34.
10. Irène Herrmann and Franziska Metzger, 'A Truculent Revenge: the Clergy and the Writing of National History', in: Porciani and Tollebeek (eds.), *Setting the Standards*, 313–29.
11. James G. Crossley and Christian Karner (eds.), *Writing History, Constructing Religion*, Aldershot: Ashgate, 2005; Mimi Hanaoka, *Authority and Identity in Medieval Islamic Historiography: Persian Histories from the Peripheries*, Cambridge: Cambridge University Press, 2016.
12. C. J. W. Parker, 'The Failure of Liberal Racialism: E. A. Freeman', in: *Historical Journal* 24 (1991), 825–46; Thomas Gerhards, *Heinrich von Treitschke: Wirkung und Wahrnehmung eines Historikers im 19. und 20. Jahrhundert*, Paderborn: Schöningh, 2013.
13. Ingo Haar and Michael Fahlbusch (eds.), *German Scholars and Ethnic Cleansing, 1920–1945*, Oxford: Berghahn Books, 2005.
14. Paul Maylam, *South Africa's Racial Past: the History and Historiography of Racism, Segregation and Apartheid*, Avebury: Ashgate, 2001.
15. Robin D. G. Kelley, '"But a Local Phase of a World Problem": Black History's Global Vision, 1883–1950', in: *Journal of American History* 86:3 (1999), 1045–77; Gérard Bouchard, *The Making of the Nations and Cultures of the New World: an Essay in Comparative History*, Montreal: McGill-Queen's University Press, 2008.
16. Thomas Welskopp, 'Clio and Class Struggle in Socialist Histories of the Nation: a Comparison of Robert Grimm's and Eduard Bernstein's Writings, 1910–1920', in: Stefan Berger and Chris Lorenz (eds.), *Nationalizing the Past: Historians and Nation Builders in Modern Europe*, Basingstoke: Palgrave Macmillan, 298–318.
17. Luther Carpenter, *G. D. H. Cole: an Intellectual Biography*, Cambridge: Cambridge University Press, 1973; Anthony Wright, *R. H. Tawney*, Manchester: Manchester University Press, 1988.
18. Miroslav Hroch, 'Regional Memory: the Role of History in (Re)Constructing Regional Identity', in: Steven G. Ellis, Raingard Esser,

Jean-François Berdah and Miloš Řezník (eds.), *Frontiers, Regions and Identities in Europe*, Pisa: Pisa University Press, 2009, 1–15.

19. Stefan Troebst (ed.), 'Geschichtsregionen: Concept and Critique', special issue of *European Review of History* 10:2 (2003).
20. Antonis Liakos, 'The Canon of European History and the Conceptual Framework of National Historiographies', in: Matthias Middell and Lluis Roura y Aulinas (eds.), *Transnational Challenges to National History Writing*, Basingstoke: Palgrave Macmillan, 2013, 315–42.
21. For Britian see Robin W. Winks (ed.), *Historiography: the Oxford History of the British Empire, vol. V*, Oxford: Oxford University Press, 1999. This trend was regardless of the fact that, well into the twentieth century and the postcolonial world, it remained more prestigious for historians to obtain higher degrees from well-known universities in the metropoles rather than at the universities of the imperial peripheries.
22. Hervé Inglebert, *Le monde, l'histoire: essai sur les histoires universelles*, Paris: Presses Universitaires de France, 2014.
23. Eric Storm, 'The Spatial Turn and the History of Nationalism: Nationalism between Regionalism and Transnational Approaches', in: Stefan Berger and Eric Storm (eds.), *Writing the History of Nationalism*, London: Bloomsbury, 2019, 215–38.
24. Andrew Mycock and Marina Loskoutova, 'Nation, State and Empire: the Historiography of "High Imperialism" in the British and Russian Empires', in: Berger and Lorenz (eds.), *Nationalizing the Past*, 233–58. See Robert Seeley, *The Expansion of England: Two Courses of Lectures*, London: Macmillan, 1895, but the idea of a 'greater Britain' was widely popularised also by James Frederick Hodgetts, *Greater England: Being a Brief Historical Sketch of the Various Possessions of Her Majesty, the Empress Queen, in Europe, Asia, Africa, America and Oceania*, London: Hatchards, 1887.
25. Gita Deneckere and Thomas Welskopp, 'The "Nation" and "Class": European National Master-Narratives and their Social "Other"', in: Stefan Berger and Chris Lorenz (eds.), *The Contested Nation: Ethnicity, Class, Religion and Gender in National Histories*, Basingstoke: Palgrave Macmillan, 2008, 135–70.
26. James C. Kennedy, 'Religion, Nation and European Representations of the Past', in: Berger and Lorenz (eds.), *The Contested Nation*, 104–34.
27. Stefan Berger, 'A Return to the National Paradigm? National History Writing in Germany, Italy, France and Britain from 1945 to the Present', in: *Journal of Modern History* 77:3 (2005), 629–78.

28. Lutz Raphael, *Geschichtswissenschaft im Zeitalter der Extreme: Theorien, Methoden, Tendenzen von 1900 bis zur Gegenwart*, Munich: C. H. Beck, 2003, 215–27.
29. Roger Fieldhouse and Richard Taylor (eds.), *E. P. Thompson and English Radicalism*, Manchester: Manchester University Press, 2013.
30. Bonnie G. Smith, *The Gender of History: Men, Women and Historical Practice*, Cambridge, MA: Harvard University Press, 1998; Billie Melman, 'Gender, History and Memory: the Invention of Women's Past in the Nineteenth and Early Twentieth Centuries', in: *History and Memory* 5:1 (1993), 5–41.
31. Jitka Malečková, 'Where are Women in National Histories?', in: Berger and Lorenz (eds.), *The Contested Nation*, 171–99.
32. The terminology has been a matter of debate and development over time. Whilst initially historians talked about 'lesbian and gay' history, the proliferation of identities ultimately led to the acronym 'LGBT'. Under the impact of queer studies, it became 'LGBTQ'. Sometimes the further proliferation of sexual identities was indicated by adding a plus sign: 'LGBTQ+' or 'LGBT+'. Of late historians have been using 'LGBTI' with the 'I' standing for 'intersexual'. Without wanting to take sides in these debates about naming, I have used 'LGBTI' throughout the text.
33. Leila J. Rupp, 'Outing the Past: US Queer History in Global Perspective', in: Leila J. Rupp and Susan K. Freeman (eds.), *Understanding and Teaching US Lesbian, Gay, Bisexual and Transgender History*, Madison, WI: University of Wisconsin Press, 2014, 24.
34. Franz Fanon, *The Wretched of the Earth*, New York: Grove Press, 2004, 239.
35. Stefan Berger, 'Introduction: Toward a Global History of National Historiographies', in: Berger (ed.), *Writing the Nation: a Global Perspective*, Basingstoke: Palgrave Macmillan, 2007, 1–29.
36. Stefan Tanaka, *Japan's Orient: Rendering Pasts into History*, Berkeley: University of California Press, 1993.
37. John S. Brownlee, *Japanese Historians and the National Myths, 1600–1945: the Age of the Gods and Emperor Jinmu*, Vancouver: University of British Columbia Press, 1997.
38. Martin S. Shanguhyia and Toyin Falola, 'Introduction', in: Shanguhyia and Falola (eds.), *The Palgrave Handbook of African Colonial and Postcolonial History*, Basingstoke: Palgrave Macmillan, 2018, 4; see also in that volume, Robert M. Maxon, 'Decolonization Histories', 643–60.
39. Dipesh Chakrabarty, *Provincializing Europe: Postcolonial Thought and Historical Difference*, Princeton: Princeton University Press, 2000, 88.

40. On the concept of Eurocentrism see Antoon de Baets, 'Eurocentrism', in: Thomas Benjamin (ed.), *Encyclopedia of Western Colonialism since 1450, vol. I*, Detroit: Thomson Gale, 2007, 456–61.
41. Vasant Kaiwar, *The Postcolonial Orient: the Politics of Differences and the Project of Provincialising Europe*, Leiden: Brill, 2014.
42. On the history of the idea of identity see Gerald Izenberg, *Identity: the Necessity of a Modern Idea*, Philadelphia: University of Pennsylvania Press, 2016.
43. Stefan Berger, 'The Rise and Fall of "Critical" Historiography? Some Reflections on the Historiographical Agenda of the Left in Britain, France and Germany at the End of the Twentieth Century', in: *European Review of History* 3:2 (1996), 213–34.
44. Jürgen Kocka, *Geschichte und Aufklärung*, Göttingen: Vandenhoeck and Ruprecht, 1989.
45. Jörn Rüsen, *Evidence and Meaning: a Theory of Historical Studies*, Oxford: Berghahn Books, 2017, 105.
46. As the director of the Institute for Advanced Studies at the University Alliance Ruhr (Kulturwissenschaftliches Institut Essen), Rüsen directed a major project on humanism which resulted, among other things in a multi-volume book series with Transcript publishers entitled 'Being Human: Caught in the Web of Cultures – Humanism in the Age of Globalization'. See, for example, Jörn Rüsen and Henner Laass (eds.), *Humanism in Intercultural Perspective: Experiences and Expectations*, Bielefeld: Transcript, 2009; Oliver Kozlarek, Jörn Rüsen and Ernst Wolff (eds.), *Shaping a Humane World: Civilizations – Axial Times – Modernities – Humanisms*, Bielefeld: Transcript, 2012. Most recently: Jörn Rüsen, *Menschsein: Grundlagen, Geschichte und Diskurse des Humanismus*, Berlin: Kadmos, 2020.
47. Donald E. Brown, 'Human Nature and History', in: *History and Theory* 38:4 (1999), 138–57; Brown, *Human Universals*, New York: McGraw Hill, 1991.
48. Rüsen, *Evidence and Meaning*, 104–6.
49. Jessica Benjamin, *Shadow of the Other: Intersubjectivity and Gender in Psychoanalysis*, London: Routledge, 1998, xiii–xiv.
50. Ibid., xv. See also: Jessica Benjamin, *The Bonds of Love: Psychoanalysis, Feminism and the Problem of Domination*, New York: Pantheon, 1988.
51. Jörn Rüsen, 'Introduction: Historical Thinking as Intercultural Discourse', in: Rüsen (ed.), *Western Historical Thinking: an Intercultural Debate*, Oxford: Berghahn Books, 2002, 1–14.
52. Arthur Alfaix Assis, *What Is History For? Johann Gustav Droysen and the Functions of Historiography*, Oxford: Berghahn Books, 2014. See

also Wilfried Nippel, *Johann Gustav Droysen: ein Leben zwischen Wissenschaft und Politik*, Munich: C. H. Beck, 2008.

53. Jörn Rüsen, 'Responsibility and Irresponsibility in Historical Studies: a Critical Consideration of the Ethical Dimension of the Historian's Work', in: David Carr, Thomas R. Flynn and Rudolf A. Makkreel (eds.), *The Ethics of History*, Evanston, IL: Northwestern University Press, 2004.
54. On the development of 'scientificity' see Heiko Feldner, 'The New Scientificity in Historical Writing around 1800', in: Stefan Berger, Heiko Feldner and Kevin Passmore (eds.), *Writing History: Theory and Practice*, 3rd edn, London: Bloomsbury, 2020, 3–21.
55. Ernst Breisach, *On the Future of History: the Postmodern Challenge and Its Aftermath*, Chicago: University of Chicago Press, 2003. Whilst Breisach's book is hugely interesting in discussing the impact of a range of thinkers on the writing of history and whilst he acknowledges that influence, I am not sure that those theorists can be summed up under the heading of postmodernism.
56. Jane Caplan, 'Postmodernism, Poststructuralism and Deconstruction: Notes for Historians', in: *Central European History* 22:3/4 (1989), 260–78.
57. For a trenchant early analysis see Peter Schöttler, 'Historians and Discourse Analysis', in: *History Workshop Journal* 27 (1989), 37–65. Thomas Pegelow Kaplan has recently provided a plea to recognise the ongoing usefulness of linguistic approaches to the study of the past. See Thomas Pegelow Kaplan, 'History and Theory: Writing Modern European Histories after the Linguistic Turn', in: Michael Meng and Adam R. Seipp (eds.), *Modern Germany in Transatlantic Perspective*, Oxford: Berghahn Books, 2017, 21–46.
58. Ethan Kleinberg, 'Haunting History: Deconstruction and the Spirit of Revision', in: *History and Theory* 46:4 (2007), 113–43.
59. For a good introduction see Ann Curthoys and John Docker, *Is History Fiction?*, 2nd edn, Sydney: UNSW Press, 2010, 279–323.
60. Siegfried Kracauer, *History: the Last Things before the Last*, Oxford: Oxford University Press, 1969.
61. These different narrative forms are lucidly explained in: Herman Paul, *Key Issues in Historical Theory*, London: Routledge, 2015, 58–9.
62. Hayden White, *Metahistory: the Historical Imagination in Nineteenth-Century Europe*, Baltimore, MD: Johns Hopkins University Press, 1973.
63. A good introduction to the intricate relationship between narrations, collective identities and historical consciousness is provided by the contributions to Jürgen Straub (ed.), *Narration,*

Identity and Historical Consciousness, Oxford: Berghahn Books, 2005.

64. See Chris Lorenz, *Konstruktion der Vergangenheit: eine Einführung in die Geschichtstheorie*, Cologne: Böhlau, 1997, 400–14, 422–36.
65. Chris Lorenz, 'Historical Knowledge and Historical Reality: a Plea for "Internal Realism"', in: *History and Theory* 33 (1994), 297–327.
66. Stefan Berger and Chris Lorenz, 'Narrativity and Historical Writing: Introductory Remarks', in: Stefan Berger, Chris Lorenz and Nicola Brauch (eds.), *Analysing Historical Narratives: On Academic, Popular and Educational Framings of the Past*, Oxford: Berghahn Books, 2021, 1–28.
67. Geoffrey Roberts (ed.), *The History and Narrative Reader*, London: Routledge, 2001. On the impact of White on historical practice see Richard T. Vann, 'The Reception of Hayden White', in: *History and Theory* 37:2 (1998), 143–61; Gabrielle Spiegel, 'Rhetorical Theory/ Theoretical Rhetoric: Some Ambiguities in the Reception of Hayden White's Work', in: Robert Doran (ed.), *Philosophy of History after Hayden White*, London: Bloomsbury, 2013, 171–82; Philippe Carrard, 'Hayden White and/in France: Receptions, Translations, Questions', in: *Rethinking History* 22:4 (2018), 1–17; Wolfgang Weber, 'Hayden White in Deutschland', in: *Storia della Storiografia* 25 (1994), 89–102; Frank Ankersmit, 'Hayden White's Appeal to the Historians', in: *History and Theory* 37:2 (1998), 182–93. It should be noted that the concrete analysis of historical narratives with the toolbox of narratology is still in its infancy. See the case studies in Berger, Lorenz and Brauch (eds.), *Analysing Historical Narratives*.
68. Frank Anskersmit, *Narrative Logic: a Semantic Analysis of the Historian's Language*, Den Haag: Nijhoff, 1983; Anskersmit, *The Reality Effect in the Writing of History: the Dynamics of Historiographical Topology*, Amsterdam: Noord-Hollandsche, 1989; Anskersmit, *Historical Representation*, Stanford: Stanford University Press, 2001. On Ankersmit see also Marek Tamm and Eugen Zeleňak, 'In a Parallel World: an Introduction to Frank Ankersmit's Philosophy of History', in: *Journal of the Philosophy of History* 12 (2018), 325–44; Herman Paul and Adriaan van Veldhuizen, 'A Retrieval of Historicism: Frank Ankersmit's Philosophy of History and Politics', in: *History and Theory* 57:1 (2018), 33–55.
69. Philippe Carrard, 'History and Narrative: an Overview', in: *Narrative Works* 5:1 (2015), 174–96; Carrard, 'Historiographic Discourse and Narratology: a Footnote to Fludernik's Work on Factual Narrative', in: Jan Alber and Greta Olson (eds.), *How to Do Things with Narrative: Cognitive and Diachronic Perspectives*, Berlin: De

Gruyter, 2018, 125–40; see also Ann Rigney, 'History as Text: Narrative Theory and History', in: Nancy Partner and Sarah Foot (eds.), *The Sage Handbook of Historical Theory*, London: Sage, 2013, 183–202.

70. Joep Leerssen and Ann Rigney (eds.), *Historians and Social Values*, Amsterdam: Amsterdam University Press, 2000.
71. Hayden White, *The Practical Past*. Evanston, IL: Northwestern University Press, 2014.
72. Nietzsche distinguished between antiquarian, monumental and critical history writing. See Friedrich Nietzsche, *The Use and Abuse of History*, New York: Cosimo, 2010 (originally published 1873).
73. On White more generally see Herman Paul, *Hayden White*, Oxford: Blackwell, 2013; Frank Ankersmit, Ewa Domanska and Hans Kellner (eds.), *Re-Figuring Hayden White*, Stanford: Stanford University Press, 2009.
74. See also my remarks on de Certeau in Chapter 5 on historical anthropology.
75. Michel de Certeau, *The Writing of History*, New York: Columbia University Press, 1988. See also Mark Poster, *Cultural History and Postmodernity: Disciplinary Readings and Challenges*, New York: Columbia University Press, 1997, 108–19.
76. Jeremy Ahearne, *Michel de Certeau: Interpretation and Its Other*, Cambridge: Polity Press, 1995.
77. On agonistic politics see the work of Chantal Mouffe, *Agonistics: Thinking the World Politically*, London: Verso, 2013; Mouffe, *The Democratic Paradox*, London: Verso, 2000.
78. Kalle Pihlainen, *The Work of History: Constructivism and a Politics of the Past*, London: Routledge, 2017.
79. Nikolaos Avgelis, 'Lakatos on the Evaluation of Scientific Theories', in: Kostas Gavroglu, Yorgos Goudaroulis and Pantelis Nicolacopoulos (eds.), *Lakatos and Theories of Scientific Change*, Dordrecht: Kluwer, 1989, 160; Hugo A. Maynell, 'Anarchy and Falsification: Feyerabend and Popper', in: Maynell, *Redirecting Philosophy: Reflections on the Nature of Knowledge from Plato to Lonergan*, Toronto: University of Toronto Press, 1998, 130–51; Paul Feyerabend, *Against Method*, 3rd edn, London: Verso, 1993.
80. Marek Tamm, 'Truth, Objectivity and Evidence in History Writing', in: *Journal of the Philosophy of History* 8:2 (2014), 265–90; see also, for an emphasis on formal criteria of the discipline, Kalle Pihlainen, 'The Confines of the Form: Historical Writing and the Desire that It Be what It Is Not', in: Kuisma Korhohnen, Tr*opes for the Past: Hayden White and the History/Literature Debate*, Amsterdam: Rodopi, 2006, 55–67.

81. Chris Lorenz, '"You Got Your History, I Got Mine": Some Reflections on Truth and Objectivity in History', in: *Österreichische Zeitschrift für Geschichtswissenschaft* 10:4 (1999), 563–84.
82. My interest in theories that have questioned the link between historical writing and essentialised forms of identity construction led me to discuss White and Foucault together as thinkers who in their different ways paved the way for the critical examination of this link. It should be noted, however, that in other ways they can also be seen as diametrically opposed to each other, especially when considering their positions on epistemology. As Peter Schöttler has argued, White belonged to a tradition emphasising that historical knowledge was based on understanding developments in the past, whereas Foucault firmly put himself into an opposite tradition demanding that historical knowledge should be about explaining those developments. See Peter Schöttler, *Nach der Angst: Geschichtswissenschaft vor und nach dem 'linguistic turn'*, Münster: Westfälisches Dampfboot, 2018, 156. However, Herman Paul, 'A Loosely Knit Network: Philosophy of History after Hayden White', in: *Journal of the Philosophy of History* 13 (2019), 3–20, has argued on 14 that White's theory of history always took the explanatory function of historical writing very seriously.
83. Michel Foucault, *Discipline and Punish: the Birth of the Prison*, New York: Vintage, 1979; Foucault, *The History of Sexuality, vol. III: the Care of the Self*, New York: Knopf, 1988.
84. T. Carlos Jacques, 'Whence Does the Critic Speak? A Study of Foucault's Genealogy', in: Barry Smart (ed.), *Michel Foucault: Critical Assessments, vol. III*, London: Routledge, 1997, 97–112. On 102 he quotes Foucault: 'In fact power produces; it produces reality ...' Bruno Latour, who is discussed in Chapter 10 below, picks up from Foucault this notion that power produces reality. See Bruno Latour, *Reassembling the Social: an Introduction to Actor-Network Theory*, Oxford: Oxford University Press, 2005.
85. Michel Foucault, *The Order of Things: an Archaeology of Human Sciences*, New York: Pantheon, 1970.
86. Michel Foucault, *The Archaeology of Knowledge*, London: Pantheon, 1972. See also Poster, *Cultural History*, 134–52.
87. Michel Foucault, 'Nietzsche, Genealogy, History', in: Paul Rabinow (ed.), *Michel Foucault: Ethics, Subjectivity and Truth*, New York: The New Press, 1994, 76–100, quote on 77.
88. Kiff Bamford, *Jean-François Lyotard: Critical Lives*, London: Reaktion Books, 2017.
89. François Dosse, *History of Structuralism, vol. II: the Sign Sets, 1967 to the Present*, Minneapolis: University of Minnesota Press, 1997,

chapter 22: 'Foucault and the Deconstruction of History (1): the Archaeology of Knowledge', 234–46.

90. Peter L. Berger and Thomas Luckmann, *The Social Construction of Reality: a Treatise in the Sociology of Knowledge*, New York: Anchor, 1967.
91. Eric Hobsbawm and Terence Ranger (eds.), *The Invention of Tradition*, Cambridge: Cambridge University Press, 1983; Benedict Anderson, *Imagined Communities: Reflections on the Origin and Spread of Nationalism*, London: Verso, 1983.
92. Pierre Bourdieu, *Outline of a Theory of Practice*, Cambridge: Cambridge University Press, 1977 (originally published in French in 1972).
93. In Bourdieu's work 'fields' describe quasi-autonomous areas with their own culturally determined conventions.
94. Pierre Bourdieu, *Distinction: a Social Critique of the Judgment of Taste*, Cambridge, MA: Harvard University Press, 1984 (originally published in French in 1979).
95. Peter Burke, *What Is Cultural History?*, 3rd edn, Cambridge: Polity Press, 2018, 58–60. See also David Swartz, *Culture and Power: the Sociology of Pierre Bourdieu*, Chicago, IL: University of Chicago Press, 1997.
96. Gary Saul Morson and Caryl Emerson, *Mikhail Bakhtin: Creation of a Prosaics*, Stanford: Stanford University Press, 1990, 32–8.
97. Alistair Renfrew, *Mikhail Bakhtin*, London: Routledge, 2015, 75–93.
98. Sue Vice, *Introducing Bakhtin*, Manchester: Manchester University Press, 1997, 18–45.
99. Tzvetan Todorov, *Mikhail Bakhtin: the Dialogical Principle*, Minneapolis: University of Minnesota Press, 1984, chapter 5: 'Intertextuality', 60–74.
100. An online version of a translation of this seminal article can be found at www.ubu.com/aspen/aspen5and6/threeEssays.html#barthes [accessed 24 March 2020].
101. Michael Moriarty, *Roland Barthes*, Stanford: Stanford University Press, 1991; Jonathan Cullen, *Roland Barthes: a Very Short Introduction*, Oxford: Oxford University Press, 2001.
102. Throughout this book I shall be using the terms 'historism' and 'historist' rather than the terms 'historicism' and 'historicist' that are more common in English. I have followed this practice ever since 1995, as it avoids confusion in English between two very different phenomena: 'historicism' and 'historism' which currently are referred to by the same word, namely 'historicism'. Whereas 'historism' (in German *Historismus*), associated, above all, with the work of Leopold von Ranke, is about an evolutionary concept that

understands all political and social order as historically developed and grown, 'historicism' (in German *Historizismus*) refers to theories that posit history following predetermined laws towards a particular end, especially those of Plato, Hegel and Marx that were examined by Karl Popper in: *The Open Society and Its Enemies*, 2 vols., London: Routledge, 1945.

103. Charles A. Beard, 'Written History as an Act of Faith', in: *American Historical Review* 39:2 (1934), 219–31; Carl Becker, 'What Are Historical Facts?', in: *Western Political Quarterly* 8:3 (1955), 327–40.
104. Marc Bloch, *The Historian's Craft*, New York: Vintage, 1964, 43.
105. E. H. Carr, *What Is History?*, Cambridge: Cambridge University Press, 1961; Jack D'Amico, Dain A. Trafton and Massimo Verdicchio (eds.), *The Legacy of Benedetto Croce: Contemporary Critical Views*, Toronto: University of Toronto Press, 1999.
106. Arthur Danto, *Analytical Philosophy of History*, Cambridge: Cambridge University Press, 1965.
107. Jacques Lacan, *Ecrits: a Selection*, New York: Norton, 1977 (originally published in French in 1966).
108. Jacques Derrida, *Of Grammatology*, Baltimore: Johns Hopkins University Press, 1997 (originally published in French in 1967); on Derrida's thinking see also Christopher Norris, *Derrida*, Cambridge, MA: Harvard University Press, 1987.
109. Kleinberg, 'Haunting History', 142.
110. Ethan Kleinberg, *Haunting History: For a Deconstructive Approach to the Past*, Stanford: Stanford University Press, 2017.
111. Judith Butler, *Gender Trouble: Feminism and the Subversion of Identity*, London: Routledge, 1990.
112. Edward Said, 'Criticism, Culture and Performance', in: Gauri Viswanathan (ed.), *Power, Politics and Culture: Interviews with Edward W. Said*, London: Bloomsbury, 2005, 99. Another voice against 'solitarist' approaches to human identity and for an acceptance that we all contain multitudes of identity has been Amartya Sen, *Identity and Violence*, London: Penguin, 2006.
113. Homi Bhabha, *The Location of Culture*, London: Routledge, 1994.
114. Ernesto Laclau and Chantal Mouffe, *Hegemony and Socialist Strategy: Towards a Radical Democratic Politics*, London: Verso, 1985.
115. Stuart Hall, 'Introduction: Who Needs Identity?', in: Stuart Hall and Paul du Gay (eds.), *Questions of Cultural Identity*, London: Sage, 1996, 1–17.
116. Lawrence Grossberg, 'History, Politics and Postmodernism: Stuart Hall and Cultural Studies', in: *Journal of Communication Enquiry* 10:2 (1986), 61–77, esp. 64–5.

117. Frederick Cooper and Rogers Brubaker, 'Identity', in: Frederick Cooper, *Colonialism in Question: Theory, Knowledge, History*, Berkeley: University of California Press, 2005, 59–91.
118. Lutz Niethammer, *Kollektive Identität: Heimliche Quellen einer unheimlichen Konjunktur*, Reinbek: rororo, 2000.
119. Chris Lorenz, 'Who Needs Collective Identity? Some Reflections on an Essentially Contested Concept', unpublished paper in English. I am grateful to the author for letting me read his paper. A version of this paper has been published in Spanish. See Chris Lorenz, 'Quién necesita de la identidad colectiva? Algunas reflexiones sobre un concepto radicalmente controvertido', in: Omar Acha, Daniel Brauer, Facundo N. Martín and Adrián Ratto (eds.), *Las Identidades Colectivas endre los Ideales y la Ficcion*, Buenos Aires: Prometeo, 2021, 31–65.
120. Stefan Berger, 'Writing the Past in the Present: an Anglo-Saxon Perspective', in: *Diogenes* 58:1/2 (2012), 5–19.
121. Thomas S. Kuhn, *The Structure of Scientific Revolution*, Chicago: University of Chicago Press, 1962.
122. Bettina Hitzer and Thomas Welskopp, 'Die "Bielefelder Schule" der westdeutschen Sozialgeschichte: Karriere eines geplanten Paradigmas?', in: Hitzer and Welskopp (eds.), *Die Bielefelder Sozialgeschichte. Klassische Texte zu einem geschichtswissenschaftlichen Programm und seinen Kontroversen*, Bielefeld: transcript, 2010, 13–32.
123. Stephen Davies, *Empiricism and History*, Basingstoke: Palgrave Macmillan, 2003.
124. Gabrielle M. Spiegel, 'The Limits of Empiricism: the Utility of Theory in Historical Thought and Writing', in: *Medieval History Journal* 22:1 (2019), 1–22. Spiegel, of course, has been hugely influential in introducing theories associated with the linguistic turn to the historical profession. See her magisterial book: *Practicing History: New Directions in Historical Writing after the Linguistic Turn*, London: Routledge, 2005. On the long tradition of constructing empiricism as scientific programme and theory, see Lorenz, *Konstruktion der Vergangenheit*, 22–8.
125. Ian Wohlfahrt, 'Et Cetera? The Historian as Chiffonier', in: *New German Critique* 39 (1986), 143–86.
126. Not least through readable introductions to the field of historical writing. One example among many is Norman J. Wilson, *History in Crisis? Recent Directions in Historiography*, 3rd edn, New York: Pearson, 2014.
127. Peter C. Hoffer, *The Historians' Paradox: the Study of History in our Time*, New York: New York University Press, 2008.
128. Ibid., 7.

129. Ethan Kleinberg, Joan Wallach Scott and Gary Wilder, *Theses on Theory and History*, http://theoryrevolt.com/download/WildOnCollective_Theses-Booklet_EN.pdf, May 2018 [accessed 19 March 2020].
130. Schöttler, *Nach der Angst*.
131. Krijn Thijs, 'The Metaphor of the Master: "Narrative Hierarchy" in National Historical Cultures of Europe', in: Berger and Lorenz (eds.), *The Contested Nation*, 60–74.
132. Bruce A. van Sledright, 'From Empathic Regard to Self-Understanding: Im/Positionality, Empathy and Historical Contextualisation', in: O. L. Davis Jr, Elizabeth Anne Yeager and Stuart J. Fosten (eds.), *Historical Empathy and Perspective: Taking in the Social Studies*, Lanham: Rowman and Littlefield, 2001, 51–68.
133. Greg Anderson, 'Retrieving the Lost Worlds of the Past: the Case for an Ontological Turn', in: *American Historical Review* 120:3 (2015), 787–810, quote on 790.
134. Laura Lee Downs, 'If "Woman" is Just an Empty Category, then Why am I Afraid to Walk Alone at Night? Identity Politics Meets the Postmodern Subject', in: *Comparative Studies in Society and History* 35:2 (1993), 414–37.
135. Francis Fukuyama, *Identity: Contemporary Identity Politics and the Struggle for Recognition*, New York: Profile Books, 2018.
136. Sceptical, for example, is Richard J. Evans, *In Defence of History*, new edn, New York: Granta, 2012 (originally published in 2001). Downright denunciatory is G. R. Elton, *Return to Essentials: Some Reflections on the Present State of Historical Study*, Cambridge: Cambridge University Press, 1991, especially the Cook lectures at the University of Michigan that are included in that volume.
137. Geoff Eley, *A Crooked Line: From Cultural History to the History of Society*, Ann Arbor: University of Michigan Press, 2005.

2 The New Political History

1. Edward Augustus Freeman, 'On the Study of History', *Fortnightly Review* 35 (1881), 319–39, quote on 320.
2. Effi Gazi, 'Theorizing and Practicing "Scientific History" in Southeastern Europe (Nineteenth and Twentieth Centuries): Spyridon Lambros and Nicolae Iorga', in: Berger and Lorenz (eds.), *Nationalizing the Past*, 198.
3. Christopher L. Hill, *National History and the World of Nations: Capital, State and the Rhetoric of History in Japan, France and the United States*, Durham, NC: Duke University Press, 2008.

4. Michael Bentley, *Modernizing England's Past: English Historiography in the Age of Modernism, 1870–1970*, Cambridge: Cambridge University Press, 2005.
5. Stefan Berger, *The Search for Normality: National Identity and Historical Consciousness in Modern Germany*, Oxford: Berghahn Books, 2nd edn, 2003 (originally published in 1997).
6. The strong attachment of Swedish historiography to royal power and the state is stressed in comparative perspective with other Nordic historiographies by Peter Aronsson, Narve Fulsås, Pertti Haapala and Bernard Eric Jensen, 'Nordic National Histories', in: Berger and Lorenz (eds.), *The Contested Nation*, 256–82.
7. Robert Gildea, *The Past in French History*, New Haven: Yale University Press, 1996.
8. Peter Novick, *That Noble Dream: the 'Objectivity Question' and the American Historical Profession*, Cambridge: Cambridge University Press, 1988, 72.
9. Margaret Mehl, *History and the State in Nineteenth-Centry Japan*, Basingstoke: Palgrave Macmillan, 1998.
10. Rodrigo Díaz-Maldonado, 'National Identity Building in Mexican Historiography during the Nineteenth Century: an Attempt at Synthesis', in: *Storia della Storiografia* 70:2 (2016), 73–93.
11. Trond Nordby, 'State and Nation-Building', in: Jan Eivind Myhre, Trond Nordby and Sølvi 'Sogner (eds.), *Making a Historical Culture: Historiography in Norway*, Oslo: Scandinavian University Press, 1995, 181–209; Effi Gazi, *Scientific National History: the Greek Case in Comparative Perspective (1850–1920)*, Bern: Peter Lang, 2000; Roumen Daskalov, *The Making of a Nation in the Balkans. Historiography of the Bulgarian Revival*, Budapest: Central European University Press, 2004.
12. Frank Hadler, 'Der Magna-Moravia Mythos zwischen Geschichtsschreibung und Politik im 19. und 20. Jahrhundert', in: Eva Behring, Ludwig Richter and Wolfgang F. Schwarz (eds.), *Geschichtliche Mythen in den Literaturen und Kulturen Ostmittel- und Südosteuropas*, Stuttgart: Franz Steiner, 1999, 275–92.
13. Patrick J. Geary and Gábor Klaniczay (eds.), *Manufacturing the Middle Ages: Entangled History of Medievalism in Nineteenth-Century Europe*, Leiden: Brill, 2013; R. J. W. Evans and Guy Marchal (eds.), *The Uses of the Middle Ages in Modern European States: History, Nationhood and the Search for Origins*, Basingstoke: Palgrave Macmillan, 2011.
14. See the respective chapters on China, India and Africa by Q. Edward Wang, 'Between Myth and History: the Construction of a National Past

in Modern East Asia', Radhika Seshan, 'Writing the Nation in India: Communalism and Historiography' and Ibrahima Thioub, 'Writing National and Transnational History in Africa: the Example of the "Dakar School"', all in: Stefan Berger (ed), *Writing the Nation: a Global Perspective*, Basingstoke: Palgrave Macmillan, 2007, 126–54, 155–78, 197–212.

15. On Europe see the contributions in Berger and Lorenz (eds.), *The Contested Nation*; for non-European spaces compare the contributions in Berger (ed.). *Writing the Nation.*
16. Lionel Gossmann, *Basel in the Age of Burckhardt: a Study in Unseasonable Ideas*, Chicago: University of Chicago Press, 2000, 201–410.
17. Peter Schöttler, 'After the Deluge: the Impact of the Two World Wars on the Historical Work of Henri Pirenne and Marc Bloch', in: Berger and Lorenz (eds.), *Nationalizing the Past*, 404–25; see also Peter Schöttler, 'Lucien Febvres Beitrag zur Entmythologisierung der rheinischen Geschichte', in: Lucien Febvre, *Der Rhein und seine Geschichte*, ed. Peter Schöttler, Frankfurt am Main: Campus, 1994, 217–63; Sarah Keymeulen and Jo Tollebeek, *Henri Pirenne, Historian: a Life in Pictures*, Leuven: University of Leuven Press, 2011, 32–5. See also Jo Tollebeek, 'At the Crossroads of Nationalism: Huizinga, Pirenne and the Low Countries in Europe', in: *European Review of History* 17:2 (2010), 187–215.
18. Ellen Frances Fitzpatrick, *History's Memory: Writing America's Past, 1880–1980*, Cambridge, MA: Harvard University Press, 2002.
19. Berger, 'Return to the National Paradigm'.
20. Stefan Berger (with Christoph Conrad), *The Past as History: National Identity and Historical Consciousness in Modern Europe*, Basingstoke: Palgrave Macmillan, 2015, 290–7.
21. Patrick Finney, *Remembering the Road to World War II: International History, National Identity, Collective Memory*, London: Routledge, 2011.
22. Carol Gluck, *Thinking with the Past: the Japanese and Modern History*, New York; Columbia University Press, 2017.
23. See the many contributions on postcolonial historiographies after 1945 in Axel Schneider and Daniel Woolf (eds.), *The Oxford History of Historical Writing, vol. V: Historical Writing since 1945*, Oxford: Oxford University Press, 2011.
24. Charles Maier, *The Unmasterable Past: History, Holocaust and National Identity*, Cambridge, MA: Harvard University Press, new edn, with a new preface by the author, 1997.
25. Carl Levy, 'Historians and the "First Republic"', in: Stefan Berger, Mark Donovan and Kevin Passmore (eds.), *Writing National*

Histories: Western Europe since 1800, London: Routledge, 1999, 265–78.

26. David Starkey, 'The English Historian's Role and the Place of History in English National Life', in: *The Historian* 71 (2001), 6–15, quote on 14.
27. Ben Wellings and Chris Gifford, 'The Past in English Euroscepticism', in: Stefan Berger and Caner Tekin (eds.), *History and Belonging: Representations of the Past in Contemporary European Politics*, Oxford: Berghahn Books, 2018, 88–105.
28. Sorin Antohi, Balázs Trencsényi and Péter Apor (eds.), *Narratives Unbound: Historical Studies in Post-Communist Eastern Europe*, Budapest: Central European University Press, 2007.
29. Thomas Martin Devine, *Independence or Union: Scotland's Past and Scotland's Present*, London: Allen Lane, 2016; Michael A. Vargas, *Constructing Catalan Identity: Memory, Imagination, and the Medieval*, Basingstoke: Palgrave Macmillan, 2018.
30. Ruth Wodak, Majid Khosravinik, and Brigitte Mral (eds.), *Right-Wing Populism in Europe: Politics and Discourse*, London: Bloomsbury, 2013; Chip Berlet and Matthew N. Lyons, *Right-Wing Populism in America: Too Close for Comfort*, New York: Guilford Press, 2000; Lars Tore Flåten, *Hindu Nationalism, History and Identity in India: Narrating a Hindu Past under BJP*, London: Routledge, 2016; Stuart Macintyre and Anna Clark, *The History Wars*, new edn, Melbourne: Melbourne University Press, 2004.
31. Susan Pedersen, 'What is Political History Now', in: David Cannadine (ed.), *What Is History Now?*, Basingstoke: Palgrave Macmillan, 2002, 36–56, quote on 36.
32. Jon Lawrence and Alexandre Campsie, 'Political History', in: Stefan Berger, Heiko Feldner and Kevin Passmore (eds.), *Writing History: Theory and Practice*, 3rd edn, London: Bloomsbury, 2020, 323–42.
33. Gerd-Rainer Horn, '1968: a Social Movement Sui Generis', in: Stefan Berger and Holger Nehring (eds.), *The History of Social Movements in Global Perspective*, Basingstoke: Palgrave Macmillan, 2017, 515–42.
34. Lawrence and Campsie, 'Political History', 327–32; see also David Craig, '"High Politics" and the "New Political History"', in: *Historical Journal* 53 (2010), 453–75.
35. This was still an approach championed, among others, by notable British political historian Maurice Cowling. See, for example, his *The Impact of Labour: the Beginning of Modern British Politics*, Cambridge: Cambridge University Press, 1971. There was certainly no

shortage of highly traditionalist attempts to define political history and restrict it to governmental institutions. See, for example, Mark H. Leff, 'Revisioning US Political History', in: *American Historical Review* 100 (1995), 829–53.

36. Miles Taylor, *The Decline of British Radicalism, 1847–1860*, Oxford: Oxford University Press, 1995; Jon Lawrence and Miles Taylor (eds.), *Party, State and Society: Electoral Behaviour in Britain since 1820*, Aldershot: Ashgate, 1997.
37. Duncan Tanner, *Political Change and the Labour Party, 1900–1918*, Cambridge: Cambridge University Press, 1990.
38. Jon Lawrence, 'Class and Gender in the Making of Urban Toryism, 1880–1914', in: *English Historical Review* 108 (1993), 629–52.
39. Michel Foucault, *Security, Territory, Population: Lectures at the Collège de France*, New York: St Martin's Press, 2009; see also Thomas Lemke, *Foucault, Governmentality and Critique*, London: Paradigm, 2012.
40. Ronald Formisano, 'The Concept of Political Culture', in: *Journal of Interdisciplinary History* 31:3 (2001), 393–426.
41. Thomas Mergel, 'Überlegungen zu einer Kulturgeschichte der Politik', in: *Geschichte und Gesellschaft* 28 (2002), 574–606.
42. Johannes Paulmann, *Pomp und Politik: Monarchenbegegnungen zwischen Ancien Regime und Erstem Weltkrieg*, Paderborn: Schöningh, 2000; see also Markus Mösslang and Torsten Riotte (eds.), *The Diplomat's World: a Cultural History of Diplomacy, 1815–1914*, Oxford: Oxford University Press, 2008.
43. Edward Said, *Orientalism*, New York: Random House, 1978.
44. Gayatri Chakravorty Spivak, 'Can the Subaltern Speak?', in: Spivak, *Towards a History of the Vanishing Present*, Cambridge, MA: Harvard University Press, 1999.
45. Ranajit Guha, *Dominance without Hegemony: History and Power in Colonial India*, Cambridge, MA: Harvard University Press, 1997.
46. Chakrabarty, *Provincializing Europe*, 12–15.
47. Fanon, *The Wretched of the Earth*, 107–48.
48. Declan Kibert, *Inventing Ireland*, Cambridge, MA: Harvard University Press, 1996.
49. Partha Chatterjee, *Empire and Nation: Selected Essays*, New York: Columbia University Press, 2010.
50. Toyin Falola (ed.), *African Historiography: Essays in Honour of Jacob Ade Ajayi*, Harlow: Longman, 1993.
51. Bernard S. Cohn, 'Representing Authority in Victorian India', in: Saurabh Dube (ed.), *Postcolonial Passages: Contemporary History-Writing on India*, Oxford: Oxford University Press, 2004, 47–69.

52. Mrinalini Sinha, *Colonial Masculinity: the 'Manly Englishman' and the 'Effeminate Bengali' in the Late Nineteenth Century*, Manchester: Manchester University Press, 1995.
53. Reinhart Koselleck, *The Practice of Conceptual History: Timing History, Spacing Concepts*, Stanford: Stanford University Press, 2002; Koselleck, *Futures Past: On the Semantics of Historical Time*, New York: Columbia University Press, 2004.
54. On the Cambridge school, compare Mark Bevir, 'The Role of Contexts in Understanding and Explanation', in: Hans-Erich Bödeker (ed.), *Begriffsgeschichte, Diskursgeschichte, Metapherngeschichte*, Göttingen: Wallstein, 2002, 159–208.
55. Willibald Steinmetz, Ingrid Gilcher-Holtey, and Heinz-Gerhard Haupt (eds.), *Writing Political History Today*, Frankfurt am Main: Campus, 2013.
56. Gareth Stedman Jones, *Languages of Class: Studies in English Working-Class History, 1832–1982*, Cambridge: Cambridge University Press, 1983.
57. Dror Wahrmann, *Imagining the Middle Class: the Political Representation of Class in Britain, c. 1780–1840*, Cambridge: Cambridge University Press, 1995.
58. Patrick Joyce, *Visions of the People: Industrial England and the Question of Class*, Cambridge: Cambridge University Press, 1991; James Vernon, *Politics and the People: a Study in English Political Culture, c. 1815–1867*, Cambridge: Cambridge University Press, 1993.
59. Eugenio Biagini, *Liberty, Retrenchment and Reform: Popular Liberalism in the Age of Gladstone, 1860–1880*, Cambridge, Cambridge University Press, 1992; Biagini, *British Democracy and Irish Nationalism, 1867–1906*, Cambridge: Cambridge University Press, 2007.
60. François Furet, *Interpreting the French Revolution*, Cambridge: Cambridge University Press, 1981; Lynn Hunt, *Politics, Culture and Class in the French Revolution*, Oakland: University of California Press, 1984; François Furet and Mona Ozouf (eds.), *A Critical Dictionary of the French Revolution*, Cambridge, MA: Harvard University Press, 1989.
61. Mona Ozouf, *Festivals and the French Revolution*, Cambridge, MA: Harvard University Press, 1988.
62. Mona Ozouf, *Varennes: la mort de la royauté (21 juin 1791)*, Paris: Gallimard, 2005.
63. On Ozouf see Harvey Chisick, 'Mono Ozouf', in: Philip Daileader and Philip Whelan (eds.), *French Historians, 1900–2000*, Oxford: Wiley-Blackwell, 2010, 461–74.
64. Kathleen Wilson, *The Sense of the People: Politics, Culture and Imperialism in England, 1715–1785*, Cambridge: Cambridge University Press, 1998.

65. Catherine Hall, Keith McClelland and Jane Rendall, *Defining the Victorian Nation: Class, Race, Gender and the Reform Act of 1867*, Cambridge: Cambridge University Press, 2000.
66. Catherine Hall, *Civilizing Subjects: Metropole and Colony in the English Imagination*, Chicago: University of Chicago Press, 2002.
67. Ross McKibbin, 'Class and Conventional Wisdom: the Conservative Party and the "Public" in Interwar Britain', in: McKibbin, *The Ideologies of Class: Social Relations in Britain, 1880–1950*, Oxford: Oxford University Press, 1990, 259–93; Alison Light, *Forever England: Feminity, Literature and Conservatism between the Wars*, London: Routledge, 1991.
68. Martin Francis, 'Tears, Tantrums and Bared Teeth: the Emotional Economy of Three Conservative Prime Ministers, 1951–1963', in: *Journal of British Studies* 41:3 (2002), 354–87.
69. Arjun Appadurai (ed.), *The Social Life of Things: Commodities in Cultural Perspective*, Cambridge: Cambridge University Press, 1996. More recently, Frank Trentmann, *Empire of Things: How We Became a World of Consumers from the Fifteenth Century to the Twenty-First*, London: Penguin, 2016.
70. See, for example, Patrick Joyce, 'Filing the Raj: Political Technologies of the Imperial British State', in: Patrick Joyce and Tony Bennett (eds.), *Material Powers: Cultural Studies, Histories and the Material Turn*, London: Routledge, 2010, chapter 5.
71. Boyd Hilton, *The Age of Atonement: the Influence of Evangelicalism on Social and Economic Thought, 1795–1865*, Oxford: Oxford University Press, 1988.
72. Jon Parry, *Democracy and Religion: Gladstone and the Liberal Party, 1867–1975*, Cambridge: Cambridge University Press, 1986.
73. Lee Trepanier, *Political Symbols in Russia: Church, State and the Quest for Order and Justice*, Lanham, MD: Lexington Books, 2007.
74. Marianne Elliott, *When God Took Sides: Religion and Identity in Ireland: Unfinished History*, Oxford: Oxford University Press, 2009.
75. Jonathan D. Spence, *The Memory Palace of Matteo Ricci*, London: Quercus, 2008.
76. Maartje Janse, 'A Dangerous Type of Politics? Politics and Religion in Early Mass Organisations: the Anglo-American World, c. 1830', in: Joost Augusteijn, Patrick Dassen and Maartje Janse (eds.), *Political Religion beyond Totalitarianism: the Sacralization of Politics in the Age of Democracy*, Basingstoke: Palgrave Macmillan, 2013, 55–76.
77. Emilio Gentile, *Politics as Religion*, Princeton: Princeton University Press, 2006.
78. Henk te Velde, 'The Dilemma of National History', in: A. in't Groen, H. J. De Jonge, E. Klaasen, H. Papma and P. van Slooten

(eds.), *Knowledge in Ferment: Dilemmas in Science, Scholarship and Society*, Leiden: Leiden University Press, 2007, 227–41, quote on 228.

79. Henk te Velde, 'Political Transfer: an Introduction', in: *European Review of History* 12: 2 (2005), 205–21.
80. Nicolas Roussellier, 'The Political Transfer of English Parliamentary Rules in the French Assemblies (1789–1848)', in: *European Review of History* 12:2 (2005), 239–48.
81. Henk te Velde and Maarte Janse and (eds.), *Organising Democracy: Reflections on the Rise of Political Organisations in the Nineteenth Century*, Basingstoke: Palgrave Macmillan, 2017.
82. Anne Heyer, 'The Making of the Democratic Party: the Emergence of the Party Organizations of the German Social Democratic Workers' Party, the British National Liberal Federation and the Dutch Anti-Revolutionary Party, 1860s–1880s', PhD thesis, University of Leiden, 2018.
83. An attempt to present global historical perspectives on social movements is Stefan Berger and Holger Nehring (eds.), *The History of Social Movements in Global Perspective*, Basingstoke: Palgrave Macmillan, 2017.
84. Pasi Ihalainen, *The Springs of Democracy: National and Transnational Debates on Constitutional Reform in the British, German, Swedish and Finnish Parliaments, 1917–1919*, Helsinki: Finnish Literature Society, 2017, open access publication: http://dx.doi.org/10.21435/sfh.24.
85. Sean Scalmer, *On the Stump: Campaign Oratory and Democracy in the United States, Britain and Australia*, Philadelphia: Temple University Press, 2018.
86. Stefan Berger and Sean Scalmer (eds.), *The Transnational Activist: Transformations and Comparisons from the Anglo-World since the Nineteenth Century*, Basingstoke: Palgrave Macmillan, 2017.
87. Stephen Howe (ed.), *The New Imperial History Reader*, London: Routledge, 2010.
88. Christopher Bayly, *Imperial Meridian: the British Empire and the World, 1780–1830*, London: Routledge, 1989.
89. Immanuel Wallerstein, Charles Lemert and Carlos Aguirre Rojas, *Uncertain Worlds: World-Systems Analysis in Changing Times*, London: Routledge, 2012.
90. Clifford Geertz, *The Interpretation of Cultures*, New York: Basic Books, 1973.
91. Arjun Appadurai, *Modernity at Large: Cultural Dimensions of Globalization*, Minneapolis: University of Minnesota Press, 1996.
92. Jürgen Osterhammel, *The Transformation of the World: a Global History of the Nineteenth Century*, Princeton: Princeton University Press, 2014, 392–468.

93. The formulation 'empire state' is Frederick Cooper's in *Colonialism in Question: Theory, Knowledge, History*, Berkeley: University of California Press, 2005, 174.
94. Stefan Berger and Alexei Miller, 'Introduction: Building Nations in and with Empires – a Reassessment', in: Berger and Miller (eds.), *Nationalizing Empires*, Budapest: Central European University Press, 2015, 1–30.
95. James Epstein, 'Introduction: New Directions in Political History', in: *Journal of British Studies* 41:3 (2002), 255–8, quote on 255.

3 The New Social, Economic and Labour History

1. John L. Harvey, 'History and the Social Sciences', in: Berger, Feldner and Passmore (eds.), *Writing History*, 105.
2. Berger (with Conrad), *The Past as History*, 173–5.
3. Nils Goldschmidt and Matthias Störring, 'Gustav Schmoller: A Socialist of the Chair', in: Stefan Berger, Ludger Pries and Manfred Wannöffel (eds.), *The Palgrave Handbook of Workers' Participation at Plant Level*, Basingstoke: Palgrave Macmillan, 2019, 91–112.
4. William Cunningham, *The Growth of English Industry and Commerce*, Cambridge: Cambridge University Press, 1882.
5. Abbot Usher, 'Sir J. H. Clapham and the Empirical Reaction in Economic History', in: *Journal of Economic History* 11:2 (1951), 148–53.
6. Kevin Morgan, *The Webbs and Soviet Communism*, London: Lawrence and Wishart, 2006.
7. Stewart A. Weaver, *The Hammonds: a Marriage in History*, Stanford: Stanford University Press, 1997.
8. Lawrence Goldman, *The Life of R. H. Tawney: Socialism and History*, London: Bloomsbury, 2013; James Kirby, 'R. H. Tawney and Christian Social Teaching: *Religion and the Rise of Capitalism* Reconsidered', in: *English Historical Review* 131:551 (2016), 793–822.
9. François Dosse, *New History in France: the Triumph of the Annales*, Urbana: University of Illinois Press, 1994 (originally published in French in 1987); Peter Burke, *The French Historical Revolution. the Annales School, 1919–1989*, Cambridge: Cambridge University Press, 1999; Stuart Clark (ed.), *The Annales School: Critical Assessments*, 4 vols., London: Routledge, 1999.
10. Welskopp, 'Clio and Class Struggle'.
11. Ian Tyrrell, *The Absent Marx: Class Analysis and Liberal History in 20th Century America*, Westport, CT: Greenwood Press, 1986.

12. Harun Yilmaz, *National Identities in Soviet Historiography: the Rise of Nations under Stalin*, London: Routledge, 2015.
13. Quoted in. in Anatole G. Mazour, *Modern Russian Historiography*, 2nd edn, Princeton: Princeton University Press, 1958, 204.
14. Yilmaz, *National Identities in Soviet Historiography.*
15. Idrit Idrizi, 'Between Subordination and Symbiosis: Historians' Relationship with Political Power in Communist Albania', in: *European History Quarterly* 50:1 (2020), 66–87.
16. Q. Edward Wang, 'Between Marxism and Nationalism: Chinese Historiography and the Soviet Influence, 1949–1963', in: *Journal of Contemporary China* 9 (2000), 95–111.
17. Juandir Malerba and Ronaldo Pereira de Jesus, 'Marxism and Brazilian Historiography', in: Q. Edward Wang and Georg G. Iggers (eds.), *Marxist Historiographies: a Global Perspective*, London: Routledge, 2016, 142–73.
18. Carpenter, *G.D.H. Cole.*
19. Harvey J. Kaye, *The British Marxist Historians*, New York: Palgrave Macmillan, 1988.
20. Harvey J. Kaye, 'Our Island Story Retold: A. L. Morton and "the People" in History', in: Kaye, *The Education of Desire: Marxists and the Writing of History*, New York: Routledge, 1992, 116–24.
21. His autobiography is an outstanding account of the rise of social history in Britain. See Harold Perkin, *The Making of a Social Historian*, London: Athena Press, 2002.
22. Stefan Berger (ed.), 'Labour and Social History in Great Britain: Historiographical Reviews and Agendas, 1990s to the Present', special issue of *Mitteilungsblatt des Instituts für soziale Bewegungen* 27 (2002).
23. Haar and Fahlbusch (eds.), *German Scholars and Ethnic Cleansing.*
24. Karen Schönwälder, ' "Taking Their Place in the Frontline" (?): German Historians during Nazism and War', in: *Tel Aviver Jahrbuch für deutsche Geschichte* 25 (1996), 205–19.
25. Thomas Etzemüller, *Sozialgeschichte als politische Geschichte: Werner Conze und die Neuorientierung der westdeutschen Geschichtswissenschaft nach 1945*, Munich: Oldenbourg, 2001.
26. Jin-Sung Chun, *Das Bild der Moderne in der Nachkriegszeit. Die westdeutsche 'Strukturgeschichte' im Spannungsfeld von Modernitätskritik und wissenschaftlicher Innovation, 1948–1962*, Munich: Oldenbourg, 2000.
27. E. H. Carr, *What Is History?*, new edn with a foreword by Richard J. Evans, Basingstoke: Palgrave Macmillan, 2001, 60.
28. Jack H. Hexter, 'Fernand Braudel and the Monde Braudelien', in: *Journal of Modern History* 44 (1972), 480–539.

29. Eric Hobsbawm, *Interesting Times: a Twentieth-Century Life*, New York: Pantheon, 2007, 314–28.
30. Nelson E. Hayes and Tanya Hayes (eds.), *Claude Lévi-Strauss: the Anthropologist as Hero*, Cambridge, MA: Harvard University Press, 1970.
31. Juan Maiguashca, 'Latin American Marxist History: Rise, Fall and Resurrection', in: Wang and Iggers (eds.), *Marxist Historiographies*, 108.
32. Curtis Anderson Gayle, 'The Importance and Legacy of Marxist History in Japan', in: Wang and Iggers (eds.), *Marxist Historiographies*, 180–1; Michihiro Okamoto, 'The Social Movement History as a Social Movement in and of Itself', in: Stefan Berger (ed.), *The Engaged Historian: Perspectives on the Intersections of Politics, Activism and the Historical Profession*, Oxford: Berghahn Books, 2019, 185–204.
33. Rochona Majumdar, 'Thinking through Transition: Marxist Historiography in India', in: Wang and Iggers (eds.), *Marxist Historiographies*, 199.
34. W. W. Rostow, *The Stages of Economic Growth*, Cambridge: Cambridge University Press, 1960.
35. See, for example, Peter Burke, *Sociology and History*, London: George Allen and Unwin, 1980.
36. Eric J. Hobsbawm, 'From Social History to the History of Society', in: *Daedalus* 100 (1971), 20–45.
37. Paul E. Lovejoy, 'The Ibadan School of Historiography and Its Critics', in: Toyin Falola (ed.), *African Historiography: Essays in Honour of Jacob Ade Ajayi*, London: Longman, 1993, 194–202.
38. Tony Judt, 'A Clown in Regal Purple: Social History and the Historians', in: *History Workshop Journal* 7 (1979), 66–94.
39. Chris Lorenz, '"Won't You Tell Me, Where Have All the Good Times Gone?" On the Advantages and Disadvantages of Modernization Theory for History', in: *Radical History Review* 10 (2006), 171–200.
40. On the key assumptions of classical Marxist historiography see Geoff Eley, 'Marxist Historiography', in: Berger, Feldner and Passmore (eds.), *Writing History*, 67–85. On Weber see Wolfgang Mommsen, 'Max Weber's Political Sociology and his Philosophy of World History', in: *International Social Science Journal* 17 (1965), 23–45.
41. Steve Rigby, *Marxism and History: a Critical Introduction*, 2nd edn, Manchester: Manchester University Press, 1998.
42. Martin Albrow, *Max Weber's Construction of Social Theory*, New York: St Martin's Press, 1990, 149–57.
43. De Certeau, *The Writing of History*, 212.

44. Pat Hudson, 'Economic History', in: Berger, Feldner and Passmore (eds.), *Writing History*, 386–404.
45. Lynn Abrams, *Oral History Theory*, London: Routledge, 2010.
46. Alf Lüdtke (ed.), *The History of Everday Life: Reconstructing Historical Experiences and Ways of Life*, Princeton: Princeton University Press, 1989.
47. Gareth Williams, *Writers of Wales: George Ewart Evans*, Cardiff: Cardiff University Press, 1991.
48. Brian Keith Axel (ed.), *From the Margins: Historical Anthropology and Its Futures*, Durham, NC: Duke University Press, 2002; Don Kalb and Herman Tak (eds.), *Critical Junctions: Anthropology and History beyond the Cultural Turn*, Oxford: Berghahn Books, 2005; Saurabh Dube, *Historical Anthropology*, Oxford: Oxford University Press, 2009; Jakob Tanner, 'Historical Anthropology', in: Berger, Feldner and Passmore, *Writing History*, 236–52.
49. Hans Medick, 'Missionaries in a Row-Boat: Ethnological Ways of Knowing as a Challenge to Social History', in: *Comparative Studies in Society and History* 29 (1987), 76–98.
50. Carlo Ginzburg, *The Cheese and the Worms: the Cosmos of a Sixteenth-Century Miller*, Baltimore: Johns Hopkins University Press, 1980 (originally published in Italian in 1976).
51. Lyndal Roper, *Oedipus and the Devil: Religion and Sexuality in Early Modern Europe*, London: Routledge, 1994.
52. Alf Lüdtke, 'Cash, Coffee Breaks, Horseplay: *Eigensinn* and Politics among Factory Workers in Germany circa 1900', in: Michael Hanagan and Charles Stevenson (eds.), *Confrontation, Class Consciousness, and the Labour Process: Studies in Proletarian Class Formation*, New York, 1986, 65–95; Alf Lüdtke, 'Polymorphous Synchrony: German Industrial Workers and the Politics of Everyday Life', in: Marcel van der Linden (ed.), *The End of Labour History*, Cambridge: Cambridge University Press, 1993, 39–84.
53. Lüdtke, 'Polymorphous Synchrony', 49.
54. Lutz Niethammer (ed.), *Lebensgeschichte und Sozialkultur im Ruhrgebiet, 1930–1960*, 3 vols., Bonn: J. W. H. Dietz Nachf., 1983/5; see also Ulrike Jureit, 'Die Entdeckung des Zeitzeugen. Faschismus- und Nachkriegserfahrungen im Ruhrgebiet', in: Jürgen Danyel, Jan Holger Kirsch and Martin Sabrow (eds.), *50 Klassiker der Zeitgeschichte*, Göttingen: Vandenhoeck and Ruprecht, 2007, 174–7.
55. Stuart Hall, 'Raphael Samuel: 1934–96', in: *New Left Review* 1:221, January–February 1997; https://newleftreview.org/I/221/stuart-hall-raphael-samuel-1934-1996 [accessed 12 February 2019].

56. Ian Gwinn, '"History Should Become Common Property": Raphael Samuel, History Workshop, and the Practice of Socialist History', in: *Socialist History* 51 (2017), 96–117.
57. Michael Wildt, 'Die grosse Geschichtswerkstattschlacht im Jahre 1992 oder: Wie Werkstatt Geschichte entstand', in: *Werkstatt Geschichte* 50 (2009), 70–7.
58. Eric Hobsbawm, 'The Forward March of Labour Halted', in: *Marxism Today*, September 1978, 279–86; http://banmarchive.org.uk/collections/mt/pdf/78_09_hobsbawm.pdf [accessed 12 February 2019].
59. E. P. Thompson, *The Making of the English Working Class*, Harmondsworth: Penguin, 1963. See also Bryan D. Palmer, *The Making of E. P. Thompson: Marxism, Humanism and History*, Toronto: New Hogtown Press, 1981.
60. Patrick Joyce, 'History and Postmodernism', in: *Past and Present* 133:1 (1991), 204–9; Joyce, 'The End of Social History', in: *Social History* 20: 1 (1995), 73–91; Joyce, 'What is the Social in Social History', in: *Past and Present* 206: 1 (2010), 213–48.
61. Geoff Eley and Keith Nield, 'Starting Over: the Present, the Postmodern and the Moment of Social History', in: Keith Jenkins (ed.), *The Postmodern History Reader*, 3rd edn, London: Routledge, 2001, 366–79.
62. Dipesh Chakrabarty, *Rethinking Working-Class History: Bengal 1890–1940*, Princeton: Princeton University Press, 1989.
63. Thomas Welskopp, *Das Banner der Brüderlichkeit. Die deutsche Sozialdemokratie vom Vormärz bis zum Sozialistengesetz*, Bonn: J. W. H. Dietz Nachf., 2000.
64. David Montgomery, *The Fall of the House of Labor: the Workplace, the State and American Labor Activism, 1865–1925*, New York: Columbia University Press, 1987; David M. Gordon, Richard C. Edwards and Michael Reich, *Segmented Work, Divided Workers: the Historical Transformation of Labor in the United States*, Cambridge, MA: Harvard University Press, 1982.
65. Robert E. Weir, *Beyond Labor's Veil: the Culture of the Knights of Labor*, University Park, PA: Pennsylvania State University Press, 1996.
66. Marcel van der Linden, 'The "Globalization" of Labour and Working-Class History and Its Consequences', in: Jan Lucassen (ed.), *Global Labour History: a State of the Art*, Bern: Peter Lang, 2006, 13–38.
67. Bourdieu, *Outline of a Theory of Practice*.
68. Victoria E. Bonnell and Lynn Hunt (eds.), *Beyond the Cultural Turn: New Directions in the Study of Society and Culture*, Berkeley: University of California Press, 1999.
69. Hudson, 'Economic History'.

70. Craig Muldrew, *The Economy of Obligation: the Culture of Credit and Social Relations in Early Modern England*, Basingstoke: Palgrave Macmillan, 1998.
71. Hudson, 'Economic History', 402–3.
72. Jürgen Kocka, 'History and the Social Sciences Today', in: Hans Joas and Barbro Klein (eds.), *The Benefit of Broad Horizons: Intellectual and Institutional Preconditions for a Global Social Science*, Leiden: Brill, 2010, 53–67. Stefan Berger, 'The Revival of German Labour History', in: German History 37:3 (2019), 277–94.
73. Thomas Welskopp, 'Social History', in: Berger, Feldner and Passmore (eds.), *Writing History*, 343–62, quote on 358.
74. Kathleen Canning, *Languages of Labor and Gender: Female Factory Work in Germany, 1850–1914*, Ithaca, NY: Cornell University Press, 1996.
75. David Roediger, 'What if Labour Were Not White and Male? Recentering Working-Class History and Reconstructing Debate on the Unions and Race', in: *International Labor and Working-Class History* 51 (1997), 72–95.
76. Jonathan Hyslop, 'The Imperial Working Class Makes itself "White": White Labourism in Britain, Australia and South Africa before the First World War', in: *Journal of Historical Sociology* 12 (1999), 398–421.
77. David R. Roediger, *The Wages of Whiteness: Race and the Making of the American Working Class*, London: Verso, 1991; on the increasing attention to constructions of class in the 1990s compare also Lenard Berlanstein (ed.), *Rethinking Labor History: Essays on Discourse and Class Analysis*, Urbana: University of Illinois Press, 1993.
78. John Belchem, *Irish, Catholic and Scouse: the History of the Liverpool Irish, 1800–1939*, Liverpool: Liverpool University Press, 2007; John C. Kulczycki, *The Polish Coal Miners' Union and the German Labour Movement in the Ruhr, 1920–1934: National and Social Solidarity*, Oxford: Berghahn Books, 1997.
79. Romain Bonnet, Amerigo Caruso, Claire Morelon and Alessandro Saluppo, 'Revolutionary Fears, Industrial Unrest and Anti-Labor Mobilisation in Austria-Hungary, Germany, France and Great Britain (1905–1914)', in: Stefan Berger and Klaus Weinhauer (eds.), *Revolutions in Global Perspective, 1905–1934*, Basingstoke: Palgrave Macmillan, 2022.
80. Lex Heerma van Voss, Patrick Pasture and Jan de Maeyer (eds.), *Between Cross and Class: Comparative Histories of Christian Labour in Europe, 1840–2000*, Bern: Peter Lang, 2005.
81. Stefan Berger, 'Difficult (Re)Alignments: Comparative Perspectives on Social Democracy and Religion from Late Nineteenth Century to

Interwar Germany and Britain', in: *Journal of Contemporary History* 53:3 (2018), 574–96.

82. Les Heerma van Voss and Marcel van der Linden (eds.), *Class and Other Identities: Gender, Religion and Ethnicity in the Writing of European Labour History*, Oxford: Berghahn Books, 2002.
83. Geoff Eley, *A Crooked Line: From Cultural History to the History of Society*, Ann Arbor: University of Michigan Press, 2005.
84. Ibid., 181.

4 The New Cultural History

1. Tracey Loughran, 'Cultural History', in: Berger, Feldner and Passmore (eds.), *Writing History*, 379.
2. Karen O'Brien, *Narratives of Enlightenment: Cosmopolitan History from Voltaire to Gibbon*, Cambridge: Cambridge University Press, 1997.
3. Etienne Balibar, 'Fictive Ethnicity and Ideal Nations', in: John Hutchinson and Anthony D. Smith (eds.), *Ethnicity*, Oxford: Oxford University Press, 1996, 162–8.
4. On the relationship of culture to ethnicity and race see Chris Lorenz, 'Representations of Identity: Ethnicity, Race, Class, Gender and Religion. An Introduction to Conceptual History', in: Berger and Lorenz (eds.), *The Contested Nation*, 24–59; also Marius Turda and Maria Sophia Quine, *Historicizing Race*, London: Bloomsbury, 2018.
5. H. B. Nisbet, 'Herder: the Nation in History', in: Michael Branch (ed.), *National History and Identity: Approaches to the Writing of National History in the North-East Baltic Region, Nineteenth and Twentieth Centuries*, Tampere: Suomalaisen Kirjallisuuden Seura, 1999, 78–96.
6. Stefan Troebst, '"Historical Meso-Region": a Concept in Cultural Studies and Historiography', in: *European History Online* (EGO), published by the Leibniz Institute of European History (IEG), Mainz, 6 March 2012; www.ieg-ego.eu/troebsts-2010-en [accessed 14 May 2020].
7. Peter Aronsson, 'National Cultural Heritage – Nordic Cultural Memory: Negotiating Politics, Identity and Knowledge', in: Bernd Henningsen, Hendriette Kliemann-Geisinger and Stefan Troebst (eds.), *Transnationale Erinnerungsorte: Nord- und südeuropäische Perspektiven*, Berlin: BWV, 2009, 71–90.
8. Jakob Burckhardt, *The Civilisation of the Renaissance in Italy*, 1878 (originally published in German in 1860), online: https://web.archive.org/web/20080921145058/http://www.boisestate.edu/courses/

hy309/docs/burckhardt/burckhardt.html [accessed 27 March 2020]; on Burckhardt see also Werner Kaegi, *Jacob Burckhardt: eine Biographie*, 2 vols., Basel: Schwabe, 1977; also Gossmann, *Basel in the Age of Burckhardt*.

9. Aram Mattioli, *Jacob Burckhardt und die Grenzen der Humanität*, Weitra: Bibliothek der Provinz, 2001.
10. Jacob Burckhardt, *Force and Freedom: Reflections on History*, New York: Pantheon, 1943 (originally published in 1905).
11. Roger Chartier, *Cultural History: Between Practices and Representations*, Ithaca, NY: Cornell University Press, 1988, 24–5. See also Drago Roksandić, Filip Šimetin Šegvić and Nikolina Šimetin Šegvić (eds.), *Annales in Perspective: Designs and Accomplishments*, Zagreb: FF Press, 2019.
12. Johan Huizinga, *The Waning of the Middle Ages: a Study of the Forms of Life, Thought and Art in France and the Netherlands in the 14th and 15th Centuries*, Harmondsworth: Penguin, 1965.
13. Robert Anchor, 'History and Play: Johan Huizinga and his Critics', in: *History and Theory* 27 (1978), 63–93.
14. Patrick Hutton, 'The History of Mentalities: the New Map of Cultural History', in: *History and Theory* 20 (1981), 237–59; David Wootton, 'Lucien Febvre and the Problem of Unbelief in the Early Modern Period', in: *Journal of Modern History* 60:4 (1988), 695–730; Carole Fink, *Marc Bloch: a Life in History*, Cambridge: Cambridge University Press, 1999.
15. Patrick H. Hutton, *Philippe Ariès and the Politics of French Cultural History*, Boston: University of Massachusetts Press, 2004, chapter 6.
16. Raymond Williams, *Keywords: a Vocabulary of Culture and Society*, Oxford: Oxford University Press, 1976, 90; also Williams, *Culture*, London: Fontana, 1981.
17. Raymond Williams, 'Culture is Ordinary', in: Williams, *Resources of Hope: Culture, Democracy, Socialism*, London: Verso, 1989, 3–14.
18. Stuart Hall, 'The Question of Cultural Identity', in: Stuart Hall, David Held and Anthony McGrew (eds.), *Modernity and Its Futures*, Cambridge: Polity Press, 1992, 274–316.
19. Stuart Hall, 'Encoding/Decoding', in: S. Hall, D. Hobson, A. Lowe and P. Willis (eds.), *Culture, Media, Language: Working Papers in Cultural Studies, 1972–1979*, London: Hutchinson, 1980, 128–38.
20. Grossberg, 'History, Politics and Postmodernism'.
21. Richard Hoggart, *The Uses of Literacy*, Harmondsworth: Penguin, 1957; Thompson, *The Making of the English Working Class*.
22. On the impact of poststructuralism on the historical profession see Kevin Passmore, 'Poststructuralist and Linguistic Methods', in: Berger, Feldner and Passmore (eds.), *Writing History*, 133–57.

23. Lynn Hunt (ed.), *The New Cultural History*, Berkeley: University of California Press, 1989.
24. Alison Moore, 'Historicising Historical Theory's History of Cultural Historiography', in: *Cosmos and History: the Journal of Natural and Social Philosophy* 12:1 (2016), 257–91.
25. Chartier, *Cultural History*, 4.
26. Ilse Nina Bulhof, *Wilhelm Dilthey: a Hermeneutic Approach to the Study of History and Culture*, The Hague: Martinus Nijhoff, 1980.
27. Paul Ricoeur, *The Conflict of Interpretations: Essays in Hermeneutics*, Evanston, IL: Northwestern University Press, 1974, 13.
28. Lawrence Stone, 'The Revival of Narrative: Reflections on a New Old History, in: *Past and Present* 85 (1979), 3–24, quote on 19.
29. Hunt (ed.), *The New Cultural History*.
30. Theodore R. Schatzki, Karin Knorr-Cetina and Eike von Savigny (eds.), *The Practice Turn in Contemporary Theory*, London: Routledge, 2001.
31. Joyce Appleby, Lynn Hunt and Margaret Jacob, *Telling the Truth about History*, New York: Norton, 1994.
32. Bonnell and Hunt (eds.), *Beyond the Cultural Turn*.
33. Linda Kalof (ed.), *Cultural History of Women*, 6 vols., London: Bloomsbury, 2016.
34. Susan Pedersen, 'The Future of Feminist History', in: *Perspectives on History*, 1 October 2000; www.historians.org/publications-and-directories/perspectives-on-history/october-2000/the-future-of-feminist-history [accessed 19 March 2019].
35. Rosalind Shaw, *Memories of the Slave Trade: Ritual and Historical Imagination in Sierra Leone*, Chicago: University of Chicago Press, 2002.
36. Jan Vansina, *Paths in the Rainforest*, Madison: University of Wisconsin Press, 1990.
37. Megan Vaughan, 'Culture', in: Ulinka Rublack (ed.), *A Concise Companion to History*, Oxford: Oxford University Press, 2011, 227–45.
38. Claudio Lomnitz, *Death and the Idea of Mexico*, New York: Zone Books, 2008.
39. Ramón Grosfoguel, *Colonial Subjects: Puerto Ricans in a Global Perspective*, Berkeley: University of California Press, 2003.
40. Shahid Amin, 'Gandhi as Mahatma: Gorakhpur District, Eastern UP, 1921–22', in: R. Guha (ed.), *Subaltern Studies, vol. III: Writings on South Asian History and Society*, Delhi: Oxford University Press, 1986, 1–61.
41. Bill Schwartz (ed.), *The Expansion of England: Race, Ethnicity and Cultural History*, London: Routledge, 1996.

42. See also David Buisseret and Steven G. Reinhardt (eds.), *Creolization in the Americas*, Arlington: University of Texas Press, 2000.
43. On histories of cultural transfers see also Stefan Berger, 'Comparative and Transnational History', in: Berger, Feldner and Passmore (eds.), *Writing History*, 292–316.
44. Border studies has become a major transdisciplinary research field in its own right. For introductions see Thomas M. Wilson and Hastings Donnan (eds.), *A Companion to Border Studies*, Oxford: Blackwell, 2012; Doris Wastl-Walter (ed.), *The Ashgate Research Companion to Border Studies*, London: Routledge, 2016.
45. There are many studies on border territories. See, for example, Peter Schöttler, 'Le Rhin comme enjeu historiographique dans l'entre-deux-guerres: vers une histoire des mentalités frontalières', *Genèses* 14 (1994), 63–82; Sharif Gemie, 'France and the Val d'Aran: Politics and Nationhood on the Pyrenean Border, 1800–25', in: *European History Quarterly* 28 (1998), 311–43.
46. Michael Werner and Bénédicte Zimmermann, 'Beyond Comparison: "Histoire Croisée" and the Challenge of Reflexivity', *History and Theory* 45:1 (2006), 30–50.
47. Michel Espagne and Michael Werner, *Transferts: les relations interculturelles dans l'espace Franco-Allemand*, Paris: Ed. Recherche sur la Civilisation, 1988.
48. Paul Gilroy, *The Black Atlantic: Modernity and Double Consciousness*, London: Verso, 1993.
49. Paul Gilroy, *After Empire: Melancholia or Convivial Culture*, London: Routledge, 2004.
50. A good introduction to Gilroy is provided by Paul Williams, *Paul Gilroy*, London: Routledge, 2013.
51. Paul Gilroy, *Against Race: Imagining Political Culture beyond the Color Line*, Cambridge, MA: Harvard University Press, 2000.
52. On the concept of the 'engaged historian', see Stefan Berger (ed.), *The Engaged Historian: Perspectives on the Intersections of Politics, Activism and the Historical Profession*, Oxford: Berghahn Books, 2019.
53. History News Network, 'Black Historians at the OAH Risked the Charge of Presentism to Show the Links between Racial Violence in 1917 and Black Lives Matter Today', in: *History News Network*, 10 May 2017, https://historynewsnetwork.org/article/165903 [accessed 2 April 2020].
54. M. M. Bakhtin, *Speech Genres and Other Late Essays*, Austin: University of Texas Press, 1986, 7.
55. Bhabha, *The Location of Culture*, 246.

56. Stephen Murray and Will Roscoe (eds.), *Boy Wives and Female Husbands: Studies of African Homosexualities*, New York: St Martin's Press, 1998.
57. R. B. Parkinson, *A Little Gay History: Desire and Diversity across the World*, New York: University of Columbia Press, 2013; Marc Stein (ed.), *Encyclopedia of Lesbian, Gay, Bisexual and Transgendered History in America*, 3 vols., New York: Charles Scribners, 2003.
58. Anna Green, *Cultural History*, Basingstoke: Palgrave Macmillan, 2008, 119.
59. Peter Burke, 'Performing History: the Importance of Occasions', in: *Rethinking History* 9:1 (2005), 35–52.
60. Ibid., 38.
61. Ibid., 41.
62. Ibid., 36.
63. Alain Corbin, *The Foul and the Fragrant: Odour and the French Social Imagination*, Cambridge, MA: Harvard University Press, 1986; Corbin, *Sound and Meaning in the Village Bells*, London: Macmillan, 1999.
64. Alain Corbin, *The Lure of the Sea: the Discovery of the Seaside in the Western World, 1750–1840*, Berkeley: University of California Press, 1994. On Corbin, generally, see also Sima Godfrey, 'Alain Corbin: Making Sense of French History', in: *French Historical Studies* 25:2 (2002), 381–98.
65. Peter Burke, 'Is There a Cultural History of Emotions?', in: Penelope Gouk and Helen Hills (eds.), *Representing Emotions*, Aldershot: Ashgate, 2005, 27–48.
66. Lucien Febvre, 'Sensibility and History: How to Reconstitute the Emotional Life of the Past', in: Peter Burke (ed.) *A New Kind of History: From the Writings of Febvre*, London: Harper and Row, 1973, 12–26 (originally published in French in *Annales* in 1941).
67. Johann Huizinga, *The Autumn of the Middles Ages*, Chicago: University of Chicago Press, 1996 (originally published in Dutch in 1919; first English translation 1924).
68. Piroska Nagy, 'History of Emotions', in: Marek Tamm and Peter Burke (eds.), *Debating New Approaches to History*, London: Bloomsbury, 2019, 189–202, esp. 192.
69. Peter N. Stearns and Carol Z. Stearns, 'Emotionology: Clarifying the History of Emotions and Emotional Standards', in: *American Historical Review* 90:4 (1985), 813–36.
70. Carolyn Pedwell, 'De-Colonising Empathy: Thinking Affect Transnationally', in: *Samyukta: a Journal of Women's Studies* 16:1 (2016), 27–49.

71. Barbara H. Rosenwein, 'Worrying about Emotions in History', in: *American Historical Review* 107:3 (2002), 821–45; see also R. Harré (ed.) *The Social Construction of Emotions*, Oxford: Blackwell, 1986.
72. William M. Reddy, 'Against Constructionism: the Historical Ethnography of Emotions', in: *Current Anthropology* 38:3 (1997), 327–40, quotes on 331, 340. On the limits of radical constructionism see also Ian Hacking, *The Social Construction of What?*, Cambridge, MA: Harvard University Press, 2000.
73. Ute Frevert, 'Comment: History of Emotions', in: Tamm and Burke (eds.), *Debating*, 202–8; see also Frevert, *Emotions in History: Lost and Found*, Budapest: Central European University Press, 2001; Frevert (ed.), *Emotional Lexicons: Continuity and Change in the Vocabulary of Feeling, 1700–2000*, Oxford: Oxford University Press, 2014.
74. Frevert, 'Comment', 204.
75. William M. Reddy, *The Making of Romantic Love: Longing and Sexuality in Europe, South Asia and Japan, 900–1200 CE*, Chicago: University of Chicago Press, 2012.
76. Kathleen Canning, 'The Body as Method? Reflections on the Place of the Body in Gender History', in: *Gender and History* 11 (1999), 499–513; Laurence Goldstein (ed.), *The Male Body: Features, Destinies, Exposures*, Ann Arbor: University of Michigan Press, 1994; Nelly Oudshoorn, *Beyond the Natural Body: an Archaeology of Sex Hormones*, London: Routledge, 1994; Irene Costera Meijer and Baukje Prins, 'Interview with Judith Butler', in: *Signs* 23 (1998), 275–86.
77. See, for example, Tim Armstrong (ed.), *American Bodies: Cultural Histories of the Physique*, Sheffield: Sheffield Academic Press, 1996.
78. Svenja Goltermann, 'Exercise and Perfection: Embodying the Nation in Ninteenth-Century Germany, in: *European Review of History* 11:3 (2004), 333–46. See also Patrizia Gentile and Jane Nicholas (eds.), *Contesting Bodies and Nation in Canadian History*, Toronto: University of Toronto Press, 2013.
79. Sander L. Gilman, *The Jew's Body*, London: Routledge, 1991; Kimberly Wallace-Sanders (ed.), *Skin Deep, Spirit Strong: the Black Female Body in American Culture*, Ann Arbor: University of Michigan Press, 2002.
80. Tony Ballantine and Antoinette Burton (eds.), *Bodies in Contact: Rethinking Colonial Encounters in World History*, Durham, NC: Duke University Press, 2005; Magali M. Carrera, *Imagining Identity in New Spain: Race, Lineage and the Colonial Body in Portraiture and Casta Paintings*, Austin: University of Texas Press, 2003.

81. Richard Sennett, *Flesh and Stone: the Body and the City in Western Civilisation*, New York: W. W. Norton, 1994.
82. Seminal in this field, inspiring many other works, was Anson Rabinbach, *The Human Motor: Energy, Fatigue and the Origins of Modernity*, New York: Basic Books, 1990. See also, for example, Carol Wolkowitz, *Bodies at Work*, London: Sage, 2006; Daniel E. Bender, *Sweated Work, Weak Bodies: Anti-Sweatshop Campaigns and Languages of Labor*, New Brunswick: Rutgers University Press, 2004.
83. Sarah Coakley (ed.), *Religion and the Body*, Cambridge: Cambridge University Press, 1997; Neil Carter, *Medicine, Sport and the Body*, London: Bloomsbury, 2012; Johanna Siméant and Christoph Traïni, *Bodies in Protest: Hunger Strikes and Angry Music*, Amsterdam: Amsterdam University Press, 2016.
84. Falko Schnicke, 'Princesses, Semen, and Separation: Masculinity and Body Politics in Nineteenth-Century German Historiography', in: *Bulletin of the German Historical Institute London* 40:1 (2018), 26–60.
85. Rob Boddice, *The History of Emotions*, Manchester: Manchester University Press, 2018, 19.
86. Richard McMahon, Joachim Eibach and Randolph Roth, 'Making Sense of Violence? Reflections on the History of Interpersonal Violence in Europe', in: *Crime, History and Societies* 17:2 (2013), 5–26.
87. See the enormous, albeit controversial, success of Timothy Snyder, *Bloodlands: Europe between Hitler and Stalin*, New York: Basic Books, 2010.
88. Stefanos Geroulanos and Todd Meyers, *The Human Body in the Age of Catastrophe: Brittleness, Integration, Science, and the Great War*, Chicago: University of Chicago Press, 2018.
89. Arturo J. Aldama (ed.), *Violence and the Body: Race, Gender and the State*, Bloomington: Indiana University Press, 2003.
90. Fabian Klose, *Human Rights in the Shadow of Colonial Violence: the Wars of Independence in Kenya and Algeria*, Philadelphia: University of Pennsylvania Press, 2013.
91. David Niremberg, *Communities of Violence: Persecution of Minorities in the Middle Ages*, Princeton: Princeton University Press, 1996.
92. Robert W. Scribner, *Popular Culture and Popular Movements in Reformation Germany*, London: Hambledon Press, 1987; on the influence of Bakhtin on cultural history more generally, see also Peter Burke, 'Bakhtin for Historians', in: *Social History* 13 (1988), 85–90.

93. Richard Jenkins, *Pierre Bourdieu*, rev. edn, London: Routledge, 2002, chapter 5: 'Symbolic Violence and Social Reproduction'.
94. Saul Newman, *Power and Politics in Poststructuralist Thought: New Theories of the Political*, London: Routledge, 2005, 51–3 on Foucault's 'microphysics of power'.
95. The studies here are legion; see, for example, Snyder, *Bloodlands*; Donald Bloxham and Robert Gerwarth (eds.), *Political Violence in Twentieth-Century Europe*, Cambridge: Cambridge University Press, 2011; Michael Mann, *The Dark Side of Democracy: Explaining Ethnic Cleansing*, Cambridge: Cambridge University Press, 2006; Norman M. Naimark, *Stalin's Genocides*, Princeton: Princenton University Press, 2010; Stathis N. Kalyvas, *The Logic of Violence in Civil War*, Cambridge, MA: Harvard University Press, 2006; Joanna Bourke, *An Intimate History of Killing: Face to Face Killing in Twentieth Century Warfare*, New York: Basic Books, 2000.
96. Zygmunt Baumann, *Modernity and Ambivalence*, Cambridge: Polity Press, 1991.
97. The diverse theoretical approaches informing nationalism studies are discussed in detail in Stefan Berger and Eric H. Storm (eds.), *Writing the History of Nationalism*, London: Bloomsbury, 2019.
98. Richard Biernacki, 'Method and Metaphor after the New Cultural History', in: Victoria E. Bonnell and Lynn Hunt (eds.), *Beyond the Cultural Turn: New Directions in the Study of Society and Culture*, Berkeley: University of California Press, 1999, 83.
99. Jill Lepore, *The Whites of Their Eyes: the Tea Party's Revolution and the Battle over American History*, Princeton: Princeton University Press, 2010; Stuart Hall and Martin Jaques (eds.), *The Politics of Thatcherism*, London: Lawrence and Wisheart, 1983.
100. Macintyre and Clarke, *The History Wars*.

5 Gender History

1. Chen Yang and Karen Offen, 'Women's History at the Cutting Edge: a Joint Paper in Two Voices', in: *Women's History Review* 27:1 (2018), 6–28, quotes on 10, 15, 24.
2. For these and more examples see Julie Des Jardins, *Women and the Historical Enterprise: Gender, Race, and the Politics of Memory*, Chapel Hill: University of Michigan Press, 2003.
3. Bonnie G. Smith, *The Gender of History: Men, Women and Historical Practice*, Cambridge, MA: Harvard University Press, 1998;

Jitka Malečková, 'Where are Women in National Histories', in: Berger and Lorenz (eds.), *The Contested Nation*, 171–99; Billie Melman, 'Gender, History and Memory: the Invention of Women's Pasts in the Nineteenth and Early Twentieth Centuries', in: *History and Memory* 5:1 (1993), 5–41; Mary Spongberg, *Women Writers and the Nation's Past, 1790–1860: Empathetic Histories*, London: Bloomsbury, 2019.

4. Ivy Pinchbeck, *Women Workers and the Industrial Revolution, 1750–1850*, London: Crofts, 1930.
5. Alice Clark, *The Working Life of Women in the Seventeenth Century*, London: Kelley, 1919; Eileen Power, *Medieval English Nunneries*, Cambridge: Cambridge University Press, 1922, Olive Schreiner, *Women and Labour*, New York: Stokes, 1911.
6. Mary R. Beard, *Woman as a Force in History: a Study in Tradition and Realities*, New York: Macmillan, 1946; Léon Abensour, *Histoire générale du féminisme des origines à nos jours*, Paris: Delagrave, 1921.
7. The title is cited in Japanese by Dorothy Ko, 'Gender', in: Ulinka Rublack (ed.), *A Concise Companion to History*, Oxford: Oxford University Press, 2011, 208–9.
8. Maxine Berg, *A Woman in History: Eileen Power, 1889–1940*, Cambridge: Cambridge University Press, 1996.
9. See, for example, Catherine Hall, *White, Male and Middle-Class: Explorations in Feminism and History*, Oxford: Oxford University Press, 1992, 15.
10. Simone de Beauvoir, *The Second Sex*, New York: Jonathan Cape, 1953.
11. Carolyn Steedman, *Landscape for a Good Woman*, Chicago: Rutgers University Press, 1987.
12. Laura Lee Downs, *Writing Gender History*, 2nd edn, London: Bloomsbury, 2010, 32.
13. This is reflected by titles such as Renate Bridenthal, Claudia Koonz and Susan Stuard (eds.), *Becoming Visible: Women in European History*, Boston: Houghton Mifflin, 1977; Sheila Rowbotham, *Hidden from History: 300 Years of Women's Oppression and the Fight against it*, London: Pluto, 1973; Gerda Lerner, *The Majority Finds its Past: Placing Women in History*, Durham, NC: University of North Carolina Press, 1979.
14. Susan Mann and Yu-Yin Cheng (eds.), *Under Confucian Eyes: Writing on Gender in Chinese History*, Berkeley: University of Berkeley Press, 2001.
15. Toyin Falola and Saheed Aderinto, *Nigeria, Nationalism and Writing History*, Rochester, NY: University of Rochester Press, 2010, 143–56.

16. Lynn M. Thomas, 'Imperial Concerns and "Women's Affairs": State Efforts to Regulate Clitorectomy and Eradicate Abortion in Meru, Kenya, c. 1910–1950', in: *Journal of African History* 39 (1998), 121–45.
17. Joan Kelly, *Women, History, and Theory*, Chicago: University of Chicago Press, 1984.
18. Sally Alexander, 'Women's Work in Nineteenth-Century London: a Study of the Years 1820–1850', in: Anne Oakley and Juliet Mitchell (eds.), *The Rights and Wrongs of Women*, Harmondsworth: Penguin, 1976, 59–112.
19. Barbara Taylor, *Eve and the New Jerusalem: Socialism and Feminism in the Nineteenth Century*, New York: Virago, 1983.
20. Jacqueline Jones, *Labor of Love, Labor of Sorrow: Black Women, Work and the Family from Slavery to the Present*, New York: Basic Books, 1985.
21. Catherine Hall, *Civilizing Subjects: Metropole and Colony in the English Imagination, 1830–1867*, Chicago: University of Chicago Press, 2002.
22. Leonore Davidoff and Catherine Hall, *Family Fortunes: Men and Women of the English Middle Class, 1750–1850*, rev. edn, London: Routledge, 2002 (originally published in 1987).
23. Michelle Rosaldo and Louise Lamphere (eds.), *Women, Culture and Society*, Stanford: Stanford University Press, 1974.
24. Linda Kerber, 'Separate Spheres, Female Worlds, Woman's Place: the Rhetoric of Women's History', in: *Journal of American History* 75 (1988), 9–39.
25. Joan W. Scott, 'Gender: a Useful Category of Historical Analysis', in: *American Historical Review* 91:5 (1986), 1053–75.
26. Elisabetta Ruspini, Jeff Hearn, Bob Pease and Keith Pringle (eds.), *Men and Masculinities around the World: Transforming Men's Practices*, Basingstoke: Palgrave Macmillan, 2011; Michael S. Kimmel, Jeff Hearn and R. W. Connell (eds.), *Handbook of Studies on Men and Masculinities*, London: Sage, 2005.
27. Robert Nye, *Masculinity and Male Codes of Honour in France*, Berkeley: University of California Press, 1992. See also Ute Frevert, *Men of Honour: a Cultural History of the Duel*, Oxford: Blackwell, 1995.
28. John Tosh, 'What Should Historians Do with Masculinity? Reflections on Ninenteenth-Century Britain', in: *History Workshop Journal* 38 (1994), 179–202.
29. Mark E. Kann, *A Republic of Men: the American Founders, Gendered Language, and Patriarchal Politics*, New York: New York University Press, 1998.

30. Showcasing some of this intriguing work is Pablo Dominguez Andersen and Simon Wendt (eds.), *Masculinities and the Nation in the Modern World: Between Hegemony and Marginalization*, Basingstoke: Palgrave Macmillan, 2015.
31. Butler, *Gender Trouble*, 7.
32. Foucault, *The History of Sexuality, vol. I.*
33. Katherine Crawford, *European Sexualities, 1400–1800*, Cambridge: Cambridge University Press, 2007.
34. Harry Cocks and Matt Houlbrook (eds.), *The Modern History of Sexuality*, Basingstoke: Palgrave Macmillan, 2005; Peter Stearns, *Sexuality in World History*, London: Routledge, 2009; Dagmar Herzog, *Sexuality in Europe: a Twentieth-Century History*, Cambridge: Cambridge University Press, 2011; Sarah Toulalan and Kate Fisher (eds.), *The Routledge History of Sex and the Body, 1500 to the Present*, London: Routledge, 2013.
35. Michelle Perrot (ed.), *History of Private Life, vol. IV: From the Fires of Revolution to the Great War*, Cambridge, MA: Harvard University Press, 1990. The five-volume series, published between the late 1980s and early 1990s in English (between 1985 and 1987 in French), was under the general editorship of Philippe Ariès and Georges Duby and covered the period from ancient history to the twentieth century.
36. Roy Porter, 'History of the Body Reconsidered', in: Peter Burke (ed.), *New Perspectives on Historical Writing*, Cambridge: Polity Press, 2001, 232–60, quote on 236.
37. Michel Foucault, 'The Birth of Bio-Power', in: P. Rabinow and N. Nose (eds.), *The Essential Foucault*, New York: The New Press, 2003, 202–7.
38. Catherine Gallagher and Thomas Laqueur (eds.), *The Making of the Modern Body: Sexuality and Society in the Nineteenth Century*, Berkeley: University of California Press, 1987.
39. Roger Cooter, 'The Turn of the Body: History and the Politics of the Corporeal', in: *Arbor: Ciencia, Pensamiento y Cultura* 743 (2010), 393–405.
40. Caroline Walker Bynum, 'Why All the Fuss about the Body? A Medievalist's Perspective', in: *Critical Enquiry* 22 (1995), 1–33.
41. Barbara Marie Stafford, *Echo Objects: the Cognitive Work of Images*, Chicago: University of Chicago Press, 2007.
42. Eelco Runia, 'Presence', in: *History and Theory* 45 (2006), 1–29; Hans-Ulrich Gumbrecht, 'Presence Achieved in Language (with Special Attention Given to the Presence of the Past', in: *History and Theory* 45 (2006), 317–27.

43. Nikolas Rose, *The Politics of Life Itself: Biomedicine, Power, and Subjectivity in the Twenty-First Century*, Princeton: Princeton University Press, 2007.
44. Jürgen Habermas, *The Structural Transformation of the Public Sphere: an Inquiry into a Category of Bourgeois Society*, Cambridge, MA: MIT Press, 1989.
45. Isabel V. Hull, *Sexuality, State and Civil Society in Germany, 1700–1815*, Ithaca, NY: Cornell University Press, 1996.
46. Mrinalini Sinha, *Specters of Mother India: the Global Restructruring of an Empire*, Durham, NC: Duke University Press, 2006.
47. Ann Laura Stoler, *Carnal Knowledge and Imperial Power: Race and the Intimate in Colonial Rule*, Berkeley: University of California Press, 2002.
48. Londa Schiebinger, *Nature's Body: Gender in the Making of Modern Science*, Boston: Harvard University Press, 1993.
49. Lisa Bloom, *Gender on Ice: American Ideologies of Polar Expeditions*, Minneapolis: University of Minnesota Press, 1993.
50. Nancy Folbre, *Greed, Lust and Gender: a History of Economic Ideas*, Oxford: Oxford University Press, 2009.
51. Jan Luiten van Zanden, 'Introduction', in: van Zanden, Auke Rijpma and Jan Kok (eds.), *Agency, Gender, and Economic Development in the World Economy, 1850–2000: Testing the Sen Hypothesis*, London: Routledge, 2017, 1–9.
52. Ida Blom, Karen Hagemann and Catherine Hall (eds.), *Gendered Nations: Nationalism and Gender Order in the Long Nineteenth Century*, Oxford: Berghahn Books, 2000.
53. Patricia Herminghouse and Magda Müller (eds.), *Gender and Germanness: Cultural Production of Nations*, Oxford: Berghahn Books, 1997.
54. Jacqueline Aquino Siapno, *Gender, Islam, Nationalism and the State in Aceh: the Paradox of Power, Co-optation and Resistance*, London: Routledge, 2002.
55. Dieter Langewiesche, *Der gewaltsame Lehrer. Europas Kriege in der Moderne*, Munich: C. H. Beck, 2019.
56. Margaret Randolph Higonnet, Jane Jenson, Sonya Michel and Margaret Collins Wietz (eds.), *Behind the Lines: Gender and the Two World Wars*, New Haven: Yale University Press,1987, a collection of essays that explicitly sought to apply Scott's insights into 'gender as a useful category for historical analysis' to the field of the history of warfare.
57. Joshua Goldstein, *War and Gender: How Gender Shapes the War System and Vice Versa*, Cambride: Cambridge University Press, 2001.

58. Karen Hagemann, Gisela Mettele and Jane Rendall (eds.), *Gender, War and Politics: Transatlantic Perspectives, 1775–1830*, Basingstoke: Palgrave Macmillan, 2010.
59. Mark Moss, *Manliness and Militarism: Educating Young Boys in Ontario for War*, Oxford: Oxford University Press, 2001.
60. Karen Hagemann and Stefanie Schüler-Springorum (eds.), *Home/Front: the Military, War and Gender in Twentieth-Century Germany*, Oxford: Berg, 2002.
61. Belinda J. Davis, *Home Fires Burning: Food, Politics and Everyday Life in World War I*, Chapel Hill: University of North Carolina Press, 2000.
62. Jad Adams, *Women and the Vote: a World History*, Oxford: Oxford University Press, 2014, chapter 10.
63. Jean Bethke Elshtain, *Women and War*, New York: Basic Books, 1987.
64. Berenice Carroll (ed.), *Liberating Women's History*, Chicago: Chicago University Press, 1976: Karen Offen, *European Feminisms, 1700–1950: a Political History*, Stanford: Stanford University Press, 2000; Gerda Lerner, *The Creation of Patriarchy*, Oxford: Oxford University Press, 1986.
65. Alice Kessler-Harris, 'A Rich and Adventurous Journey: the Transnational Journey of Gender History in the United States', in: *Journal of Women's History* 19:1 (2007), 153–9.
66. Clare Midgley, Alison Twells and Julie Carter, 'Introduction', in: Midgley, Twells and Carter (eds.), *Women in Transnational History: Connecting the Local and the Global*, London: Routledge, 2016, 4.
67. Gayatri Chakravorty Spivak, 'The Rani of Sirmur: an Essay in Reading the Archives', in: *History and Theory* 24:3 (1985), 247–72.
68. See Nupur Chaudhuri and Margaret Strobl (eds.), *Western Women and Imperialism: Complicity and Resistance*, Bloomington: Indiana University Press, 1992; Ruth Roach Pierson and Nupur Chaudhuri (eds.), *Nation, Empire, Colony: Historicizing Gender and Race*, Bloomington: Indiana University Press, 1998.
69. Pamela S. Nadell and Kate Haulman (eds.), *Making Women's Histories: Beyond National Perspectives*, New York: New York University Press, 2013.
70. Karen Garner, *Women and Gender in International History: Theory and Practice*, London: Bloomsbury, 2018.
71. Oliver Janz and Daniel Schönpflug, 'Introduction', in: Janz and Schönpflug (eds.), *Gender History in a Transnational Perspective*, Oxford: Berghahn Books, 2014, 2.
72. Nancy F. Cott, *The Grounding of Modern Feminism*, New Haven: Yale University Press, 1987: Leslie Heywood and Jennifer Drake

(eds.), *Third Wave Agenda: Being Feminist, Doing Feminism*, Minneapolis: University of Minnesota Press, 1997.

73. Carroll Smith-Rosenberg, *Disorderly Conduct: Visions of Gender in American History*, Oxford: Oxford University Press, 1985, 11.
74. Françoise Thébaut, 'Writing Women's and Gender History in France: a National Narrative?', in: *Journal of Women's History* 19:1 (2007), 167–72.
75. Joanna de Groot, 'Women's History in Many Places: Reflections on Plurality, Diversity and Polyversality', in: *Women's History Review* 27:1 (2018), 109–19.
76. Chandra Talpade Mohanty, *Feminism without Borders: Decolonizing Theory, Practising Solidarity*, Durham, NC: Duke University Press, 2003.
77. Estelle Freedman, *No Turning Back: the History of Feminism and the Future of Women*, New York: Random House, 2002.
78. Natalie Zemon Davis, 'Women's History in Transition: the European Case', in: *Feminist Studies* 3:3/4 (1976), 83–103, quote on 90.
79. Theories of intersectionality are often sourced to Kimberlé Crenshaw, 'Mapping the Margins: Intersectionality, Identity Politics, and Violence against Women of Color', in: *Stanford Law Review* 43:6 (1991), 1241–99; see also, from a more historical perspective: Kathleen Canning, *Gender History in Practice: Historical Perspectives on Bodies, Class and Citizenship*, Ithaca, NY: Cornell University Press, 2006.
80. Alice Kessler-Harris, *In Pursuit of Equity: Women, Men, and the Quest for Economic Citizenship in Twentieth-Century America*, Oxford: Oxford University Press, 2001.
81. Lynn M. Thomas, *Politics of the Womb: Women, Reproduction and the State in Kenya*, Berkeley: University of California Press, 2003.
82. Kathryn Burns, *Colonial Habits: Convents and the Spiritual Economy of Cuzco, Peru*, Durham, NC: University of North Carolina Press, 1999.
83. Lata Mani, *The Debate on Sati in Colonial India*, Berkeley: University of California Press, 1998.
84. Ifi Amadiume, Ma*le Daughters, Female Husbands: Gender and Sex in an African Society*, London: Zed Books, 1987; Oyeronke Oyewumi, *The Invention of Women: Making an African Sense of Western Gender Discourses*, Minneapolis: University of Minnesota Press, 1997.
85. Michèle Barrett, *Imagination in Theory: Essays on Writing and Culture*, Cambridge: Polity Press, 1999, 111–23.
86. Butler, *Gender Trouble.*
87. Judith Butler, *Bodies that Matter: on the Discursive Limits of 'Sex'*, London: Routledge, 1993.

88. Lorenzo Bernini, *Queer Theories: an Introduction – from Mario Mieli to the Antisocial Turn*, London: Routledge, 2020; for the concept of 'compulsory heterosexuality' see Adrienne Rich, 'Reflections on "Compulsory Heterosexuality"', in: *Journal of Women's History* 16:1 (2004), 9–11.
89. Colleen Walsh, 'Stonewall Then and Now: Harvard Scholars Reflect on the History and Legacy of the Milestone Gay Rights Demonstrations Triggered by a Police Raid at a Dive Bar in New York', in: *Harvard Gazette*, 27 June 2019; https://news.harvard.edu/gazette/story/2019/06/harvard-scholars-reflect-on-the-history-and-legacy-of-the-stonewall-riots/ [accessed 2 April 2020].
90. John D'Emilio, *Sexual Politics, Sexual Communities: the Making of a Homosexual Minority in the United States, 1940–1970*, Chicago: University of Chicago Press, 1983.
91. Marc Stein, 'Theoretical Politics, Local Communities: the Making of US LGBT Historiography',in: *GLQ: a Journal of Lesbian and Gay Studies* 11 (2005), 605–25.
92. Afsaneh Najmabadi, *Women with Mustaches and Men without Beards: Gender and Sexual Anxieties of Iranian Modernity*, Berkeley: University of California Press, 2005.
93. A good overview is provided by Leila J. Rupp and Susan K. Freeman, *US Lesbian, Gay, Bisexual and Transgender History*, Madison: University of Wisconsin Press, 2014; on Britain compare Brian Lewis (ed.), *British Queer History: New Approaches and Perspectives*, Manchester: Manchester University Press, 2013.
94. Howard H. Chiang, 'On the Historiographical Politics of Queer Sexuality: Thinking across the Post-Colonial and LGBTQ Subjects of History', in: *Ex Historia* 1 (2009): 1–24; https://humanities.exeter.ac.uk/media/universityofexeter/collegeofhumanities/history/exhistoria/volume1/HowardHChiangessay.pdf [accessed 17 June 2021].
95. Thomas Laqueur, *Making Sex: Bodies and Gender from the Greeks to Freud*, Cambridge, MA: Harvard University Press, 1990.
96. Joan W. Scott, 'The Evidence of Experience', in: *Critical Inquiry* 17:4 (1991), 773–97, quote on 778.
97. Ibid., 780.
98. Ibid.
99. Ibid., 781.
100. Ibid., 782.
101. Ibid., 787.
102. Denise Riley, *Am I that Name? Feminism and the Category of Women in History*, Basingstoke: Macmillan, 1988.
103. Scott, 'Evidence of Experience', 792.

104. Spiegel (ed.), *Practicing History*, 200.
105. Virginia Woolf in *Times Literary Supplement*, 18 March 1920.
106. Downs, *Writing Gender History*, 187.

6 Historical Anthropology

1. There are several introductions to historical anthropology penned in German. See, for example, Gert Dressel, *Historische Anthropologie. Eine Einführung*, Cologne: Böhlau, 1996; Richard van Dülmen, *Historische Anthropologie. Entwicklung, Probleme, Aufgaben*, Cologne: UTB, 2004; Jakob Tanner, *Historische Anthropologie zur Einführung*, Hamburg: Junus, 2004. There are, however, also many books in English that carry the term 'historical anthropology' in their titles. See, for example, Axel, *From the Margins*.
2. Foucault, *Archaeology of Knowledge*.
3. Geertz, *Interpretation of Cultures*.
4. Ibid., 89.
5. Lucien Febvre, *Das Gewissen des Historikers*, Frankfurt am Main: Suhrkamp, 1990, 18.
6. Bloch, *The Historian's Craft*, 75.
7. Emmanuel LeRoy Ladurie, *Montaillou: Cathars and Catholics in a French village, 1294–1324*, London: Scholar Press, 1978; Jacques LeGoff (ed.), *The Medieval World*, London: Collins, 1990.
8. Dosse, *New History in France*, 140.
9. Nobert Elias, *The Civilising Process, vol. I: the History of Manners*, Oxford: Blackwell, 1969. The second volume entitled *State Formation and Civilisation* was published only much later by the same publisher, in 1982.
10. Howard Zinn, *A People's History of the United States: 1492 to the Present*, New York: Harper Collins, 1980; see also Martin Duberman, *Howard Zinn: a Life on the Left*, New York: The New Press, 2012.
11. Jürgen Habermas, *Anthropologie* [1958], in: Habermas, *Kultur und Kritik. Verstreute Aufsätze*, Frankfurt am Main: Suhrkamp, 1973, 89–111.
12. Clifford Geertz, 'Deep Play: Notes on the Balinese Cock-Fight', republished in: Alan Dundes (ed.), *The Cock-Fight: a Case Book*, Madison: University of Wisconsin Press, 1994, 94–132 (originally published in 1972); see also Jeffrey C. Alexander, Philip Smith and Matthew Norton (eds.), *Interpreting Clifford Geertz: Cultural Investigation in the Social Sciences*, Basingstoke: Palgrave Macmillan, 2011; Marshall Sahlins, *How 'Natives' Think: About Captain Cook, For Example*, Chicago: University of Chicago Press, 1995;

Nancy C. Lutkehaus, *Margaret Mead: the Making of an American Icon*, Princeton: Princeton University Press, 2008; Victor Turner, *The Ritual Process: Structure and Anti-Structure*, London: Routledge, 2017 (originally published in 1969).

13. On de Saussure's ideas being foundational to poststructuralism, see Kevin Passmore, 'Poststructuralist and Linguistic Methods', in: Berger, Feldner and Passmore (eds.), *Writing History*, 135–7.
14. See also Clifford Geertz, *Negara: the Theatre State in Nineteenth-Century Bali*, Princeton: Princeton University Press, 1980.
15. Marshall Sahlins, 'Individual Experience and Cultural Order', in: Sahlins, *Culture in Practice: Selected Essays*, New York: Zone Books, 2000, 277–91.
16. Brian Keith Axel, 'Introduction: Historical Anthropology and Its Vicissitudes', in: Axel (ed.), *From the Margins*, 8.
17. Keith Snell, 'English Historical Continuity and the Culture of Capitalism: the Work of Alan Macfarlane', in: *History Workshop Journal* 27:1 (1989), 154–63; Stephen D. White and Richard T. Vann, 'The Invention of English Individualism: Alan Macfarlane and the Modernization of Pre-Modern England', in: *Social History* 8:3 (1983), 345–63. Whilst his work led to debates about the exceptionalism of the English and also to accusations that he was contributing to a political project associated with Thatcherism in the United Kingdom, this shall not interest us here, where we are more interested in his contribution to bringing the disciplines of anthropology and history closer together.
18. All of the quotes are from Alan Macfarlane, 'Historical Anthropology' in: *Cambridge Anthropology* 3:3 (1977), in: http://www.alanmacfarlane.com/TEXTS/frazerlecture.pdf [accessed 15 May 2019].
19. Lüdtke (ed.), The *History of Everyday Life.*
20. Raphael Samuel, 'History Workshop 1966–1980', in: Samuel (ed.), *People's History and Socialist Theory*, London: Routledge, 1981, 408–22; Bill Schwarz, 'History on the Move: Reflections on History Workshop', in: *Radical History Review* 57 (1993), 202–20.
21. *History Workshop Journal*, 'Editorial', in: *History Workshop Journal* 1 (1965), 2; see also Gwinn, 'History Should Become Common Property'.
22. For a comparison of the British and the German history workshop movements see Ian Gwinn, '"A Different Kind of History is Possible": the History Workshop Movement and the Politics of British and West German Historical Practice', PhD dissertation, University of Liverpool, 2016.
23. Giovanni Levi, 'On Microhistory', in: Peter Burke (ed.), *New Perspectives on Historical Writing*, Cambridge: Polity Press, 1991, 93–113.

24. Lizette Jacinto, 'Micro-History', in: Bloomsbury Digital Resource on Historical Theory and Historiography, launched in September 2021 (manuscript in the possession of the author).
25. Carlo Ginzburg and Bruce Lincoln, *Old Thiess: a Livonian Werewolf: a Classic Case in Comparative Perspective*, Chicago: University of Chicago Press, 2020.
26. Sirurður Gylfi Magnússon and István M. Szijártó, *What is Microhistory? Theory and Practice*, London: Routledge, 2013. See also Zoltán Boldizsár Simon, 'Microhistory: In General', in: *Journal of Social History* 49:1 (2015), 237–48; John-Paul Ghobrial (ed.), *Global History and Microhistory, Past and Present*, supplement 14, Oxford: Oxford University Press, 2019; Hans Medick, 'Turning Global? Microhistory in Extension', in: *Historische Anthropologie* 24:2 (2016), 241–52.
27. Thomas Lindenberger and Michael Wildt, 'Radical Plurality: History Workshops as a Practical Critique of Knowledge', in: *History Workshop Journal* 33 (1992), 73–99.
28. Jacques Rancière, *Proletarian Nights: the Workers' Dream in Nineteenth-Century France*, London: Verso, 2012 (originally published in French in 1981).
29. Jacques Rancière, *The Names of History: On the Poetics of Knowledge*, Minneapolis: University of Minnesota Press, 1994. Interestingly Hayden White wrote an approving foreword to the English translation that was first published in French in 1992.
30. Oliver Davis, *Jacques Rancière*, Cambridge: Polity Press, 2010.
31. Medick, 'Missionaries in the Row Boat'.
32. *Historische Anthropologie*, 'Editorial', in: *Historische Anthropologie* 1: 1 (1993), 1–3.
33. André Burguière, 'L'anthropologie historique', in: Jacques Le Goff, Roger Chartier and Jacques Revel (eds.), *La nouvelle histoire*, Paris: Retz, 1978, 37–61, quotes on 44. On the development of historical anthropologies in different countries see also Alexandre Coello de la Rosa and Josep Luís Mateo Dieste, *In Praise of Historical Anthropology: Perspectives, Methods and Applications to the Study of Power and Colonialism*, London: Routledge, 2020, chapter 1: 'Anthropology and History: Uncomfortable Dance Partners'.
34. Bill Schwarz has recently discussed the strange lack of dialogue between the British history workshop movement and the Subaltern Studies movement, concluding also that the two had much in common. See Bill Schwarz, 'Subaltern Histories', in: *History Workshop Journal* 89 (2019), 90–107.

35. Vinayak Chaturvedi (ed.), *Mapping Subaltern Studies and the Postcolonial*, London: Verso, 2000.
36. Bernard S. Cohn, *An Anthropologist among the Historians and Other Essays*, Oxford: Oxford University Press, 1987, 44.
37. Rajajit Guha and Gayatri C. Spivak (eds.), *Selected Subaltern Studies*, Oxford: Oxford University Press, 1988.
38. The term is Ann Laura Stoler's. See her article 'In Cold Blood: Hierarchies of Credibility and the Politics of Colonial Narratives', in: *Representations* 37 (1992), 151–89.
39. Ann Laura Stoler, *Capitalism and Confrontation in Sumatra's Plantation Belt, 1870–1979*, New Haven: Yale University Press, 1985.
40. Ann Laura Stoler, *Race and the Education of Desire: Foucault's History of Sexuality and the Colonial Order of Things*, Durham, NC: Duke University Press, 1995.
41. Stoler, *Carnal Knowledge and Imperial Power*.
42. Jacques Derrida, *Archive Fever: a Freudian Impression*, Chicago: University of Chicago Press, 1996 (originally published in French in 1995).
43. Ann Laura Stoler, *Along the Archival Grain: Epistemic Anxieties and Colonial Common Sense*, Princeton: Princeton University Press, 2008.
44. Ann Laura Stoler, *Duress: Imperial Durabilities in Our Times*, Durham, NC: Duke University Press, 2016.
45. Eley, *A Crooked Line*, 132.
46. Axel (ed.), *From the Margins*.
47. Walter L. Adamson, *Hegemony and Revolution: a Study of Antonio Gramsci's Political and Cultural Theory*, Berkeley: University of California Press, 1980.
48. Adrian Randall and Andrew Charlesworth (eds.), *Moral Economy and Popular Protest: Crowds, Conflicts, Authority*, Basingstoke: Palgrave Macmillan, 2000.
49. E. P. Thompson, 'History and Anthropology', in: Thompson, *Persons and Polemics: Historical Essays*, London: Merlin Press, 1994, 201–27.
50. Tanner, 'Historical Anthropology'.
51. William M. Reddy, 'Anthropology and the History of Culture', in: Lloyd Kramer and Sarah Maza (eds.), *A Companion to Western Historical Thought*, Oxford: Blackwell, 2002, 277–96.
52. Geertz, *The Interpretation of Cultures*, 363.
53. William H. Sewell Jr., 'A Theory of Structure: Duality, Agency, and Transformation', in: *American Journal of Sociology* 98 (1992), 1–29.
54. Bourdieu, *Outline of a Theory of Practice*.
55. Michel de Certeau, *The Practice of Everyday Life*, Berkeley: University of Berkeley Press, 1984 (originally published in French in 1980).

56. Michel de Certeau, *The Possession at Loudon*, Chicago: University of Chicago Press, 1996 (originally published in French in 1970).
57. De Certeau, *Practice*, 11.
58. On de Certeau see also Poster, *Cultural History and Postmodernity*, 120–6; Burke, *What Is Cultural History?*, 76–8.
59. William H. Sewell Jr, 'The Concept(s) of Culture', in: Gabrielle M. Spiegel (ed.), *Practicing History: New Directions in Historical Writing after the Linguistic Turn*, London: Routledge, 2005, 76–96.
60. E. P. Thompson, 'The Moral Economy of the English Crowd in the Eighteenth Century', in: *Past and Present* 50 (1971), 76–136.
61. Natalie Zemon Davis, 'The Reasons for Misrule: Youth Groups and Charivaris in Sixteenth-Century France', in: *Past and Present* 50:1 (1971), 41–75; E. P. Thompson, '"Rough Music": le Charivari Anglais', in: *Annales* 27:2 (1972), 285–312. See also the intriguing exchange of letters between Davis and Thompson published by Alexandra Walsham, 'Rough Music and Charivari: Letters between Natalie Zemon Davis and Edward Thompson, 1970–1972', in: *Past and Present* 235 (2017), 243–62.
62. Robert Darnton, *The Great Cat Massacre: And Other Episodes in French Cultural History*, New York: Basic Books, 1984; see also Burke, *What Is Cultural History?*, 37.
63. James Clifford and George E. Marcus (eds.), *Writing Culture: the Poetics and Politics of Ethnography*, Berkeley: University of California Press, 1986.
64. Jan Goldstein (ed.), *Foucault and the Writing of History*, Oxford: Blackwell, 1994.
65. Nicholas Dirks (ed.), *Near Ruins: Cultural Theory at the End of the Century*, Minneapolis: University of Minnesota Press, 1998.
66. Edna G. Bay, *Wives of the Leopard: Gender, Politics, and Culture in the Kingdom of Dahomey*, Charlottesville: University of Virgina Press, 1998.
67. Van Dülmen, *Historische Anthropologie*.
68. Rhys Isaacs, *The Transformation of Virginia, 1740–1790*, Chapel Hill: North Carolina University Press, 1982.
69. Ildikó Beller-Hann, *Community Matters in Xinjiang, 1880–1949: Towards a Historical Anthropology of the Uyghur*, Leiden: Brill, 2008.
70. David Cressy, *Birth, Marriage and Death: Ritual, Religion and the Life Cycle in Tudor and Stuart England*, Oxford: Oxford University Press, 1997.
71. Keith Thomas, *Religion and the Decline of Magic*, London: Weidenfeld and Nicolson, 1971; Edward E. Evans-Pritchard, *Witchcraft, Oracles and Magic among the Azande*, Oxford: Oxford University Press, 1976

(originally published in 1937). On the influence of anthropology on Thomas see also Burke, *What Is Cultural History?*, 34.

72. Natalie Zemon Davis, 'The Rites of Violence: Religious Riot in Sixteenth-Century France', in: *Past and Present* 59 (1973), reprinted in Davis, *Society and Culture in Early Modern France*, Stanford: Stanford University Press, 1975, 152–88.
73. Roman Loimeier, *Muslim Societies in Africa: a Historical Anthropology*, Bloomington: Indiana University Press, 2013.
74. Tanner, 'Historical Anthropology'; see also Paul Rabinow, *Essays on the Anthropology of Reason*, Princeton: Princeton University Press, 1996.
75. Christoph Wulf, 'On Historical Anthropology: an Introduction', in: *The Senses and Society* 11:1 (2016), 7–23, quote on 11.
76. Steven G. Ellis and Lud'a Klusáková (eds.), *Frontiers and Identities: Exploring the Research Area*, Pisa: Pisa University Press, 2006; Steven G. Ellis and Lud'a Klusáková (eds.), *Imagining Frontiers. Contesting Identities*, Pisa: Pisa University Press, 2007.
77. Gunter Gebauer and Christoph Wulf, *Mimesis: Culture, Art, Society*, Berkeley: California University Press, 1995.
78. Margrit Pernau, 'The Indian Body and Unani Medicine: Body History as Entangled History', in: Axel Michaels and Christoph Wulf (eds.), *Images of the Body in India*, London: Routledge, 2011, 97–108.
79. Chakrabarty, *Provincializing Europe*.
80. Steven Feierman, 'Colonizers, Scholars, and the Creation of Invisible Histories', in: Victoria E. Bonnell and Lynn Hunt (eds.), *Beyond the Cultural Turn: New Directions in the Study of Society and Culture*, Berkely: University of California Press, 1999, 182–216, quote on 186.
81. John Pemberton, *On the Subject of 'Java'*, Ithaca, NY: Cornell University Press, 1994.
82. David Sabean, *Property, Production and Family in Neckarhausen, 1700–1870*, Cambridge: Cambridge University Press, 1987.
83. Lynn Hunt, 'Introduction', in: Hunt (ed.), *The New Cultural History*, 1–22, quote on 11.

7 The History of Memory

1. Good introductions to the field are provided by Siobhan Kattagoo (ed.), *The Ashgate Companion to Memory Studies*, Farnham: Ashgate, 2015; Astrid Erll, *Memory in Culture*, Basingstoke: Palgrave Macmillan, 2011; Astrid Erll and Ansgar Nünning (eds.), *Cultural Memory Studies: an International and Interdisciplinary Handbook*, Berlin: De

Gruyter, 2008. More specificially on memory history is Stefan Berger and Bill Niven (eds.), *Writing the History of Memory*, London: Bloomsbury, 2014, and Stefan Berger and Jeffrey K. Olick (eds), A Cultural History of Memory, 6 vols, London: Bloomsbury, 2020. See also Nicolas Pethes, *Cultural Memory Studies: an Introduction*, Cambridge: Cambridge Scholars, 2019.

2. On the interdisciplinarity of memory studies, see Henry L. Roediger and James V. Wertsch, 'Creating a New Discipline of Memory Studies', in: *Memory Studies* 1:1 (2008), 9–22.
3. Ibid., 19.
4. On the interrelatedness of past, present and future and the problem of understanding the past in terms of linear time see Berber Bevernage and Chris Lorenz (eds.), *Breaking up Time: Negotiating the Borders between Past, Present and Future*, Göttingen: Vandenhoeck and Ruprecht, 2013.
5. On 'agonistic memory' see Anna Cento Bull and Hans Lauge Hansen, 'On Agonistic Memory', in: *Memory Studies* 9:4 (2016), 390–404.
6. Pierre Nora, *Les lieux de mémoire*, Paris: Gallimard, 1984–92. See also the three-volume translation into English entitled *Realms of Memory: Rethinking the French Past*, ed. Lawrence D. Kritzman, New York: Columbia University Press, 1996–8.
7. Maurice Halbwachs, *On Collective Memory*, trans. Lewis A. Koser, Chicago: Chicago University Press, 1992.
8. Benoit Majerus, 'Lieux de Mémoirs: a European Transfer Story', in: Berger and Niven (eds.), *Writing the History of Memory*, 157–72; Stefan Berger and Joana Seiffert, 'Erinnerungsorte – ein Erfolgskonzept auf dem Prüfstand', in: Berger and Seiffert (eds.), *Erinnerungsorte: Chancen, Grenzen und Perspektiven eines Erfolgskonzeptes in den Kulturwissenschaften*, Essen: Klartext, 2014, 11–36.
9. Lucette Valensi, 'Histoire nationale, histoire monumental: les lieux de mémoirs', in: *Annales* 50:6 (1995), 1271–7. Similarly critical are Ben Mercer, 'The Moral Rearmament of France: Pierre Nora, Memory and the Crisis of Republicanism', in: *French Politics, Culture and Society* 31 (2013), 102–15; Jean-Paul Willaime, 'De la sacralisation de la France: lieux de mémoire et imaginaire national', in: *Archives de Science Sociales des Religions* 66 (1988), 125–45.
10. Wulf Kansteiner, 'Finding Meaning in Memory: a Methodological Critique of Collective Memory Studies', in: *History and Theory* 41:2 (2002), 179–197.
11. Thoughtful critiques of Nora's project are: Huet Tam Ho Tai, 'Remembered Realms: Pierre Nora and French National Memory', in: *American Historical Review* 106: 3 (2001), 906–22; Tony Judt, 'À la

Recherche du Temps Perdue', in: *New York Review of Books* 45:19 (1998), 51–8.

12. Raphael Samuel, *Theatres of Memory*, 2vols., London: Verso, 1994–8.
13. On the history workshop movement, see Chapter 3 on social history and Chapter 6 on historical anthropology.
14. Bertrand Taithe, 'Monuments aux morts? Reading Nora's Realms of Memory and Samuel's Theatres of Memory', in: *History of the Human Sciences* 12:2 (1999), 123–39.
15. Jan Assmann, *Cultural Memory and Early Civilisation: Writing: Remembrance and Political Imagination*, Cambridge: Cambridge University Press, 2011; Aleida Assman, *Cultural Memory and Western Civilisation: Functions, Media, Archives*, Cambridge: Cambridge University Press, 2011.
16. On Warburg compare Ernst H. Gombrich, *Aby Warburg: an Intellectual Biography*, Chicago: University of Chicago Press, 1986.
17. In the German historians' controversy of the mid-1980s, attempts by right-of centre historians to use history in the service of strengthening German national identity had been successfully rebuffed by left-of centre historians. On the controversy see Richard J. Evans, *In Hitler's Shadow: West German Historians and the Attempt to Escape from the Nazi Past*, London: Pantheon, 1989.
18. Daniel Levy and Natan Sznaider, 'Memory Unbound: the Holocaust and the Formation of Cosmopolitan Memory', in: *European Journal of Social Theory* 5:1 (2002), 87–106; Levy and Sznaider, *The Holocaust and Memory in the Global Age*, Philadelphia: Temple University Press, 2005.
19. For some of these debates see James E. Young, *The Texture of Memory: Holocaust Memorials and Meaning*, New Haven: Yale University Press, 1993.
20. Elazar Barkan, *The Guilt of Nations. Restitution and Negotiating Historical Injustices*, New York: W. W. Norton, 2000.
21. Https://humanrightscolumbia.org/about/about-our-institute [accessed 23 August 2019].
22. Paul Ricoeur, *Memory, History, Forgetting*, Chicago: University of Chicago Press, 2004.
23. Kwame Anthony Appiah, 'Cosmopolitan Patriots', in: Martha Craven Nussbaum and Joshua Cohen (ed.), *For Love of Country?*, New York: Beacon Press, 2002, 21–9.
24. Paul Gilroy, *Postcolonial Melancholia*, New York: Columbia University Press, 2005. On Gilroy see also Chapter 4.
25. Robert Aldrich, 'Colonial Museums in a Postcolonial Europe', in: Dominic Thomas (ed.), *Museums in Postcolonial Europe*, London: Routledge, 2009, chapter 1.

26. Herman Lebovics, 'Will the Musée du Quai Branly Show France the Way to Postcoloniality?', in: Thomas (ed.), *Museums*, chapter 7.
27. Etienne Achille, Charles Forsdick and Lydie Moudileno, 'Introduction: Postcolonizing Lieux de Mémoire', in: Achille, Forsdick and Moudileno (eds.), *Postcolonial Realms of Memory: Sites and Symbols in Modern France*, Liverpool: Liverpool University Press, 2020, 1–22, quote on 15.
28. C. Sarah Soh, *The Comfort Women: Sexual Violence and Postcolonial Memory in Korea and Japan*, Chicago: University of Chicago Press, 2008.
29. Jay Winter, *War beyond Words: Languages of Remembrance from the Great War to the Present*, Cambridge: Cambridge University Press, 2017; Winter, *Remembering War: the Great War between Memory and History in the Twentieth Century*, New Haven: Yale University Press, 2006.
30. Cristian Cercel, Nina Parish and Eleanor Rowley, 'War in the Museum: the Historial of the Great War in Péronne and the Military History Museum in Dresden', in: *Journal of War and Culture Studies* 12:2 (2019), 194–214.
31. John Bodmar, *Remaking America: Public Memory, Commemoration and Patriotism in the Twentieth Century*, Princeton: Princeton University Press, 1992.
32. Jennifer L. Allen, 'National Commemoration in an Age of Transnationalism';, in: *Journal of Modern History* 91:1 (2019), 109–48.
33. James E. Young, 'The Counter-Monument: Memory against itself in Germany Today', in: *Critiqual Inquiry* 18:2 (1992), 267–96.
34. Andreas Huyssen, 'The Voids of Berlin', in: *Critical Inquiry* 24:1 (1997), 57–81.
35. Rudy Koshar, *From Monuments to Traces: Artefacts of German Memory, 1870–1990*, Berkeley: University of California Press, 2000.
36. Allen, 'National Commemoration', 137–43.
37. Ibid., 143.
38. Ibid., 144.
39. Www.memorystudiesassociation.org/about_the_msa/ [accessed 23 August 2019].
40. Michael Rothberg, *Multidirectional Memory: Remembering the Holocaust in the Age of Decolonisation*, Stanford: Stanford University Press, 2009.
41. Jeffrey K. Olick and Daniel Levy, 'Collective Memory and Cultural Constraint: Holocaust Myth and Rationality in German Politics', in: *American Sociological Review* 32:6 (1997), 921–36.
42. Jeffrey K. Olick, In *the House of the Hangman: the Agonies of German Defeat, 1943–1949*, Chicago: University of Chicago Press, 2005; Olick, *The Politics of Regret: on Collective Memory and Historical Responsibility*, London: Routledge, 2007.
43. Jeffrey K. Olick, *The Sins of the Fathers: Germany, Memory, Method*, Chicago: University of Chicago Press, 2017, 12–16.

44. The influence of narrativism more generally and Hayden White in particular is also emphasized in Patrick Hutton, 'Recent Scholarship on Memory and History', in: *The History Teacher* 33:4 (2000), 533–48, especially 535–6.
45. James V. Wertsch, *Voices of Collective Remembering*, Cambridge: Cambridge University Press, 2002.
46. Alon Confino, 'Collective Memory and Cultural History: Problems of Method', in: *American Historical Review* 102:5 (1997), 1386–403, especially 1395–9.
47. Iryna Vushko, 'Historians at War: History, Politics and Memory in Ukraine', in: *Contemporary European History* 27:1 (2018), 112–24.
48. Jakob Tanner, 'Narratives', in: Kathrin Fahlenbrach, Martin Klimke and Joachim Scharloth (eds.), *Protest Cultures: a Companion*, Oxford: Berghahn Books, 2016, 137–45.
49. James Green, *Taking History to Heart: the Power of the Past in Building Social Movements*, Amherst: University of Massachusetts Press, 2000.
50. See www.terrorhaza.hu/en [accessed 23 August 2019].
51. An excellent recent example is Constantin Iordachi and Péter Apor (eds.), *Occupation and Communism in East European Museums: Re-Visualizing the Recent Past*, London: Bloomsbury, 2021.
52. James Mark, *The Unfinished Revolution: Making Sense of the Unfinished Past in East Central Europe*, New Haven: Yale University Press, 2010.
53. Attila Pók, 'On the Memory of Communism in Eastern and Central Europe', in: Berger and Niven (eds.), *Writing the History of Memory*, 173–98.
54. Rubie S. Watson (ed.), *History, Memory and Opposition under State Socialism*, Santa Fe: School of American Research Press, 1994; Grant Evans, *The Politics of Ritual and Remembrance: Laos since 1975*, Honolulu: University of Hawaii Press, 1998; Marc Andre Matten (ed.), *Places of Memory in Modern China: History, Politics and Identity*, Leiden: Brill, 2012.
55. Stefan Berger, 'History and Forms of Collective Identity in Europe: Why Europe Cannot and Should Not be Built on History', in: Laura Rorato and Anna Saunders (eds.), *The Essence and the Margin: National Identities and Collective Memories in Contemporary European Culture*, Amsterdam: Rodopi, 2009, 21–36. To what extent the EU has actively been driving a process of constructing a European identity is a controversial subject. Sam Pryke has surveyed the different positions and arrives at the conclusion that a growing Europeanism is the result of the discursive construction of

Europeanness through a great variety of different actors and debates surrounding European citizenship and the Europeanisation of everyday life. See Sam Pryke, 'National and European Identity', in: *National Identities* 22:1 (2020), 91–105.

56. Jan Gross, *Neighbors: the Destruction of the Jewish Community in Jedwabne, Poland*, Princeton: Princeton University Press, 2001.
57. Antony Polonsky and Joanna B. Michlic (eds.), *The Neighbors Respond: the Controversy over the Jedwabne Massacre in Poland*, Princeton: Princeton University Press, 2004.
58. Marta Bucholc and Maciej Komornik, 'The Polish "Holocaust Law" Revisited: the Devastating Effects of Prejudice Mongering', in: *Cultures of History Forum*, 19 Febuary 2019; www.cultures-of-history.uni-jena.de/politics/poland/the-polish-holocaust-law-revisited-the-devastating-effects-of-prejudice-mongering/ [accessed 15 April 2020].
59. Nikolay Koposov, *Memory Laws, Memory Wars: the Politics of the Past in Europe and Russia*, Cambridge: Cambridge University Press, 2018.
60. Tony Judt, *Post-War: a History of Europe since 1945*, London: Heinemann, 2005.
61. Onni Gust, 'The Brexit Syllabus: British History for Brexiteers', 5 September 2016, in: *History Workshop Journal*; www.historyworkshop.org.uk/the-brexit-syllabus-british-history-for-brexiteers/ [accessed 24 August 2019].
62. See the roundtable articles and discussions on Brexit in *Contemporary European History* 28:1 (2019), 1–81.
63. Andrew Bonnell, 'Europhobia in the New Tory Historiography', in: John Milfull (ed.), *Britain in Europe: Prospects for Change*, Aldershot: Ashgate, 1999, 207–25.
64. Wellings and Gifford, 'The Past in English Euroscepticism'.
65. Ben Wellings, 'Our Island Story: England, Europe and the Anglophone Alternative', in: *Political Studies Review* 14:3 (2016), 368–77, quote on 369. See also Ben Wellings, *English Nationalism and Euroscepticism: Losing the Peace*, Bern: Peter Lang, 2012. A fascinating comparison between very different memorialisations of empire in Britain and France is provided by Robert Gildea, *Empires of the Mind: the Colonial Past and the Politics of the Present*, Cambridge: Cambridge University Press, 2019.
66. On the European memory space, more generally, and its many contestations see Małgorzata Pakier and Bo Stråth (eds.), *A European Memory? Contested Histories and Politics of Remembrance*, Oxford: Berghahn Books, 2010.
67. John Ramsden, *Don't Mention the War: the British and the Germans since 1890*, London: Abacus, 2006, 363–5.

68. Gurminder Bhambra, 'Brexit, Empire and Decolonisation', 19 December 2018, in: *History Workshop Journal*; http://www.historyworkshop.org.uk /brexit-empire-and-decolonization/ [accessed 24 August 2019].
69. Linda Colley, *Acts of Union and Disunion: What has Held the United Kingdom Together and What is Dividing it?*, London: Profile, 2014, 132.
70. Kalypso Nikolaïdis, Berny Sèbe and Gabrielle Maas, 'Echoes of Empire: the Present of the Past', in: Nikolaïdis, Sèbe and Maas (eds.), *Echoes of Empire: Memory, Identity and Colonial Legacies*, London: I. B. Tauris, 2015, 7.
71. R. Ovendale, 'The End of Empire', in: R. English and M. Kenny (eds.), *Rethinking British Decline*, Basingstoke: Palgrave Macmillan, 2000, 274.
72. Niall Ferguson, *Empire: How Britain Made the Modern World*, London: Penguin, 2003; it led Catherine Hall to call him 'the self-proclaimed protagonist of capitalism and empire' in her article on ' Edward Said', in: *History Workshop Journal* 57:1 (2004), 235–43.
73. Wendy Ugolini, '"When Are You Going Back?" Memory, Ethnicity and the British Home Front', in: Lucy Noakes and Juliette Pattinson (eds.), *British Cultural Memory and the Second World War*, London: Bloomsbury, 2014, 89–110.
74. Sarah E. Gardner, 'What We Talk about When We Talk about Confederate Monuments', in: *Origins: Current Events in Historical Perspectives*, 11:5 (2018);http://origins.osu.edu/article/what-we-talk-about-when-we-talk-about-confederate-monuments [accessed 24 August 2019]. Histories of the memory of the civil war are many and they clearly have shown how deeply the memory in the south was connected to ongoing racism, the Jim Crow system and white supremacy. See, for example, William Blair, *Cities of the Dead: Contesting the Memory of the Civil War in the South, 1865–1914*, Chapel Hill: University of North Carolina Press, 2004; W. Fitzhugh Brundage, *The Southern Past: a Clash of Race and Memory*, Cambridge, MA: Harvard University Press, 2008; Caroline E. Janney, *Remembering the Civil War: Reunion and the Limits of Reconciliation*, Chapel Hill: University of North Caroline Press, 2013. There are, of course, many other debates surrounding monuments, where historians have been to the fore to deconstruct the racist undertones of these monuments. In Britain, for example, the debate about the Cecil Rhodes statue in Oxford is a good example. See Roseanne Chantiluke, Brian Kwoba and Athinagamso Nkopo (eds.), *Rhodes Must Fall: the Struggle to Decolonise the Racist Heart of Empire*, London: Zed Books, 2018.
75. Leigh Raiford and Renee C. Romano, 'Introduction: the Struggle over Memory', in: Renee C. Romano and Leigh Raiford (eds.), *The Civil Rights Movement in American Memory*, Athens, GA: University of Georgia Press, 2006, xii.

76. Ibid., xv.
77. Audrey R. Chapman and Hugo van der Merwe (eds.), *Truth and Reconcilation in South Africa: Did the TRC Deliver?*, Philadelphia: University of Pennsylvania Press, 2008.
78. Sarah Nuttal and Carli Coetzee (eds.), *Negotiating the Past: the Making of Memory in South Africa*, Oxford: Oxford University Press, 1998; Sabine Marschall, *Landscape of Memory: Commemorative Monuments, Memorials and Public Statuary in Post-Apartheid South Africa*, Leiden: Brill, 2010; Mamadou Diawara, Bernard Lategan and Jörn Rüsen (eds.), *Historical Memory in Africa: Dealing with the Past, Reaching for the Future in an Intercultural Context*, Oxford: Berghahn Books, 2010; Gary Baines, *South Africa's 'Border War': Contested Narratives and Conflicted Memories*, London: Bloomsbury, 2014; Christopher J. Colvin, *Traumatic Story-Telling and Memory in Post-Apartheid South Africa: Performing Signs of Injury*, London: Routledge, 2019.
79. Annie E. Coombes, *History after Apartheid: Visual Culture and Public Memory in a Democratic South Africa*, Durham, NC: Duke University Press, 2003.
80. Aleida Assmann, 'Erinnerung, Identität, Emotionen: Die Nation neu denken', in: *Blätter für deutsche und internationale Politik*, no. 3 (2020), 73–86. Assmann's keynote lecture at the 2019 Memory Studies Congress in Madrid made a similar argument. She developed her argument in book-length in Aleida Assmann, Die Wiedererfindung der Nation: warum wir sie fuerchten und warum wir sie brauchen, Munich: C.H. Beck 2020.
81. Bull and Hansen. 'Agonistic Memory'.
82. For the UNREST programme see its website: www.unrest.eu; the results of the programme have been summarised in Stefan Berger and Wulf Kansteiner (eds.), *Agonistic Memory and the Legacy of Twentieth-Century Wars in Europe*, Basingstoke: Palgrave Macmillan, 2022.
83. The theatre play entitled *Where the Forest Thickens* was performed by the Spanish theatre company Micomicon and can be watched at: www.youtube.com/watch?v=DtJg2jZmdHg [accessed 22 August 2020]; on the exhibition see the exhibition catalogue: Stefan Berger, Heinrich Theodor Grütter and Wulf Kansteiner (eds.), *Krieg. Macht. Sinn: War and Violence in European Memory*, Essen: Klartext, 2019.
84. On Bakhtin see my remarks in Chapter 1.
85. Anna Cento Bull and Daniela De Angeli, 'Emotions and Critical Thinking at a Dark Heritage Site: Investigating Visitors' Reaction to a First World War Museum in Slovenia', in: Journal of Heritage Tourism16:3 (2021), 263–280.
86. Stefan Berger, Anna Cento Bull, Cristian Cercel, David Clarke, Nina Parish, Eleanor Rowley and Zofia Woyczicka, 'Memory Cultures of

War in European War Museums', in: Berger and Kansteiner (eds.), *Agonistic Memory*.

87. Mihaela Mihai, 'Theorizing Agonistic Emotions', in: *Parallax* 20:2 (2014), 31–48.
88. G. M. Savenije and de Bruijn, 'Historical Empathy in the Museum: Uniting Contextualisation and Emotional Engagement', in: *International Journal of Heritage Studies* 23:4 (2017), 832–45. See also Alex Drago, 'The Emotional Museum', in: Jenny Kidd, Sam Cairns, Alex Drago, Amy Ryall and Miranda Stearn (eds.), *Challenging History in the Museum: International Perspectives*, London: Routledge, 2014, 23–86.
89. Cristian Cercel, 'The Military History Museum in Dresden: Between Forum and Temple', in: *History and Memory* 30:1 (2018), 3–39.
90. Francisco Ferrándiz and Marije Hristova, 'The Production of Memory Modes during Mass Grave Exhumations in Contemporary Europe', in: Berger and Kansteiner (ed.), *Agonistic Memory*.
91. Stefan Berger, 'Introduction: Historical Writing and Civic Engagement: a Symbiotic Relationship', in: Berger (ed.), *The Engaged Historian*, 1–32.
92. Hutton, 'Recent Scholarship', 545.

8 The History of Concepts

1. For a good introduction, albeit one restricted to Europe, see Willibald Steinmetz, Michael Freeden and Javier Fernández-Sebastián (eds.), *Conceptual History in the European Space*, Oxford: Berghahn Books, 2017; for more global perspectives see Margrit Pernau and Dominic Sachsenmaier (eds.), *Global Conceptual History: a Reader*, London: Bloomsbury, 2016.
2. Melvin Richter, 'Pocock, Skinner, and the *Geschichtliche Grundbegriffe*', in: *History and Theory* 14:1 (1990), 38–70.
3. Skinner explicitly rejected the methodological approach of 'basic concepts' in: 'Intellectual History, Liberty and Republicanism: an Interview with Quentin Skinner', in: *Contributions to the History of Concepts* 3 (2007), 113–15; on the positions of Pocock and Koselleck see their respective contributions to Hartmut Lehmann and Melvin Richter (eds.), *The Meaning of Historical Terms and Concepts: New Studies on Begriffsgeschichte*, Washington, DC: German Historical Institute, 1996.
4. Arthur Lovejoy, *The Great Chain of Being: the Study of the History of an Idea*, Cambridge, MA: Harvard University Press, 1936.

5. Annabel Brett, 'What Is Intellectual History Now?', in: David Cannadine (ed.), *What Is History Now?*, Basingstoke: Palgrave Macmillan, 2002, 114.
6. Donald Kelley, 'What is Happening to the History of Ideas?', in: *Journal of the History of Ideas* 51:1 (1990), 3–25.
7. Seminal for the rethinking of intellectual history was Dominick La Capra, *Rethinking Intellectual History: Texts, Contexts, Language*, Ithaca, NY: Cornell University Press, 1983.
8. Reinhard Koselleck, *The Practice of Conceptual History: Timing History, Spacing Concepts*, Stanford: Stanford University Press, 2002; Koselleck, *Futures Past: On the Semantics of Historical Time*, New York: Columbia University Press, 2004.
9. Otto Brunner, Werner Conze and Reinhart Koselleck (eds.), *Geschichtliche Grundbegriffe: historisches Lexikon zur politisch-sozialen Sprache in Deutschland*, 9 vols., Stuttgart: Klett-Cotta, 1972–97. For an English translation of the introduction and prefaces to the *Geschichtliche Grundbegriffe* see *Contributions to the History of Concepts* 6: 1 (2011), 1–38.
10. A good introduction to diverse aspects of Koselleck's work is Hans Joas and Peter Vogt (eds.), *Begriffene Geschichte Beiträge zum Werk Reinhart Kosellecks*, Frankfurt am Main: Suhrkamp, 2011.
11. Christian Geulen, 'Plädoyer für eine Geschichte der Grundbegriffe des 20. Jahrhunderts', in: *Zeithistorische Forschungen/Studies in Contemporary History* 7 (2010), 79–97. It prompted a vigorous debate among conceptual historians. See the roundtable '*Geschichtliche Grundbegriffe* Reloaded: Writing the Conceptual History of the Twentieth Century', in: *Contributions to the History of Concepts* 7: 1 (2012), 78–128.
12. Niklas Olsen, *History in the Plural: an Introduction to the Work of Reinhart Koselleck*, Oxford: Berghahn Books, 2012, 171.
13. Lucian Hölscher, 'Theoretische Grundlagen der historischen Zukunftsforschung', in: Hölscher (ed.), *Die Zukunft des 20. Jahrhunderts. Dimensionen einer historischen Zukunftsforschung*, Frankfurt am Main: Campus, 2017, 7–38. See also Hölscher, *Die Entdeckung der Zukunft*, 2nd edn, Göttingen: Wallstein, 2016.
14. Ernst Müller and Falko Schmieder, 'Reinhart Kosellecks Begriffe und Denkfiguren', in: Müller and Schmieder (eds.), *Begriffsgeschichte und historische Semantik: ein kritisches Kompendium*, Frankfurt am Main: suhrkamp, 2016, 278–337.
15. It should be noted that both White and Koselleck were distinctively appreciative of each other's work. Thus White contributed a warm foreword to Koselleck's *The Practice of Conceptual History*, and

Koselleck was ready to accept the significance of White's tropological theory. See Reinhart Koselleck, 'Introduction to Hayden White's *Tropics of Discourse*', in: Kosselleck, *The Practice of Conceptual History*, 38–44.

16. Reinhart Koselleck, 'A Response to Comments on the *Geschichtliche Grundbegriffe*', in: Lehmann and Richter (eds.), *The Meaning of Historical Terms and Concepts*, 59–70.
17. Andreas Huyssen, *Present Pasts: Urban Palimpsests and the Politics of Memory*, Stanford: Stanford University Press, 2003.
18. Peter Laslett (ed.), *John Locke's Two Treatises of Government: a Critical Edition with an Introduction and Apparatus Criticus*, Cambridge: Cambridge University Press, 1960.
19. Quentin Skinner, *Reason and Rhetoric in the Philosophy of Hobbes*, Cambridge: Cambridge University Press, 1996. Critical of Skinner's attempt to put Hobbes studies on a new intellectual footing is Martyn Thompson, *Michael Oakeshott and the Cambridge School on the History of Political Thought*, London: Routledge, 2019, chapter 6.
20. Quentin Skinner, 'Meaning and Understanding in the History of Ideas', in: *History and Theory* 8:1 (1969), 3–53.
21. A good introduction to Quentin Skinner is provided by Kari Palonen, *Quentin Skinner: History, Politics, Rhetoric*, Cambridge: Polity Press, 2003. Speech act theory is associated in particular with the work of J. L. Austin and J. R. Searle. See J. L. Austin, *How to Do Things with Words*, Oxford: Oxford University Press, 1962; J. R. Searle, *Speech Acts: an Essay in the Philosophy of Language*, Cambridge: Cambridge University Press, 1969. Both drew heavily from the work of the philosopher Ludwig Wittgenstein.
22. Quentin Skinner, 'Retrospect: Studying Rhetoric and Conceptual Change', in: Skinner, *Visions of Politics, vol. I: Regarding Method*, Cambridge: Cambridge University Press, 2002, 175–87.
23. Quentin Skinner, 'A Genealogy of the Modern State', in: *Proceedings of the British Academy* 162 (2009), 325–70; Skinner, *Liberty before Liberalism*, Cambridge: Cambridge University Press, 1998; Skinner, *Hobbes and Republican Liberty*, Cambridge: Cambridge University Press, 2008.
24. One area where this has been very visible is in the intellectual history of religion, where Skinner's ideas had a strong influence. See Alister Chapman, John Coffey and Brad S. Gregory (eds.), *Seeing Things Their Way: Intellectual History and the Return of Religion*, Notre Dame: University of Notre Dame Press, 2009.
25. Quentin Skinner, *The Foundations of Modern Political Thought, vol. I: the Renaissance; vol. II: the Age of the Reformation*, Cambridge: Cambridge University Press, 1978.

26. Annabel Brett and James Tully (eds.), *Rethinking the Foundations of Modern Political Thought*, Cambridge: Cambridge University Press, 2007.
27. J. G. A. Pocock, 'The History of Political Thought: a Methodological Enquiry', in: Peter Laslett and Walter Runciman (eds.), *Philosophy, Politics and Society*, 2nd ser., Oxford: Oxford University Press, 1962, 183–202.
28. J. G. A. Pocock, *The Machiavellian Moment: Florentine Political Thought and the Atlantic Republican Tradition*, Princeton: Princeton University Press, 1975.
29. Samuel James, 'J. G. A. Pocock and the Idea of the "Cambridge School" in the History of Political Thought', in: *History of European Ideas* 45:1 (2019), 83–98.
30. J. G. A. Pocock, *Barbarism and Religion*, 6vols., Cambridge: Cambridge University Press, 1999–2016.
31. Mark Bevir, 'The Role of Contexts in Understanding and Explanation', in: Hans Erich Bödeker (ed.), *Begriffsgeschichte, Diskursgeschichte, Metapherngeschichte*, Göttingen: Wallstein, 2002, 159–208.
32. R. G. Collingwood, *The Idea of History*, Oxford: Oxford University Press, 1961.
33. Margrit Pernau and Imke Rajamani, 'Emotional Translations: Conceptual History beyond Language', in: *History and Theory* 55 (2016), 46–65.
34. One example among many is Thomas Dixon, *Weeping Britannia: Portrait of a Nation in Tears*, Oxford: Oxford University Press, 2015.
35. Robert Darnton, *The Forbidden Best-Sellers of Pre-Revolutionary France*, New York: Norton, 1995.
36. Mary Elizabeth Berry, *Japan in Print: Information and Nation in the Early Modern Period*, Berkeley: University of California Press, 2006.
37. Anthony Grafton, *The Footnote: a Curious History*, Cambridge, MA: Harvard University Press, 1999.
38. Pim den Boer, 'National Cultures, Transnational Concepts: *Begriffsgeschichte* beyond Conceptual Nationalism', in: Javier Fernández Sebastian (ed.), *Political Concepts and Time: New Approaches to Conceptual History*, Santander: Cantabria University Press, 2011, 205–22.
39. Jörn Leonhard, *Liberalismus: zur historischen Semantik eines europäischen Deutungsmusters*, Munich: Oldenbourg, 2001; in English see Leonhard, 'From European Liberalism to the Languages of Liberalism: the Semantics of Liberalism in European Comparison', in: *Yearbook of Political Thought and Conceptual History* 8 (2004), 17–51.
40. Annabel Patterson, *Early Modern Liberalism*, Cambridge: Cambridge University Press, 1997.

41. Uday Singh Mehta, *Liberalism and Empire: a Study in Nineteenth-Century British Liberal Thought*, Chicago: University of Chicago Press, 1999.
42. Christopher A. Bayly, *Recovering Liberties: Indian Thought in the Age of Liberalism and Empire*, Cambridge: Cambridge University Press, 2012.
43. Andrew Sartori, *Liberalism in Empire: an Alternative History*, Berkeley: Yale University Press, 2014.
44. Duncan Bell, *Reordering the World: Essays on Liberalism and Empire*, Princeton: Princeton University Press, 2016.
45. Iain Hampsher-Monk, Karen Tilmans and Frank van Vree (eds.), *History of Concepts: Comparative Approaches*, Amsterdam: University of Amsterdam Press, 1998.
46. Maria Todorova, *Imagining the Balkans*, Oxford: Oxford University Press, 1997.
47. Larry Wolff, *Inventing Eastern Europe: the Map of Civilisation on the Mind of the Enlightenment*, Stanford: Stanford University Press, 1994.
48. Diana Mishkova, 'The Politics of Regionalist Science: the Balkans as a Supranational Space in Late Nineteenth to Mid-Twentieth Century Academic Projects', in: *East Central Europe* 39 (2012), 266–303.
49. Balázs Trencsényi, 'Balkans *Baedecker* for *Übermensch* Tourists: Janko Janev's Popular Historiography', in: Stefan Berger, Billie Melman and Chris Lorenz (eds.), *Popularizing National Pasts: 1800 to the Present*, London: Routledge, 2012, 149–68.
50. For the Balkans and Eastern Europe see the excellent work of Balázs Trencsényi, Michael Kopeček, Luka Lisjak Gabrijelčič, Maria Falina, Mónika Baár and Maciej Janowski, *A History of Modern Political Thought in East Central Europe*, 2 vols., Oxford: Oxford University Press, 2018. For Scandinavia and the concept of 'Norden', which would be another example of a transnational region and its role in the construction of sets of competing identities, see Marja Jalava and Bo Stråth, 'Scandinavia/Norden', in: Diana Mishkova and Balázs Trencsényi (eds.), *European Regions and Boundaries: a Conceptual History*, Oxford: Berghahn Books, 2017, 36–56. See also Bo Stråth, '"Norden" as a European Region: Demarcation and Belonging', in: J. P. Arnason (ed.), *Domains and Divisions of European History*, Liverpool: Liverpool University Press, 2009, 198–215.
51. Riccardo Bavaj and Martina Steber, 'Introduction – Germany and "the West": the Vagaries of a Modern Relationship', in: Bavaj and Steber (eds.), *Germany and 'the West': a Conceptual History*, Oxford: Berghahn Books, 2015, 1–40, quote on 1.
52. See, for example, Mehmet Hacisalihoglu, 'Borders, Maps and Censuses: the Politicization of Geography and Statistics in the Multiethnic

Ottoman Empire', in: Jörn Leonhard and Ulrike von Hirschhausen (eds.), *Comparing Empires: Encounters and Transfers in the Long Nineteenth Century*, Göttingen: Vandenhoeck and Ruprecht, 2011, 171–210.

53. Helge Jordheim, 'The Nature of Civilization: the Semantics of Civilization and Civility in Scandinavia', in: Margrit Pernau and Helge Jordheim (eds.), *Civilizing Emotion: Concepts in Nineteenth-Century Asia and Europe*, Oxford: Oxford University Press, 2015, 25–44.
54. Patrick Pasture, *Imagining European Unity since 1000 AD*, Basingstoke: Palgrave Macmillan, 2015.
55. Ulrich Maier, Martin Papenheim and Willbald Steinmetz, *Semantiken des Politischen: vom Mittelalter bis ins 20. Jahrhundert*, Göttingen: Wallstein, 2012.
56. Jan Ifversen, 'Myth in the Writing of European History', in: Stefan Berger and Chris Lorenz (eds.), *Nationalizing the Past: Historians as Nation-Builders in Modern Europe*, Basingstoke: Palgrave Macmillan, 2010, 452–79.
57. Jan Ifversen, 'A Guided Tour into the European Question', in: Marjet Brolsma, Robin de Bruin and Matthijas Lok (eds.), *Eurocentrism in European History and Memory*, Amsterdam: Amsterdam University Press, 2019, 195–222.
58. Rhiannon Stephens and Axel Fleisch, 'Theories and Methods of African Conceptual History', in: Axel Fleisch and Rhiannon Stephens (eds.), *Doing Conceptual History in Africa*, Oxford: Berghahn Books, 2016, 3–5.
59. Peter Burke, *Languages and Communities in Early Modern Europe*, Cambridge: Cambridge University Press, 2004.
60. Anna Wierzbicka, *Imprisoned in English: the Hazards of English as a Default Language*, Oxford: Oxford University Press, 2014.
61. Johann Wolfgang Unger, Michal Krzyzanowski and Ruth Wodak (eds.), *Multilingual Encounters in Europe's Institutional Spaces*, London: Bloomsbury, 2014.
62. László Kontler, 'Concepts, Contests and Contexts: Conceptual History and the Problem of Translatability', in: Steinmetz, Freeden and Fernández-Sebastián (eds.), *Conceptual History*, 197–211.
63. Christopher L. Hill, 'Conceptual Universalization in the Transnational Nineteenth Century', in: Samuel Moyn and Andrew Sartori (eds.), *Global Intellectual History*, New York: Columbia University Press, 2013, 134–58.
64. Ernesto Laclau, *Emancipation(s)*, London: Verso, 1996, 47–8; Gurminder K. Bhambra, 'Whither Europe', *Interventions* 18:2 (2016), 187–202.

65. Henrik Stenius, 'Concepts in the Nordic Periphery', in: Steinmetz, Freeden and Fernández-Sebastián (eds.), *Conceptual History*, 263–80.
66. The idea of key concepts owes much to Williams, *Keywords*. On Williams see also Chapter 4. Historical linguistics have been trying to push this agenda much further. See Anna Wierzbicka, *Understanding Cultures through Their Key Words: English, Russian, Polish, German, and Japanese*, Oxford: Oxford University Press, 1997.
67. Ihalainen, *The Springs of Democracy*.
68. Bo Stråth, 'Ideology and Conceptual History', in: Michael Freeden, Lyman Tower Sargent and Marc Stears (eds.), *The Oxford Handbook of Political Ideologies*, Oxford: Oxford University Press, 2013, 3–19.
69. Joel Isaac and Duncan Bell (eds.), *Uncertain Empire: American History and the Idea of the Cold War*, Oxford: Oxford University Press, 2015.
70. Frank Ninkovich, *The Global Republic: America's Inadvertent Rise to World Power*, Chicago: University of Chicago Press, 2014.
71. Edoardo Zimmermann, 'Translations of the "American Model" in Nineteenth-Century Argentina: Constitutional Culture as a Global Legal Entanglement', in: Thomas Duve (ed.), *Entanglements in Legal History: Conceptual Approaches*, Frankfurt am Main: Max Planck Institute for European Legal History, 2014, 385–426.
72. Philip Gleason, 'Pluralism and Assimilation: a Conceptual History', in: John Edwards (ed.), *Linguistic Minorities, Policies and Pluralism*, London: Academic Press, 1984, 221–58.
73. Geoff Eley and Keith Nield, *The Future of Class in History: What's Left of the Social*, Ann Arbor: University of Michigan Press, 2007.
74. Mike Savage, 'Class and Labour History', in: Lex Heerma van Voss and Marcel van der Linden (eds.), *Class and Other Identities: Gender, Religion and Ethnicity in the Writing of European Labour History*, Oxford: Berghahn Books, 2002, 55–72.
75. Myoung-Kyu Park, 'How Concepts Met History in Korea's Complex Modernization: New Concepts of Economy and Society and their Impact', in: Hagen Schulz-Forberg (ed.), *A Global Conceptual History of Asia, 1860–1940*, London: Routledge, 2014, 25–42.
76. Lucian Hölscher, 'Religion im Wandel: von Begriffen des religiösen Wandels zum Wandel religiöser Begriffe', in: Wilhelm Gräb (ed.), *Religion als Thema der Theologie: Geschichte, Standpunkte und Perspektiven der theologischen Religionskritik und Religionsbegründung*, Gütersloh: Gütersloher Verlagshaus, 1999, 45–62. See also the contributions in Lucian Hölscher (ed.), *Baupläne der sichtbaren Kirche: sprachliche Konzepte religiöser Vergemeinschaftung in Europa*, Göttingen: Wallstein, 2007.

77. Lucian Hölscher, 'Konfessionspolitik in Deutschland zwischen Glaubensstreit und Koexistenz', in: Hölscher (ed.), *Baupläne*, 11–52.
78. Talal Assad, *Genealogies of Religion: Discipline and Reasons of Power in Christianity and Islam*, Baltimore: Johns Hopkins University Press, 1993.
79. James Carson, *The Columbian Covenant: Race and the Writing of American History*, Basingstoke: Palgrave Macmillan, 2015.
80. Elazar Barkan, *The Retreat of Scientific Racism: Changing Concepts of Race in Britain and the United States between the World Wars*, Cambridge: Cambridge University Press, 1992.
81. David Theo Goldberg, *Racial Subjects: Writing on Race in America*, New York: Routledge, 1997, 18.
82. Barbara Ransby, *Making All Black Lives Matter: Reimagining Freedom in the Twenty-First Century*, Oakland: University of California Press, 2018.
83. Sinha, *Colonial Masculinity*.
84. Anna Kelk Mager, 'Tracking the Concept of "Work" on the North-Eastern Cape Frontier, South Africa', in: Fleisch and Stephens (eds.), *Doing Conceptual History*, 73–90, espec. 78–9.
85. Pamela Khanakwa, 'Male Circumcision among the Bagisu of Eastern Uganda: Practices and Conceptualisations', in: Fleisch and Stephens (eds.), *Doing Conceptual History*, 115–37.
86. Jussi Kurunmäki, Jeppe Nevers and Henk te Velde (eds.), *Democracy in Modern Europe: a Conceptual History*, Oxford: Berghahn Books, 2018; see also John Dunn (ed.), *Democracy: the Unfinished Journey*, Oxford: Oxford University Press, 1992.
87. Ian Adams, *Ideology and Politics in Britain Today*, Manchester: Manchester University Press, 1998, esp. chapter 2: 'British Liberal Democracy'.
88. Paul Cartledge, *Democracy: a Life*, Oxford: Oxford University Press, 2016.
89. Joanna Innes and Mark Philp (eds.), *Re-imagining Democracy in the Age of Revolutions: America, France, Britain, Ireland, 1750–1850*, Oxford: Oxford University Press, 2013.
90. Achille Mbembe, *Politiques de l'inimité*, Paris: Edition la Découverte, 2016; see also Mbembe, *Critique of Black Reason*, Durham, NC: Duke University Press, 2017 (originally published in French in 2013).
91. The indeterminacy of concepts in political languages has been emphasised by Michael Freeden, *The Political Theory of Political Thinking: the Anatomy of a Practice*, Oxford: Oxford University Press, 2013.

92. Michael Freeden, 'Conceptual History, Ideology and Language', in: Steinmetz, Freeden and Fernández-Sebastián (eds.), *Conceptual History*, 125.
93. Nick Fairclough, *Language and Power*, London: Longman, 2001.
94. Ana Lúcia Sá, 'The Concept of "Land" in Bioko: "Land as Property" and "Land as Country"', in: Fleisch and Stephens (eds.), *Doing Conceptual History*, 138–61.
95. See also Chapter 11 on transnational history.
96. Margrit Pernau and Dominic Sachsenmaier, 'History of Concepts and Global History', in: Pernau and Sachsenmaier (eds.), *Global Conceptual History: a Reader*, London: Bloomsbury, 2016, 4.

9 The Visual Turn

1. Stephen Bann, 'Face-to-Face with History', in: *New Literary History* 29 (1998), 235–46. Bann himself, of course, has done much to bring about the visual turn in history writing by being among the first to consider visual evidence next to textual in his books on the development of historical consciousness during the nineteenth century. See especially Stephen Bann, *The Clothing of Clio: a Study of the Representation of History in Nineteenth-Century Britain and France*, Cambridge: Cambridge University Press, 1984; Bann, *Romanticism and the Rise of History*, New York: Twayne Publishers, 1995. It is also interesting to note that Bann's writing has been influenced by White, Barthes and Foucault – key theorists discussed in Chapter 1 of this volume.
2. Matthew Rampley, 'Introduction', in: Matthew Rampley, Thierry Lenain, Hubert Locher, Andrea Pinotti, Charlotte Schoell-Glass and Kitty Zijlmans (eds.), *Art History and Visual Studies in Europe: Transnational Discourses and National Frameworks*, Leiden: Brill, 2012, 7. See also the exhibition catalogue *Velazquez, Rembrandt, Vermeer: Miradas afines*, Madrid: Museo Nacional del Prado, 2019.
3. Michael Baxandall, *Painting and Experience in Fifteenth-Century Italy: a Primer in the Social History of Pictorial Style*, Oxford: Oxford University Press, 1972.
4. C. Guichard, 'Connoisseurship and Artistic Experience: London and Paris, 1600–1800', in: C. Rabier (ed.), *Fields of Expertise: a Comparative History of Expert Procedures in Paris and London, 1600 to the Present*, Cambridge: Cambridge Scholars, 2007, 173–91.
5. Svetlana Alpers, *The Art of Describing: Dutch Art in the Seventeenth Century*, Chicago: University of Chicago Press, 1983.

6. James Elkins, *The Domain of Images*, Ithaca, NY: Cornell University Press, 2001.
7. Kenneth Winetrout, 'The New Age of the Visible: a Call to Study', in: *AV Communication Review* 12:1 (1964), 46–52.
8. Marshall McLuhan, *Understanding Media: the Extensions of Man*, New York: McGraw-Hill, 1964.
9. Horst Bredekamp, *Image Acts: a Systematic Approach to Visual Agency*, Berlin: De Gruyter, 2018; see also W. J. T. Mitchell, *What Do Pictures Want?*, Chicago: University of Chicago Press, 2005.
10. See, for example, the skilful interweaving of autobiographical images in Marianne Hirsch, *Family Frames: Photography, Narrative and Postmemory*, Cambridge, MA: Harvard University Press, 1997.
11. On those theorists see Chapter 1.
12. Walter Benjamin, 'The Work of Art in the Age of Mechanical Reproduction' (originally published in German in 1935; for a translation see: www.marxists.org/reference/subject/philosophy/works/ge/benjamin.htm [accessed 24 April 2020]); see also Vanessa R. Schwartz, 'Walter Benjamin for Historians', in: *American Historical Review* 106:5 (2001), 1721–43.
13. See, for example, Chris Jenks, 'The Centrality of the Eye in Western Culture', in: Jenks (ed.), *Visual Culture*, London: Routledge, 1995, 16; Irit Rogoff, 'Studying Visual Culture', in: Nicholas Mirzoeff (ed.), *The Visual Culture Reader*, London: Routledge, 1998, 18. See also Richard Howells and Joaquim Negreiros (eds.), *Visual Culture*, Cambridge: Polity Press, 2012; Nicholas Mirzoeff, *An Introduction to Visual Culture*, London: Routledge, 1999.
14. Foucault, *Discipline and Punish*. On Foucault see also Chapter 1 above.
15. Gil Bartholeyns, 'History of Visual Culture', in: Marek Tamm and Peter Burke (eds.), *Debating New Approaches to History*, London: Bloomsbury 2019, 251–2.
16. Peter Burke, *The Fabrication of Louis XIV*, New Haven: Yale University Press, 1992.
17. Nicolas Mirzoeff, *The Right to Look: a Counter-History of Visuality*, Durham, NC: Duke University Press, 2011.
18. Nathalie Heinich, *De la visibilité: excellence et singularité en régime médiatheque*, Paris: Gallimard, 2012.
19. Martin Jay, 'Scopic Regimes of Modernity Revisited', in: Ian Heywood and Barry Sandywell (eds.), *The Handbook of Visual Culture*, London: Bloomsbury, 2011, 102–13.
20. Jonathan Crary, *Techniques of the Observer: On Vision and Modernity in the Nineteenth Century*, Cambridge, MA: MIT Press, 1990.

21. Bruno Latour, 'Visualisation and Cognition: Thinking with Eyes and Hands', in: *Knowledge and Society: Studies in the Sociology of Culture Past and Present* 6 (1986), 1–40, quote on 9. Latour, of course, was heavily influenced by some of the ideas surrounding narrativism and poststructuralism discussed in Chapter 1 above.
22. W. J. T. Mitchell, 'Showing Seeing: a Critique of Visual Culture', in: *Journal of Visual Culture* 1:2 (2002), 165–85.
23. Norman Bryson, 'Visual Culture and the Dearth of Images', in: *Journal of Visual Culture* 2:2 (2003), 229–32. The distinction between 'normal' and 'deviant' owed much to Foucault.
24. Jean Baudrillard, *The Gulf War Did Not Take Place*, Bloomington: Indiana University Press, 1995 (originally published in French in 1991).
25. Christian Hartmann, Johannes Hürter and Ulrike Jureit (eds.), *Verbrechen der Wehrmacht: Bilanz einer Debatte*, Munich: C. H. Beck, 2005.
26. Peter Lord, *The Visual Culture of Wales, vol. I: Industrial Society*, *Cardiff*: University of Wales Press, 1998; Lord, *The Visual Culture of Wales, vol. II: Imaging the Nation*, Cardiff: University of Wales Press, 2000; Lord, *The Visual Culture of Wales, vol. III: Medieval Vision*, Cardiff: University of Wales Press, 2003.
27. James A. Cook, Joshua Goldstein, Matthew D. Johnson and Sigrid Schmalzer (eds.), *Visualizing Modern China: Image, History and Memory, 1750 to the Present*, Lanham, MD: Lexington Books, 2014.
28. James A. Cook, Joshua Goldstein, Matthew D. Johnson and Sigrid Schmalzer, 'Introduction', in: ibid., 6.
29. Jennifer A. Watts (ed.), *Maynard L. Parker: Modern Photography and the American Dream*, New Haven: Yale University Pres, 2012.
30. Jennifer Watts, 'Picture Taking in Paradise: Los Angeles and the Creation of Regional Identity, 1880–1920', in: Vanessa R. Schwartz and Jeannene M. Przyblyski (eds.), *The Nineteenth-Century Visual Culture Reader*, London: Routledge, 2004, 218–32, quote on 218.
31. Wolfram Hartmann, Jeremy Silvester and Patricia Hayes (eds.), *The Colonising Camera: Photographs in the Making of Namibian History*, Cape Town: University of Cape Town Press, 1998.
32. Ibid., 18, 164–70.
33. Richard Vokes and Darren Newbury, 'Photography and African Futures', in: *Visual Studies* 33:1 (2018), 1–10, quote on 1.
34. Drew A. Thompson, 'Visualizing FRELIMO's Liberated Zones in Mozambique, 1962–1974', in: *Social Dynamics* 39:1 (2013), 24–50.
35. Vanessa Watson, 'African Urban Fantasies: Dreams or Nightmares?', in: *Environment and Urbanization* 26:1 (2014), 215–31.

36. Carol Quirke, *Eyes on Labor: News Photography and America's Working Class*, Oxford: Oxford University Press, 2012.
37. John Gorman, *Banner Bright: an Illustrated History of Trade Union Banners*, London: Scorpion, 1986.
38. Annie Ravenhill-Johnson, *The Art and Ideology of the Trade Union Emblem, 1850–1925*, ed. Paula James, London: Anthem Press, 2013.
39. Weir, *Beyond Labor's Veil.*
40. Victoria Bonnell, *Iconography of Power: Soviet Political Posters under Lenin and Stalin*, Berkeley: University of California Press, 1997.
41. Peter Burke, 'Representing Women's Work in Early Modern Italy', in: Josef Ehmer and Catharina Lis (eds.), *The Idea of Work in Europe from Antiquity to Modern Times*, Farnham: Ashgate, 2009, 177–90.
42. Felicitas Hentschke and James Williams (eds.), *To Be at Home: House, Work, and Self in the Modern World*, Berlin: De Gruyter, 2018.
43. Nitin Varma, 'Servant Testimonies and Anglo-Indian Homes in Nineteenth-Century India', in: Hentschke and Williams (eds.), *To Be at Home*, 219–28.
44. June Namias, *White Captives: Gender and Ethnicity on the American Frontier*, Chapel Hill: University of North Carolina Press, 1993.
45. Kirk Savage, 'Molding Emancipation: John Quincy Adams Ward's *The Freedman* and the Meaning of the Civil War', in: Schwartz and Przyblyski (eds.), *Nineteenth-Century Visual Culture*, 262–75.
46. Sarah Dellmann, *Images of Dutchness: Popular Visual Culture, Early Cinema and the Emergence of a National Cliché, 1800–1914*, Amsterdam: Amsterdam University Press, 2018.
47. Ardis Cameron (ed.), *Looking for America: the Visual Production of Nation and People*, Oxford: Blackwell, 2005.
48. Ardis Cameron, 'Sleuthing towards America: Visual Detection in Everyday Life', in: Cameron (ed.), *Looking for America*, 17–41.
49. Don Nardo, *Migrant Mother: How a Photograph Defined the Great Depression*, Mankato, MN: Compass Point, 2011.
50. Shawn Michelle Smith, 'Photographing the "American Negro": Nation, Race and Photography at the Paris Exhibition in 1900', in: Cameron (ed.), *Looking for America*, 61–93.
51. Stuart Cosgrove, 'The Zoot-Suit and Style Warfare', in: Cameron (ed.), *Looking for America*, 264–80.
52. Ardis Cameron, 'Introduction', in: Cameron (ed.), *Looking for America*, 1–2.
53. Darcy Grimaldo Grigsby, 'Revolutionary Sons, White Fathers and Creole Difference: Guillaume Guillon-Lethière's *Oath of the Ancestors* (1822)', in: Schwartz and Przyblyski (eds.), *Nineteenth-Century Visual Culture*, 249–61.

54. Jane Lydon, *The Flash of Recognition: Photography and the Emergence of Indigenous Rights*, Sydney: New South Publishing, 2012.
55. Amos Morris-Reich, *Race and Photography: Racial Photography as Scientific Evidence, 1876–1980*, Chicago: University of Chicago Press, 2016.
56. Christopher Pinney, *Camera Indica: the Social Life of Indian Photographs*, Chicago: University of Chicago Press, 1997, especially chapter 1 entitled '"Stern Fidelity" and "Penetrating Certainty"', 17–71.
57. Deborah Poole, *Vision, Race and Modernity: a Visual Economy of the Andean Image World*, Princeton: Princeton University Press, 1997.
58. Ibid., 24.
59. Christraud M. Geary, *In and out of Focus: Images from Central Africa*, London: Philip Wilson, 2002.
60. Michael J. Wintle, *The Image of Europe: Visualizing Europe in Cartography and Iconography*, Cambridge: Cambridge University Press, 2009.
61. Richard Vokes, 'The Chairman's Photographs: the Politics of an Archive in South-Western Uganda', in: Christopher Morton and Darren Newbury (eds.), *The African Photographic Archive: Research and Curatorial Strategies*, London: Bloomsbury, 2015, 95–112.
62. Michelle Lamuniere, *You Look Beautiful Like That: the Portrait Photographs of Seydou Keïta and Malick Sidibé*, New Haven: Yale University Press, 2001.
63. Mark Nash, *Red Africa: Affective Communities and the Cold War*, London: Black Dog Publishing, 2016.
64. Jean-Claude Schmitt, *Le corps des images: essais sur la culture visuelle au moyen âge*, Paris: Gallimard, 2002.
65. David Morgan, *The Forge of Vision: a Visual History of Modern Christianity*, Oakland: University of California Press, 2015.
66. Serge Gruzinski, *Images at War: Mexico from Columbus to Blade Runner (1492–2019)*, Durham, NC: Duke University Press, 2001.
67. Paul Jenkins, 'The Earliest Generation of Missionary Photographers in West Africa and the Portrayal of Indigenous People and Culture', in: *History in Africa* 20 (1993), 89–118.
68. Ibid., 110.
69. Michael Godby, 'The Photograph Album of an Unknown American Missionary in Natal, c. 1930: the Good News and the Bad', in: *South African Historical Journal* 61:2 (2009), 357–71.
70. Jane Lydon, *Photography, Humanitarianism, Empire*, London: Bloomsbury, 2016.

71. Darren Newbury, '"Window on the West Indies": the Photographic Imagination of the Society for the Propagation of the Gospel', in: *Visual Studies* 33:1 (2018), 41–56.
72. Benjamin Städter, *Verwandelte Blicke: eine Visual History von Kirche und Religion in der Bundesrepublik, 1945–1980*, Frankfurt am Main: Campus, 2011.
73. Joan B. Landes, *Visualizing the Nation: Gender, Representation and Revolution in Eighteenth Century France*, Ithaca, NY: Cornell University Press, 2001.
74. Lisa Tickner, 'Banners and Banner Making', in: Schwartz and Przyblyski (eds.), *Nineteenth-Century Visual Culture*, 341–7.
75. Wolfram Hartmann, 'Performing Gender, Staging Colonialism: Camping it up/Acting it out in Ovamboland', in: Hartmann, Silvester and Hayes (eds.), *The Colonising Camera*, 156–63.
76. Elizabeth Vlossak, 'Gender Approaches to the History of Nationalism', in: Berger and Storm (eds.), *Writing the History of Nationalism*, 191–214.
77. Sumathi Ramaswamy, *The Goddess and the Nation*, Durham, NC: Duke University Press, 2010.
78. Mariatte C. Denman, 'Visualizing the Nation: Madonnas and Mourning Mothers in Postwar Germany', in: Patricia Herminghouse and Magda Mueller (eds.), *Gender and Germanness: Cultural Production of Nation*, Oxford, Berghahn Books, 1997, 189–201.
79. Ingeborg Majer O'Sickey, 'Framing the *Unheimlich*: Heimatfilm and Bambi', in: Herminghouse and Mueller (eds.), *Gender and Germanness*, 202–16.
80. Francis Haskell, *History and its Images: Art and the Interpretation of the Past*, Yale: Yale University Press, 1993.

10 The History of Material Culture

1. Carl Knappett and Lambros Malafouris (eds.), *Material Agency: Towards a Non-Anthropocentric Approach*, Boston: Springer, 2008.
2. Timothy J. LeCain, *The Matter of History: How Things Create the Past*, Cambridge: Cambridge University Press, 2017, 7.
3. Ian Hodder, *The Archaeological Process: an Introduction*, Oxford: Blackwell, 1999; Tony Bennett and Patrick Joyce (eds.), *Material Powers: Cultural Studies, History and the Material Turn*, London: Routledge, 2010.
4. Anne Gerritsen and Giorgio Riello, 'History and Material Culture', in: Berger, Feldner and Passmore (eds.), *Writing History*, 274. See also

Henry H. Glassie, *Material Culture*, Bloomington: Indiana University Press, 1999.

5. Chris Tilley, Webb Keane, Susanne Küchler, Mike Rowlands and Patricia Spyer (eds.), *Handbook of Material Culture*, London: Sage, 2006.
6. Franciso Ferrándiz, 'Exhuming the Defeated: Civil War Mass Graves in 21st Century Spain', in: *American Ethnologist* 40:1 (2013), 38–54; Ewa Domanska, 'The Material Presence of the Past', in: *History and Theory* 45:3 (2006), 337–48.
7. Gerritsen and Riello, 'Material Culture', 275–6.
8. Rosemary Sweet, *Antiquaries: the Discovery of the Past in Eighteenth-Century Britain*, London: Hambledon, 2004.
9. Leora Auslander, 'Beyond Words', in: *American Historical Review* 110:4 (2005), 1015–45.
10. Appadurai (ed.), *The Social Life of Things*.
11. Asa Briggs, *Victorian Things*, Harmondsworth: Penguin, 1988.
12. Michael Dietler, 'Consumption', in: Dan Hicks and Mary C. Beaudry (eds.), *The Oxford Handbook of Material Culture Studies*, Oxford: Oxford University Press, 2010, 209–28.
13. Fank Trentmann, *Empire of Things*.
14. Sidney Minz, *Sweetness and Power: the Place of Sugar in Modern History*, Harmondsworth: Penguin, 1985.
15. Loretta Lees, Tom Slater and Elvin Wyly, *Gentrification*, London: Routledge, 2008; Juliana Mansveld, *Geographies of Consumption*, London: Sage, 2008; Steven Hinchliffe, *Geographies of Nature: Societies, Environments, Ecologies*, London: Sage, 2007; Sarah Whatmore, *Hybrid Geographies: Natures, Cultures, Spaces*, London: Sage, 2002.
16. Bill Brown, *A Sense of Things*, Chicago: University of Chicago Press, 2004.
17. Lyn Pykett, 'The Material Turn in Victorian Studies', in: *Literature Compass* 1:1 (2003),https://doi.org/10.1111/j.1741-4113.2004.00020.x [accessed 29 April 2020].
18. Jane Bennett, *The Enchantment of Modern Life: Attachments, Crossings and Ethics*, Princeton: Princeton University Press, 2001.
19. Alex Preda, 'The Turn to Things: Arguments for a Sociological Theory of Things', in: *Sociological Quarterly* 40:2 (1999), 347–66.
20. Momin Rahman and Anne Witz, 'What Really Matters? The Elusive Quality of the Material in Feminist Thought', in: *Feminist Theory* 4:3 (2003), 243–61.
21. As famously claimed by Derrida, *Of Grammatology*.
22. Benjamin K. Bergen, *Louder than Words: the New Science of How the Mind Makes Meaning*, New York: Basic Books, 2012.

23. Christopher Tilley (ed.), *Reading Material Culture: Structuralism, Hermeneutics and Post-Structuralism*, Oxford: Blackwell, 1990; Ian Woodward, *Understanding Material Culture*, London: Sage, 2007; Allison Paige Burkette, *Language and Material Culture*, Amsterdam: John Benjamins, 2015.
24. See also above, 97–99 and 113 f.
25. Iris Clever and Wilhelmijn Ruberg, 'Beyond Cultural History? The Material Turn, Praxiography and Body History', in: *Humanities* 3 (2014), 546–66.
26. James Raven, Naomi Tadmor and Helen Small (eds.), *The Practice and Representation of Reading in England*, Cambridge: Cambridge University Press, 1996.
27. Tracey Chapman Hamilton and Mariah Proctor-Tiffany, 'Women and the Circulation of Material Culture: Crossing Boundaries and Connecting Spaces', in: Hamilton and Proctor-Tiffany (eds.), *Moving Women, Moving Objects (400–1500)*, Leiden: Brill, 2019, 1–12.
28. Foucault, *The Order of Things*.
29. Laurel Thatcher Ulrich, Ivan Gaskell, Sara J. Schechner and Sarah Anne Carter, 'Introduction: Thinking with Things', in: Ulrich, Gaskell, Schechner and Carter (eds.), *Tangible Things: Making History through Objects*, Oxford: Oxford University Press, 2015.
30. Ivan Gaskell, 'History of Things', in: Marek Tamm and Peter Burke (eds.), *Debating New Approaches to History*, London: Bloomsbury, 2019, 222–3.
31. Bruno Latour, *The Pasteurisation of France*, Cambridge, MA: Harvard University Press, 1988, 193.
32. Ben Anderson and John Wylie, 'On Geography and Materiality', in: *Environment and Planning A: Economy and Space* 41:2 (2009), 318–35.
33. Nigel Thrift, *Non-Representational Theory: Space, Politics, Affect*, London: Routledge, 2008.
34. Eva Horn and Hannes Bergthaller, *The Anthropocene: Key Issues for the Humanities*, London: Routledge, 2019; Christophe Bonneuil and Jean-Baptiste Fressoz, *The Shock of the Anthropocene: the Earth, History and Us*, London: Verso, 2016.
35. Marek Tamm and Zoltán Boldizsár Simon, 'More-than-Human History: Philosophy of History at the Time of the Anthropocene', in: J. M. Kuukkanen (ed.), *Philosophy of History: Twenty-First Century Perspectives*, London: Bloomsbury 2020, 198–215.
36. Dipesh Chakrabarty, 'Human Agency in the Anthropocene', in: *Perspectives on History* 50:12 (2012), www.historians.org/publications-and-directories/perspectives-on-history/december-2012/human-agency-in

-the-anthropocene [accessed 22 January 2020]; see also Dipesh Chakrabarty, 'Anthropocene Time', in: *History and Theory* 57:1 (2018), 5–32.

37. LeCain, *The Matter of History*, chapter 2.
38. Chris Otter, *Diet for a Large Planet: Industrial Britain, Food Systems, and World Ecology*, Chicago: University of Chicago Press, 2020.
39. Ann Brower Stahl, 'Material Histories', in: Hicks and Beaudry (eds), *Handbook of Material Culture*, 150–72.
40. Bruno Latour, *We Have Never Been Modern*, Cambridge, MA: Harvard University Press, 1993 (originally published in French in 1991).
41. LeCain, *The Matter of History*, 15.
42. Bjørnar Olsen, 'Comment', in: Tamm and Burke (eds.), *Debating*, 238.
43. Gretchen M. Hermann, 'Gift or Commodity: What Changes Hands in the US Garage Sale?', in: Daniel Miller (ed.), *Consumption: Critical Concepts in the Social Sciences, vol. II: the History and Regional Development of Consumption*, London: Routledge, 2001, 72–101.
44. On Bourdieu, see Chapter 1.
45. LeCain, *The Matter of History*, chapters 4–6.
46. Mark Fiege, *The Republic of Nature: an Environmental History of the United States*, Seattle: University of Washington Press, 2012.
47. An introduction is provided by Grégory Quenet, 'Environmental History', in: Tamm and Burke (eds.), *Debating New Approaches*, 75–100.
48. Dipesh Chakrabarty, 'The Climate of History: Four Theses', in: *Critical Enquiry* 35 (2009), 197–122; see also idem, 'The Human Significance of the Anthropocene', in: Bruno Latour (ed.), *Reset Modernity!*, Cambridge, MA: MIT Press, 2016, 189–99.
49. Lloyd Price, 'Environmental and Animal History', in: Berger, Feldner and Passmore (eds.), *Writing History*, 253–59.
50. See, for example, Ken S. Coates, *A Global History of Indigenous Peoples: Struggle and Survival*, Basingstoke: Palgrave Macmillan, 2004; Frederick A. Hoxie (ed.), *The Oxford Handbook of American Indian History*, Oxford: Oxford University Press, 2016.
51. Ngahuia Te Awekotuku with L. W. Nikora, *Mau Moko: The World of Māori Tattoo*, Honolulu: University of Hawaii Press, 2007.
52. Annabel Cooper, Lachy Paterson and Angela Wanhalla, 'Introduction: a Scheme of Things', in: Cooper, Paterson and Wanhalla (eds.), *The Lives of Colonial Objects*, Dunedin: Otago University Press, 2015, 13.
53. Susan M. Pearce, *Museums, Objects and Collections: a Cultural Study*, Leicester: Leicester University Press, 1992; Pearce (ed.), *Interpreting*

Objects and Collections, London: Routledge, 1992; Pearce, *Experiencing Material Culture in the Western World*, Leicester: Leicester University Press, 1997.

54. Kathleen M. Adams, 'Identity, Heritage and Memorialization: the Toraja Tongkonan of Indonesia', in: Anne Gerritsen and Giorgio Riello (eds.), *Writing Material Culture History*, London: Bloomsbury, 2015, 93–100.
55. Ann Brower Stahl, *Making History in Banda: Anthropological Visions of Africa's Past*, Cambridge: Cambridge University Press, 2001.
56. Frank Dikötter, *Exotic Commodities: Modern Objects and Everyday Life in China*, New York: Columbia University Press, 2007.
57. Michel de Certeau, Luce Giard and Pierre Mayol, *The Practice of Everyday Life: Living and Cooking, vol. II*, Minneapolis: University of Minnesota Press, 1998, 256. On de Certeau, see also Chapters 1 and 6 above.
58. Javier Gimeno-Martinez, *Design and National Identity*, London: Bloomsbury, 2016.
59. Lawrence J. Vale, *Architecture, Power and National Identity*, 2nd edn, London: Routledge, 2008.
60. Helen Berry, 'Regional Identity and Material Culture', in: Karen Harvey (ed.), *History and Material Culture*, London: Routledge, 2009, 139–57.
61. Stefan Berger, Ulrich Borsdorf, Ludger Claβen, Heinrich Theodor Grütter and Dieter Nellen (eds.), *Zeit-Räume Ruhr: Erinnerungsorte des Ruhrgebiets*, Essen: Klartext, 2019; see also Stefan Berger, 'Industrial Heritage and the Ambiguities of Nostalgia for an Industrial Past in the Ruhr Valley, Germany' in: *Labor: Studies in Working-Class History* 16:1 (2019), 37–64.
62. Thomas G. Andrews, *Killing for Coal: America's Deadliest Labor War*, Cambridge, MA: Harvard University Press, 2008; for a direct relationship between work, environment and class consciousness see also Chad Montrie, *Making a Living: Work and Environment in the United States*, Chapel Hill: University of North Carolina Press, 2008.
63. Manuel Charpy, 'How Things Shape Us: Masterial Culture and Identity in the Industrial Age', in: Gerritsen and Riello (eds.), *Writing Material Culture History*, 199–222.
64. Valerie Steele, *Corset: a Cultural History*, New Haven: Yale University Press, 2001.
65. Adeline Masquelier (ed.), *Dirt, Undress and Difference: Critical Perspectives on the Body's Surface*, Bloomington: Indiana University Press, 2005.
66. Arlette Klaric, 'Gustav Stickley's Designs for the Home: an Activist Aesthetic for the Upwardly Mobile', in: Patricia Johnston (ed.), *Seeing*

High and Low: Representing Social Conflict in American Visual Culture, Berkeley: University of California Press, 2006, 177–93.

67. Charpy, 'How Things Shape Us'.
68. Stacy Alaimo and Susan Hekman (eds.), *Material Feminisms*, Bloomington: Indiana University Press, 2008.
69. Karen Barad, 'Posthuman Performativity: Toward an Understanding of How Matter Comes to Matter', in: *Signs* 28 (2003), 801–31.
70. Hannah Greig, Jane Hamlett and Leonie Hannan, 'Introduction: Gender and Material Culture', in: Greig, Hamlett and Hannan (eds.), *Gender and Material Culture in Britain since 1600*, Basingstoke: Palgrave Macmillan, 2015, 1.
71. Ibid., 5.
72. Stella Moss, 'Manly Drinkers: Masculinity and Material Culture in the Interwar Public House', in: Greig, Hamlett and Hannan (eds.), *Gender and Material Culture*, 138–52.
73. Nira Wickramasinghe, *Dressing the Colonised Body: Politics, Clothing and Identity in Colonial Sri Lanka*, London: Longman, 2003.
74. Uthara Suvrathan, 'Spoiled for Choice? The Sacred Landscape of Ancient and Early Medieval Banavasi', in: *South Asian Studies* 30:2 (2014), 206–29.
75. Ibid., 227.
76. See www.bbc.co.uk/programmes/b00nrtd2/episodes/downloads [accessed 5 January 2020].
77. See www.bbc.co.uk/ahistoryoftheworld/about/transcripts/episode1/ [accessed 22 January 2020].
78. Neil MacGregor, *A History of the World in 100 Objects*, London: Penguin, 2010.
79. Giorgio Riello, *Cotton: the Fabric that Made the Modern World*, Cambridge: Cambridge University Press, 2013.
80. LeCain, *The Matter of History*, 21.
81. Gerritsen and Riello, 'Introduction', in: Gerritsen and Riello (eds.), *Writing Material Culture History*, 7.

11 Transnational, Comparative and Global History

1. See, for example, Merry E. Wiesner-Hanks (general editor), *The Cambridge World History*, 9 vols., Cambridge: Cambridge University Press, 2015; Akira Iriye and Jürgen Osterhammel (general editors), *A History of the World*, 6 vols., Cambridge, MA: Harvard University Press, 2012–20.

2. Sven Beckert and Dominic Sachsenmaier (eds.), *Global History Globally: Research and Practice around the World*, London: Bloomsbury, 2018. A very good introduction to global history, its promises and perils, is provided by Sebastian Conrad, *What is Global History?*, Princeton: Princeton University Press, 2016.
3. Michael Geyer and Charles Bright, 'World History in a Global Age', in: *American Historical Review* 100:4 (1995), 1034–60; Roland Axtman, 'Society, Globalization and the Comparative Method', *History of the Human Sciences* 6 (1993), 53–74.
4. Kenneth Pomeranz, 'Histories for a Less National Age', in: *American Historical Review* 119:1 (2014), 1–22.
5. Berger, 'Comparative and Transnational History'. See also Willibald Steinmetz (ed.), *The Force of Comparison: New Perspective on Modern European History and the Contemporary World*, Oxford: Berghahn Books, 2019.
6. Maxine Berg (ed.), *Writing the History of the Global: Challenges for the Twenty-First Century*, Oxford: Oxford University Press, 2013.
7. David A. Hollinger, 'The Historian's Use of the United States and Vice Versa', in: Thomas Bender (ed.), *Rethinking American History in a Global Age*, Berkeley: University of California Press, 2002, 381–96.
8. On the long-term trajectories of global history see Inglebert, *Le monde, l'histoire*; Katja Naumann, 'Long-Term and Decentred Trajectories of Doing History from a Global Perspective: Institutionalization, Postcolonial Critique, and Empiricist Approaches, before and after the 1970s', in: *Journal of Global History* 14: 3 (2019), 335–54; Benedikt Stuchtey and Eckhardt Fuchs (eds.), *Writing World History, 1800–2000*, Oxford: Oxford University Press, 2003.
9. Matthias Middell and Katja Naumann, 'Historians and International Organization(s): the International Committee of Historical Sciences (CISH)', in: Danile Laqua, Christophe Verbruggen and Wouter van Acker (eds.), *International Organizations and Global Civil Society: Histories of the Union of International Assocations*, London: Bloomsbury, 2019, 133–51.
10. Pascale Rabault-Feuerbahn, '"Les grandes assises de l'orientalisme": la question interculturell dans les Congrès internationaux des orientalistes (1873–1912)', in: *Revue Germanique Internationale* 12 (2010), 47–68.
11. On Renan see Said, *Orientalism*, 132.
12. Chakrabarty, *Provincializing Europe*.
13. Kwame Anthony Appiah, *Lines of Descent: W. E. B. Du Bois and the Emergence of Identity*, Cambridge, MA: Harvard University Press, 2014.

14. Nico Slate, *Colored Cosmopolitanism: the Shared Struggle for Freedom in the United States and India*, Cambridge, MA: Harvard University Press, 2012; Slate, *The Prism of Race: W. E. B. Du Bois, Langston Hughes, Paul Robeson, and the Colored World of Cedric Dover*, Basingstoke: Palgrave Macmillan, 2014.
15. C. L. R. James, *The Black Jacobins*, London: Secker and Warburg, 1938.
16. Arnold Toynbee, *A Study of History*, 12 vols., Oxford: Oxford University Press, 1934–61.
17. William McNeill, *The Rise of the West: a History of the Human Community*, Chicago: Chicago University Press, 1963.
18. William McNeill, *Plagues and People*, New York: Anchor Press, 1976; McNeill, *The Human Condition: an Ecological and Historical View*, Princeton: Princeton University Press, 1980; McNeill, *The Pursuit of Power: Technology, Armed Forces, and Society*, Chicago: Chicago University Press, 1982.
19. William McNeill, *Arnold Toynbee: a Life*, Oxford: Oxford University Press, 1989.
20. Katja Naumann, *Laboratorien der Weltgeschichtsschreibung: Lehre und Forschung an den Universitäten Chicago, Columbia and Harvard, 1918–1968*, Göttingen: Vandenhoeck and Ruprecht, 2019.
21. Michael Adas, 'The Virtues of Rigorous Comparison: Peter Stearns's Contributions to Global History', in: *Journal of Social History* 51:3 (2018), 457–66.
22. This is particularly true for his three-volume nineteenth-century history but also his one-volume twentieth-century one and his many articles on labour history that often had a keen transnational and comparative eye. On Hobsbawm see Richard J. Evans, *Eric Hobsbawm: a Life in History*, New York: Little Brown, 2019.
23. On various traditions of twentieth-century scholarship in world history see Jerry H. Bentley, *Shapes of World History in Twentieth-Century Scholarship*, Washington, DC: American Historical Association, 2003. In many ways continuing Hobsbawm's project of a world social history is John Coatsworth, Juan Cole, Michael Hanagan, Peter C. Perdue, Charles Tilly and Louise Tilly, *Global Connections: Politics, Exchange, and Social Life in World History, vol. II: Since 1500*, Cambridge: Cambridge University Press, 2015.
24. Immanuel Wallerstein, *The Modern World System*, 4 vols., Berkeley: University of California Press, 2011. Volume I originally appeared in 1974, volume II followed in 1980, vol. III in 1989 and volume IV had to wait until 2011, when the University of California Press re-issued the whole set.

25. Ian Tyrrell, 'American Exceptionalism in an Age of International History', in: *American Historical Review* 96:4 (1991), 1031–55.
26. Annette C. Palmer and Lawrence A. Peskin, 'What in the World is "America and the World"'?, in: *Perspectives on History*, 1 November 2011; www.historians.org/publications-and-directories/perspectives-on-history/november-2011/what-in-the-world-is-america-and-the-world [accesssed 17 May 2020].
27. Werner and Zimmermann, 'Beyond Comparison', 30. On the origins of cultural transfer studies, see also Espagne and Werner, *Transferts*.
28. Lucien Febvre, *Le Rhin: histoire, mythes et réalité*, Paris: Perrin, 1997; see also Schöttler, 'Le Rhin comme enjeu historiographique'.
29. Kapil Raj, *Relocating Modern Science: Circulation and the Construction of Knowledge in South Asia and Europe, 1650–1900*, Basingstoke: Palgrave Macmillan, 2007.
30. Philipp Ther, 'Beyond the Nation: the Relational Basis of a Comparative History of Germany and Europe', in: *Central European History* 36:1 (2003), 45–73; see also Deborah Cohen and Maua O'Connor (eds.), *Comparison and History: Europe in Cross-National Perspective*, London: Routledge, 2004; Gabriele Lingelbach, 'Comparative History, Intercultural Transfer Studies and Global History: Three Modes of Conceptualizing History beyond the Nation State', in: *Yearbook of Transnational History* 2 (2019), 1–20; Angelika Epple, Walter Erhart, and Johannes Grave (eds.), *Practices of Comparing: Towards a New Understanding of a Fundamental Human Practice*, Bielefeld: Bielefeld University Press, 2020.
31. Simon MacDonald, 'Transnational History: a Review of Past and Present Scholarship', https://www.ucl.ac.uk/centre-transnational-history/objectives/simon_macdonald_tns_review.pdf [accessed 29 December 2018].
32. Liise Lehtsalu, 'Comparison as a Method of Transregional and Global History', *European History Quarterly* 48:4 (2018), 714.
33. Sven Beckert, C. A. Bayly, Sven Eckert, Matthew Connelly, Isabel Hofmeyr, Wendy Kozol and Patricia Seed, 'AHR Conversation on Transnational History', *American Historical Review* 111:5 (2006), 1459. See also Patricia Clavin, 'Defining Transnationalism', *Contemporary European History* 14:4 (2005), 421–39. Good examples of how networks and experts have shaped the transnational are provided by David Rodogno, Bernhard Struck and Jakob Vogel (eds.), *Shaping the Transnational Sphere: Experts, Networks, and Issues from the 1840s to the 1930s*, Oxford: Berghahn Books, 2014.
34. As argued by Heinz-Gerhard Haupt and Jürgen Kocka, 'Preface', in: Haupt and Kocka (eds.), *Comparative and Transnational History:*

Central European Approaches and New Perspectives, Oxford: Berghahn Books, 2009, vii.

35. Madeleine Herren, Martin Rüsch and Christiane Sibille (eds.), *Transcultural History: Theories, Methods, Sources*, Berlin: Springer, 2012.
36. Angelika Epple, 'Calling for a Practice Turn in Global History: Practices as Drivers of Globalization', in: *History and Theory* 57:3 (2018), 390–407.
37. Arif Dirlik, 'Performing the World: Reality and Representation in the Making of World Histor(ies)', in: *Journal of World History* 16:4 (2005), 391–410.
38. Matthias Middell (ed.), *Cultural Transfers, Encounters and Connections in the Global Eighteenth Century*, Leipzig: Leipziger Universitätsverlag, 2014.
39. On both fields, the history of migration and economic history, see Amit Kumar Mishra, 'Global Histoires of Migration(s)', and Kenneth Pomeranz, 'Scale, Scope and Scholarship: Regional Practices and Global Economic Histories', both in: Beckert and Sachsenmaier (eds.), *Global History*, 195–214, 163–94.
40. Akira Iriye, *Global and Transnational History: the Past, Present and Future*, Basingstoke: Palgrave Macmillan, 2013. Also Jerry H. Bentley, 'The World History Project: Global History in the North American Context', in: Beckert and Sachsenmaier (eds.), *Global History*, 127–42; Marnie Hughes-Warrington, 'Writing World History', in: David Christian (ed.), *The Cambridge World History, vol. I*, Cambridge: Cambridge University Press, 2015, 41–55; Jürgen Osterhammel, 'World History', in: Axel Schneider and Daniel Woolf (eds.), *The Oxford History of Historical Writing, vol. V: Historical Writing since 1945*, Oxford: Oxford University Press, 2011, 93–112; Eric Vanhaute, *World History: an Introduction*, London: Routledge, 2012.
41. Daniel Lord Smail, *On Deep History and the Brain*, Berkeley: University of California Press, 2008.
42. Ibid., 124–5.
43. Andrew Shryock and Daniel Lord Smail (eds.), *Deep History: the Architecture of Past and Present*, Berkeley: University of California Press, 2011.
44. David Christian, *Maps of Time: an Introduction to Big History*, Berkeley: University of California Press, 2004; Eric Chaisson, *Epic of Evolution: Seven Ages of the Cosmos*, New York: Columbia University Press, 2006; Cynthia Stokes Brown, *Big History: From the Big Bang to the Present*, New York: The New Press, 2007;

Fred Spier, *The Structure of Big History: from the Big Bang until Today*, Amsterdam: Amsterdam University Press, 1996; Spier, *Big History and the Future of Humanity*, 2nd edn, Oxford: Wiley-Blackwell, 2015.

45. See https://bighistory.org [accessed 28 January 2021].
46. Craig Benjamin, Esther Quaedackers and David Baker (eds.), *The Routledge Companion to Big History*, London: Routledge, 2020.
47. David Christian, 'What is Big History?', in: Benjamin, Quaedackers and Baker (eds.), *Companion*, 16–34.
48. Wilson and Donnan (eds.), *Companion to Border Studies*.
49. Mary Louise Pratt, *Imperial Eyes: Travel Writing and Transculturation*, London: Routledge, 1992.
50. Bhabha, *The Location of Culture*.
51. Gloria Anzaldúa, *Borderlands/La Frontera: the New Mestiza*, San Franciso: Aunt Lute Books, 1987.
52. Sunil Amrith, 'Struggles for Citizenship around the Bay of Bengal', and Bhavani Raman, 'The Postwar "Returnee", Tamil Culture and the Bay of Bengal', both in: Gyan Prakash, Nikhil Menon and Michael Laffan (eds.), *The Postcolonial Moment in South and South-East Asia*, London: Bloomsbury, 2018, 107–21, 121–40.
53. Thomas Lahusen (ed.), 'Harbin and Manchuria: Place, Space and Identity', special issue of the *South Atlantic Quarterly* 99:1 (2000).
54. Jack Goody, *The Oriental, the Ancient and the Primitive: Systems of Marriage and the Family in Pre-Industrial Societies of Eurasia*, Cambridge: Cambridge University Press, 1990.
55. Thomas Adam, *Intercultural Transfers and the Making of the Modern World, 1800–2000: Sources and Contexts*, Basingstoke: Palgrave Macmillan, 2012.
56. Silke Strickrodt, '"Afro-Brazilians" of the Western Slave Coast in the Nineteenth Century', in: José C. Curto and Paul E. Lovejoy (eds.), *Enslaving Connections: Changing Cultures of Africa and Brazil during the Era of Slavery*, New York: Humanity Books, 2004, 213–44.
57. Benedict Anderson, 'Long-Distance Nationalism', in: Anderson, *The Spectre of Comparisons: Nationalism, Southeast Asia and the World*, London: Verso, 1998, 58–74.
58. Eric Pécout, 'The International Armed Volunteers: Pilgrims of a Transnational Risorgimento', in: *Journal of Modern Italian Studies* 14:4 (2009), 413–26.
59. Jie-Hyun Lim, 'World History, Nationally: How Has the National Appropriated the Transnational in East-Asian Historiography', in: Beckert and Sachsenmaier (eds.), *Global History*, 251–68.

60. Xupeng Zhang, 'National Histoires in Chinese Global Histories', in: Stefan Berger, Chris Lorenz and Nicola Brauch (eds.), *Analysing Historical Narratives: On Academic, Popular and Educational Framings of the Past*, Oxford: Berghahn Books, 2021.
61. Dominic Sachsenmaier, *Global Perspectives on Global History: Theories and Approaches in a Connected World*, Cambridge: Cambridge University Press, 2011, where he deals overwhelmingly with US, German and Chinese perspectives on global history.
62. Hartmut Kaelble, 'Social History of European Integration', in Clemens Wurm (ed.), *Western Europe and Germany: the Beginnings of European Integration, 1945–1960*, Oxford: Berghahn Books, 1995, 219–47.
63. Gerard Delanty, *Inventing Europe: Idea, Identity, Reality*, Basingstoke: Palgrave Macmillan, 1995.
64. This is particularly strong in countries with strong doses of Euroscepticism, such as Britain. See, for example, Starkey, 'The English Historians''.
65. Berger, 'History and Forms of Collective Identity in Europe'.
66. Jörn Leonhard, 'Comparison, Transfer and Entanglement, or: How to Write Modern European History Today?', in: *Journal of Modern European History* 14:2 (2016)149–63.
67. Omar Gueye, 'African History and Global History: Revisiting Paradigms', in: Beckert and Sachsenmaier (eds.), *Gobal History*, 83–108.
68. Frederick Jackson Turner, *The Frontier in American History*, New York: Holt, 1920.
69. Hans-Ulrich Wehler, *The German Empire*, Oxford: Berg, 1985.
70. Peter Mathias, *The First Industrial Nation: the Economic History of Britain, 1700–1914*, London: Methuen, 1969.
71. Neville Kirk, *Labour and Socialism in Britain and the USA*, 2 vols., Avebury: Ashgate, 1994.
72. On the impact of the *Sonderweg* debate on German historical writing and explicitly on furthering comparative studies, see Berger, *The Search for Normality*, 117–20.
73. Sidney Pollard, *Peaceful Conquests: the Industrialisation of Europe, 1760–1970*, Oxford: Oxford University Press, 1981.
74. Roumen Daskalov and Tchavdar Marinov (eds.), *Entangled Histories of the Balkans, vol. I: National Ideologies and Language Policies*, Leiden: Brill, 2013; Roumen Daskalov and Diana Mishkova (eds.), *Entangled Histories of the Balkans, vol. II: Transfers of Political Ideologies and Institutions*, Leiden: Brill, 2013; Roumen Daskalov

and Alexander Vezenkov (eds.), *Entangled Histories of the Balkans, vol. III: Shared Pasts, Disputed Legacies*, Leiden: Brill, 2015; Roumen Daskalov, Diana Mishkova, Tchavdar Marinov and Alexander Vezenkov (eds.), *Entangled Histories of the Balkans, vol. IV: Concepts, Approaches and (Self-)Representations*, Leiden: Brill, 2017.

75. Werner Sombart, *Why Is There No Socialism in the United States?*, London: Routledge, 2019 (originally published in German in 1906). For Britain, see also Ross McKibbin, 'Why Was There No Marxism in Great Britain?', in: *English Historical Review* 99 (1984), 297–331.
76. Stefan Berger, 'European Labour Movements and the European Working Class in Comparative Perspective', in Berger and David Broughton (eds.), *The Force of Labour*, Oxford: Berg, 1995, 245–62.
77. John Breuilly, *Labour and Liberalism in Nineteenth-Century Europe: Essays in Comparative History*, Manchester: Manchester University Press, 1992, chapters 6 and 7.
78. Andy Croll, 'The Impact of Postmodernism on Modern British Social History', in Stefan Berger (ed.), *Labour and Social History in the United Kingdom: Historiographical Reviews and Agendas, 1990 to the Present*, special edition of the *Mitteilungsblatt des Instituts für soziale Bewegungen* 28 (2002), 137–52.
79. Jan Lucassen (ed.), *Global Labour History: a State of the Art*, Bern: Peter Lang, 2008.
80. Leon Fink, 'Preface', in Fink (ed.), *Workers across the Americas: the Transnational Turn in Labor History*, New York: Oxford University Press, 2011, x–xi.
81. Kelley, 'But a Local Phase of a World Problem'.
82. On Gilroy see also above, 91, 157, 257.
83. Gilroy, *The Black Atlantic*.
84. Peter Linebaugh and Marcus Rediker, *The Many-Headed Hydra: Sailors, Slaves, Commoners, and the Hidden History of the Revolutionary Atlantic*, Boston: Beacon Press, 2000.
85. Marilyn Lake, 'White Man's Country: the Trans-National History of a National Project', in: *Australian Historical Studies* 34:122 (2003), 346–63.
86. Marilyn Lake and Henry Reynolds, *Drawing the Global Colour Line: White Men's Countries and the International Challenge of Racial Equality*, Cambridge: Cambridge University Press, 2008.
87. Madeline Y. Hsu, 'Transnationalism and Asian-American Studies as Migration-Centred Project', in: *Journal of Asian American Studies* 11:2 (2008), 185–97.

88. Radhika Viyas Mongia, 'Race, Nationality, Mobility: a History of the Passport', in: Antoinette Burton (ed.), *After the Imperial Turn: Thinking with and through the Nation*, Durham, NC: Duke University Press, 2003, 196–216, quotes on 196.
89. Margot Canady, 'Thinking Sex in the Transnational Turn: an Introduction', in: *American Historical Review* 114:5 (2009), 1250–7.
90. Fiona Paisley, *Glamour in the Pacific: Cultural Internationalism and Race Politics in the Women's Pan-Pacific*, Honolulu: University of Hawaii Press, 2009.
91. Philippa Levine (ed.), *Gender and Empire*, Oxford: Oxford University Press, 2004.
92. Susan Zimmermann, 'The Challenge of Multinational Empire for the Internatinal Women's Movement: the Habsburg Monarchy and the Development of Feminist Inter/National Politics', in: *Journal of World History* 16 (2004), 87–172.
93. On transnational activism see Berger and Scalmer (eds.), *The Transnational Activist.* Transnational history has indeed pointed to the importance of many transnational biographies in the modern world. See Desley Deacon, Penny Russell and Angela Woolacott (eds.), *Transnational Lives: Biographies of Global Modernity*, Basingstoke: Palgrave Macmillan, 2010.
94. Johanna Gehmacher, 'Invisible Transfers: Translation as a Crucial Practice in Transnational Women's Movements around 1900', in: *Bulletin of the German Historical Institute London* 41:2 (2019), 3–44.
95. Ann Rigney, 'Remembering Hope: Transnational Activism beyond the Traumatic', in: *Memory Studies* 11:3 (2018), 368–80; Stefan Berger, Sean Scalmer and Christian Wicke (eds.), *Remembering Social Movements*: Activism and Memory, London: Routledge, 2021; Yifat Gutman and Jenny Wuestenberg (eds.), *Handbook on Memory Activism*, Oxford: Blackwell, 2022.
96. Gisela Bock and Pat Thane (eds.), *Maternity and Gender Policies: Women and the Rise of the European Welfare States, 1880–1950*, London: Routledge, 1991; Laura J.Shepherd, *Gender Matters in Global Politics: a Feminist Introduction to International Relations*, London: Routledge, 2009.
97. Midgley, Twells and Carlier, 'Introduction'.
98. Said, *Orientalism.*
99. Chakrabarty, *Provincializing Europe.*
100. Margrit Pernau and Helge Jordheim, 'Introduction', in Pernau and Jordheim (eds.), *Civilizing Emotions: Concepts in Nineteenth-Century Asia and Europe*, Oxford: Oxford University Press, 2015, 5.

101. Ann Laura Stoler and Frederick Cooper, 'Between Metropole and Colony: Rethinking a Research Agenda', in: Stoler and Cooper (eds.), *Tensions of Empire: Colonial Cultures in a Bourgeois World*, Los Angeles: University of California Press, 1997. On empires as intensely transnational affairs see also Stuart Ward, 'Transcending the Nation? A Global Imperial History', in: Burton (ed.), *After the Imperial Turn*, 44–56.
102. Cemil Aydin, *The Politics of Anti-Westernism in Asia: Visions of World Order in Pan-Islamic and Pan-Asian Thought*, New York: Columbia University Press, 2019.
103. Pierre-Yves Saunier, 'Going Transnational? News from Down Under: Transnational History Symposium, Canberra, ANU, September 2004', *Historical Social Research* 31:2 (2006), 128; see also Akira Iriye and Pierre-Yves Saunier (eds.), *The Palgrave Dictionary of Transnational History*, Basingstoke: Palgrave Macmillan, 2009.
104. Lynn Hunt, *Writing History in the Global Era*, New York: Norton, 2014.
105. Thomas Adam, 'Transnational History: a Programme for Research, Publishing and Teaching', in: *Yearbook for Transnational History* 1 (2018), 1–10, quote on 2.
106. Fernand Braudel, *The Mediterranean and the Mediterranean World in the Age of Philipp II*, 2 vols., Berkeley: University of California Press, 1995(originally published in French in 1949).
107. Paul Duedahl, 'Selling Mankind: UNESCO and the Invention of Global History, 1945–1976', in: *Journal of World History* 22:1 (2011), 101–33.
108. Paul Betts, 'Humanity's New Heritage: UNESCO and the Rewriting of World History', in: *Past and Present* 228 (2015), 249–83, quote on 253.
109. Jan Rüger, 'OXO, or: The Challenges of Transnational History', in: *European History Quarterly* 40:4 (2010), 656–68.
110. Thomas Bender, *A Nation among Nations: America's Place in World History*, New York: Hill and Wang, 2006.
111. Matthias Middell and Katja Naumann, 'Global History and the Spatial Turn: From the Impact of Area Studies to the Study of Critical Junctures of Globalization', in: *Journal of Global History* 5:1 (2010), 149–70, quote on 160.
112. Ibid., 161.
113. Barney Warf and Santa Arias (eds.), *The Spatial Turn: Interdisciplinary Perspectives*, London: Routledge, 2009.
114. Antoinette Burton, 'Introduction: On the Inadequacy and Indispensability of the Nation', in: Burton (ed.), *After the Imperial Turn*, 1–26.
115. Pierre-Yves Saunier, *Transnational History*, Basingstoke: Palgrave Macmillan, 2013, 140.

116. See, for example, Stéphane Gerson (ed.), *France in the World: a New Global History*, New York: Other Press, 2019(originally published in French and edited by Patrick Boucheron in 2017); Xose Manuel Nunez Seixas, *Historia mundial de Espana*, Barcelona: Ediciones Destino, 2018; Gabriele Lingelbach is preparing a similar undertaking for Germany, provisionally entitled *Deutschland in der Welt – die Welt in Deutschland: Globalgeschichte Deutschland sim 19. und 20. Jahrhundert.*
117. Fiona Paisley and Pamela Scully, *Writing Transnational History*, London: Bloomsbury, 2019, 3–4.
118. Gilles Deleuze and Félix Guattari, *A Thousand Plateaus*, London: Continuum, 2004 (originally published in French in 1980).
119. Middell and Naumann, 'Global History', 161.

12 Conclusion: Problematising History and Identity

1. Michael Bentley, *Modern Historiography: an Introduction*, London: Routledge, 1999, 140.
2. See, for example, the diverse contributions to the forum 'After Narrativism' published in the flagship journal of the theory of history: *History and Theory* 54:2 (2015), 153–309.
3. Jouni-Matti Kuukkanen, *Post-Narrativist Philosophy of Historiography*, Basingstoke: Palgrave Macmillan, 2015.
4. In my reading, Chris Lorenz's work has for some time moved along this path. See, for example, Lorenz, '"You Got Your History, I Got Mine"'.
5. Chris Lorenz, Stefan Berger and Nicola Brauch, 'Narrativity and Historical Writing: Introductory Remarks', in: Stefan Berger, Nicola Brauch and Chris Lorenz (eds), Analyzing Historical Narratives: on Academic, Popular and Educational Framings of the Past, Oxford: Berghahn Books, 2021, 1–28.
6. Donald Bloxham, *Why History? A History*, Oxford: Oxford University Press, 2020, especially chapter 8 entitled 'Justifying History Today'.
7. Anderson, *Imagined Communities*.
8. Charles Maier, 'Consigning the Twentieth Century to History: Alternative Narratives for the Modern Era', in: *American Historical Review* 105:3 (2000), 807–31, especially 816.
9. Poster, *Cultural History and Postmodernity*, 154.
10. Robert Berkhofer, *Beyond the Great Story: History as Text and Discourse*, Cambridge, MA: Harvard University Press, 1995.
11. The Network of Concerned Historians and its guiding spirit, Antoon de Baets, have, for many years now, highlighted cases of historians who have been persecuted, silenced and in some cases even murdered by

political regimes seeking to streamline the past to serve their political ends in the present. See: www.concernedhistorians.org/content/home.html [accessed 8 May 2020]; see also Antoon de Baets, *Crimes against History*, London: Routledge, 2018, which is the latest of a series of books by de Baets highlighting the impact of censorship and persecution of historians across the globe.

12. Marjorie Dryburgh, 'Life Histories and National Narratives: Remembering Occupied Manchuria in Postwar China', in: *History Workshop Journal* 88 (2019), 229–51.
13. Joan W. Scott, 'After History?', in: *Common Knowledge* 5 (1996), 10.
14. Hall, 'Introduction: Who Needs Identity?'.
15. On the concept of a 'delayed break' see Berger, 'A Return to the National Paradigm'. On the concept of 'critical' historiography see Stefan Berger, '"Critical" Historiography in Crisis? Some Comparative Remarks on the Historiographical Agenda of the Left in Britain, France and Germany in the 1990s', in: *European Review of History* 3:2 (1996), 213–32.
16. A powerful book in this respect, albeit sadly not translated into English, is Niethammer, *Kollektive Identität.*
17. Berger, 'Writing the Past in the Present'.
18. One example among many is Elizabeth A. Clark, *History, Theory, Text: Historians and the Linguistic Turn*, Cambridge, MA: Harvard University Press, 2004. Clark, who made her mark as one of the foremost historians of late ancient Christianity, wrote this book in the hope of making fellow historians more aware of the offerings of the linguistic turn to their historical practice.
19. Michel Foucault, *The Foucault Effect: Studies in Governmentality*, Chicago: University of Chicago Press, 1991. The book is based on lectures and interviews by Foucault during the years 1977 to 1979.
20. Robert J. C. Young, *Empire, Colony, Postcolony*, Oxford: Wiley Blackwell, 2015.
21. Victor Roudometof, *Glocalization: a Critical Introduction*, London: Routledge, 2016.
22. David Harlan, *The Degradation of American History*, Chicago: University of Chicago Press, 1997.
23. On the ongoing manifold influences of Thompson see also the contributions in Madeleine Davis and Kevin Morgan (eds.), '"Causes that were Lost"? Fifty Years of E. P. Thompson's *The Making of the English Working Class* as Contemporary History', special issue of: *Contemporary British History* 28: 4 (2014), 373–533.

24. James W. Cook, 'The Kids Are All Right: On the "Turning" of Cultural History', in: *American Historical Review* 117:3 (2012), 746–71.
25. Charles Stewart (ed.), *Creolization: History Ethnography, Theory*, Walnut Creek, Ca.: Left Coast Press, 2006; Peter Burke, *Cultural Hybridity*, Cambridge: Polity Press, 2009.
26. Some of her most important essays have been collected in Joan Wallach Scott, *Gender and the Politics of History*, 30th Anniversary Edition, New York: Columbia University Press, 2018.
27. Kathy Davis, 'Embody-ing Theory: Beyond Modernist and Postmodernist Readings of the Body', in: David (ed.), *Embodied Practices: Feminist Perspectives on the Body*, London: Sage, 1997, 1–27.
28. Jenny Wüstenberg and Aline Sierp (eds.), *Agency in Transnational Memory Politics*, Oxford: Berghahn Books, 2020.
29. Gary Browning, *A History of Modern Political Thought: the Question of Interpretation*, Oxford: Oxford University Press, 2016, chapter 4: 'Quentin Skinner, the Cambridge School and Contextualism', 67–88.
30. On perspectivism as a transdisciplinary concept in the sciences see Michela Massimi and Casey D. McCoy (eds.), *Understanding Perspectivism: Scientific Challenges and Methodological Prospects*, London: Routledge, 2019.
31. Geraldine Heng, *The Invention of Race in the European Middle Ages*, Cambridge: Cambridge University Press, 2018; see also Robert Bartlett, 'Medieval and Modern Concepts of Race and Ethnicity', in: *Journal of Medieval and Early Modern Studies* 31:1 (2001), 39–56.
32. Erle C. Ellis, *Anthropocene: a Very Short Introduction*, Oxford: Oxford University Press, 2018.
33. On the concept of logocentrism see Valentine Cunningham, 'Logocentrism', in: Irina R. Makaryk (ed.), *Encyclopedia of Contemporary Literary Theory: Approaches, Scholars, Terms*, Toronto: University of Toronto Press, 1993, 583–5.
34. George Vasilev, 'Methodological Nationalism and the Politics of History-Writing: How Imaginary Scholarship Perpetuates the Nation', in: *Nations and Nationalism* 25:2 (2019), 499–522.
35. On the notion of an 'engaged scholarship', see Stefan Berger, 'Historical Writing and Civic Engagement: a Symbiotic Relationship', in: Berger (ed.), *The Engaged Historian*, 1–32.
36. László Vörös, 'The Social Function of Historical Knowledge and Scholarly History Writing in the 21st Century', in: *Historický Casopis* 65:5 (2017), 785–97 has argued that much scholarly writing remains wedded to the construction of collective identities, despite the fact that in the theory of history such endeavours have long been criticised as untenable.
37. Macintyre and Clark, *The History Wars*.

38. Mary O'Dowd, 'Australian Identity, History and Belonging: the Influence of White Australian Identity on Racism and the Non-Acceptance of the History of Colonisation of Indigenous Australians', in: *International Journal of Diversity in Organisations, Communities and Nations* 10:6 (2011), 29–43.
39. Péter Vágó, 'The Politics of History in Hungary after 2010', in: Katarzyna Kącka and Ralph Schattkowsky (eds.), *History and Politics: Remembrance as Legitimation*, Cambridge: Cambridge Scholars, 2017, 281–92.
40. Marek Tamm, 'The Republic of Historians: Historians as Nation-Builders in Estonia (late 1980s to early 1990s)', in: *Rethinking History* 20:2 (2016), 154–71.
41. On East-Central and Eastern Europe see Alexei Miller and Maria Lipman (eds.), *The Convolutions of Historical Politics*, Budapest: Central European University Press, 2012.
42. Neeladri Bhattacharya, 'Memory, History and the Politics of the Hindu Right', in: Thomas Maissen and Niels F. May (eds.), *National History and New Nationalism in the Twenty-First Century: a Global Comparison*, London: Routledge, 2020, 302–20.
43. Sylvia Paletschek (ed.), *Popular Historiographies in the Nineteenth and Twentieth Centuries*, Oxford: Berghahn Books, 2011.
44. Scott, 'After History?', 23.
45. Kathleen Burk, *Troublemaker: the Life and History of A. J. P. Taylor*, New Haven: Yale University Press, 2002.
46. Chris Lorenz, 'If You Are So Smart, Why Are You under Surveillance? Universities, Neoliberalism and New Public Management', in: *Critical Enquiry* 38:3 (2012), 599–629.
47. O. L. Davis Jr., Elizabeth Anne Yeager and Stuart J. Foster (eds.), *Historical Empathy and Perspective Taking in the Social Studies*, Lanham, MD: Rowman and Littlefield, 2001.
48. Roy Rosenzweig and David Thelen, *The Presence of the Past: Popular Uses of History in American Life*, New York: Columbia University Press, 1998.
49. James B. Gardner and Paula Hamilton (eds.), *The Oxford Handbook of Public History*, Oxford: Oxford University Press, 2017; Thomas Cauvin, *Public History: a Textbook of Practice*, London: Routledge 2016; Faye Sayer, *Public History: a Practical Guide*, London: Bloomsbury, 2015.
50. Hilda Kean and Paul Ashton, 'Introduction: People and their Pasts and Public History Today', in: Paul Ashton and Hilda Kean (eds.), *People and Their Pasts: Public History Today*, Basingstoke: Palgrave Macmillan, 2009, 1.

51. This is an important sub-theme in Cherstin M. Lyon, Elizabeth M. Nix and Rebecca K. Shrum, *Introduction to Public History: Interpreting the Past, Engaging Audiences*, Lanham: Rowman and Littlefield, 2017.
52. Berger (ed.), *The Engaged Historian.*
53. Jo Guldi and David Armitage, *The History Manifesto*, Cambridge: Cambridge University Press, 2014.
54. Deborah Cohen and Peter Mandler, 'The History Manifesto: a Critique', in: *American Historical Review* (2015), 530–42, quote on 542.
55. White, *The Practical Past.*
56. Georg G. Iggers, *The Conception of German History: the National Tradition of Historical Thought from Herder to the Present*, rev. edn, Middletown, CT: Wesleyan University Press, 1983 (originally published in 1968).
57. On Iggers' life, which was inextricably linked to that of his wife Wilma, see their double autobiography: Georg and Wilma Iggers, *Two Lives in Uncertain Times: Facing the Challenges of the Twentieth Century as Scholars and Citizens*, Oxford: Berghahn Books, 2006.
58. See Chapter 5 above, on the pathbreaking book she penned together with Leonore Davidoff.
59. Catherine Hall (ed.), *Cultures of Empire: a Reader: Colonizers in Britain and the Empire in the Nineteenth and Twentieth Century*, Manchester: Manchester University Press, 2000; Catherine Hall and Sonya Rose (eds.), *At Home with the Empire: Metropolitan Culture and the Imperial World*, Cambridge: Cambridge University Press, 2006.
60. Catherine Hall, *Macaulay and Son: Architects of Imperial Britain*, New Haven: Yale University Press, 2012.
61. See www.ucl.ac.uk/lbs/ [accessed 20 May 2020].
62. Dosse, *New History in France*, 4.
63. Matthew S. Champion, 'The History of Temporalities: an Introduction', in: *Past and Present* 243 (2019), 247–54, quote on 247. See also Chris Lorenz and Berber Bevernage (eds.), *Breaking up Time: Negotiating the Borders between Present, Past and Future*, Göttingen: Vandenhoeck and Ruprecht, 2013; Marek Tamm and Laurent Olivier (eds.), *Rethinking Historical Time: New Approaches to Presentism*, London: Bloomsbury, 2019; Vanessa Ogle, *The Global Transformation of Time, 1870–1950*, Cambridge, MA: Harvard University Press, 2015; Jonathan Martineau, *Time, Capitalism and Alienation: a Socio-Historical Inquiry into the Making of Modern Time*, Leiden: Brill, 2015.
64. Stuart Woolf, 'The Changing Role of History and of Historians over the Past Half Century', in: *Storial della Storiografia* 52 (2007), 3–30.
65. Andrew Zimmermann, 'History, Theory, Poetry', in: *History of the Present: a Journal of Critical History* 10:1 (2020), 183–6.

Bibliography

Abensour, Léon, *Histoire générale du féminisme des origines à nos jours*, Paris: Delagrave, 1921.

Abrams, Lynn, *Oral History Theory*, London: Routledge, 2010.

Achille, Etienne, Charles Forsdick and Lydie Moudileno, 'Introduction: Postcolonizing Lieux de Mémoire', in: Etienne Achille, Charles Forsdick and Lydie Moudileno (eds.), *Postcolonial Realms of Memory: Sites and Symbols in Modern France*, Liverpool: Liverpool University Press, 2020, pp. 1–22.

Adam, Thomas, *Intercultural Transfers and the Making of the Modern World, 1800–2000: Sources and Contexts*, Basingstoke: Palgrave Macmillan, 2012.

'Transnational History: a Programme for Research, Publishing and Teaching', in: *Yearbook for Transnational History* 1 (2018), pp. 1–10.

Adams, Ian, *Ideology and Politics in Britain Today*, Manchester: Manchester University Press, 1998.

Adams, Jad, *Women and the Vote: a World History*, Oxford: Oxford University Press, 2014.

Adams, Kathleen M., 'Identity, Heritage and Memorialization: the Toraja Tongkonan of Indonesia', in: Anne Gerritsen and Giorgio Riello (eds.), *Writing Material Culture History*, London: Bloomsbury, 2015, pp. 93–100.

Adamson, Walter L., *Hegemony and Revolution: a Study of Antonio Gramsci's Political and Cultural Theory*, Berkeley, CA: University of California Press, 1980.

Adas, Michael , 'The Virtues of Rigorous Comparison: Peter Stearns's Contributions to Global History', in: *Journal of Social History* 51:3 (2018), pp. 457–66.

Ahearne, Jeremy, *Michel de Certeau: Interpretation and its Other*, Cambridge: Polity Press, 1995.

Alaimo, Stacy, and Susan Hekman (eds.), *Material Feminisms*, Bloomington: Indiana University Press, 2008.

Albrow, Martin, *Max Weber's Construction of Social Theory*, New York: St Martin's Press, 1990.

Aldama, Arturo J. (ed.), *Violence and the Body: Race, Gender and the State*, Bloomington: Indiana University Press, 2003.

Aldrich, Robert, 'Colonial Museums in a Postcolonial Europe', in: Dominic Thomas (ed.), *Museums in Postcolonial Europe*, London: Routledge, 2009, pp. 12–32.

Alexander, Jeffrey C., Philip Smith and Matthew Norton (eds.), *Interpreting Clifford Geertz: Cultural Investigation in the Social Sciences*, Basingstoke: Palgrave Macmillan, 2011.

Alexander, Sally, 'Women's Work in Nineteenth-Century London: a Study of the Years 1820–1850', in: Anne Oakley and Juliet Mitchell (eds.), *The Rights and Wrongs of Women*, Harmondsworth: Penguin, 1976, pp. 59–112.

Allen, Jennifer L., 'National Commemoration in an Age of Transnationalism', in: *Journal of Modern History* 91:1 (2019), pp. 109–48.

Alpers, Svetlana, *The Art of Describing: Dutch Art in the Seventeenth Century*, Chicago: University of Chicago Press, 1983.

Amadiume, Ifi , *Male Daughters, Female Husbands: Gender and Sex in an African Society*, London: Zed Books, 1987.

Amin, Shahid, 'Gandhi as Mahatma: Gorakhpur District, Eastern UP, 1921–22', in: R. Guha (ed.), *Subaltern Studies, vol. III: Writings on South Asian History and Society*, Delhi: Oxford University Press, 1986, pp. 1–61.

Amrith, Sunil, 'Struggles for Citizenship around the Bay of Bengal', in: Gyan Prakash, Nikhil Menon and Michael Laffan (eds.), *The Postcolonial Moment in South and South-East Asia*, London: Bloomsbury, 2018, pp. 107–20.

Anchor, Robert, 'History and Play: Johan Huizinga and his Critics', in: *History and Theory* 27 (1978), pp. 63–93.

Anderson, Ben, and John Wylie, 'On Geography and Materiality', in: *Environment and Planning A: Economy and Space* 41:2 (2009), pp. 318–35.

Anderson, Benedict, *Imagined Communities: Reflections on the Origin and Spread of Nationalism*, London: Verso, 1983; rev. edn, 2006.

'Long-Distance Nationalism', in: Anderson, *The Spectre of Comparisons: Nationalism, Southeast Asia and the World*, London: Verso, 1998, pp. 58–74.

Anderson, Greg, 'Retrieving the Lost Worlds of the Past: the Case for an Ontological Turn', in: *American Historical Review* 120:3 (2015), pp. 787–810.

Andrews, Thomas G., *Killing for Coal: America's Deadliest Labor War*, Cambridge, MA: Harvard University Press, 2008.

Ankersmit, Frank, 'Hayden White's Appeal to the Historians', in: *History and Theory* 37:2 (1998), pp. 182–93.

Historical Representation, Stanford: Stanford University Press, 2001.

Narrative Logic: a Semantic Analysis of the Historian's Language, Den Haag: Nijhoff, 1983.

The Reality Effect in the Writing of History: the Dynamics of Historiographical Topology, Amsterdam: Noord-Hollandsche, 1989.

Ankersmit, Frank, Ewa Domanska and Hans Kellner (eds.), *Re-Figuring Hayden White*, Stanford: Stanford University Press, 2009.

Antohi, Sorin, Balázs Trencsényi and Péter Apor (eds.), *Narratives Unbound: Historical Studies in Post-Communist Eastern Europe*, Budapest: Central European University Press, 2007.

Anzaldúa, Gloria, *Borderlands/La Frontera: the New Mestiza*, San Franciso: Aunt Lute Books, 1987.

Appadurai, Arjun, *Modernity at Large: Cultural Dimensions of Globalization*, Minneapolis: University of Minnesota Press, 1996.

Appadurai, Arjun (ed.), *The Social Life of Things: Commodities in Cultural Perspective*, Cambridge: Cambridge University Press, 1986.

Appiah, Kwame Anthony, 'Cosmopolitan Patriots', in: Martha Craven Nussbaum and Joshua Cohen (eds.), *For Love of Country?*, New York: Beacon Press, 2002, pp. 21–9.

Lines of Descent: W. E. B. Du Bois and the Emergence of Identity, Cambridge, MA: Harvard University Press, 2014.

Appleby, Joyce, Lynn Hunt and Margaret Jacob, *Telling the Truth about History*, New York: Norton, 1994.

Aristotle, *Metaphysics*, Santa Fe: Green Lion Press, 2002.

Armstrong, Tim (ed.), *American Bodies: Cultural Histories of the Physique*, Sheffield: Sheffield Academic Press, 1996.

Aronsson, Peter, 'National Cultural Heritage – Nordic Cultural Memory: Negotiating Politics, Identity and Knowledge', in: Bernd Henningsen, Hendriette Kliemann-Geisinger and Stefan Troebst (eds.), *Transnationale Erinnerungsorte: Nord- und südeuropäische Perspektiven*, Berlin: BWV, 2009, pp. 71–90.

Aronsson, Peter, Narve Fulsås, Pertti Haapala and Bernard Eric Jensen, 'Nordic National Histories', in: Stefan Berger and Chris Lorenz (eds.), *The Contested Nation: Ethnicity, Class, Religion and Gender in National Histories*, Basingstoke: Palgrave Macmillan, 2008, pp. 256–82.

Assad, Talal, *Genealogies of Religion: Discipline and Reasons of Power in Christianity and Islam*, Baltimore: Johns Hopkins University Press, 1993.

Assis, Arthur Alfaix, *What Is History For? Johann Gustav Droysen and the Functions of Historiography*, Oxford: Berghahn Books, 2014.

Assman, Aleida, *Cultural Memory and Western Civilisation: Functions, Media, Archives*, Cambridge: Cambridge University Press, 2011.

'Erinnerung, Identität, Emotionen: Die Nation neu denken', in:*Blätter für deutsche und internationale Politik*, 3 (2020), pp. 73–86.

Die Wiedererfindung der Nation: warum wir sie fuerchten und warum wir sie brauchen, Munich: C.H. Beck, 2020.

Assmann, Jan, *Cultural Memory and Early Civilisation: Writing: Remembrance and Political Imagination*, Cambridge: Cambridge University Press, 2011.

Auslander, Leora, 'Beyond Words', in: *American Historical Review* 110:4 (2005), pp. 1015–45.

Austin, J. L., *How to Do Things with Words*, Oxford: Oxford University Press, 1962

Avgelis, Nikolaos, 'Lakatos on the Evaluation of Scientific Theories', in: Kostas Gavroglu, Yorgos Goudaroulis and Pantelis Nicolacopoulos (eds.), *Lakatos and Theories of Scientific Change*, Dordrecht: Kluwer, 1989, pp. 157–67.

Axel, Brian Keith, 'Introduction: Historical Anthropology and its Vicissitudes', in: Axel (ed.), *From the Margins: Historical Anthropology and its Futures*, Durham, NC: Duke University Press, 2002, pp. 1–44.

Axel, Brian Keith (ed.), *From the Margins: Historical Anthropology and its Futures*, Durham, NC: Duke University Press, 2002.

Axtman, Roland, 'Society, Globalization and the Comparative Method', in: *History of the Human Sciences* 6 (1993), pp. 53–74.

Aydin, Cemil, *The Politics of Anti-Westernism in Asia: Visions of World Order in Pan-Islamic and Pan-Asian Thought*, New York: Columbia University Press, 2019.

Baines, Gary, *South Africa's 'Border War': Contested Narratives and Conflicted Memories*, London: Bloomsbury, 2014

Bakhtin, M. M., *Speech Genres and Other Late Essays*, Austin: University of Texas Press, 1986.

Balibar, Etienne, 'Fictive Ethnicity and Ideal Nations', in: John Hutchinson and Anthony D. Smith (eds.), *Ethnicity*, Oxford: Oxford University Press, 1996, pp. 162–8.

Ballantine, Tony, and Antoinette Burton (eds.), *Bodies in Contact: Rethinking Colonial Encounters in World History*, Durham, NC: Duke University Press, 2005.

Bamford, Kiff, *Jean-François Lyotard: Critical Lives*, London: Reaktion Books, 2017.

Bann, Stephen, *The Clothing of Clio: a Study of the Representation of History in Nineteenth-Century Britain and France*, Cambridge: Cambridge University Press, 1984.

'Face-to-Face with History', in: *New Literary History* 29 (1998), pp. 235–46.
Romanticism and the Rise of History, New York: Twayne, 1995.

Barad, Karen, 'Posthuman Performativity: Toward an Understanding of How Matter Comes to Matter', in: *Signs* 28 (2003), pp. 801–31.

Barclay, Katie, *The History of Emotions: a Student Guide to Methods and Sources*, Basingstoke: Palgrave Macmillan, 2020.

Barkan, Elazar, *The Guilt of Nations: Restitution and Negotiating Historical Injustices*, New York: W. W. Norton, 2000.
The Retreat of Scientific Racism: Changing Concepts of Race in Britain and the United States between the World Wars, Cambridge: Cambridge University Press, 1992.

Barlow, Paul, 'Facing the Past and Present: the National Portrait Gallery and the Search for "Authentic" Portraiture', in: Joanna Woodall (ed.), *Portraiture: Facing the Subject*, Manchester: Manchester University Press, 1997, pp. 219–38.

Barrett, Michèle , *Imagination in Theory: Essays on Writing and Culture*, Cambridge: Polity Press, 1999, pp. 111–23.

Bartholeyns, Gil, 'History of Visual Culture', in: Marek Tamm and Peter Burke (eds.), *Debating New Approaches to History*, London: Bloomsbury 2019, pp. 247–76.

Bartlett, Robert, 'Medieval and Modern Concepts of Race and Ethnicity', in: *Journal of Medieval and Early Modern Studies* 31:1 (2001), pp. 39–56.

Baudrillard, Jean, *The Gulf War Did Not Take Place*, Bloomington: Indiana University Press, 1995 (originally published in French in 1991).

Baumann, Zygmunt, *Modernity and Ambivalence*, Cambridge: Polity Press, 1991.

Bavaj, Riccardo, and Martina Steber, 'Introduction – Germany and "the West": the Vagaries of a Modern Relationship', in: Riccardo Bavaj and Martina Steber (eds.), *Germany and 'the West': a Conceptual History*, Oxford: Berghahn Books, 2015, pp. 1–40.

Baxandall, Michael, *Painting and Experience in Fifteenth-Century Italy: a Primer in the Social History of Pictorial Style*, Oxford: Oxford University Press, 1972.

Bay, Edna G., *Wives of the Leopard: Gender, Politics, and Culture in the Kingdom of Dahomey*, Charlottesville: University of Virgina Press, 1998.

Bayly, Christopher, *Imperial Meridian: the British Empire and the World, 1780–1830*, London: Routledge, 1989.
Recovering Liberties: Indian Thought in the Age of Liberalism and Empire, Cambridge: Cambridge University Press, 2012.

Beard, Charles A., 'Written History as an Act of Faith', in: *American Historical Review* 39:2 (1934), pp. 219–31.

Beard, Mary R., *Woman as a Force in History: a Study in Tradition and Realities*, New York: Macmillan, 1946.

Becker, Carl, 'What are Historical Facts?', in: *Western Political Quarterly* 8:3 (1955), pp. 327–40.

Beckert, Sven, and Dominic Sachsenmaier (eds.), *Global History Globally: Research and Practice around the World*, London: Bloomsbury, 2018.

Beckert, Sven, C. A. Bayly, Sven Eckert, Matthew Connelly, Isabel Hofmeyr, Wendy Kozol and Patricia Seed, 'AHR Conversation on Transnational History', *American Historical Review* 111:5 (2006), pp. 1441–64.

Belchem, John, *Irish, Catholic and Scouse: the History of the Liverpool Irish, 1800–1939*, Liverpool: Liverpool University Press, 2007.

Bell, Duncan, *Reordering the World: Essays on Liberalism and Empire*, Princeton: Princeton University Press, 2016.

Beller-Hann, Ildikó, *Community Matters in Xinjiang, 1880–1949: Towards a Historical Anthropology of the Uyghur*, Leiden: Brill, 2008.

Bender, Daniel E., *Sweated Work, Weak Bodies: Anti-Sweatshop Campaigns and Languages of Labor*, New Brunswick: Rutgers University Press, 2004.

Bender, Thomas, *A Nation among Nations: America's Place in World History*, New York: Hill and Wang, 2006.

Benjamin, Craig, Esther Quaedackers and David Baker (eds.), *The Routledge Companion to Big History*, London: Routledge, 2020.

Benjamin, Jessica, *The Bonds of Love: Psychoanalysis, Feminism and the Problem of Domination*, New York: Pantheon, 1988.

Shadow of the Other: Intersubjectivity and Gender in Psychoanalysis, London: Routledge, 1998.

Benjamin, Walter, 'The Work of Art in the Age of Mechanical Reproduction' (originally published in German in 1935; for a translation see: www.marxists.org/reference/subject/philosophy/works/ge/benjamin.htm [accessed 24 April 2020]).

Bennett, Jane, *The Enchantment of Modern Life: Attachments, Crossings and Ethics*, Princeton: Princeton University Press, 2001.

Bennett, Tony, and Patrick Joyce (eds.), *Material Powers: Cultural Studies, History and the Material Turn*, London: Routledge, 2010.

Bentley, Jerry H., *Shapes of World History in Twentieth-Century Scholarship*, Washington, DC: American Historical Association, 2003.

'The World History Project: Global History in the North American Context', in: Sven Beckert and Dominic Sachsenmaier (eds.), *Global History Globally: Research and Practice around the World*, London: Bloomsbury, 2018, pp. 127–42.

Bentley, Michael, *Modern Historiography: an Introduction*, London: Routledge, 1999.

Modernizing England's Past: English Historiography in the Age of Modernism, 1870–1970, Cambridge: Cambridge University Press, 2005.

Berg, Maxine, *A Woman in History: Eileen Power, 1889–1940*, Cambridge: Cambridge University Press, 1996.

Berg, Maxine (ed.), *Writing the History of the Global: Challenges for the Twenty-First Century*, Oxford: Oxford University Press, 2013.

Bergen, Benjamin K., *Louder than Words: the New Science of How the Mind Makes Meaning*, New York: Basic Books, 2012.

Berger, Peter L., and Thomas Luckmann, *The Social Construction of Reality: a Treatise in the Sociology of Knowledge*, New York: Anchor, 1967.

Berger, Stefan, 'Border Regions, Hybridity and National Identity: the Cases of Alsace and Masuria', in: Q. Edward Wang and Franz L. Fillafer (eds.), *The Many Faces of Clio: Cross-Cultural Approaches to Historiography*, Oxford: Berghahn Books, 2007, pp. 366–81.

'Comparative and Transnational History', in: Stefan Berger, Heiko Feldner and Kevin Passmore (eds.), *Writing History: Theory and Practice*, 3rd edn, London: Bloomsbury, 2020, pp. 290–313.

'"Critical" Historiography in Crisis? Some Comparative Remarks on the Historiographical Agenda of the Left in Britain, France and Germany in the 1990s', in: *European Review of History* 3:2 (1996), pp. 213–32.

'Difficult (Re)Alignments: Comparative Perspectives on Social Democracy and Religion from Late Nineteenth Century to Interwar Germany and Britain', in: *Journal of Contemporary History* 53:3 (2018), pp. 574–96.

'European Labour Movements and the European Working Class in Comparative Perspective', in Stefan Berger and David Broughton (eds.), *The Force of Labour*, Oxford: Berg, 1995, pp. 245–62.

'History and Forms of Collective Identity in Europe: Why Europe Cannot and Should not be Built on History', in: Laura Rorato and Anna Saunders (eds.), *The Essence and the Margin: National Identities and Collective Memories in Contemporary European Culture*, Amsterdam: Rodopi, 2009, pp. 21–36.

'Industrial Heritage and the Ambiguities of Nostalgia for an Industrial Past in the Ruhr Valley, Germany', in: *Labor: Studies in Working-Class History* 16:1 (2019), pp. 37–64.

'Introduction: Historical Writing and Civic Engagement: a Symbiotic Relationship', in: Stefan Berger (ed.), *The Engaged Historian: Perspectives on the Intersections of Politics, Activism and the Historical Profession*, Oxford: Berghahn Books, 2020, pp. 1–32.

'Introduction: Toward a Global History of National Historiographies', in: Stefan Berger (ed.), *Writing the Nation: a Global Perspective*, Basingstoke: Palgrave Macmillan, 2007, pp. 1–29.

(with Christoph Conrad), *The Past as History: National Identity and Historical Consciousness in Modern Europe*, Basingstoke: Palgrave Macmillan, 2015.

'Professional and Popular Historians: 1800–1900–2000', in: Barbara Korte and Sylvia Paletschek (eds.), *Popular History Now and Then: International Perspectives*, Bielefeld: Transcript, 2012, pp. 13–30.

'A Return to the National Paradigm? National History Writing in Germany, Italy, France and Britain from 1945 to the Present', in: *Journal of Modern History* 77:3(2005), pp. 629–78.

'The Revival of German Labour History', in: *German History* 37:3 (2019), pp. 277–94.

'The Rise and Fall of "Critical" Historiography? Some Reflections on the Historiographical Agenda of the Left in Britain, France and Germany at the End of the Twentieth Century', in: *European Review of History* 3:2 (1996), pp. 213–34.

The Search for Normality: National Identity and Historical Consciousness in Modern Germany, Oxford: Berghahn Books, 2nd edn, 2003 (originally published in 1997).

'Writing the Past in the Present: an Anglo-Saxon Perspective', in: *Diogenes* 58:1/2 (2012), pp. 5–19.

Berger, Stefan (ed.), *The Engaged Historian: Perspectives on the Intersections of Politics, Activism and the Historical Profession*, Oxford: Berghahn Books, 2019.

(ed.), 'Labour and Social History in Great Britain: Historiographical Reviews and Agendas, 1990s to the Present', special issue of *Mitteilungsblatt des Instituts für soziale Bewegungen* 27 (2002).

Berger, Stefan, Anna Cento Bull, Cristian Cercel, David Clarke, Nina Parish, Eleanor Rowley and Zofia Woyczicka, 'Memory Cultures of War in European War Museums', in: Stefan Berger and Wulf Kansteiner (eds.), *Agonistic Memory and the Legacy of Twentieth-Century Wars in Europe*, Basingstoke, Palgrave Macmillan, 2022.

Berger, Stefan, and Antoon de Baets, 'Reflections on Exile Historiography', in: Stefan Berger and Antoon de Baets (eds.), 'Writing History in Exile', special issue of *Storia della Storiografia* 69:1 (2016), pp. 11–26.

Berger, Stefan, and Wulf Kansteiner, 'Antagonistic, Cosmopolitan and Agonistic Memories of War', in: Stefan Berger, Heinrich Theodor Grütter and Wulf Kansteiner (eds.), *Krieg. Macht. Sinn: War and Violence in European Memory*, Essen: Klartext, 2019, pp. 17–35.

'Introduction: the Memory of War in Contemporary Europe: Antagonism, Cosmopolitanism and Agonism', in: Stefan Berger and Wulf Kansteiner (eds.), *Memory and the Legacy of Twentieth-Century Wars in Europe*, Basingstoke: Palgrave Macmillan, 2022.

Berger, Stefan, and Wulf Kansteiner (eds.), *Agonistic Memory and the Legacy of Twentieth-Century Wars in Europe*, Basingstoke: Palgrave Macmillan, 2022.

Berger, Stefan, Nicola Brauch and Chris Lorenz (eds), Analyzing Historical Narratives: on Academic, Popular and Educational Framings of the Past, Oxford: Berghahn Books, 2021.

Berger, Stefan, and Chris Lorenz (eds.), *The Contested Nation: Ethnicity, Class, Religion and Gender in National Histories*, Basingstoke: Palgrave Macmillan, 2008.

Berger, Stefan, and Alexei Miller, 'Introduction: Building Nations in and with Empires: a Reassessment', in: Stefan Berger and Alexei Miller (eds.), *Nationalizing Empires*, Budapest: Central European University Press, 2015, pp. 1–30.

Berger,Stefan, and Alexei Miller (eds.), *Nationalizing Empires*, Budapest: Central European University Press, 2015.

Berger, Stefan, and Holger Nehring (eds.), *The History of Social Movements in Global Perspective*, Basingstoke: Palgrave Macmillan, 2017.

Berger, Stefan, and Bill Niven (eds.), *Writing the History of Memory*, London: Bloomsbury, 2014.

Berger, Stefan, and Jeffrey Olick (eds.), *A Cultural History of Memory*, 6 vols., London: Bloomsbury, 2020.

Berger, Stefan, and Sean Scalmer, and Christian Wicke (eds.), Remembering Social Movements: Activism and Memory, London: Routledge, 2021.

(eds.), *The Transnational Activist: Transformations and Comparisons from the Anglo-World since the Nineteenth Century*, Basingstoke: Palgrave Macmillan, 2018.

Berger, Stefan, and Joana Seiffert, 'Erinnerungsorte – ein Erfolgskonzept auf dem Prüfstand', in: Stefan Berger and Joana Seiffert (eds.),*Erinnerungsorte: Chancen, Grenzen und Perspektiven eines Erfolgskonzeptes in den Kulturwissenschaften*, Essen: Klartext, 2014, pp. 11–36.

Berger, Stefan, and Eric H. Storm (eds.), *Writing the History of Nationalism*, London: Bloomsbury, 2019.

Berger, Stefan, Ulrich Borsdorf, Ludger Claβen, Heinrich Theodor Grütter and Dieter Nellen (eds.), *Zeit-Räume Ruhr: Erinnerungsorte des Ruhrgebiets*, Essen: Klartext, 2019.

Berkhofer, Robert, *Beyond the Great Story: History as Text and Discourse*, Cambridge, MA: Harvard University Press, 1995.

Berlanstein, Lenard (ed.), *Rethinking Labor History: Essays on Discourse and Class Analysis*, Urbana: University of Illinois Press, 1993.

Berlet, Chip, and Matthew N. Lyons, *Right-Wing Populism in America: Too Close for Comfort*, New York: Guilford Press, 2000.

Berlin, Isaiah, *Four Essays on Liberty*, Oxford: Oxford University Press, 1969.

Bernini, Lorenzo, *Queer Theories: an Introduction – from Mario Mieli to the Antisocial Turn*, London: Routledge, 2020.

Berry, Helen, 'Regional Identity and Material Culture', in: Karen Harvey (ed.), *History and Material Culture*, London: Routledge, 2009, pp. 139–57.

Berry, Mary Elizabeth, *Japan in Print: Information and Nation in the Early Modern Period*, Berkeley, CA: University of California Press, 2006.

Betts, Paul , 'Humanity's New Heritage: UNESCO and the Rewriting of World History', in: *Past and Present* 228 (2015), pp. 249–83.

Bevernage, Berber, and Chris Lorenz (eds.), *Breaking up Time: Negotiating the Borders between Past, Present and Future*, Göttingen: Vandenhoeck and Ruprecht, 2013.

Bevir, Mark, 'The Role of Contexts in Understanding and Explanation', in: Hans-Erich Bödeker (ed.), *Begriffsgeschichte, Diskursgeschichte, Metapherngeschichte*, Göttingen: Wallstein, 2002, pp. 159–208.

Bhaba, Homi, *The Location of Culture*, London: Routledge, 1994.

Bhambra, Gurminder, 'Brexit, Empire and Decolonisation', in: *History Workshop Journal*, 19 December 2018; www.historyworkshop.org.uk/brexit-empire-and-decolonization/ [accessed 24 August 2019].

'Whither Europe', *Interventions* 18:2 (2016), pp. 187–202.

Bhattacharya, Neeladri, 'Memory, History and the Politics of the Hindu Right', in: Thomas Maissen and Niels F. May (eds.), *National History and New Nationalism in the Twenty-First Century: a Global Comparison*, London: Routledge 2020, pp. 302–20.

Biagini, Eugenio, *British Democracy and Irish Nationalism, 1867–1906*, Cambridge: Cambridge University Press, 2007.

Liberty, Retrenchment and Reform: Popular Liberalism in the Age of Gladstone, 1860–1880, Cambridge, Cambridge University Press, 1992.

Biernacki, Richard, 'Method and Metaphor after the New Cultural History', in: Victoria E. Bonnell and Lynn Hunt (eds.), *Beyond the Cultural Turn: New Directions in the Study of Society and Culture*, Berkeley: University of California Press, 1999, pp. 62–94.

Billington, Ray Allen, *Frederick Jackson Turner: Historian, Scholar, Teacher*, Oxford: Oxford University Press, 1973.

Blair, William, *Cities of the Dead: Contesting the Memory of the Civil War in the South, 1865–1914*, Chapel Hill: University of North Carolina Press, 2004.

Bloch, Marc, *Feudal Society*, Chicago: University of Chicago Press, 1961.

The Historian's Craft, Manchester: Manchester University Press, 2008.

'Pour une histoire comparée des sociétées européenne', in; *Revue de Synthèse Historique* 46 (1928), pp. 15–50.

Blom, Ida, Karen Hagemann and Catherine Hall (eds.), *Gendered Nations: Nationalism and Gender Order in the Long Nineteenth Century*, Oxford: Berghahn Books, 2000.

Bloom, Lisa, *Gender on Ice: American Ideologies of Polar Expeditions*, Minneapolis: University of Minnesota Press, 1993.

Bloxham, Donald, *Why History? A History*, Oxford: Oxford University Press, 2020.

Bloxham, Donald, and Robert Gerwarth (eds.), *Political Violence in Twentieth-Century Europe*, Cambridge: Cambridge University Press, 2011.

Bock, Gisela, and Pat Thane (eds.), *Maternity and Gender Policies: Women and the Rise of the European Welfare States, 1880–1950*, London: Routledge, 1991.

Boddice, Rob, *The History of Emotions*, Manchester: Manchester University Press, 2018.

Bodmar, John, *Remaking America: Public Memory, Commemoration and Patriotism in the Twentieth Century*, Princeton: Princeton University Press, 1992.

Bonnell, Andrew, 'Europhobia in the New Tory Historiography', in: John Milfull (ed.), *Britain in Europe: Prospects for Change*, Aldershot: Ashgate, 1999, pp. 207–25.

Bonnell, Victoria, *Iconography of Power: Soviet Political Posters under Lenin and Stalin*, Berkeley: University of California Press, 1997.

Bonnell, Victoria E., and Lynn Hunt (eds.), *Beyond the Cultural Turn: New Directions in the Study of Society and Culture*, Berkeley: University of California Press, 1999.

Bonnet, Romain, Amerigo Caruso, Claire Morelon and Alessandro Saluppo, 'Revolutionary Fears, Industrial Unrest and Anti-Labor Mobilisation in Austria-Hungary, Germany, France and Great Britain (1905–1914)', in: Stefan Berger and Klaus Weinhauer (eds.), *Revolutions in Global Perspective, 1905–1934*, Basingstoke: Palgrave Macmillan, 2022.

Bonneuil, Christophe, and Jean-Baptiste Fressoz, *The Shock of the Anthropocene: the Earth, History and Us*, London: Verso, 2016.

Bouchard, Gérard, *The Making of the Nations and Cultures of the New World: an Essay in Comparative History*, Montreal: McGill-Queen's University Press, 2008.

Bourdieu, Pierre, *Distinction: a Social Critique of the Judgment of Taste*, Cambridge, MA: Harvard University Press, 1984.

Outline of a Theory of Practice, Cambridge: Cambridge University Press, 1977 (originally published in French in 1972).

Bourke, Joanna, *An Intimate History of Killing: Face to Face Killing in Twentieth Century Warfare*, New York: Basic Books, 2000.

Braudel, Fernand, *The Mediterranean and the Mediterranean World in the Age of Philip II*, 2 vols., Berkeley: University of California Press, 1995 (originally published in French in 1949).

Bredekamp, Horst, *Image Acts: a Systematic Approach to Visual Agency*, Berlin: De Gruyter, 2018.

Breisach, Ernst, *On the Future of History: the Postmodern Challenge and Its Aftermath*, Chicago: University of Chicago Press, 2003.

Brett, Annabel, 'What Is Intellectual History Now?', in: David Cannadine (ed.), *What Is History Now?*, Basingstoke: Palgrave Macmillan, 2002, pp. 113–31.

Brett, Annabel, and James Tully (eds.), *Rethinking the Foundations of Modern Political Thought*, Cambridge: Cambridge University Press, 2007.

Breuilly, John, *Labour and Liberalism in Nineteenth-Century Europe: Essays in Comparative History*, Manchester: Manchester University Press, 1992.

Bridenthal, Renate, Claudia Koonz and Susan Stuard (eds.), *Becoming Visible: Women in European History*, Boston: Houghton Mifflin, 1977.

Briggs, Asa, *Victorian Things*, Harmondsworth: Penguin, 1988.

Brown, Bill, *A Sense of Things*, Chicago: University of Chicago Press, 2004.

Brown, Cynthia Stokes, *Big History: From the Big Bang to the Present*, New York: The New Press, 2007.

Brown, Donald E., 'Human Nature and History', in: *History and Theory* 38:4 (1999), pp. 138–57.

Human Universals, New York: McGraw-Hill, 1991.

Browning, Gary, *A History of Modern Political Thought: the Question of Interpretation*, Oxford: Oxford University Press, 2016.

Brownlee, John S., *Japanese Historians and the National Myths, 1600–1945: the Age of the Gods and Emperor Jinmu*, Vancouver: University of British Columbia Press, 1997.

Brundage, Anthony, *The People's Historian: John Richard Green and the Writing of History in Victorian England*, Westport, CT: Greenwood Press, 1994.

Brundage, W. Fitzhugh, *The Southern Past: a Clash of Race and Memory*, Cambridge, MA: Harvard University Press, 2008.

Brunner, Otto, Werner Conze and Reinhart Koselleck (eds.), *Geschichtliche Grundbegriffe: historisches Lexikon zur politisch-sozialen Sprache in Deutschland*, 9 vols., Stuttgart: Klett-Cotta, 1972–97.

Bryson, Norman, 'Visual Culture and the Dearth of Images', in: *Journal of Visual Culture* 2:2 (2003), pp. 229–32.

Bucholc, Marta, and Maciej Komornik, 'The Polish "Holocaust Law" Revisited: the Devastating Effects of Prejudice Mongering', in: *Cultures of History Forum*, 19 February 2019; www.cultures-of-history.uni-jena.de/politics/poland/the-polish-holocaust-law-revisited-the-devastating-effects-of-prejudice-mongering/ [accessed 15 April 2020].

Buisseret, David, and Steven G. Reinhardt (eds.), *Creolization in the Americas*, Arlington: University of Texas Press, 2000.
Bulhof, Ilse Nina, *Wilhelm Dilthey: a Hermeneutic Approach to the Study of History and Culture*, The Hague: Martinus Nijhoff, 1980.
Burckhardt, Jakob, *Briefe*, 3rd edn, Leipzig: Dieterich, 1938.
The Civilisation of the Renaissance in Italy, 1878 (originally published in German in 1860); https://web.archive.org/web/20080921145058/http://www.boisestate.edu/courses/hy309/docs/burckhardt/burckhardt.html [accessed 27 March 2020].
Force and Freedom: Reflections on History, New York: Pantheon, 1943 (originally published in 1905).
'Über das Studium der Geschichte', in: Burckhardt, *Weltgeschichtliche Betrachtungen*, Munich: Steiner, 1982, p. 402 (originally published in 1868).
Burguière, André, 'L'anthropologie historique', in: Jacques Le Goff, Roger Chartier and Jacques Revel (eds.), *La nouvelle histoire*, Paris: Retz, 1978, pp. 37–61.
Burk, Kathleen, *Troublemaker: the Life and History of A. J. P. Taylor*, New Haven: Yale University Press, 2002.
Burke, Peter, 'Bakhtin for Historians', in: *Social History* 13 (1988), pp. 85–90.
Cultural Hybridity, Cambridge: Polity Press, 2009.
The Fabrication of Louis XIV, New Haven: Yale University Press, 1992.
The French Historical Revolution: the Annales School, 1919–1989, Cambridge: Cambridge University Press, 1999.
'Is There a Cultural History of Emotions?', in: Penelope Gouk and Helen Hills (eds.), *Representing Emotions*, Aldershot: Ashgate, 2005, pp. 27–48.
Languages and Communities in Early Modern Europe, Cambridge: Cambridge University Press, 2004.
'Performing History: the Importance of Occasions', in: *Rethinking History* 9:1 (2005), pp. 35–52.
The Renaissance Sense of the Past, London: Edward Arnold, 1969.
'Representing Women's Work in Early Modern Italy', in: Josef Ehmer and Catharina Lis (eds.), *The Idea of Work in Europe from Antiquity to Modern Times*, Farnham: Ashgate, 2009, pp. 177–90.
Sociology and History, London: George Allen and Unwin, 1980.
What Is Cultural History?, 3rd edn, Cambridge: Polity Press, 2018.
Burkette, Allison Paige, *Language and Material Culture*, Amsterdam: John Benjamins, 2015.
Burns, Kathryn, *Colonial Habits: Convents and the Spiritual Economy of Cuzco, Peru*, Durham, NC: University of North Carolina Press, 1999.

Burton, Antoinette, 'Introduction: On the Inadequacy and Indispensability of the Nation', in: Antoinette Burton (ed.), *After the Imperial Turn: Thinking with and Through the Nation*, Durham, NC: Duke University Press, 2003, pp. 1–26.

Bury, J. P., *The Idea of Progress: an Enquiry into Its Origin and Growth*, London: Macmillan, 1920.

Butler, Judith, *Bodies that Matter: on the Discursive Limits of 'Sex'*, London: Routledge, 1993.

Gender Trouble: Feminism and the Subversion of Identity, London: Routledge, 1990.

Cameron, Ardis, 'Sleuthing towards America: Visual Detection in Everyday Life', in: Cameron, Ardis (ed.), *Looking for America: the Visual Production of Nation and People*, Oxford: Blackwell, 2005, pp. 17–41.

Cameron, Ardis (ed.), *Looking for America: the Visual Production of Nation and People*, Oxford: Blackwell, 2005.

Cameron, Rondo, 'Comparative Economic History', *Research in Economic History*, supplement 1 (1977), pp. 287–305.

Canady, Margot, 'Thinking Sex in the Transnational Turn: an Introduction', in: *American Historical Review* 114:5 (2009), pp. 1250–7.

Canning, Kathleen, 'The Body as Method? Reflections on the Place of the Body in Gender History', in: *Gender and History* 11 (1999), pp. 499–513.

Gender History in Practice: Historical Perspectives on Bodies, Class and Citizenship, Ithaca, NY: Cornell University Press, 2006.

Languages of Labor and Gender: Female Factory Work in Germany, 1850–1914, Ithaca, NY: Cornell University Press, 1996.

Caplan, Jane, 'Postmodernism, Poststructuralism and Deconstruction: Notes for Historians', in: *Central European History* 22: 3/4 (1989), pp. 260–78.

Carpenter, Luther P., *G. D. H. Cole: an Intellectual Biography*, Cambridge: Cambridge University Press, 1973.

Carr, E. H., *What Is History?*, Cambridge: Cambridge University Press, 1961; new edn with a foreword by Richard J. Evans, Basingstoke: Palgrave Macmillan, 2001.

Carrard, Philippe, 'Hayden White and/in France: Receptions, Translations, Questions', in: *Rethinking History* 22:4 (2018), pp. 1–17.

'Historiographic Discourse and Narratology: a Footnote to Fludernik's Work on Factual Narrative', in: Jan Alber and Greta Olson (eds.), *How to Do Things with Narrative: Cognitive and Diachronic Perspectives*, Berlin: De Gruyter, 2018, pp. 125–40.

'History and Narrative: an Overview', in: *Narrative Works* 5:1 (2015), pp. 174–96.

Carrera, Magali M., *Imagining Identity in New Spain: Race, Lineage and the Colonial Body in Portraiture and Casta Paintings*, Austin: University of Texas Press, 2003.

Carroll, Berenice (ed.), *Liberating Women's History*, Chicago: University of Chicago Press, 1976.

Carson, James, *The Columbian Covenant: Race and the Writing of American History*, Basingstoke: Palgrave Macmillan, 2015.

Carter, Neil, *Medicine, Sport and the Body*, London: Bloomsbury, 2012.

Cartledge, Paul, *Democracy: a Life*, Oxford: Oxford University Press, 2016.

Cauvin, Thomas, *Public History: a Textbook of Practice*, London: Routledge, 2016.

Cento Bull, Anna and Daniela de Angeli, 'Emotions and Critical Thinking at a Dark Heritage Site: Reactions to a First World War Museum in Slovenia', in: Journal of Heritage Tourism 16:3 (2021), pp. 263–280.

Cento Bull, Anna and Hans Lauge Hansen, 'On Agonistic Memory', in: Memory Studies 9:4 (2016), pp. 390–404.

Cercel, Cristian, 'The Military History Museum in Dresden: Between Forum and Temple', in: *History and Memory* 30:1 (2018), pp. 3–39.

Cercel, Cristian, Nina Parish, and Eleanor Rowley, 'War in the Museum: the Historial of the Great War in Péronne and the Military History Museum in Dresden', in: *Journal of War and Culture Studies* 12:2 (2019), pp. 194–214.

Chaisson, Eric, *Epic of Evolution: Seven Ages of the Cosmos*, New York: Columbia University Press, 2006.

Chakrabarty, Dipesh, 'Anthropocene Time', in: *History and Theory* 57:1 (2018), pp. 5–32.

'The Climate of History: Four Theses', in: *Critical Enquiry* 35 (2009), 197–222.

'Human Agency in the Anthropocene', in: *Perspectives on History* 50:12 (2012); www.historians.org/publications-and-directories/perspectives-on-history/december-2012/human-agency-in-the-anthropocene [accessed 22 January 2020].

'The Human Significance of the Anthropocene', in: Bruno Latour (ed.), *Reset Modernity!*, Cambridge, MA: MIT Press, 2016, 189–99.

Provincializing Europe: Postcolonial Thought and Historical Difference, Princeton: Princeton University Press, 2000; 2nd edn, 2008.

Rethinking Working-Class History: Bengal, 1890–1940, Princeton: Princeton University Press, 1989.

Champion, Matthew S., 'The History of Temporalities: an Introduction', in: *Past and Present* 243 (2019), pp. 247–54.

Chantiluke, Roseanne, Brian Kwoba and Athinagamso Nkopo (eds.), *Rhodes Must Fall: the Struggle to Decolonise the Racist Heart of Empire*, London: Zed Books, 2018.

Chapman, Alister, John Coffey and Brad S. Gregory (eds.), *Seeing Things Their Way: Intellectual History and the Return of Religion*, Notre Dame: University of Notre Dame Press, 2009.

Chapman, Audrey R., and Hugo van der Merwe (eds.), *Truth and Reconcilation in South Africa: Did the TRC Deliver?*, Philadelphia: University of Pennsylvania Press, 2008.

Charpy, Manuel, 'How Things Shape us: Material Culture and Identity in the Industrial Age', in: Anne Gerritsen and Giorgio Riello (eds.), *Writing Material Culture History*, London: Bloomsbury, 2015, pp. 199–222.

Chartier, Roger, *Cultural History: Between Practices and Representations*, Ithaca, NY: Cornell University Press, 1988.

Chatterjee, Partha, *Empire and Nation: Selected Essays*, New York: Columbia University Press, 2010.

Chaturvedi, Vinayak (ed.), *Mapping Subaltern Studies and the Postcolonial*, London: Verso, 2000.

Chaudhuri, Nupur, and Margaret Strobl (eds.), *Western Women and Imperialism: Complicity and Resistance*, Bloomington: Indiana University Press, 1992.

Chiang, Howard H., 'On the Historiographical Politics of Queer Sexuality: Thinking across the Post-Colonial and LGBTQ Subjects of History', in:, in: *Ex Historia* 1 (2009): 1–24; https://humanities.exeter.ac.uk/media/universityofexeter/collegeofhumanities/history/exhistoria/volume1/HowardHChiangessay.pdf [accessed 17 June 2021]

Chickering, Roger, *Karl Lamprecht: a German Academic Life*, Atlantic Highlands, NJ: Humanities Press, 1993.

Chisick, Harvey, 'Mono Ozouf', in: Philip Daileader and Philip Whelan (eds.), *French Historians, 1900–2000*, Oxford: Wiley-Blackwell, 2010, pp. 461–74.

Christian, David, *Maps of Time: an Introduction to Big History*, Berkeley: University of California Press, 2004.

'What is Big History?', in: Craig Benjamin, Esther Quaedackers and David Baker (eds.), *The Routledge Companion to Big History*, London: Routledge, 2020, 16–34.

Chun, Jin-Sung, *Das Bild der Moderne in der Nachkriegszeit. Die westdeutsche 'Strukturgeschichte' im Spannungsfeld von Modernitätskritik und wissenschaftlicher Innovation, 1948–1962*, Munich: Oldenbourg, 2000.

Clark, Alice, *The Working Life of Women in the Seventeenth Century*, London: Kelley, 1919.

Clark, Elizabeth A., *History, Theory, Text: Historians and the Linguistic Turn*, Cambridge, MA: Harvard University Press, 2004.

Clark, Stuart (ed.), *The Annales School: Critical Assessments*, 4 vols., London: Routledge, 1999.

Clark, William, *Academic Charisma and the Origins of the Research University*, Chicago: University of Chicago Press, 2006.

Clavin, Patricia, 'Defining Transnationalism', in: *Contemporary European History* 14:4 (2005), pp. 421–39.

Clever, Iris, and Wilhelmijn Ruberg, 'Beyond Cultural History? The Material Turn, Praxiography and Body History', in: *Humanities* 3 (2014), pp. 546–66.

Clifford, James, and George E. Marcus (eds.), *Writing Culture: the Poetics and Politics of Ethnography*, Berkeley: University of California Press, 1986.

Coakley, Sarah (ed.), *Religion and the Body*, Cambridge: Cambridge University Press, 1997.

Coates, Ken S. , *A Global History of Indigenous Peoples: Struggle and Survival*, Basingstoke: Palgrave Macmillan, 2004.

Coatsworth, John, Juan Cole, Michael P. Hanagan, Peter C. Perdue, Charles Tilly and Louise Tilly, *Global Connections: Politics, Exchange, and Social Life in World History, vol. II: Since 1500*, Cambridge: Cambridge University Press, 2015.

Cocks, Harry, and Matt Houlbrook (eds.), *The Modern History of Sexuality*, Basingstoke: Palgrave Macmillan, 2005.

Coello de la Rosa, Alexandre, and Josep Luís Mateo Dieste, *In Praise of Historical Anthropology: Perspectives, Methods and Applications to the Study of Power and Colonialism*, London: Routledge, 2020.

Cohen, Deborah, and Peter Mandler, 'The History Manifesto: a Critique', in: *American Historical Review* (2015), pp. 530–42.

Cohen, Deborah and Maua O'Connor (eds.), *Comparison and History: Europe in Cross-National Perspective*, London: Routledge, 2004.

Cohn, Bernard S., *An Anthropologist among the Historians and Other Essays*, Oxford: Oxford University Press, 1987.

'India as a Racial, Linguistic and Cultural Area', in: Milton Singer (ed.), *Introducing India in Liberal Education*, Chicago: University of Chicago Press, 1957, pp. 51–62.

'Representing Authority in Victorian India', in: Saurabh Dube (ed.), *Postcolonial Passages: Contemporary History-Writing on India*, Oxford: Oxford University Press, 2004, pp. 47–69.

Colley, Linda, *Acts of Union and Disunion: What Has Held the United Kingdom Together and What Is Dividing It?*, London: Profile, 2014.

Collingwood, R. G., *The Idea of History*, Oxford: Oxford University Press, 1961.

Colvin, Christopher J., *Traumatic Story-Telling and Memory in Post-Apartheid South Africa: Performing Signs of Injury*, London: Routledge, 2019.

Confino, Alon, 'Collective Memory and Cultural History: Problems of Method', in: *American Historical Review* 102:5 (1997), pp. 1386–403.

Conrad, Sebastian, *What is Global History?*, Princeton: Princeton University Press, 2016.

Cook, James W. , 'The Kids Are All Right: On the "Turning" of Cultural History', in: *American Historical Review* 117:3 (2012), pp. 746–71.

Cook, James A., Joshua Goldstein, Matthew D. Johnson and Sigrid Schmalzer (eds.), *Visualizing Modern China: Image, History and Memory, 1750 to the Present*, Lanham, MD: Lexington Books, 2014.

Coombes, Annie E., *History after Apartheid: Visual Culture and Public Memory in a Democratic South Africa*, Durham, NC: Duke University Press, 2003.

Cooper, Annabel, Lachy Paterson and Angela Wanhalla, 'Introduction: a Scheme of Things', in: Annabel Cooper, Lachy Paterson and Angela Wanhalla (eds.), *The Lives of Colonial Objects*, Dunedin: Otago University Press, 2015, pp. 13–19.

Cooper, Frederick, *Colonialism in Question: Theory, Knowledge, History*, Berkeley: University of California Press, 2005.

Cooper, Frederick, with Rogers Brubaker, 'Identity', in: Frederick Cooper, *Colonialism in Question: Theory, Knowledge, History*, Berkeley: University of California Press, 2005, pp. 59–91.

Cooter, Roger, 'The Turn of the Body: History and the Politics of the Corporeal', in: *Arbor: Ciencia, Pensamiento y Cultura* 743 (2010), pp. 393–405.

Corbin, Alain, *The Foul and the Fragrant: Odour and the French Social Imagination*, Cambridge, MA: Harvard University Press, 1986.

The Lure of the Sea: the Discovery of the Seaside in the Western World, 1750–1840, Berkeley: University of California Press, 1994.

Sound and Meaning in the Village Bells, London: Macmillan, 1999.

Cosgrove, Stuart, 'The Zoot-Suit and Style Warfare', in: Ardis Cameron (ed.), *Looking for America: the Visual Production of Nation and People*, Oxford: Blackwell, 2005, pp. 264–80.

Cott, Nancy F., *The Grounding of Modern Feminism*, New Haven: Yale University Press, 1987.

Cowling, Maurice, *The Impact of Labour: the Beginning of Modern British Politics*, Cambridge: Cambridge University Press, 1971.

Craig, David, '"High Politics" and the "New Political History"', in: *Historical Journal* 53 (2010), pp. 453–75.

Crary, Jonathan, *Techniques of the Observer: On Vision and Modernity in the Nineteenth Century*, Cambridge, MA: MIT Press, 1990.

Crawford, Katherine, *European Sexualities, 1400–1800*, Cambridge: Cambridge University Press, 2007.

Crenshaw, Kimberlé, 'Mapping the Margins: Intersectionality, Identity Politics, and Violence against Women of Color', in: *Stanford Law Review* 43:6 (1991), pp.1241–99

Cressy, David, *Birth, Marriage and Death: Ritual, Religion and the Life Cycle in Tudor and Stuart England*, Oxford: Oxford University Press, 1997.

Croll, Andy, 'The Impact of Postmodernism on Modern British Social History', in Stefan Berger (ed.), 'Labour and Social History in the United Kingdom: Historiographical Reviews and Agendas 1990 to the Present', special edition of *Mitteilungsblatt des Instituts für soziale Bewegungen* 28 (2002), pp. 137–52.

Crossley, James G., and Christian Karner (eds.), *Writing History, Constructing Religion*, Aldershot: Ashgate, 2005.

Cullen, Jonathan, *Roland Barthes: a Very Short Introduction*, Oxford: Oxford University Press, 2001.

Cunningham, Valentine, 'Logocentrism', in: Irina R. Makaryk (ed.), *Encyclopedia of Contemporary Literary Theory: Approaches, Scholars, Terms*, Toronto: University of Toronto Press, 1993, pp. 583–5.

Cunningham, William, *The Growth of English Industry and Commerce*, Cambridge: Cambridge University Press, 1882.

Curthoys, Ann, and John Docker, *Is History Fiction?*, 2nd edn, Sydney: UNSW Press, 2010.

D'Amico, Jack, Dain A. Trafton and Massimo Verdicchio (eds.), *The Legacy of Benedetto Croce: Contemporary Critical Views*, Toronto: University of Toronto Press, 1999.

Danto, Arthur, *Analytical Philosophy of History*, Cambridge: Cambridge University Press, 1965.

Darnton, Robert, *The Forbidden Best-Sellers of Pre-Revolutionary France*, New York: Norton, 1995.

The Great Cat Massacre: And Other Episodes in French Cultural History, New York: Basic Books, 1984.

Daskalov, Roumen, *The Making of a Nation in the Balkans: Historiography of the Bulgarian Revival*, Budapest: Central European University Press, 2004.

Daskalov, Roumen, and Tchavdar Marinov (eds.), *Entangled Histories of the Balkans, vol. I: National Ideologies and Language Policies*, Leiden: Brill, 2013.

Daskalov, Roumen, and Diana Mishkova (eds.), *Entangled Histories of the Balkans, vol. II: Transfers of Political Ideologies and Institutions*, Leiden: Brill, 2013.

Daskalov, Roumen, and Alexander Vezenkov (eds.), *Entangled Histories of the Balkans, vol. III: Shared Pasts, Disputed Legacies*, Leiden: Brill, 2015.

Daskalov, Roumen, Diana Mishkova, Tchavdar Marinov and Alexander Vezenkov (eds.), *Entangled Histories of the Balkans, vol. IV: Concepts, Approaches and (Self-)Representations*, Leiden: Brill, 2017.

Davidoff, Leonore, and Catherine Hall, *Family Fortunes: Men and Women of the English Middle Class, 1750–1850*, rev. edn, London: Routledge, 2002.

Davies, Stephen, *Empiricism and History*, Basingstoke: Palgrave Macmillan, 2003.

Davis, Belinda J., *Home Fires Burning: Food, Politics and Everyday Life in World War I*, Chapel Hill: University of North Carolina Press, 2000.

Davis, Kathy, 'Embody-ing Theory: Beyond Modernist and Postmodernist Readings of the Body', in: Kathy Davis (ed.), *Embodied Practices: Feminist Perspectives on the Body*, London: Sage, 1997, pp. 1–27.

Davis, Madeleine, and Kevin Morgan (eds.), '"Causes that were Lost"? Fifty Years of E. P. Thompson's *The Making of the English Working Class* as Contemporary History', special issue of:*Contemporary British History* 28:4 (2014), pp. 373–533.

Davis, Natalie Zemon, 'The Reasons for Misrule: Youth Groups and Charivaris in Sixteenth-Century France', in: *Past and Present* 50:1 (1971), pp. 41–75.

'The Rites of Violence: Religious Riot in Sixteenth-Century France', in: *Past and Present* 59 (1973); reprinted in Davies, *Society and Culture in Early Modern France*, Stanford: Stanford University Press, 1975, pp. 152–88.

'Women's History in Transition: the European Case', in: *Feminist Studies* 3:3/4 (1976), pp. 83–103.

Davis, O. L. , Jr, Elizabeth Anne Yeager and Stuart J. Foster (eds.), *Historical Empathy and Perspective Taking in the Social Studies*, Lanham, MD: Rowman and Littlefield, 2001.

Davis, Oliver, *Jacques Rancière*, Cambridge: Polity Press, 2010.

de Baets, Antoon, *Crimes against History*, London: Routledge, 2018.

'Eurocentrism', in: Thomas Benjamin (ed.), *Encyclopedia of Western Colonialism since 1450, vol. I*, Detroit: Thomson Gale, 2007, pp. 456–61.

de Beauvoir, Simone, *The Second Sex*: New York: Jonathan Cape, 1953.

de Certeau, Michel, *The Possession at Loudon*, Chicago: University of Chicago Press, 1996 (originally published in French in 1970).

The Practice of Everyday Life, Berkeley: University of California Press, 1984 (originally published in French in 1980).

The Writing of History, New York: Columbia University Press, 1988.

de Certeau, Michel, Luce Giard and Pierre Mayol, *The Practice of Everyday Life: Living and Cooking, vol. II*, Minneapolis: University of Minnesota Press, 1998.

de Groot, Joanna , 'Women's History in Many Places: Reflections on Plurality, Diversity and Polyversality', in: *Women's History Review* 27:1 (2018), pp. 109–19.

Deacon, Desley, Penny Russell and Angela Woolacott (eds.), *Transnational Lives: Biographies of Global Modernity, 1700 to the Present*, Basingstoke: Palgrave Macmillan, 2010.

Delanty, Gerard, *Inventing Europe: Idea, Identity, Reality*, Basingstoke: Palgrave Macmillan, 1995.

Deleuze, Gilles, and Félix Guattari, *A Thousand Plateaus*, London: Continuum, 2004 (originally published in French in 1980).

Dellmann, Sarah, *Images of Dutchness: Popular Visual Culture, Early Cinema and the Emergence of a National Cliché, 1800–1914*, Amsterdam: Amsterdam University Press, 2018.

D'Emilio, John, *Sexual Politics, Sexual Communities: the Making of a Homosexual Minority in the United States, 1940–1970*, Chicago: University of Chicago Press, 1983.

den Boer, Pim , 'National Cultures, Transnational Concepts: Begriffsgeschichte beyond Conceptual Nationalism', in: Javier Fernández Sebastian (ed.), *Political Concepts and Time: New Approaches to Conceptual History*, Santander: Cantabria University Press, 2011, pp. 205–22.

Deneckere, Gita, and Thomas Welskopp, 'The "Nation" and "Class": European National Master-Narratives and their Social "Other"', in: Stefan Berger and Chris Lorenz (eds.), *The Contested Nation: Ethnicity, Class, Religion and Gender in National Histories*, Basingstoke: Palgrave Macmillan, 2008, pp. 135–70.

Denman, Mariatte C., 'Visualizing the Nation: Madonnas and Mourning Mothers in Postwar Germany', in: Patricia Herminghouse and Magda Mueller (eds.), *Gender and Germanness: Cultural Production of Nation*, Oxford, Berghahn Books, 1997, pp. 189–201.

Derrida, Jacques, *Archive Fever: a Freudian Impression*, Chicago: University of Chicago Press, 1996.

Of Grammatology, Baltimore: Johns Hopkins University Press, 1997.

Des Jardins, Julie, *Women and the Historical Enterprise: Gender, Race, and the Politics of Memory*, Chapel Hill: University of Michigan Press, 2003.

Devine, Thomas Martin, *Independence or Union: Scotland's Past and Scotland's Present*, London: Allen Lane, 2016.

Diawara, Mamadou, Bernard Lategan and Jörn Rüsen (eds.), *Historical Memory in Africa: Dealing with the Past, Reaching for the Future in an Intercultural Context*, Oxford: Berghahn Books, 2010.

Díaz-Maldonado, Rodrigo, 'National Identity Building in Mexican Historiography during the Nineteenth Century: an Attempt at Synthesis', in: *Storia della Storiografia* 70:2 (2016), pp. 73–93.

Dietler, Michael, 'Consumption', in: Dan Hicks and Mary C. Beaudry (eds.), *The Oxford Handbook of Material Culture Studies*, Oxford: Oxford University Press, 2010, pp. 209–28.

Dikötter, Frank, *Exotic Commodities: Modern Objects and Everyday Life in China*, New York: Columbia University Press, 2007.

Dirks, Nicholas (ed.), *Near Ruins: Cultural Theory at the End of the Century*, Minneapolis: University of Minnesota Press, 1998.

Dirlik, Arif, 'Performing the World: Reality and Representation in the Making of World Histor(ies)', in: *Journal of World History* 16:4 (2005), pp. 391–410.

Dixon, Thomas, *Weeping Britannia: Portrait of a Nation in Tears*, Oxford: Oxford University Press, 2015.

Djokić, Dejan (ed.), *Yugoslavism: Histories of a Failed Idea, 1918–1992*, London: Hurst, 2003.

Domanska, Ewa, 'The Material Presence of the Past', in: *History and Theory* 45:3 (2006), pp. 337–48.

Dominguez Andersen, Pablo, and Simon Wendt (eds.), *Masculinities and the Nation in the Modern World: Between Hegemony and Marginalization*, Basingstoke: Palgrave Macmillan, 2015.

Dosse, François, *History of Structuralism, vol. II: the Sign Sets, 1967 to the Present*, Minneapolis: University of Minnesota Press, 1997.

New History in France: the Triumph of the Annales, Urbana: University of Illinois Press, 1994 (originally published in French in 1987).

Downs, Laura Lee, 'If "Woman" is Just an Empty Category, then Why am I Afraid to Walk Alone at Night? Identity Politics Meets the Postmodern Subject', in: *Comparative Studies in Society and History* 35:2 (1993), pp. 414–37.

Writing Gender History, 2nd edn, London: Bloomsbury, 2010.

Drago, Alex, 'The Emotional Museum', in: Jenny Kidd, Sam Cairns, Alex Drago, Amy Ryall and Miranda Stearn (eds.), *Challenging*

History in the Museum: International Perspectives, London: Routledge, 2014, pp. 23–86.

Dressel, Gert, *Historische Anthropologie. Eine Einführung*, Cologne: Böhlau, 1996.

Dryburgh, Marjorie, 'Life Histories and National Narratives: Remembering Occupied Manchuria in Postwar China', in: *History Workshop Journal* 88 (2019), pp. 229–51.

Dube, Saurabh, *Historical Anthropology*, Oxford: Oxford University Press, 2009.

Duberman, Martin, *Howard Zinn: a Life on the Left*, New York: New Press, 2012.

Duedahl, Paul, 'Selling Mankind: UNESCO and the Invention of Global History, 1945–1976', in: *Journal of World History* 22:1(2011), pp. 101–33.

Dunn, John (ed.), *Democracy: the Unfinished Journey*, Oxford: Oxford University Press, 1992.

Durkheim, Émile, *The Rules of Sociological Method and Selected Texts on Sociology and its Method*, London: Simon and Schuster, 1982.

Eley, Geoff, *A Crooked Line: From Cultural History to the History of Society*, Ann Arbor: University of Michigan Press, 2005.

'Marxist Historiography', in: Stefan Berger, Heiko Feldner and Kevin Passmore (eds.), *Writing History: Theory and Practice*, 3rd edn, London: Bloomsbury, 2020, pp. 67–85.

'Starting Over: the Present, the Postmodern and the Moment of Social History', in: Keith Jenkins (ed.), *The Postmodern History Reader*, 3rd edn, London: Routledge, 2001, pp. 366–79.

Eley, Geoff, and Keith Nield, *The Future of Class in History: What's Left of the Social*, Ann Arbor: University of Michigan Press, 2007.

Elias, Nobert, *The Civilising Process, vol. I: the History of Manners*, Oxford: Blackwell, 1969.

Elkins, James, *The Domain of Images*, Ithaca, NY: Cornell University Press, 2001.

Elliott, Marianne, *When God Took Sides: Religion and Identity in Ireland: Unfinished History*, Oxford: Oxford University Press, 2009.

Ellis, Erle C., *Anthropocene: a Very Short Introduction*, Oxford: Oxford University Press, 2018.

Ellis, Steven G., and Lud'a Klusáková (eds.), *Frontiers and Identities: Exploring the Research Area*, Pisa: Pisa University Press, 2006.

(eds.), *Imagining Frontiers: Contesting Identities*, Pisa: Pisa University Press, 2007.

Elshtain, Jean Bethke, *Women and War*, New York: Basic Books, 1987.

Elton, G. R., *Return to Essentials: Some Reflections on the Present State of Historical Study*, Cambridge: Cambridge University Press, 1991.

Epple, Angelika, 'Calling for a Practice Turn in Global History: Practices as Drivers of Globalization', in: *History and Theory* 57:3 (2018), pp. 390–407.

Epple, Angelika, Walter Erhart and Johannes Grave (eds.), *Practices of Comparing: Towards a New Understanding of a Fundamental Human Practice*, Bielefeld: Bielefeld University Press, 2020.

Epstein, James, 'Introduction: New Directions in Political History', in: *Journal of British Studies* 41:3 (2002), pp. 255–8.

Erll, Astrid, *Memory in Culture*, Basingstoke: Palgrave Macmillan, 2011.

Erll, Astrid, and Ansgar Nünning (eds.), *Cultural Memory Studies: an International and Interdisciplinary Handbook*, Berlin: De Gruyter, 2008.

Espagne, Michel, and Michael Werner, *Transferts: les relations interculturelles dans l'espace Franco-Allemand*, Paris: Ed. Recherche sur le Civilisations, 1988.

Etzemüller, Thomas, *Sozialgeschichte als politische Geschichte: Werner Conze und die Neuorientierung der westdeutschen Geschichtswissenschaft nach 1945*, Munich: Oldenbourg, 2001.

Evans, Grant, *The Politics of Ritual and Remembrance: Laos since 1975*, Honolulu: University of Hawaii Press, 1998.

Evans, R. J. W., and Guy P. Marchal (eds.), *The Uses of the Middle Ages in Modern European States: History, Nationhood and the Search for Origins*, Basingstoke: Palgrave Macmillan, 2011.

Evans, Richard J., *Eric Hobsbawm: a Life in History*, New York: Little Brown, 2019.

In Defence of History, new edn, New York: Granta, 2012 (originally published in 2001).

In Hitler's Shadow: West German Historians and the Attempt to Escape from the Nazi Past, London: Pantheon, 1989.

Evans-Pritchard, Edward E., *Witchcraft, Oracles and Magic among the Azande*, Oxford: Oxford University Press, 1976 (originally published in 1937).

Fairclough, Nick, *Language and Power*, London: Longman, 2001.

Falola, Toyin (ed.), *African Historiography: Essays in Honour of Jacob Ade Ajayi*, Harlow: Longman, 1993.

Falola, Toyin, and Saheed Aderinto, *Nigeria, Nationalism and Writing History*, Rochester, NY: University of Rochester Press, 2010, pp. 143–56.

Fanon, Franz, *The Wretched of the Earth*, New York: Grove Press, 2004.

Febvre, Lucien, *Das Gewissen des Historikers*, Frankfurt am Main: Suhrkamp, 1990.

Le Rhin: histoire, mythes et réalité, Paris: Perrin, 1997.

'Sensibility and History: How to Reconstitute the Emotional Life of the Past', in: Peter Burke (ed.), *A New Kind of History: From the Writings of Febvre*, London: Harper and Row, 1973, pp. 12–26 (originally published in French in *Annales* in 1941).

Feierman, Steven, 'Colonizers, Scholars, and the Creation of Invisible Histories', in: Victoria E. Bonnell and Lynn Hunt (eds.), *Beyond the Cultural Turn: New Directions in the Study of Society and Culture*, Berkeley: University of California Press, 1999, pp. 182–216.

Feldner, Heiko, 'The New Scientificity in Historical Writing around 1800', in: Stefan Berger, Heiko Feldner and Kevin Passmore (eds.), *Writing History: Theory and Practice*, 3rd edn, London: Bloomsbury, 2020, pp. 3–21.

Ferguson, Niall, *Empire: How Britain Made the Modern World*, London: Penguin, 2003.

Ferrándiz, Franciso, 'Exhuming the Defeated: Civil War Mass Graves in 21st Century Spain', in: *American Ethnologist* 40:1 (2013), pp. 38–54.

Ferrándiz, Francisco, and Marije Hristova, 'The Production of Memory Modes during Mass Grave Exhumations in Contemporary Europe', in: Stefan Berger and Wulf Kansteiner (eds.), *Agonistic Memory and the Legacy of Twentieth-Century Wars in Europe*, Basingstoke: Palgrave Macmillan, 2022.

Fewster, Derek, '"Braves Step Out of the Night of the Barrows": Regenerating the Heritage of Early Medieval Finland', in: R. J. W. Evans and Guy P. Marchal (eds.), *The Uses of the Middle Ages in Modern European States: History, Nationhood and the Search for Origins*, Basingstoke: Palgrave Macmillan, 2011, pp. 31–51.

Feyerabend, Paul, *Against Method*, 3rd edn, London: Verso, 1993.

Fiege, Mark, *The Republic of Nature: an Environmental History of the United States*, Seattle: University of Washington Press, 2012.

Fieldhouse, Roger, and Richard Taylor (eds.), *E. P. Thompson and English Radicalism*, Manchester: Manchester University Press, 2013.

Fink, Carole, *Marc Bloch: a Life in History*, Cambridge: Cambridge University Press, 1999.

Fink, Leon, 'Preface', in: Leon Fink (ed.), *Workers across the Americas: the Transnational Turn in Labor History*, New York: Oxford University Press, 2011, pp. x–xi.

Finney, Patrick, *Remembering the Road to World War II: International History, National Identity, Collective Memory*, London: Routledge, 2011.

Fitzpatrick, Ellen Frances, *History's Memory: Writing America's Past, 1880–1980*, Cambridge, MA: Harvard University Press, 2002.

Flåten, Lars Tore, *Hindu Nationalism, History and Identity in India: Narrating a Hindu Past under BJP*, London: Routledge, 2016.

Fleisch, Axel, and Rhiannon Stephens (eds.), *Doing Conceptual History in Africa*, Oxford: Berghahn Books, 2016.

Folbre, Nancy, *Greed, Lust and Gender: a History of Economic Ideas*, Oxford: Oxford University Press, 2009.

Formisano, Ronald P., 'The Concept of Political Culture', in: *Journal of Interdisciplinary History* 31:3 (2001), pp. 393–426.

Foucault, Michel, *The Archaeology of Knowledge*, London: Pantheon, 1972.

'The Birth of Bio-Power', in: P. Rabinow and N. Nose (eds.), *The Essential Foucault*, New York: The New Press, 2003, pp. 202–7.

Discipline and Punish: the Birth of the Prison, New York: Pantheon, 1977.

The Foucault Effect: Studies in Governmentality, Chicago: University of Chicago Press, 1991.

The History of Sexuality, vol. I: Introduction, New York: Random House, 1978.

The History of Sexuality, vol. III: the Care of the Self, New York: Knopf, 1988.

'Nietzsche, Genealogy, History', in: Paul Rabinow (ed.), *Michel Foucault: Ethics, Subjectivity and Truth*, New York: The New Press, 1994, pp. 76–100.

The Order of Things: an Archaeology of Human Sciences, New York: Pantheon, 1970.

Security, Territory, Population: Lectures at the Collège de France, New York: St Martin's Press, 2009.

Francis, Martin, 'Tears, Tantrums and Bared Teeth: the Emotional Economy of Three Conservative Prime Ministers, 1951–1963', in: *Journal of British Studies* 41:3(2002), pp. 354–87.

Freeden, Michael, 'Conceptual History, Ideology and Language', in: Willibald Steinmetz, Michael Freeden and Javier Fernández-Sebastián (eds.), *Conceptual History in the European Space*, Oxford: Berghahn Books, 2017, pp. 118–38.

The Political Theory of Political Thinking: the Anatomy of a Practice, Oxford: Oxford University Press, 2013.

Freedman, Estelle, *No Turning Back: the History of Feminism and the Future of Women*, New York: Random House, 2002.

Freeman, Edward Augustus, 'On the Study of History', in: *Fortnightly Review* 35 (1881), pp. 319–39.

Frevert, Ute, 'Comment: History of Emotions', in: Marek Tamm and Peter Burke (eds.), *Debating New Approaches to History*, London: Bloomsbury 2019, pp. 202–8.

Emotions in History: Lost and Found, Budapest: Central European University Press, 2001.

Men of Honour: a Cultural History of the Duel, Oxford: Blackwell, 1995.

Frevert, Ute (ed.), *Emotional Lexicons: Continuity and Change in the Vocabulary of Feeling, 1700–2000*, Oxford: Oxford University Press, 2014.

Friese, Heidrun (ed.), *Identities: Time, Difference and Boundaries*, Oxford: Berghahn Books, 2002.

Fukuyama, Francis, *Identity: Contemporary Identity Politics and the Struggle for Recognition*, New York: Profile Books, 2018.

Furet, François, *Interpreting the French Revolution*, Cambridge: Cambridge University Press, 1981.

Furet, François, and Mona Ozouf (eds.), *A Critical Dictionary of the French Revolution*, Cambridge, MA: Harvard University Press, 1989.

Gallagher, Catherine, and Thomas Laqueur (eds.), *The Making of the Modern Body: Sexuality and Society in the Nineteenth Century*, Berkeley: University of California Press, 1987.

Gardner, James B., and Paula Hamilton (eds.), *The Oxford Handbook of Public History*, Oxford: Oxford University Press, 2017.

Gardner, Sarah E., 'What We Talk about When We Talk about Confederate Monuments', in:*Origins: Current Events in Historical Perspectives* 11:5 (2018), http://origins.osu.edu/article/what-we-talk-about-when-we-talk-about-confederate-monuments [accessed 24 August 2019].

Garner, Karen, *Women and Gender in International History: Theory and Practice*, London: Bloomsbury, 2018.

Gaskell, Ivan, 'History of Things', in: Marek Tamm and Peter Burke (eds.), *Debating New Approaches to History*, London: Bloomsbury, 2019, pp. 217–31.

Gayle, Curtis Anderson, 'The Importance and Legacy of Marxist History in Japan', in: Q. Edward Wang and Georg G. Iggers (eds.), *Marxist Historiographies: a Global Perspective*, London: Routledge, 2016, pp. 174–90.

Gazi, Effi, *Scientific National History: the Greek Case in Comparative Perspective (1850–1920)*, Bern: Peter Lang, 2000.

'Theorizing and Practising "Scientific" History in South-Eastern Europe: Spyridon Lambros and Nicolae Iorga', in: Stefan Berger and Chris Lorenz (eds.),*Nationalizing the Past: Historians as Nation-Builders in Modern Europe*, Basingstoke: Palgrave Macmillan, 2010, pp. 192–208.

Geary, Christraud M., *In and out of Focus: Images from Central Africa*, London: Philip Wilson, 2002.

Geary, Patrick J., and Gábor Klaniczay (eds.), *Manufacturing the Middle Ages: Entangled History of Medievalism in Nineteenth-Century Europe*, Leiden: Brill, 2013.

Gebauer, Gunter, and Christoph Wulf, *Mimesis: Culture, Art, Society*, Berkeley: University of California Press, 1995.

Geertz, Clifford, 'Deep Play: Notes on the Balinese Cock-Fight', re-published in: Alan Dundes (ed.), *The Cock-Fight: a Case Book*, Madison: University of Wisconsin Press, 1994, pp. 94–132.

The Interpretation of Cultures, New York: Basic Books, 1973.

Negara: the Theatre State in Nineteenth-Century Bali, Princeton: Princeton University Press, 1980.

Gehmacher, Johanna , 'Invisible Transfers: Translation as a Crucial Practice in Transnational Women's Movements around 1900', in: *Bulletin of the German Historical Institute London* 41:2 (2019), pp. 3–44.

Gemie, Sharif, 'France and the Val d'Aran: Politics and Nationhood on the Pyrenean Border, 1800–25', in: *European History Quarterly* 28 (1998), pp. 311–43.

Gentile, Emilio, *Politics as Religion*, Princeton: Princeton University Press, 2006.

Gentile, Patrizia, and Jane Nicholas (eds.), *Contesting Bodies and Nation in Canadian History*, Toronto: University of Toronto Press, 2013.

Gerhards, Thomas, *Heinrich von Treitschke: Wirkung und Wahrnehmung eines Historikers im 19. und 20. Jahrhundert*, Paderborn: Schöningh, 2013.

Geroulanos, Stefanos, and Todd Meyers, *The Human Body in the Age of Catastrophe: Brittleness, Integration, Science, and the Great War*, Chicago: University of Chicago Press, 2018.

Gerritsen, Anne, and Giorgio Riello, 'History and Material Culture', in: Stefan Berger, Heiko Feldner and Kevin Passmore (eds.), *Writing History: Theory and Practice*, 3rd edn, London: Bloomsbury, 2020, pp. 273–91.

'Introduction', in Anne Gerritsen and Giorgio Riello (eds.), *Writing Material Culture History*, London: Bloomsbury, 2015, pp. 1–14.

Gerson, Stéphane (ed.), *France in the World: a New Global History*, New York: Other Press, 2019. (originally published in French and edited by Patrick Boucheron in 2017).

Geulen, Christian, 'Plädoyer für eine Geschichte der Grundbegriffe des 20. Jahrhunderts', in: *Zeithistorische Forschungen/Studies in Contemporary History* 7 (2010), pp. 79–97.

Geyer, Michael, and Charles Bright, 'World History in a Global Age', in: *American Historical Review* 100:4 (1995), pp. 1034–60.

Ghobrial, John-Paul (ed.), *Global History and Microhistory, Past and Present* supplement 14, Oxford: Oxford University Press, 2019.

Gildea, Robert, *Empires of the Mind: the Colonial Past and the Politics of the Present*, Cambridge: Cambridge University Press, 2019.

The Past in French History, New Haven: Yale University Press, 1996.

Gilman, Sander L., *The Jew's Body*, London: Routledge, 1991.

Gilroy, Paul, *After Empire: Melancholia or Convivial Culture*, London: Routledge, 2004.

Against Race: Imagining Political Culture beyond the Color Line, Cambridge, MA: Harvard University Press, 2000.

The Black Atlantic: Modernity and Double Consciousness, London: Verso, 1993.

Postcolonial Melancholia, New York: Columbia University Press, 2005.

Gimeno-Martinez, Javier, *Design and National Identity*, London: Bloomsbury, 2016.

Ginzburg, Carlo, *The Cheese and the Worms: the Cosmos of a Sixteenth-Century Miller*, Baltimore: Johns Hopkins University Press, 1980 (originally published in Italian in 1976).

Ginzburg, Carlo, and Bruce Lincoln, *Old Thiess: a Livonian Werewolf: a Classic Case in Comparative Perspective*, Chicago: University of Chicago Press, 2020.

Glassie, Henry H., *Material Culture*, Bloomington: Indiana University Press, 1999.

Gleason, Philip, 'Pluralism and Assimilation: a Conceptual History', in: John Edwards (ed.), *Linguistic Minorities, Policies and Pluralism*, London: Academic Press, 1984, pp. 221–58.

Gluck, Carol, *Thinking with the Past: the Japanese and Modern History*, New York; Columbia University Press, 2017.

Godby, Michael , 'The Photograph Album of an Unknown American Missionary in Natal, c. 1930: the Good News and the Bad', in: *South African Historical Journal* 61:2(2009), pp. 357–71.

Godfrey, Sima, 'Alain Corbin: Making Sense of French History', in: *French Historical Studies* 25:2 (2002), pp. 381–98.

Goldberg, David Theo, *Racial Subjects: Writing on Race in America*, New York: Routledge, 1997.

Goldman, Lawrence, *The Life of R. H. Tawney: Socialism and History*, London: Bloomsbury, 2013.

Goldschmidt, Nils, and Matthias Störring, 'Gustav Schmoller: a Socialist of the Chair', in: Stefan Berger, Ludger Pries and Manfred Wannöffel (eds.), *The Palgrave Handbook of Workers' Participation at Plant Level*, Basingstoke: Palgrave Macmillan, 2019, pp. 91–112.

Goldstein, Jan (ed.), *Foucault and the Writing of History*, Oxford: Blackwell, 1994.

Goldstein, Joshua, *War and Gender: How Gender Shapes the War System and Vice Versa*, Cambride: Cambridge University Press, 2001.

Goldstein, Laurence (ed.), *The Male Body: Features, Destinies, Exposures*, Ann Arbor: University of Michigan Press, 1994.

Goltermann, Svenja, 'Exercise and Perfection: Embodying the Nation in Ninteenth-Century Germany, in: *European Review of History* 11:3 (2004), pp. 333–46.

Gombrich, Ernst H., *Aby Warburg: an Intellectual Biography*, Chicago: University of Chicago Press, 1986.

Goody, Jack, *The Oriental, the Ancient and the Primitive: Systems of Marriage and the Family in Pre-Industrial Societies of Eurasia*, Cambridge: Cambridge University Press, 1990.

Gordon, David M., Richard C. Edwards and Michael Reich, *Segmented Work, Divided Workers: the Historical Transformation of Labor in the United States*, Cambridge, MA: Harvard University Press, 1982.

Gorman, John, *Banner Bright: an Illustrated History of Trade Union Banners*, London: Scorpion, 1986.

Gossmann, Lionel, *Basel in the Age of Burckhardt: a Study in Unseasonable Ideas*, Chicago: University of Chicago Press, 2000.

Grafton, Anthony, *The Footnote: a Curious History*, Cambridge, MA: Harvard University Press, 1999.

'The Power of Ideas', in: Ulinka Rublack (ed.),*A Concise Companion to History*, Oxford: Oxford University Press, 2011, pp. 355–79.

Green, Anna, *Cultural History*, Basingstoke: Palgrave Macmillan, 2008.

Green, James, *Taking History to Heart: the Power of the Past in Building Social Movements*, Amherst: University of Massachusetts Press, 2000.

Greenfeld, Liah, *Nationalism: Five Roads to Modernity*, Cambridge, MA: Harvard University Press, 1992.

Greig, Hannah, Jane Hamlett and Leonie Hannan, 'Introduction: Gender and Material Culture', in: Hannah Greig, Jane Hamlett and Leonie Hannan (eds.), *Gender and Material Culture in Britain since 1600*, Basingstoke: Palgrave Macmillan, 2015, pp. 1–15.

Grell, Chantal, *L'histoire entre erudition et philosophie: étude sur la conaissance historique à l'âge des Lumières*, Paris: Presses Universitaires de France, 1993.

Grigsby, Darcy Grimaldo, 'Revolutionary Sons, White Fathers and Creole Difference: Guillaume Guillon-Lethière's *Oath of the Ancestors* (1822)', in: Vanessa R. Schwartz and Jeannene M. Przyblyski (eds.), *The Nineteenth-Century Visual Culture Readers*, London: Routledge, 2004, pp. 249–61.

Grosfoguel, Ramón, *Colonial Subjects: Puerto Ricans in a Global Perspective*, Berkeley: University of California Press, 2003.

Gross, Jan, *Neighbors: the Destruction of the Jewish Community in Jedwabne, Poland*, Princeton: Princeton University Press, 2001.

Grossberg, Lawrence, 'History, Politics and Postmodernism: Stuart Hall and Cultural Studies', in: *Journal of Communication Enquiry* 10:2 (1986), pp. 61–77.

Grothe, Ewald, 'Otto Hintze: "Staatenbildung und Verfassungsentwicklung"', in: Detlef Lehnert (ed.), *Verfassungsdenker: Deutschland und Österreich, 1870–1970*, Berlin: Metropol, 2017, pp. 47–62.

Gruzinski, Serge, *Images at War: Mexico from Columbus to Blade Runner (1492–2019)*, Durham, NC: Duke University Press, 2001.

Gueye, Omar, 'African History and Global History: Revisiting Paradigms', in: Sven Beckert and Dominic Sachsenmaier (eds.), *Global History Globally: Research and Practice around the World*, London: Bloomsbury, 2018, pp. 83–108.

Guha, Ranajit, *Dominance without Hegemony: History and Power in Colonial India*, Cambridge, MA: Harvard University Press, 1997.

Guha, Rajajit, and Gayatri C. Spivak (eds.), *Selected Subaltern Studies*, Oxford: Oxford University Press, 1988.

Guichard, C., 'Connoisseurship and Artistic Experience: London and Paris, 1600–1800', in: C. Rabier (ed.), *Fields of Expertise: a Comparative History of Expert Procedures in Paris and London, 1600 to the Present*, Cambridge: Cambridge Scholars, 2007, pp. 173–91.

Guldi, Jo, and David Armitage, *The History Manifesto*, Cambridge: Cambridge University Press, 2014.

Gumbrecht, Hans-Ulrich, 'Presence Achieved in Language (with Special Attention Given to the Presence of the Past', in:*History and Theory* 45 (2006), pp. 317–27.

Gust, Onni, 'The Brexit Syllabus: British History for Brexiteers', 5 Sept. 2016, in: *History Workshop Journal*; www.historyworkshop.org.uk/the-brexit-syllabus-british-history-for-brexiteers/ [accessed 24 August 2019].

Gutman, Yifat, and Jenny Wuestenberg (eds.), *Handbook on Memory Activism*, Oxford: Blackwell, 2022.

Gwinn, Ian, '"A Different Kind of History is Possible": the History Workshop Movement and the Politics of British and West German Historical Practice', PhD dissertation, University of Liverpool, 2016.

'"History Should Become Common Property": Raphael Samuel, History Workshop, and the Practice of Socialist History, 1966–1980', in: *Socialist History* 51 (2017), pp. 96–117.

Haar, Ingo, and Michael Fahlbusch (eds.), *German Scholars and Ethnic Cleansing, 1920–1945*, Oxford: Berghahn Books, 2005.

Habermas, Jürgen, *Anthropologie* [1958], in: Jürgen Habermas (ed.), *Kultur und Kritik. Verstreute Aufsätze*, Frankfurt am Main: Suhrkamp, 1973, pp. 89–111.

The Structural Transformation of the Public Sphere: an Inquiry into a Category of Bourgeois Society, Cambridge, MA: MIT Press, 1989.

Hacisalihoglu Mehmet, 'Borders, Maps and Censuses: the Politicization of Geography and Statistics in the Multiethnic Ottoman Empire', in: Jörn Leonhard and Ulrike von Hirschhausen (eds.), *Comparing Empires: Encounters and Transfers in the Long Nineteenth Century*, Göttingen: Vandenhoeck and Ruprecht, 2011, pp. 171–210.

Hacking, Ian, *The Social Construction of What?*, Cambridge, MA: Harvard University Press, 2000.

Hadler, Frank, 'Der Magna-Moravia Mythos zwischen Geschichtsschreibung und Politik im 19. und 20. Jahrhundert', in: Eva Behring, Ludwig Richter and Wolfgang F. Schwarz (eds.), *Geschichtliche Mythen in den Literaturen und Kulturen Ostmittel- und Südosteuropas*, Stuttgart: Franz Steiner, 1999, pp. 275–92.

Hagemann, Karen, and Stefanie Schüler-Springorum (eds.), *Home/Front: the Military, War and Gender in Twentieth-Century Germany*, Oxford: Berg, 2002.

Hagemann, Karen, Gisela Mettele and Jane Rendall (eds.), *Gender, War and Politics: Transatlantic Perspectives, 1775–1830*, Basingstoke: Palgrave Macmillan, 2010.

Halbwachs, Maurice, *On Collective Memory*, trans. Lewis A. Koser, Chicago: University of Chicago Press, 1992.

Hall, Catherine, *Civilizing Subjects: Metropole and Colony in the English Imagination, 1830–1867*, Chicago: University of Chicago Press, 2002.

'Edward Said', in: *History Workshop Journal* 57:1 (2004), 235–43.

Keith McClelland and Jane Rendall, Defining the Victorian Nation: Class, Race, Gender and the Reform Act of 1867, Cambridge: Cambridge University Press, 2000.

Macaulay and Son: Architects of Imperial Britain, New Haven: Yale University Press, 2012.

White, Male and Middle-Class: Explorations in Feminism and History, Oxford: Oxford University Press, 1992.

Hall, Catherine (ed.), *Cultures of Empire: a Reader: Colonizers in Britain and the Empire in the Nineteenth and Twentieth Century*, Manchester: Manchester University Press, 2000.

Hall, Catherine, and Sonya Rose (eds.), *At Home with the Empire: Metropolitan Culture and the Imperial World*, Cambridge: Cambridge University Press, 2006.

Hall, Stuart, 'Encoding/Decoding', in: S. Hall, D. Hobson, A. Lowe and P. Willis (eds.), *Culture, Media, Language: Working Papers in Cultural Studies, 1972–1979*, London: Hutchinson, 1980, pp. 128–38.

'Introduction: Who Needs Identity?', in: Stuart Hall and Paul du Gay (eds.), *Questions of Cultural Identity*, London: Sage, 1996, pp. 1–17.

'The Question of Cultural Identity', in: Stuart Hall, David Held and Anthony McGrew (eds.), *Modernity and its Futures*, Cambridge: Polity Press, 1992, pp. 274–316.

'Raphael Samuel: 1934–96', in: *New Left Review* 1:221 (January–February 1997); https://newleftreview.org/I/221/stuart-hall-raphael-samuel-1934-1996 [accessed 12 February 2019]

Hall, Stuart, and Martin Jaques (eds.), *The Politics of Thatcherism*, London: Lawrence and Wisheart, 1983.

Hamilton, Tracey Chapman, and Mariah Proctor-Tiffany, 'Women and the Circulation of Material Culture: Crossing Boundaries and Connecting Spaces', in: Tracey Chapman Hamilton and Mariah Proctor-Tiffany (eds.), *Moving Women, Moving Objects (400–1500)*, Leiden: Brill, 2019, pp. 1–12.

Hampsher-Monk , Iain, Karen Tilmans and Frank van Vree (eds.), *History of Concepts: Comparative Approaches*, Amsterdam: University of Amsterdam Press, 1998.

Hanaoka, Mimi, *Authority and Identity in Medieval Islamic Historiography: Persian Histories from the Peripheries*, Cambridge: Cambridge University Press, 2016.

Harlan, David, *The Degradation of American History*, Chicago: University of Chicago Press, 1997.

Harré, R. (ed.), *The Social Construction of Emotions*, Oxford: Blackwell, 1986.

Hartmann, Christian, Johannes Hürter and Ulrike Jureit (eds.), *Verbrechen der Wehrmacht: Bilanz einer Debatte*, Munich: C. H. Beck, 2005.

Hartmann, Wolfram, 'Performing Gender, Staging Colonialism: Camping it up/Acting it out in Ovamboland', in: Wolfram Hartmann, Jeremy Silvester and Patricia Hayes (eds.), *The Colonising Camera: Photographs in the Making of Namibian History*, Cape Town: University of Cape Town Press, 1998, pp. 156–63.

Hartmann, Wolfram, Jeremy Silvester and Patricia Hayes (eds.), *The Colonising Camera: Photographs in the Making of Namibian History*, Cape Town: University of Cape Town Press, 1998.

Harvey, John L., 'History and the Social Sciences', in: Stefan Berger, Heiko Feldner and Kevin Passmore (eds.), *Writing History: Theory and Practice*, 3rd edn, London: Bloomsbury, 2020, pp. 86–112.

Harvey, Karen (ed.), *History and Material Culture*, London: Routledge, 2009.

Haskell, Francis, *History and its Images: Art and the Interpretation of the Past*, Yale: Yale University Press, 1993.

Haupt, Heinz-Gerhard, and Jürgen Kocka, 'Preface', in: Heinz-Gerhard Haupt and Jürgen Kocka (eds.), *Comparative and Transnational History: Central European Approaches and New Perspectives*, Oxford: Berghahn Books, 2009, pp. vii–viii.

Hay, Denys, 'The Place of Hans Baron in Renaissance Studies', in: Anthony Molho and John A. Tedeschi (eds.), *Renaissance: Studies in Honour of Hans Baron*, Florence: G. C. Sansoni, 1971, pp. 11–29.

Hayes, Nelson E., and Tanya Hayes (eds.), *Claude Lévi-Strauss: the Anthropologist as Hero*, Cambridge, MA: Harvard University Press, 1970.

Heerma van Voss, Lex, and Marcel van der Linden (eds.), *Class and Other Identities: Gender, Religion and Ethnicity in the Writing of European Labour History*, Oxford: Berghahn Books, 2002.

Heerma van Voss, Lex, Patrick Pasture and Jan de Maeyer (eds.), *Between Cross and Class: Comparative Histories of Christian Labour in Europe, 1840–2000*, Bern: Peter Lang, 2005.

Heinich, Nathalie, *De la visibilité: excellence et singularité en régime médiatheque*, Paris: Gallimard, 2012.

Heng, Geraldine, *The Invention of Race in the European Middle Ages*, Cambridge: Cambridge University Press, 2018.

Hentschke, Felicitas, and James Williams (eds.), *To Be at Home: House, Work, and Self in the Modern World*, Berlin: De Gruyter, 2018.

Hermann, Gretchen M., 'Gift or Commodity: What Changes Hands in the US Garage Sale?', in: Daniel Miller (ed.), *Consumption: Critical Concepts in the Social Sciences, vol. II: the History and Regional Development of Consumption*, London: Routledge, 2001, pp. 72–101.

Herminghouse, Patricia, and Magda Müller (eds.), *Gender and Germanness: Cultural Production of Nations*, Oxford: Berghahn Books, 1997.

Herren, Madeleine, Martin Rüsch and Christiane Sibille (eds.), *Transcultural History: Theories, Methods, Sources*, Berlin: Springer, 2012.

Herrmann, Irène, and Franziska Metzger, 'A Truculent Revenge: the Clergy and the Writing of National History', in: Ilaria Porciani and Jo Tollebeek (eds.), *Setting the Standards: Institutions, Networks and Communities of National Historiography*, Basingstoke: Palgrave Macmillan, 2012, pp. 313–29.

Herzog, Dagmar, *Sexuality in Europe: a Twentieth-Century History*, Cambridge: Cambridge University Press, 2011.

Hexter, Jack H., 'Fernand Braudel and the Monde Braudelien', in: *Journal of Modern History* 44 (1972), pp. 480–539.

Heyer, Anne, 'The Making of the Democratic Party: the Emergence of the Party Organizations of the German Social Democratic Workers' Party, the British National Liberal Federation and the Dutch Anti-Revolutionary Party, 1860s–1880s', PHD thesis, University of Leiden, 2018.

Heywood,Ian, and Barry Sandywell (eds.), *The Handbook of Visual Culture*, London: Bloomsbury, 2011.

Heywood, Leslie, and Jennifer Drake (eds.), *Third Wave Agenda: Being Feminist, Doing Feminism*, Minneapolis: University of Minnesota Press, 1997.

Higonnet, Margaret Randolph, Jane Jenson, Sonya Michel and Margaret Collins Wietz (eds.), *Behind the Lines: Gender and the Two World Wars*, New Haven: Yale University Press,1987.

Hill, Alette Olin, Boyd H. Hill, William H. Sewell and Sylvia L. Thruppe, 'Marc Bloch and Comparative History', in: *American Historical Review* 85 (1980), pp. 828–57.

Hill, Christopher L., 'Conceptual Universalization in the Transnational Nineteenth Century', in: Samuel Moyn and Andrew Sartori (eds.), *Global Intellectual History*, New York: Columbia University Press, 2013, pp. 134–58.

National History and the World of Nations: Capital, State and the Rhetoric of History in Japan, France and the United States, Durham, NC: Duke University Press, 2008.

Hilton, Boyd, *The Age of Atonement: the Influence of Evangelicalism on Social and Economic Thought, 1795–1865*, Oxford, Oxford University Press, 1988.

Hinchliffe, Steven, *Geographies of Nature: Societies, Environments, Ecologies*, London: Sage, 2007.

Hirsch, Marianne, *Family Frames: Photography, Narrative and Postmemory*, Cambridge, MA: Harvard University Prss, 1997.

Historische Anthropologie, 'Editorial', in: *Historische Anthropologie* 1:1 (1993), pp. 1–3.

History News Network, 'Black Historians at the OAH Risked the Charge of Presentism to Show the Links between Racial Violence in 1917 and Black Lives Matter Today', in: History News Network, 10 May 2017, https://historynewsnetwork.org/article/165903 [accessed 2 April 2020].

History and Theory, 'Forum: After Narrativism', in: *History and Theory* 54:2 (2015), pp. 153–309.

History Workshop Journal, 'Editorial', in: History Workshop Journal 1 (1965), pp. 1–3.

Hitzer, Bettina, and Thomas Welskopp, 'Die "Bielefelder Schule" der westdeutschen Sozialgeschichte: Karriere eines geplanten Paradigmas?', in: Bettina Hitzer and Thomas Welskopp (eds.), *Die Bielefelder*

Sozialgeschichte. Klassische Texte zu einem geschichtswissenschaftlichen Programm und seinen Kontroversen, Bielefeld:Transcript, 2010, pp. 13–32.

Ho Tai, Huet Tam, 'Remembered Realms: Pierre Nora and French National Memory', in: *American Historical Review* 106:3 (2001), pp. 906–22.

Hobsbawm, Eric, 'The Forward March of Labour Halted', in : *Marxism Today* (September 1978), pp. 279–86; http://banmarchive.org.uk/collections/mt/pdf/78_09_hobsbawm.pdf [accessed 12 February 2019].

'From Social History to the History of Society', in: *Daedalus* 100 (1971), pp. 20–45.

Interesting Times: a Twentieth-Century Life, New York: Pantheon, 2007.

Hobsbawm, Eric, and Terence Ranger (eds.), *The Invention of Tradition*, Cambridge: Cambridge University Press, 1983.

Hodder, Ian, *The Archaeological Process: an Introduction*, Oxford: Blackwell, 1999.

Hodgetts, James Frederick, *Greater England: Being a Brief Historical Sketch of the Various Possessions of Her Majesty, the Empress Queen, in Europe, Asia, Africa, America and Oceania*, London: Hatchards, 1887.

Hoffer, Peter C., *The Historians' Paradox: the Study of History in our Time*, New York: New York University Press, 2008.

Hoggart, Richard, *The Uses of Literacy*, Harmondsworth: Penguin, 1957.

Hollinger, David A., 'The Historian's Use of the United States and Vice Versa', in: Thomas Bender (ed.), *Rethinking American History in a Global Age*, Berkeley: University of California Press, 2002, pp. 381–96.

Hölscher, Lucian, *Die Entdeckung der Zukunft*, 2nd edn, Göttingen: Wallstein, 2016.

'Konfessionspolitik in Deutschland zwischen Glaubensstreit und Koexistenz', in Lucian Hölscher (ed.), *Baupläne der sichtbaren Kirche: sprachliche Konzepte religiöser Vergemeinschaftung in Europa*, Göttingen: Wallstein, 2007, pp. 11–52.

'Religion im Wandel: von Begriffen des religiösen Wandels zum Wandel religiöser Begriffe', in: Wilhelm Gräb (ed.), *Religion als Thema der Theologie: Geschichte, Standpunkte und Perspektiven der theologischen Religionskritik und Religionsbegründung*, Gütersloh: Gütersloher Verlagshaus, 1999, pp. 45–62.

'Theoretische Grundlagen der historischen Zukunftsforschung', in: Hölscher (ed.), *Die Zukunft des 20. Jahrhunderts. Dimensionen einer historischen Zukunftsforschung*, Frankfurt am Main: Campus, 2017, pp. 7–38.

Hölscher, Lucian (ed.), *Baupläne der sichtbaren Kirche: sprachliche Konzepte religiöser Vergemeinschaftung in Europa*, Göttingen: Wallstein, 2007.

Horn, Eva, and Hannes Bergthaller, *The Anthropocene: Key Issues for the Humanities*, London: Routledge, 2019.

Horn, Gerd-Rainer, '1968: a Social Movement Sui Generis', in: Stefan Berger and Holger Nehring (eds.), *The History of Social Movements in Global Perspective*, Basingstoke: Palgrave Macmillan, 2017, pp. 515–42.

Howe, Stephen (ed.), *The New Imperial History Reader*, London: Routledge, 2010.

Howells, Richard, and Joaquim Negreiros (eds.), *Visual Culture*, Cambridge: Polity Press, 2012.

Hoxie, Frederick A. (ed.), *The Oxford Handbook of American Indian History*, Oxford: Oxford University Press, 2016.

Hroch, Miroslav, 'Regional Memory: the Role of History in (Re) Constructing Regional Identity', in: Steven G. Ellis, Raingard Esser, Jean-François Berdah and Miloš Řezník (eds.), *Frontiers, Regions and Identities in Europe*, Pisa: Pisa University Press, 2009, pp. 1–15.

Hsu, Madeline Y., 'Transnationalism and Asian-American Studies as Migration-Centred Project', in: *Journal of Asian American Studies* 11:2 (2008), pp. 185–97.

Hudson, Pat, 'Economic History', in: Stefan Berger, Heiko Feldner and Kevin Passmore (eds.), *Writing History: Theory and Practice*, 3rd edn, London: Bloomsbury, 2020, pp. 386–404.

Hughes-Warrington, Marnie, 'Writing World History', in: David Christian (ed.), *The Cambridge World History, vol. I*, Cambridge: Cambridge University Press, 2015, pp. 41–55

Huizinga, Johann, *The Autumn of the Middles Ages*, Chicago: University of Chicago Press, 1996.

The Waning of the Middle Ages: a Study of the Forms of Life, Thought and Art in France and the Netherlands in the 14th and 15th Centuries, Harmondsworth: Penguin, 1965.

Hull, Isabel V., *Sexuality, State and Civil Society in Germany, 1700–1815*, Ithaca, NY: Cornell University Press, 1996.

Hunt, Lynn, 'Introduction', in: Lynn Hunt (ed.), *The New Cultural History*, Berkeley: University of California Press, 1989, pp. 1–22.

Politics, Culture and Class in the French Revolution, Oakland: University of California Press, 1984.

Writing History in the Global Era, New York: Norton, 2014.

Hunt, Lynn (ed.), *The New Cultural History*, Berkeley: University of California Press, 1989.

Hutton, Patrick, 'The History of Mentalities: the New Map of Cultural History', in: *History and Theory* 20 (1981), pp. 237–59

Philippe Ariès and the Politics of French Cultural History, Boston: University of Massachusetts Press, 2004.

'Recent Scholarship on Memory and History', in: *History Teacher* 33:4 (2000), pp. 533–48.

Huyssen, Andreas, *Present Pasts: Urban Palimpsests and the Politics of Memory*, Stanford: Stanford University Press, 2003.

'The Voids of Berlin', in: *Critical Inquiry* 24:1 (1997), pp. 57–81.

Hyslop, Jonathan, 'The Imperial Working Class Makes itself "White": White Labourism in Britain, Australia and South Africa before the First World War', in: *Journal of Historical Sociology* 12 (1999), pp. 398–421.

Idrizi, Idrit, 'Between Subordination and Symbiosis: Historians' Relationship with Political Power in Communist Albania', in: *European History Quarterly* 50:1 (2020), pp. 66–87.

Ifversen, Jan, 'A Guided Tour into the European Question', in: Marjet Brolsma, Robin de Bruin and Matthijas Lok (eds.), *Eurocentrism in European History and Memory*, Amsterdam: Amsterdam University Press, 2019, pp. 195–222.

'Myth in the Writing of European History', in: Stefan Berger and Chris Lorenz (eds.), *Nationalizing the Past: Historians as Nation-Builders in Modern Europe*, Basingstoke: Palgrave Macmillan, 2010, pp. 452–79.

Iggers, Georg G., *The German Conception of History: the National Tradition of Historical Thought from Herder to the Present*, rev. edn, Middletown, CT: Wesleyan University Press, 1983.

The Theory and Practice of History: Leopold von Ranke, London: Routledge, 2011.

Iggers, Georg, and Wilma Iggers, *Two Lives in Uncertain Times: Facing the Challenges of the Twentieth Century as Scholars and Citizens*, Oxford: Berghahn Books, 2006.

Ihalainen, Pasi, *The Springs of Democracy: National and Transnational Debates on Constitutional Reform in the British, German, Swedish and Finnish Parliaments, 1917–1919*, Helsinki: Finnish Literature Society, 2017.

Inglebert, Hervé, *Le monde, l'histoire: essai sur les histoires universelles*, Paris: Presses Universitaires de France, 2014.

Innes, Joanna, and Mark Philp (eds.), *Re-imagining Democracy in the Age of Revolutions: America, France, Britain, Ireland, 1750–1850*, Oxford: Oxford University Press, 2013.

Iordachi, Constantin, and Péter Apor (eds.), *Occupation and Communism in East European Museums: Re-Visualizing the Recent Past*, London: Bloomsbury, 2021.

Iriye, Akira, *Global and Transnational History: the Past, Present and Future*, Basingstoke: Palgrave Macmillan, 2013.

Iriye, Akira, and Jürgen Osterhammel (eds.), *A History of the World*, 6 vols., Cambridge, MA: Harvard University Press, 2012– 20.

Iriye, Akira, and Pierre-Yves Saunier (eds.), *The Palgrave Dictionary of Transnational History*, Basingstoke: Palgrave Macmillan, 2009.

Isaac, Joel, and Duncan Bell (eds.), *Uncertain Empire: American History and the Idea of the Cold War*, Oxford: Oxford University Press, 2015.

Isaacs, Rhys, *The Transformation of Virginia, 1740–1790*, Chapel Hill: University of North Carolina Press, 1982.

Izenberg, Gerald, *Identity: the Necessity of a Modern Idea*, Philadelphia: University of Pennsylvania Press, 2016.

Jacques, T. Carlos, 'Whence Does the Critic Speak? A Study of Foucault's Genealogy', in: Barry Smart (ed.), *Michel Foucault: Critical Assessments, vol. III*, London: Routledge, 1997, pp. 97–112.

Jalava, Marja, and Bo Stråth , 'Scandinavia/Norden', in: Diana Mishkova and Balázs Trencsényi (eds.), *European Regions and Boundaries: a Conceptual History*, Oxford: Berghahn Books, 2017, pp. 36–56.

James, C. L. R., *The Black Jacobins*, London: Secker and Warburg, 1938.

James, Samuel, 'J. G. A. Pocock and the Idea of the "Cambridge School" in the History of Political Thought', in: *History of European Ideas* 45:1 (2019), pp. 83–98.

Janney, Caroline E., *Remembering the Civil War: Reunion and the Limits of Reconciliation*, Chapel Hill: University of North Carolina Press, 2013.

Janse, Maartje, 'A Dangerous Type of Politics? Politics and Religion in Early Mass Organisations: the Anglo-American World, c. 1830', in: Joost Augusteijn, Patrick Dassen and Maartje Janse (eds.), *Political Religion beyond Totalitarianism: the Sacralization of Politics in the Age of Democracy*, Basingstoke: Palgrave Macmillan, 2013, pp. 55–76.

Janz, Oliver, and Daniel Schönpflug, 'Introduction', in: Oliver Janz and Daniel Schönpflug (eds.), *Gender History in a Transnational Perspective*, Oxford: Berghahn Books, 2014, pp. 1–24.

Jay, Martin , 'Scopic Regimes of Modernity Revisited', in: Ian Heywood and Barry Sandywell (eds.), *The Handbook of Visual Culture*, London: Bloomsbury, 2011, pp. 102–13.

Jenkins, Paul, 'The Earliest Generation of Missionary Photographers in West Africa and the Portrayal of Indigenous People and Culture', in: *History in Africa* 20 (1993), pp. 89–118.

Jenkins, Richard, *Pierre Bourdieu*, rev. edn, London: Routledge, 2002.

Jenks, Chris, 'The Centrality of the Eye in Western Culture', in: Chris Jenks (ed.), *Visual Culture*, London: Routledge, 1995, pp. 1–25.

Joas, Hans, and Peter Vogt (eds.), *Begriffene Geschichte. Beiträge zum Werk Reinhart Kosellecks*, Frankfurt am Main: Suhrkamp, 2011.

Jones, Gareth Stedman, *Languages of Class: Studies in English Working-Class History, 1832–1982*, Cambridge: Cambridge University Press, 1983.

Jones, Jacqueline, *Labor of Love, Labor of Sorrow: Black Women, Work and the Family from Slavery to the Present*, New York: Basic Books, 1985.

Jordheim, Helge, 'The Nature of Civilization: the Semantics of Civilization and Civility in Scandinavia', in: Margrit Pernau and Helge Jordheim (eds.), *Civilizing Emotion: Concepts in Nineteenth-Century Asia and Europe*, Oxford:Oxford University Press, 2015, pp. 25–44.

Joyce, Patrick, 'The End of Social History', in: *Social History* 20:1 (1995), pp. 73–91.

'Filing the Raj: Political Technologies of the Imperial British State', in: Patrick Joyce and Tony Bennett (eds.), *Material Powers: Cultural Studies, Histories and the Material Turn*, London: Routledge, 2010, pp. 144–84.

'History and Postmodernism', in: *Past and Present* 133:1 (1991), pp. 204–9.

Visions of the People: Industrial England and the Question of Class, Cambridge: Cambridge University Press, 1991.

'What is the Social in Social History?', in: *Past and Present* 206:1 (2010), pp. 213–48.

Judt, Tony, 'À la recherche du temps perdue', in : *New York Review of Books* 45:19 (1998), pp. 51–8.

'A Clown in Regal Purple: Social History and the Historians', in: *History Workshop Journal* 7 (1979), pp. 66–94.

Post-War: a History of Europe since 1945, London: Heinemann, 2005.

Jureit, Ulrike, 'Die Entdeckung des Zeitzeugen. Faschismus- und Nachkriegserfahrungen im Ruhrgebiet', in: Jürgen Danyel, Jan Holger Kirsch and Martin Sabrow (eds.), *50 Klassiker der Zeitgeschichte*, Göttingen: Vandenhoeck and Ruprecht, 2007, pp. 174–7.

Kaegi, Werner, *Jacob Burckhardt: eine Biographie*, 2 vols., Basel: Schwabe, 1977.

Kaelble, Hartmut, 'Social History of European Integration', in Clemens Wurm (ed.), *Western Europe and Germany: the Beginnings of European Integration, 1945–1960*, Oxford: Berghahn Books, 1995, pp. 219–47.

'Vergleichende Sozialgeschichte im 19. und 20. Jahrhundert. Forschungen europäischer Historiker', in: *Jahrbuch für Wirtschaftsgeschichte* 1 (1993), pp. 173–200.

Kaiwar, Vasant, *The Postcolonial Orient: The Politics of Differences and the Project of Provincialising Europe*, Leiden: Brill, 2014.

Kalb, Don, and Herman Tak (eds.), *Critical Junctions: Anthropology and History Beyond the Cultural Turn*, Oxford: Berghahn Books, 2005.

Kalof, Linda (ed.), *Cultural History of Women*, 6 vols., London: Bloomsbury, 2016.

Kalyvas, Stathis N., *The Logic of Violence in Civil War*, Cambridge, MA: Harvard University Press, 2006.

Kann, Mark E., *A Republic of Men: the American Founders, Gendered Language, and Patriarchal Politics*, New York: New York University Press, 1998.

Kansteiner, Wulf , 'Finding Meaning in Memory: a Methodological Critique of Collective Memory Studies', in: *History and Theory* 41:2 (2002), pp. 179–97.

Kaplan, Thomas Pegelow, 'History and Theory: Writing Modern European Histories after the Linguistic Turn', in: Michael Meng and Adam R. Seipp (eds.), *Modern Germany in Transatlantic Perspective*, Oxford: Berghahn Books, 2017, pp. 21–46.

Kattagoo, Siobhan (ed.), *The Ashgate Companion to Memory Studies*, Farnham: Ashgate, 2015.

Kaye, Harvey J., *The British Marxist Historians*, New York: Palgrave Macmillan, 1988.

'Our Island Story Retold: A. L. Morton and "the People" in History', in: Kaye, *The Education of Desire: Marxists and the Writing of History*, New York: Routledge, 1992, pp. 116–24.

Kean, Hilda, and Paul Ashton, 'Introduction: People and their Pasts and Public History Today', in: Paul Ashton and Hilda Kean (eds.), *People and their Pasts: Public History Today*, Basingstoke: Palgrave Macmillan, 2009, pp. 1–20.

Kelley, Donald, 'What Is Happening to the History of Ideas?', in: *Journal of the History of Ideas* 51:1 (1990), pp. 3–25.

Kelley, Robin D. G., "But a Local Phase of a World Problem": Black History's Global Vision, 1883–1950, in: *Journal of American History* 86:3(1999), pp. 1045–77.

Kelly, Joan, *Women, History, and Theory*, Chicago: University of Chicago Press, 1984.

Kennedy, James C., 'Religion, Nation and European Representations of the Past', in: Stefan Berger and Chris Lorenz (eds.), *The Contested Nation: Ethnicity, Class, Religion and Gender in National Histories*, Basingstoke:Palgrave Macmillan, 2007, pp. 104–34.

Kerber, Linda, 'Separate Spheres, Female Worlds, Woman's Place: the Rhetoric of Women's History', in: *Journal of American History* 75 (1988), pp. 9–39.

Kessler, Joseph A., 'Turanism and Pan-Turanism in Hungary, 1890–1945', PHD thesis, University of California, Berkeley, 1967.

Kessler-Harris, Alice, *In Pursuit of Equity: Women, Men, and the Quest for Economic Citizenship in Twentieth-Century America*, Oxford: Oxford University Press, 2001.

'A Rich and Adventurous Journey: the Transnational Journey of Gender History in the United States', in: *Journal of Women's History* 19:1 (2007), pp. 153–9.

Keymeulen, Sarah, and Jo Tollebeek , *Henri Pirenne, Historian: a Life in Pictures*, Leuven: University of Leuven Press, 2011.

Khanakwa, Pamela, 'Male Circumcision among the Bagisu of Eastern Uganda: Practices and Conceptualisations', in: Axel Fleisch and Rhiannon Stephens (eds.), *Doing Conceptual History in Africa*, Oxford: Berghahn Books, 2016, pp. 115–37.

Kibert, Declan, *Inventing Ireland*, Cambridge, MA: Harvard University Press, 1996.

Kimmel, Michael S., Jeff Hearn and R. W. Connell (eds.), *Handbook of Studies on Men and Masculinities*, London: Sage, 2005.

Kirby, James, 'R. H. Tawney and Christian Social Teaching: *Religion and the Rise of Capitalism* Reconsidered', in: *English Historical Review* 131:551 (2016), pp. 793–822.

Kirk, Neville, *Labour and Socialism in Britain and the USA*, 2 vols., Avebury: Ashgate, 1994.

Klaric, Arlette, 'Gustav Stickley's Designs for the Home: an Activist Aesthetic for the Upwardly Mobile', in: Patricia Johnston (ed.), *Seeing High and Low: Representing Social Conflict in American Visual Culture*, Berkeley: University of California Press, 2006, pp. 177–93.

Kleinberg, Ethan, 'Haunting History: Deconstruction and the Spirit of Revision', in: *History and Theory* 46:4 (2007), pp. 113–43.

Haunting History: For a Deconstructive Approach to the Past, Stanford: Stanford University Press, 2017.

Kleinberg, Ethan, Joan Wallach Scott and Gary Wilder, 'Theses on Theory and History', http://theoryrevolt.com/download/WildOnCollective_Theses-Booklet_EN.pdf, May 2018 [accessed 19 March 2020].

Klose, Fabian, *Human Rights in the Shadow of Colonial Violence: the Wars of Independence in Kenya and Algeria*, Philadelphia: University of Pennsylvania Press, 2013.

Knappett, Carl, and Lambros Malafouris (eds.), *Material Agency: Towards a Non-Anthropocentric Approach*, Boston: Springer, 2008.

Ko, Dorothy, 'Gender', in: Ulinka Rublack (ed.), *A Concise Companion to History*, Oxford: Oxford University Press, 2011, pp. 203–25.

Kocka, Jürgen, *Geschichte und Aufklärung*, Göttingen: Vandenhoeck and Ruprecht, 1989.

'History and the Social Sciences Today', in: Hans Joas and Barbro Klein (eds.), *The Benefit of Broad Horizons: Intellectual and Institutional Preconditions for a Global Social Science*, Leiden: Brill, 2010, pp. 53–67.

Kontler, László, 'Concepts, Contests and Contexts: Conceptual History and the Problem of Translatability', in: Willibald Steinmetz, Michael Freeden, and Javier Fernández-Sebastián (eds.), *Conceptual History in the European Space*, Oxford: Berghahn Books, 2017, pp. 197–211.

Koposov, Nikolay, *Memory Laws, Memory Wars: the Politics of the Past in Europe and Russia*, Cambridge: Cambridge University Press, 2018.

Koselleck, Reinhart, *Futures Past: On the Semantics of Historical Time*, New York: Columbia University Press, 2004.

'Introduction to Hayden White's *Tropics of Discourse*', in: Reinhart Koselleck , *The Practice of Conceptual History: Timing History, Spacing Concepts*, Stanford: Stanford University Press, 2002, pp. 38–44.

The Practice of Conceptual History: Timing History, Spacing Concepts, Stanford: Stanford University Press, 2002.

'A Response to Comments on the *Geschichtliche Grundbegriffe*', in: Hartmut Lehmann and Melvin Richter (eds.), *The Meaning of Historical Terms and Concepts*, Washington, DC: German Historical Institute, 1996, pp. 59–70.

Koshar, Rudy, *From Monuments to Traces: Artefacts of German Memory, 1870–1990*, Berkeley: University of California Press, 2000.

Kozlarek, Oliver, Jörn Rüsen and Ernst Wolff (eds.), *Shaping a Humane World: Civilizations – Axial Times – Modernities – Humanisms*, Bielefeld: Transcript, 2012.

Kracauer, Siegfried, *History: the Last Things before the Last*, Oxford: Oxford University Press, 1969.

Krieger, Leonard, *The German Idea of Freedom: History of a Political Tradition*, Boston: Beacon Press, 1957.

Kuhn, Thomas S., *The Structure of Scientific Revolution*, Chicago: University of Chicago Press, 1962.

Kulczycki, John C., *The Polish Coal Miners' Union and the German Labour Movement in the Ruhr, 1920–1934: National and Social Solidarity*, Oxford: Berghahn Books, 1997.

Kurunmäki, Jussi, Jeppe Nevers and Henk te Velde (eds.), *Democracy in Modern Europe: a Conceptual History*, Oxford: Berghahn Books, 2018.

Kuukkanen, Jouni-Matti, *Post-Narrativist Philosophy of Historiography*, Basingstoke: Palgrave Macmillan, 2015.

La Capra, Dominick, *Rethinking Intellectual History: Texts, Contexts, Language*, Ithaca, NY: Cornell University Press, 1983.

Lacan, Jacques, *Ecrits: a Selection*, New York: Norton, 1977.

Laclau, Ernesto, *Emancipation(s)*, London: Verso, 1996.

Laclau, Ernesto, and Chantal Mouffe, *Hegemony and Socialist Strategy: Towards a Radical Democratic Politics*, London: Verso, 1985.

Ladurie, Emmanuel LeRoy, *Montaillou: Cathars and Catholics in a French Village, 1294–1324*, London: Scholar Press, 1978.

Lahusen, Thomas (ed.), 'Harbin and Manchuria: Place, Space and Identity', special issue of *South Atlantic Quarterly* 99:1 (2000).

Lai, Cheng-Chung, *Braudel's Historiography Reconsidered*, Lanham, MD: University Press of America, 2004.

Lake, Marilyn, 'White Man's Country: the Trans-National History of a National Project', in: *Australian Historical Studies* 34:122 (2003), pp. 346–63.

Lake, Marilyn, and Henry Reynolds, *Drawing the Global Colour Line: White Men's Countries and the International Challenge of Racial Equality*, Cambridge: Cambridge University Press, 2008.

Lamuniere, Michelle, *You Look Beautiful Like That: the Portrait Photographs of Seydou Keïta and Malick Sidibé*, New Haven: Yale University Press, 2001.

Landes, Joan B., *Visualizing the Nation: Gender, Representation and Revolution in Eighteenth Century France*, Ithaca, NY: Cornell University Press, 2001.

Langewiesche, Dieter, *Der gewaltsame Lehrer. Europas Kriege in der Moderne*, Munich: C. H. Beck, 2019.

Lapore, Jill, *The Whites of their Eyes: the Tea Party's Revolution and the Battle over American History*, Princeton: Princeton University Press, 2010.

Laqueur, Thomas, *Making Sex: Bodies and Gender from the Greeks to Freud*, Cambridge, MA: Harvard University Press, 1990.

Laslett, Peter (ed.), *John Locke's Two Treatises of Government: a Critical Edition with an Introduction and Apparatus Criticus*, Cambridge: Cambridge University Press, 1960.

Latour, Bruno, *The Pasteurisation of France*, Cambridge, MA: Harvard University Press, 1988.

Reassembling the Social: an Introduction to Actor-Network Theory, Oxford: Oxford University Press, 2005.

'Visualisation and Cognition: Thinking with Eyes and Hands', in: *Knowledge and Society: Studies in the Sociology of Culture Past and Present* 6 (1986), pp. 1–40.

We Have Never Been Modern, Cambridge, MA: Harvard University Press, 1993. (originally published in French in 1991).

Lawrence, Jon, and Alexandre Campsie, 'Political History', in: Stefan Berger, Heiko Feldner and Kevin Passmore (eds.), *Writing History: Theory and Practice*, 3rd edn, London: Bloomsbury, 2020, pp. 323–42.

Lawrence, Jon, 'Class and Gender in the Making of Urban Toryism, 1880–1914', in: *English Historical Review* 108 (1993), pp. 629–52.

Lawrence, Jon, and Miles Taylor (eds.), *Party, State and Society: Electoral Behaviour in Britain since 1820*, Aldershot: Ashgate, 1997.

Lebovics, Herman, 'Will the Musée du Quai Branly Show France the Way to Postcoloniality?', in: Dominic Thomas (ed.), *Museums in Postcolonial Europe*, London: Routledge, 2009, pp. 101–14.

LeCain, Timothy J., *The Matter of History: How Things Create the Past*, Cambridge: Cambridge University Press, 2017.

Leerssen, Joep, and Ann Rigney (eds.), *Historians and Social Values*, Amsterdam: Amsterdam University Press, 2000.

Lees, Loretta, Tom Slater and Elvin Wyly, *Gentrification*, London: Routledge, 2008.

Leff, Mark H. , 'Revisioning US Political History', in: *American Historical Review* 100 (1995), pp. 829–53.

LeGoff, Jacques (ed.), *The Medieval World*, London: Collins, 1990.

Lehmann, Hartmut, and Melvin Richter (eds.), *The Meaning of Historical Terms and Concepts: New Studies on Begriffsgeschichte*, Washington, DC: German Historical Institute, 1996.

Lehtsalu, Liise, 'Comparison as a Method of Transregional and Global History', in: *European History Quarterly* 48:4 (2018), pp. 714–19.

Lemke, Thomas, *Foucault, Governmentality and Critique*, London: Paradigm, 2012.

Leonhard, Jörn, 'Comparison, Transfer and Entanglement, or: How to Write Modern European History Today?', in:*Journal of Modern European History* 14:2 (2016), pp. 149–63.

'From European Liberalism to the Languages of Liberalism: the Semantics of Liberalism in European Comparison', in: *Yearbook of Political Thought and Conceptual History* 8 (2004), pp. 17–51.

Liberalismus: zur historischen Semantik eines europäischen Deutungsmusters, Munich: Oldenbourg, 2001.

Lepore, Jill, *The Whites of Their Eyes: the Tea Party's Revolution and the Battle over American History*, Princeton: Princeton University Press, 2010.

Lerner, Gerda, *The Creation of Patriarchy*, Oxford: Oxford University Press, 1986.

The Majority Finds its Past: Placing Women in History, Durham, NC: University of North Carolina Press, 1979.

Levi, Giovanni, 'On Microhistory', in: Peter Burke (ed.), *New Perspectives on Historical Writing*, Cambridge: Polity Press, 1991, pp. 93–113.

Levine, Philippa, *The Amateur and the Professional: Antiquarians, Historians and Archaeologists in Victorian England, 1838–1886*, Cambridge: Cambridge University Press, 1986.

Levine, Philippa (ed.), *Gender and Empire*, Oxford: Oxford University Press, 2004.

Levy, Carl, 'Historians and the "First Republic"', in: Stefan Berger, Mark Donovan and Kevin Passmore (eds.), *Writing National Histories: Western Europe since 1800*, London: Routledge, 1999, pp. 265–78.

Levy, Daniel, and Natan Sznaider, *The Holocaust and Memory in the Global Age*, Philadelphia: Temple University Press, 2005.

'Memory Unbound: the Holocaust and the Formation of Cosmopolitan Memory', in: *European Journal of Social Theory* 5:1 (2002), pp. 87–106.

Lewis, Brian (ed.), *British Queer History: New Approaches and Perspectives*, Manchester: Manchester University Press, 2013.

Liakos, Antonis, 'The Canon of European History and the Conceptual Framework of National Historiographies', in: Matthias Middell and Lluis Roura y Aulinas (eds.), *Transnational Challenges to National History Writing*, Basingstoke: Palgrave Macmillan, 2013, pp. 315–42.

Light, Alison, *Forever England: Feminity, Literature and Conservatism between the Wars*, London: Routledge, 1991.

Lim, Jie-Hyun, 'World History, Nationally: How Has the National Appropriated the Transnational in East-Asian Historiography', in: Sven Beckert and Dominic Sachsenmaier (eds.), *Global History Globally: Research and Practice around the World*, London: Bloomsbury, 2018, pp. 251–68.

Lindenberger, Thomas, and Michael Wildt, 'Radical Plurality: History Workshops as a Practical Critique of Knowledge', in: *History Workshop Journal* 33 (1992), pp. 73–99.

Linebaugh, Peter, and Marcus Rediker, *The Many-Headed Hydra: Sailors, Slaves, Commoners, and the Hidden History of the Revolutionary Atlantic*, Boston: Beacon Press, 2000.

Lingelbach, Gabriele, 'Comparative History, Intercultural Transfer Studies and Global History: Three Modes of Conceptualizing History beyond the Nation State', in: *Yearbook of Transnational History* 2 (2019), pp. 1–20.

Loimeier, Roman, *Muslim Societies in Africa: a Historical Anthropology*, Bloomington: Indiana University Press, 2013.

Lomnitz, Claudio, *Death and the Idea of Mexico*, New York: Zone Books, 2008.

Lord, Peter, *The Visual Culture of Wales, vol. I: Industrial Society*, Cardiff: University of Wales Press, 1998.

The Visual Culture of Wales, vol. II: Imaging the Nation, Cardiff: University of Wales Press, 2000.

The Visual Culture of Wales, vol. III: Medieval Vision, Cardiff: University of Wales Press, 2003.

Lorenz, Chris, 'Historical Knowledge and Historical Reality: a Plea for "Internal Realism"', in: *History and Theory* 33 (1994), pp. 297–327.

'If You Are So Smart, Why Are You under Surveillance? Universities, Neoliberalism and New Public Management', in: *Critical Enquiry* 38:3 (2012), pp. 599–629.

Konstruktion der Vergangenheit: eine Einführung in die Geschichtstheorie, Cologne: Böhlau, 1997.

'Quién necesita de la identidad colectiva? Algunas reflexiones sobre un concepto radicalmente controvertido', in: Omar Acha, Daniel Brauer, Facundo N. Martín and Adrián Ratto (eds.), *Las Identidades colectivas entre los ideales y la ficción*, Estudios de filosofía de la historia, Buenos Aires: Prometeo, 2021, 31–65.

'Representations of Identity: Ethnicity, Race, Class, Gender and Religion. An Introduction to Conceptual History', in: Stefan Berger and Chris Lorenz (eds.), *The Contested Nation: Ethnicity, Class, Religion and Gender in National Histories*, Basingstoke: Palgrave Macmillan, 2008, pp. 24–59.

'Who Needs Collective Identity? Some Reflections on an Essentially Contested Concept', unpublished paper.

'"Won't You Tell Me, Where Have All the Good Times Gone?" On the Advantages and Disadvantages of Modernization Theory for History', in: *Radical History Review* 10 (2006), pp. 171–200.

'"You Got Your History, I Got Mine": Some Reflections on the Possibility of Truth and Objectivity in History', in:*Österreichische Zeitschrift für Geschichtswissenschaft* 10:4 (1999), pp. 563–84.

Lorenz, Chris, Stefan Berger and Nicola Brauch, 'Narrativity and Historical Writing: Introductory Remarks', in: Stefan Berger, Nicola Brauch and Chris Lorenz (eds), Analyzing Historical Narratives: on Academic, Popular and Educational Framings of the Past, Oxford: Berghahn Books, 2021, pp. 1–28.

Lorenz, Chris, and Berber Bevernage (eds.), *Breaking up Time: Negotiating the Borders between Present, Past and Future*, Göttingen: Vandenhoeck and Ruprecht, 2013.

Loughran, Tracey, 'Cultural History', in: Stefan Berger, Heiko Feldner and Kevin Passmore (eds.), *Writing History: Theory and Practice*, 3rd edn, London: Bloomsbury, 2020, pp. 363–85.

Lovejoy, Arthur, *The Great Chain of Being: the Study of the History of an Idea*, Cambridge, MA: Harvard University Press, 1936.

Lovejoy, Paul E., 'The Ibadan School of Historiography and its Critics', in: Toyin Falola (ed.), *African Historiography: Essays in Honour of Jacob Ade Ajayi*, London: Longman, 1993, pp. 194–202.

Lucassen, Jan (ed.), *Global Labour History: a State of the Art*, Bern: Peter Lang, 2008.

Lüdtke, Alf, 'Cash, Coffee Breaks, Horseplay: *Eigensinn* and Politics among Factory Workers in Germany circa 1900', in: Michael Hanagan and Charles Stevenson (eds.), *Confrontation, Class Consciousness, and the Labour Process: Studies in Proletarian Class Formation*, New York, 1986, pp. 65–95.

'Polymorphous Synchrony: German Industrial Workers and the Politics of Everyday Life', in: Marcel van der Linden (ed.), *The End of Labour History*, Cambridge: Cambridge University Press, 1993, pp. 39–84.

Lüdtke, Alf (ed.), *The History of Everyday Life: Reconstructing Historical Experiences and Ways of Life*, Princeton: Princeton University Press, 1989.

Lutkehaus, Nancy C., *Margaret Mead: the Making of an American Icon*, Princeton: Princeton University Press, 2008.

Lydon, Jane, *The Flash of Recognition: Photography and the Emergence of Indigenous Rights*, Sydney: New South Publishing, 2012.

Photography, Humanitarianism, Empire, London: Bloomsbury, 2016.

Lyon, Cherstin M., Elizabeth M. Nix and Rebecca K. Shrum, *Introduction to Public History: Interpreting the Past, Engaging Audiences*, Lanham, MD: Rowman and Littlefield, 2017.

McClellan, Steven , 'German Economic and Social Sciences between the National and the Transnational: the Verein für Sozialpolitik, 1872–1952', in: *Blackwell History Compass* 15:2 (2017), https://doi.org/10.1111/hic3.12354 [accessed 15 May 2020].

MacDonald, Simon, 'Transnational History: a Review of Past and Present Scholarship', https://www.ucl.ac.uk/centre-transnational-history/objectives/simon_macdonald_tns_review.pdf [accessed 29 December 2018].

Macfarlane, Alan, 'Historical Anthropology', in: *Cambridge Anthropology* 3:3 (1977), in: www.alanmacfarlane.com/TEXTS/frazerlecture.pdf [accessed 15 May 2019].

MacGregor, Neil, *A History of the World in 100 Objects*, London: Penguin, 2010.

Macintyre, Stuart, and Anna Clark, *The History Wars*, rev. edn, Melbourne: Melbourne University Press, 2004.

McKibbin, Ross, 'Class and Conventional Wisdom: the Conservative Party and the "Public" in Interwar Britain', in: McKibbin, *The Ideologies of*

Class: Social Relations in Britain, 1880–1950, Oxford: Oxford University Press, 1990, pp. 259–93.

'Why Was There no Marxism in Great Britain?', in: *English Historical Review* 99 (1984), pp. 297–331.

McLuhan, Marshall, *Understanding Media: the Extensions of Man*, New York: McGraw-Hill, 1964.

McMahon, Richard, Joachim Eibach and Randolph Roth, 'Making Sense of Violence? Reflections on the History of Interpersonal Violence in Europe', in: *Crime, History and Societies* 17:2 (2013), pp. 5–26.

McNeill, William, *Arnold Toynbee: a Life*, Oxford: Oxford University Press, 1989.

The Human Condition: an Ecological and Historical View, Princeton: Princeton University Press, 1980

Plagues and People, New York: Anchor Press, 1976.

The Pursuit of Power: Technology, Armed Forces, and Society, Chicago: University of Chicago Press, 1982.

The Rise of the West: a History of the Human Community, Chicago: University of Chicago Press, 1963.

Mager, Anna Kelk, 'Tracking the Concept of "Work" on the North-Eastern Cape Frontier, South Africa', in: Axel Fleisch and Rhiannon Stephens (eds.), *Doing Conceptual History in Africa*, Oxford: Berghahn Books, 2016, pp. 73–90.

Maier, Charles, 'Consigning the Twentieth Century to History: Alternative Narratives for the Modern Era', in: *American Historical Review* 105:3 (2000), pp. 807–31.

The Unmasterable Past: History, Holocaust and National Identity, new edn, with a new preface by the author, Cambridge, MA: Harvard University Press, 1997.

Maier, Ulrich, Martin Papenheim and Willbald Steinmetz, *Semantiken des Politischen: vom Mittelalter bis ins 20. Jahrhundert*, Göttingen: Wallstein, 2012.

Maiguashca, Juan, 'Latin American Marxist History: Rise, Fall and Resurrection', in: Q. Edward Wang and Georg G. Iggers (eds.), *Marxist Historiographies: a Global Perspective*, London: Routledge, 2016, pp. 104–24.

Majerus, Benoit, 'Lieux de Mémoirs: a European Transfer Story', in: Stefan Berger and Bill Niven (eds.), *Writing the History of Memory*, London: Bloomsbury, 2014, pp. 157–72.

Majumdar, Rochona, 'Thinking through Transition: Marxist Historiography in India', in: Q. Edward Wang and Georg G. Iggers (eds.), *Marxist Historiographies: a Global Perspective*, London: Routledge, 2016, pp. 193–218.

Malečková, Jitka, 'Where are Women in National Histories', in: Stefan Berger and Chris Lorenz (eds.), *The Contested Nation: Ethnicity, Class, Religion and Gender in National Histories*, Basingstoke: Palgrave Macmillan, 2007, pp. 171–99.

Malerba, Juandir, and Ronaldo Pereira de Jesus, 'Marxism and Brazilian Historiography', in: Q. Edward Wang and Georg G. Iggers (eds.), *Marxist Historiographies: a Global Perspective*, London: Routledge, 2016, pp. 142–73.

Mangnússon, Siurður Gylfi, and István M. Szijártó, *What is Microhistory? Theory and Practice*, London: Routledge, 2013.

Mani, Lata, *The Debate on Sati in Colonial India*, Berkeley: University of California Press, 1998.

Mann, Michael, *The Dark Side of Democracy: Explaining Ethnic Cleansing*, Cambridge: Cambridge University Press, 2006.

Mann, Susan, and Yu-Yin Cheng (eds.), *Under Confucian Eyes: Writing on Gender in Chinese History*, Berkeley: University of Berkeley Press, 2001.

Mansveld, Juliana, *Geographies of Consumption*, London: Sage, 2008.

Mark, James, *The Unfinished Revolution: Making Sense of the Unfinished Past in East Central Europe*, New Haven: Yale University Press, 2010.

Marschall, Sabine, *Landscape of Memory: Commemorative Monuments, Memorials and Public Statuary in Post-Apartheid South Africa*, Leiden: Brill, 2010.

Martineau, Jonathan, *Time, Capitalism and Alienation: a Socio-Historical Inquiry into the Making of Modern Time*, Leiden: Brill, 2015.

Masquelier, Adeline (ed.), *Dirt, Undress and Difference: Critical Perspectives on the Body's Surface*, Bloomington: Indiana University Press, 2005.

Massimi, Michela, and Casey D. McCoy (eds.), *Understanding Perspectivism: Scientific Challenges and Methodological Prospects*, London: Routledge, 2019.

Mathias, Peter, *The First Industrial Nation: the Economic History of Britain, 1700–1914*, London: Methuen, 1969.

Matten, Marc Andre (ed.), *Places of Memory in Modern China: History, Politics and Identity*, Leiden: Brill, 2012.

Mattioli, Aram, *Jacob Burckhardt und die Grenzen der Humanität*, Weitra: Bibliothek der Provinz, 2001.

Maurer, Kathrin, *Visualizing the Past: the Power of the Image in German Historicism*, Berlin: De Gruyter, 2013.

Maylam, Paul, *South Africa's Racial Past: the History and Historiography of Racism, Segregation and Apartheid*, Avebury: Ashgate, 2001.

Maynell, Hugo A., 'Anarchy and Falsification: Feyerabend and Popper', in: Maynell, *Redirecting Philosophy: Reflections on the Nature of*

Knowledge from Plato to Lonergan, Toronto: University of Toronto Press, 1998, pp. 130–51.

Mazour, Anatole G., *Modern Russian Historiography*, 2nd edn, Princeton: Princeton University Press, 1958.

Mbembe, Achille, *Critique of Black Reason*, Durham, NC: Duke University Press, 2017 (originally published in French in 2013).

Politiques de l'Inimité, Paris: Edition La Découverte, 2016.

Meade, Teresa A., and Merry E. Wiesner-Hanks (eds.), *Companion to Gender History*, Oxford: Blackwell, 2004.

Medick, Hans, 'Missionaries in the Row Boat? Ethnological Ways of Knowing as a Challenge to Social History', in: *Comparative Studies in Society and History* 29 (1987), pp. 76–98.

'Turning Global? Microhistory in Extension', in: *Historische Anthropologie* 24:2 (2016), pp. 241–52.

Megill, Allan, 'Historical Representations: Identity, Allegiance', in: Stefan Berger, Linas Eriksonas and Andrew Mycock (eds.), *Narrating the Nation. Representations in History, Media and the Arts*, Oxford: Berghahn Books, 2008, pp. 19–34.

Mehl, Margaret, *History and the State in Nineteenth-Centry Japan*, Basingstoke: Palgrave Macmillan, 1998.

Meijer, Irene Costera, and Baukje Prins, 'Interview with Judith Butler', in: *Signs* 23 (1998), pp. 275–86.

Meinecke, Friedrich, *Cosmopolitanism and the Nation-State*, Princeton: Princeton University Press, 1970 (originally published in German in 1908).

Historism: the Rise of a New Historical Outlook, London: Routledge, 1972.

Machiavellism: the Doctrine of Raison d'État and its Place in Modern History, New Haven: Yale University Press, 1957.

Melman, Billie, 'Gender, History and Memory: the Invention of Women's Pasts in the Nineteenth and Early Twentieth Centuries', in: *History and Memory* 5:1 (1993), pp. 5–41.

Mercer, Ben , 'The Moral Rearmament of France: Pierre Nora, Memory and the Crisis of Republicanism', in: *French Politics, Culture and Society* 31 (2013), pp. 102–15

Mergel, Thomas, 'Überlegungen zu einer Kulturgeschichte der Politik', in: *Geschichte und Gesellschaft* 28 (2002), pp. 574–606.

Middell, Matthias, *Weltgeschichtsschreibung im Zeitalter der Verfachlichung und Professionalisierung. Das Leipziger Institut für Kultur- und Universalgeschichte, 1890–1990*, 3 vols., Leipzig: Akademische Verlagsanstalt, 2005.

Middell, Matthias (ed.), *Cultural Transfers, Encounters and Connections in the Global Eighteenth Century*, Leipzig: Leipziger Universitätsverlag, 2014.

Middell, Matthias, and Katja Naumann, 'Global History and the Spatial Turn: From the Impact of Area Studies to the Study of Critical Junctures of Globalization', in:*Journal of Global History* 5:1 (2010), pp. 149–70.

'Historians and International Organization(s): the International Committee of Historical Sciences (CISH)', in: Danile Laqua, Christophe Verbruggen and Wouter van Acker (eds.), *International Organizations and Global Civil Society: Histories of the Union of International Assocations*, London: Bloomsbury, 2019, pp. 133–51.

Midgley, Clare, Alison Twells and Julie Carlier, 'Introduction', in Clare Midgley, Alison Twells and Julie Carlier (eds.), *Women in Transnational History: Connecting the Local and the Global*, London: Routledge, 2016, pp. 1–10.

Mihai, Mihaela, 'Theorizing Agonistic Emotions', in: *Parallax* 20:2 (2014), pp. 31–48.

Miller, Alexei, and Maria Lipman (eds.), *The Convolutions of Historical Politics*, Budapest: Central European University Press, 2012.

Miller, Perry, *Life of the Mind in America: From the Revolution to the Civil War*, Cambridge, MA: Harvard University Press, 1965.

Minz, Sidney, *Sweetness and Power: the Place of Sugar in Modern History*, Harmondsworth: Penguin, 1985.

Mirzoeff, Nicholas, *An Introduction to Visual Culture*, London: Routledge, 1999.

The Right to Look: a Counter-History of Visuality, Durham, NC: Duke University Press, 2011.

Mishkova, Diana, 'The Politics of Regionalist Science: the Balkans as a Supranational Space in Late Nineteenth to Mid-Twentieth Century Academic Projects', in: *East Central Europe* 39 (2012), pp. 266–303.

Mishra, Amit Kumar, 'Global Histoires of Migration(s)', in: Sven Beckert and Dominic Sachsenmaier (eds.), *Global History Globally: Research and Practice around the World*, London: Bloomsbury, 2018, pp. 195–214.

Mitchell, W. J. T., 'Showing Seeing: a Critique of Visual Culture', in: *Journal of Visual Culture* 1:2 (2002), pp. 165–85.

What Do Pictures Want?, Chicago: University of Chicago Press, 2005.

Mohanty, Chandra Talpade , *Feminism without Borders: Decolonizing Theory, Practising Solidarity*, Durham, NC: Duke University Press, 2003.

Mommsen, Wolfgang J., 'Max Webers Begriff der Universalgeschichte', in: Jürgen Kocka (ed.), *Max Weber, der Historiker*, Göttingen: Vandenhoeck and Ruprecht, 1986, pp. 51–72.

'Max Weber's Political Sociology and his Philosophy of World History', in: *International Social Science Journal* 17 (1965), pp. 23–45.

Mongia, Radhika Viyas, 'Race, Nationality, Mobility: a History of the Passport', in: Antoinette Burton (ed.), *After the Imperial Turn: Thinking with and through the Nation*, Durham, NC: Duke University Press, 2003, pp. 196–216.

Montgomery, David, *The Fall of the House of Labor: the Workplace, the State and American Labor Activism, 1865–1925*, New York: Columbia University Press, 1987.

Montrie, Chad, *Making a Living: Work and Environment in the United States*, Chapel Hill: University of North Carolina Press, 2008.

Moore, Alison, 'Historicising Historical Theory's History of Cultural Historiography', in: *Cosmos and History: the Journal of Natural and Social Philosophy* 12:1 (2016), pp. 257–91.

Morgan, David, *The Forge of Vision: a Visual History of Modern Christianity*, Oakland: University of California Press, 2015.

Morgan, Kevin, *The Webbs and Soviet Communism*, London: Lawrence and Wishart, 2006.

Moriarty, Michael, *Roland Barthes*, Stanford: Stanford University Press, 1991.

Morris-Reich, Amos, *Race and Photography: Racial Photography as Scientific Evidence, 1876–1980*, Chicago: University of Chicago Press, 2016.

Morson, Gary Saul, and Caryl Emerson, *Mikhail Bakhtin: Creation of a Prosaics*, Stanford: Stanford University Press, 1990.

Moss, Mark, *Manliness and Militarism: Educating Young Boys in Ontario for War*, Oxford: Oxford University Press, 2001.

Moss, Stella, 'Manly Drinkers: Masculinity and Material Culture in the Interwar Public House', in: Hannah Greig, Jane Hamlett and Leonie Hannan (eds.), *Gender and Material Culture in Britain since 1600*, Basingstoke: Palgrave Macmillan, 2015, pp. 138–52.

Mösslang, Markus, and Torsten Riotte (eds.), *The Diplomat's World: a Cultural History of Diplomacy, 1815–1914*, Oxford: Oxford University Press, 2008.

Mouffe, Chantal, *Agonistics: Thinking the World Politically*, London: Verso, 2013.

The Democratic Paradox, London: Verso, 2000.

Muldrew, Craig, *The Economy of Obligation: the Culture of Credit and Social Relations in Early Modern England*, Basingstoke: Palgrave Macmillan, 1998.

Müller, Ernst, and Falko Schmieder, 'Reinhart Kosellecks Begriffe und Denkfiguren', in: Ernst Müller and Falko Schmieder (eds.), *Begriffsgeschichte und historische Semantik: ein kritisches Kompendium*, Frankfurt am Main: Suhrkamp, 2016, pp. 278–337.

Murray, Stephen, and Will Roscoe (eds.), *Boy Wives and Female Husbands: Studies of African Homosexualities*, New York: St Martin's Press, 1998.

Musgrow, Charles D., 'Monumentality in Nationalist Nanjing: Purple Mountain's Changing Views', in: James A. Cook, Joshua Goldstein, Matthew D. Johnson and Sigrid Schmalzer (eds.), *Visualizing Modern China: Image, History and Memory, 1750 to the Present*, Lanham, MD: Lexington Books, 2014pp. 87–106.

Mycock, Andrew, and Marina Loskoutova, 'Nation, State and Empire: the Historiography of "High Imperialism" in the British and Russian Empires', in: Stefan Berger and Chris Lorenz (eds.), *Nationalizing the Past: Historians and Nation Builders in Modern Europe*, Basingstoke: Palgrave Macmillan, 2010, pp. 233–58.

Nadell, Pamela S., and Kate Haulman (eds.), *Making Women's Histories: Beyond National Perspectives*, New York: New York University Press, 2013.

Nagy, Piroska, 'History of Emotions', in: Marek Tamm and Peter Burke (eds.), *Debating New Approaches to History*, London: Bloomsbury, 2019, pp. 189–202.

Naimark, Norman M., *Stalin's Genocides*, Princeton: Princenton University Press, 2010.

Najmabadi, Afsaneh, *Women with Mustaches and Men without Beards: Gender and Sexual Anxieties of Iranian Modernity*, Berkeley: University of California Press, 2005.

Namias, June, *White Captives: Gender and Ethnicity on the American Frontier*, Chapel Hill: University of North Carolina Press, 1993.

Nardo, Don, *Migrant Mother: How a Photograph Defined the Great Depression*, Mankato, MN: Compass Point, 2011.

Nash, Mark, *Red Africa: Affective Communities and the Cold War*, London: Black Dog, 2016.

Naumann, Katja, *Laboratorien der Weltgeschichsschreibung: Lehre und Forschung an den Universitäten Chicago, Columbia and Harvard, 1918–1968*, Göttingen: Vandenhoeck and Ruprecht, 2019.

'Long-Term and Decentred Trajectories of Doing History from a Global Perspective: Institutionalization, Postcolonial Critique, and Empiricist Approaches, before and after the 1970s', in: *Journal of Global History* 14:3 (2019), pp. 335–54

Neumann, Victor, *The Temptation of Homo Europaeus*, New York: Columbia University Press, 1993.

Newbury, Darren, '"Window on the West Indies": the Photographic Imagination of the Society for the Propagation of the Gospel', in: *Visual Studies* 33:1 (2018), pp. 41–56.

Newman, Saul, *Power and Politics in Poststructuralist Thought: New Theories of the Political*, London: Routledge, 2005.

Niethammer, Lutz, *Kollektive Identität: Heimliche Quellen einer unheimlichen Konjunktur*, Reinbek: rororo, 2000.

Niethammer, Lutz (ed.), *Lebensgeschichte und Sozialkultur im Ruhrgebiet, 1930–1960*, 3 vols., Bonn: J.W.H. Dietz Nachf., 1983–5.

Nietzsche, Friedrich, *The Use and Abuse of History*, New York: Cosimo, 2010 (originally published in 1873).

Nikolaïdis, Kalypso, Berny Sèbe and Gabrielle Maas , 'Echoes of Empire: the Present of the Past', in: Kalypso Nikolaïdis, Berny Sèbe and Gabrielle Maas (eds.), *Echoes of Empire: Memory, Identity and Colonial Legacies*, London: I. B. Tauris, 2015, pp. 1–18.

Ninkovich, Frank, *The Global Republic: America's Inadvertent Rise to World Power*, Chicago: University of Chicago Press, 2014.

Nippel, Wilfried, *Johann Gustav Droysen: ein Leben zwischen Wissenschaft und Politik*, Munich: C. H. Beck, 2008.

Niremberg, David, *Communities of Violence: Persecution of Minorities in the Middle Ages*, Princeton: Princeton University Press, 1996.

Nisbet, H. B., 'Herder: the Nation in History', in: Michael Branch (ed.), *National History and Identity: Approaches to the Writing of National History in the North-East Baltic Region, Nineteenth and Twentieth Centuries*, Tampere: Suomalaisen Kirjallisuuden Seura, 1999, pp. 78–96.

Nora, Pierre, *Les lieux de mémoire*, Paris: Gallimard, 1984–92.

Nora, Pierre (ed.), *Realms of Memory: Rethinking the French Past*, 3 vols., English language edition by Lawrence D. Kritzman, trans. Arthur Goldhammer, New York: Columbia University Press, 1996–8.

Nordby, Trond, 'State and Nation-Building', in: Jan Eivind Myhre, Trond Nordby and Sølvi 'Sogner (eds.), *Making a Historical Culture: Historiography in Norway*, Oslo: Scandinavian University Press, 1995, pp. 181–209.

Norris, Christopher, *Derrida*, Cambridge, MA: Harvard University Press, 1987.

Novick, Peter, *That Noble Dream: the 'Objectivity Question' and the American Historical Profession*, Cambridge: Cambridge University Press, 1988.

Núñez-Seixas, Xosé-Manuel, 'History of Civilisation: Transnational or Post-Imperial? Some Iberian Perspectives (1860–1930)', in: Stefan Berger and Chris Lorenz (eds.), *Nationalizing the Past: Historians and Nation Builders in Modern Europe*, Basingstoke: Palgrave Macmillan, 2010, pp. 384–403.

Historia Mundial de Espagna, Barcelona: Ediciones Distino, 2018.

Nuttal, Sarah, and Carli Coetzee (eds.), *Negotiating the Past: the Making of Memory in South Africa*, Oxford: Oxford University Press, 1998

Nye, Robert, *Masculinity and Male Codes of Honour in France*, Berkeley: University of California Press, 1992.

O'Brien, Karen, *Narratives of Enlightenment: Cosmopolitan History from Voltaire to Gibbon*, Cambridge: Cambridge University Press, 1997.

O'Dowd, Mary, 'Australian Identity, History and Belonging: the Influence of White Australian Identity on Racism and the Non-Acceptance of the History of Colonisation of Indigenous Australians', in: *International Journal of Diversity in Organisations, Communities and Nations* 10:6 (2011), pp. 29–43.

O'Sickey, Ingeborg Majer, 'Framing the Unheimlich: Heimatfilm and Bambi', in: Patricia Herminghouse and Magda Müller (eds.), *Gender and Germanness: Cultural Production of Nations*, Oxford: Berghahn Books, 1997, pp. 202–16.

Offen, Karen, *European Feminisms, 1700–1950: a Political History*, Stanford: Stanford University Press, 2000.

Offen, Karen and Chen Yan (eds.), 'Women's History at the Cutting Edge', special issue of *Women's History Review* 27:1 (2018).

Ogle, Vanessa, *The Global Transformation of Time, 1870–1950*, Cambridge, MA: Harvard University Press, 2015.

Okamoto, Michihiro, 'The Social Movement History as a Social Movement in and of Itself', in: Stefan Berger (ed.), *The Engaged Historian: Perspectives on the Intersections of Politics, Activism and the Historical Profession*, Oxford: Berghahn Books, 2019, pp. 185–204.

Olick, Jeffrey K., *In the House of the Hangman: the Agonies of German Defeat, 1943–1949*, Chicago: University of Chicago Press, 2005.

The Politics of Regret: On Collective Memory and Historical Responsibility, London: Routledge, 2007.

The Sins of the Fathers: Germany, Memory, Method, Chicago: University of Chicago Press, 2017.

Olick, Jeffrey K., and Daniel Levy, 'Collective Memory and Cultural Constraint: Holocaust Myth and Rationality in German Politics', in: *American Sociological Review* 32:6 (1997), pp. 921–36.

Olsen, Bjørnar, 'Comment', in: Marek Tamm and Peter Burke (eds.), *Debating New Approaches to History*, London: Bloomsbury, 2019, pp. 232–8.

Olsen, Niklas, *History in the Plural: an Introduction to the Work of Reinhart Koselleck*, Oxford: Berghahn Books, 2012.

Osterhammel, Jürgen, *The Transformation of the World: a Global History of the Nineteenth Century*, Princeton: Princeton University Press, 2014.

'World History', in: Axel Schneider and Daniel Woolf (eds.), *The Oxford History of Historical Writing, vol. V: Historical Writing since 1945*, Oxford: Oxford University Press, 2011, pp. 93–112.

Otter, Chris, *Diet for a Large Planet: Industrial Britain, Food Systems, and World Ecology*, Chicago: University of Chicago Press, 2020.

Oudshoorn, Nelly, *Beyond the Natural Body: an Archaeology of Sex Hormones*, London: Routledge, 1994

Ovendale, R., 'The End of Empire', in: R. English and M. Kenny (eds.), *Rethinking British Decline*, Basingstoke: Palgrave Macmillan, 2000, pp. 257–78.

Oyewumi, Oyeronke, *The Invention of Women: Making an African Sense of Western Gender Discourses*, Minneapolis: University of Minnesota Press, 1997.

Ozouf, Mona, *Festivals and the French Revolution*, Cambridge, MA: Harvard University Press, 1988.

Varennes: la mort de la royauté (21 juin 1791), Paris: Gallimard, 2005.

Paisley, Fiona, *Glamour in the Pacific: Cultural Internationalism and Race Politics in the Women's Pan-Pacific*, Honolulu: University of Hawaii Press, 2009.

Paisley, Fiona, and Pamela Scully, *Writing Transnational History*, London: Bloomsbury, 2019.

Pakier, Małgorzata, and Bo Stråth (eds.), *A European Memory? Contested Histories and Politics of Remembrance*, Oxford: Berghahn Books, 2010.

Paletschek, Sylvia (ed.), *Popular Historiographies in the Nineteenth and Twentieth Centuries*, Oxford: Berghahn Books, 2011.

Palmer, Annette C., and Lawrence A. Peskin, 'What in the World is "America and the World"?', in: *Perspectives on History* (1 November 2011); www.historians.org/publications-and-directories/perspectives-on-history/november-2011/what-in-the-world-is-america-and-the-world [accesssed 17 May 2020].

Palmer, Bryan D., *The Making of E. P. Thompson: Marxism, Humanism and History*, Toronto: New Hogtown Press, 1981.

Palonen, Kari, *Quentin Skinner: History, Politics, Rhetoric*, Cambridge: Polity Press, 2003.

Park, Myoung-Kyu, 'How Concepts Met History in Korea's Complex Modernization: New Concepts of Economy and Society and their Impact', in: Hagen Schulz-Forberg (ed.), *A Global Conceptual History of Asia, 1860–1940*, London: Routledge, 2014, pp. 25–42.

Parker, C. J. W., 'The Failure of Liberal Racialism: E. A. Freeman', in: *Historical Journal* 24 (1991), pp. 825–46.

Parkinson, R. B., *A Little Gay History: Desire and Diversity across the World*, New York: University of Columbia Press, 2013.

Parry, Jon, *Democracy and Religion: Gladstone and the Liberal Party, 1867–1975*, Cambridge: Cambridge University Press, 1986.

Passmore, Kevin, 'Poststructuralist and Linguistic Methods', in: Stefan Berger, Heiko Feldner and Kevin Passmore (eds.), *Writing History: Theory and Practice*, 3rd edn, London: Bloomsbury, 2020, pp. 133–57.

Pasture, Patrick, *Imagining European Unity since 1000 AD*, Basingstoke: Palgrave Macmillan, 2015.

Patterson, Annabel, *Early Modern Liberalism*, Cambridge: Cambridge University Press, 1997.

Paul, Herman, *Hayden White*, Oxford: Blackwell, 2013.

Key Issues in Historical Theory, London: Routledge, 2015.

'A Loosely Knit Network: Philosophy of History after Hayden White', in: *Journal of the Philosophy of History* 13 (2019), pp. 3–20.

Paul, Herman, and Adriaan van Veldhuizen, 'A Retrieval of Historicism: Frank Ankersmit's Philosophy of History and Politics', in: *History and Theory* 57:1 (2018), pp. 33–55.

Paulmann, Johannes, *Pomp und Politik: Monarchenbegegnungen zwischen Ancien Regime und Erstem Weltkrieg*, Paderborn: Schöningh, 2000.

Pearce, Susan M., *Experiencing Material Culture in the Western World*, Leicester: Leicester University Press, 1997.

Museums, Objects and Collections: a Cultural Study, Leicester: Leicester University Press, 1992.

Pearce, Susan M. (ed.), *Interpreting Objects and Collections*, London: Routledge, 1992.

Pécout, Eric, 'The International Armed Volunteers: Pilgrims of a Transnational Risorgimento', in: *Journal of Modern Italian Studies* 14:4 (2009), pp. 413–26.

Pedersen, Susan, 'The Future of Feminist History', in: *Perspectives on History* (1 October 2000); www.historians.org/publications-and-directories/perspectives-on-history/october-2000/the-future-of-feminist-history [accessed 19 March 2019].

'What is Political History Now', in: David Cannadine (ed.), *What Is History Now?*, Basingstoke: Palgrave Macmillan, 2002, pp. 36–56.

Pedwell, Carolyn, 'De-Colonising Empathy: Thinking Affect Transnationally', in: *Samyukta: a Journal of Women's Studies* 16:1 (2016), pp. 27–49.

Pemberton, John, *On the Subject of 'Java'*, Ithaca, NY: Cornell University Press, 1994.

Perkin, Harold, *The Making of a Social Historian*, London: Athena Press, 2002.

Pernau, Margrit, 'The Indian Body and Unani Medicine: Body History as Entangled History', in: Axel Michaels and Christoph Wulf (eds.), *Images of the Body in India*, London: Routledge, 2011, pp. 97–108.

Pernau, Margrit, and Helge Jordheim, 'Introduction', in: Margrit Pernau and Helge Jordheim (eds.), *Civilizing Emotions: Concepts in Nineteenth-Century Asia and Europe*, Oxford: Oxford University Press, 2015, pp. 1–24.

Pernau, Margrit, and Imke Rajamani, 'Emotional Translations: Conceptual History beyond Language', in: *History and Theory* 55 (2016), pp. 46–65.

Pernau, Margrit, and Dominic Sachsenmaier, 'History of Concepts and Global History', in: Margrit Pernau and Dominic Sachsenmaier (eds.), *Global Conceptual History: a Reader*, London: Bloomsbury, 2016, pp. 1–28.

Pernau, Margrit, and Dominic Sachsenmaier (eds.), *Global Conceptual History: a Reader*, London: Bloomsbury, 2016.

Perrot, Michelle (ed.), *History of Private Life, vol. IV: From the Fires of Revolution to the Great War*, Cambridge, MA: Harvard University Press, 1990.

Pethes, Nicolas, *Cultural Memory Studies: an Introduction*, Cambridge: Cambridge Scholars, 2019.

Pierson, Ruth Roach, and Nupur Chaudhuri (eds.), *Nation, Empire, Colony: Historicizing Gender and Race*, Bloomington: Indiana University Press, 1998.

Pihlainen, Kalle, 'The Confines of the Form: Historical Writing and the Desire that It Be What It Is Not', in: Kuisma Korhohnen, *Tropes for the Past: Hayden White and the History/Literature Debate*, Amsterdam: Rodopi, 2006, pp. 55–67.

The Work of History: Constructivism and a Politics of the Past, London: Routledge, 2017.

Pinchbeck, Ivy, *Women Workers and the Industrial Revolution, 1750–1850*, London: Crofts, 1930.

Pinney, Christopher, *Camera Indica: the Social Life of Indian Photographs*, Chicago: University of Chicago Press, 1997.

Pittock, Murray, 'Historiography', in: Alexander Broadie (ed.), *Cambridge Companion to the Scottish Enlightenment*, Cambridge: Cambridge University Press, 2003, pp. 258–79.

'History and the Teleology of Civility in the Scottish Enlightenment', in: Peter France and Susan Manning (eds.), *Enlightenment and Emancipation*, Lewisburg, PA: Bucknell University Press, 2006, pp. 81–96.

Pocock, J. G. A., *Barbarism and Religion*, 6 vols., Cambridge: Cambridge University Press, 1999–2016.

'The History of Political Thought: a Methodological Enquiry', in: Peter Laslett and Walter Runciman (eds.), *Philosophy, Politics and Society*, 2nd ser., Oxford: Oxford University Press, 1962.

The Machiavellian Moment: Florentine Political Thought and the Atlantic Republican Tradition, Princeton: Princeton University Press, 1975.

Pók, Attila, 'On the Memory of Communism in Eastern and Central Europe', in: Stefan Berger and Bill Niven (eds.), *Writing the History of Memory*, London: Bloomsbury, 2014, pp. 173–98.

Pollard, Sidney, *Peaceful Conquests: the Industrialisation of Europe, 1760–1970*, Oxford: Oxford University Press, 1981.

Polonsky, Antony, and Joanna B. Michlic (eds.), *The Neighbors Respond: the Controversy over the Jedwabne Massacre in Poland*' Princeton: Princeton University Press, 2004.

Pomeranz, Kenneth, 'Histories for a Less National Age', in: *American Historical Review* 119:1 (2014), pp. 1–22.

'Scale, Scope and Scholarship: Regional Practices and Global Economic Histories', in: Sven Beckert and Dominic Sachsenmaier (eds.), *Global History Globally: Research and Practice around the World*, London: Bloomsbury, 2018, pp. 163–94.

Poole, Deborah, *Vision, Race and Modernity: a Visual Economy of the Andean Image World*, Princeton: Princeton University Press, 1997.

Popper, Karl, *The Open Society and its Enemies*, 2 vols., London: Routledge, 1945.

Porciani, Ilaria, and Jo Tollebeek (eds.), *Setting the Standards. Institutions, Networks and Communities of National Historiography*, Basingstoke: Palgrave Macmillan, 2012.

Porciani, Ilaria, and Lutz Raphael (eds.), *Atlas of European Historiography: the Making of a Profession, 1800–2005*, Basingstoke: Palgrave Macmillan, 2010.

Porter, Roy, 'History of the Body Reconsidered', in: Peter Burke (ed.), *New Perspectives on Historical Writing*, Cambridge: Polity Press, 2001, pp. 232–60.

Poster, Mark, *Cultural History and Postmodernity: Disciplinary Readings and Challenges*, New York: Columbia University Press, 1997.

Power, Eileen, *Medieval English Nunneries*, Cambridge: Cambridge University Press, 1922.

Pratt, Mary Louise, *Imperial Eyes: Travel Writing and Transculturation*, London: Routledge, 1992.

Preda, Alex, 'The Turn to Things: Arguments for a Sociological Theory of Things', in: *Sociological Quarterly* 40:2 (1999), pp. 347–66.

Prellwitz, Jens, *Jüdisches Erbe, sozialliberales Ethos, deutsche Nation: Gustav Mayer im Kaiserreich und in der Weimarer Republik*, Mannheim: Palatium, 1998.

Price, Lloyd, 'Environmental and Animal History', in: Stefan Berger, Heiko Feldner and Kevin Passmore (eds.), *Writing History: Theory and Practice*, 3rd edn, London: Bloomsbury, 2020, pp. 253–9.

Pryke, Sam, 'National and European Identity', in: *National Identities* 22:1 (2020), pp. 91–105.

Pykett, Lyn, 'The Material Turn in Victorian Studies', in: *Literature Compass* 1:1 (2003), https://doi.org/10.1111/j.1741-4113.2004.00020.x [accessed 29 April 2020].

Quenet, Grégory, 'Environmental History', in: Marek Tamm and Peter Burke (eds.), *Debating New Approaches to History*, London: Bloomsbury, 2019, pp. 75–100.

Quirke, Carol, *Eyes on Labor: News Photography and America's Working Class*, Oxford: Oxford University Press, 2012.

Rabault-Feuerbahn, Pascale, '"Les grandes assises de l'orientalisme": la question interculturell dans les Congrès internationaux des orientalistes (1873–1912)', in: *Revue Germanique Internationale* 12 (2010), pp. 47–68.

Rabinbach, Anson, *The Human Motor: Energy, Fatigue and the Origins of Modernity*, New York: Basic Books, 1990.

Rabinow, Paul, *Essays on the Anthropology of Reason*, Princeton: Princeton University Press, 1996.

Rabinowitz, Paula, 'Margaret Bourke-White's Red Coat; or, Slumming in the Thirties', in: Ardis Cameron (ed.), *Looking for America: the Visual Production of Nation and People*, Oxford: Blackwell, 2005, pp. 149–70.

Rafael, Vicente L., *The Promise of the Foreign: Nationalism and the Techniques of Translation in the Spanish Philippines*, Durham, NC: Duke University Press, 2005.

Rahman, Momin, and Anne Witz, 'What Really Matters? The Elusive Quality of the Material in Feminist Thought', in: *Feminist Theory* 4:3 (2003), pp. 243–61.

Raiford, Leigh, and Renee C. Romano, 'Introduction: the Struggle over Memory', in: Renee C. Romano and Leigh Raiford (eds.), *The Civil Rights Movement in American Memory*, Athens, GA: University of Georgia Press, 2006, pp. 1–12.

Raj, Kapil, *Relocating Modern Science: Circulation and the Construction of Knowledge in South Asia and Europe, 1650–1900*, Basingstoke: Palgrave Macmillan, 2007.

Raman, Bhavani, 'The Postwar "Returnee", Tamil Culture and the Bay of Bengal', in: Gyan Prakash, Nikhil Menon and Michael Laffan (eds.), *The Postcolonial Moment in South and South-East Asia*, London: Bloomsbury, 2018, pp. 121–40.

Ramaswamy, Sumathi, *The Goddess and the Nation*, Durham, NC: Duke University Press, 2010.

Rampley, Matthew, 'Introduction', in: Matthew Rampley, Thierry Lenain, Hubert Locher, Andrea Pinotti, Charlotte Schoell-Glass and Kitty Zijlmans (eds.), *Art History and Visual Studies in Europe: Transnational Discourses and National Frameworks*, Leiden: Brill, 2012, pp. 1–13.

Ramsden, John, *Don't Mention the War: the British and the Germans since 1890*, London: Abacus, 2006, pp. 363–5.

Rancière, Jacques, *The Names of History: On the Poetics of Knowledge*, Minneapolis: University of Minnesota Press, 1994.

Proletarian Nights: the Workers' Dream in Nineteenth-Century France, London: Verso, 2012. (originally published in French in 1981).

Randall, Adrian, and Andrew Charlesworth (eds.), *Moral Economy and Popular Protest: Crowds, Conflicts, Authority*, Basingstoke: Palgrave Macmillan, 2000.

Ransby, Barbara, *Making All Black Lives Matter: Reimagining Freedom in the Twenty-First Century*, Oakland: University of California Press, 2018.

Raphael, Lutz, *Geschichtswissenschaft im Zeitalter der Extreme: Theorien, Methoden, Tendenzen von 1900 bis zur Gegenwart*, Munich: C. H. Beck, 2003, pp. 215–27.

Raven, James, Naomi Tadmor and Helen Small (eds.), *The Practice and Representation of Reading in England*, Cambridge: Cambridge University Press, 1996.

Ravenhill-Johnson, Annie, *The Art and Ideology of the Trade Union Emblem, 1850–1925*, ed. Paula James, London: Anthem Press, 2013.

Reddy, William M., 'Against Constructionism: the Historical Ethnography of Emotions', in: *Current Anthropology* 38:3 (1997), pp. 327–40

'Anthropology and the History of Culture', in: Lloyd Kramer and Sarah Maza (eds.), *A Companion to Western Historical Thought*, Oxford: Balckwell, 2002, pp. 277–96.

The Making of Romantic Love: Longing and Sexuality in Europe, South Asia and Japan, 900–1200 CE, Chicago: University of Chicago Press, 2012.

Renfrew, Alistair, *Mikhail Bakhtin*, London: Routledge, 2015.

Rich, Adrienne, 'Reflections on "Compulsory Heterosexuality"', in: *Journal of Women's History* 16:1 (2004), pp. 9–11.

Richter, Melvin, 'Pocock, Skinner, and the *Geschichtliche Grundbegriffe*', in: *History and Theory* 14:1 (1990), pp. 38–70.

Ricoeur, Paul, *The Conflict of Interpretations: Essays in Hermeneutics*, Evanston, IL: Northwestern University Press, 1974.

Memory, History, Forgetting, Chicago: University of Chicago Press, 2004.

Riello, Giorgio, *Cotton: the Fabric that Made the Modern World*, Cambridge: Cambridge University Press, 2013.

Rigby, Steve, *Marxism and History: a Critical Introduction*, 2nd edn, Manchester: Manchester University Press, 1998.

Rigney, Ann, 'History as Text: Narrative Theory and History', in: Nancy Partner and Sarah Foot (eds.), *The Sage Handbook of Historical Theory*, London: Sage, 2013, pp. 183–202.

'Remembering Hope: Transnational Activism beyond the Traumatic', in: *Memory Studies* 11:3 (2018), pp. 368–80.

Riley, Denise, *Am I that Name? Feminism and the Category of Women in History*, Basingstoke: Macmillan, 1988.

Roberts, Geoffrey (ed.), *The History and Narrative Reader*, London: Routledge, 2001.

Rodogno, David, Bernhard Struck and Jakob Vogel (eds.), *Shaping the Transnational Sphere. Experts, Networks, and Issues from the 1840s to the 1930s*, Oxford: Berghahn Books, 2014.

Roediger, David R., *The Wages of Whiteness: Race and the Making of the American Working Class*, London: Verso, 1991.

'What if Labour Were Not White and Male? Recentering Working-Class History and Reconstructing Debate on the Unions and Race', in: *International Labor and Working-Class History* 51 (1997), pp. 72–95.

Roediger, Henry L., and James V. Wertsch, 'Creating a New Discipline of Memory Studies', in: *Memory Studies* 1:1 (2008), pp. 9–22.

Rogoff, Irit, 'Studying Visual Culture', in: Nicholas Mirzoeff (ed.), *The Visual Culture Reader*, London: Routledge, 1998, pp. 24–36.

Roksandić, Drago, Filip Šimetin Šegvić and Nikolina Šimetin Šegvić (eds.), *Annales in Perspective: Designs and Accomplishments*, Zagreb: FF Press, 2019.

Roper, Lyndal, *Oedipus and the Devil: Religion and Sexuality in Early Modern Europe*, London: Routledge, 1994.

Rosaldo, Michelle, and Louise Lamphere (eds.), *Women, Culture and Society*, Stanford: Stanford University Press, 1974.

Rose, Nikolas, *The Politics of Life Itself: Biomedicine, Power, and Subjectivity in the Twenty-First Century*, Princeton: Princeton University Press, 2007.

Rose,Sonya O., *What is Gender History?*, Cambridge: Polity Press, 2010.

Rosenwein, Barbara H., 'Worrying about Emotions in History', in: *American Historical Review* 107:3 (2002), pp. 821–45.

Rosenzweig, Roy, and David Thelen, *The Presence of the Past: Popular Uses of History in American Life*, New York: Columbia University Press, 1998.

Rostow, W. W., *The Stages of Economic Growth*, Cambridge: Cambridge University Press, 1960.

Rothberg, Michael, *Multidirectional Memory: Remembering the Holocaust in the Age of Decolonisation*, Stanford: Stanford University Press, 2009.

Roudometof, Victor, *Glocalization: a Critical Introduction*, London: Routledge, 2016.

Roundtable, '*Geschichtliche Grundbegriffe* Reloaded: Writing the Conceptual History of the Twentieth Century', in: *Contributions to the History of Concepts* 7:1 (2012), pp. 78–128.

Roussellier, Nicolas, 'The Political Transfer of English Parliamentary Rules in the French Assemblies (1789–1848)', in: *European Review of History* 12:2 (2005), pp. 239–48.

Rowbotham, Sheila, *Hidden from History: 300 Years of Women's Oppression and the Fight against It*, London: Pluto, 1973.

Rüger, Jan, 'OXO, or: The Challenges of Transnational History', in: *European History Quarterly* 40:4 (2010), pp. 656–68.

Runia, Eelco, 'Presence', in: *History and Theory* 45 (2006), pp. 1–29.

Rupp, Leila J., 'Outing the Past: US Queer History in Global Perspective', in: Leila J. Rupp and Susan K. Freeman (eds.), *Understanding and Teaching US Lesbian, Gay, Bisexual and Transgender History*, Madison: University of Wisconsin Press, 2014, pp. 17–30.

Rupp, Leila J. , and Susan K. Freeman, *US Lesbian, Gay, Bisexual and Transgender History*, Madison: University of Wisconsin Press, 2014.

Rüsen, Jörn, *Evidence and Meaning: a Theory of Historical Studies*, Oxford: Berghahn Books, 2017.

'Introduction: Historical Thinking as Intercultural Discourse', in: Rüsen (ed.), *Western Historical Thinking: an Intercultural Debate*, Oxford: Berghahn Books, 2002, pp. 1–14.

Menschsein: Grundlagen, Geschichte und Diskurse des Humanismus, Berlin: Kadmos, 2020.

'Responsibility and Irresponsibility in Historical Studies: a Critical Consideration of the Ethical Dimension of the Historian's Work', in: David Carr, Thomas R. Flynn and Rudolf A. Makkreel (eds.), *The Ethics of History*, Evanston, IL: Northwestern University Press, 2004.

Rüsen, Jörn, and Henner Laass (eds.), *Humanism in Intercultural Perspective: Experiences and Expectations*, Bielefeld: Transcript, 2009.

Ruspini, Elisabetta, Jeff Hearn, Bob Pease and Keith Pringle (eds.), *Men and Masculinities around the World: Transforming Men's Practices*, Basingstoke: Palgrave Macmillan, 2011.

Sá, Ana Lúcia, 'The Concept of "Land" in Bioko: "Land as Property" and "Land as Country"', in: Axel Fleisch and Rhiannon Stephens (eds.),

Doing Conceptual History in Africa, Oxford: Berghahn Books, 2016, pp. 138–61.

Sabean, David, *Property, Production and Family in Neckarhausen, 1700–1870*, Cambridge: Cambridge University Press, 1987.

Sabrow, Martin, *Das Diktat des Konsenses: Geschichtswissenschaft in der DDR, 1949–1969*, Munich: Oldenbourg, 2001.

Sachsenmaier, Dominic, *Global Perspectives on Global History: Theories and Approaches in a Connected World*, Cambridge: Cambridge University Press, 2011.

Sahlins, Marshall, *How 'Natives' Think: About Captain Cook, For Example*, Chicago: University of Chicago Press, 1995.

'Individual Experience and Cultural Order', in: Marshall Sahlins (ed.), *Culture in Practice: Selected Essays*, New York: Zone Books, 2000, pp. 277–91.

Said, Edward, 'Criticism, Culture and Performance', in: Gauri Viswanathan (ed.), *Power, Politics and Culture: Interviews with Edward W. Said*, London: Bloomsbury, 2005.

Orientalism, New York: Random House, 1978.

Samuel, Raphael, 'History Workshop 1966–1980', in: Raphael Samuel (ed.), *People's History and Socialist Theory*, London: Routledge, 1981, pp. 408–22.

Theatres of Memory, 2 vols., London: Verso, 1994–8.

Sandberg, John, 'Religion and the Enlightenment(s)', in: *History Compass* 8:11 (2010), pp. 1291–8.

Sartori, Andrew, *Liberalism in Empire: an Alternative History*, Berkeley: Yale University Press, 2014.

Saunier, Pierre-Yves, 'Going Transnational? News from Down Under: Transnational History Symposium, Canberra, ANU, September 2004', *Historical Social Research* 31:2 (2006), pp. 118–31.

Transnational History, Basingstoke: Palgrave Macmillan, 2013.

Savage, Kirk, 'Molding Emancipation: John Quincy Adams Ward's *The Freedman* and the Meaning of the Civil War', in: Vanessa R. Schwartz and Jeannene M. Przyblyski (eds.), *The Nineteenth-Century Visual Culture Reader*, London: Routledge, 2004, pp. 262–75.

Savage, Mike, 'Class and Labour History', in: Lex Heerma van Voss and Marcel van der Linden (eds.), *Class and Other Identities: Gender, Religion and Ethnicity in the Writing of European Labour History*, Oxford: Berghahn Books, 2002, pp. 55–72.

Savenije, G. M., and P. de Bruijn, 'Historical Empathy in the Museum: Uniting Contextualisation and Emotional Engagement', in: *International Journal of Heritage Studies* 23:4 (2017), pp. 832–45.

Sayer, Faye, *Public History: a Practical Guide*, London: Bloomsbury, 2015.

Scalmer, Sean, *On the Stump: Campaign Oratory and Democracy in the United States, Britain and Australia*, Philadelphia: Temple University Press, 2018.

Schatzki, Theodore R., Karin Knorr-Cetina and Eike von Savigny (eds.), *The Practice Turn in Contemporary Theory*, London: Routledge, 2001.

Schiebinger, Londa, *Nature's Body: Gender in the Making of Modern Science*, Boston: Harvard University Press, 1993.

Schmitt, Jean-Claude, *Le corps des images: essais sur la culture visuelle au moyen âge*, Paris: Gallimard, 2002.

Schneider, Axel, and Daniel Woolf (eds.), *The Oxford History of Historiography, vol. V: Historical Writing since 1945*, Oxford: Oxford University Press, 2011.

Schnicke, Falko, 'Princesses, Semen, and Separation: Masculinity and Body Politics in Nineteenth-Century German Historiography', in: *Bulletin of the German Historical Institute London* 40:1 (2018), pp. 26–60.

Schönwälder, Karen, '"Taking their Place in the Frontline" (?): German Historians during Nazism and War', in: *Tel Aviver Jahrbuch für deutsche Geschichte* 25 (1996), pp. 205–19.

Schöttler, Peter (ed.), *Marc Bloch: Historiker und Widerstandskämpfer*, Frankfurt am Main: Campus, 1999.

Schöttler, Peter, 'After the Deluge: the Impact of the Two World Wars on the Historical Work of Henri Pirenne and Marc Bloch', in: Stefan Berger and Chris Lorenz (eds.), *Nationalizing the Past: Historians and Nation Builders in Modern Europe*, Basingstoke: Palgrave Macmillan, 2010, pp. 404–25

'Historians and Discourse Analysis', in: *History Workshop Journal* 27 (1989), pp. 37–65.

'Lucien Febvres Beitrag zur Entmythologisierung der rheinischen Geschichte', in: *Lucien Febvre, Der Rhein und seine Geschichte*, ed. Peter Schöttler, Frankfurt am Main: Campus, 1994, pp. 217–63

Nach der Angst: Geschichtswissenschaft vor und nach dem 'linguistic turn', Münster: Westfälisches Dampfboot, 2018.

'Le Rhin comme enjeu historiographique dans l'entre-deux-guerres: vers une histoire des mentalités frontalières', *Genèses* 14 (1994), pp. 63–82.

Schreiner, Olive, *Women and Labour*, New York: Stokes, 1911.

Schultz, Hans-Dietrich, and Wolfgang Natter, 'Imagining Mitteleuropa: Conceptualisations of "its" Space in and outside German Geography', in: *European Review of History* 10:2 (2003), pp. 273–92.

Schwarz, Bill, 'History on the Move: Reflections on History Workshop', in: *Radical History Review* 57 (1993), pp. 202–20.

'Subaltern Histories', in: *History Workshop Journal* 89 (2019), pp. 90–107.

Schwarz, Bill (ed.), *The Expansion of England: Race, Ethnicity and Cultural History*, London: Routledge, 1996.

Schwartz, Vanessa R., 'Walter Benjamin for Historians', in: *American Historical Review* 106:5 (2001), pp. 1721–43.

Scott, Joan W., 'After History?', in: *Common Knowledge* 5 (1996), pp. 9–26.

'The Evidence of Experience', in: *Critical Inquiry* 17:4 (1991), pp. 773–97.

Gender and the Politics of History, 30th Anniversary Edition, New York: Columbia University Press, 2018.

'Gender: a Useful Category of Historical Analysis', in: *American Historical Review* 91:5 (1986), pp. 1053–75.

Scribner, Robert W., *Popular Culture and Popular Movements in Reformation Germany*, London: Hambledon Press, 1987.

Searle, J. R., *Speech Acts: an Essay in the Philosophy of Language*, Cambridge: Cambridge University Press, 1969.

Sebastian, Javier Fernández (ed.), *Political Concepts and Time: New Approaches to Conceptual History*, Santander: Cantabria University Press, 2011.

Seeley, Robert, *The Expansion of England: Two Courses of Lectures*, London: Macmillan, 1895.

Sen, Amartya, *Identity and Violence*, London: Penguin, 2006.

Sennett, Richard, *Flesh and Stone: the Body and the City in Western Civilisation*, New York: W. W. Norton, 1994.

Seshan, Radhika, 'Writing the Nation in India: Communalism and Historiography', in: Stefan Berger (ed), *Writing the Nation: a Global Perspective*, Basingstoke: Palgrave Macmillan, 2007, pp. 155–78.

Sewell, William H., Jr, 'The Concept(s) of Culture', in: Gabrielle M. Spiegel (ed.), *Practicing History: New Directions in Historical Writing after the Linguistic Turn*, London: Routledge, 2005, pp. 76–96.

'A Theory of Structure: Duality, Agency, and Transformation', in: *American Journal of Sociology* 98 (1992), pp. 1–29.

Shanguhyia, Martin S., and Toyin Falola, 'Introduction', in: Martin S. Shanguhyia and Toyin Falola (eds.), *The Palgrave Handbook of African Colonial and Postcolonial History*, Basingstoke: Palgrave Macmillan, 2018, pp. 1–39.

Shaw, Rosalind, *Memories of the Slave Trade: Ritual and Historical Imagination in Sierra Leone*, Chicago: University of Chicago Press, 2002.

Shepherd, Laura J., *Gender Matters in Global Politics: a Feminist Introduction to International Relations*, London: Routledge, 2009.

Shryock, Andrew, and Daniel Lord Smail (eds.), *Deep History: the Architecture of Past and Present*, Berkeley: University of California Press, 2011

Siapno, Jacqueline Aquino , *Gender, Islam, Nationalism and the State in Aceh: the Paradox of Power, Co-optation and Resistance*, London: Routledge, 2002.

Siméant, Johanna, and Christoph Traïni, *Bodies in Protest: Hunger Strikes and Angry Music*, Amsterdam: Amsterdam University Press, 2016.

Simon, Zoltán Boldizsár, 'Microhistory: in General', in: *Journal of Social History* 49:1 (2015), pp. 237–48.

Singh Mehta, Uday, *Liberalism and Empire: a Study in Nineteenth-Century British Liberal Thought*, Chicago: University of Chicago Press, 1999.

Sinha, Mrinalini, *Colonial Masculinity: the 'Manly Englishman' and the 'Effeminate Bengali' in the Late Nineteenth Century*, Manchester: Manchester University Press, 1995.

Specters of Mother India: the Global Restructruring of an Empire, Durham, NC: Duke University Press, 2006.

Sizgorich, Thomas, 'Religious History', in: Sara Foot and Chase F. Robinson (eds.), *The Oxford History of Historical Writing, vol. II: 400–1400*, Oxford: Oxford University Press, 2012, pp. 604–28.

Skinner, Quentin, *The Foundations of Modern Political Thought, vol. I: the Renaissance; vol. II: the Age of the Reformation*, Cambridge: Cambridge University Press, 1978.

'A Genealogy of the Modern State', in: *Proceedings of the British Academy* 162 (2009), pp. 325–70.

Hobbes and Republican Liberty, Cambridge: Cambridge University Press, 2008.

'Intellectual History, Liberty and Republicanism: an Interview with Quentin Skinner', in: *Contributions to the History of Concepts* 3 (2007), pp. 113–15.

Liberty before Liberalism, Cambridge: Cambridge University Press, 1998.

'Meaning and Understanding in the History of Ideas', in: *History and Theory* 8:1 (1969), pp. 3–53.

Reason and Rhetoric in the Philosophy of Hobbes, Cambridge: Cambridge University Press, 1996.

'Retrospect: Studying Rhetoric and Conceptual Change', in: Skinner, *Visions of Politics, vol. I: Regarding Method*, Cambridge: Cambridge University Press, 2002, pp. 175–87.

Slate, Nico, *Colored Cosmopolitanism: the Shared Struggle for Freedom in the United States and India*, Cambridge, MA: Harvard University Press, 2012.

The Prism of Race: W. E. B. Du Bois, Langston Hughes, Paul Robeson, and the Colored World of Cedric Dover, Basingstoke: Palgrave Macmillan, 2014.

Smail, Daniel Lord, *On Deep History and the Brain*, Berkeley: University of California Press, 2008.

Smith, Bonnie G., *The Gender of History: Men, Women and Historical Practice*, Cambridge, MA: Harvard University Press, 1998.

Smith, Shawn Michelle, 'Photographing the "American Negro": Nation, Race and Photography at the Paris Exhibition in 1900', in: Ardis Cameron (ed.), *Looking for America: the Visual Production of Nation and People*, Oxford: Blackwell, 2005, pp. 61–93.

Smith-Rosenberg, Carroll, *Disorderly Conduct: Visions of Gender in American History*, Oxford: Oxford University Press, 1985.

Snell, Keith, 'English Historical Continuity and the Culture of Capitalism: the Work of Alan Macfarlane', in: *History Workshop Journal* 27:1 (1989), pp. 154–63.

Snyder, Timothy, *Bloodlands. Europe between Hitler and Stalin*, New York: Basic Books, 2010.

Soh, C. Sarah, *The Comfort Women: Sexual Violence and Postcolonial Memory in Korea and Japan*, Chicago: University of Chicago Press, 2008.

Sombart, Werner, *Why Is There No Socialism in the United States?*, London: Routledge, 2019 (originally published in German in 1906).

Spence, Jonathan D., *The Memory Palace of Matteo Ricci*, London: Quercus, 2008.

Spiegel, Gabrielle M., 'Historical Thought in Medieval Europe', in: Lloyd Kramer and Sarah Maza (eds.), *A Companion to Western Historical Thought*, Oxford: Blackwell, 2002, pp. 78–98.

The Limits of Empiricism: the Utility of Theory in Historical Thought and Writing', in: *Medieval History Journal* 22:1 (2019), pp. 1–22.

Gabrielle M., *Practicing History: New Directions in Historical Writing after the Linguistic Turn*, London: Routledge, 2005.

'Rhetorical Theory/Theoretical Rhetoric: Some Ambiguities in the Reception of Hayden White's Work', in: Robert Doran (ed.), *Philosophy of History after Hayden White*, London: Bloomsbury, 2013, pp. 171–82

Spier, Fred, *Big History and the Future of Humanity*, 2nd edn, Oxford: Wiley-Blackwell, 2015.

The Structure of Big History: from the Big Bang until Today, Amsterdam: Amsterdam University Press, 1996.

Spivak, Gayatri Chakravorty, 'The Rani of Sirmur: an Essay in Reading the Archives', in: *History and Theory* 24:3 (1985), pp. 247–72.

Spivak, Gayatri Chakravorty (ed.), *Towards a History of the Vanishing Present*, Cambridge, MA: Harvard University Press, 1999.

Spongberg, Mary, *Women Writers and the Nation's Past, 1790–1860: Empathetic Histories*, London: Bloomsbury, 2019.

Städter, Benjamin, *Verwandelte Blicke: eine Visual History von Kirche und Religion in der Bundesrepublik, 1945–1980*, Frankfurt am Main: Campus, 2011.

Stafford, Barbara Marie, *Echo Objects: the Cognitive Work of Images*, Chicago: University of Chicago Press, 2007.

Stahl, Ann Brower, *Making History in Banda: Anthropological Visions of Africa's Past*, Cambridge: Cambridge University Press, 2001.

'Material Histories', in: Dan Hicks and Mary C. Beaudry (eds.), *The Oxford Handbook of Material Culture Studies*, Oxford: Oxford University Press, 2010, pp. 150–72.

Starkey, David, 'The English Historian's Role and the Place of History in English National Life', in: *The Historian* 71 (2001), pp. 6–15.

Stearns, Peter, *Sexuality in World History*, London: Routledge, 2009.

Stearns, Peter N., and Carol Z. Stearns, 'Emotionology: Clarifying the History of Emotions and Emotional Standards', in: *American Historical Review* 90:4 (1985), pp. 813–36.

Steedman, Carolyn, *Landscape for a Good Woman*, Chicago, IL: Rutgers University Press, 1987.

Steele, Valerie, *Corset: a Cultural History*, New Haven: Yale University Press, 2001.

Stein, Marc, 'Theoretical Politics, Local Communities: the Making of US LGBT Historiography', in: *GLQ: a Journal of Lesbian and Gay Studies* 11 (2005), 605–25.

Stein,Marc (ed.), *Encyclopedia of Lesbian, Gay, Bisexual and Transgendered History in America*, 3 vols., New York: Charles Scribners, 2003.

Steinmetz, Willibald (ed.), *The Force of Comparison: New Perspective on Modern European History and the Contemporary World*, Oxford: Berghahn Books, 2019.

Steinmetz, Willibald, Michael Freeden and Javier Fernández-Sebastián (eds.), *Conceptual History in the European Space*, Oxford: Berghahn Books, 2017.

Steinmetz, Willibald, Ingrid Gilcher-Holtey and Heinz-Gerhard Haupt (eds.), *Writing Political History Today*, Frankfurt am Main: Campus, 2013.

Stelzel, Philipp, *History after Hitler: a Transatlantic Enterprise*, Philadelphia: University of Pennsylvania Press, 2019.

Stenius, Henrik, 'Concepts in the Nordic Periphery', in: Willibald Steinmetz, Michael Freeden and Javier Fernández-Sebastián (eds.), *Conceptual*

History in the European Space, Oxford: Berghahn Books, 2017, pp. 263–80.

Stephens, Rhiannon, and Axel Fleisch, 'Theories and Methods of African Conceptual History', in: Axel Fleisch and Rhiannon Stephens (eds.), *Doing Conceptual History in Africa*, Oxford: Berghahn Books, 2016, pp. 3–5.

Stewart, Charles (ed.), *Creolization: History Ethnography, Theory*, Walnut Creek, CA: Left Coast Press, 2006.

Stoler, Ann Laura, *Along the Archival Grain: Epistemic Anxieties and Colonial Common Sense*, Princeton: Princeton University Press, 2008.

Capitalism and Confrontation in Sumatra's Plantation Belt, 1870–1979, New Haven: Yale University Press, 1985.

Carnal Knowledge and Imperial Power: Race and the Intimate in Colonial Rule, Berkeley: University of California Press, 2002.

Duress: Imperial Durabilities in Our Times, Durham, NC: Duke University Press, 2016.

'In Cold Blood: Hierarchies of Credibility and the Politics of Colonial Narratives', in: *Representations* 37 (1992), pp. 151–89.

Race and the Education of Desire: Foucault's History of Sexuality and the Colonial Order of Things, Durham, NC: Duke University Press, 1995.

Stoler, Ann Laura, and Frederick Cooper, 'Between Metropole and Colony: Rethinking a Research Agenda', in: Ann Laura Stoler and Frederick Cooper (eds.), *Tensions of Empire: Colonial Cultures in a Bourgeois World*, Los Angeles: University of California Press, 1997, pp. 1–56.

Stone, Lawrence, 'The Revival of Narrative: Reflections on a New Old History', in: *Past and Present* 85 (1979), pp. 3–24.

Storm, Eric, 'The Spatial Turn and the History of Nationalism: Nationalism between Regionalism and Transnational Approaches', in: Stefan Berger and Eric Storm (eds.), *Writing the History of Nationalism*, London: Bloomsbury, 2019, pp. 215–38.

Stråth, Bo, 'Ideology and Conceptual History', in: Michael Freeden, Lyman Tower Sargent and Marc Stears (eds.), *The Oxford Handbook of Political Ideologies*, Oxford: Oxford University Press, 2013, pp. 3–19.

'"Norden" as a European Region: Demarcation and Belonging', in: J. P. Arnason (ed.), *Domains and Divisions of European History*, Liverpool: Liverpool University Press, 2009, pp. 198–215.

Straub, Jürgen (ed.), *Narration, Identity and Historical Consciousness*, Oxford: Berghahn Books, 2005.

Strickrodt, Silke, '"Afro-Brazilians" of the Western Slave Coast in the Nineteenth Century', in: José C. Curto and Paul E. Lovejoy (eds.), *Enslaving Connections: Changing Cultures of Africa and Brazil during the Era of Slavery*, New York: Humanity Books, 2004, pp. 213–44.

Stuchtey, Benedikt, and Eckhardt Fuchs (eds.), *Writing World History, 1800–2000*, Oxford: Oxford University Press, 2003.

Suvrathan, Uthara, 'Spoiled for Choice? The Sacred Landscape of Ancient and Early Medieval Banavasi', in: *South Asian Studies* 30:2 (2014), pp. 206–29.

Swartz, David, *Culture and Power: the Sociology of Pierre Bourdieu*, Chicago: University of Chicago Press, 1997.

Sweet, Rosemary, *Antiquaries: the Discovery of the Past in Eighteenth-Century Britain*, London: Hambledon, 2004.

Taithe, Bertrand, 'Monuments aux Morts? Reading Nora's *Realms of Memory* and Samuel's *Theatres of Memory*', in: *History of the Human Sciences* 12:2 (1999), pp. 123–39.

Tamm, Marek, 'The Republic of Historians: Historians as Nation-Builders in Estonia (late 1980s to early 1990s)', in: *Rethinking History* 20:2 (2016), pp. 154–71.

'Truth, Objectivity and Evidence in History Writing', in: *Journal of the Philosophy of History* 8:2 (2014), pp. 265–90.

Tamm, Marek, and Peter Burke (eds.), *Debating New Approaches to History*, London: Bloomsbury, 2019.

Tamm, Marek, and Laurent Olivier (eds.), *Rethinking Historical Time: New Approaches to Presentism*, London: Bloomsbury, 2019.

Tamm, Marek, and Zoltán Boldizsár Simon, 'More-than-Human History: Philosophy of History at the Time of the Anthropocene', in: J. M. Kuukkanen (ed.), *Philosophy of History: Twenty-First Century Perspectives*, London: Bloomsbury 2020, pp. 198–215.

Tamm, Marek, and Eugen Zeleňak, 'In a Parallel World: an Introduction to Frank Ankersmit's Philosophy of History', in: *Journal of the Philosophy of History* 12 (2018), pp. 325–44.

Tanaka, Stefan, *Japan's Orient: Rendering Pasts into History*, Berkeley: University of California Press, 1993.

Tanner, Duncan, *Political Change and the Labour Party, 1900–1918*, Cambridge: Cambridge University Press, 1990.

Tanner, Jakob, 'Historical Anthropology', in: Stefan Berger, Heiko Feldner and Kevin Passmore (eds.), *Writing History: Theory and Practice*, 3rd edn, London: Bloomsbury, 2020, pp. 236–52.

Historische Anthropologie zur Einführung, Hamburg: Junus, 2004.

'Narratives', in: Kathrin Fahlenbrach, Martin Klimke and Joachim Scharloth (eds.), *Protest Cultures: a Companion*, Oxford: Berghahn Books, 2016, pp. 137–45.

Taylor, Barbara, *Eve and the New Jerusalem: Socialism and Feminism in the Nineteenth Century*, New York: Virago, 1983.

Taylor, Miles, *The Decline of British Radicalism, 1847–1860*, Oxford: Oxford University Press, 1995.

Te Awekotuku, Ngahuia, and L. W. Nikora, *Mau Moko: the World of Māori Tattoo*, Honolulu: University of Hawaii Press, 2007.

te Velde, Henk, 'The Dilemma of National History', in: A.in't Groen, H. J. De Jonge, E. Klaasen, H. Papma and P. van Slooten (eds.), *Knowledge in Ferment: Dilemmas in Science, Scholarship and Society*, Leiden: Leiden University Press, 2007, pp. 227–41.

'Political Transfer: an Introduction', in: *European Review of History* 12:2 (2005), pp. 205–21.

te Velde, H., and Maarte Janse (eds.), *Organising Democracy: Reflections on the Rise of Political Organisations in the Nineteenth Century*, Basingstoke: Palgrave Macmillan, 2017.

Thébaut, Françoise, 'Writing Women's and Gender History in France: a National Narrative?', in: *Journal of Women's History* 19:1 (2007), pp. 167–72.

Ther, Philipp, 'Beyond the Nation: the Relational Basis of a Comparative History of Germany and Europe', in: *Central European History* 36:1 (2003), pp. 45–73.

Thijs, Krijn, 'The Metaphor of the Master: "Narrative Hierarchy" in National Historical Cultures of Europe', in: Stefan Berger and Chris Lorenz (eds.), *The Contested Nation: Ethnicity, Class, Religion and Gender in National Histories*, Basingstoke: Palgrave Macmillan, 2008, pp. 60–74.

Thioub, Ibrahima , 'Writing National and Transnational History in Africa: the Example of the "Dakar School"', in: Stefan Berger (ed), *Writing the Nation: a Global Perspective*, Basingstoke: Palgrave Macmillan, 2007, pp. 197–212.

Thomas, Keith, *Religion and the Decline of Magic*, London: Weidenfeld and Nicolson, 1971.

Thomas, Lynn M., 'Imperial Concerns and "Women's Affairs": State Efforts to Regulate Clitorectomy and Eradicate Abortion in Meru, Kenya, c. 1910–1950', in: *Journal of African History* 39 (1998), pp. 121–45.

Politics of the Womb: Women, Reproduction and the State in Kenya, Berkeley: University of California Press, 2003.

Thompson, Drew A., 'Visualizing FRELIMO's Liberated Zones in Mozambique, 1962–1974', in: *Social Dynamics* 39:1(2013), pp. 24–50.

Thompson, E. P., 'History and Anthropology', in: Thompson, *Persons and Polemics: Historical Essays*, London: Merlin Press, 1994, pp. 201–27.

The Making of the English Working Class, Harmondsworth: Penguin, 1963.

'The Moral Economy of the English Crowd in the Eighteenth Century', in: *Past and Present* 50 (1971), pp. 76–136.

'"Rough Music": le Charivari Anglais', in: *Annales* 27:2 (1972), pp. 285–312.

Thompson, Martyn P., *Michael Oakeshott and the Cambridge School on the History of Political Thought*, London: Routledge, 2019.

Thorstendahl, Rolf, *The Rise and Propagation of Historical Professionalism*, London: Routledge, 2015.

Thrift, Nigel, *Non-Representational Theory: Space, Politics, Affect*, London: Routledge, 2008.

Tickner, Lisa, 'Banners and Banner Making', in: Vanessa R. Schwartz and Jeannene M. Przyblyski (eds.), *The Nineteenth-Century Visual Culture Reader*, London: Routledge, 2004, pp. 341–7.

Tilley, Christopher (ed.), *Reading Material Culture: Structuralism, Hermeneutics and Post-Structuralism*, Oxford: Blackwell, 1990.

Tilley, Christopher, Webb Keane, Susanne Küchler, Mike Rowlands and Patricia Spyer (eds.), *Handbook of Material Culture*, London: Sage, 2006.

Tilly, Charles, *Big Structures, Large Processes, Huge Comparisons*, New York: Sage, 1985, pp. 81–143.

Todorov, Tzvetan, *Mikhail Bakhtin: the Dialogical Principle*, Minneapolis: University of Minnesota Press, 1984.

Todorova, Maria, *Imagining the Balkans*, Oxford: Oxford University Press, 1997.

Tollebeek, Jo, 'At the Crossroads of Nationalism: Huizinga, Pirenne and the Low Countries in Europe', in: *European Review of History* 17:2 (2010), pp. 187–215.

Tosh, John, 'What Should Historians Do with Masculinity? Reflections on Ninenteenth-Century Britain', in: *History Workshop Journal* 38 (1994), pp. 179–202.

Toulalan, Sarah, and Kate Fisher (eds.), *The Routledge History of Sex and the Body, 1500 to the Present*, London: Routledge, 2013.

Toynbee, Arnold, *A Study of History*, 12 vols., Oxford: Oxford University Press, 1934–61.

Trencsényi, Balázs, 'Balkans *Baedecker* for *Übermensch* Tourists: Janko Janev's Popular Historiography', in: Stefan Berger, Billie Melman and Chris Lorenz (eds.), *Popularizing National Pasts: 1800 to the Present*, London: Routledge, 2012, pp. 149–68.

Trencsényi, Balázs, Michael Kopeček, Luka Lisjak Gabrijelčič, Maria Falina, Mónika Baár and Maciej Janowski, *A History of Modern Political Thought in East Central Europe*, 2 vols., Oxford: Oxford University Press, 2018.

Trentmann, Frank, *Empire of Things: How We Became a World of Consumers from the Fifteenth Century to the Twenty-First*, London: Allen Lane, 2016.

Trepanier, Lee, *Political Symbols in Russia: Church, State and the Quest for Order and Justice*, Lanham, MD: Lexington Books, 2007.

Troebst, Stefan, '"Historical Meso-Region": a Concept in Cultural Studies and Historiography', in: *European History Online* (EGO), published by the Leibniz Institute of European History (IEG), Mainz, 6 March 2012; www.ieg-ego.eu/troebsts-2010-en [accessed 14 May 2020].

'Slavizität: Identitätsmuster, Analyserahmen, Mythos', in: *Osteuropa* 59:12 (2009), pp. 7–20.

Troebst, Stefan (ed.), 'Geschichtsregionen: Concept and Critique', special issue of *European Review of History* 10:2 (2003).

Turda, Marius, and Maria Sophia Quine, *Historicizing Race*, London: Bloomsbury, 2018.

Turner, Frederick Jackson, *The Frontier in American History*, New York: Holt, 1920.

Turner, Victor, *The Ritual Process: Structure and Anti-Structure*, London: Routledge, 2017.

Tyrrell, Ian, *The Absent Marx: Class Analysis and Liberal History in 20th Century America*, Westport, CT: Greenwood Press, 1986.

'American Exceptionalism in an Age of International History', in: *American Historical Review* 96:4 (1991), pp. 1031–55.

Ugolini, Wendy, '"When Are You Going Back?" Memory, Ethnicity and the British Home Front', in: Lucy Noakes and Juliette Pattinson (eds.), *British Cultural Memory and the Second World War*, London: Bloomsbury, 2014, pp. 89–110.

Ulrich, Laurel Thatcher, Ivan Gaskell, Sara J. Schechner and Sarah Anne Carter, 'Introduction: Thinking with Things', in: Laurel Thatcher Ulrich, Ivan Gaskell, Sara J. Schechner and Sarah Anne Carter (eds.), *Tangible Things: Making History through Objects*, Oxford: Oxford University Press, 2015, pp. 1–20.

Unger, Johann Wolfgang, Michal Krzyzanowski and Ruth Wodak (eds.), *Multilingual Encounters in Europe's Institutional Spaces*, London: Bloomsbury, 2014.

Usher , P. Abbot, 'Sir J. H. Clapham and the Empirical Reaction in Economic History', in: *Journal of Economic History* 11:2 (1951), pp. 148–53.

Vágó, Péter, 'The Politics of History in Hungary after 2010', in: Katarzyna Kącka and Ralph Schattkowsky (eds.), *History and Politics: Remembrance as Legitimation*, Cambridge: Cambridge Scholars, 2017, pp. 281–92.

Vale, Lawrence J., *Architecture, Power and National Identity*, 2nd edn, London: Routledge, 2008.

Valensi, Lucette, 'Histoire nationale, histoire monumental: les lieux de mémoirs', in: *Annales* 50:6 (1995), pp. 1271–7.

van der Linden, Marcel, 'The "Globalization"of Labour and Working-Class History and its Consequences', in: Jan Lucassen (ed.), *Global Labour History: a State of the Art*, Bern: Peter Lang, 2006, pp. 13–38.

van Dülmen, Richard, *Historische Anthropologie: Entwicklung, Probleme, Aufgaben*, Cologne: UTB, 2004.

van Sledright, Bruce A., 'From Empathic Regard to Self-Understanding: Im/Positionality, Empathy and Historical Contextualisation', in: O. L. Davis Jr, Elizabeth Anne Yeager and Stuart J. Fosten (eds.), *Historical Empathy and Perspective-Taking in the Social Studies*, Lanham, MD: Rowman and Littlefield, 2001, pp. 51–68.

van Zanden, Jan Luiten, 'Introduction', in: Jan Luiten van Zanden, Auke Rijpma and Jan Kok (eds.), *Agency, Gender, and Economic Development in the World Economy, 1850–2000: Testing the Sen Hypothesis*, London: Routledge, 2017, pp. 1–9.

Vanhaute, Eric, *World History: an Introduction*, London: Routledge, 2012.

Vann, Richard T., 'The Reception of Hayden White', in: *History and Theory* 37:2 (1998), pp. 143–61

Vansina, Jan, *Paths in the Rainforest*, Madison: University of Wisconsin Press, 1990.

Vargas, Michael A., *Constructing Catalan Identity: Memory, Imagination, and the Medieval*, Basingstoke: Palgrave Macmillan, 2018.

Varma, Nitin, 'Servant Testimonies and Anglo-Indian Homes in Nineteenth-Century India', in: Felicitas Hentschke and James Williams (eds.), *To Be at Home: House, Work, and Self in the Modern World*, Berlin: De Gruyter, 2018, pp. 219–28.

Vasilev, George, 'Methodological Nationalism and the Politics of History-Writing: How Imaginary Scholarship Perpetuates the Nation', in: *Nations and Nationalism* 25:2 (2019), pp. 499–522.

Vaughan, Megan, 'Culture', in: Ulinka Rublack (ed.), *A Concise Companion to History*, Oxford: Oxford University Press, 2011, pp. 227–45.

Vergara, Alejandro, *Velazquez, Rembrandt, Vermeer: miradas afines*, Madrid: Museo Nacional del Prado, 2019.

Vernon, James, *Politics and the People: a Study in English Political Culture, c. 1815–1867*, Cambridge: Cambridge University Press, 1993.

Vice, Sue, *Introducing Bakhtin*, Manchester: Manchester University Press, 1997.

Vlossak, Elizabeth, 'Gender Approaches to the History of Nationalism', in: Stefan Berger and Eric Storm (eds.), *Writing the History of Nationalism*, London: Bloomsbury, 2019, pp. 191–214.

Vokes, Richard, 'The Chairman's Photographs: the Politics of an Archive in South-Western Uganda', in: Christopher Morton and Darren Newbury (eds.), *The African Photographic Archive: Research and Curatorial Strategies*, London: Bloomsbury, 2015, pp. 95–112.

Vokes, Richard, and Darren Newbury, 'Photography and African Futures', in: *Visual Studies* 33:1 (2018), pp. 1–10.

Volpe, Andrea L., 'Cartes des Visite Portrait Photographs and the Culture of Class Formation', in: Ardis Cameron (ed.), *Looking for America: the Visual Production of Nation and People*, Oxford: Blackwell, 2005, pp. 42–58.

von Ranke, Leopold, *Über die Epochen der neueren Geschichte*, Darmstadt: Wissenschaftliche Buchgesellschaft, 1982 (originally published in 1854).

Vörös, László, 'The Social Function of Historical Knowledge and Scholarly History Writing in the 21st Century', in: *Historický Casopis* 65:5 (2017), pp. 785–97.

Vushko, Iryna, 'Historians at War: History, Politics and Memory in Ukraine', in: *Contemporary European History* 27:1 (2018), pp. 112–24.

Wahrmann, Dror, *Imagining the Middle Class: the Political Representation of Class in Britain, c. 1780–1840*, Cambridge: Cambridge University Press, 1995.

Walker Bynum, Caroline, 'Why All the Fuss about the Body? A Medievalist's Perspective', in: *Critical Enquiry* 22 (1995), pp. 1–33.

Wallace-Sanders, Kimberly (ed.), *Skin Deep, Spirit Strong: the Black Female Body in American Culture*, Ann Arbor: University of Michigan Press, 2002.

Wallerstein, Immanuel, *The Modern World System*, 4 vols., Berkeley: University of California Press, 2011.

Wallerstein, Immanuel, Charles Lemert and Carlos Aguirre Rojas, *Uncertain Worlds: World-Systems Analysis in Changing Times*, London: Routledge, 2012.

Walsh, Colleen, 'Stonewall Then and Now: Harvard Scholars Reflect on the History and Legacy of the Milestone Gay Rights Demonstrations Triggered by a Police Raid at a Dive Bar in New York', in: *Harvard Gazette* (27 June 2019); https://news.harvard.edu/gazette/story/2019/06/harvard-scholars-reflect-on-the-history-and-legacy-of-the-stonewall-riots/ [accessed 2 April 2020].

Walsham, Alexandra, 'Rough Music and Charivari: Letters between Natalie Zemon Davis and Edward Thompson, 1970–1972', in: *Past and Present* 235 (2017), pp. 243–62.

Wang, Edward Q., 'Between Marxism and Nationalism: Chinese Historiography and the Soviet Influence, 1949–1963', in: *Journal of Contemporary China* 9 (2000), pp. 95–111.

'Between Myth and History: the Construction of a National Past in Modern East Asia', in: Stefan Berger (ed), *Writing the Nation: a Global Perspective*, Basingstoke: Palgrave Macmillan, 2007, pp. 126–54.

Ward, Stuart, 'Transcending the Nation? A Global Imperial History', in: Antoinette Burton (ed.), *After the Imperial Turn: Thinking with and through the Nation*, Durham, NC: Duke University Press, 2003, pp. 44–56.

Warf, Barney, and Santa Arias (eds.), *The Spatial Turn: Interdisciplinary Perspectives*, London: Routledge, 2009.

Wastl-Walter, Doris (ed.), *The Ashgate Research Companion to Border Studies*, London: Routledge, 2016.

Watson, Rubie S. (ed.), *History, Memory and Opposition under State Socialism*, Santa Fe: School of American Research Press, 1994.

Watson, Vanessa, 'African Urban Fantasies: Dreams or Nightmares?', in: *Environment and Urbanization* 26:1 (2014), pp. 215–31.

Watts, Jennifer, 'Picture Taking in Paradise: Los Angeles and the Creation of Regional Identity, 1880–1920', in: Vanessa R. Schwartz and Jeannene M. Przyblyski (eds.), *The Nineteenth Century Visual Culture Reader*, London: Routledge, 2004, pp. 218–32.

Watts, Jennifer A. (ed.), *Maynard L. Parker: Modern Photography and the American Dream*, New Haven: Yale University Pres, 2012.

Weaver, Stewart A., *The Hammonds: a Marriage in History*, Stanford: Stanford University Press, 1997.

Weber, Wolfgang, 'Hayden White in Deutschland', in: *Storia della Storiografia* 25 (1994), pp. 89–102.

Wehler, Hans-Ulrich, *The German Empire*, Oxford: Berg, 1985.

Weir, Robert E., *Beyond Labor's Veil: the Culture of the Knights of Labor*, University Park, PA: Pennsylvania State University Press, 1996.

Wellings, Ben, *English Nationalism and Euroscepticism: Losing the Peace*, Bern: Peter Lang, 2012.

'Our Island Story: England, Europe and the Anglophone Alternative', in: *Political Studies Review* 14:3 (2016), pp. 368–77.

Wellings, Ben, and Chris Gifford, 'The Past in English Euroscepticism', in: Stefan Berger and Caner Tekin (eds.), *History and Belonging: Representations of the Past in Contemporary European Politics*, Oxford: Berghahn Books, 2018, pp. 88–105.

Welskopp, Thomas, *Das Banner der Brüderlichkeit. Die deutsche Sozialdemokratie vom Vormärz bis zum Sozialistengesetzt*, Bonn: J. W. H. Dietz Nachf., 2000.

'Clio and Class Struggle in Socialist Histories of the Nation: a Comparison of Robert Grimm's and Eduard Bernstein's Writings, 1910–1920', in:

Stefan Berger and Chris Lorenz (eds.), *Nationalizing the Past: Historians and Nation Builders in Modern Europe*, Basingstoke: Palgrave Macmillan, 2010, pp. 298–318.

'Social History', in: Stefan Berger, Heiko Feldner and Kevin Passmore (eds.), *Writing History: Theory and Practice*, 3rd edn, London: Bloomsbury, 2020, pp. 343–62.

Werner, Michael, and Bénédicte Zimmermann, 'Beyond Comparison: "Histoire Croisee" and the Challenge of Reflexivity', *History and Theory* 45:1 (2006), pp. 30–50.

Wertsch, James V., *Voices of Collective Remembering*, Cambridge: Cambridge University Press, 2002.

Whatmore, Sarah, *Hybrid Geographies: Natures, Cultures, Spaces*, London: Sage, 2002.

White, Hayden, *Metahistory: the Historical Imagination in Nineteenth-Century Europe*, Baltimore: Johns Hopkins University Press, 1973.

The Practical Past, Evanston, IL: Northwestern University Press, 2014.

White, Stephen D., and Richard T. Vann, 'The Invention of English Individualism: Alan Macfarlane and the Modernization of Pre-Modern England', in: *Social History* 8:3 (1983), pp 345–63.

Wickramasinghe, Nira, *Dressing the Colonised Body: Politics, Clothing and Identity in Colonial Sri Lanka*, London: Longman, 2003.

Wierzbicka, Anna, *Imprisoned in English: the Hazards of English as a Default Language*, Oxford: Oxford University Press, 2014.

Understanding Cultures through Their Key Words: English, Russian, Polish, German, and Japanese, Oxford: Oxford University Press, 1997.

Wiesner-Hanks, Merry E. (ed.), *The Cambridge World History*, 9 vols., Cambridge: Cambridge University Press, 2015.

Wildt, Michael, 'Die grosse Geschichtswerkstattschlacht im Jahre 1992 oder: Wie Werkstatt Geschichte entstand', in: *Werkstatt Geschichte* 50 (2009), pp. 70–7.

Willaime, Jean-Paul, 'De la sacralisation de la France: lieux de mémoire et imaginaire national', in: *Archives de Science Sociales des Religions* 66 (1988), pp. 125–45.

Williams, Gareth, *Writers of Wales: George Ewart Evans*, Cardiff: Cardiff University Press, 1991.

Williams, Paul, *Paul Gilroy*, London: Routledge, 2013.

Williams, Raymond, *Culture*, London: Fontana, 1981.

'Culture is Ordinary', in: Williams, *Resources of Hope: Culture, Democracy, Socialism*, London: Verso, 1989, pp. 3–14.

Keywords: a Vocabulary of Culture and Society, Oxford: Oxford University Press, 1976.

Wilson, Kathleen, *The Sense of the People: Politics, Culture and Imperialism in England, 1715–1785*, Cambridge: Cambridge University Press, 1998.

Wilson, Norman J., *History in Crisis? Recent Directions in Historiography*, 3rd edn, New York: Pearson, 2014.

Wilson, Thomas M., and Hastings Donnan (eds.), *Companion to Border Studies*, Oxford: Blackwell, 2012.

Wimmer, Andreas, and Nina Glick-Schiller, 'Methodological Nationalism and Beyond: Nation-State Building, Migration and the Social Sciences', in: *Global Networks* 2:4 (2002), pp. 301–34.

Winetrout, Kenneth, 'The New Age of the Visible: a Call to Study', in: *AV Communication Review* 12:1 (1964), pp. 46–52.

Winks, Robin W. (ed.), *Historiography: the Oxford History of the British Empire, vol. V*, Oxford: Oxford University Press, 1999.

Winter, Jay, *Remembering War: the Great War between Memory and History in the Twentieth Century*, New Haven: Yale University Press, 2006.

War beyond Words: Languages of Remembrance from the Great War to the Present, Cambridge: Cambridge University Press, 2017.

Wintle, Michael J., *The Image of Europe: Visualizing Europe in Cartography and Iconography*, Cambridge: Cambridge University Press, 2009.

Wodak, Ruth, Majid Khosravinik and Brigitte Mral (eds.), *Right-Wing Populism in Europe: Politics and Discourse*, London: Bloomsbury, 2013.

Wollff, Larry, *Inventing Eastern Europe: the Map of Civilisation on the Mind of the Enlightenment*, Stanford: Stanford University Press, 1994.

Wohlfahrt, Ian, 'Et Cetera? The Historian as Chiffonier', in: *New German Critique* 39 (1986), pp. 143–86.

Wolkowitz, Carol, *Bodies at Work*, London: Sage, 2006.

Woodward, Ian, *Understanding Material Culture*, London: Sage, 2007.

Woolf, Daniel, *A Global History of History*, Cambridge: Cambridge University Press, 2011.

Woolf, Stuart, 'The Changing Role of History and of Historians over the Past Half Century', in: *Storial della Storiografia* 52 (2007), pp. 3–30.

Wootton, David, 'Lucien Febvre and the Problem of Unbelief in the Early Modern Period', in: *Journal of Modern History* 60:4 (1988), pp. 695–730.

Wright, Anthony, *R. H. Tawney*, Manchester: Manchester University Press, 1988.

Wright, Johnson Kent, 'Historical Thought in the Era of the Enlightenment', in: Lloyd Kramer and Sarah Maza (eds.), *A Companion to Western Historical Thought*, Oxford: Blackwell, 2002, pp. 123–42.

Wrightson, Keith, 'The Enclosure of English Social History', in: Adrian Wilson (ed.), *Rethinking Social History: English Society, 1570-*

1920 and its Interpretation, Manchester: Manchester University Press, 1993, pp. 59–77.

Wulf, Christoph, 'On Historical Anthropology: an Introduction', in: *The Senses and Society* 11:1 (2016), pp. 7–23.

Wüstenberg, Jenny, and Aline Sierp (eds.), *Agency in Transnational Memory Politics*, Oxford: Berghahn Books, 2020.

Yan, Chen, and Karen Offen, 'Women's History at the Cutting Edge: a Joint Paper in Two Voices', in: *Women's History Review* 27:1 (2018), pp. 6–28.

Yilmaz, Harun, *National Identities in Soviet Historiography: the Rise of Nations under Stalin*, London: Routledge, 2015.

Young, James E., 'The Counter-Monument: Memory against Itself in Germany Today', in: *Critiqual Inquiry* 18:2 (1992), pp. 267–96.

The Texture of Memory: Holocaust Memorials and Meaning, New Haven: Yale University Press, 1993.

Young, Robert J. C., *Empire, Colony, Postcolony*, Oxford: Wiley Blackwell, 2015.

Zhang, Xupeng, 'National Histories in Chinese Global Histories', in: Stefan Berger, Nicola Brauch and Chris Lorenz (eds.), *Analysing Historical Narratives: On Academic, Popular and Educational Framings of the Past*, Oxford: Berghahn Books, 2021, pp. 259–281.

Zimmermann, Andrew, 'History, Theory, Poetry', in: *History of the Present: a Journal of Critical History* 10:1 (2020), pp. 183–6.

Zimmermann, Edoardo, 'Translations of the "American Model" in Nineteenth-Century Argentina: Constitutional Culture as a Global Legal Entanglement', in: Thomas Duve (ed.), *Entanglements in Legal History: Conceptual Approaches*, Frankfurt am Main: Max Planck Institute for European Legal History, 2014, pp. 385–426.

Zimmermann, Susan, 'The Challenge of Multinational Empire for the International Women's Movement: the Habsburg Monarchy and the Development of Feminist Inter/National Politics', in: *Journal of World History* 16 (2004), pp. 87–172.

Zinn, Howard, *A People's History of the United States: 1492 to the Present*, New York: Harper Collins, 1980.

Index

Abensour, Léon, 106
abolition of slavery, 52
absolutism, 185, 207
Adam, Thomas, 271, 279
Adams, Kathleen, 250
Adorno, Theodor W., 140
Africa, 3, 4, 9, 38, 46, 51, 82, 88, 92, 108, 133, 143, 146, 160, 163, 171–2, 193, 198, 215, 225, 228, 241, 249, 250, 261, 264, 272, 275, 296, 297
see also South Africa *Age of Atonement, The* (1988)
Ajayi, Jacob Ade, 46
Alaimo, Stacey, 256
Albania, 62
Allen, Jennifer, 160
Alpers, Svetlana, 205
American civil war, the, 170, 220, 247
American Historical Assocation, the, 261
American revolution, 106
Amin, Shahid, 88
anarchism, 4
Anderson, Ben, 241
Anderson, Benedict, 20, 271
Anderson, Greg, 30
Ankersmit, Frank, 15, 285
Annales (journal), 61, 155
Annales school, 64–5, 80, 83, 130, 132, 150, 154, 265, 269, 309
  mentalities, 87, 130, 180
anthropocentrism, 242
anthropologists, 11, 92, 130, 131, 132, 136, 138, 141, 142, 144, 149, 150, 236, 294
anthropology
  cultural, 129, 141
  feminist, 109
  historical, 32, 55, 69, 129–50
antiquarianism, 16
anti-Semitism, 4, 163, 165, 167
  Anti-Semitism Dispute, 4
anti-Westernism, 278
Anzaldúa, Gloria, 270
Appadurai, Arjun, 56, 237
Appiah, Kwame Anthony, 157
Appleby, Joyce, 86
Argentina, 160
Ariès, Philippe, 84
Asia, 3, 261, 270, 296
  East, 272
  South, 147
  South-East, 136
Assad, Talal, 196
Assmann, Aleida, 173
Assmann, Jan, 156
Austin, John, 93
Australia, 40, 41, 54, 65, 133, 249, 258, 275, 296, 301
  indigenous people, 102, 225
  Sydney, 61
Austria, 160
  Habsburg empire, 37, 190
authoritarianism, 60, 172, 199
Awe, Bolanle, 107

Bacon, Francis, 207
Bakhtin, Mikhail, 22, 23, 70, 75, 92, 100, 141, 161, 289, 292
  heteroglossia, 22–3, 27
  polyglossia, 22–3, 75
  polyphonic concept, 22
  unfinalisability, 22, 23, 289
Bangladesh, 37, 252
Barad, Karen, 256
Barkan, Elazar, 156, 197
Barthes, Roland, 23, 206, 232, 289
Batatu, Hanna, 65
Baudrillard, Jean, 210, 296

Baumann, Zygmunt, 100
Bavaj, Riccardo, 191
Baxandall, Michael, 205
Bay, Edna, 143
Bayly, Christopher, 55, 189
Beard, Charles, 23
Beard, Mary, 106
Becker, Carl, 23
Beckert, Sven, 266
Begriffsgeschichte, 47
Begum, Gulbadan, 106
Belgium, 39
Bellér-Hann, Ildikó, 144
Benjamin, Jessica, 11, 31
Benjamin, Walter, 134, 206
Bennett, Jane, 237
Bennett, Tony, 235
Bentham, Jeremy, 207
Bentley, Michael, 284
Berger, Peter L., 20
Berkhofer, Robert, 286
Berlin, 167, 233
Berry, Graham, 55
Berry, Helen, 253
Berry, Mary Elizabeth, 187
Beuys, Joseph, 160
Beyond the Cultural Turn (1999), 86, 102
Bhabha, Homi, 25, 89, 92, 270, 290
Bhambra, Gurminder, 168
Biagini, Eugenio, 48
Bible, 271
Bielefeld
  school of social history, 28
  university, 47
Biernacki, Richard, 102
Black Atlantic, The (1993), 275
Black Lives Matter campaign, 197
Blainey, Geoffrey, 102, 301
Bloch, Marc, 23, 39, 61, 83, 130, 261
Bloom, Lisa, 116
Bloxham, Donald, 285
Boddice, Rob, 99
Bodnar, John, 159
Bolshevik revolution, 54, 62
Bonnell, Andrew, 168
Bonnell, Victoria, 74, 86, 218
border, 4, 39, 53, 118, 146, 239, 299
  cultural, 90, 141, 201
Borderlands/ La Frontera (1987), 270
Bourdieu, Pierre, 21, 51, 74, 93, 95, 98, 100, 139, 206, 207, 244, 289, 294, 299
  'habitus', 21, 98
bourgeoisie, 21, 94
Braudel, Fernand, 64, 264, 269, 279, 307
Brazil, 62, 271
Breuilly, John, 100, 274
Brexit, 40, 167–9, 172, 199
Briggs, Asa, 237
Britain, 5, 38, 42, 48, 50, 53, 56, 59–61, 62, 63, 70, 75, 109, 133, 156, 172, 189, 194, 197, 199, 236, 273, 304, 308
see also England; United Kingdom
British empire, 40, 55, 109, 167, 169, 189
British parliamentary system, 43
Brown, Bill, 237
Brown, Cynthia Stokes, 268
Brubaker, Rogers, 26
Brunner, Otto, 181
Brussels, 40, 167, 192, 193
Buddhism, 96, 257
Bulgaria, 37, 38
Bull, Anna Cento, 173
Burckhardt, Jakob, 38, 82, 290
Burguière, André, 135
Burke, Peter, 92–4, 219
Burrow, J. W., 47
Burton, Antoinette, 281
Butler, Judith, 25, 111, 122, 289
Butterfield, Herbert, 186
Bynum, Caroline Walker, 113

Cambridge
  school of intellectual history, 181, 183, 184, 186, 295
  university, 47, 179, 181, 183, 295
Canada, 40, 102
Canning, Kathleen, 76
capital
  cultural, 21, 289
  social, 21, 207
  symbolical, 21
capitalism, 4, 7, 60–1, 62, 65, 74, 88, 98, 109, 218
  free trade, 56
  pre-capitalist, 73

Carr, E. H., 64, 180
Caribbean islands, 308
Carson, James, 197
Catalonia, 40
Catholicism, 6, 38, 52, 53, 77
Cercel, Cristian, 176
Cerutti, Simona, 133
Chaisson, Eric, 268
Chakrabarty, Dipesh, 9, 45, 73, 242
Chamberlain, Houston Steward, 3
Champion, Matthew, 309
Chartier, Roger, 85
Chartism, 47, 133
Chatterjee, Partha, 45
Chiang, Howard H., 123
Chicago, university, 132, 264
  Committee on the Comparative Study of New Nations, 132
Chile, 171
China, 38, 52, 62, 107, 164, 211, 249–51, 258, 261, 299, 308
  Confucianism, 52
  eastern, 144
  empire, 37
  Uyghurs, 144
Christian, David, 268, 269
Christianity, 51–2, 197, 227, 229
citizenship, citizen, 81, 113, 159, 166, 218, 223
civil society, 71, 215, 234, 251
Civilizing Subjects (2002), 50
Cixous, Hélène, 25
Clapham, John, 60
Clark, Alice, 106
class, 7, 9, 11, 149, 195, 216–25, 254–7, 274–5, 291–300
  consciousness, 10
  and gender, 108, 120
  language of class, 5
  middle, 7, 48, 198, 199, 213, 217, 254–5
  subaltern, 9, 45, 136, 292, 299
  working, 48, 74, 76–7, 134, 216, 253
  see also identity
Clay, Henry, 54
Cohen, Deborah, 307
Cohn, Bernard S., 46, 136
Cold War, 62, 163, 167, 195, 199, 213, 215, 227, 233, 261, 264, 308
Cole, G. D. H., 5, 62
Colley, Linda, 169
Collingwood, R. G., 186, 242
colonial subjects, 9, 88, 198
colonialism, 8, 16, 38, 45, 46, 108, 136, 138, 155, 158–9, 198, 213, 215, 231, 262, 266, 276, 300, 308
  decolonisation, 9, 45, 266, 273
Columbia University, 156
communication, 31, 47, 50, 56, 84, 99, 280, 309
communism, 4, 40, 62, 144, 163–5, 167, 199, 229, 273, 286, 308
  anti-communism, 165
  post-communism, 165, 166, 302
Conception of German History, The (1968), 308
conceptual history, 47, 183, 191–3, 195, 197, 201, 295
Confino, Alon, 162
conservatism, 43, 53
constitutionalism, 185, 194
constructionism, 28, 130, 183
constructivism, 12, 21, 27, 95, 102, 122, 123, 150, 284, 285, 289, 292, 296, 300
  social, 20
contextualism, 186, 295
Conze, Werner, 64, 181
Cook, James W., 292
Coombe, Annie, 172
Cooper, Frederick, 26, 278
Cooter, Roger, 113
Corbin, Alain, 93
cosmopolitan universalism, 12
cosmopolitanism, 156, 157, 263, 280, 294
Cotton: the Fabric that Made the Modern World (2013), 258
Crary, Jonathan, 207
creolisation, 89, 282
Cressy, David, 144
Croce, Benedetto, 23
Crockett, Davy, 54
Cuba, 164
cultural history, 75–107
Cultural History of Women (2016), 87
culture
  cultural diversity, 11
  cultural transfer, 89–90

cultural turn, 33, 51, 73, 75, 80, 85, 86, 89, 95, 100, 103, 150, 178, 238, 292
national. *see* national, culture
public, 111
Cultures of Empire (2000), 308
Cunningham, William, 60

D'Emilio, John, 123
Dakar school of historical writing, 38
Darnton, Robert, 141, 187
Davidoff, Leonore, 107, 109
Davis, Natalie Zemon, 121, 146
de Beauvoir, Simone, 107
de Certeau, Michel, 15–17, 70, 93, 124, 134, 139–41, 160, 251, 289, 294
de Riello, Giorgio, 236
de Saussure, Ferdinand, 24, 131, 185
decisionism, 17
Defining the Victorian Nation (2000), 50
Deleuze, Gilles, 282
democracy, 53, 55, 73, 192, 199, 200, 207, 264, 296
liberal, 64, 114, 173, 174
mass, 54
parliamentary, 54, 168
Democracy and Religion (1986), 52
demonology, 218
den Boer, Pim, 189
Derrida, Jacques, 13, 23–6, 138, 289
Descartes, René, 180
determinism, 49, 66, 73, 150
ecological, 247
diaspora, 91, 211, 251, 270
Díaz-Maldonado, Rodrigo, 37
Dickmann, René, 231
Dikötter, Frank, 250
Dilthey, Wilhelm, 85
Diop, Cheikh Anta, 38, 272
Dirlik, Arif, 266
discrimination, 4, 7, 31, 47, 81, 87–8, 91, 92, 98, 169, 197, 301, 307
Dobb, Maurice, 63
Domanska, Eva, 236
Dosse, François, 130, 309
Douglass, H. Ford, 275
Downs, Laura Lee, 31
Droysen, Johann Gustav, 12
Du Bois, W.E.B., 263, 276
Duffy, Charles Gavan, 55
Dülmen, Richard von, 135
Dunn, John, 184
Durckheim, Émile, 61
Duress: Imperial Durabilities in Our Times (2016), 138

eclecticism, 33, 290
Economy of Obligation (1998), 75
Ehmer, Josef, 219
Eleanor of Aquitaine, 239
Eley, Geoff, 33, 72, 78, 138
Elias, Norbert, 99, 130
Elkins, James, 205
empire, 3, 5, 35, 37, 38, 55, 56, 109, 111, 114, 126, 146, 168–70, 190, 199, 214, 227, 250, 266, 276, 293, 308
empiricism, 28
Engels, Friedrich, 4
England, 4, 6, 35, 40, 50, 60, 63, 72, 77, 89, 129, 184, 188, 253, 275, 297, 308
see also Britain; United Kingdom
Enlightenment, 2, 10, 81, 186, 190, 280
Kantian, 11
epistemology, 31, 143, 285, 318
Epstein, James, 309
equality, 39, 71, 81, 92, 101, 171, 189, 225
inequality, 78, 149
Espagne, Michel, 265
essentialism, 76, 91, 93, 95, 101, 102, 113, 125, 138, 161, 162, 163, 166, 167, 170, 172, 192, 258, 259, 263, 288
anti-essentialism, 24, 33, 267
de-essentialised, 46, 146, 288
non-essentialist, 124
ethnic minorities, 4, 31
ethnicity, 43, 50, 56, 76, 77, 82, 121, 190, 195, 196, 220, 222, 224, 233, 275, 292
ethnic cleansing, 4, 6, 157
ethnocentrism, 10, 12, 135
ethnography, 75
ethnology, 82, 161
Eurocentrism, 9, 135, 138, 193

Europe
early modern, 36, 220
East-Central, 164, 165, 190
Eastern, 4, 39, 40, 62, 163, 164, 165, 166, 167, 174, 190, 191
Europhobia, 168
history. *see* history
interwar, 39
medieval, 227, 239
non-European others, 5
post-war, 6, 233
South-Eastern, 190
Western, 53, 129, 165, 167, 172, 174
European Union, 40, 156, 165, 167, 168, 192, 199, 272, 305
Europeanisation, 40
Euroscepticism, 40, 168
Evans, George Ewart, 69
Evans-Pritchard, Edward E., 146
Eve and the New Jerusalem (1983), 108
evolutionary biology, 268
exceptionalism, 273

fake news, 29
Falola, Toyin, 9
Fanon, Franz, 8, 44, 45
fascism, 40, 164, 165, 199, 207
Febvre, Lucien, 39, 61, 83, 94, 130, 265
Feierman, Steven, 147
Felice, Renzo de, 40
feminism, 7, 107, 126, 133, 276
Ferguson, Adam, 2
Ferguson, Niall, 169, 304
Ferrándiz, Paco, 236
feudalism, 4
Feyerabend, Paul, 17
Fiege, Mark, 246
Finland, 53, 54, 194
First World War, 4, 5, 6, 16, 36, 39, 40, 50, 51, 54, 59, 60, 61, 62, 64, 84, 94, 99, 117, 130, 154, 159, 163, 166–9, 175, 194, 210, 229, 232, 278, 297
Fitzpatrick, Ellen, 39
Folbre, Nancy, 116
folk tales, 107
Foucault, Michel, 18–19, 20, 25, 26, 43, 70, 73, 74, 84, 93–4, 95, 98, 100, 110, 111–13, 115, 124, 129, 137, 140, 180, 206–7, 224, 225, 239, 289, 290, 293–4, 298
'archaeology of knowledge', 129
'biopower', 113
governmentality, 43, 70, 98, 290
foundationalism, 30, 124, 138, 146, 197, 294
Foundations of Modern Political Thought, *The* (1978), 185
France, 39, 41, 50, 61–2, 65, 83, 85, 93–4, 130, 133, 134, 146, 154–5, 158, 159, 172, 196, 207, 225, 263, 265, 309
Francophone world, 55
pre-revolutionary, 187
Rassemblement National, 172
Francis, Martin, 50
Frankfurt school, the, 140
Freeden, Michael, 200
Freeman, Edward Augustus, 4, 34
French revolution, 35, 49, 139, 154, 199
Freud, Sigmund, 180
Frevert, Ute, 96
Fukuyama, Francis, 31, 286
functionalism, 66, 73
fundamentalism, 303
Christian, 3
Furet, François, 48

Gallagher, Catherine, 113
Gardner, Sarah E., 170
Gebauer, Gunter, 147
Geertz, Clifford, 56, 69, 129, 131, 293
Gellner, Ernest, 100
genealogy, 20, 196
genocide, 4, 6, 99, 157, 163, 166, 192, 248
Georgia, 170
Gerittsen, Anne, 236
Germanic cultures, 39
Germany, 4, 10, 28, 35–6, 38, 39, 44, 47, 53, 60, 61, 63, 64, 70, 73, 76, 77, 129, 130, 133–4, 135, 160, 173, 188, 191, 194, 196, 199, 210, 232, 233, 253, 265, 274, 299, 307
Alltagsgeschichte, 129
Alternative für Deutschland, 41, 172
Federal Republic, 70, 156, 233
Historical School of Economics, 60

Nazi Germany, 6, 154, 165, 168
pan-Germanism, 5, 82
Prussia, 36
reunification, 168
Volksgeschichte, 4
Weimar Germany, 44, 64
West, 40, 64, 229, 233
Geschichtswerkstatt, 70
Geulen, Christian, 182
Geuss, Raymond, 184
Ghana, 228, 250
Gibbon, Edward, 186
Giddens, Anthony, 86, 266
Gifford, Chris, 168
Gilroy, Paul, 91, 157, 275
Gimeno-Martinez, Javier, 251
Ginzburg, Carlo, 69, 133
Gladstone, William, 55
Gladstonian Liberal Party, 48
Gleason, Philip, 195
globalisation, 118, 119, 261, 262, 279, 280, 300
Gobineau, Joseph Arthur de, 3
Goffman, Erving, 93
Goody, Jack, 270
governmentality, 51
Grafton, Anthony, 187
Gramsci, Antonio, 26, 84, 136
Great Depression, 222
Greece/Greek, 35, 37, 38, 147, 272
Green, Anna, 92
Greig, Hannah, 256
Grieben, Theresa, 220
Grimm, Robert, 61
Gross, Jan, 166
Gruzinski, Serge, 227
Guattari, Félix, 282
Guha, Ranajit, 44, 136

Habermas, Jürgen, 114, 130
hagiography, 218
Haiti, 225, 263
Halbwachs, Maurice, 154
Hall, Catherine, 50, 109, 308
Hall, Stuart, 26, 31, 46, 83–4, 91, 101, 102, 124, 249, 288, 290, 301, 308, 309
Hamlett, Jane, 256
Hanna, Leonie, 256
Hansen, Hans Lauge, 173
Harlan, David, 291
Harrison, Roydon, 63
Hartmann, Wolfram, 231
Harvey, John L., 59
Hayes, Carlton, 100
Hegel, Wilhelm Friedrich, 180
hegemony, 26, 27, 44, 138, 167, 190, 194
Heidegger, Martin, 237
Hekmans, Susan, 256
Heng, Geraldine, 297
Herder, Johann Gottfried, 82
heritage, 153, 156, 213, 306
of everyday, 155
industrial, 305
medieval, 305
national, 166
prehistorical, 305
war, 305
hermeneutic tradition, 74, 85
Hill, Christopher, 35, 63
Hilton, Boyd, 51
Hilton, Rodney, 63
Hinduism, 37, 38, 96, 122, 231, 302
Hintze, Otto, 261
Hispanic world, 55
Historian's Craft, The (1964), 23
historians
amateur, 32
Annales, 39, 84, 130, 180, 290
Bulgarian, 37
Chinese, 37
conservative, 5
Enlightenment, 2
German, 40
Indian, 37
Liberal, 4
Norwegian, 37
pessimistic, 14
popular, 303
professional, 2–3, 5, 20, 27, 31–2, 36, 134, 302, 303, 304
progressive, 62
Slovak, 37
historical consciousness, 10, 100
historical profession, 2, 6, 9, 13, 17, 28–9, 32, 62, 120, 130, 133, 242, 286, 287–8, 290, 300, 306, 308

historical thinking, 15, 30, 233
historiography
  American, 39
  British, 62, 63
  class, 9
  Enlightenment, 262
  German, 64, 308
  German nationalist, 39
  history of, 1, 31–3, 99
  Mexican, 36
  nationalist, 275
  non-Western, 9
  Western, 44, 64
Historische Anthropologie (journal), 135
history
  African, 250
  American, 39, 195, 197, 246, 247, 265
  animal, 247
  anti-colonial, 8, 46, 228
  apologetic national history, 8
  architectural, 251
  art, 203, 205
  Australian, 102, 301
  of biocultures, 267
  and biology, 3, 113
  black, 30, 101
  black American, 275
  of the body, 80, 97, 98, 103, 113, 238, 287, 292
  British political, 43
  church, 2
  of civil society, 114
  class, 5, 72, 81
  of concepts, 178, 179, 181, 184, 185, 186, 187, 188, 191, 195, 201, 291
  conceptual, 28, 32, 189, 287
  cultural, 1, 32, 34, 39, 43, 44, 46, 47, 66, 97, 100–3, 105, 106, 125, 143, 195, 196, 203, 205, 259, 280, 287, 292, 293, 294, 298
  design, 251
  ecclesiastical, 3
  economic, 1–33, 60, 61, 71, 74–6, 78, 116, 126, 267, 293
  of emotions, 80, 94–7, 103, 287, 292
  of empire, 5, 55, 267
  environmental, 247, 249, 264, 280
  European, 5, 6
  of everyday life, 28, 68
  feminist, 71, 87, 106, 109, 120
  French, 48
  gender, 1, 7, 30, 32, 43, 76, 97, 105–10, 112, 113, 116, 118–27, 150, 229, 287, 292–3
  German, 90, 149, 273
  global, 1, 5, 32, 35, 43, 118, 119, 134, 258, 261, 262, 264, 266, 267, 272, 275, 279, 299, 300
  imperial, 6
  indigenous, 30, 102, 249
  intellectual, 35, 47, 179, 181, 186, 295, 308
  of international conflict and revolutions, 99
  Italian, 40
  labour, 5, 7, 59, 61–4, 65, 71–5, 79, 81, 101, 108, 274, 291, 292, 299
  LGBTI, 7, 8, 123, 124
  Marxisant social, 49
  Marxist, 63
  of material culture, 1, 28, 32, 50, 187, 188, 235, 236, 237, 238, 244, 249, 251–3, 257–9, 287, 298
  of medicine, 264
  memory, 1, 32, 150, 154, 159, 164, 210, 253, 287
  Mexican, 88
  micro/macro, 5, 55, 66, 68, 72, 131, 133, 134, 281, 294, 295, 307
  military, 264
  national, 5, 20, 39, 40, 56, 155, 162, 210, 250, 262, 265, 275, 280, 302, 308
  of nationalism, 80, 92, 293
  natural, 247
  new cultural, 80–103
  new histories, 28
  new political, 34, 42–56, 291, 309
  new social, 74
  non-Western, 9, 30, 37, 44, 45, 82, 96, 106, 107, 129, 261, 262, 264
  oral, 69, 70, 133, 306
  pan-histories, 5, 6
  people's, 129
  philosophy of, 4, 11, 15, 29

political, 5, 28, 34–56, 64, 66, 71, 78, 89, 114, 126, 130, 133, 290–2, 293, 309
of political thought, 179, 181, 185, 295
of pollution, 247
post-colonial, 8, 25, 46, 108, 214, 215, 262
public, 304–7
racial, 6
of religion, 196, 309
of science, 115, 126, 280, 287, 293
science of, 8, 12
of violence, 80, 99, 103, 292
of sexualities, 111, 114, 126, 293
social, 5, 7, 28, 43, 48, 65–8, 72, 73, 74, 76, 78–9, 81, 83, 86, 103, 105, 133, 138, 139, 149, 180, 195, 288, 291, 292, 309
of social movements, 99
spatial, 6
transnational, 70, 118, 119, 264, 266, 272, 273, 275, 279–80, 281, 282, 287, 295
visual, 1, 187, 203, 206, 207, 210, 216, 219, 224, 230, 238, 287
Whiggish, 32
world, 82, 130, 261, 262, 264, 267, 269, 273, 281
history from below, 28, 45, 66, 68, 69, 70, 129, 134, 149, 249, 306
History of Mankind – UNESCO, 280
History of Sexuality (1978), 111
History Workshop Journal, 70, 133
history workshop movement. *see* movements
Hitler–Stalin pact, 165
Hobbes, Thomas, 184
Hobsbawm, Eric, 20, 63, 64, 65, 71, 100, 101, 264, 307
Hodder, Ian, 235
Hoffer, Hence, 29
Hoffer, Peter C., 29
Hoggart, Richard, 85
holism, 284
holocaust, the, 86, 156, 163, 165, 166
Auschwitz, 165
Hölscher, Lucian, 182, 196
homogeneity, 7, 82, 89, 222, 301
homosexuality, 112, 304
Howard, John, 301
Hroch, Miroslav, 100
Hsu, Y. Madeline, 276
Hudson, Pat, 74–6, 334
Huizinga, Johan, 83, 94
Hull, Isabell, 114
human rights, 99, 156, 171, 174–6, 177, 225
humanism, 10, 91, 157, 166–7, 176, 243, 314
humanitarianism, 48, 99, 173, 229
Hungary, 4, 164, 172, 199, 301
hunger strikes, 99
Hunt, Lynn, 48, 74, 86, 149, 279
Hutchinson, John, 100
Hutton, Patrick, 177
Huyssen, Andreas, 160, 183
hypernationalism, 6, 8, 39

Iberianism, 5, 82
Idea of Work in Europe from Antiquity to Modern Times, The (2009), 219
identity
anti-colonial, 8
black, 4, 31, 41, 90, 91, 98, 102, 108, 120, 169–70, 221, 222, 225, 226, 227, 229, 263, 264, 273, 275, 304
class, 4, 5, 26, 32, 50, 73, 76, 77, 79, 81, 109, 222, 255, 288, 290, 309
collective, 136, 195, 198, 199, 201, 203, 204, 210, 213, 216, 220
colonised, 10, 136, 137, 148, 214
gender, 76
Islamophobic identitarian discourses, 3
LGBTI, 7, 8
minority, 10
national, 1, 6
non-spatial, 200
of 'self', 11
oppressed, 8, 10
postcolonial, 8
religious, 2, 3, 146, 227, 257, 296
sexual, 7, 10, 112, 124, 293
spatial, 1, 5, 32, 35, 89, 98, 190, 191, 192, 194, 195, 200, 201, 256, 272, 274, 281, 288
sub-national, 5
transnational, 5, 295
identity politics, 26, 31, 120, 121, 138, 167, 249, 290

Idrizi, Idrit, 62
Ifversen, Jan, 192
Iggers, Georg G., 307
Ihalainen, Pasi, 53, 194
Images of the Body in India (2011), 147
Imperial Meridian (1989), 55
imperialism, 8, 38, 40, 47, 50, 56, 119, 138, 158, 192, 198, 200, 207, 215, 218, 266, 279
  ecological, 248
  Japanese, 8
India, 9, 37, 38, 41, 44, 46, 47, 65, 72, 96, 114, 122, 136, 173, 189, 199, 225, 231, 233, 302
  BJP, 41
  Mayo controversy, 114
  sati, 122
  south, 257
Indian Mutiny (1857), the, 46
Indian national movement, the, 37
indigeneity/indigenous, 248, 249, 296
indigenous populations, 16, 227, 301
individualism, 99, 114, 196
Indonesia, 117, 250, 299
industrial revolution, 60
International Big History Association, 269
International Committee of the Historical Sciences, 262
International Public History (journal), 306
internationalism, 48, 118
Inventing Ireland (1996), 45
Invention of Tradition, The (1983), 101
Iran, 123
see also Islamic Republic
Iraq, 65
Ireland, 3, 52
  Irish, 52, 77, 211
Isaac, Rhys, 144
Islam, 3, 38, 117, 197
Islamic Republic of Iran, 3
Islamic world, 3
Italian Renaissance, 82
Italy, 35, 40, 61, 69, 129, 133, 205
  microstoria, 129, 133

Jacob, Margaret, 86
Jamaica, 275
James, C. L. R., 44, 263
Japan, 8, 35, 36, 38, 40, 65, 96, 97, 106, 187, 196, 246, 258, 299
  Meiji period, 36
  Shintoism, 38
Jay, Martin, 207
Jenkins, Paul, 228
Jewish community, 98, 166, 224, 297
Johnson, Boris, 172
Jones, Gareth Stedman, 47
Jordheim, Helge, 191
Joyce, Patrick, 48, 72, 236
Judt, Tony, 66, 167

Kann, Mark E., 111
Kedourie, Elie, 100
Kelley, Donald, 180
Kenya, 108
Kessler-Harris, Alice, 121
Kiberd, Declan, 45
Kiernan, Viktor, 63
Kleinberg, Ethan, 12, 13, 25, 29, 320, 322
knowledge, historical, 15, 23, 24, 105, 127, 138
Kocka, Jürgen, 10
Kohl, Helmut, 40, 233
Kollwitz, Käthe, 233
Koposov, Nikolay, 166
Korea, 159, 196
Koselleck, Reinhart, 47, 179–84, 187–8, 295, 377–8
Kracauer, Siegfried, 13
Kristeva, Julia, 25
Kuhn, Thomas, 27
Kuukkanen, Jouni-Matti, 284
Kuwait, 252

Labour History Review (journal), 63
labour movement. *see* movements
Lacan, Jacques, 24, 25, 26, 75, 289
Laclau, Ernesto, 26, 290
Lakatos, Imre, 17
Lake, Marilyn, 275
Lambros, Spyridon, 35
Lancaster, university, 63
Landes, Joan, 229
Landscape for a Good Woman (1950), 107
Languages of Class (1983), 47
Laos, 164

Laqueur, Thomas, 113, 124
Laslett, Peter, 184
Latin America, 3, 38, 65, 121, 195, 228, 229, 297
Latour, Bruno, 206, 210, 241, 296
Lawrence, Jon, 42, 43
LeCain, Tim, 235, 243, 246
Lehtsalu, Liise, 266
Leonhard, Jörn, 189, 272
Levi, Giovanni, 133
Lévi-Strauss, Claude, 65, 141
Levy, Daniel, 156, 161, 359
LGBTI. *see* identity
liberalism, 43, 52, 53, 189, 279
Lincoln, Abraham, 221
Lincoln, Bruce, 134
Lindenberger, Thomas, 134
linguistic turn, 28, 80, 130, 131, 133, 201, 238, 239, 259, 289
Lis, Catharina, 219
literature, 8, 12, 13, 23, 35, 73, 74, 88, 157, 162, 237, 243, 289
  anti-colonial, 8
  modernist, 13
Locke, John, 184
Loimeier, Roman, 146
London, 61, 72, 107, 257
London School of Economics, 61, 106
Lopata, Andy, 216
Lorenz, Chris, 14, 18, 26, 289
Los Angeles, 88
Loughran, Tracey, 80
Louis XIV, 2, 207
Louis XVI, 49
Lovejoy, Arthur, 180
Luckmann, Thomas, 20
Lüdtke, Alf, 69, 135
Ly, Abdoulaye, 272
Lydon, Jane, 225
Lyotard, Jean-François, 20

Macfarlane, Alan, 132, 293
Machiavellian Moment, The (1975), 186
MacGregor, Neil, 257
Macintyre, Stuart, 65
McKibbin, Ross, 50
McLuhan, Marshall, 205
McNeill, William, 264
Magna Carta, 36, 199
Maier, Charles, 285
Making of the English Working Class, The (1963), 7, 72
Making of the Modern Body, The (1987), 113
Mandler, Peter, 307
Māori culture, 249
  Māori Land Court Record, 249
Mark, James, 164
Marriot, McKim, 132
Marx, Karl, 4, 65, 78, 130, 180, 182
Marxism, 4, 26, 49, 62, 63, 65, 66, 73, 78, 84, 100, 129, 130, 138, 139, 149, 262, 274
  historical materialism, 4, 74, 130, 243
  neo-Marxism, 63
Marxism Today (journal), 84
mass media, 43
Mayo, Katherine, 114
Mbembe, Achille, 200
Mead, Margaret, 131
Medick, Hans, 135
medieval era, 37, 83, 84, 93, 96, 106, 111, 185, 211, 257, 297, 305
see also Middle Ages
Megill, Allan, 1
Meinecke, Friedrich, 100
memory
  of activism, 277
  agonistic, 153, 173–7
  British war memory, 168
  cosmopolitan, 156–77
  European memory culture, 167
  holocaust, 161
  national. *see* national, memory
  palimpsestic, 183
  postcolonial, 158
memory history. *see* history
Memory Palace of Matteo Ricci (2008), 52
memory studies, 152, 159, 160, 162, 177, 210, 294
  collective memory, 153–4, 155, 161, 162
  cultural memory, 152–4, 161
  historical memory, 152, 155, 172
  Realms of Memory project, 154
  social memory, 152–4

Memory Studies Association, 161
Memory Studies (journal), 152, 161
Memory, History, Forgetting (2000), 157
men's studies, 110, 126
Mergel, Thomas, 44
Metahistory (1973), 14
Mexico, 88, 227, 270
Michaels, Axel, 147
Middell, Matthias, 280
Middle Ages, 36, 83, 116
Mierzoeff, Nicholas, 207
Mihai, Mihaela, 176
minority
  ethnic, 101, 169, 223, 249, 288, 301
  identities, 8, 71, 101, 176, 250, 301
Minz, Sidney, 237
Mitchell, W. J. T., 210
modernity, 8, 20, 24, 35, 42, 47, 64, 78, 88, 91, 100, 117, 180, 181, 198, 199, 207, 210, 213, 215, 225, 237, 246, 248, 251
  critiques, 183
Modi, Narendra, 173, 199, 302
Mohanty, Chandra Talpade, 120
Mongia, Radhika Viyas, 276
Moore, Alison, 85
Moravian empire, 37
Morgan, David, 227
Morton, A. L., 63
Moss, Stella, 256
Mother India (1927), 114
Mouffe, Chantal, 26, 290
movements
  anti-slavery, 53
  Black Lives Matter, 91
  civil rights, 169–71
  environmental, 53, 108
  global student, 71
  history workshop, 132–6
  labour, 5, 61, 69, 73, 74, 77, 216–18, 274
  LGBTI, 123, 124
  peace, 53, 108
  reproductive rights, 108
  social, xi, 31, 42, 53, 81, 102, 108, 118, 120, 301
  women's, 53, 106–7, 118, 133
Mozambique, 215
Mughal empire, 38, 46, 106
Muldrew, Craig, 75
multiculturalism, 91, 102, 158, 168, 251, 280
multi-lingualism, 193
Murray, Stephen, 92
museums
  British Museum, London, 257
  Bundeswehr Military Museum, Dresden, 176
  District 6 Museum, Cape Town, 172
  First World War Museum, Kobarid, 175
  First World War Museum, Peronne, 159
  House of Terror, Budapest, 164
  Quai Branly Museum, Paris, 158
Muslims, 37, 144, 146, 280
mythology, 21, 37–8, 107, 134, 154–5, 192, 232, 273, 286

Nagy, Piroska, 94
Najmabadi, Afsaneh, 123
Namias, June, 220
Namibia, 213, 214, 231
Napoleonic era, 191
Nardo, Don, 222
narrativism, 12, 15, 20, 21, 27, 28, 72, 73, 81, 102, 103, 118, 130, 133, 150, 157, 183, 284, 285, 289, 294, 296, 300
  grand narratives, 20, 21, 22, 143, 244, 279, 286, 289, 305
narrativity, 15, 17, 41, 69, 74, 78, 80, 85, 153, 162
national
  character, 2, 38, 89, 199
  community, 154
  cultures, 82, 89, 251
  identities, 20, 35, 38, 39, 40, 42, 45, 76, 81, 89, 191, 222, 246, 250, 265, 271, 309
  memory, 89, 155, 158–60, 166, 173, 262
  symbols, 251
National Association for the Advancement of Colored People (NAACP), 307
national associations for public history, 306

national historical master narratives, 6, 60, 62, 63, 264
National Socialism (Nazism), 64, 70, 165, 168, 197
nationalism, 6, 10, 21, 45, 46, 52, 62, 100, 101, 103, 108, 116, 126, 160, 166, 173, 229, 231, 261, 262, 265, 271, 279, 299, 301, 302
 anti-communist, 165
 cultural, 91
 English, 168
 historiographical, 6, 9, 273, 288, 290
 Indian, 45, 231
 methodological, 3
 nascent, 3
 new, 35
nation-state, 3, 6, 42, 56, 160
Naumann, Katja, 280
Nazism. *see* National Socialism
neoliberalism, 71
Netherlands, 52, 222
New Cultural History, *The* (1989), 86, 149
New Delhi, 252
new histories, 28, 76, 152, 237, 290, 293, 295, 296, 298, 299, 301, 307
New Left Review (journal), 84
New York, 123, 156, 220
New Zealand, 249, 299
Newbury, Darren, 215
Nield, Keith, 72
Niethammer, Lutz, 26, 69, 70
Nigeria, 46, 66, 107, 271
Nigerian Women in Historical Perspective (1992), 108
Ninkovich, Frank, 195
Niremberg, David, 99
Nobel Peace Prize, 168
Nora, Pierre, 154, 155, 156
normativity, 15, 20, 120
Nye, Robert, 110

occasionalism, 93
Offen, Karen, 105
Olick, Jeffrey, 161
On Deep History and the Brain (2008), 267
ontological turn, 30
Order of Things, *The* (1970), 19
orientalism, 44, 278
Origins of Modern English Society, 1780–1880, *The* (1969), 63
Osterhammel, Jürgen, 56
others, 5, 10–12, 24, 117, 167, 190
Otter, Chris, 242
Ottoman empire, 38
Oxford, university, 62
Ozouf, Mona, 48

Paisley, Fiona, 281
Pakistan, 37, 38
pan-movements, 5
pan-Slavism, 5, 82, 190
Papua New Guinea, 252
Paris, 64, 142, 158–9, 222
Parker, Maynard L., 211
parliamentarism, 53, 194
parochialism, 266
Parry, Jon, 52
Parsons, Talcott, 66
Past and Present (journal), 63
Pasture, Patrick, 191
patriotism, 53, 102, 157, 166, 272
Patterson, Annabel, 189
Paulmann, Johannes, 44
peasants, 45, 88, 94, 218
Pécout, Eric, 271
Pedersen, Susan, 41, 87
Pedwell, Carolyn, 95
Pelling, Henry, 63
Pemberton, John, 149
Pernau, Margrit, 147, 187, 201
perspectivalism, 15, 24, 207–8
photography, 187, 205, 206, 213, 215, 216, 220, 222, 223, 226, 228, 296
physiology, 95
Pihlainen, Kalle, 17
Pinchbeck, Ivy, 106
Pirenne, Henri, 39, 61
pluralism, 195
plurality, 7, 14, 19, 23, 139, 140, 146, 152, 160, 182, 183, 186, 201, 207, 234, 294, 296
pluralisation, 17, 27, 30, 41, 42, 130, 133, 229
Pocock, J. G. A., 47, 179, 181, 184, 185, 186, 187, 295
poetry, 107, 218, 309
Pók, Attila, 164
Poland, 6, 164, 166, 172, 199, 272

polyphony, 22, 23, 25, 134, 155, 266, 289
Pomeranz, Kenneth, 261
Porter, Roy, 113
positivism, 23, 29
Postcolonial Melancholia (2005), 157
postcolonial theory, 44, 45, 159
postcolonialism, 9, 12, 44, 159, 292
Poster, Mark, 286
Postmodern Condition, The (1979), 20
postmodernism, 12, 25, 31, 86, 284, 289, 307
poststructuralism, 12, 20, 31, 85, 95, 102, 103, 105, 110, 114, 118, 123, 131, 137, 143, 150, 155, 183, 189, 195, 238, 248, 267, 274, 282, 285, 289, 292, 293, 294, 296, 300
Power, Eileen, 106
Prakash, Gyan, 123
Pratt, Mary Louise, 270
Preda, Alex, 237
prehistory, 107, 185, 305
presentationalism, 113
presentism, 120
primitivism, 213
Princeton University, 141, 151
progress, 2, 14, 28, 35, 66, 73, 122, 127, 190, 199, 214, 215, 227, 229, 248, 261, 262, 291, 293
Protestantism, 6, 38, 52
Proust, Marcel, 13
Prussian school of historiography, 36
psychology, 11, 95, 98, 99, 268
Puerto Rico, 88
Putin, Vladimir, 41, 199
Pykett, Lyn, 237

Queen Victoria, 46
Quirke, Carol, 216

race/racism, 3, 4, 5, 11, 30, 31, 32, 50, 56, 64, 71, 76, 77, 81, 82, 84, 88, 91, 98, 103, 108, 109, 115, 118, 119, 121, 127, 137, 169, 171, 177, 197, 200, 218–25, 233, 249, 256, 263, 267, 275, 276, 278, 282, 292, 295, 296, 297, 299, 301, 304, 308, 309
  anti-racist, 46, 167, 197, 308
  anti-white, 171
  Aryan, 6
radicalism, 43, 47
  Chartist, 48
Rahman, Momin, 237
Raiford, Leigh, 170
Rajamani, Imke, 187
Ramaswamy, Sumathi, 231
Ramsden, John, 168
Rancière, Jacques, 134, 303
Ranger, Terence, 20, 101
Ranke, Leopold von, 13
Rassemblement National, 41
Ravenhill-Johnson, Annie, 217
Reddy, William M., 95, 96
Redfield, Robert, 132
Reform Act (1867), 50
relativism, 15, 17, 18, 23, 27, 86, 95, 141, 183, 284
  cultural, 135
religion, 3, 7, 30, 32, 35, 38, 42, 49, 51–2, 61, 73, 77, 83, 87, 145, 190, 197, 294
  historians, 77
  see also identity
Religion and the Decline of Magic (1971), 146
Rembrandt van Rijn, 213
Renaissance, 19, 83, 185, 208
Renan, Ernest, 262
Rendal, Jane, 50
representation, 15, 46, 49, 50, 69, 85, 87, 88, 230, 231, 291, 294
  symbolic, 110
representationalism, 284
republicanism, 82, 154, 185, 186, 229
Reynolds, Henry, 276
Rhine (river), 39, 265
Ricoeur, Paul, 85, 157
Riello, Giorgio, 258
Riley, Denise, 125
Rise of the West, The (1963), 264
ritualism, 44, 52, 73, 88, 90, 100, 141, 144–8, 196, 198, 211, 218, 227, 237, 250
Robertson, William, 2
Roediger, Henry L., 152
Romania, 6, 164
  Institute of National Memory, 164
Romano, Renee Christine, 170

romanticism, 94
Roper, Lyndal, 69
Roscoe, Will, 92
Rose, Nikolas, 113
Rosenzweig, Roy, 305
Rothberg, Michael, 161
Rousseau, Jean-Jacques, 180
Rudé, George, 63
Ruhr region, 70, 253, 299
  mnemohistory, 253
Runciman, David, 184
Rupp, Leila, 8
Rüsen, Jörn, 10–12, 289
Russia, 6, 41, 52, 160, 166, 199
Rwanda, 147

Sá, Ana Lúcia, 200
Sabean, David, 149
Sachsenmaier, Dominic, 201, 272
Sahlins, Marshall, 131, 293
Said, Edward, 25, 44, 278
Samuel, Raphael, 63, 70, 155
Saunier, Pierre-Yves, 279, 281
Savage, Kirk, 220
Savage, Mike, 196
Saville, John, 63
Scalmer, Sean, 54
Scandinavia, 6, 82, 189, 295
scepticism, 26, 64, 68, 73, 186
Schiebinger, Londa, 116
Schmoller, Gustav, 60
Schreiner, Olive, 106
Schulte, Regina, 135
Schwartz, Bill, 88
sciences
  historical, 17, 30, 41, 150, 204, 268, 281
  Western, 8, 116, 236
scientificity
  of history, 12, 13, 15, 30, 67, 68, 286, 291
Scotland/Scottish, 2, 40
Scott, Joan W., 29, 110, 124, 286, 293, 303
Scribner, Bob, 100
Scully, Pamela, 281
Second Sex (1949), 183
  Second World War, 107
secularisation, 42
Seeley, J. R., 6
self-determination, 275
Sen, Amartya, 116
Senegal, 38
Sense of the People, The (1995), 50
Sexual Politics, Sexual Communities (1983), 123
sexuality
  discourse, 111–16, 123, 137, 238, 278, 304
  history of. *see* history
Shanguhija, Martin S., 9
Shils, Edward, 132
Shryock, Andrew, 268
Singer, Milton, 132
Sinha, Mrinalini, 46, 114, 327
Skinner, Quentin, 47, 179, 181, 184, 295
Slate, Nico, 263
slaves/slavery, 4, 88, 90, 91, 143, 170, 263, 274, 275, 303, 308
  slave-led revolution (1791), 263
Slovenia, 175
Smail, Daniel Lord, 267
Smith, A.D., 100
Smith, Shawn, 222
Smith-Rosenberg, Carroll, 119
social
  class. *see* identity, class
  Darwinism, 3, 82
  democracy, 54, 73, 194, 218
  justice, 71, 176, 306
  mobility, 196
  reforms, 54, 60, 62, 78
social history, 59–79
social injustice, 4
Social Life of Things, The (1986), 237
social sciences, 59
socialism, 53, 62, 108, 133, 274
  ethical, 4
  liberal, 4
  religious, 4
sociology, 61, 64, 65, 66, 80, 86, 95, 98, 107, 131, 210, 237, 298
Soh, Sarah, 159
Sombart, Werner, 274
sophisticated falsification, theory of, 17
South Africa,
sovereignty, 3, 207
Soviet Union, 62, 164, 195, 218
Spain, 3, 6, 40, 236

spatial turn, 28, 281
Spence, Jonathan, 52
Spiegel, Gabrielle, 28
Spier, Fred, 268
Spivak, Gayatri Chakravorty, 44, 123, 136
Springs of Democracy (2017), 53
Sri Lanka, 38, 252, 256
Städter, Benjamin, 229
Stahl, Ann Brower, 250
Stalin, Josef, 62
Starkey, David, 40, 304
Stearns, Peter, 65, 264
Steber, Martina, 191
Steedman, Carolyn, 31, 107
Steele, Valerie, 255
Stoler, Ann Laura, 114, 136, 137, 278
Stone, Lawrence, 86
Study of History, A (1934–61), 264, 294–6
structuralism, 66, 73, 291
Strukturgeschichte, 64
Stürmer, Michael, 40
subaltern studies, 44, 72, 88
Subaltern Studies Group, 44, 72, 136
Suvrathan, Uthara, 257
Sweden, 36, 53, 194
Sznajder, Natan, 156

Taiwan, 258
Takamure, Itsue, 106
Tamm, Marek, 18
Tanner, Duncan, 43
Tawney, R. H., 5, 61, 307
Taylor, A. J. P., 304
Taylor, Barbara, 108
te Velde, Henk, 52
teleology, 73, 78, 150, 279
terrorism, 100
Thébaud, Françoise, 120
Thelen, David, 305
Theodora of Byzantium (empress), 239
theology, 2, 297
Theses on Theory and History (2018), 29
Thomas, Keith, 146
Thomas, Lynn, 108
Thompson, E. P., 7, 63, 72, 85, 139, 141, 292
Thrift, Nigel, 241
Tickner, Lisa, 231
Todorova, Maria, 190
Torr, Dona, 63
Tosh, John, 111
totalitarianism, 174
  anti-totalitarianism, 167
Toynbee, Arnold, 264
trade unionism, 73, 224
trade unions, 5, 77, 216, 217
traditionalists, 122
transgender, 8, 101
transnationalism, 264, 273, 275
Treitschke, Heinrich von, 4
Trump, Donald, 41, 172
Tully, James, 184
Turner, Frederic Jackson, 248
Turner, Victor, 131, 144, 250
Tyrrell, Ian, 264

Ukraine, 162
Unani medicine, 147
UNESCO, 280
unionism, 61, 73
United Kingdom, 102, 167–9, 174
see also Britain; England
United States of America, 4, 35, 36, 38, 39, 54, 60, 61, 64, 65, 66, 68, 91, 102, 111, 133, 144, 159, 163, 170, 172, 186, 195, 197, 207, 220–4, 246–9, 253, 262–70, 274, 275, 280, 299, 307
universalism, 194, 278
university. *see* individual universities
utopianism, 49

Vale, Lawrence, 252
Valensi, Lucette, 154
van Zanden, Jan Luiten, 116
Vansina, Jan, 88
Varennes: the Death of the Monarchy (2005), 49, 204
Varma, Nitin, 220
Velázquez, Diego, 204
Versailles, Treaty of, 64
Vietnam, 164, 308
Villard, Léonie, 126
visual turn, 28, 32, 203, 206, 233, 296
Vokes, Richard, 215
Volksgeschichte, 64
Voltaire, 2

Wales, 211
  University of, 211
Ward, John Quincy Adams, 220
Warren, Mercy Otis, 106
Washington, DC, 252
Watts, Jennifer A., 211
Weber, Max, 61, 65, 66, 67, 78, 237
Weir, Robert E., 73
welfare state, 76, 194, 277
Wellings, Ben, 168
Werkstatt Geschichte, 70
Werner, Michael, 90, 265
Wertsch, James V., 152
West Indies, 114, 229
Western universalism, 108
Western-centrism, 9, 30, 278
Westminster parliament, 53
What Is History? (1961), 64, 180
White, Hayden, 11–18, 20, 85, 93, 135, 157, 162, 183, 232, 285, 289
  'practical past', 15, 189
Wickramasinghe, Nira, 257
Wilder, Gary, 29
Wildt, Michael, 134
Williams, Raymond, 84, 86
Wilson, Kathleen, 50
Windschuttle, Keith, 102, 301
Winetrout, Kenneth, 205
Wissenschaft, 12
Witz, Anne, 237
Women in Transnational History (2016), 278
women's movement. *see* movements
Women's Research and Documentation Centre, 107
women's history. *see* history
Woolf, Stuart, 309
Woolf, Virginia, 13, 126
working class, 6, 61, 71, 72, 73, 78, 130, 134, 216
World History Conferences, 262
World War. *see* First World War; Second World War
Wretched of the Earth (1961), 8
Writing of History, The (1975), 45
Writing Transnational History (2019), 281
Wulf, Christoph, 146, 147
Wylie, John, 241

xenophobia, 199

Young, James, 160
Yugoslavia, 3
Yugoslavism, 82

Zimmermann, Andrew, 309
Zimmermann, Bénédicte, 90, 265
Zimmermann, Edoardo, 195
Zinn, Howard, 130
Zolberg, Aristide, 132

CPSIA information can be obtained
at www.ICGtesting.com
Printed in the USA
LVHW080053310123
738277LV00014B/1299

9 781107 648845